Thirty Years in the South Seas

Dreißig Jahre in der Südsee

Land und Leute, Sitten und Gebräuche im Bismarckarchipel und auf den deutschen Salomoinseln

Von

R. Parkinson

Herausgegeben von Dr. B. Ankermann, Direktorial-Assistent am Königlichen Museum für Völkerkunde zu Berlin

Mit 56 Tafeln, 4 Karten und 141 Textabbildungen

Stuttgart
Verlag von Strecker & Schröder
1907

Thirty Years in the South Seas

Land and People, Customs and Traditions in the
Bismarck Archipelago and on the German Solomon Islands

by

R. Parkinson

Edited by **Dr B. Ankermann**, Assistant Director
Königliches Museum für Völkerkunde, Berlin

With 56 plates, 4 maps and 141 figures

Translated by
John Dennison

Translation edited by
J. Peter White

SYDNEY UNIVERSITY PRESS

Dedicated to
His Majesty
King Wilhelm II of Württemberg
the High Patron of Science
and the Arts
with deep respect
from the author

Subtitle-page photograph: Richard R.H. Parkinson, born
13 November 1844, died 24 July 1909. Parkinson is buried near
Kokopo, New Britain, in a forgotten and neglected grave.

Published 2010 by Sydney University Press
SYDNEY UNIVERSITY PRESS
University of Sydney Library
Fisher Library F03
The University of Sydney
NSW 2006 AUSTRALIA
Email: sup.info@sydney.edu.au
sydney.edu.au/sup

© Sydney University Press 2010

First edition published in 1907 by Verlag von Streder & Schröder, Stuttgart

This edition is based on the 1999 hardcover edition published by Crawford House Publishing, Bathurst in association with Oceania Publications, University of Sydney

The digital version of this book is freely available through the Sydney eScholarship Repository at:
ses.library.usyd.edu.au/handle/2123/6248

National Library of Australia Cataloguing-in-Publication entry
Author: Parkinson, Richard, 1844-1909.

Title: Thirty years in the South Seas : land and people, customs and traditions in the Bismarck Archipelago and on the German Solomon Islands / Richard Parkinson ; edited by Dr B. Ankermann ; translated by John Dennison and translation edited by J. Peter White.

Edition: Reprinted ed.

ISBN: 9781920899639 (pbk.)

Notes: Includes bibliographical references and index.

Subjects: Parkinson, Richard, 1844-1909.
Ethnology--Oceania.
Oceania--Description and travel.
Bismarck Archipelago (Papua New Guinea)--Social life and customs.

Other Authors/Contributors:
Ankermann, B.
White, J. Peter (John Peter), 1937-
Dennison, John D.

Dewey Number: 919.5

Contents

Editor's Preface		xii
Translator's Preface		xiv
'The German Professor': Richard Parkinson		xv
Author's Foreword		xxxiii
Editor's Foreword		xxxv

I	**New Britain with the French Islands and the Duke of Yorks**		1
	1.	The Land	1
	2.	The Inhabitants	19
		a. The Natives of the North-east of the Gazelle Peninsula	27
		b. The Baining	68
		c. The Taulil and Butam	74
		d. The Tribes of the Central Part of New Britain	76
		e. The Tribes of Western New Britain and the French Islands	87
II	**New Ireland, New Hanover and their Offshore Islands**		111
	1.	The Land	111
	2.	The Natives	117
III	**St Matthias and the Neighbouring Islands**		139
IV	**The Admiralty Islands**		155
V	**The Western Islands**		183
	1.	Wuwulu and Aua	183
	2.	Ninigo, Luf and Kaniet	191
VI	**The German Solomon Islands, together with Nissan and the Carteret Islands**		199
VII	**The Eastern Islands (Nuguria, Tauu and Nukumanu)**		225
VIII	**Secret Societies, Totemism, Masks and Mask Dances**		247
IX	**Stories and Fables**		295
X	**Languages**		311
	1.	The Languages of the Coastal Dwellers of the Northern Gazelle Peninsula	311
	2.	The Duke of York Language	317
	3.	The Baining Language	322
	4.	The Sulka Language	328
	5.	The Nakanai Language	335
XI	**Cultigens and Useful Plants, Domesticated and Hunted Animals**		341
XII	**History of Discovery**		349

Index	371

List of Figures, Plates and Maps

Figures

1	Coral limestone rock, coast of St George's Channel	2
2	Kaije volcano overlooking Blanche Bay	7
3	River valley of the Karo, Baining Mountains	8
4	Waterfall in a neighbouring valley of the Karo, Baining Mountains	10
5	Möwehafen	12
6	Party at the Pulié River, 10 kilometres from the mouth	14
7	Women of the Gazelle Peninsula	23
8	Men of the Baining	25
9	Women of the Baining	27
10	Youth from the Möwehafen region	28
11	Mother and child. Gazelle Peninsula	34
12	Mother and child. Gazelle Peninsula	35
13	Woman in mourning. Gazelle Peninsula	36
14	Rooster mask. Gazelle Peninsula	43
15	Prow of the *kakala*	47
16	Prow of the *pongpong*	47
17	Trepanned skulls from the Gazelle Peninsula	49
18	Trepanned skulls from the Gazelle Peninsula	49
19	Boy with deep scars on his forehead	50
20	Ornamental objects from the Gazelle Peninsula	64
21	Village scene in the Baining territory	69
22	Baining objects	75
23	Group of women from the 'Liebliche Inseln'	88
24	Men of Möwehafen	93
25	Decorations and other items from the French Islands	94
26	Items of decoration from the Willaumez Peninsula and the adjacent coast	97
27	Items of decoration from the south coast of New Britain	98
28	Decoration of a *Trochus* amulet	99
29	Men of Mérite. French Islands	99
30	Cords of *Nassa* snails for wrapping the spear shaft	101
31	Attachment of the barbs to the spear by binding	101
32	Clubs of the Sulka and O Mengen	102
33	Clubs from the region between Jacquinot Bay and Montague Bay	103
34	Stone axe from the Normanby Islands	103
35	Sulka shield	104
36	O Mengen shield	105
37	Shield and spears from the French Islands	106
38	Shield from South Cape	107
39	Stone axe blade from Willaumez	107
40	Village scene at Kombiuß ('Liebliche Inseln'). House of the Kaiser Wilhelmsland type	108
41	Probable shape of Australia at the beginning of the Tertiary Period	109
42	Northern tip of the island of Nusa (Raised coral reefs)	114
43	Musical instrument from New Ireland	126

44	Ornamented part of a spear from New Hanover	127
45	Decoration of a club from New Ireland	128
46	Chest ornament (*kapkap*)	130
47	Armring of *Trochus* shell	131
48	Canoe prow from southern New Ireland	133
49	Apparatus for shark-catching. New Ireland	133
50	Facial tattooing in Siara	137
51	Map of St Matthias	141
52	Men of St Matthias	142
53	Woman from St Matthias	142
54	Woman from St Matthias	142
55	Objects from St Matthias and Emirau	144
56	Decoration on spears and dance sticks	146
57	Decoration on spears and dance sticks	149
58	Group of men from Squally Island	151
59	Group of men from Squally Island	152
60	Group on Lou Island [*sic*]	155
61	Spears from the Admiralty Islands	157
62	Wooden bowl from the Admiralty Islands	158
63	Wooden bowl in the shape of a bird. Admiralty Islands	159
64	Wooden bowl in the form of a four-footed animal. Admiralty Islands	159
65	Decorations of ladles, water containers, and so on, of the Admiralty Islanders	160
66	Aprons from the Admiralty Islands	162
67	Drum from the Admiralty Islands	164
68	Lalobé pole village of the Moánus tribe	170
69	Youths from Wuwulu	185
70	Weapons from Wuwulu and Aua	187
71	Women from Aua	188
72	Wooden bowl from Wuwulu	189
73	Axe-shaped spatula, Wuwulu	189
74	Men of Wuwulu	189
75	Canoe prow. Hermit Islands	194
76	Banniu harbour. North coast of Bougainville	200
77	Cremation of a corpse in Kieta on Bougainville	212
78	Very rare chief's ornament of small shell discs	215
79	Stone tools from the Solomon Islands (pestles)	217
80	Stone tools from the Solomon Islands (axe blades)	217
81	Stone tools from the Solomon Islands (stone axes with handles)	218
82	Spears from the Solomon Islands	220
83	Girls of Nukumanu (Tasman Islands)	226
84	Boys of Nukumanu (Tasman Islands)	226
85	Ancestral image of Pau-Pau. Nukumanu	229
86	Memorial of Loatu, Tauu	230
87	Tattooing on Nukumanu. (Man, posterior and anterior aspects)	232
88	Tattooing on Nukumanu. (Woman, posterior and anterior aspects)	233
89	*Ruvettus* hook from Nukumanu	235
90	Canoe prow from Tauu	235
91	Wooden vessels. Eastern islands	236
92	Pounders. Eastern islands	236
93	Multi-pronged spears from Nukumanu	236
94	Whalebone club from Nukumanu	237
95	Shovel from Nuguria	237
96	Women of the Greenwich Islands	239
97	Weaver at work	240
98	Loom from Nukumanu	241
99	Stone bowl found on Mount Varzin, Gazelle Peninsula	244
100	Stone pestle, found on Uatom	244
101	Stone bowl found on Nusa	244
102	Stone vessel found on Nusa	244

103	The *duk-duk* assembled for a public dance	249
104	The *duk-duk* on the *taraiu*	250
105	The *duk-duk* presents itself on the water	254
106	The *duk-duk* lands on the beach	255
107	Skull masks from the Gazelle Peninsula	258
108	Painted piece of bark of the Baining	269
109	Various patterns of painted bark	271
110	Various patterns of painted bark	271
111	Various patterns of painted bark	271
112	Mask from Cape Orford	272
113	Mask from Cape Orford	273
114	Mask from Cape Orford	274
115	Mask from the circumcision ceremonies. 'Liebliche Inseln' and Möwehafen	276
116	Kneeling mask-wearer from the French Islands	277
117	*Tatanua* mask from New Ireland	278
118	Mask, New Ireland	279
119	Mask, New Ireland	279
120	*Matua* mask, front and side views	280
121	*Totok* or *kulibu* carving	281
122	Carving as a memorial to the dead	283
123	Stone figures from southern New Ireland	284
124	Mask from Bougainville	284
125	Mask from Nissan	285
126	Fragment of a map of the western hemisphere, by Th. de Bry (1596)	350
127	Part of a map by Witfliet (1597)	351
128	Part of a map by Herrera (1601)	352
129	Schouten and Le Maire's map	352
130	*De Eendracht*, Schouten and Le Maire's ship	352
131	Tasman's chart	353
132	*Heemskerk* and *Zeehaen*, Tasman's two ships	356
133	Natives of New Ireland	356
134	Facsimile of Tasman's log with his personal signature	358
135	William Dampier	359
136	Dampier's map	359
137	Facsimile of Dampier's coastal survey of New Britain	360
138	Dalrymple's map	363
139	Part of a map put together in 1785 for orientation of the Count de la Pérouse	363
140	L.C.D. Fleurieu's map (1790)	364
141	Admiralty Islanders	364

Plates

1	Gorge at Möwehafen	xxxviii
2	Robert Koch Spring on the Willaumez Peninsula	9
3	A group on the island of Aveleng	16
4	Men of the Arawa Islands	24
5	The laying out of a corpse. Gazelle Peninsula	31
6	Sinking fish baskets (*wup na tatakia*), Gazelle Peninsula	32
7	New Guinea type of canoe on the 'Lieblichen Inseln'	45
8	Clubs. Gazelle Peninsula	57
9	Baining women bearing loads	58
10	Sulka men in front of their huts; on the left is a rich harvest of taro tubers	67
11	Group of Sulka men	72
12	Group of women from the 'Liebliche Inseln'	79
13	Village scene at Nakanai	83
14	Youth from Unea (French Islands)	90
15	Village on the French Islands (Naraga)	100
16	Village scene on the 'Liebliche Inseln'	108
17	Girl from northern New Ireland	114

18	The house in which a young girl is incarcerated before marriage	123
19	Spears from St Matthias and Emirau	129
20	Dance sticks of the St Matthias women	136
21	Village scene on Squally Island	143
22	Pole village of the Moánus on Ndruval	150
23	Men's house in the village of the Matánkor on Lou	156
24	Moánus women from Lalobé with their children	163
25	Matánkor women of the island of Lou	171
26	Matánkor village on Lou	178
27	Men of the Moánus tribe from the village of Lalobé	184
28	Natives of the Matánkor tribe on the island of Lou	191
29	Village scene on Aua	196
30	Sailing canoe from the Hermit Islands	203
31	Outrigger of a canoe. Hermit Islands	210
32	Village scene at Ernst-Gunther-Hafen, northern Bougainville	216
33	Buka women	222
34	Village scene on Nissan	231
35	Shell money (*kuamanu*) from the island of Nissan. Various stages of preparation	238
36	Clubs from Buka and Bougainville	245
37	Village scene on Nukumanu	251
38	Women on Nukumanu	257
39	Group of men on Nukumanu	264
40	Artistically laid out taro garden on Nukumanu	270
41	Village scene on Tauu	278
42	The surviving population of the island of Tauu	285
43	The *tubuan* renders the last rites to the deceased	291
44	Dancers, representing spirits	297
45	The *mabucha* dance of the Baining	304
46	The *gifu* mask of the Sulka tribe	310
47	Dance at a circumcision ceremony. South coast of New Britain	317
48	Mask house on New Ireland	323
49	*Turu* carving from the Fischer Islands	331
50	Masked men from Lihir	339
51	*Matasesén* from northern Bougainville	345
52	Coconut plantation at Ralum	351
53	Grotto in raised coral rock on Mioko	358
54	Waterfall in the Karo valley. Baining	360
55	Forest path on the Gazelle Peninsula. Breadfruit and *canari* trees, bananas	365
56	HIMS *Möwe* in Peterhafen, French Islands	368

Maps

The Bismarck Archipelago	4
New Britain	20
New Ireland	112
The Admiralty Islands	166

Preface to the New Edition

The production of an electronic edition of this translation, ten years after its printed version, puts it within reach of anyone with an internet connection. This does not totally remove all barriers to access, but we hope that this free online version will now be available to many more descendants of the people whom Parkinson described.

We thank Sydney University Press and Agata Mrva-Montoya in particular for their help in creating this new version.

J. Peter White
26 January 2010

Editor's Preface

Of the considerable volume of German ethnographic reporting prior to World War I, Richard Parkinson's *Thirty Years in the South Seas* is probably the best known, despite the fact that it has never been fully translated into English. Originally published in 1907, the book now commands a very high price, and Parkinson's work is thus doubly inaccessible to the descendants of the people he described. Translating his work from the German has removed one of these barriers, but the publishers are unfortunately not in a position to remove the cost barrier altogether, although we have considerably reduced it.

In common with Sack and Cusack (1979:xiii), we would like to stress that '... a translation is always an interpretation ... it is essential to go back to the original if an argument turns on a particular word or phrase...'. As John Dennison makes clear, however, this translation tries to adhere as closely to the original as is possible while producing readable English.

We, like Sack and Cusack, have found that German geographic names were a major problem. In general, the names of larger places (for example, Neupommern: New Britain) have been put into English, while the smaller, many of which no longer exist as settlements with English names, have been retained in German. Readers seeking precise locations will find Scheps and Liedtke (1992) helpful, along with Sack and Cusack (1979). But, with the latter, '... we refuse responsibility for sorting out the mess of geographical names...' (1979:383).

In this translation we have retained the figure and plate numbering of the original publication.

Works such as this would be impossible without assistance from many people and organisations. In this case our major acknowledgment must be to John Dennison, who has laboured over the translation for more than five years, and who has been a pleasure to work with throughout. His generosity in undertaking this enormous translation has few parallels. Three others must also be especially thanked: Ann Dennison, who proofread the original translation for its phrasing and spelling; Marta Towe, who checked the entire translation; and Andrew Wilson, who undertook the original formatting of the entire volume. In the spirit of noting that what may seem a small favour to the giver can solve a major problem for the recipient, we thank, in no particular order, Rob Welsch, Robin Torrence, Margaret Clunies Ross, John Clifton-Everest, Mike Gunn, Wulf Schiefenhovel, Deirdre Koller, and the Computer Access Section of Fisher Library.

The project has been partly financed by Oceania Publications, University of Sydney.

J. Peter White
30 November 1998

References

Sack, P., and Cusack, D. 1979. *German New Guinea: The Annual Reports*. Australian National University Press, Canberra.

Scheps, B., and Liedtke, W. 1992. *Bibliography of German Colonial Literature for References of Ethnology and History of the Populations of Kaiser Wilhelms Land, the Bismarck Archipelago and the German Solomon Islands 1880-1914, Annotated*. Staatliches Museum fur Volkerkunde, Dresden.

Translator's Preface

The 1907 edition of Parkinson's *Dreißig Jahre in der Südsee* was described in C. R. H. Taylor's *A Pacific Bibliography* (1965) as magnificent.

I started translation of it early in 1982, but translation halted abruptly upon receiving a telex and a following letter from Peter White telling me that a publication of a translation of this 876-page work was imminent. No further action was taken until, in 1991, a chance comment by a colleague engaged in the Lapita Homelands Project jogged my memory.

I contacted Peter, and learned that nothing further had been heard of the other translation. I resumed my task, with the assistance of much-improved word-processing technology – the final draft of these 876 pages plus supplementary text travelled to Sydney on two 1.3 MB diskettes (it was felt that direct line transmission of such a valuable text was too risky).

This translation project has taken a long time, being interleaved with the other projects and duties of a physical anthropologist and teacher, as well as those of a professional translator. Translation is never an easy task, because you are very aware that you are interpreting the thoughts of someone else, in this instance, of someone who arrived on New Britain more than 100 years ago, in 1882. Allowance must be made for changes in the meaning, and therefore translation, of words over time, and so I used the earliest dictionary that I could find, published in 1945. I have retained the text form and have tried to preserve the style of the author. Where place names were German borrowings of English names, I have used the original English form. Otherwise I have preserved Parkinson's spellings of place names (while comparing them with the versions given in the *Pacific Islands Pilot*), as these have historical significance in their own right.

Many long hours were spent on this work. I cannot express gratitude enough to my wife, Ann, who gave up her husband to a computer terminal, and then painstakingly reviewed his draft translation, turning it into readable English. Ann, and our daughter Sarah, endured much while I laboured. I am most grateful to J. Peter White, who gave me the opportunity to carry out this task, waited patiently while I drip-fed him diskettes, and then meticulously amended the drafts, before passing them to Marta Towe, who painstakingly checked the accuracy of the translation. I am also grateful to the staff of the University of Otago Geography Department, which gave me access to maps of the region, to aid my understanding. I thank you all for your support.

To the readers of this translation, Richard Parkinson has left us a legacy in his writing. I hope you enjoy reading his words as much as I have enjoyed translating them. I wish you well in your research.

K. J. Dennison
Dunedin, December 1997

References

Army Air Forces. March 1944. *Bismarck Archipelago, New Britain*. Chart No. 58. 1st ed. S400–E15145–50/55. Reproduced by 955th Engr. Topo. Co., 4th Photo Gp. RCN.

Breul, K. 1945. *Cassell's German and English Dictionary*. 5th ed. Cassell and Company Limited, London.

Division of National Mapping. 1969. *Territory of Papua and New Guinea*. Map 9202. NMP/65/138. Department of National Development, Canberra.

Hydrographic Department. 1908. *Pacific Islands Pilot*. Vol. 1, 4th ed. His Majesty's Stationery Office, London.

———. 1943. *Pacific Islands Pilot*. Vol. 2, 7th ed. His Majesty's Stationery Office, London.

———. 1971. *Pacific Islands Pilot*. Vol. 1, 9th ed. Her Majesty's Stationery Office, London.

'The German Professor': Richard Parkinson

Ninety years after its first appearance, Richard Parkinson's classic work *Dreißig Jahre in der Südsee* (1907a) now enters its fourth phase.[1] First published in 1907, it went through an abbreviated reissue in 1926, which was subsequently translated into English (Parkinson n.d.); and now an English translation of the original version is finally available. The book, however, is only part of a bigger story about an unusual man in an unusual time and place. Unlike Nikolai Mikloucho-Maclay, who has had several biographers and many commentators (for example, Greenop 1944; Sentinella 1974; Webster 1984), little has been published about Parkinson. Obtaining reliable facts about some aspects of his early years is surprisingly difficult; even the date of his death is frequently misquoted. There are times when he seems a shadow, and at other times he appears as a person of substance. He was already halfway through his life when he arrived in the Pacific Islands, yet we know little about his years before that time. Even his life in the Pacific was overshadowed by other people and events, and rarely does he emerge as a fully developed character in his own right. This essay is a preliminary and incomplete introduction to the man, and to the people and events surrounding him during his time in the Bismarck Archipelago between 1882 and 1909.[2]

Richard Heinrich Robert Parkinson wrote in German and is usually considered to have been of German origin. He was born on 13 November 1844 in the Duchy of Schleswig, which was then and is now in Denmark. His nationality was questioned in later years when Germany laid claim to the Bismarck Archipelago, in what is now Papua New Guinea. In part this was because throughout the 19th century the Duchy of Schleswig alternated between Danish and Prussian (later German) control, and its position was not finally settled until 1920, when the Danish affiliation of Northern Schleswig was settled by referendum following the Treaty of Versailles. Following Germany's establishment of its Pacific Islands colonies in the late 19th century, Parkinson was officially recognised by the colonial authorities as being German (Richard Parkinson (RP) to G.R. Le Hunte, 20 March 1886, ML CYA 3141).

Parkinson's biological father is generally regarded as having been the Duke of Augustenborg, on the island of Als. His mother was Louise Sophie Caroline Brüning, daughter of a local shoemaker and a lady-in-waiting to the duke's wife. Rather than have to admit to the illegitimate child, the duke is said to have forced the English-born manager of his horse stud, Richard Parkinson, to marry Louise. Parkinson senior did so, but immediately moved on, possibly encouraged by the duke. In due course, the duke took an interest in the upbringing of the young Richard (Mead 1964:183), who attended school in Augustenborg Castle.

Parkinson may have attended a university or received other formal tertiary training. He taught English in Heligoland (Mead 1964:191), and at some stage met Johann S. Kubary, who worked in the Caroline Islands 'as a collector and naturalist' (Sack and Clark 1983:94) for the German trading and plantation company Godeffroy und Sohn, which had its own museum and publication series (Schmeltz and Krause 1881). The meeting with Kubary changed Parkinson's life, because he applied for employment with the company, and was accepted as a plantation manager and surveyor in Samoa. Just when and where he acquired surveying skills is not known, but they proved invaluable later when he moved with his wife, Phebe, to New Britain. Perhaps it was before meeting Kubary that Parkinson visited Africa (Mead 1964:191), but there are no details about when, where or what he did there.

Parkinson arrived in Samoa in 1876 (Andree 1901:239; Thiel 1909:113; Anon. 1909:211). He encountered what can best be described as a colourful scene of political intrigue between Germans, Americans, Samoans and others. (Robson (1965) provides a popular account of the time; Kennedy (1974) provides a more academic view.) Parkinson's work exposed him to the Polynesian Samoans and the indentured plantation labourers from Melanesia (Andree 1901:239; Thiel 1909:114; cf. Meleisea 1980). He became involved with the local political and social scenes, and in 1879 married Phebe Clotilda Coe, daughter

---

1. All in-text references to Parkinson's publications refer to the list of his publications that precedes the main references.

2. This account of Parkinson's life is based on several sources, particularly letters from Arthur Vaag of Mandø, Denmark, to R.W. Robson in Sydney, dated 24 September and 24 October 1968; and six letters between Christopher Legge, at the Field Museum of Natural History, Chicago, and Robert Langdon in Canberra from 26 February to 14 April 1970. Vaag published an account of Parkinson's early life based on the information in these letters in *Sønderjysk Manedsskrift* no. 4, 1971, which is cited by Robson (1973:169; 1979:236) but which I have not seen. An English summary of Vaag's story can be found in *Pacific Islands Monthly*, January 1972. The biographical details contained in Margaret Mead's interview with

of Jonas Coe and sister to Emma Coe, later known in New Britain as 'Queen Emma'. At that time, Parkinson was thirty-six years old, and Phebe only sixteen.

In 1879, Emma (now Forsayth) and her lover-cum-business partner, Thomas Farrell, moved to Mioko, in the Duke of York Islands, between New Britain and New Ireland in the Bismarck Archipelago, to recruit labour and trade throughout the islands (Robson 1965:95-8). The area at that time had few European settlers, though survivors from the ill-fated Nouvelle France project of the Marquis de Rays on New Ireland were soon to increase the white population (Niaux 1936). The first trader had tried to set up business at Port Hunter in the Duke of York Islands in 1872, and in 1873 two traders moved on to Matupit Island and the New Britain mainland, but were soon driven out by the local people (Corris 1973:xxv-xxvi, 286). In 1875, George Brown arrived to establish the first missionary station, at Port Hunter on the main Duke of York Island (Brown 1908:88), and later in the same year Eduard Hernsheim visited Brown and began a trading station near his mission (Sack and Clark 1983:29-30). It was logical for Emma and Farrell to set up business near these two; Emma had known George Brown well during his time in Samoa (Robson 1965:100), and, no doubt, there was safety in numbers. The main items sought by trade with the islanders were coconuts for processing into copra. At that time the trade depended heavily on village people being willing to collect and process the coconuts. This did not provide as regular or reliable a supply as the traders needed, and it became obvious to Emma and Farrell that the best way to develop the business was to establish their own coconut plantations, along the lines of those in Samoa. Accordingly, they set up the Western Pacific Plantation and Trading Company, which was registered in Sydney (Finsch 1888:22).

Parkinson resigned from the Godeffroy company around 1880-81 after an altercation with one of the company's principals in Samoa (Robson 1965:117). Emma invited him and Phebe to join her and Farrell in the Duke of York Islands, which they did in late 1882. Emma gave Parkinson responsibility for setting up the first of her plantations on the mainland of New Britain. After a reconnaissance along the coast of the Gazelle Peninsula on New Britain, he selected an area at Ralum, on the south side of Blanche Bay, and set up the first coconut plantation in the New Guinea area (Robson 1965:117, 125). In April 1883, Hernsheim, now based on Matupit Island, near present-day Rabaul, offered the wry comment: 'Parkinson plantation: maize, cotton, very small beginnings; land too dry' (Sack and Clark 1983:148). Later that month, Farrell and Parkinson visited Hernsheim, and Farrell told him that they would stop trading and concentrate on developing plantations.

At this time, Hernsheim had a cool relationship with Parkinson, and a poor one with Emma and Farrell (Sack and Clark 1983:155, 157), probably because he perceived their trading and recruiting activities as threats to his business (Firth 1979). These poor relationships and Parkinson's ancestry came to the surface in May 1884, when Emma and Parkinson discussed with Hernsheim, then acting as German consul, their plans for recruiting men to work on the plantations. Farrell could not get a recruiting licence in Sydney, and so Emma wanted to transfer the registration of her ship *Bella Brandon* to Parkinson, under the German flag. Hernsheim's diary comments: 'naturally refuse, as Parkinson's nationality is not known to me'. This was probably as much due to Hernsheim's dislike for Farrell as it was against Parkinson, for later that year the animosity between Hernsheim and Parkinson was resolved (Sack and Clark 1983:178). Parkinson subsequently acknowledged Hernsheim in his foreword to *Dreißig Jahre*, where he thanked Hernsheim for providing him with many opportunities to travel and learn about many peoples and places (Parkinson 1907a:xvii).

The small European community in the Duke of York Islands and on New Britain was slowly increasing in numbers (Schnee (1904:353) records that in 1883 the white population was only thirty persons; by 1894 this had risen to 112). The community was a mixed bag of people of different backgrounds and nationalities, with little cohesion and often with conflicting interests, but was a busy centre for visiting vessels – especially government and naval vessels. Among these was Otto Finsch on the Samoa (Finsch 1888), who was visiting various parts of the western Pacific to buy land for possible coaling stations for the German navy while collecting artifacts (Parkinson was later quite scathing in his criticism of Finsch's anthropological work; see Tschauder and Swadling 1979:36-7). Hugh Romilly, the British deputy high commissioner for the western Pacific, made several official visits to the archipelago from 1881 onwards (Romilly 1886). These visits by Finsch and Romilly were part of the international political manoeuvring in the Pacific at that time, as Britain and Germany vied with each other for control of the various island groups. The German government declared a protectorate over the archipelago in November 1884.

The German takeover of the archipelago once more brought to the surface the question of Parkinson's nationality. In March 1886, Parkinson wrote to G. Ruthven Le Hunte, the administrator of British New Guinea, who had visited the Parkinsons, that:

> Since we became Germanised the authorities all at once claim me as a German subject. A few years ago there was a great blarney about my German citizenship ... all at once they inform me that I am a real good German subject

---

Parkinson's widow, Phebe, in 1929 are an invaluable source of information not otherwise available. Other details are derived from Robson's (1965) account of Queen Emma, Phebe's sister, though Robson rarely indicates the sources of his information. Dutton (1976) presents a less factual version of Emma and her associates. Other biographical information is drawn from letters between Parkinson and the Field Columbian Museum (later the Field Museum of Natural History), Chicago, and the Australian Museum, Sydney; from a letter from Richard Parkinson to G.R. Le Hunte in the Mitchell Library, State Library of NSW; and from Richard Andree's (1901) appreciation of Parkinson. More sources, undoubtedly, remain to be revealed; I have not been able, for example, to consult the article 'Erinnerungen an den alten Parkinson' in *Kolonie und Heimat* (1908-09, 26:11-15).

and citizen and that as such I am entitled to hold office in this new Government ... This is because I am the only one that at present really knows anything about the country and they think they can make use of me. [RP to G.R. Le Hunte, 20 March 1886, ML CYA 3141; quoted in full in Dutton 1976]

Early in 1884 the Parkinsons had moved into a new home at Malapau near Ralum on the New Britain mainland, where they raised their family until their move to nearby Kuradui in 1907 (see an undated photograph in Moore et al. 1984:26). Richard began in earnest to develop the plantation side of Emma's business, as well as his own plantations, particularly trying potential new crops. He had already introduced tobacco from Samoa in 1883, and the Tolai people quickly accepted it into their gardening practices (Salisbury 1970:111). By 1884 he was planning to bring in coffee, and later cocoa as well. Despite Hernsheim's comment recorded in 1883, Parkinson stated in his letter to Le Hunte quoted above:

I have around 210 acres under cotton and coconuts each, 30 acres planted with various plants on trial; 5 acres under Coffee, 5 acres under Rice, 10 acres under Millet ... and 10 acres as general botanical garden with all sorts of knick-knacks. [RP to Le Hunte, 20 March 1886, ML CYA 3141]

By 1896 the plantations had about 1200 acres under cotton and 1600 acres under coconuts (Salisbury 1970:80). Parkinson was also interested in experimenting with introduced animals. According to Robson (1965:165), he was responsible for introducing horses, donkeys, cattle (including the Brahman variety), sheep, goats, pigs and poultry (perhaps to improve the local strains), as well as various grasses to grow fodder for them.

Kubary, who had inspired Parkinson to leave Europe and take up a life in the Pacific, arrived on Matupit in late 1885 or early 1886 to work for Hernsheim, and renewed his friendship with Parkinson (Sack and Clark 1983:94, 108). After a period with Hernsheim, Kubary joined the Deutsch Neu Guinea Compagnie, which managed the colony on behalf of the German government (Sack and Clark 1979:6). In 1890, Parkinson had a disagreement with Emma about the amount of time he spent on collecting natural-history specimens and on ethnological studies instead of concentrating on his plantation work. Parkinson left E.E. Forsayth & Co., the company formed by Emma after Farrell's death in 1887, and joined Kubary in the Deutsch Neu Guinea Compagnie, as a surveyor and collector (Anon. 1890:49; Sack and Clark 1983:108). Phebe took over his role in running the plantations (Robson 1965:168).

The work with the Deutsch Neu Guinea Compagnie provided Parkinson with many opportunities to travel and collect artifacts and information in the Bismarck Archipelago. He also travelled to India and Europe in 1893 (Mead 1964:200), and it was possibly in connection with his employment in the company that he arranged for six Tolai dancers to go to the Colonial Exhibition of 1896 in Berlin (Salisbury 1970:34). But the company did not prosper and in 1900 Parkinson rejoined Emma after the German government took over management of the colony.

It was about this time that Parkinson had a serious illness or accident (Australian Museum Archives AMS6 852/1899), the effects of which remained with him for the rest of his life. In an interview with Mead (1964:193), Phebe referred to his 'lingering illness', which severely affected his work for about a decade: 'it was not malaria but something internal', she said. Parkinson now spent much time on ships, recruiting for Emma's plantations and collecting ethnographical items for museums in Australia, USA and Europe. He accompanied Acting Governor Hahl to the Caroline Islands in 1901 to recuperate and 'to add to his collections and to his ethnological knowledge' (Sack and Clark 1980:80).

Parkinson maintained a long and friendly correspondence with the Australian Museum between 1884 and 1904. He borrowed books from the museum, provided natural-history and artifact collections, and exchanged information with the curator, Edward Ramsay, and his successor, Robert Etheridge Jr. He was also in contact with Charles Hedley, a zoologist at the museum, who, like Parkinson, had broad interests including ethnology. Hedley was clearly impressed by Parkinson, and in 1904 proposed him as president of the Ethnographical Section at the Dunedin meeting of the Australasian Association of Science. Parkinson declined, because he would be in the Caroline Islands at that time, but he told Etheridge that he would be very happy to accept such an invitation if a meeting of the association were to be held in Australia (Australian Museum Archives, AMS9 P33/1903). The opportunity, however, did not arise again.

The correspondence with the Australian Museum ended soon after this, though why is not known. Parkinson's last letter to Etheridge appears to be that dated 20 December 1903, and in it he states, 'I am only to glad' [sic] to help Etheridge with information about the Tolai *iniet* society (Australian Museum Archives, AMS9 P3/1904). Whatever had happened terminated the contact between the Australian Museum and Parkinson. Etheridge did not even know about Parkinson's death in 1909, and wrote to him in 1912, receiving the news in a polite and helpful reply from Phebe (Australian Museum Archives, AMS9 P34/1912).

Parkinson's link with the Field Columbian Museum in Chicago began in 1898 with a sale of fifty-two human skulls. It was renewed in 1905 through an intermediary, Bryan Lathrap of York Harbor, Maine.

Lathrap wrote to F.V. Skiff, the museum director, after a conversation with Linzee Tilden about 'an English merchant' in the Pacific who wanted to sell his private collection of artifacts so that he could retire. The asking price was US$3,500, and Lathrap enclosed a catalogue of it, which was to be returned to Tilden (Lathrap to Skiff, 5 September 1905). Skiff contacted Tilden who told Skiff (25 October 1905) that he had met Parkinson and seen his collection during a visit to New Britain in the northern spring of 1905:

> The owner and collector feels he is getting old, and is desirous of clearing up such impedimenta as might cause annoyance to his family, or work for his executor in case he should die, or be free to move to Sydney to live on account of his children.

George Dorsey, chief curator of Anthropology at the Field Columbian Museum, strongly recommended purchase, but Skiff wanted the collection to be inspected first. Parkinson declined to send it to Chicago 'on refusal', but sent photographs of selected items and assured Skiff that each item was well-identified to village and function (RP to Skiff, 20 February 1906). The correspondence dragged on, with Parkinson complaining about the lack of response from Chicago (RP to Skiff, 31 August 1906). Skiff eventually replied (14 November 1906) that he wanted to buy the collection, but insisted that the collection first be sent to Chicago for inspection. The matter was finally resolved by Dorsey arranging to visit Parkinson in New Britain. Parkinson welcomed this suggestion, adding that after the end of 1907, he would 'have a good deal of time to spend in travelling' and he could buy artifacts on behalf of the Field Museum of Natural History (as it had been renamed in November 1905) (RP to Dorsey, 14 November 1906). This reference to 'a good deal of time' referred to Emma's plans to sell her New Britain interests and move to Sydney, which she did in 1907 (Robson 1965:222).

Parkinson finally gave in to Skiff and sent eight cases of artifacts and one of human skulls to Chicago. He did not send everything, retaining in New Britain enough artifacts to fill at least another four large cases (RP to Fisk, 2 July 1907). Parkinson added that he would write a separate letter with a proposal to act as a buyer for the museum, since 'many things that today are placed on the marked [sic] are made for sale by the natives and are in fact valueless'.

Dorsey inspected the items sent to Chicago and recommended that the museum acquire them, but only after he had inspected the items retained by Parkinson. Dorsey arrived in New Britain around mid-1908, and wrote to Skiff (7 August 1908) to confirm his recommendation for acquisition. He added that at this time the Hamburg Wissenschaftliche Stiftung's Südsee Expedition was in the Bismarck Archipelago, and its leader, Dr Friedrich Fülleborn, told Dorsey that they would have bought the entire collection at once. The sale to the Field Museum, however, caused bad feeling among some of the Hamburg group, which considered the price paid by the museum to be extremely low compared to the prices that they had to pay for artifacts, while the fact that the collection had gone to the USA, and not Germany, aroused patriotic passions (Fischer 1981:117). Fischer notes particularly that Wilhelm Müller, the physical anthropologist on the Südsee Expedition, complained that Dorsey left after only a few weeks with at least 10,000 artifacts, whereas the expedition with its ten scholars and two years in the western Pacific went home with far fewer items.

After Dorsey returned to Chicago, Parkinson's health deteriorated. He wrote to Dorsey (27 October 1908) that Dr Fülleborn 'stepped in and undertook an operation which seems to have been of great benefit. I am still as limp as an old towel …'. Parkinson had another four or five cases of artifacts to send to Chicago, and would pack them 'as soon as I feel my leg serviceable'. An undated photograph of the Parkinson family shows Richard sitting on a *chaise longue* with his right leg extended, though there is no indication from Parkinson, Phebe or Dorsey which leg was causing him trouble (Moore et al. 1984:26).

Parkinson obviously formed a good opinion of Dorsey, and his subsequent letters to him display an intimacy missing from his earlier correspondence with Ramsay, Etheridge and Skiff. He expressed pleasure at hearing that Dorsey had 'made a good harvest during your trip' to German New Guinea. He appears to have been less impressed, however, by the two Hamburg expeditions then in the Bismarck Archipelago and along the north coast of New Guinea. The Südsee Expedition, first under Fülleborn and then Augustin Krämer, lasted for two years. It had a steam vessel, the *Peiho*, at its disposal; no fewer than ten scientists with skills in ethnology, zoology, physical anthropology, and linguistics; funding of 600,000 Marks; and specific aims to collect for the Hamburg Museum für Völkerkunde (Fischer 1981). The Deutsche Marine Expedition, from Hamburg and initially under Stefan and, following Stefan's death, Krämer (Sack and Clark 1979:294), was also in the Bismarck Archipelago at that time. The resources of these two expeditions were no doubt a richness to be envied by Parkinson, who had by this time spent twenty-six years trying to fit his ethnographic studies in between his work responsibilities.

There is little evidence of much professional contact between Parkinson and the expeditioners, other than the use of Fülleborn's services as a surgeon. At least one of the expeditioners on the Südsee Expedition was known to Parkinson: Franz Hellwig had been a trader in the islands, and had worked for several trading companies, including E.E. Forsayth & Co. and Hernsheim & Co. (Fischer 1981:71; cf. Parkinson 1907a:414). Parkinson may have been disappointed about not being included in the Bismarck Archipelago section of the expeditions, though his own poor health would have prevented this. Similarly, it is not clear what contact Parkinson had with Richard Thurnwald, who spent two years in the colony, including some time at Herbertshöhe (Pullen-Burry 1909:48-9, 51, 134-7; Sack and Clark 1979:295; cf. Thurnwald 1910). Thurnwald also spent time in the Vunakokor-Toma-Paparatava areas inland from Ralum, where he collected 741 stone *iniet* figures for the Berlin museum (Koch 1982:28). One wonders whether there was any jealousy or animosity between Thurnwald the professional ethnographer and Parkinson the planter and amateur ethnographer.

The days of the amateur were under threat, as professionals such as Thurnwald, Albert Buell Lewis, and the members of the Hamburg expeditions and others moved into the field.[3] Parkinson may have been spurned by some of them, for he told Dorsey (27 October 1908), perhaps with a touch of bitterness, that, 'The Hamburgers have had all kinds of troubles that would not have occurred to you or to me but to them seemed to be great obstacles.' Parkinson then proceeded to list health problems encountered by the naval expedition. Schlaginhaufen and his ethnographers 'have had 3 weeks in hospital', and Krämer was soon to arrive to replace Stefan. In a rather sardonic touch of humour, he added:

> Sapper gone home. I am afraid that if he had stopped here a month longer he would have been quite mummified. He was a regular wandering skeleton and could without any fear have gone into the worst cannibal country.

But Parkinson had to stop writing the letter, because 'writing troubles me more than I had expected'.

During his visit to Parkinson, Dorsey had organised for him to act as a collector for the Field Museum. Dorsey requested (22 December 1908) 'big collections representative of every phase of culture from the important localities in your territory'. He later advised Parkinson (13 January 1909) that US$3,000 had been appropriated for Parkinson to collect for the museum. Dorsey specified items from the Roviana group in the Solomon Islands, stone figures from southern New Ireland, *malagan* carvings from the Tabar Islands to the east of New Ireland, masks from the south coast of New Britain and, from the Gazelle Peninsula of New Britain, *duk-duk* masks of the Tolai, and various items from the Baining. Even before Dorsey's letter reached Parkinson, Parkinson's illness was worsening (RP to Dorsey, 3 February 1909):

> I got a very bad relapse of my illness and was unable to write or to do anything at all. The last lot [of artifacts] Mrs Parkinson managed to get away; none of these things are labelled but as most of them are dublicates [sic] you will find your way through ... In consequence of the relapse, I had suffered very severe pain and the Doctor [Fülleborn?] has performed one more operation. I am therefore still prostrate in bed and helpless as a log of wood. What is still worse is that when I ever get over my illness which I begin to doubt very much, I shall be a cripple for the rest of my life.

Parkinson was obviously not going to do much collecting for the museum, and so he returned an advance that Dorsey had given him. However, he was willing to provide whatever help he could to anyone whom Dorsey might send out to collect. Because of the illness, Parkinson advised Dorsey not to 'send the Kodak and the films, as they will be of no use now to me'. After complaining that he had not yet received payment for the large collection sold to the museum, Parkinson noted that a recent government expedition up the Sepik River reached only 240 miles from the mouth, '40 miles less than I and a party reached in 1887'. Worse still in Parkinson's eyes, no collections were made because of 'a gentleman on board being otherwise occupied during the trip'. The letter ends on a note of despair. His daughter was writing the letter for him, but, he said, 'even dictation irritates my nerves, and I feel, that I have to break off any communication ... All my life I have been accustomed to activity. I am now reduced to utter helplessness.'

Parkinson hoped to get better, or experience 'the great ending up of all our human troubles'. Dorsey replied (12 April 1909), regretting Parkinson's illness and forced withdrawal as a collector. He sought Parkinson's assistance for A.B. Lewis, who was about to undertake a major collecting trip to German New Guinea for the Field Museum. The good news from Dorsey was that the payment for Parkinson's collection was on its way. Parkinson's patience must have been sorely tried, however, for barely one month later Skiff wrote to him (11 May 1909) that 'at this time the Museum has no funds from which an appropriation can be made for the purchase of your collection'. This meant that Parkinson was now free to offer the collection to anyone else, but he would still have to pay US$110.74 for the freight bill to Chicago. The non-payment put Parkinson in a difficult situation, but despite this and the troubles with his illness, he was still trying to obtain artifacts for the museum. He ordered *tumbuan* and *duk-duk* masks at 50 Marks each, and had

> also entered a contract with a trader at Lagunabange, New Ireland, who will deliver to me all what he can get at the next Malagene. This place is at present the one in which the old carving tradition is best preserved ... I hope to get about 200 specimens together, all in good order, and without much European material.

3. Klaus Neumann rightly reminds me (*in litt*. 6 January 1998) that the missionary contributions continued well beyond the takeover of New Guinea by Australia. In many respects, their writings may be more accurate, since most learned their local languages and were thus able to discuss matters directly with the local peoples, rather than through a third language such as pidgin English.

Parkinson, however, was still bedridden, though 'fortunately the pain has lately been less, but I cannot do without morphine' (RP to Dorsey, 14 May 1909). Eventually the museum sent the cheque for US$3,500 (less part of the freight bill) on 14 July 1909, nearly four years after the collection had first been offered. The long-awaited cheque arrived too late. Parkinson died in Hebertshöhe hospital on 24 July 1909 (Thiel 1909:113).[4]

The Collector

Both Richard and Phebe Parkinson were heavily involved in collecting all kinds of natural-history specimens – land snails, insects, butterflies, mammals, birds, frogs, marine molluscs, plants – as well as artifacts. He was well-known overseas for natural-history collections, and visiting scientists often stayed with the Parkinsons. Yet his interests were focused firmly on the human side.

According to Phebe, Parkinson was less interested in the money that might be gained from selling specimens than in the new knowledge that they might contribute to science (Mead 1964:199). Consequently, he sent many items to museums as gifts or for exchanges (Mead 1964:201). His duties with the Deutsch Neu Guinea Compagnie included collecting artifacts, presumably to enhance German museums. Interestingly, whereas Parkinson occasionally remarks in *Dreißig Jahre* about artifacts that he obtained for the German museums, there is no mention of the Australian Museum. The sale of his personal collection to the Field Museum of Natural History took place after the book was published, and one of the features of the collection that attracted Dorsey was that many items were illustrated in the book (Dorsey to Skiff, 7 August 1908). Some of those illustrated, however, were in mission collections, and in the 1970s the Hiltrup Museum of the Mission of the Sacred Heart sold several of the bark cloths illustrated.

Between 1882 and 1909, Farrell (died 1887), Parkinson (died 1909) and Emma (died 1913) sold or donated thousands of artifacts to the Australian Museum, the Field Museum, and museums in Dresden, Stuttgart, Berlin and elsewhere in Germany (the precise number of artifacts is not known, but must have exceeded 10,000). It is no wonder that artifacts from the Bismarck Archipelago soon became scarce and expensive. Even so, Emma, now Mrs Kolbe, could write to the Australian Museum in 1897 (Australian Museum Archives, AMS9 K9/1897) that: 'A German Proffessor [sic] named Dahl left us last steamer with a tremendous assortment of specimens of all kinds – he was a government official.'

When the Parkinsons reached the Duke of York Islands in 1882, Farrell and Emma were already exploiting the trade in artifacts. Emma, as Mrs Farrell, sold a collection of 250 items to the Australian Museum in 1881 (Australian Museum Archives, AMS7 C:10:81:10). Farrell himself was a partner in the Sydney trading company Mason Bros, which included artifacts among its wares (Langdon 1968:5). It was to this company that the Australian Museum turned in 1883 to help re-build its Pacific Islands collections after the Garden Palace fire of 1882 destroyed virtually the entire artifact collection of the museum (Specht 1980; Bolton et al. 1979).

At the beginning of January 1884, Farrell wrote to Ramsay, curator of the Australian Museum, advising him that 'Mr Parkinson is now fairly settled' (at Ralum), and that from now on any collections that Farrell sent would be jointly with Parkinson (Australian Museum Archives, AMS8 55/84). This meant that henceforth the museum should keep its payment to them separate from the funds paid to Farrell for an 1882 transaction. In the meantime, Parkinson had a collection of birds' eggs and nests for the museum, but did not yet have the birds. Farrell asked the museum to send equipment to help their collecting; specifically, he wanted small and large collecting jars, preserving fluid, 4 pounds of naphthalene or camphor, and boxes for butterflies and paper for spreading them. The museum met his request, with slight modifications.

Parkinson's contact with the Australian Museum appears to have begun in middle 1884 (Australian Museum Archives, AMS8 224/1884), when he advised Ramsay that a consignment of zoological and ethnological specimens was on its way to Sydney. Whereas the zoological specimens were in exchange for a book, the museum paid Farrell and Parkinson £19 11s for artifacts from Manus, New Ireland and New Britain (Australian Museum Archives, AMS55 29/1884).

In April 1889, Parkinson wrote to the museum advising that he had despatched a consignment of human skulls from the Ralum area to Sydney (Australian Museum Archives, AMS9 P13/1889). The skulls were not received until November 1890 because the ship on which they were consigned had been re-routed to Java (Australian Museum Archives, AMS9 P21/1890). Ramsay wanted more human remains, especially complete skeletons, for Parkinson advised him that:

> If it is worthwhile I will take the trouble to procure some. But if it is not I do not like to grope about for Native bones which is not very interesting and as a rule not without great danger. One has to do such work oneself, else the skeletons are not complete.

4. Although Robson correctly cites Parkinson's date of death on the caption of Parkinson's portrait (1965: opp. page 160), which is taken from the 1926 edition of *Dreißig Jahre*, his text places it in the wrong year, 1907. Other authors have followed Robson (for example, West 1972:890), and Salisbury (1970:39) sets the date prior to the publication of *Dreißig Jahre*. The cause of Parkinson's death is not clear, and Parkinson's letters to Dorsey do not identify the nature of his leg problem.

To this Ramsay replied that he wanted skeletons 'as fresh as possible so that the bones can be whitened. Any history concerning the individuals, their names, tribe, etc will render them more acceptable' (Australian Museum Archives, AMS6 946/1890). Ramsay further asked him to keep sinews on the hands and feet to prevent 'small bones going astray', and to keep the scalp and hair on the skull. Given the freshness of the remains that these conditions would require, it is hardly surprising that Parkinson considered there to be 'great danger' in acquiring skeletons. For this danger, Ramsay offered Parkinson between £5 and £10 for each male and female pair in good, unstained condition. This was a good price, but Parkinson did not take up Ramsay's offer.

Parkinson's involvement with human remains continued. Following the opening of negotiations in 1905 for Parkinson to sell his personal collection of artifacts to the museum, Dorsey wrote to him (11 November 1905) asking about the availability of human skulls and skeletons. Parkinson replied (19 February 1906) that skulls from the Gazelle Peninsula could be obtained 'without delay', and he could probably send fifty skulls from other areas 'within three or four months' (Parkinson (1907a:593-5) noted how easy it was to obtain human skulls). The Gazelle skulls would cost US$2.50 each, but those from other areas would be more expensive, as they would be harder to get. Complete skeletons could be difficult to obtain, 'as natives could not be trusted with the collecting and a skilled white man would have to be employed [sic]'. Dorsey strongly recommended (19 April 1906) to his director, F.V. Skiff, that they accept Parkinson's offer, and for an unlimited number:

> it is only a question of a few years when the skulls of Melanesians can be obtained only at a great price, if at all ... we could easily use to great advantage as many thousand skulls as he could send at that price.

Even Parkinson could not fill such an order, but advised Dorsey (14 November 1906) that he had a case of seventy-five skulls waiting for his visit to New Britain.[5]

As far as artifacts were concerned, Parkinson appears to have acquired them in various ways, though it is usually difficult or impossible to identify how a particular item was obtained. Some he acquired himself while on his travels. In 1901 he accompanied Acting Governor Hahl on a visit to Pohnpei (Ponape) to recuperate from an unspecified problem and 'to add to his collections and knowledge' (Sack and Clark 1980:80). On the Gazelle Peninsula and in New Ireland, he might wait until there was a major ceremony, after which he would attempt to acquire, either himself or through one of the E.E. Forsayth & Co. or Deutsch Neu Guinea Compagnie agents, the masks and other ceremonial items. Etheridge, however, had to wait for a pair of Tolai *duk-duk* masks. Parkinson initially expected to get them in mid-1903, but was still waiting at the end of the year (Australian Museum Archives, AMS9 P21/1903; AMS9 P43/1903).

In *Dreißig Jahre*, Parkinson describes (1907a:635) how in early 1901 an E.E. Forsayth & Co. schooner brought a large collection of masks from the Sulka area on the south coast of New Britain. Parkinson does not provide any information on how the schooner came to have such a cargo; one can only assume that there had been a major ceremony. Parkinson appears to have depended on local people to bring him specific zoological specimens (Australian Museum Archives, AMS9 P39/1900), though whether he requested them to make specific kinds of artifacts is uncertain.

Examination of some Parkinson items in the Australian Museum suggests another possible way that he obtained artifacts. In his foreword to *Dreißig Jahre*, Parkinson stated (1907a:xv) that having workers from many different parts of the archipelago and the north Solomons provided opportunities for him to expand and improve his knowledge of their cultures. Among these workers were up to 150 men from Buka Island, an island that appears unusually well-represented in the collections the Australian Museum purchased from him and Farrell. There are more than 300 dance wands and paddles, some of which appear to be unfinished. Spiegel (1967:35) thought that these had a special sepia staining, but their surfaces display charring, possibly to facilitate carving. It seems unusual that Parkinson and Farrell should have purchased items in such an unfinished state on Buka, and it is possible that they were made by some of Parkinson's men at Ralum. Would it be going too far to suggest that Farrell or Parkinson commissioned these men to make them, and then sent them to Sydney without explanation? In this context, it is worth recalling the comments by Farrell, Parkinson and others on the increasing scarcity of artifacts from about 1884 onwards, and yet they were still able to collect thousands for museums around the world. Parkinson assured Skiff (20 February 1906), many years later, that 'I have always collected choice and perfect specimens, a great many of which at the present time are obsolete and extremely rare in ethnological collections'.

Did he keep the best for himself, and occasionally send to some museums not so much the second best, but items which he commissioned especially for them?

The Author and Ethnographer

Parkinson's writing career started with a slender and less well-known book, *Im Bismarck-Archipel* (Parkinson 1887a), which covers a curious miscellany of diverse topics ranging from the climate and geography of

---

5. The obsession among museum curators at that time for obtaining human remains may have been a contributing factor to an action taken by the Australian administration after it took over the management of former German New Guinea. The Australian administration banned the disturbing, collecting or excavating of human remains; anyone finding remains was required to report them immediately to the relevant district officer (Australia 1924:40-1). Neumann (1991:75) also points out that in the late 19th century, the skulls of Tolai 'big men' were dug up for ceremonial purposes (Parkinson 1907a:81). In the case of ToKede, however, Neumann's informant, Stanley ToMarita, recalled that it was an associate of Queen Emma (Parkinson?) who proposed digging up ToKede's skull. After the appropriate ceremonies, ToKede's skull was sent to a German museum (Neumann 1991:267, fn 2).

the Gazelle Peninsula to the labour trade, plantations and commerce on New Britain, customs and beliefs of the peoples of the Gazelle Peninsula, missions and missionaries, European colonial politics in the Pacific Islands, and the Ten Commandments translated into vernaculars by missionaries Brown and Danks. It was to this book, rather than to *Dreißig Jahre*, that Richard Salisbury turned, fifty years after Parkinson's death, for basic information about aspects of Tolai life and culture at the time of European colonisation, for his study of Vunamami, the village centred on the plantation area of Queen Emma's 'empire' (Salisbury 1970). *Im Bismarck-Archipel* was the first of more than forty-two publications by Parkinson (sole author of thirty-six papers and two books, two jointly authored papers, two jointly authored/edited/illustrated volumes, and an unknown number of newspaper articles and letters), spanning twenty years and almost all in German (see bibliography at the end of this paper). Several papers dealt with tropical agriculture (Parkinson 1887b, 1897a, 1898a), a topic otherwise of little interest to the early white settlers (Sack 1980:14), but the rest focused on the geography (including sailing directions) and people of the archipelago and northern Solomon Islands. As Sack (1980:17) notes, the late 19th century was a period of colonial exploration and description in this region, and it was to the literature on these themes that Parkinson made his major contributions.

Initially Parkinson planned to write regional overviews of his studies, and in 1899 informed Robert Etheridge Jr, curator of the Australian Museum, that his study on the north-west Solomon Islands (Parkinson 1898d) was 'part of a series of similar works which I have in hand at present' (Australian Museum Archives, AMS9 P56/1899). Parkinson changed his mind. Rather than the 'series of similar works', he later advised Etheridge (Australian Museum Archives, AMS9 P20/1903) that:

> I am at present trying my hands at a Descriptive Ethnographie [sic] of the Bismarck Archipel but find to my great dismay how really very little we at present know and how much is entirely dark to us. I plot [sic] on as best I can but I am not at all satisfied with my work.

In the foreword to *Dreißig Jahre*, Parkinson (1907a:xv) noted the opportunities he had had to travel and see peoples and places. In 1894 he had accompanied A. Bastian on a trip to the mainland of New Guinea as an employee of the Deutsch Neu Guinea Compagnie. During this trip, Bastian encouraged Parkinson to publish, and the advice did not fall on deaf ears. Parkinson hoped (1907a:xvi) that the critics would not be too harsh on his efforts, but he was conscious of the rapid cultural changes that had taken place throughout the region following white settlement. This theme of rapid change was a longstanding and continuing one, for as early as 1884 Thomas Farrell had advised Etheridge's predecessor, Ramsay (Australian Museum Archives, AMS8 55/1884) that:

> ethnographical things begin to get rather scarce on account of new things getting introduced and the original arms and implements taken away by labor vessels and trading vessels to various places.

This situation did not improve, for in 1905 Governor Hahl of German New Guinea wrote to von Luschan, director of the Berlin Museum für Völkerkunde, that 'Die Ethnologika werden selten und teuer' (cited by Koch 1982:28). In a letter to Skiff, director of the Field Museum, dated 20 February 1906, Parkinson observed that the artifact collection that he was offering for sale to the museum included 'choice and perfect' objects, 'a great many of which at the present time are obsolete and extremely rare in ethnological collections'. Later, George Dorsey wrote to Skiff (7 August 1908) from Herbertshöhe, during his visit to Parkinson, that:

> Native culture in some of the islands represented [in the Parkinson collection offered to the Field Museum] has almost or entirely disappeared – in some cases the natives themselves are gone.

So how well did Parkinson observe and record? This is a difficult question to answer, since he allows us to know little about how he conducted his 'fieldwork'. There is no evidence that he was academically trained in ethnography or related disciplines; indeed, these disciplines were then only in their infancy. His works have little theoretical content, though Richard Feinberg (1986:3) notes 'an unacceptable propensity to account for behavioural variation in terms of biological differences'. Parkinson did not learn local languages or even stay long in any one place (other than the plantation at Ralum), but the nature of his contacts with the Tolai people allowed him to engage in a form of 'participant observation'. Feinberg's advice (1986:3) is 'to take parts of his account with a healthy dose of scepticism', but even he acknowledges that Parkinson was a keen, intelligent observer who 'gained a wealth of information, belying Hogbin's glib dismissal of his ethnographic acumen'.

There is no detailed critique of Parkinson's writings by people from the societies that he placed on record. In part, this is because his works were mostly published in German, some printed in Gothic script, and written in a formal and often complex style. This has made them largely inaccessible to most non-German speakers (to compound the problem, both of his books have been out of print for so long that they are difficult to find and are priced at the upper end of the market). Only three of his works have been translated into English (1897b, 1900c, 1907a).

Parkinson's study (1897b) of the Aitape-Vanimo coast and adjacent islands of the New Guinea mainland (an area not covered by *Dreißig Jahre*) has been translated into English (Tschauder and Swadling 1979), with commentaries by scholars from two of the societies covered by this work. Woichom (1979) found a number of points where Parkinson's work needed correction or clarification, but both he and Deklin (1979) regarded such points as minor and welcomed the opportunity to gain access to what is essentially an historical document. Both agree that Parkinson's main failings are his generalisations and lack of detail, and on both points they provide useful additional information.

The third work by Parkinson that has been translated into English is his summary study of the Polynesian outlier islands of Nukuria, Nukumanu, Takuu, and Ontong Java (Feinberg 1986). This translation has annotations by Feinberg and A. Howard, both non-indigenous commentators.

The only commentary by a person from the area covered by *Dreißig Jahre* appears to be that of Simet (1977), who discusses aspects of the *tumbuan* society among the Tolai people of the north-east Gazelle Peninsula of East New Britain. Simet's published appreciation of non-Tolai commentators on this society is restrained, without criticism of specific authors. One of Simet's major points, and an important one for understanding the *tumbuan* society, is that the authors generally misunderstood the relationship between the *tumbuan* and its associated *duk-duk* by assigning them gender roles (*tumbuan* = female, *duk-duk* = male). Rather, the *duk-duk* should be seen as the child of the *tumbuan* (Simet 1977:2). Parkinson did not make this mistake. He clearly identified the *tumbuan* as female (1907a:578), and identified the *duk-duk* as her child (1907a:584). Simet's unpublished doctoral thesis (Simet 1991) provides a much longer and more detailed description of the *tumbuan* society, but does not provide a critique of earlier authors, though he notes (Simet 1991:314) Parkinson's 'harsh' appreciation of the society and its activities.

Indigenous commentators from other societies covered by *Dreißig Jahre* would probably echo the criticisms of Woichom and Deklin about the generalisations and lack of detail. This criticism, however, could be levelled at virtually every outside observer, and is not in itself a criticism of Parkinson alone. It leads us, however, to inquire how Parkinson obtained his information. In the absence of clear statements by Parkinson himself, we must piece together a rough and incomplete picture from the various hints and comments available to us. We must acknowledge that he was a self-taught man, without anthropological training, who thought it worthwhile to make a record, however inadequate he felt it was. Even this inadequate record was better than the little that most traders and planters of that era left for posterity (Biskup 1974:4).

Parkinson himself gives a few clues as to how he obtained information. During his visits to the Aitape-Vanimo coast of New Guinea in 1898 and 1899, he noted with approval (Tschauder and Swadling 1979: 36) that:

> Here and there one encounters locals who have worked for Europeans and who can now act as interpreters. This means that it is now easier to obtain certain information than was the case in 1895 [his first visit to this area]. At that time the only means of communication was sign language ...

In her interview with Margaret Mead, Parkinson's wife, Phebe, stated that Parkinson did not speak pidgin English, though she did not indicate how he communicated with the local people (Mead 1964:200). Missionaries such as Brown and Danks learned their respective local languages to be able to translate the Bible and to conduct religious teaching, but Parkinson's work brought him into contact with a wide range of languages. The labour force on the New Britain plantations was drawn from throughout the islands of the Bismarck Archipelago and north Solomons, and proved to be a rich source of information (Parkinson 1907a:xv). Given the diversity of languages spoken on the plantations, it is surprising that Parkinson did not find pidgin English useful. It seems unlikely, however, that he relied solely 'on gestures, and the bayonets of his Buka bodyguards to make his wishes known' (Robson 1965:168). Perhaps it was a case of the labourers learning enough English or German for Parkinson to communicate with them. He was able to discuss various topics with them, such as the discussion he had with a man from Ontong Java who had been at Ralum 'for many years' about how to catch the *palu* (*Ruvettus*) fish (Australian Museum Archives, AMS9 P28/1900).

Parkinson relied heavily on Phebe, who had a good command of pidgin English as well as fluency in the Tolai language (Thiel 1909:114). She spent much time with Tolai people, and helped Parkinson record their names and other information (Mead 1964:184). May Macfarlane (1925:20) later claimed that, 'Much of the actual labour of collecting the information which he used was done by Mrs Parkinson. Mrs Parkinson has frequently acted as guide and safeguard for visiting scientific observers.' Phebe held regular 'markets' with Tolai women to buy food for the plantation workers, and probably as much as anyone helped Parkinson to obtain detailed information about the Tolai people. An undated photograph shows Parkinson writing while Phebe talks to a man, presumably translating for Parkinson (Overell 1923: plate opp. 178;

reproduced in Gash and Whittaker 1975:43, plate 77). His text, however, does not acknowledge this, for in the sections dealing with the Gazelle Peninsula, he frequently observes that he was told the information directly. According to Klaus Neumann (*in. litt.* 6 January 1998), Parkinson probably had sufficient command of Kuanua (the Tolai language) to at least understand what was said. While it is questionable whether Phebe assisted much with the obtaining of information about secret and sacred male activities, we can be almost certain that it was through her that Parkinson was able to include in his book so much about Tolai women.

Phebe's contribution went beyond merely acting as an interpreter, for she was heavily involved in organising the collection and stuffing of animals, as well as shipping these and artifacts to overseas museums (Mead 1964:200). She was clearly well-informed about local customs, for when Etheridge wrote to Parkinson in 1912, not knowing he was dead, she was able to provide him with the information he sought about the use of decorated paddles and staffs from Buka (Australian Museum Archives AMS9 P34/1912). Perhaps it was Phebe's influence, and Samoan origins, which contributed to the success of their negotiations with the Tolai for the purchase of use rights to their land through the Tolai practice of *totokom* (a form of reciprocity; cf. Salisbury 1970:72, 77). Parkinson understood many customs, such as *kamara* ('payback' or compensation), sufficiently well to employ them in his dealings with villagers (1907a:60-1). His view on *kamara* differed from that of Hahl, who felt it was too harsh a practice to incorporate into the judicial system then being developed by the German administration (Rowley 1966:36-7; cf. Parkinson 1907a:61).

Parkinson was a Protestant (Mead 1964:193), but this did not stop him from developing a close relationship with the Catholic missionaries operating out of Vunapope, just down the road from Ralum and Kuradui. This contact, however, was more scientific than spiritual, for Parkinson (1907a:xvii) particularly thanked them for sharing with him information about the islanders. Not only were the missionaries living close to the people and learning their languages, but like Parkinson they were observing, recording and publishing aspects of indigenous lifestyles and beliefs. Some are acknowledged directly by Parkinson, particularly in the section of *Dreißig Jahre* dealing with languages (Parkinson 1907a:724), which was written with the help of Fathers Bley and Rascher; it also drew on the language work of the Methodist missionaries Brown, Rickard and Danks (Parkinson 1907a:723). Similarly, the discussion about Sulka masks and rituals was based on information from Brother Hermann Müller (Parkinson 1907a:176), who had learned the Sulka language: 'und nachdem dies nun gelungen, bin ich imstande gewesen, einige Aufschlüsse über die Masken zu erhalten' (Parkinson 1907a:635).

Dreißig Jahre, however, is not just a record of what Parkinson saw or was told by others. He was a widely read person, who used the works of others to fill gaps in his information or to place it in a wider context. While his early writings were breaking new ground, by the time Parkinson wrote his major work there was a wide-ranging literature by missionaries, travellers, visiting scholars and government officials. He cites many of these works, mostly as sources of information, but occasionally to correct or amplify their statements. He adopted a comparative approach, and drew upon Codrington, Woodford, Haddon, Fison, and MacGregor (the administrator of British New Guinea) for his broad-ranging discussion about religion and totemism. His reading went beyond the boundaries of the island world to include the works of Spencer and Gillen and Howitt on the Australian Aboriginal peoples (Parkinson 1907a:674-5). Thiel (1909:114) also notes that Parkinson was a corresponding member of scientific societies in Germany, Italy, Sweden, England and Australia.

In short, Parkinson was probably as well read and informed, if not better, than many of his contemporaries in the islands. The 'German Professor', as he was called by Farrell (Robson 1965:167), sought out new literature wherever he could. When he sent a collection of human skulls to the Australian Museum in 1889, he asked that they be exchanged for a copy of the *Pictorial Atlas of Australia,* a book about which he had heard (Australian Museum Archives P13/1889). Later, he asked Etheridge to send him the latest parts of the Australian Museum's *Memoir* series on Funafuti – he already had parts 1 to 7 – and any other Australian Museum publications on the Pacific Islands. He thanked Etheridge for sending a copy of his 'work on the ornamentation of the Dilly Baskets'. Parkinson had already read it, and was considering a similar study of string bags and netting of the New Guinea coast (Australian Museum Archives P56/1899). Etheridge responded by sending parts 8 and 9 of the Funafuti report. Parkinson read them closely and wrote to Etheridge to correct Hedley's (1897:272-6) misunderstanding about a large fishhook used on Funafuti. This was not, said Parkinson, for catching sharks, but for catching the *palu* fish (*Ruvettus*). He added that the drawings by Hedley and 'Mr Waite' (scientific assistant at the museum) showing the way the hook was used 'are excellent but I do not think they are complete' (see Hedley 1897:272-6). He referred Etheridge to a drawing in his own account (Parkinson 1897b), itself 'not shown very clearly', so Parkinson included for Etheridge a better drawing. This is almost identical to that from Nukumanu subsequently included in *Dreißig Jahre,* but in mirror image (Parkinson 1907a:537, fig. 89). Parkinson (1907b) was also able to amplify some observations by Edge-Partington on Polynesian outlier basketry published in *Man*.

Parkinson's access to a wide range of literature is well demonstrated in the final section of *Dreißig Jahre*, in which he provided an overview of European exploration of the Pacific Islands, including the German annexation of the Bismarck Archipelago (Parkinson 1907a:811-58). Some of this information he may have obtained from books in his possession, but the correspondence between Parkinson and Etheridge reveals that he also borrowed books from the Australian Museum (Australian Museum Archives AMS9 P39/1900), such as the accounts of Cook's three voyages in the Pacific. This was the Hawkesworth edition; the museum apologised for not being able to send Dalrymple as well, since it was not held in the museum library (Australian Museum Archives AMS6 190/1900). For Etheridge, such loans yielded a gain in the form of information. Etheridge used Parkinson as a source of information about artifacts in the museum collections, some of them received from Parkinson himself. In 1903, Etheridge sent him a photo of an item from the Duke of York Islands. Parkinson replied (Australian Museum Archives, AMS9 P20/1903) that he had inquired at Port Hunter and at 'other places in the Duke of York Islands', and everyone agreed that it was a float for a large seine net, and not a mark of rank, other than that the owner of such a net 'is generally a person of some importance'. Parkinson goes on to correct Hunter's speculation (1793:215; cf. Calaby 1989: plate 97) that such items were a mark of high rank and were carried in canoes of chiefs.

The above discussion shows Parkinson as generally a meticulous, perhaps punctilious, recorder of facts at a time when anthropological theory and practice were still being developed. He was willing to check a detail with several people, rather than rely on the testimony of one alone; indeed, in his book he occasionally indicates whether a piece of information came from one man or several, or whether the information presented was current or belonged to the past (for example, Parkinson 1907a:66 – 'Alte Leute sagen, dass in früheren Zeiten ...'). His long residence and wide travels in the archipelago allowed many of his statements to be based on repeated observations. This allowed him to use specific examples to illustrate a general point, as in the case of the burial of an *agala*, which he witnessed some years before writing *Dreißig Jahre* (Parkinson 1907a:74-5), rather than to rely solely on generalisation.

It is interesting to compare briefly his approach with that taken by the missionary George Brown in compiling his book. Brown (1910:vi) used the *Anthropological Notes and Queries* first put out by the British Association for the Advancement of Science in 1874 as a guide to the kinds of information that he recorded. Parkinson, on the other hand, seems not to have had such a systematic approach, recording what he could without necessarily trying to be comprehensive. As a result, while *Dreißig Jahre* focuses strongly on some matters, such as the use of shell money by the Tolai people and often detailed accounts of male material culture, it has little to offer about other subjects, such as trade or pottery-making.

Inevitably, there are errors or misinterpretations in Parkinson's work. When dealing with the south coast societies from Kandrian westwards, Parkinson states (1907a:212-13) that the wooden bowls seen on the south coast between South Cape and Cape Merkus may have been made in the area, and that the Tami Islanders were eager to obtain them. He also noted that wooden bowls were being made on the islands at Kandrian. In view of later studies, neither statement is likely to be true. The Tami Islanders were the original bowl-makers and traded these to New Britain; in more recent times this role was taken over by some of the Siassi Islanders lying between New Britain and New Guinea (cf. Harding 1967).

Parkinson was very interested in people and their ritual lives, and engaged in a long speculation about the origin of the Polynesians and their relationship to people of the archipelago (1907a:551-64). Yet he omitted several topics that one might have expected him to include. Part XI of the 1907 version of *Dreißig Jahre* deals briefly with the cultivation of plants, domestic animals and hunting, and ends with a curious short section in which pottery-making in the Admiralty Islands and the northern Solomon Islands receive summary mention. This is followed by an equally puzzling commentary on some uses of obsidian, which to some extent duplicates previous references. The entire section is awkwardly positioned, and may have been a late addition when Parkinson realised that he had omitted discussion of these matters. The few words on these topics do no justice to them, and do more to draw attention to the omissions than to resolve them. It is surprising that the man who was so meticulous in describing the correct function and use of the *palu* fishhook should pay so little attention to such important economic and social activities. Perhaps it was because some of these aspects fell into the female domain, whereas Parkinson would have spent most of his time in the company of men. Even so, we could reasonably expect that he might have sought the assistance of Phebe in filling such gaps, had she accompanied him on his travels.

Parkinson's first book (1887a) contained only rather amateurish drawings and lithographs, presumably by Parkinson himself. At some subsequent stage he acquired skills in the new art of photography, and collaborated with A.B. Meyer to produce a magnificent two-volume 'Album' of 'Papuan types' of people and scenes in the New Guinea-Bismarck Archipelago area (Meyer and Parkinson 1894, 1900). His images also appeared in the annual reports for German New Guinea (for example, Anon. 1890), and the 1907 edition of *Dreißig Jahre* is richly illustrated with 197 photographs presumed to be by him. His photos remained a major source of visual information long after his death, appearing in works such as the New Guinea-Bismarck Archipelago section of Buschan's (1923) worldwide review of tribal peoples.

Conclusion

In presenting this summary account of Parkinson's anthropological activities in the Bismarck Archipelago, I have ranged widely across several of his fields of interest and his contacts with museums and scholars around the world. What emerges is that although Parkinson spent much of his time in the archipelago working for Queen Emma and the Deutsch Neu Guinea Compagnie, his dedication to learning about the indigenous peoples was the overriding theme of the thirty years referred to in his book title.

Dreißig Jahre in der Südsee was the synthesis needed to bring together the detail of his earlier writings into a single comparative study. It was the culmination of his writing career, though three papers appeared after it, one posthumously (Parkinson 1908a, 1908b, 1910).

One of the driving forces behind the book was Parkinson's awareness of the rapid cultural change that had taken place during his time in the archipelago. *Dreißig Jahre* (and Parkinson's other writings) is more than just a description of 'interesting peoples' (1907a:xv) in the Bismarck Archipelago; it is a record of lifestyles that were being abandoned or lost – a recurring theme in his writings. It is about a changing world recorded by an outsider who was never a member of the societies he observed and described, and to whose cultural change he contributed as much as anyone in his role as trader, recruiter and planter.

Compared with the compendious volumes of the Hamburg Südsee Expedition, which focus on a single island or island group, *Dreißig Jahre* is somewhat unbalanced. The Tolai people, among whom he lived, receive the majority of his attention, but his accounts of many other groups are often the first available for them. No other single author could have attempted such an overview, and none has since. The Hamburg teams spent several months in the archipelago, but Parkinson brought years of experience, observation and understanding to his work. In some respects he is less academic as an author than the Hamburg specialists, and despite his matter-of-fact descriptive style and almost obsessive attention to detail, the individuality of his experiences gives his writings a personal touch that is lacking among the Hamburgers and many other writers of that period.

Dreißig Jahre is unparalleled in the literature of the Bismarck Archipelago. It is an incomparable picture of a time and place now long past. An English-language review of his book offered little more than a summary of Parkinson's foreword and bits of his text, but its author acknowledged that 'no one is better qualified to write about this *terra incognita* than Herr Parkinson' (A.H.Q. 1908). Similarly, another reviewer saw it as an 'ornament' to the German ethnographic literature (Andree 1907:320). On reading this new English translation, others, it is hoped, will agree that it is 'a magisterial guide to the region' (Firth 1986:164), 'a massive and authoritative ethnography' (Salisbury 1970:39), and 'für alle Zeiten eine reiche Fundgrube, ein Thesaurus für alle sein wird' (Anon. 1909:211).

Jim Specht
Australian Museum

Acknowledgements

In preparing this essay I received assistance and advice from Robert Langdon, formerly executive officer of the Pacific Manuscripts Bureau, Australian National University, Canberra, who allowed me access to unpublished documentary material in his possession. I thank him for his permission to use these documents, especially his correspondence with Christopher Legge in Chicago. Robert also kindly read an early draft of this essay, but has no responsibility for any shortcomings of the final version. I am indebted to Klaus Neumann, Australian National University, Canberra, for his critical comments and suggestions, as a result of which several omissions have been corrected and additional observations have been possible.

Michael Wilkins of Sydney assisted in tracing published and archival materials about Parkinson. Julie Gleaves, formerly in the Australian Museum Research Library and Archives, tracked down additional archival material within the museum, and Samantha Fenton (library manager) helped find several German-language publications. Jan Brazier (manager of Archives and Records in the museum) commented on a draft and advised on citation conventions for archival materials. Janice Klein, registrar at the Field Museum, Chicago, checked several matters relating to the correspondence between Dorsey, Skiff and Parkinson. Wal Ambrose, Australian National University, Canberra, allowed me to consult his copy of the 1926 edition of *Dreißig Jahre,* and Glenn Summerhayes, also Australian National University, Canberra, generously let me explore his library and discover Pullen-Burry (1909).

Antje Sonntag, Division of Anthropology at the Australian Museum, drew my attention to Hans Fischer's account of the 1908-10 Hamburg Südsee Expedition, obtained a copy of Thiel's obituary of Parkinson, and assisted with translation of several German texts. I am grateful for her assistance. Christian Kaufmann, Museum der Kulturen, Basel, kindly tracked down and copied for me Richard Andree's appreciation (1901) of Parkinson.

Ewan Maidment, executive officer of the Pacific Manuscripts Bureau, and Alison Pilger, director of the *Australian Dictionary of Biography,* both based in the Australian National University, Canberra, advised on possible additional sources of information.

I thank the Australian Museum, the Field Museum, and the Mitchell Library, State Library of New South Wales, for permission to cite manuscript materials held in each institution.

None of the above, however, is responsible for specific interpretations, any factual errors or omissions that remain.

Bibliography of R.H.R. Parkinson

The following list of publications by Parkinson is the most comprehensive yet assembled, and is compiled from several sources, especially Sack (1980) for the German-language items. Sack's list has been compared with, and added to as a result, those provided by Anon. (1968), Edridge (1985), and Hanson and Hanson (1984). Thiel (1909:114) records that Parkinson was a correspondent with newspapers such as *Norddeutsche Allgemeine Zeitung, Hamburger Nachrichten* and *Ostasiatischer Lloyd.* I have not examined these, and list only two, one of which (1894b) is quoted by Neumann (1991:132), who also cites (1991:270, fn 8) several other Parkinson documents. Thiel also notes (1909:114) that Parkinson was a corresponding member of scientific societies in Berlin, Stuttgart, Rome, Stockholm, London and Australia. I have not conducted a search of the publications of these societies, but three of Parkinson's papers in their journals are included below (Parkinson 1904b, 1907b, 1908b).

1887a. *Im Bismarck-Archipel. Erlebnisse und Beobachtungen auf der Insel Neu-Pommern (Neu-Britannien).* F.A. Brockhaus, Leipzig.

1887b. Plantagen in Neu-Pommern. *Deutsche kolonialzeitung.* 4(22):693-6.

1888. Ein Ausflug nach dem Kaiserin-Augusta-Strom in Kaiser Wilhelmsland. *Norddeutsche Allgemeine Zeitung.* 179.

1889a. Waffe, Signalrohr oder Tabakspfeife? *Internationales Archiv für Ethnographie.* 2:168.

1889b. Beiträge zur Kenntniss des deutschen Schutzgebietes in der Südsee. *Geographische Gesellschaft Hamburg, Mitteilungen.* 1887-88:201-81.

1890. Segeldirektion für die König-Albert-Strasse. *Nachrichten über Kaiser Wilhelms-land und den Bismarck-Archipel.* 6:49.

1892. Über Tätowierung der Eingebornen im Distrikt Siarr auf der Ostküste von Neu-Mecklenburg (Neu-Irland). *Internationales Archiv für Ethnographie.* 5:76-8.

1894a. Über das Durchbohren von Muschelplatten, behufs Herstellung von Armringen, etc. *Internationales Archiv für Ethnographie.* 7:89.

1894b. Article in *Norddeutsche Allgemeine Zeitung.* 22 February.

1895. Zur Ethnographie der Matty-Insel. *Internationales Archiv für Ethnographie.* 8:248.

1896a. Beiträge zur Ethnographie der Matty- und Durour-Inseln. *Internationales Archiv für Ethnographie.* 9:195-203.

1896b. Bougainville. *Deutsches kolonialblatt.* 46-8.

1896c. Bismarck-Archipel. *Globus.* 69:146.

1897a. Pflanzungen im Bismarckarchipel. *Der Tropenpflanzer.* 254-5.

1897b. Zur Ethnographie der Ontong Java- und Tasman-Inseln, mit Einigen Bemerkungen über die Marquesen- und Abgarris-Inseln. *Internationales Archiv für Ethnographie.* 10:104-18, 137-51.

1898a. Kaffeekultur im Bismarck-Archipel. *Der Tropenpflanzer.* 335-6.

1898b. "Koppensnellen" in der Südsee. *Deutsche kolonialzeitung.* 87-8.

1898c. Nachtrage zur Ethnographie der Ontong-Java-Inseln. *Internationales Archiv für Ethnographie.* 11:194-209.

1898d. Zur Ethnographie der nordwestlichen Salomo-Inseln. *Zoologisches und anthropologisch-ethnographisches Museum, Dresden, Abhandlungen und Berichte.* 7(6):1-35.

1899. Die Ballonmützen auf Bougainville (Salomo-Inseln). *Globus.* 75:243.

1900a. Durchfahrt zwischen Buka und Bougainville. *Deutsches kolonialblatt.* 71.

1900b. Die Schiffsschnäbel der Salomonen. (Berichtigung). *Globus.* 78:19.

1900c. Die Berlinhafen-Section. Ein Beitrag zur Ethnographie der Neu-Guinea-Küste. *Internationales Archiv für Ethnographie.* 13:18-54.

1901a. Die Einwohner der Insel St. Matthias. *Globus.* 79:229-33, 256.
1901b. Die Insel St. Matthias. *Globus.* 79:256.
1901c. Mit der "Möwe" im Bismarck-Archipel. Berall. 3:86.
1904a. Tätowierung der Mogemokinsulaner. *Globus.* 84:15.
1904b. A rice-sheller from Nusa. *Man.* 4:117.
1905a. Ein Besuch auf den Admiralitäts-Inseln. *Globus.* 87(13):238.
1905b. St. Matthias und die Inseln Kerue und Tench. *Globus.* 88(5):69-72.
1905c. Baumrindenkleidung in Deutsch Neu Guinea. *Internationales Archiv für Ethnographie.* 17:222.
1907a. *Dreißig Jahre in der Südsee. Land und Leute, Sitten und Gebräuche im Bismarckarchipel und auf den deutschen Salomoinseln.* Strecker & Schröder, Stuttgart. Reissued in 1926 in a condensed version edited by A. Eichhorn and published by Strecker & Schröder, Stuttgart.
1907b. Notes on Solomon Islands baskets and on Lord Howe's group. *Man.* 7:183-6.
1907c. Die Gazellehalbinsel. *Deutsches kolonialblatt.* 519.
1907d. Heilkunst im Bismarck-Archipel. *Medizinisch-Chirugisches Centralblatt.* 598.
1907e. Heilkunst im Bismarck-Archipel. *Medizinische Blätter.* 578.
1908a. Tanz und Gesang im Bismarck Archipel. *Deutsche Rundschau für Geographie und Statistik.* 30:402.
1908b. Totemism in Melanesia and its probable origin. *Australian and New Zealand Association for the Advancement of Science, Report of the 11th Meeting 1907.* 11:209-16.
1910. Die Lieblichen Inseln. *Deutsche kolonialzeitung.* 341-2.
n.d. Thirty Years in the South Seas. The Bismarck Archipelago. Land, Natives and Customs. Translated and edited by N.C. Barry. Mimeographed.

The second edition and the Barry translation

Noel C. Barry, a resident of Rabaul, was not an anthropologist, and it is unclear why he undertook the translation of *Dreißig Jahre* (Parkinson n.d.). According to Mead (1964:178), who had read the 1907 edition as a graduate student, Barry was starting the translation of the 1926 edition when she visited New Britain in 1928-29. He completed it before the outbreak of the Pacific War and gave it to Phebe. She in turn gave it to a member of the Archbold Expedition, who took it back to the USA (Robson 1965:222). After the war, Robson retrieved the typescript from the USA; presumably, this was the original top copy of the typescript. The Australian Museum holds a carbon copy of a typescript similar to the Barry version, with the exception of only a few minor typing errors; it is uncertain whether this is a copy of Barry's original typed version or from a later version. Robson placed the rescued copy in the Australian School of Pacific Administration in Sydney and, some time later, copies were made and placed in several major libraries, including that of the Australian Museum. For many people, this Barry translation became the sole avenue into Parkinson's book.

The 1926 edition of *Dreißig Jahre* translated by Barry was edited by August Eichhorn of the Staatliche Museum für Völkerkunde in Berlin. Some changes to the 1907 edition were necessary, for Parkinson wrote before World War I, in which Germany lost its Pacific possessions. Thus, 'die deutschen Salomoinseln' became 'die früher' or 'die vormals deutschen Salomoninseln'.

Eichhorn's version has the same list of contents as the 1907 original, but he begins with the history of European exploration of the Bismarck Archipelago. In the 1907 version, Parkinson placed this section at the end of the book as section XII. Eichhorn does not explain why he made this switch, nor does he explain why some passages – paragraphs and whole pages – of the 1907 text were omitted. Examination of the 1926 text suggests that Eichhorn may have felt that Parkinson occasionally included material of little or no direct relevance to the main topic of the book. For example, a missing paragraph of page 812 discusses matters relating to Asian and European histories that, strictly speaking, have no relevance to the main text.

Some omissions, then, can be supported on the grounds of irrelevance, but others cannot be so explained, such as Parkinson's pages 857-58 dealing with German mapping of the archipelago, and pages 40-2, which discuss matters such as European traders in the Bismarck Archipelago. Eichhorn also omitted Parkinson's account (1907a:25-6) of a visit to Möwehafen (Kandrian) in 1896, during which Parkinson walked inland some distance and visited a palisaded settlement of two houses. Eichhorn may have felt that this was redundant, since the incident is referred to again in a later section.

Eichhorn condensed parts of the original, sometimes so badly that the meaning is corrupted. The original pages 24-5 discuss the Willaumez Peninsula on the north coast of New Britain, and then move to consideration of the south coast. Eichhorn's compression of the text, however, loses the critical transition from north to south, so that his text attributes south-coast features to the Willaumez Peninsula. In another condensing exercise, more than two pages of Parkinson's text (1907a:35-7) are condensed into a single paragraph (see Parkinson n.d.:49-50).

The net result of these omissions and compression is that whereas the original 1907 book had 858 pages of text, in the 1926 version the text is reduced to 347 pages, less than half of the original length. The illustrations were also reduced in the 1926 version, from 197 plus four maps, to 158 plus four maps, and their sequence was changed. Photos originally inserted into the 1907 text were sometimes combined in the 1926 edition to make a separate full-page plate (for example, 1907a, plates 129, 132 and 133, were combined onto one page, 1926, plates 1 to 3). Partly in line with the abbreviated text, the index of Eichhorn's version is much shorter than that of 1907. But it is also less complete. The 1907 index lists twenty-two sub-entries under 'Baining', whereas there are only three in the 1926 edition, even though the topics covered by the 1907 entries remain in the 1926 text.

Barry exerted little editorial control over his translation. He added (Parkinson n.d.:34) a footnote to Parkinson's discussion of the circumstances surrounding the German takeover of Kaiser Wilhelmsland and the Bismarck Archipelago (Parkinson 1907a:854-5), pointing out that an alternative interpretation is possible.

While these examples demonstrate how necessary it is for anyone using Barry's translation and the 1926 Eichorn edition to crosscheck with the original Parkinson text, there is unfortunately another good reason: that of accuracy. Parkinson (1907a:20) speculated on the future of Australia's population, suggesting that in 100 years' time the population could reach about 30 million people. Barry (n.d.:45), however, got his numbers mixed up and attributed to Parkinson the suggestion that the population would reach 100 million! Further on, Barry (n.d.:164) states that the missionary George Brown visited 'Henry Reid Bay' in New Britain in 1873. Since Brown did not even arrive in the Duke of York Islands until 1875, we accept Parkinson's (1907a:175) original attribution of 1878.

These are minor deficiencies, however, and Barry's work has served a useful purpose over several decades. We do not know why he translated the book, or what he intended to do with it on completion. That he gave it to Phebe Parkinson, who passed it on to someone else, can have several explanations. Perhaps Barry hoped that she would check and correct the translation. Perhaps Phebe hoped that the visiting American might help her find a publisher. We do not know, and may never know, what their intentions were. All we can say is that Robson's recovery of the typescript from the USA rescued it from obscurity and possible loss, and allowed several generations of non-German readers to access Richard Parkinson's major work.

By making *Dreißig Jahre* more accessible to non-German readers, however, Barry inadvertently gave Parkinson's book prominence over works by other contemporary German writers, especially those of the Catholic missionaries. For many non-German readers, Barry's version of Parkinson became the standard reference, and discouraged them from reading and appraising independently the writings of Parkinson's contemporaries. It is hoped that this new translation will not reinforce this situation, but will encourage exploration of those other writers, many of whom provide more detailed appreciations and interpretations of topics covered only briefly by Parkinson's book.

Co-authored works

Meyer, A.B., and R.H.R. Parkinson. 1894. *Album von Papua-Typen. Neu Guinea und Bismarck Archipel.* Stengel & Markert, Dresden.

———. 1895. Schnitzereien und Masken vom Bismarck Archipel und Neu Guinea. *Zoologisches und anthropologisch-ethnographisches Museum, Dresden, Publikationen 10.*

———. 1900. *Album von Papua-Typen. II. Nord Neu Guinea, Bismarck Archipel, Deutsche Salomo Inseln.* Stengel & Co., Dresden.

Parkinson, R.R.H., and W. Foy. 1899. Die Volksstämme Neu-Pommerns. *Zoologisches und anthropologisch-ethnologisches Museum, Dresden, Abhandlungen und Berichte. 7(5).*

References

Archival Materials

I have consulted documents in the Australian Museum Archives (Sydney), the Field Museum (Chicago), and the Mitchell Library, State Library of NSW (Sydney). Documents from five series in the Australian Museum Archives are referenced in the text by the series and document numbers; for example, Australian Museum Archives AMS9 P34/1904 refers to a letter from Phebe Parkinson in 1912 held in series 9 of the archives. The documents cited are:

Australian Museum Archives, AMS6: Outward Letter Books 1837-1923
AMS6, 946/1890. Edward Ramsay to Richard Parkinson, 20 November 1890.
AMS6, 852/1899. Robert Etheridge Jr to Richard Parkinson, 20 November 1899.

AMS6, 190/1900. Robert Etheridge Jr to Richard Parkinson, 14 March 1900.
Australian Museum Archives, AMS7: Letters Received 1853-1883
AMS7, C:10:81:10. Thomas Farrell to Edward Ramsay, 19 December 1881.
Australian Museum Archives, AMS8: Letters Received 1883-1888
AMS8, 55/1884. Thomas Farrell to Edward Ramsay, 14 January 1884.
AMS8, 224/1884. Richard Parkinson to Edward Ramsay, 11 June 1884.
Australian Museum Archives: AMS9: Letters Received 1889-1926
AMS9, P13/1889. Richard Parkinson to Edward Ramsay, 20 April 1889.
AMS9, P21/1890. Richard Parkinson to Edward Ramsay, 28 July 1890.
AMS9, K9/1897. Emma *kol*be to Robert Etheridge, 29 April 1897.
AMS9, P56/1899. Richard Parkinson to Robert Etheridge, 5 October 1899.
AMS9, P28/1900. Richard Parkinson to Robert Etheridge, 2 April 1900.
AMS9, P39/1900. Richard Parkinson to Robert Etheridge, 28 May 1900.
AMS9, P20/1903. Richard Parkinson to Robert Etheridge, 11 May 1903.
AMS9, P21/1903. Richard Parkinson to Robert Etheridge, 27 May 1903.
AMS9, P33/1903. Richard Parkinson to Robert Etheridge, 25 September 1903.
AMS9, P43/1903. Richard Parkinson to Robert Etheridge, 10 November 1903.
AMS9, P3/1904. Richard Parkinson to Robert Etheridge, 20 December 1903.
AMS9, P34/1912. Phebe Parkinson to Robert Etheridge, 27 June 1912.
Australian Museum Archives: AMS55: Purchase Schedules 1883-1924
AMS55, 29/1884. Schedule of purchases from Richard Parkinson, 8 August 1884.

Documents in the Field Museum, Chicago, Anthropology Archives Correspondence Files, are not catalogued. Each item is identified by the date of the letter only where it is obvious who was writing to whom; in other instances, the citation provides the names the author and the recipient, followed by the date of the letter; the abbreviation 'RP' refers to Richard Parkinson. The correspondence cited is as follows:

Bryan Lathrap to F.V. Skiff, 5 September 1905.
Linzee Tilden to F.V. Skiff, 25 October 1905.
George Dorsey to Richard Parkinson, 11 November 1905.
Richard Parkinson to George Dorsey, 19 February 1906.
Richard Parkinson to F.V. Skiff, 20 February 1906.
George Dorsey to F.V. Skiff, 19 April 1906.
Richard Parkinson to F.V. Skiff, 31 August 1906.
F.V. Skiff to Richard Parkinson, 14 November 1906.
Richard Parkinson to George Dorsey, 14 November 1906.
Richard Parkinson to 'Mr Fisk', 2 July 1907.
George Dorsey to F.V. Skiff, 7 August 1908.
Richard Parkinson to George Dorsey, 27 October 1908.
George Dorsey to Richard Parkinson, 22 December 1908.
George Dorsey to Richard Parkinson, 13 January 1909.
Richard Parkinson to George Dorsey, 3 February1909.
George Dorsey to Richard Parkinson. 12 April 1909.
F.V. Skiff to Richard Parkinson, 11 May 1909.
Richard Parkinson to George Dorsey, 14 May 1909.

One original document in the Mitchell Library, State Library of New South Wales, is cited. This is a letter from Richard Parkinson to Sir George Ruthven Le Hunte in Port Moresby dated 20 March 1886, in the collection of papers of Sir Hubert Murray volume 4, and is catalogued as ML ref. CYA 3141.

Copies of the correspondence between Arthur Vaag and R.W. Robson and between Christopher Legge and Robert Langdon are held by Langdon in Canberra. The relevant ones are:

Arthur Vaag to R.W. Robson, 24 September 1968.
Arthur Vaag to R.W. Robson, 24 October 1968.
Christopher Legge to Robert Langdon, 26 February 1970.
Christopher Legge to Robert Langdon, undated, but probably early March 1970.
Christopher Legge to Robert Langdon, 11 March 1970.
Robert Langdon to Christopher Legge, 18 March 1970.
Christopher Legge to Robert Langdon, 30 March 1970.
Christopher Legge to Robert Langdon, 14 April 1970.

Published materials

A.H.Q. 1908. Melanesia: Parkinson. Review of *Dreißig Jahre in der Südsee*. *Man*. 8(6):94-6.

Andree, R. 1901. R. Parkinson. *Globus*. 79:238-40.

———. 1907. Review of R. Parkinson, *Dreißig Jahre in der Südsee*. *Globus*. 92:320-1.

Anon. 1890. *Nachrichten über Kaiser Wilhelms-Land und den Bismarck-Archipel*. Vol. 6. Neu Guinea Compagnie, Berlin.

Anon. 1909. [Notice of Parkinson's death in the 'Kleine Nachrichten' section.] *Globus*. 96:211.

Anon. 1968. *An Ethnographic Bibliography of New Guinea*. Department of Anthropology and Sociology, Australian National University, Canberra.

Australia. 1924. *Report to the League of Nations on the Administration of the Territory New Guinea, from 1st July 1922 to 30th June, 1923*. Parliament of the Commonwealth of Australia, Government Printer, Melbourne.

Biskup, P. 1974. *The New Guinea Diaries of Jean Baptiste Octave Mouton*. Australian National University Press, Canberra.

Bolton, L., O'Donnell, G., and Wade, J. 1979. Lost Treasures of the Garden Palace. *Australian Natural History*. 19(12):414-19.

Brown, G. 1908. *George Brown, M.D. Pioneer-Missionary and Explorer*. Hodder and Stoughton, London.

———. 1910. *Melanesians and Polynesians*. Macmillan & Co., London.

Buschan, G. (ed.). 1923. *Illustrierte Völkerkunde*. Strecker und Schröder, Stuttgart.

Calaby, J. 1989. *The Hunter Sketchbook*. National Library of Australia, Canberra.

Corris, P. 1973. *William T. Wawn: The South Sea Islanders and the Queensland Labour Trade*. University Press of Hawaii, Honolulu.

Deklin, F. 1979. A review of Richard Parkinson's 1900 paper on the Aitape Coast – from a Vanimo viewpoint. *Records of the National Museum and Art Gallery* (Papua New Guinea). 7:30-4.

Dutton, G. 1976. *Queen Emma of the South Seas*. Macmillan, Melbourne.

Edridge, S. 1985. *Solomon Islands Bibliography to 1980*. Institute of Pacific Studies, Suva; Alexander Turnbull Library, Wellington; Solomon Islands National Library, Honiara.

Feinberg, R. 1986. Ethnography of Ontong Java and Tasman Islands with Remarks re. the Marqueen and Tasman Islands by R. Parkinson. *Pacific Studies*. 9(3):1-31.

Finsch, O. 1888. *Samoafahrten. Reise in Kaiser Wilhelmsland und Englisch Neu-Guinea in den Jahren 1884 und 1885 an bord des Deutschen Dampfer "Samoa"*. Hirt und Sohn, Leipzig.

Firth, S. 1979. Captain Hernsheim: Pacific Venturer, Merchant Prince. In D. Scarr (ed.), *More Pacific Islands Portraits*, pp. 115-130. Australian National University Press, Canberra.

———. 1986. *New Guinea under the Germans*. Web Books, Port Moresby.

Fischer, H. 1981. *Die Hamburger Südsee-Expedition: Über Ethnographie und kolonialismus*. Syndikat, Frankfurt am Main.

Gash, N., and Whittaker, J. 1975. *Pictorial History of New Guinea*. Jacaranda Press, Milton, Queensland.

Greenop, F. 1944. *Who Travels Alone*. K.G. Murray, Sydney.

Hanson, L., and Hanson, F.A. 1984. *The Art of Oceania: A Bibliography*. G.K. Hall & Co., Boston, Mass.

Harding, T.G. 1967. *Voyagers of the Vitiaz Strait*. University of Washington Press, Seattle.

Hedley, C. 1897. The ethnology of Funafuti. *Memoirs of the Australian Museum*. III, part XI:227-304.

Hunter, J. 1793. *Historical Journal of the Transactions at Port Jackson and Norfolk Island, including the Journals of Governors Phillip and King, since the Publication of the Previous Voyage*. J. Stockdale, London.

Kennedy, P.M. 1974. *The Samoan Tangle: A Study in Anglo-German-American Relations 1878-1900*. Irish University Press, Dublin.

Koch, G. 1982. *Iniet: Geister in Stein*. Museum für Völkerkunde, Berlin, Neue Folge 39, Abteilung XI.

Langdon, R. (ed.). 1968. The papers in "Squeaker" Hamilton's trunk. *PAMBU*. 3:5 [newsletter of the Pacific Manuscripts Bureau, Australian National University, Canberra].

Macfarlane, M. 1925. *Australian Women's Mirror*. 19 November:20.

Mead, M. 1964. Weaver of the Border. In: J.B. Casagrande (ed), *In the Company of Man: Twenty Portraits of Anthropological Informants*, pp. 175-210. Harper and Row, New York (first published 1960).

Meleisea, M. 1980. *O Tama Ulu: Melanesians in Samoa*. Institute of Pacific Studies, University of the South Pacific, Suva.

Moore, C., Griffin, J. and Griffin, A. 1984. *Colonial Intrusion: Papua New Guinea ... 1884*. Papua New Guinea Centennial Committee, Port Moresby.

Neumann, K. 1991. *Not the Way It Really Was: Constructing the Tolai Past*. University of Hawaii Press, Honolulu.

Niaux, J.H. 1936 *The Phantom Paradise*. Angus & Robertson, Sydney.

Overell, L. 1923. *A Woman's Impressions of German New Guinea*. Dodd, Mead & Co., New York.

Pullen-Burry, B. 1909. *In a German Colony, or Four Weeks in New Britain.* Methuen & Co., London.

Robson, R.A.W. 1965. *Queen Emma.* Pacific Publications, Sydney. (Also see revised editions of 1971, 1973, 1979.)

Romilly, H.H. 1886. *The Western Pacific and New Guinea.* John Murray, London.

Rowley, C. 1966. *The New Guinea Villager.* Pall Mall Press, London.

Sack, P. (ed.). 1980. *German New Guinea: A Bibliography.* Department of Law, Research School of Social Sciences, Australian National University, Canberra.

Sack, P. and Clark, D. (eds and trans). 1979. *German New Guinea: The Annual Reports.* Australian National University Press, Canberra.

———. 1980. *Albert Hahl: Governor in New Guinea.* Australian National University Press, Canberra.

———. 1983. *Eduard Hernsheim: South Sea Merchant.* Institute of Papua New Guinea Studies, Boroko.

Salisbury, R.A.F. 1970. *Vunamami. Economic Transformations in a Traditional Society.* Melbourne University Press, Melbourne.

Schmeltz, J.D.E., and Krause, R. 1881. *Die ethnographische-anthropologische Abtheilung des Museum Godeffroy in Hamburg; ein Beitrag zur Kunde der Südsee-Völker.* Friederichsen & Co., Hamburg.

Schnee, H. 1904. *Bilder aus der Südsee. Unter den kannibalischen Stämmen des Bismarck-Archipels.* Reimer, Berlin.

Sentinella, C.L. 1974. *Miklouho-Maklai: The New Guinea Diaries.* Kirsten Press, Madang.

Simet, J. 1977. *The Future of the Tumbuan Society.* Institute of Papua New Guinea Studies, Discussion Paper 24.

Simet, J. 1991. Tabu: Analysis of a Tolai ritual object. PhD thesis. Australian National University, Canberra.

Specht, J. 1980. 'Lasting Memorials': the early years at the Australian Museum. *Kalori.* 58:7-11.

Spiegel, H. 1967. A study of Buka-Passage (Solomon Islands) ceremonial paddles. *Records of the Australian Museum.* 27(3):33-78.

Thiel, M. 1909. Nachruf: Richard Parkinson. *Amtsblatt für Neuguinea.* 15:113-115.

Thurnwald, R. 1910. Im Bismarckarchipel und auf den Salomoinseln 1906-1909. *Zeitschrift für Ethnologie.* 1:98-147.

Tschauder, J.J., and Swadling, P. (trans). 1979. The Aitape Coast. *Records of the National Museum and Art Gallery* (Papua New Guinea). 7:35-107.

Webster, E.M. 1984. *The Moon Man.* Melbourne University Press, Melbourne.

West, F. 1972. Parkinson, Richard (1844-1907). In P. Ryan (ed.), *Encyclopaedia of Papua New Guinea,* vol. 2, p. 890. Melbourne University Press, Melbourne.

Woichom, J. 1979. A review of Richard Parkinson's 1900 paper on the Aitape Coast – The viewpoint of an Ali Islander. *Records of the National Museum and Art Gallery* (Papua New Guinea). 7:13-29.

Author's Foreword

A thirty-year stay on various South Sea islands has made me familiar with the land and people. From 1875 to 1882, I became acquainted with Samoa through the Polynesians living around me, and after I had settled on the Gazelle Peninsula in the latter year and been surrounded on all sides by Melanesians, I endeavoured to study this interesting people also, during the course of numerous longer journeys and short excursions.

I was able to complete my observations not only through repeated visits to individual places, but also from questioning the natives working on the plantations in all parts of the Bismarck Archipelago and the Solomon Islands. A wealth of material was available, which enabled me to control and expand my observations. Thus, over the years my records have accumulated, from which individual sections have occasionally been revised and published.

From many quarters I have been called upon to begin the revision of my entire observations and experiences. The late Geheimrat Bastian, with whom I was accustomed to having frequent, long discussions on the usages and customs of the Melanesians, during a visit to Germany in 1894, persuaded me at that time to undertake the work. While this has not seen the light of day until now, it so happened that the more I progressed with the revision, the more aware I became of how fragmentary and incomplete my records largely were. Gaps that could not be filled in were discovered everywhere; throughout, doubts persisted whether this or that record was entirely accurate. Thus for a time the work became loathsome to me, and the manuscript lay for months in a drawer, to appear once more, largely due to the exhortations of my friends in Europe. However, nobody knows better than the author how much is still to be retrieved before we are totally familiar with the natives, their customs and traditions, and their spiritual life.

Nevertheless, I hope that the critics will not judge me too harshly. I would all too happily have given a rounded whole instead of a defective sketch, but despite everything, what I offer to the reader will contain many a new thing and will lay aside old errors. Many customs and traditions are rapidly vanishing through the influence of the Europeans, whether they be missionaries, assistant judges or other colonists. Tools and weapons find their way into national museums, and modern European items take their place. Already natives are coming to me with their sons, to show their descendants the old objects preserved in my collection. When a further twenty-five years pass, in the ethnological museums of Europe one will be able to show the astonished natives of New Britain or New Ireland objects that their forefathers used in war and peace, which will appear just as strange to their descendants as the stone axes and spear tips of their ancestors do to present Europeans. The numerous gaps will only be filled in after we have made closer contact with the individual tribes with which we have only cursorily become acquainted until now; especially after becoming competent in their language. There are still, as much on New Britain as on New Ireland and Bougainville, tribes of whose language we do not know a single word, with whom we have never come into contact. It remains for later researchers to fill in all these gaps.

I do not need to say much about the figures accompanying the text. They are reproduced from individual photographs and will contribute much to the illustration of the contents. Those who desire further pictorial material will find this in the two-volume *Papua Album* that I have published in conjunction with my friend Geheimrat A.B. Meyer of Dresden.

In conclusion, I must express my gratitude to those who made their observations available to me, thereby placing me in a position to complete the description of the natives, their customs and traditions. First in line are the missionaries of the Mission of the Sacred Heart, who so very willingly gave me information and records for perusal. Also I must thank the commanders of visiting German warships for the courtesy of offering me, from time to time, the opportunity during their cruises to visit such parts of the archipelago as otherwise lie beyond the usual trade routes. I must likewise thank the firms E.E. Forsayth and Hernsheim & Co. for the many opportunities they gave me to get to know the land and people of the archipelago on the voyages of their ships to the various islands.

Bismarck Archipelago, 1906
R. Parkinson

Editor's Foreword

This book would not have required an editor had not the great distance of the author from his homeland made it impossible for him to undertake the tasks involved with the printing. The manuscript that Herr Parkinson submitted was ready for press; it certainly appeared, as one may still perceive in the text, that it was not written in one piece but originated piecemeal as the investigations of the author progressed and expanded. It might have been more convenient to arrange the material more pertinently and systematically; but the editor too could not justify what the author had not deemed necessary. Thus everything has remained essentially as the author wrote it; only stylistic unevenness and repetitions, explicable by the nature of the origin of the book, have been removed, as far as possible. Nowhere have I undertaken factual changes, not even in those instances where I have not been in agreement with the author. This is particularly so in theoretical discussions. Situations have another perspective when one is personally confronted with them in real life, rather than when one critically examines them in one's study. Advantages and disadvantages are found on both sides. Whoever lives in the open among the children of nature knows the conditions better than the scholar at home; but he judges the origin and development of these conditions one-sidedly, because the possibility of comparison with related phenomena is lacking, which only an extensive knowledge of the literature would provide. Thus Herr Parkinson's theories – for example, on the origin of the secret societies – do not find overall agreement with the experts. Despite this, I have let everything remain unaltered, even the daring hypothesis that argues its way back to a manifesto of anthropological similarities between the inhabitants of New Britain and the Australians, from an apparent connection of both regions at the beginning of the Tertiary Period. One can at the very least call the hypothesis courageous, since until now even the most highly fanciful anthropologist has not once attempted to date the existence of mankind generally, not to mention a mankind already differentiated into races, further back than the beginning of the Tertiary Period. Whether mankind existed even at the end of this period is still disputed by the experts.

However, such hypotheses should not form an absolute in knowledge; they are only there to bring together for the first time an entangled mass of evidence into a provisional form. By their subjective nature they have more value to their authors than to others, and like all hypotheses, are judged accordingly, to be cast off by others as knowledge progresses. Similarly, in this book also, they are only non-essential parts, the chief value lying in the large amount of factual material that it contains, which forms a veritable mine of information for ethnologists. Certainly the book is not intended to give a scientific, exhaustive presentation of the ethnology of the Bismarck Archipelago – specialist works of the author published earlier contain more details on their defined areas – it is not directed exclusively to scholars but predominantly to a broader circle that has an interest in our colonies and their inhabitants. We have only few such books; the earlier, vigorous interest in land and ethnological reading has sunk markedly since the end of the period of the great journeys of discovery, and only arises anew in direct connection with colonial politics.

The new colonial-political era has not been without influence on the character of this literature. With the now completed partitioning of the earth among the civilised states of Europe and America, the scientific investigation of the earth also has become more and more nationalised, so to speak. The states had primarily the intention only of securing the economic exploitation of certain regions; but after the division of economic and commercial zones there soon followed the division of scientific work. It was, of course, also natural that the scholars whose interests had previously indiscriminately covered the entire earth, now turned in preference to the overseas colonies of their own fatherlands. The time of great world journeys, the traversing of entire continents – the crossings of Africa have already been reduced to sports – have passed, on the one hand because the earth is largely known, and there is no longer anything major to discover, but also because each of the great civilised nations have secured a portion of the earth's surface for themselves and confined themselves to it. They are beginning to look around their property and establish themselves domestically.

In the process, the scientific study of land and people has remained firmly in the background; practical needs, the demands of merchants and planters had to be considered first. Above all, the security and convenience of commerce, improvement of sanitary conditions, the supply of a labour force, and so on, had to be taken care of. Naturally, there was much profit for science in this. Good maps were a first requirement, and we know how excellently many officers of our protectorate forces have performed in this area; no less important were the exploration of the soil and mineral treasures, and the knowledge of useful plants. These investigations have brought rich gains to geography, geology and botany. However, this scientific exploitation resulted more fortuitously and incidentally; the dominant feature was immediate, practical usefulness. Thus it came about that the sciences that promised no direct benefit were neglected, primarily the science of mankind and his culture, anthropology and ethnology.

It has certainly been stressed often enough that successful colonial politics, which are yet based to a great extent on a proper, purposeful treatment of the natives, are only possible on the basis of thorough ethnological knowledge. One must first of all get to know a people that one wishes to rule; one cannot expect that a primitive people become familiar with the complicated structures of our civilisation, with our fine understanding of completely foreign perceptions of justice or moral concepts, rather we must endeavour to understand their culture, their thoughts and their sentiments. However, despite the various activities that are often the ultimate cause of native revolts, through the violation of customs or perceptions that appear laughable or absurd to us but are sacred to them, one has mostly preached to deaf ears. Ethnology is still an unappreciated, but for the first time growing, science, which is studied neither in schools nor in universities, and therefore even among the educated only seldom finds real understanding. The ethnographic museums are still collections of curiosities to lay people; that the stored rarities might have another purpose than the pleasure of passing curiosity, comes least to mind.

This lack of interest and understanding can not, of course, be remedied overnight. However, nothing is more appropriate for dragging meaningful participation in ethnological problems out of the narrow circle of specialists into the broader popular circle than the universally understandable books of this present type. Nobody who is aware with what loving zeal he has studied the life of the natives during the entire thirty years of his stay in the South Seas is in any doubt that Herr Parkinson was the appropriate person to write such a book on the Bismarck Archipelago and its inhabitants. Witnesses to this are his numerous scientific essays, and no less so the many beautiful artifacts for which the German museums, particularly those of Dresden and Berlin, are obliged to his collecting zeal.

One can therefore only wish that the book finds its merited success with the German public, and that the opportunity will soon be given to the author to remove the deficiencies adherent to a first attempt, in a second edition.

The illustrations that adorn the book are for the most part taken from the author's original photographs; some of them, however, are from photographs of objects in the Berliner Museum für Völkerkunde. These are illustrations numbers 61 to 64, 66, 70, 82, 102, 117 to 119, and 123 to 125.

The pen drawings in the Berlin Museum were similarly produced, partly from Parkinson's pencil sketches, partly from illustrations in the author's earlier publications, and partly from originals in the Berlin Museum.

Table 49 and the text illustrations numbers 120 to 122 are reproduced from the splendid tables in the *Publikationen aus dem Königlichen Ethnographischen Museum zu Dresden,* volumes 10 and 13, with kind permission of the publishers, von Stengel & Co. in Dresden, and of the editor, Geheimrat A.B. Meyer, to whom at this point I express my deep gratitude.

The maps were drawn by Dr M. Groll in Berlin, from the map of the Bismarck Archipelago in the *Großer Deutscher kolonialatlas,* which was provided by Herr Parkinson with amendments and modifications.

Finally I must state my thanks to the publishers, Herren Strecker & Schröder, for the willing cooperation they have given me in the editing, and particularly, in the production of the book.

Berlin, September 1907
B. Ankermann

Plate 1 Gorge at Möwehafen. Fissure in a raised coral reef, widened by erosion

1 New Britain with the French Islands and the Duke of Yorks

1. The Land

The main island of the Bismarck Archipelago is unquestionably the island of New Britain. From its northernmost point, Cape Stephens, it stretches first in a southerly direction about 100 kilometres to the isthmus that joins this northern part, the Gazelle Peninsula, to the main island. Then the land extends about 200 kilometres to the south-west to a second constriction between Jacquinot Bay to the south and Commodore Bay to the north. From there the rest of the island runs mainly westward, a distance of about 270 kilometres, the broad Willaumez Peninsula jutting out towards the north. The total length of the island is about 560 kilometres. The breadth is quite variable; from Cape Lambert in the north-west as far as Cape Gazelle in the north-east the breadth is about 90 kilometres, while the isthmus that joins the peninsula to the main island would not be much more than 20 kilometres. The greatest breadth of the island occurs between the northernmost point of Willaumez Peninsula and South Cape, approximately 145 kilometres; a narrower part is found further on, between Jacquinot Bay and the north coast, about 50 kilometres. The surface area of the island and the small neighbouring groups is approximately 34,000 square kilometres; that is, about as much as the Grand Duchy of Baden and the Kingdom of Württemburg put together. The preceding measurements make no claim to absolute accuracy. A precise survey of the island was undertaken by the Imperial Navy a few years ago, and at the conclusion other values were most probably provided, since the earlier measurements and cartographical representations which form the basis of the values given here are admittedly very superficial and imperfect.

As far as we know, two main geological formations appear to predominate in the island's structure, namely volcanic lava and coral formations; the latter raised high above sea level by the strength of the volcanic activity. Volcanic action continues today, although compared with earlier times it has undoubtedly declined significantly. Along the entire line from Cape Gloucester in the west to Cape Stephens in the north-west, there stretches a number of active volcanoes arranged in groups, and numerous extinct craters bear witness to the strength of the subterranean fire. Earthquakes are not infrequent today, although they cause less trouble; they are, however, still strong enough to arouse feelings of anxiety at their onset, and to be a reminder that one day they could bring about an unexpected, calamitous catastrophe, against which people are powerless. Several of the earthquakes that I have experienced during my many years' stay in the archipelago would have been, in spite of their short duration, strong enough to devastate a European town thoroughly; the solid stone buildings at home would have collapsed inwards, while out here the natives' huts and the settlers' houses built of wood indeed creak and groan in truly every joint, and thus shake so severely that standing upright actually becomes extremely difficult, yet because of their style of construction, they do not collapse.

The most well-known area up to now is the northern part of the island, the Gazelle Peninsula; that is, we know fairly thoroughly only the region lying east, north and north-west from Vunakokor (Varzinberg). In recent years the high mountain range forming the western edge of the peninsula, usually called the Baining Mountains, is starting to become better known to us, thanks to the Catholic mission that has been established there. Beyond Vunakokor the area really is still completely unexplored, and for the remainder of the island our total knowledge shrinks to the coastal strip and the offshore islands, and here too we must regretfully concede that our knowledge is only sketchy.

However, every excursion, no matter how small, into these unknown regions, steadily brings us new and unexpected discoveries and experiences. For later travellers and explorers there will still remain much to do, and a series of interesting surprises certainly lies ahead of them. Over the years the basic survey of the island by the Imperial Navy will also bring us much information about the inhabitants.

As the mail steamer from Australia approaches the coast of New Britain, the eye picks up, chiefly far to the north-west and west, hazy blue mountains whose peaks are frequently covered in thick cloud. Gradually the outlines become sharper; the high Cape Orford with the mountain range behind stands out clearly, and also to the north-east the outlines of high mountains stand out against the skyline – the highlands of southern New Ireland. Soon St George's Channel is clearly marked by the high land of New Britain in the west and New Ireland to the east. The direction of this inlet, roughly 35 kilometres wide at the middle, is approximately along a north-south line. On pre-1890 charts navigators were warned of unknown dangers there; we have known for a very long time now that the navigable waters of St George's Channel are deep and without any hindrance to navigation, although from time to time, depending on the prevailing wind, a strong current sets through the strait, alternating between northerly and southerly, against which sailing ships are almost powerless.

The east coast of the Gazelle Peninsula presents itself to the beholder from St George's Channel as a high, mountainous land. The isthmus that forms the connection with the main island is significantly lower; it is formed from raised coral limestone. The same formation predominates on the east coast of the main island, with outcrops of volcanic rock inland. The mountains in the south of the peninsula are wooded throughout, rounded in form, with not very steep slopes, so that they seem well suited for establishing plantations. Numerous streams, large and small, furrow through the valleys, several of which cut deeply into the land. Into the small, Henry Reid Bay in the south of the peninsula flows quite a large stream, navigable by boats for a fair distance upstream from the mouth. The sea depth increases rapidly off the beach, and good anchorages are not available here. Henry Reid Bay is an exception, but even it offers a secure mooring only during a north-west wind.

As soon as Cape Palliser is passed, the scenery changes. To begin with, the mountains retreat somewhat and the slopes become more gentle; the uniform dark green of the tropical forest is interrupted by larger or smaller, grassy, pale-green shimmering fields, and the further north we go, the more these fields increase in extent, interrupted by patches of forest and traversed by deep, wooded ravines.

A little north of Cape Palliser lies a small bay, protected by an offshore coral reef with two small islets, and forming a good harbour even if only for small vessels. The natives call the place Mutlar and visit it occasionally to hunt turtles. A little north lies a small, concealed harbour, Rügenhafen (Putput to the natives), that I discovered in 1884 on a boat trip along the coast. The entrance is narrow, so that only one ship at a time can pass through; branches of the mighty forest trees, which extend from both sides over the narrow channel, brush the ship's sides here and there with their foliage. Yet nowhere in the entrance is the water depth less than 13 metres, and in the basin which opens beyond this pass, a great number of vessels find room to anchor in depths of 11 to 12 metres. Vessels lie absolutely securely here, and since Rügenhafen and Mutlarhafen are the only safe harbours on the eastern side of the Gazelle Peninsula, they are certain to become of no lesser importance over the course of years when the establishment of plantations has opened up the hinterland. At present the shoreline still consists of a thick, tropical forest flora; nothing stirs on the surface of the crystal-clear basin,

Fig. I Coral limestone rock, coast of St George's Channel

screeching cockatoos greet the visitor, and flocks of pigeons inhabit the treetops. Far and wide, deep, silent, forest tranquillity reigns, for the entire region is uninhabited; from time to time natives come from far away to exploit the abundance of fish in the harbour here.

About 4 kilometres north of Rügenhafen, a broad, deep valley cuts far into the land. Here is the mouth of one of the largest waterways of the peninsula, the Warangoi, which is named Karawat further inland. The fall is steep and the amount of water during the dry period of the year is not significant; in the rainy season it is transformed into a foaming, rushing, mountain torrent which can only be navigated with great difficulty upstream as well as downstream. Years ago, in the company of Bishop Couppé and the surveyor Herr Rocholl, I travelled the river by boat from the mouth to a point just south of Vunakokor. We covered this distance in a four-day journey, not without great exertion. From time to time the boats had to be dragged over shallow sandbanks, then fallen, mighty forest trees barred the way, from bank to bank, forming a barrier over which the pent-up water rushed, foaming and thundering; here and there were open stretches with deeper water so that paddles could be used, but even here we proceeded only slowly and with the utmost effort, for the current was a very strong one. The river ran in a bed that, with many bends, twined itself sometimes between steep banks that jutted out like bastions, and sometimes through reedy lowlands. Here and there mighty trees arched a leafy canopy over the surface of the water, or slender bamboo canes, united into mighty stands, stretched their fine, delicate foliage far over the banks, and between them shone the pale, columnar trunks of the imposing eucalyptus trees (*Eucalyptus naudiniana*), characteristic of the vegetation of New Britain.

The scenery is quite magnificent, and changes at each of the numerous bends, so that the four days during which we advanced upstream seemed to us to pass rapidly. But even more rapid was the return journey, for the distance that we had covered upstream in four days of hard work, we accomplished downstream in a four-hour journey. In a headlong rush our three boats raced downstream, driven solely by the strong current which was further enhanced by a torrential downpour that caught us unawares at our last camp site. The paddlers sat there helplessly; the entire effort fell on the helmsman, who had to maintain a steady eye and powerful arms to dodge huge boulders or tree stumps and skirt steep rocky banks, in guiding our fragile craft safely downstream during the raging journey. To be sure, every one of us was relieved when the thundering of the breakers proclaimed that the mouth of the Warangoi was nearby and our wild journey was at an end.

At the river mouth the New Guinea Company had set up a sawmill a few years ago, to exploit the abundant stands of timber, especially the valuable stand of eucalyptus.

Onward from the mouth of the Warangoi the landscape creates an increasingly pleasing and agreeable impression. The coconut groves become thicker, in places forming a dense border to the beach, and on the hills their tops project above the forest; extensive cultivated fields reveal the presence of people, whose grass-covered huts peep out of the greenery on the beach, and also on the high plateau and its slopes.

Inland the peak of Vunakokor, or Varzinberg, rises approximately 600 metres above the land, and ascending clouds of smoke, large clearings, as well as other signs, proclaim that population numbers cannot be small.

As we penetrate further northwards into the channel, initially we notice individual treetops looming like small black mounds on the northern horizon; they increase rapidly, and form a seemingly low, continuous wall; soon, however, we distinguish tree trunks and treetops, and then the white sandy beach and the shining foam of the surf on the coral reef; nearer still we recognise individual islands, the islands of the Duke of York group.

We round a low, wooded spur, Cape Gazelle, and there extending before us is a portion of the north coast of the Gazelle Peninsula; in the background the deep Blanche Bay towered over by the mountains of the Mother peninsula. On the right, lie two small islets, the Credner Islands; they are thickly wooded, and rise only a few metres above sea level. As a consequence of their isolated position, they were proposed by the administration as a quarantine station, and one could only with great difficulty find a more suitable site.

In the channel, signs of white settlement are sparse, but from Cape Gazelle onwards they increase rapidly. A few kilometres westward, at the small bay of Kabakaul, brightly shining, corrugated iron-roofed dwellings and warehouses become visible, and around about, extensive clearings and the beginnings of plantations betray the presence of white settlers. A little further on still, the number of buildings grows quickly; from the shore far inland stretch palm plantations; dead straight and at regular intervals, the rows of planted coconut palms march over mountains and through valleys; the virgin forest and grassy plains have long disappeared, and far along the shore, as inland, the eye perceives palm top upon palm top. The stately settlement of the Catholic Mission of the Sacred Heart with a twin-towered chapel and a number of single- and multi-storey large dwellings and school buildings comes next into view. The settlement, which was named Vunapope (foundation or root of the papacy) by the missionaries, is at the

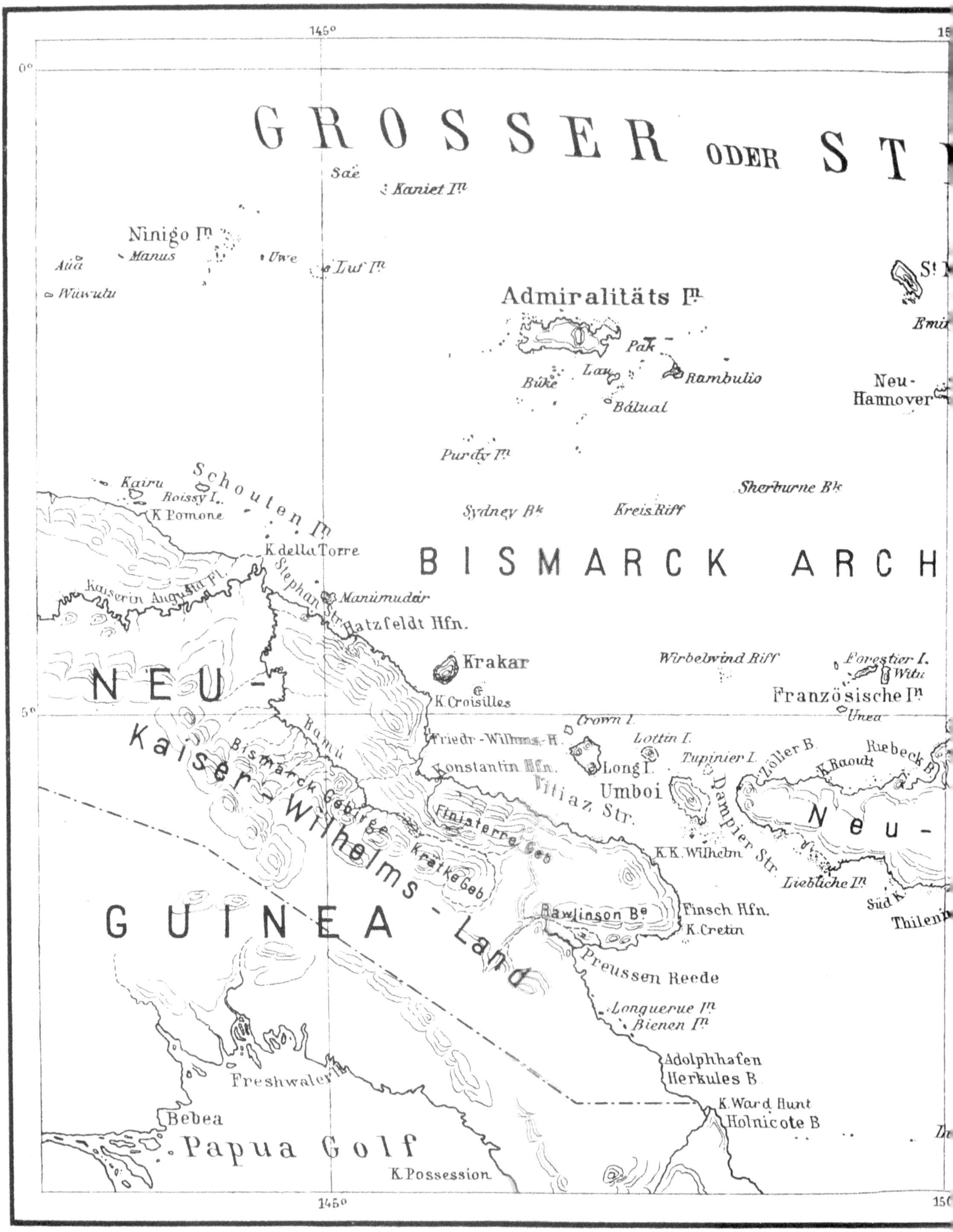

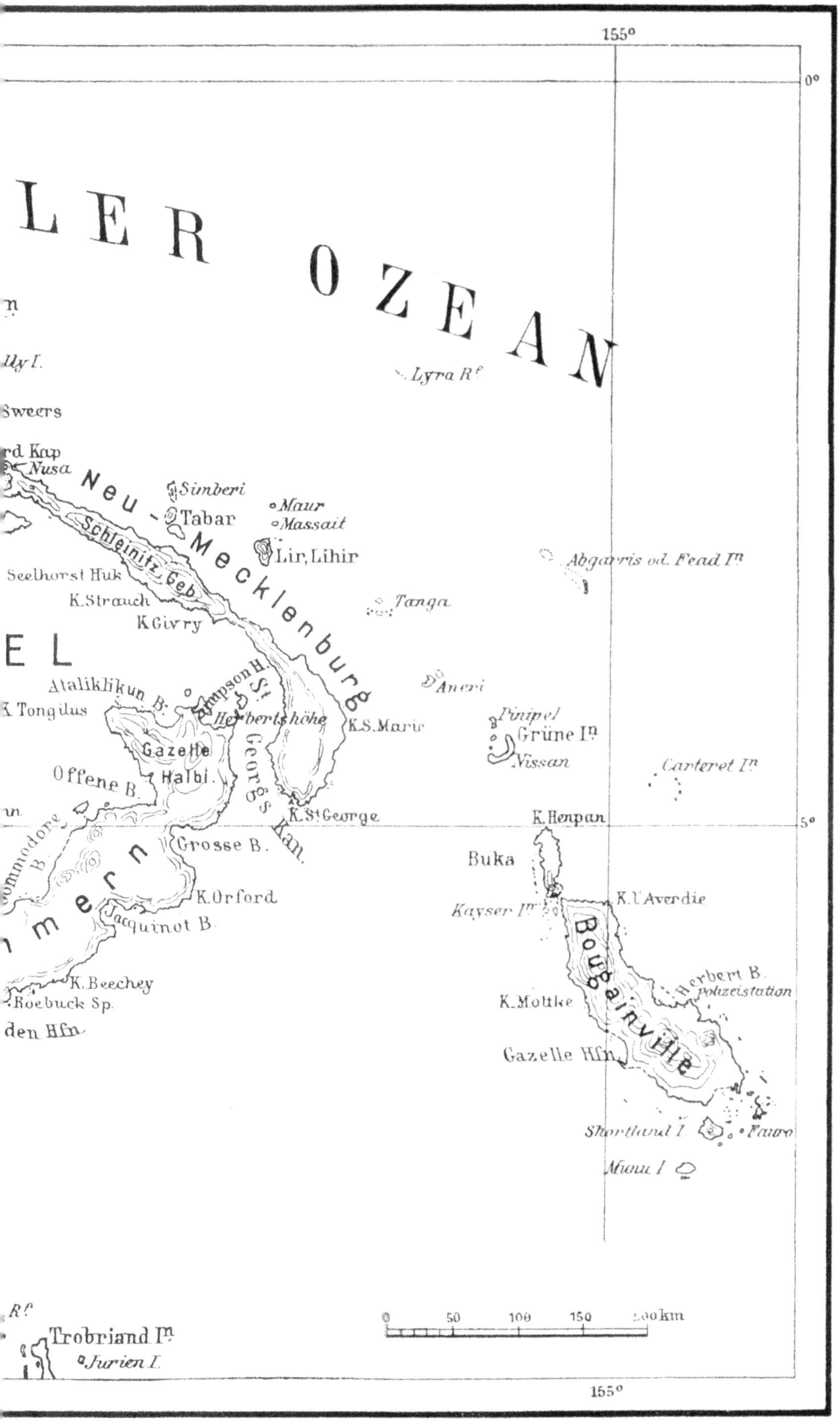

NEW BRITAIN WITH THE FRENCH ISLANDS AND THE DUKE OF YORKS

Map 1 The Bismarck Archipelago

same time the seat of the Catholic bishop of the Diocese of New Britain.

A little beyond the mission station, actually bordering it, is the Herbertshöhe plantation of the New Guinea Company with the settlement of the same name, and here also is the seat of the imperial administration. The stately home of the imperial governor, on a dominating hill, towers over a large number of dwellings, offices and warehouses that belong partly to the New Guinea Company and partly to the imperial administration, and following this are the extensive areas of the great Ralum plantation, which stretch along the beach towards Schulze Point, with their various annexes and plantation buildings.

Off Herbertshöhe one almost always finds a larger or smaller assembly of ships; beside stately German warships and the packet boats of Norddeutsche Lloyd, lie larger and smaller vessels belonging to the colony's merchant and plantation firms, which maintain settlements on the various islands of the archipelago. A suitable harbour is not, however, available, yet the spacious roadstead is fairly protected and offers excellent anchor ground with moderate depth.

If we go ashore, we find broad, well-maintained roads which have been constructed, not without great cost, in part by the imperial administration and in part by the plantation owners. These roads lead inland from Herbertshöhe, and connect the individual plantation stations with their central bases and with one another; however, they also lead out over the plantation region, and year by year the roading system is further improved and extended. The young colony stands in other ways on the path of progress, as is revealed by a stately, two-storey courthouse, spacious hotels, narrow gauge railways, telephone wires, and so on.

Blanche Bay itself begins about 8 kilometres west of Herbertshöhe. It is bounded to the west and south by a high plateau that slopes steeply to the beach; in the north and north-east the boundary is the volcanic peninsula with the three extinct volcanoes North Daughter (Tavanumbattir or Balnatoman), Mother (Kombiu) and South Daughter (Turanguna). At the foot of Mother rise a further two low craters, the more northerly of which is extinct and covered with vegetation right to the floor, while the southern one with its adjacent crater Kaije is still mildly active. The inwardly collapsed crater rim allows a view right inside; in a ditch-like depression in its floor is a ponding of water, and on the sides, rising sulphur vapour has covered the stones here and there with yellow sulphur crystals. Kaije is a smaller crater on the rim of the above-mentioned one, and in 1878 was still in full activity; since then a quiet period has set in, and it is apparently becoming extinct, although in odd places hot sulphur vapour wells up between the lava blocks and the rocks feel hot. When I settled in the Bismarck Archipelago in 1882, one of my first trips was to the peak, or more precisely to the crater rim, of Kaije. At that time, numerous traces of the most recent eruption were still evident. Scorched tree trunks surrounded the foot and the lower half of the mountain, nowhere was there a green stalk visible, the volcano loomed black and barren over its surroundings. Only with the greatest care could one walk on the inner slope of the crater, the intense heat of the rock, and the rising, foul-smelling hydrogen sulphide gas quickly drove the visitor back to the windward crater wall. Today the sides of the mountain are almost entirely covered with vegetation, even the inner walls of the crater are beginning to be covered with pale green, and the rock has already cooled to the extent that one can walk about inside the crater without burning the soles of one's boots. In the depths the volcanic hearth is still not yet extinguished, as demonstrated among other things by the numerous hot sulphur springs that pour from the foot of the volcano into Blanche Bay. One of these, situated beside the Hernsheim farm, Rabaul, has recently been used successfully for treating rheumatic pains.

From the peak of Mother, approximately 770 metres, which can be reached in a climb of about three hours from the beach, the visitor is offered a vista of incomparable beauty. Within a narrow field of view lie the sides of the mountain with the huge, deep gullies to the north, and with the maze of forested ravines and precipices. The highest peak itself, with the slight depression, the remains of the former crater, is overgrown with rank grass. To the south we peer into the smaller craters described above, and gaze upon the wooded South Daughter, approximately 530 metres tall.

Out of the clear waters of Blanche Bay rises the small, flat island of Matupi, and between the greenery of the coconut palms peep the corrugated iron roofs of the Hernsheim trading settlement. The ships that lie at anchor in the small safe harbour of Matupi look like miniatures. Beyond Matupi opens the broad basin of Blanche Bay with its dark blue water, above which tower two isolated masses of rock which, because of their shape, have been given the name the Beehives. Not far from the opposite shore, in the southern half of the basin, we notice a flat island about as large as the island of Matupi; this is Vulcan Island which in 1878, at the same time as the eruption of Kaije, rose from the depths of the sea, and is today already covered with vegetation. Seen from our vantage point, Blanche Bay gives the overall impression of being an earlier mighty crater, with an opening to the east through which the sea has broken. Around it the shore slopes steeply, in many places almost vertically, to the sea; especially in the southern half of the bay where the sea floor also drops steeply into the

Fig. 2 Kaije volcano overlooking Blanche Bay

depths, and consequently no anchor grounds are available here. The shores of the inner, northern part of the bay, Simpson Harbour, are less steep. There is also a lesser depth of water, and because of its spaciousness and sheltered position, as well as on account of the totally safe entrance, this would appear to be suitable as a fleet station, the more so as on its shores extensive flat land is available for the erection of coal depots, buildings and other installations. The Bremen Norddeutsche Lloyd has recently established a large installation here, which will serve as the main base for the company's steamers travelling in the archipelago.

Wandering further south, the eye then glimpses the broad, high plateau of the northern Gazelle Peninsula from which Vunakokor rises like an isolated cone. This part of the peninsula especially, when seen from our high vantage point, gives the perfect impression of an English park, with green lawns, isolated trees, small and large copses, and extensive woodlands. In the south and west this giant park is enclosed by high, shimmering blue mountains, the Baining Mountains.

Yet the scenic beauties are still not exhausted. If we turn to the east, before us lie both small Credner Islands (Balakuwor and Nanuk), also named the big and the little Pigeon Islands because of the pigeons that occasionally roost there. A little further on we espy the entire Duke of York group in a bird's eye view; we can clearly distinguish the narrow arms of the sea that separate the individual islands, and wind like irridescent silver strips through the dark portions of land. Away over on the far side of St George's Channel, like a spectacular backdrop to a magnificent landscape, rise the mighty mountains of New Ireland, to disappear as far to the south as to the north, in the bluish haze.

Once more, the picture changes when we gaze towards the west. The entire north coast of the peninsula lies at our feet with its offshore islands, the most significant of which is the extinct, wildly rugged crater Uatom or Watom (Man Island). Extensive coconut stands stretch from the beach up to the plateau, and between these, rising columns of smoke reveal the presence of dense population. Regular plantation establishment is just developing in this area, and only merchants and missionaries dwell at short distances along the shore. Actual harbours are not available here, and the anchorages, which according to the site offer greater or lesser security, are inferior. The broad bay which cuts into the land further westwards is Weberhafen; adjoining it, a splendid, wooded, well watered plain, running to the south and south-east, extends right behind Vunakokor, bordered in the west and south by the gently rising foothills of the Baining Mountains. This plain is expected in time to become of high economic significance, for the soil is deeper and better here than on the pumice plateau north of Vunakokor, where only coconut palms will be able to be cultivated successfully. The imperial

Fig. 3 River valley of the Karo, Baining Mountains

administration is also endeavouring to connect this part of the peninsula by a road system with the seat of government in Herbertshöhe and the main landing place of ships there, since Weberhafen too offers no absolute protection.

Beyond the plain the high, rugged Baining Mountains cut off the view.

The preceding description offers only a slight impression of the magnificent view. In the wonderful combination of land and sea I know of only one view that can compare, that from the peak of Vesuvius. However, when the image that is offered to the eye from the crater rim of Vesuvius is compared with a landscape sketched in bold strokes, I would similarly compare the view from the peak of Mother with one of those prize exhibits in which the artist has reproduced each small detail with love and care. This is conveyed by the wonderful transparency of the air: at a distance where objects seen from Vesuvius are already disappearing into indefinite outlines, from Mother in a favourable light we can still perceive very clearly the feathery crowns of the palms on distant heights, or the trunks of forest trees on the steeply sloping mountain sides.

To the west of Weberhafen the Baining Mountains approach the beach ever more closely, and the flat shore margin becomes narrower, finally disappearing completely after the small island of Masava. This islet lies on a coral reef, and with this

Plate 2 Robert Koch Spring on the Willaumez Peninsula

and the coast of the peninsula it forms a small, fairly safe harbour for smaller vessels. Close by lies a second small island called Masikonápuka, today still densely populated. Both islets were, right up until a short time ago, a type of stronghold from which the inhabitants made their raids, especially on the Baining Mountains, partly to capture slaves who were then traded on further to the east, and partly to seize *virua;* that is, human flesh. These events are now understood to be dying out as a result of the influence of the Catholic mission and the imperial administration.

From both previously mentioned islands onwards, the Baining Mountains come right down to the shore and rapidly rise to a significant height. Fertile valleys, through which foaming brooks flow, lie scattered among the mountains; for example, the valley of the Karo stream with its cascades and waterfalls. Inland about 8 kilometres from the beach the Catholic mission station of St Paul lies as a temporary, forward post, in a charming hollow surrounded by high, forest-crowned mountains.[1]

The character of the coastline does not change until Cape Lambert (Tongilus), the north-western corner of the Gazelle Peninsula. Before we reach here, however, we pass a group of small, uninhabited islands, the Scilly Islands (Talele). Once past the cape, we notice that the Baining Mountains, falling steeply right to the shore, appear as a coastal range that continues in a south-easterly direction. The mountains, soaring to a height of about 1,500 metres are wooded right up to the peaks. Out of the leafy green, waterfalls shimmer, and fairly full streams pour into the sea. The most significant of these watercourses, the Toriu (Holmes River) runs into the sea about 55 kilometres south-east of Cape Lambert. Here in recent years, the Catholic mission has established a steam sawmill which is at the forefront as quite the furthest advanced outpost of colonisation on the Gazelle Peninsula.

From the mouth of the Toriu onwards, the mountains gradually retreat, and the direction of the range which was, up until now south-easterly, alters and takes a more easterly course. This eastwards-extending range is apparently split from the mountain block in the north-west by a deep valley basin. From the peak of Vunakokor, and from Open Bay, this depression is clearly visible. Our knowledge of this mountainous district, although it lies not even 30 kilometres south of Herbertshöhe, is, however, still totally nonexistent; we do not even know whether the population of this mountain range is identical with the people of the north-western range, or whether one tribe differs significantly from the other.

From Weberhafen on to Cape Lambert and further along the coast from there, the sea voyage is quite dangerous, because of the many offshore coral reefs and sandbanks. However, the excellent annual surveys by HIMS *Möwe* are eliminating a great proportion of the dangers; however, coastal voyaging here still requires the greatest care and attention. Anchorages are available here and there along the coast, but only one single good harbour offers excellent protection. This is Powell Harbour (*Tava na tangir*), somewhat north of the isthmus.

1. On 13 August 1904 the founder of this station, Father Mathäus Rascher, who is frequently mentioned in this work, together with four other missionaries and five sisters of the Order of the Sacred Heart, was slain by the natives.

Fig. 4 Waterfall in a neighbouring valley of the Karo, Baining Mountains

It is deep and spacious, and protected against all winds; in the inner corner flows a quite significant stream which is navigable by boat for a distance inland. The shores of the harbour, however, are swampy and covered with extensive mangrove forest, but with increasing cultivation of the extensive hinterland, this problem too might be overcome.

If I have described the Gazelle Peninsula in some detail in the preceding pages, it is because this part of New Britain is by far the most important on the island; I would even go so far as to say the most important part of the entire Bismarck Archipelago. The Gazelle Peninsula flourishes economically year by year, and will maintain its importance in this direction for many years to come. Through its central position, it is eminently suitable for serving as a starting point for cultural undertakings in other parts of the archipelago, and its harbours form important support bases for sea travel. The significance of the roadstead at Herbertshöhe and the small harbour of Matupi, as well as Simpson Harbour, has been growing for years. Imaginary dangers for shipping, designated on earlier charts of this region, caused navigators to give it a wide berth. Through the Imperial Navy's reconnoitering, however, it has turned out that the greatest part of the alleged dangers do not exist, and since the archipelago is situated on the direct route between Australia and East Asia, each year more and more ships decide to take this closer route rather than going through the dangerous Torres Strait, full of reefs and other obstacles to shipping. Coal depots on the island of Matupi form an important supply point for steam traffic on this leg. This traffic has risen from year to year, in proportion to the expansion of the colony and with the growth of the young Australian confederation. From the recent population census one may assume that in about 100 years Australia will have a population of around 30 million people. This combined with the enormous traffic with East Asia, which is likewise constantly increasing in significance, must definitely have a beneficial effect on the Bismarck Archipelago. New, easily accessible trading areas for tropical products will be created, and the archipelago, within a few days' travel of Australia, will be in a position to cover a great part of these requirements.

Today, all this still lies in the distant future, but from one decade to another conditions change for the better. In 1882 traffic with the outside world was limited to the voyages of several small sailing ships, which the resident firms retained for their trading undertakings; from time to time, at long intervals a larger sailing ship also appeared, to ship out the assembled products; warships occasionally called in and were only too happy when they could steam out again. Postal connections with Australia occurred three or four times a year. All of this has already changed. Regularly voyaging saloon steamers of Bremen Lloyd and an Australian line take the mail and freight between the archipelago, Sydney, Singapore, Hong Kong and Japan; settlers and settlements increase, and the import of wares, like the export of colonial products, yield higher values year by year.

In spite of this, the German spirit of enterprise which at other times turned eagerly towards all newly opened-up regions of the world, has so far denied the islands of the Bismarck Archipelago the attention that they merit so highly, in spite of all the favourable circumstances. The reason for this is in part the superficial and inaccurate knowledge of the archipelago, which prevails in all circles of German society, and partly the bad experiences that the Berlin New Guinea Company had gone through years ago in Kaiser Wilhelmsland. The Protectorate of the New Guinea Company had almost always been mentioned in conjunction with sad and disheartening news, and even rose-coloured portrayals like those of Dr Finsch and more especially those of Herr Hugo Zöller, were unable to blot out the painful impression induced by the incessant bad news from the protectorate. Since the Bismarck Archipelago was included in the encompassing title, 'Protectorate of the New Guinea Company', the evil reputation of the German part of New Guinea had consequently extended to the island region as well, an inference as illogical as it was unfounded, although certainly excusable in view of the superficial knowledge of our most important South Sea colony.

The plantations of the Gazelle Peninsula consist almost exclusively of coconut palms. The long-fibre, silky type of cotton was produced as a by-product years ago and still is to a limited extent today, appearing on the market as Sea Island Cotton; however, since cotton prices have fallen, this secondary cultivation is dying out. In the area where the larger plantations are currently found, on the high plateau stretching southwards from the shore up to Vunakokor, other products would scarcely yield a remunerative profit. The thin layer of humus which covers the pumice layers from earlier volcanic eruptions is insufficient for other cultivation requiring a deep, heavy soil; for example, cocoa and coffee. These have found a soil suitable to them on the eastern and southern slopes and in the valleys of the Baining Mountains, and in the extensive region that stretches from Weberhafen to Vunakokor and beyond. In these regions there await many thousands of hectares of profitable cultivation; stretches just as extensive are accessible for coconut cultivation. Beyond Vunakokor the population is sparse, and one does not run the risk of troubling or restricting the natives in their settlements.

The southern part of New Britain adjacent to the Gazelle Peninsula appears to be of lesser significance, at least as far as our current acquaintance with this region justifies an opinion of it. This part, having the same surface area as the Gazelle Peninsula, to which it is connected by a hilly isthmus, forms roughly a square with sides of 80 kilometres, including Duportail Island on the north-west corner. In the south-west a second constriction links this part of the island with the western part of New Britain. The entire eastern, northern and southern flanks slope steeply to the sea and have no absolutely safe anchorage. In Jacquinot Bay in the south, good anchorage is found during the season of the nor'-westers, whereas the harbour is only partially protected during the period of the south-east wind.

The entire central part of this section consists of a high mountain range which comes right to the shore almost everywhere, showing several flat or gently rising plateaus predominantly in the north-east. The western flank consists of a series of moderately high volcanoes whose three highest peaks are found on the north-west corner: the volcanoes North Son (Golau) about 600 metres high, Father (Ulavun) some 2,000 metres high, and South Son (Bamus) about 1,600 metres high. The offshore island, Duportail (Namisoko or Lolobau), is also volcanic. Golau is extinct; on the other hand Ulavun and Bamus, and one crater on Namisoko are still active. From time to time powerful eruptions occur; their glow is visible at night over a wide area. In 1898 I was able to witness such an eruption quite clearly, south-west of Sandwich Island;[2] that is, at a distance of about 210 kilometres from the eruption site. The following year, as a result of an eruption by Ulavun, a broad strip of mud was visible, extending from the peak to beach level; in the lower, wooded zone of the mountain the devastation from this eruption was seen most clearly; here the vegetation had been totally ravaged by the hot mud: barren, dead tree trunks protruded from the already dried-up bed of mud, and in amongst this, huge lumps of rock debris, broken-off tree trunks, and so on, had piled up into insurmountable barriers. In 1896 [sic] no trace of this eruption remained. Further south of Bamus still other craters rise up along the coast, some active, others extinct, but of far smaller size and significance. This series of volcanoes, which takes up the entire western shore of Cape Quass, is separated from the central range by a deep depression which can be clearly observed from Open Bay to the north, and cuts deeply inland to the south-south-west. This depression receives the runoff from the series of volcanoes in the west and from the high mountain chain to the east; its confluence forms a rushing mountain torrent flowing into the so-called Hixon Bay, named Langalanga by the natives.

Of this part of the island too, we still really know very little. Seen from Wide Bay, the land seems to be well-populated from the beach to the mountain range, if we can draw any conclusion on the population size from the number and extent of the cultivations laid out everywhere, and from the rising columns of smoke. The steep plunge to the Langalanga valley in the west seems less populated.

2. On the west coast of northern New Ireland.

Fig. 5 Möwehafen

On the beach flats at the foot of the western side of the series of volcanoes, quite a large number of villages have been established; their inhabitants were, however, decimated by smallpox in 1897.

The northern shore towards Open Bay is named Nakanai by the inhabitants of the north of the Gazelle Peninsula. Years ago there were a few pitiful villages here, but these had disappeared by 1900. The coastline at the foot of the volcano is apparently called Wittau.

The only venture into the interior was undertaken in 1897 by Dr Hahl, Dr Danneil and Father Rascher. These three set out into the hinterland from the then-existing village of Watu on Open Bay, and after an arduous six-hour trek reached a village in the mountains. They were successful in establishing amicable relations with the natives, and, from their accounts and from the ethnographic articles brought back, which are the same as those that I have seen or bartered for on the eastern side, I have come to the conclusion that this population belongs to the same tribe that inhabits the eastern and southern coasts and the high mountain ranges, while the Nakanai and Wittau people belong to another tribe. The mountain inhabitants with whom the above-mentioned gentlemen came into contact were called Paleawe by the Nakanai people.

Economically, it seems that not a lot can be expected from this part of the island. It may be then that the Langalanga valley and the plains at the foot of the volcanoes should be given over to cultivation. In recent years there has been some success in establishing friendly exchanges with the natives of the northern and eastern coasts, with the result that a number of them were recruited as plantation workers. From the dense population there, one might anticipate obtaining a portion of the workers employed on the Gazelle Peninsula plantations in future. The Catholic mission is planning to set up a station there very shortly, and we may then hope to get to know these, in many ways highly interesting people, more closely.

The subsequent part of the island, between Jacquinot and Montague bays in the south and Cape Quass and Commodore Bay in the north, is on average about 50 kilometres wide. Here too the land is mountainous, and only on the northern side are larger, flat and gently rising stretches of outstanding soil condition available, mostly on the shore, enclosed by a border of mangrove trees.

We have now reached the large part of the island stretching to the west, with the Willaumez Peninsula extending northwards. The interior of this significant and interesting stretch of land is as good as totally unknown to us. The coasts have not yet been fully visited, but in the stretches explored thus far, a whole series of harbours have been identified on the southern side; a number of these must be designated as quite superb. On the stretch between the flat Cape Roebuck in the east and South Cape to the west, are, first of all, a number of smaller, sheltered harbours and anchorages, which form outstanding departure points for the cultivation of the stretches of land lying next to them as well as beyond. The latter exhibit overall the features of a gradually rising tableland upon which is based the not very high mountain range inland.

Offshore lie a number of small islands that show a terraced structure almost throughout. They are formed from coral limestone. Similar terraces are also to be observed on the coast of the main island, but these are frequently interrupted by watercourses and valleys, so that they do not appear so clearly here as on the small islands. Much further to the west, on the coast of Kaiser Wilhelmsland, this terrace formation comes into view particularly clearly and magnificently. Here, five to nine terraces are arranged one above the other, and these – for example, on Fortification Point – are so sharply pronounced that they might have been laid out by human hand with pick and shovel. While the terraces on Kaiser Wilhelmsland are to a large extent overgrown with grass, in New Britain both the terraces and their steeply sloping walls carry a lush forest vegetation.

Many of the islands are inhabited, and here, as on the coast of the main island, numerous, if not large, settlements are to be found. In the interior a more dense population seems to dwell, but we do not know much about that either.

A little westwards of the so-called South Cape (Cape Balli), north of the two small Ross Islands (Aveleng), lies a splendid harbour with several entrances, which was closely examined years ago by HIMS *Möwe* and has since then borne the name Möwehafen. It is formed from a series of three terraced islands which skirt the coast in such a way that, between coast and islands with the fringing coral reefs, a large basin is formed, offering ships of all sizes a totally safe anchorage, protected from all winds. Möwehafen is of paramount importance for the south coast of this part of the island: in future it will undoubtedly become the main trading centre for the western part of the island, as Blanche Bay is for the northern part of the island. A stream running into Möwehafen supplies superb drinking water throughout the year.

In 1896 I undertook a small excursion from Möwehafen that led me several kilometres inland. On a somewhat steeply rising path at an altitude of about 75 metres I and my companions came to a tableland, which bore signs of extensive, old, native cultivations. A well-trodden, broad path led inland, and following this we soon encountered great taro patches. The natives working on the cultivations promptly fled hastily into the protecting thickets at the sight of us; however, after several efforts we were able to entice the most stout-hearted out of their concealment. After initial communications had been established, still more natives joined us, until we were surrounded by about twenty of them, apparently the men working in the gardens. They led us to a small compound, comprising two huts, surrounded by a double palisade wall made of tree trunks. They indicated to us that they dwelt partly on the islands in the harbour and partly on the tableland, and after a while we heard drum signals from inland, a sign that there was a settlement there. We did not succeed in reaching it, however, although we followed the path leading there for a time and stumbled upon natives working. The soil was superb throughout, to which the large taro tubers grown in the cultivations bore ample witness. At several places I had a view over the tableland which apparently extended far to left and right, and only at a considerable distance inland was it bordered by high mountains. Möwehafen also therefore seemed to me to be very suitable as a start-off point for establishing agriculture.

The coast bore the same characteristics further to the west.

Between Möwehafen and Cape Merkus (Mulus) assorted good anchorages are available. Also, a number of quite significant watercourses empty here; the Pulié River, which pours into the sea not far from Cape Merkus, is of special importance because, in contrast with the general rule with local rivers, it has no bar beyond its mouth; this yields a water depth of 5 to 6 metres. Inside the mouth the river is 7 to 10 metres deep, and can be navigated for at least 20 kilometres inland by steamers up to 300 tonnes. Even in rainy times the current is insignificant, and the water never seems to overflow its banks. The soil on both sides of the river is superb, and appears to form a river flat, extending far inland.

Herr von Schleinitz, who navigated this river years ago as the first European, says about it: 'This river, besides the Augusta River (Kaiser Wilhelmsland), is the most significant of all the rivers discovered and explored up till now, and surpasses even the Ottilien River (Ramu) with regard to navigation.' I agree wholeheartedly with this opinion.

The forest on both banks of the river is certainly dense, but cannot be compared with almost impenetrable virgin forest and its giant trees. Deforestation would incur neither great difficulty nor expense, and the soil must, in my opinion, be suitable for every kind of tropical agriculture. I saw great stretches, that by clearing of the forest could easily be transformed into cocoa plantations. Also, the river flats do not bear the character of an absolute, low-lying area, but are sprinkled with small hills and ranges of hills, which seem eminently suitable for the establishment of settlements. The necessary construction materials could be sawn on the spot using water power without costly outlay, and I would, without exaggeration, designate the bank of this river as the most suitable site for settlement in the entire Bismarck Archipelago.

South-west of Cape Merkus lies a small, inhabited island group, 'Liebliche Inseln' on the maps. They are fairly densely covered with palms, and a few years ago the firm of E.E. Forsayth set up a small station here for the purpose of planting, but more especially for establishing friendly relations with the local natives, and persuading them to hire themselves out as plantation labourers. Gradually this undertaking seems on the way to being crowned with success, for natives from Cape Merkus right up to South Cape have gradually lost their fear of white people, and already work in the Ralum plantation of the above-mentioned firm.

From Cape Merkus onwards, the coast is fringed

Fig. 6 Party on the Pulié River, 10 kilometres from the mouth

with numerous islets, and, between these and the mainland, lies a splendid, protected harbour. Here too the coast offers numerous starting points for setting up cultivation, although the rivers are only of minor significance; for the most part they efficiently drain the system of high volcanic mountains, which start here and climb to imposing heights towards the west. The mountain range nears the coast the further westwards we go, and finally forms moderately wooded bluffs, 30 to 80 metres high.

The western tip of New Britain is surmounted by two high volcanoes, the mountains Below and Hunstein. Both of these volcanoes, the former of which is still active, together with a number of smaller volcanoes (some active, some extinct), form the nucleus of the entire western end of the island. Mount Below falls from its peak to its base in a continuous slope, and has the shape of an almost regular cone. The coast has various small bays which have more or less good anchorages according to the prevailing wind direction; proper harbours are lacking here.

On 18 March 1888, this region was the stage for a destructive natural event. In the early morning of that day, a tidal wave poured onto the shore and spread so rapidly along the coast that shortly after 7 a.m. its presence was felt in the far north of the island, in Blanche Bay on the Gazelle Peninsula. It was driven onto New Britain as far northwards as southwards; the north-running wave reached Blanche Bay first, the one running along the south coast not fully ten minutes later. In the inner corner of Blanche Bay the united waves reached 2 metres high, and for about two hours there was a continuous flooding and receding of the sea; at the western end of New Britain measurement established that the wave had reached 12 metres tall.

It was established later that the tidal wave had been caused by an explosion of volcanic Ritter Island in Dampier Strait.

The wave destroyed a large part of the low-lying coast of the island. Broad stretches were totally devastated; in places the coastline was completely razed and covered with trees tumbled over one another, broken coral limestone, sand and rotting sea creatures for up to a kilometre inland. Numerous native villages were swept away, and a great proportion of the population must have lost their lives through the suddenness of the catastrophe.

Two Europeans, von Below and Hunstein, together with a number of their coloured attendants, also met their deaths in this natural event. They were returning from an inland expedition, and were camping on the beach that morning, awaiting the arrival of the steamer that would take them back to Finschhafen. The steeply rising terrain behind the camp was probably brought down by the tidal wave, and the tumbling masses of earth and rock overwhelmed both the camp and its inhabitants. In spite of the most exhaustive searches the camp site could no longer be found.

From the western end of the island a broad flat stretches along the northern shore as far as the Willaumez Peninsula. The coastline has various deep bays, as well as several quite good harbours and numerous, more or less important rivers. The most significant of these flows into the sea not far from the Willaumez Peninsula, but even today its course is totally unexplored. Off the coast are extensive coral reefs, endangering shipping; several small islands also lie here but are of little significance. Extensive stretches of shoreline could with time be opened up for cultivation; yet today there is still not one single white settlement. Of course the rivers are all closed by bars to navigation by larger ships, although smaller vessels may go far upriver.

In several places the mountain range of the interior is of insignificant height, so that the northern and southern shores of the island could be connected by a road network without great difficulty or expense. Such a road system would extend out roughly from the lowlands of the river whose mouth is not far from Cape Merkus on the south side. It could traverse the entire length, across fertile stretches of land. The produce could then be transported to loading sites on the river bank.

Herr von Schleinitz, who explored this coast, incidentally expressed his opinion as follows:

> What I considered particularly important, is the fact that I ... came across larger low-lying areas, especially on New Britain. The low plain on New Britain, which is situated between the volcanic mountains of the western tip and those of the central part of the island, and runs from the north coast to the south coast, was estimated to cover an area of 4,000 square kilometres. It has, as far as I could examine, fertile soil watered by navigable streams, two of which I explored more closely by travelling 5 to 6 nautical miles upstream by boat. In fact they have an easily avoidable bar, about 1 metre deep off the mouth at low water, but beyond this they have navigable water to a depth of 4 to 12 metres for as far as I was able to travel upstream by rowboat. I thought it likely that these rivers had navigable waters of 4 to 5 metres for many miles still, further upstream.
>
> The plain ... has undoubtedly a great future, even if a portion of it should comprise swampy ground, indications of which were, however, not discernible.

So runs the account of Herr von Schleinitz in 1887 in the *Nachrichten aus Kaiser Wilhelms-Land* without so much as a single part of it having been adopted, so far, to take advantage of the indications given therein.

The reader will recognise from the above that I attribute the greatest significance to this western part of New Britain. Should the colony, as we might suppose and hope, develop further over the years, the western part of New Britain will rapidly outstrip the northern part, the Gazelle Peninsula – not only in consequence of the greater extent of the fertile stretches of land, but also because of easier access by means of navigable rivers and more secure harbours. Herr von Schleinitz estimated the flat land on the north coast at 4,000 square kilometres. However, by bringing the fertile land on the south coast into consideration as well, we would confidently estimate the total extent as double. The native population, as far as we could discover at present, is not exceedingly dense; in any case it is nowhere near as dense as on the Gazelle Peninsula where the administration is already experiencing difficulty in settling the natives on predetermined sites, so that areas of land surplus to their food requirements can be developed for efficient plantation enterprises by whites. The natives there cultivate mainly taro and to a very limited extent coconut palms. They can therefore be relocated to dwelling sites much more easily than those who grow mainly coconut palms, as on the Gazelle Peninsula, and who are naturally less inclined to give up their ownership of profitable resources and lay out new cultivations that would yield a profit only after a considerable number of years. For natives who cultivate taro it is all the same where their dwellings are moved to, provided they find suitable soil there, and the necessary protection against possible land-grabbing by colonial settlers.

The Willaumez Peninsula, a part of western New Britain connected with the main island to the south by a broad base, stretches northwards, with a north-south length of about 65 kilometres. Up to 1889 maps showed a number of raised volcanic islands here, separated from each other and the main island by broad arms of the sea. Herr von Schleinitz finally pointed out that what had previously been regarded as individual islands were actually high mountains connected by low-lying land. Exploration by HIMS *Möwe*, as well as expeditions by various private individuals, have recently established the precise shape of the peninsula. From not too far away it appears as if one is faced with an archipelago of volcanoes of varying heights. None of them is active today; however, if we imagine that all of these craters were actually active at one time, this must have been a sight, the like of which may scarcely be found on the rest of the earth's surface.

On the eastern side of the peninsula the spacious Hannamhafen offers a safer anchorage. The extinct volcanoes form a broad semi-circle around it. In particular, the regular, cone-shaped peaks of the Pyramidenberg, Zweigipfelberg, du Faureberg, Giquelberg, Raoulberg and Willaumezberg rise above their numerous smaller volcanic colleagues. Today idyllic calm pervades; the flanks of the fire-belchers have become overgrown with vegetation part-way up to the peaks over the years, but the fact that the subterranean fire is active even today is evident in the north-western corner of Hannamhafen.

On the occasion of a reconnoitre by HIMS *Möwe* in 1900, in which the author participated, together with Geheimrat Dr Koch, Governor von Bennigsen, and Dr Alex Pflüger from Bonn, white steam clouds were noticed towards evening in the inner corner of the harbour, rising at regular intervals above the treetops. Since general curiosity was aroused, an excursion to the spot was undertaken very early the following morning.

Right on the beach small streams of boiling water bubbled out of the sand, and beyond a narrow sand

Plate 3 A group on the island of Aveleng. Raised coral banks

barrier a small swamp of hot mud and water had formed. On skirting this swamp, we reached a wall of piled-up sinter blocks about 10 metres tall, over which we clambered for about ten minutes, forcing our way through the undergrowth and thickets. On emerging from the bush we saw before us, in a basin-like hollow surrounded by forest, a sinter field roughly 250 metres long and 150 metres wide, free of vegetation, from which several geysers hurled their boiling water and their columns of steam into the air. We carefully worked our way forwards over the hot and, in many places, very porous and brittle surface, past bubbling mud pools and hot springs, up to the larger, active geyser situated roughly in the middle of the field. In the interval of approximately two minutes it erupted for about a minute and spouted considerable amounts of water up high. Not far from this larger geyser was a smaller one which gushed water about 1 metre high in the same period.

It was extremely interesting to peer down into the throat of the larger geyser. When the water jet was perceived to have collapsed, one could step right up to the rim of the irregular, broad opening. Water, like steam, disappeared just as suddenly as it had been flung up; in the end there still remained a small film of steam at the bottom of the throat, where boiling water fell foaming and seething over mighty sinter blocks. This lasted for a few seconds, then it suddenly gurgled and roared in the depths, boiling water again broke forth vigorously out of every fissure, steam columns raged up and veiled everything that was going on further inside the throat, and in the middle of the steam cloud rose a water jet about 1.5 metres wide, that soared to about 5 metres and then separated into countless droplets which were hurled as a fountain about 10 metres high.

Beyond these two geysers, further back in the sinter field, lies a third, very large geyser. During our time there, this one sent no column of water skywards, and the intervals between the periods of activity could not be determined. However, there were indications that this geyser is active too, albeit at longer intervals. The sinter cone is very well preserved; we were able to go right to the edge of the throat, where we observed mighty volumes of boiling water bubbling wildly in the depths.

In the field there are also a number of small, hot springs, solfataras and mud volcanoes with masses of boiling, grey mud.

The boiling water thrown up had a strong salt content, with a pronounced acidic taste.

The subterranean hearth must lie very deep, as testified by the forest enclosing the sinter field. Mighty forest trees grew round about, right up to the edge of the field and stretched their green branches far out over it, indicating that soil temperature must be normal here, otherwise all vegetation would have died.

This geyser field is probably the remnant of once greater geyser activity, for round about, on later excursions into the virgin forest, we found sinter blocks of all sizes and stages of decomposition at altitudes up to 100 metres, and at one site a type of soil that Dr Pflüger identified as porcelain clay.

Although there are larger low-lying areas between the volcanoes, where cultivation might be very profitable, the peninsula can never be the stage for great undertakings because of its ground formation. Apart from that, the numerous volcanoes in their uneasy quiescence do not create an impression inspiring trust, and one involuntarily asks oneself the question: When will this place be the scene of a terrible catastrophe?

About 80 kilometres north-west of the outermost tip of the Willaumez Peninsula lies a small group of islands, indicated on maps as the Französische Inseln (French Islands). These comprise a northerly group, of which the island of Deslacs or Witu is the largest, the island of Forestier or Mundua the next largest, while about 50 kilometres to the south-west lies the isolated island of Mérite or Unea.

All of the islands consist in part of raised coral formations; however, the greatest part is volcanic rock. On the so-called North Island there are hot springs, and a not inconsiderable geyser, which develops significant activity right on the seashore, separated only by a sinter wall. This, however, does not appear to be regular. Right at the time I was there, the water fountain rose only about 1 metre; however, according to the natives' comments, the geyser could from time to time hurl a jet of water up to 10 metres high, and from the signs around this seemed not unlikely. Moreover the natives have the boiling water from this bubbling spring at their disposal, using it for cooking their food; it is seen to be surrounded by natives virtually all day long.

The island of Deslacs has two harbours that should not remain unmentioned here. One, Johann Albrecht Hafen, is big and spacious but of little value, because of its considerable depth of water. On the other hand, the second, Peterhafen, although much smaller, is of decided importance for the island group. Both harbours are the remains of former craters, the walls of which have collapsed in places, so that the sea has poured in and filled the crater with water. The small one in particular, the really charming Peterhafen, demonstrates this most clearly. It forms an oblong with steeply falling slopes on the landward side, rising to a height of about 150 metres. To seaward a sand spit juts out, concealing the entire harbour from the sea, so that even ships sailing past close inshore would never suspect such a harbour. In front of this crater harbour an offshore coral reef with a wide, deep entrance forms a good, outer harbour. Peterhafen itself is not very spacious; on the other hand even during the strongest winds it is as calm and still as a millpond. From the high crater rim there is a splendid view over the little basin and the blue tides of the outer harbour, bordered with a white crown of foaming breakers that roll over the coral reef.

The island group, which is in part the property of the New Guinea Company, exports a fairly large quantity of copra and therefore the company maintains an agent here who exploits the coconut crop. When I visited these islands for the first time years ago, they were heavily populated; today only a small remnant of the population is left. Numerous natives were struck down by a smallpox epidemic which ravaged the New Guinea coast in 1897 and also extended to New Britain and several of the smaller islands. The epidemic was introduced to the French Islands from the Willaumez Peninsula and proceeded in a terrible way, particularly on Deslacs. The smaller islands suffered to a lesser degree, and only Mérite seems to have been spared.

About 60 nautical miles west of the French Islands lies an extensive coral reef, Whirlwind Reef, which in 1899 almost caused a disaster for the imperial cruiser *Kormorant*. En route from Kaiser Wilhelmsland to the Bismarck Archipelago the cruiser, because of a shift in the strong current, ran onto the coral reef. Although the ship had not been holed, the forward section had embedded so deeply into the reef that initially all attempts to float her off by steam power proved fruitless. They therefore proceeded to lighten ship; the major part of the coal supply was thrown overboard; then followed all heavier items that could be disposed of for the present: chains, part of the ballast, torpedoes, munitions, steam winches, and so on. The cannon were held back right till the last critical moment. Fortunately they were saved, for on the seventh day, due to never-failing presence of mind and prudence, the commanding officer Lieutenant-Commander Emsmann, and his officers, supported by an efficient crew who carried out the necessary steps for saving the ship with unflagging and exacting effort during the worrying time, finally succeeded in refloating the cruiser.

The heroic saving of the ship from going down is one of those deeds of our German navy which is acknowledged far too little at home. The attention of the greater public is only aroused when a tragic catastrophe occurs, like the sinking of a ship. If the good Germans at home were more familiar with the doings of our fleet, particularly overseas, they might perhaps be less inclined to deny expenditure on the navy. While every triviality at home is discussed as widely as possible, those events that are not accessible to the ordinary reporter are given only quite casual mention; at the most, a brief telegram announces the casualties.

The Neulauenburg group (previously Duke of York) is a group consisting of several smaller, and one larger, islands in St George's Channel, about

8 nautical miles north of Cape Gazelle and 20 nautical miles west of the New Ireland coast. On modern maps the old, inconsistent names Amakata, and so on, once resplendent on older maps as island names, are gradually disappearing.

This brings me to the distressing question of geographical nomenclature. I am totally on the side of Herr von Luschan, the meritorious promoter of this question, when he turns against renaming, where good indigenous names exist. The Bismarck Archipelago and Kaiser Wilhelmsland in particular are brimming over with new-found names that hopefully over time will yield to the indigenous names, the more so since several of these are so ill-defined in position that it causes doubt for the traveller or seafarer where precisely the point in question lies. Thus, for example, it is extremely difficult to differentiate between the numerous points jutting out from the New Ireland coast: Kap Strauch, Ahlefeldspitze, Rittmeierhuk, and so on. The natives obviously do not know the names given by the Europeans, and the latter know the native designations just as little, and consequently it has come about that natives, adrift in their canoes, who finally arrived at a settlement, could not be sent back to their homeland because the name that they gave to their dwelling place was totally unknown. As a rule the origins of such natives have been determined from the type of construction of their canoes, from the weapons they carried, or from their decoration. Now, however, in a lot of cases it is quite difficult, even with the best will in the world, to discover the affiliations of the natives. With the tangle of languages predominating in Melanesia it is impossible for one individual to communicate with all the tribes; questions put forward are incorrectly comprehended by the natives and a false answer results, haunting the maps for further long years. The name Amakata, for example, certainly originated in this manner, by pointing, for clearer understanding. The native had understood that a name was wanted; he followed the direction of the outstretched hand with his eyes and gave the name of the particular island that had been directly pointed to. The answer accordingly ran *a makata* (*a* is the article), the name of one of the islands, and the inquirer made of this Amakata, as the principal designation of the entire group. This has no collective name at all, likewise the main island has no individual name. The earlier name of New Ireland, Tombara, arose similarly. It is an erroneous rendering of the word *taubar*, the direction from which the south-east wind comes, and therefore probably arose because someone indicated that direction with the hand. The number of similar examples can be multiplied without difficulty.

A further difficulty is that the natives have a particular name for a particular place or for a particular small island where they live, while distant natives know the place by a totally different name. During my brief stay on the islands of Durour and Matty I could not discover the local designations. A native of Ninigo who had lived there a long time designated them as Huen and Popolo. However, after we had got to know the natives of both small islands better, it turned out that the natives call their islands Aua and Wuwulu, and that Huen and Popolo are special designations of the Ninigo people. This example too can be multiplied *ad infinitum*.

As a rule, it can be defined thus: whole mountains and mountain ranges are given no collective names by the natives, but on the other hand individual peaks worthy of note have different designations in the various regions round about. Large islands that cannot be perceived or distinguished as such all at once, likewise have no designation; they are as a rule divided into individual districts or regions, whose names are also known to distant dwelling natives, and these are subdivided into villages or districts with unique names; the individual areas of the village on the other hand are recognised under special names by the residents. Inhabitants of neighbouring islands frequently have other designations for coasts, districts and villages of the islands nearby, that are never used by the locals. Parts of the sea, bays, harbours and straits have, as a rule, no special name, but are named for the nearest islands. Detached reefs seldom have a native designation. Characteristic foothills, prominences and mountain peaks, as well as rivers and streams have as a rule individual, independent names.

It can be seen from this that it is not always easy to establish the correct designation, apart from the difficulty that the written rendering of the name often provides for the European; and that in spite of the best intentions, we always come back to the embarrassing situation of inventing names and designations for localities that have none, and which nevertheless we perforce must name, because otherwise significant gaps would arise in the nomenclature, which might be regarded most disagreeably by travellers, seafarers and settlers.

Recently native place names have increased, which is as it should be, but it will still be a long time before we have done away with names like Herbertshöhe, Hannamhafen, and so on. Out of respect for the names and memories of old seafarers and discoverers, many of these names will still be retained, in spite of the natives' designations ascertained in the meantime.

After this digression I will return to the Duke of York group.

It has a surface area of 75 square kilometres, and in 1900 the population numbers, from a census by the then Imperial Judge Dr Schnee, amounted to 3,373 individuals: 1,060 men, 935 women, 772 boys and 606 girls. The number of births came to 253, deaths 212. From this it would seem that the population is in a state of growth; however, this is not the case, for during my long stay in the archipelago the population has decreased markedly, and is being augmented continually by newcomers from New Ireland and the Gazelle Peninsula.

The islands consist entirely of raised coral formations that form steep shorelines, especially in the north and west. Repeated raising, interrupted by periods of sinking, can clearly be detected in places, and we can conclude from this that the same also occurred on the neighbouring islands. The highest elevations are the two hills on the island of Makada, 80 and 100 metres high. Otherwise, the islands are flat and covered with thick forest.

South of the main island of the Duke of Yorks lie a number of smaller islands, three of which, Ulu, Utuan and Mioko, form the splendid Miokohafen that provides a completely safe anchorage, protected against all winds. Two practicable entrances, the Levinson and the north-west passes, lead into the harbour and permit sailing ships to enter or leave the harbour by one or other pass, depending on the prevailing wind. South of Ulu the two small islands of Kabokon and Kerawara likewise form a harbour, but of lesser significance. At the north-west end of the group lies the island of Makada, separated from the main island by a strait which forms a somewhat protected anchorage. As a continuation of the big island to a certain extent, several small islets lacking particular importance lie off its extreme north-western corner. Also worthy of mention is the small Hunterhafen, close to the north-west corner, scarcely, however, of any consequence to shipping.

Although the harbour of Mioko must be regarded as quite outstanding, it is of little value for the future development of the archipelago because of its remote, insular position. In earlier years it had played a major role, and was for a time the starting-point for further commercial undertakings in the archipelago after the Hamburg firm of J.C. Godeffroy & Son established a station there in the mid-1870s. Also, the firm of Hernsheim & Co. founded their first settlement on Makada, relocating to Matupi in Blanche Bay a short time later. The original Godeffroy station on Mioko later passed into the hands of the Deutsche Handels- und Plantagengesellschaft which still runs it. It participated only to a limited extent in the commerce of the archipelago and has contributed little to its development over its many years of operation. The company's main aim today is to recruit about 250 workers annually for its plantations in Samoa; thus creating markedly unpleasant competition for the archipelago, which annually requires an increasing number of workers for the inexorably expanding plantations, and coming very close to causing direct damage. Hopefully the administration in Samoa will gradually succeed in overcoming the laziness that has become second nature to the Samoans, to the point where that colony will be in a position to produce its own workers. The commercial undertakings of the company are taken care of by a staff of Chinese merchants, for whom one or two whites act as overseers on Mioko, as representatives of the parent company.

As in earlier times trade developed outwards from Mioko, so was Hunterhafen the starting-point of the first Christian mission, having its main seat there until 1900. However, since then, it has withdrawn to the island of Ulu in Miokohafen and founded a secondary school under the guidance of a white missionary, for the education of native mission teachers.

In spite of early colonisation by whites, and in spite of a splendid harbour and a fertile soil, plantation agriculture only began to exploit this group of islands in 1901. The Catholic mission has acquired the southern end of the main island from the Deutsche Handels- und Plantagengesellschaft and set up a plantation there; the Methodist mission is cultivating Ulu, and the island of Kabokon belongs to a private citizen who has brought it into palm cultivation.

On the island of Kerawara the first station of the New Guinea Company in the Bismarck Archipelago vegetated for a while, setting its administrative apparatus in motion from here on outwards, in its own time. One could hardly have chosen a less favourable site, and accordingly in 1890 the company saw the need to transfer to the present-day Herbertshöhe.

2. The Inhabitants

Just as the island of New Britain can be divided geographically into various main divisions, it may also be divided ethnographically into several provinces that exhibit only a superficial, loose connection with one another. It remains to be seen whether these ethnographical provinces coincide quite precisely with the principal geographical divisions, and whether one might establish beyond doubt an original connection. Wherever we go on the island, we come across the effect of volcanic forces that have taken an active part in the mighty accretions of loose rock, and in the uplifting and sinking of the earth. Because of this the surface of New Britain, like its outlines, must, from time to time, have undergone great changes, and these changes have affected the population: dispersed tribes, erected barriers between some, and linked others again by bridges. These changes have not taken place slowly and steadily, but in fits and starts, in some places suddenly, in the form of mighty volcanic eruptions. All of this has, over the course of millennia, left its mark on the population, and the most cursory observer will notice the difference immediately

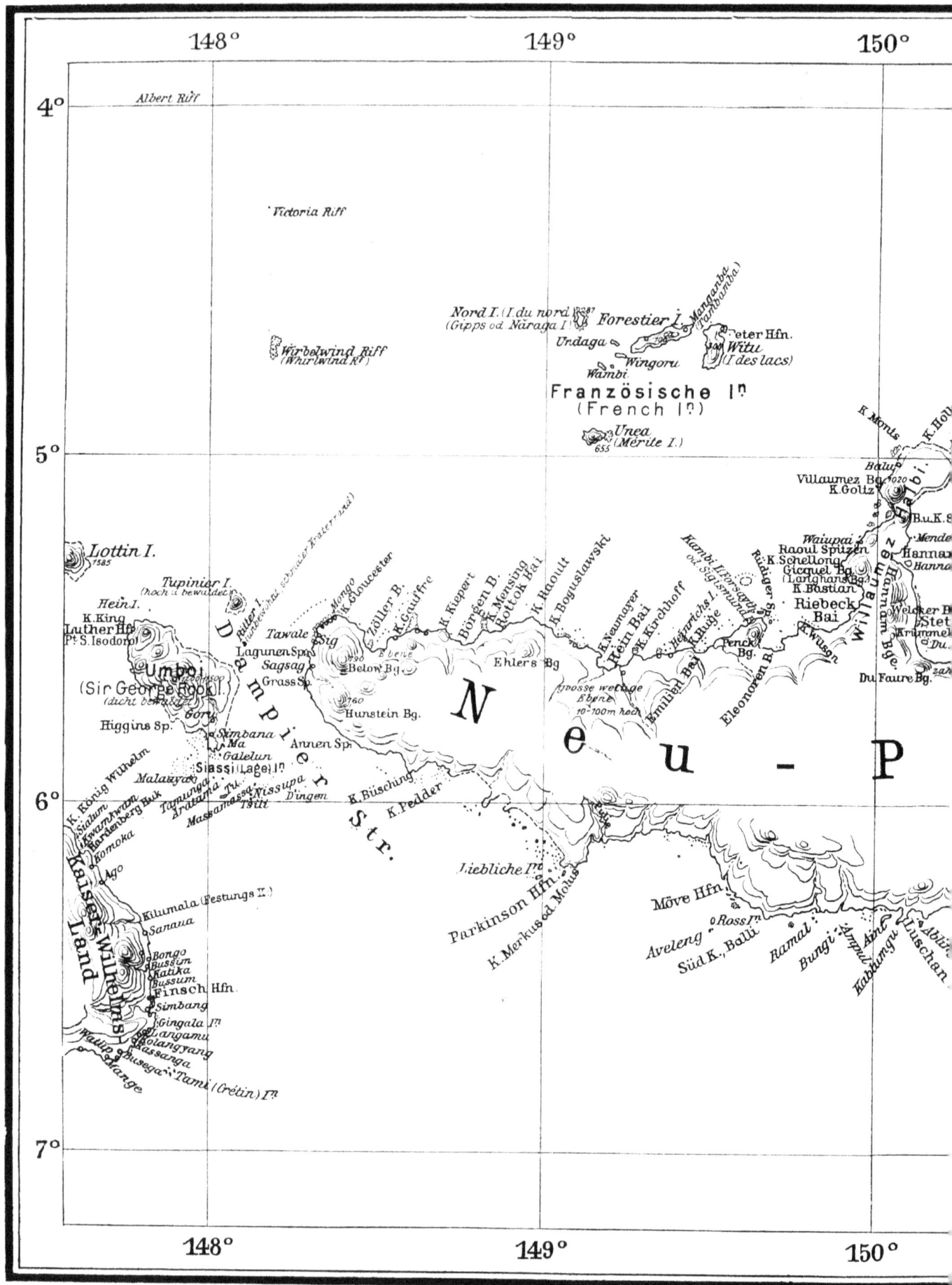

Map 2 New Britain

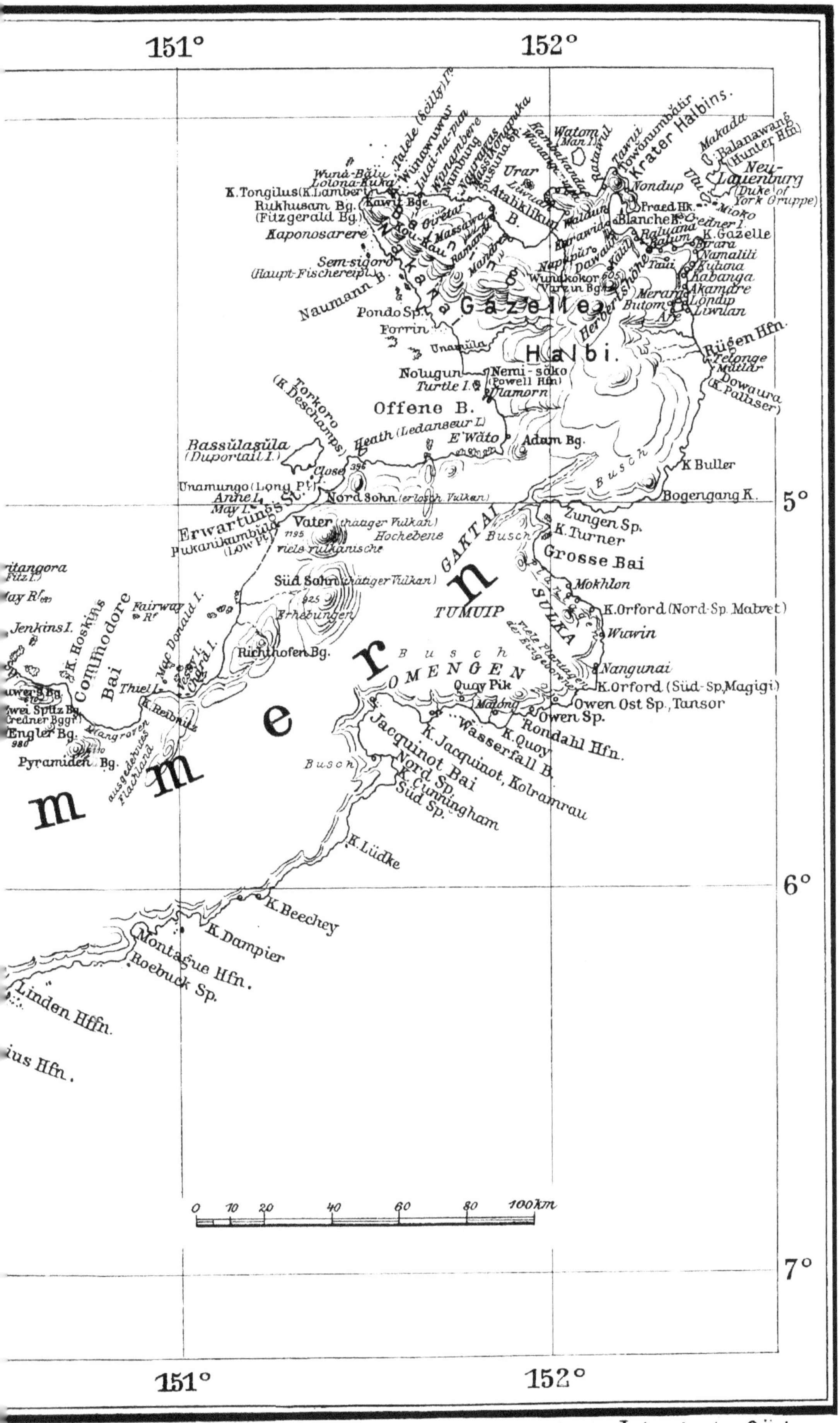

Beilage zu Parkinson Dreissig Jahre in der Südsee

when, for example, he sees a native from the Herbertshöhe area alongside one from South Cape or from the western end of the island.

The northern part of the island, the Gazelle Peninsula, comprises as I have already mentioned, two main parts: the Baining Mountains with their foothills, and the north-eastern plateau, separated from each other by a depression cutting deeply into the land from Weberhafen, frequently traversed by the rivulets and streams which pour out of the mountains. This land depression stretches through the entire Gazelle Peninsula, from Weberhafen, out beyond Vunakokor, right to St George's Channel, in this latter part forming the sunken valley of the Karawat or Warangoi River. The north-eastern plateau comprises deposited volcanic material: pumice, ash, blocks of obsidian, lava debris, and so on. This deposition did not originate suddenly from a catastrophe, as is indicated by steep slopes where one can clearly observe the laying down of strata over different periods; moreover major uplifting and sinking must have taken place alternately, because many of the strata were unquestionably deposited beneath the sea, then, after an uplift, covered by erupted material from the volcanoes, before sinking back into the sea. The source of this great volcanic activity is probably to be found in present-day Blanche Bay with its still partially active volcanic system, as well as in the far older volcano, Vunakokor (Varzinberg).

Before this mighty catastrophe, which may have stretched over a long period of time, the Gazelle Peninsula was undoubtedly inhabited by the same tribe. The volcanic activity buried part of the then surface under huge eruptions or sank other parts under the sea. Those who didn't lose their lives immediately took flight, and found sanctuary in those areas that lay beyond the range of the volcanic activity. One such region was the present-day Baining Mountains with their foothills.

Even today therefore we find here the descendants of the original inhabitants of the Gazelle Peninsula, who by their isolation have indeed largely retained their original peculiar characteristics and their language. They were named Baining by their neighbours to the north-east. They know no *tabu* (shell money), have no *duk-duks*, and are not seafarers. They manufacture stone clubs with a heavy, perforated stone head, a skill that we find again only in a few areas of New Guinea. I have extensively discussed their characteristic dances, with curious, mask-like headgear, in another section. Physically too they differ from their neighbours in their solid physique; they are considerably inferior to them intellectually, and in this respect they probably belong among the most inferior tribes of the archipelago. Right up to the most recent times they were the objects of systematically organised slave raids with associated cannibal feasts.

Now where do the inhabitants of the north-eastern Gazelle Peninsula originate? It doesn't seem difficult to answer this question with some certainty.

It must have taken a long time before the expanses covered with volcanic rubble clothed themselves with vegetation to the point where they formed a suitable dwelling place for human existence. Analogous cases demonstrate to a lesser extent that, both from the beach and from those areas spared from being overwhelmed, vegetation soon spreads over the barren ground and rapidly forms a continually developing plant cover. The weathering of rock is thereby promoted and expedited, and slowly an upper fertile layer of humus develops. The small volcanic cone, Kaije, on the Mother peninsula and the small volcanic island in Blanche Bay that rose above the surface of the sea in 1878 show this very clearly. When I visited these places in 1882 the already-developing vegetation was still quite sparse. Year by year it became thicker, and now covers not only the outside of the crater but is gradually creeping inside. On the volcanic island this has become even more obvious. Today the major part of it is covered with dense undergrowth, mostly casuarina, and recently a great number of trees and shrubs indigenous to the littoral zone have been added. In a few years' time a dense stand of forest will exist here, and then the humus layer will increase rapidly year by year.

Roughly midway between the Gazelle Peninsula and New Ireland lies the small Duke of York group, formed from raised coral reefs. In my opinion it was already inhabited at the time of the great volcanic eruptions, the deposits of which did not reach this far, by a tribe that had immigrated from New Ireland opposite. Even if this was not the case, and had the island emerged simultaneously with the volcanic eruptions of the Gazelle Peninsula, and if the uplifting and sinking occurred at the same time, this would not be proof against my claim. An alternating uplifting and sinking also occurred in the Duke of Yorks; however, after the ensuing calm these small islands must have been covered with vegetation much more quickly than the Gazelle Peninsula opposite, and would have served the New Ireland people to some extent as a first stage on their migration. The present Duke of York people are today still in active communication with New Ireland opposite, and are closely related in speech and customs to the natives there. To a great extent the New Ireland people have gradually extended their expeditions outwards from the Duke of York group to the coasts of the Gazelle Peninsula opposite, and as they found them suitable for settlements they finally settled down there.

The original inhabitants, the Baining, who had settled in the mountains, offered no resistance to the intruders; between the coast and the mountains

Fig. 7 Women of the Gazelle Peninsula

at the time there still lay a broad region turned into a wasteland by volcanic lava flows, which only in more recent times became suitable for settlement and cultivation. It is therefore easy to understand that the immigrants were able to settle unhindered on the coast, which was gradually becoming ever more hospitable.

These first pioneers associated little by little with tribally related locals from New Ireland; and a consequence of this is that the present inhabitants of the north-eastern part of the Gazelle Peninsula, the descendants of these immigrants, are extremely similar in many respects to the inhabitants of the southern half of New Ireland. On St George's Channel and in the villages on the slopes of Mother the inhabitants regard themselves as relatives of the population on New Ireland opposite.

It might be going too far, to present all the similarities between the people of southern New Ireland and the inhabitants of the north-eastern Gazelle Peninsula. I will give, as an example, the affinity in language. Hundreds of words are the same in both regions; for example, *mal* = object, *lakut* = cloud, *torom* = to serve, *tir* = to ask, *kuare* = string, *buk* = to cook, *kogo* = to cough, *matuane* = uncle, *tamane* = father, *mate* = hole, *bung* = day, *kapul* = cuscus, *nana* = mother, *palina* = bark, and so on. Over the course of time alterations have occurred; and so almost all the words that are written with an 'h' on New Ireland have changed on the Gazelle Peninsula into a 'v' or 'w'; for example, *hudu* becomes *wudu* = banana, *hahina* becomes *wawina* = woman, *hat* becomes *wat* = stone, *harubu* becomes *warubu* = to fight, *taha* becomes *tawa* = water, *hilau* becomes *wilau* = to run, and so on; many words on the Gazelle Peninsula leave out the 's', thus *lamas* becomes *lama* = coconut, *ngas* becomes *nga* = path, *kis* becomes *ki* = to sit, *pas* becomes *pa* = taro, *balus* becomes *balu* = pigeon, *mis* becomes *mi* = to smoke, *saring* becomes *aring* = to beg, and so on. The Wesleyan mission, which has maintained settlements on New Ireland as well as in the Duke of Yorks and on the Gazelle Peninsula since 1875, taught in the local dialects in all three places during the first fifteen years. However, during this period it became clear to the mission leaders that it was only a matter of dealing with one single language, split into various, not very different, dialects. The mission in recent times therefore established the dialect of the Gazelle Peninsula as a universal language, both in the Duke of Yorks and on southern New Ireland, and finds no difficulty with this.

As differences in the language developed over the course of time, after the importation of new settlers had ceased so also did other characteristics develop. When we observe today in southern New Ireland those characteristics that are missing in the closely related inhabitants of the Gazelle Peninsula, they may be based on influences from northern New Ireland and from the north-western Solomon Islands, which asserted themselves once immigration to the Gazelle Peninsula had largely ceased. Consequently these influences must have remained confined to southern New Ireland and not disseminated as far as the Gazelle Peninsula.

Slowly the immigrants spread inland from the beach on the Gazelle Peninsula. By the time they had reached as far as Mount Vunakokor (Varzin), the original inhabitants, advancing from their mountain refuges, had regained possession of a portion of their former dwelling places, and there now developed a struggle between both tribes, which continues to this day. The new arrivals were certainly strong enough to hold on to their chosen dwelling sites, but the original inhabitants also possessed sufficient ability to resist, thus preventing further expansion. Today the invaders inhabit the coast up to about 12 nautical miles south of Cape Gazelle, as well as the entire north coast as far as Weberhafen; inland they do not go far over the Varzinberg. The small islands of Masava and Masikonápuka, west of Weberhafen, form several outlying colonies to the west. Their inhabitants had established themselves on the opposite coast only within the last forty years, and maintain a narrow coastal strip there today. The natives of these outposts, as well as their tribal relatives on Weberhafen, Cape Livuan and on the islands of Urara and Uatom, have been enterprising seafarers since time immemorial. They have for many years, long before the European discovery of New Britain, maintained contact with the natives living further to the south, in the region of the three volcanoes (Father and

Plate 4 Men of the Arawa Islands

Fig. 8 Men of the Baining

the two Sons), from where they brought the *Nassa* snails which are so highly prized by the people of their land and have a particular value as currency (*tabu*) on the high plateau. Through this trade these colonists lying out to the west have acquired many things from the natives living further southwards, with whom they came into contact. However, the mutual influence has always remained only slight, since the superficial trading of both tribes never led to closer, friendly ties.

The Baining who inhabit the mountain range on the western side of the Gazelle Peninsula (whom I shall designate as the North Baining), and the Baining who occupy the mountain range on the southern half of the peninsula, belong to the same tribe insofar as we can judge today. On the shore of St George's Channel I came into contact with the latter; that is, we shouted back and forth over a short distance, because the natives were too fearful to await my approach. They had spears and clubs in their hands and wore bark loin-cloths decorated with bright patterns, whereas the North Baining, and, before the arrival of the white people, the other inhabitants of the peninsula, at least the men, wore no clothing. It is therefore not impossible that these South Baining are, or were, in contact with the natives living further to the south on the main island, and acquired various customs from there, as, for example, clothing. They are, however, different from them in that like the North Baining they have no boats and are therefore not seafarers, and also have no shields. I therefore tend to the opinion that they are to be regarded as tribally very closely related to the North Baining. Father Rascher, to whom we are grateful for so much useful information about the Baining, tells me that at Cape Buller and Cape Bogengang (St George's Channel) he encountered the South Baining and found no difficulty in conversing with them: further evidence that the South Baining and North-west Baining belong to one and the same tribes. Also, south-west of Varzin the father came into contact with the South Baining, and ascertained that they belonged with the North Baining.

In various accounts of the natives of the Gazelle Peninsula, mention is made of a tribe that dwells in the interior of the peninsula south-west of Vunakokor, and is designated by the name Taulil. The Taulil are fought both by the Baining and the north-eastern inhabitants, and are in the process of dying out. A related tribe, the Butam, was totally wiped out a few years ago. From this hostility, and from the fact that both tribes have a divergent language, one came to the conclusion that they were totally different from the north-eastern inhabitants. However, this is not the case: they are scattered tribes of the population that occupies St George's Channel still today, and which also immigrated from New Ireland, though from the more southerly part of the island, which to this day is different in language from the northern districts. The later immigrants, pressing onwards, drove the Butam and Taulil from their original dwelling places, and subsequently annihilated the former.

The remnants of the Taulil tribe number about 300 individuals. Later in the general review I will assemble the little that is known so far about the Taulil, from which it appears that they are a member of the great north-eastern tribe.

South of the Gazelle Peninsula, and connected to it by a relatively narrow isthmus, stretches the mountain region that we have come to know in the descriptive section, with a series of volcanoes, still active in places, on the western shore.

In the mountain region we meet a tribe that has begun only recently to become known to us. Incomplete and full of gaps as our knowledge may be, it still entitles us to the assumption that we are dealing with a tribe that has little in common with the neighbouring tribes in the north, and stands on a higher level intellectually. It possesses superbly crafted clubs, some with round or oval heads, some with the striking end in the shape of a pineapple. We also find a club of peculiar shape, of which Powell[3] gives a very poor illustration (page 109, certainly drawn from memory), the like of which is not found anywhere else in the region, neither in the Bismarck Archipelago nor New Guinea. Then we find peculiar mask dances and masks of the most diverse forms, which certainly show distant similarities with the *duk-duk* but are otherwise quite different. Furthermore, we find painstakingly constructed large boats with artistic painting. All of this seems to me sufficient to give this tribe a separate position.

In an earlier work (Die Volkstämme Neupommerns, in *Abhandlungen und Berichte des Königlichen Museums zu Dresden*, Festschrift 1899, No. 5), in consequence of the imprecise knowledge of this tribe at that time, I presented it as related to the Baining; however, this relationship stretches indeed only as far as the South Baining, and that too is a very tenuous one.

To the west, past Jacquinot Bay and as far as Montague Bay there occurs an admixture with the tribes on the opposite, north coast of the island, manifested, for example, in the current type of shields, which strongly call to mind Willaumez Peninsula and Nakanai. However, on the whole the influence of the inhabitants of the high mountains predominates.

The further westwards we proceed from Montague Bay, the more clear it becomes that this entire western part of the island is inhabited by a tribe that is closely related to the coastal population of New Guinea. However, from Cape Roebuck beyond Möwehafen to about Cape Merkus, there is a tribe that apparently differs greatly from the neighbours. Namely, in this region the skull is artificially deformed, so that it takes on a receding, strongly conical shape. The custom is not universal, however, and natives of this area without deformed skulls have the greatest affinity with neighbours dwelling further to the west, as with the natives on the New Guinea coast opposite, Rook Island. Trade still takes place today between the people around Finschhafen, the Tami Island people, and the natives of Rook Island and the natives of New Britain up to east of Möwehafen. I have come upon Tami boats with pottery in the region of the South Cape, and Rook canoes in the Arawa Islands.

On the northern side of the island the affinity with New Guinea is even more obvious. On the north coast the tribe has spread further to the east than on the south coast; it occupies the entire coastal region as far as Open Bay, where it has established its most recent outlying colonies; also, the natives of the island of Duportail, as well as those of the French Islands, belong to the same tribe.

Right at the western end of the island, the resemblance of the inhabitants with those of the coast of New Guinea opposite is at its most clear. Reciprocal trade exists with Rook Island, and in custom, as in language and in physical features, the greatest similarity prevails.

It follows from the above that we can distinguish four tribes on the island of New Britain, namely:

1. The north-eastern inhabitants of the Gazelle Peninsula, who in all probability have immigrated from southern New Ireland;
2. the Baining, the original inhabitants of the Gazelle Peninsula, who through volcanic events were driven back into the mountains of the west and south of the peninsula;
3. the tribes on the extension of the main island, south of the Gazelle Peninsula, and;
4. the tribes closely related to the inhabitants of the coast of New Guinea opposite, which occupy the entire western part of the island, and are differentiated from the other tribes on the south coast by deformed skulls.

The differences between the given tribes can easily be explained, in that they have lived in isolation from one another, and had no, or at best very little, communication. The fairly recent immigration from New Ireland satisfactorily explains the difference between the immigrants and the Baining. They were previously separated from each other by a broad arm of the sea, and when trade took place it could be one way only, since at that time the Baining had boats just as small as they are now.

The difference between the Baining and the inhabitants of the mountain region south of present-day Gazelle Peninsula can be explained similarly. The relatively low isthmus, which connects both parts today, is formed from raised coral formations, and where there is now an isthmus, a strait certainly existed earlier, separating the Baining highlands from the southern highlands. A similar divide may have been present between

3. Wanderings in a Wild Country, London, 1884.

the southern highlands and the great western part of the island.

The mighty volcanic activity which in stages raised Rook Island out of the sea off the New Guinea coast, so that from the shape of the terraces we are still able to establish precisely the number and extent of the upheavals, also extended to New Britain. Here too we can follow the terrace formation, even if not to the same extent as, for example, on Fortification Point in New Guinea. Nevertheless, these terrace-shaped upliftings can be followed right to the isthmus that separates the Gazelle Peninsula from the main island. Besides these upheavals, volcanic eruptions, combined with vast deposits of erupted material, have made their contribution toward the island's present form. The southern half of New Ireland, the Baining Mountains of the Gazelle Peninsula, the plateau lying to the south of it, and the western end of New Britain were indeed at one time separate islands. Their inhabitants had little to do with one another; and even after the individual islands were partially connected by upliftings of the earth, they preserved their special position and their peculiarities.

a. The Natives of the North-east of the Gazelle Peninsula

In the following account of the inhabitants, their usages and customs, I am following the previously presented organisation of the tribes, according to which clearly different ethnographic provinces can be defined. The first of these provinces encompasses the area of the Gazelle Peninsula, insofar as it is inhabited by immigrant tribes from New Ireland, and its borders have already been given.

However, from the outset I must emphasise that within this province, as within the provinces mentioned later, the traditions and customs are not universal, nor is the language. Peculiarities continue from district to district, but on closer acquaintance a common origin cannot fail to be recognised.

The whole region is divided into a number of greater and smaller districts, each as a rule with its own name. Within these districts lie the individual settlements (*qunan*) usually comprising only a small number of huts, seldom more than ten. Here dwells a family, in the narrow sense. Should the family enlarge, then several members split off and form a new *qunan*. Thus develops a colony, dominated by a particular sib. A district seldom contains several sibs near one another.

Within the individual sibs, *niurana*, there are always several prominent people who are regarded as leaders and regents. The highest eminence is that of the *a gala* (g = ng), which means literally 'the great one'. However, situations occur where the members of the sib simply depose the *a gala* because he does not show himself to be equal to his role, particularly if administering the family property badly or wastefully. His successor is always the next brother in succession or the next matrilineal nephew. These are also his successors on his death. The *a gala* then, is the actual chief and exercises the authority of a chief as far as it serves the benefit or the needs of the whole sib. He buys wives for the youths, who must subsequently pay back his outlay by working for him. He is the treasurer for the entire sib, and the family wealth in shell money – *tabu* – is held in his house. If he is an enterprising man, then he will encourage his people in the establishment of large gardens. It is then customary for him to pay for their support from the family wealth. However, the sum advanced, plus a bonus decided upon, is repaid to him after the sale of the harvest, to be deposited in the *tabu* house. Should the sib be a large one, and a great quantity of *tabu* be entrusted to him, this causes him quite a lot of trouble. The large coils of *tabu* can be distinguished easily; but in addition there are numerous bigger and smaller bundles and baskets, which all appear the same to an outsider, but they all have different owners, who must be remembered by the *a gala*.

Fig. 9 Women of the Baining

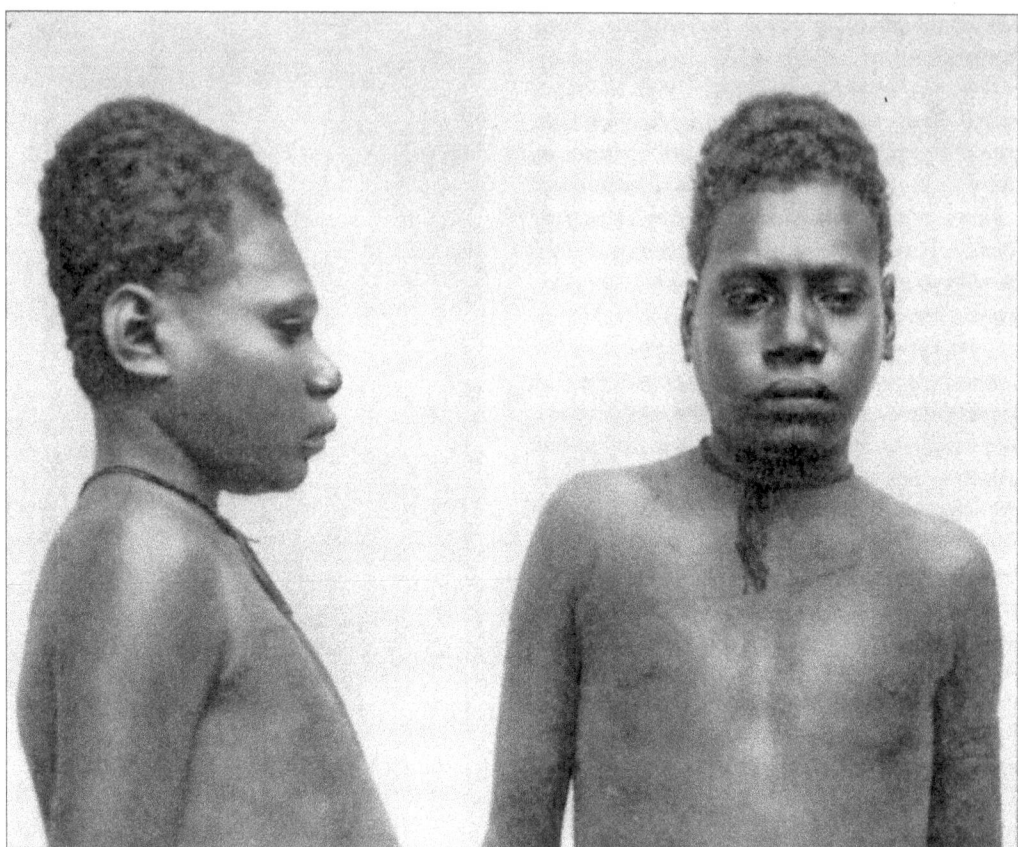

Fig. 10 Youth from the Möwehafen region

However, he never makes a mistake in the administration, although difficult problems not infrequently make demands on his memory. His claim over family land and property is no greater than that of any other family member; however, he can alienate pieces of family land, but must consult with the owners first in order to obtain their consent. He hands over the proceeds to the owners on conclusion of the sale, or deposits it with the sib funds. As the *a gala* is usually a financial wizard, he not infrequently acquires a quite considerable fortune on his own account, from the funds entrusted to him, and is then designated also as *uviana*, rich man.

After the *a gala*, the rank of *luluai* is the most important. The *luluai* is the war leader of the tribe. Not infrequently the positions of *a gala* and *luluai* are vested in one person, but the designation is received by an individual who distinguishes himself in battle, and to whose leadership the other members of the tribe will willingly submit, if need arises, because his courage and ability are recognised by them. When the *a gala* grows old and is no longer able to lead his people into battle, he summons one or more of his *luluai* who must now take over supreme command from him. In return, this person enjoys certain privileges. He may, for example, retain a greater portion of the shell money captured on war expeditions, and he can keep his own property in his own house and deal with it as he sees fit. The *luluai* therefore has the opportunity of being able, in time, to become an *uviana*, from which the rank of an *a gala* is also attainable.

There is no outward identification of these honours; ornaments seen at times on the head, neck, chest and elsewhere, are not marks of distinction, but solely a means of beautifying the body.

All the affairs of the group are discussed in council. Either a particular day and a particular place is determined in advance or, in cases where the situation is urgent, the men are called together by signal on the wooden drum. It is astonishing the speed with which the warriors will assemble at the permanently established meeting place, usually the *qunan* or the compound of the *a gala*, after the drum signal has sounded far through the forest. The purpose of the meeting is then made known to those present, and an individual can offer his opinion. Not infrequently violent debates take place, and, if the affair is not exactly very urgent, they even break up without having resolved the matter. However, if the situation is of great importance – for example, if an invasion is threatened, or a member of the tribe has been slain or a woman has been raped – then resolution is achieved with astonishing speed and they proceed forthwith to carry it out. Let us suppose that an invasion is threatened. In this case, if they feel that they are not strong enough to repel the attack, the shell money is made safe immediately. Men and women silently load themselves up with the tribal treasure and carry it either to a friendly neighbouring tribe or, if it is already too late, they bury the money in a remote, predetermined spot in the forest. Under the leadership of the *luluai*, the men capable of bearing weapons lie in ambush, or advance to meet the enemy, in order to engage him on open ground if possible.

If the cause of such a mobilisation is not of absolutely vital importance, then the parties on both sides nominate mediators from neighbouring tribes, and these then bring the situation to a conclusion by thoroughly discussing the case, and decree a payment of shell money to the injured party. Only extremely rarely do the condemned ones disobey this sentence. After payment of the blood-money, the old men of both parties come together, exchange lime and betel nuts, and thus peace is restored. In particular cases – for example when a member of the tribe is slain by another tribe, or indeed eaten – peace is not so easily restored. The honour of the tribe requires in certain cases that the deed be avenged, and a state of war exists until the other tribe is paid back in the same coin. If the latter tribe is then intent on further reprisals, these feuds can carry on for a long time. When the need to negotiate a peace exists on both sides, it is the task of the mediator to prepare a way for this; each party pays the other compensation for the numbers killed during the time of war; after the ensuing payment betel nuts are exchanged and chewed, and the peace is then a lasting one, in any event as long-lasting as our European peace treaties.

It may also happen that a tribe feels too weak to avenge the wrong perpetrated against it. In this case a quite specific custom has developed, which of course must now yield gradually to the influence of the white man. This custom consists of somebody causing damage to the property of a totally disinterested person, compelling him to seek satisfaction from the original evildoer. This custom is called *kamara*. When I settled in New Britain in the early 1880's, this custom was universally recognised. However, this seldom went as far as killing; although I know of one such case, which was quickly brought to an end when the man who had interpreted this custom in too broad a sense was killed by his own tribal members. On the other hand *kamara* was always practised when one tribe had damaged the property of another and was not quick enough in paying the atonement due.

In a few instances I myself have been compelled to practise *kamara*. Right when I first settled here, sundry items, especially tools, were stolen from me quite frequently, without my being able to identify the thief. Several elderly native friends therefore advised me to make use of *kamara*, and so I became familiar with this institution. When such a theft occurred, I used to go calmly to my wealthy and influential neighbours, one of whom was one of the abovementioned advisers, take their canoes away, tell them of the theft that had taken place, and leave it to them to seek out the thief. This was successfully accomplished regularly, and we remained the best of friends in spite of it. Of course the canoes found their way back to their owners as soon as the stolen item, or compensation, was handed over to me, but so firmly rooted was the universal custom of *kamara* that my old friend did not consider blaming me for taking his means of transport, even though I had to use this method four times in one month in order to prevent further encroachments. I learned many years later, that at the time of the regularly held market days he posted spies everywhere, to watch carefully that nothing was stolen from me, and if the need arose, to be able to catch the thief quickly.

It is true that the practice of *kamara* did not go so well for everyone. The dog belonging to a trader living not far from me was killed. As he did not know the perpetrator, he endeavoured, relying on the *kamara*, to obtain compensation for himself by taking away a coil of *tabu* from a neighbouring *luluai* in his absence. However, the latter interpreted the situation in reverse, pushed the trader around in front of his house, smashed the planking of the boat drawn up on the beach and demanded the return of his property.

As the *a gala* is the head of the tribe, so every married, native man, whether he have one or several wives, is absolute master of them. The wife is his property and must work for him; if this property right is infringed by a third person, the husband is entitled to claim compensation from the latter, and this is in most cases determined in advance according to certain rules and customs. Adultery is not always punished by death, but on the other hand incest, *pulu*, always is; this includes not only sexual connection between natural brothers and sisters, but also between persons of the same tribal sign, or as we say, the same totem. However, the husband's right does not extend to his being the executor of the death penalty in these cases; this right is reserved solely for the brother of the adultress, or her maternal uncle. In earlier times this right was almost always exercised, but under the influence of settlers, the missionary societies, and administrative authorities, the practice is waning. Of course this is not without regret on the part of the natives, who view such transgressions by women quite differently from white people, and fear, not unreasonably, that when their old law vanishes one day, the excesses of the women will increase. As a matter of fact they are quite right, for the women now know full well that in cases of adultery the authorities will protect their lives, and they are consequently less moral than was formerly the case. Adultery is therefore on the increase. This is one of the cases where we, with our progressive laws and humane views, interfere seriously in the life of the natives and cause infinite harm that spreads increasingly. In our efforts to set up the new, we break down the old, without replacing it with anything better. Compensation for the dead wife is paid to the husband in shell money by the one who carries out the punishment. It is usually the purchase price paid at the betrothal.

After marriage, the wife still remains a member of her own family, to whom she can return if the marriage is nullified by the death of her husband. In this event she is again sold by the relatives, should an admirer appear. But even during the husband's lifetime she frequently returns to her family and stays there for a shorter or longer time. Should a separation occur by mutual agreement of the married couple, the family reimburses the husband the cost of purchase, and the marriage is thereby dissolved. Such separations are quite frequent, and they are increasing in recent times in order to avoid problems, partly within the family and partly with the authorities.

However, there are extraordinarily many cases in which the marriage is a lasting union for life. Petty quarrels between the married couple are of course the norm, and the wronged or aggrieved wife then goes to her relatives, to give expression to her anger; but such minor marital quarrels are not of long duration, providing no more serious grounds exist. After a few days, when her wrath has subsided, the wife comes back again, or the husband makes amends and sends small gifts, through friends or relations, as evidence of his good will.

It is quite common for the *a gala* to buy girls in very early childhood, in order to marry them off later at marriageable age to one or other of his young men, on repayment of all outstanding expenses. The rule is that the young man does not select the wife himself; she is chosen by his parents, his maternal uncle, or by his relatives. In more mature youth it may happen that a marriage based on mutual affection can be contracted for the people in question, and this is then enduring; usually this marriage is preceded by an optional marriage which must then be dissolved before the true marriage can take place.

The marriage of a very young couple, or more correctly their engagement, proceeds under prescribed ceremonies. These are almost universally the same and follow a defined order.

Mother and father, or the uncle in their place, go to the parents of the girl and hand over about ten fathoms of *tabu* to her father, who divides them up among the girl's relatives. Then the girl goes with the purchasers to their dwelling, and here the father or uncle distributes *tabu* once more, to the people who have accompanied him. The girl's parents then choose a certain day for a visit to the parents or the uncle of the boy (*murvartulai*). On this occasion they bring prepared food, which the other party accepts, and pays for with *tabu*. Moreover, they in turn are given prepared food, for which they pay an equivalent amount of *tabu*. During the subsequent feasting a day is chosen on which the young man, who should not be present at these ceremonies, is presented to the future in-laws. For this presentation the male relatives of the youth practise a dance, and the female relatives on the bride's side do likewise. On the appointed day, the men present their dance first; then follows the presentation by the women, during which time the youth and those who have accompanied him form the audience. The bride's parents then bring a present of about ten fathoms of *tabu* to the future son-in-law, and the parents or the uncle of the youth make a similar gift to the parents or the uncle of the girl.

That marks the beginning of the engagement of the young couple in a way. When both parties are still in their childhood, as frequently happens, the girl remains with her parents or relatives until reaching marriageable age, and likewise the boy or youth with his. Although both realise that in later life they will live together as man and wife, in chance meetings they act as if they had never seen each other before, indeed they are forbidden to look at each other or gaze after each other, or to mention the future union to others.

When the girl is old enough to marry, the mother of the youth sends an older woman to the future daughter-in-law's home to fetch her. The woman envoy holds the summoned girl by the hand and flings betel nuts at the young man who is there, calling out: 'Here are so and so's betel nuts!' The other men present gather up the betel nuts and eat them. The aim of this ceremony is to establish the acquaintance of both parties, and make it possible for them to look at each other from now on at chance encounters. The ceremony itself is called *varabibir na buai* (*varabibir* = the throwing, the stoning).

In some districts it is done a little differently. When the parties have agreed on the marriage, the friends of the bridegroom seize him, and hold him firmly on the ground while the parents or the uncle of the youth distribute *tabu* among the men and the weeping women present; this is the *warakinim*. On the day of the *warakinim* it is expressly forbidden for the young man concerned to bathe in the sea. Afterwards he is taken to a house that lies apart, in the forest, and here he is kept concealed for a period, *paraparau*. Several friends keep him company during this concealment, and relatives bring them meals, *waralupa*. During this hide-and-seek the wife is bought (*warakukul*), and only then may the bridegroom see her, when all the costs of the previously described ceremonies have been paid. When the bridegroom returns from the *paraparau*, he is splendidly adorned, with a plume of feathers in his hair, forehead-bands and armbands, he holds a special club (*bagat*) richly adorned with plumes of feathers, and an ornamental basket, plaited from

Plate 5 The laying out of a corpse. Gazelle Peninsula

palm fronds and adorned with feathers and bright foliage, is slid under his arm.

The ceremonies then ensue as previously described. If the acquaintance of both young people has taken place through the *warabibir na buai*, then the relatives arrange a further approach. For this purpose the young men, on inducement from the women, seize the bridegroom and bring him by night to the dwelling of his father or uncle, while at the same time the women bring the bride to the same place with a gift for the bridegroom of two fathoms of *tabu*; the men repay this gift by handing over the same amount of *tabu* to the bride, in the name of the bridegroom; although the bridegroom often delivers the present to the bride in person. After this exchange of gifts, the bride remains in the house of her in-laws and the bridegroom takes himself off to the bachelors' house. Two or three days later, the bridegroom, accompanied by one of his friends, visits the bride once more, and she sets food before them; this ceremony is called *tultuluai* and is repeated from day to day, in order for the bride and groom to become accustomed to each other. If his future bride does not please the young gentleman, he demonstrates this by rejecting the gifts offered and by not touching the food set before him; the bride shows her aversion to the bridegroom by offering betel nuts or food to the young man only under compulsion. As a conclusive trial, on a certain day a fire is made in front of the hut. Bride and bridegroom sit opposite each other at the fire. If the bride turns her face to the bridegroom, this is a sign of consent; should she turn her face away, she is indicating her aversion. The bridegroom expresses his antipathy either by remaining very far away or by sending a young man to act as his spokesman. Nevertheless, the people are seldom dissuaded by this insubordination, the women must persuade and soothe, and should this not help either, then a battery of magical means is seized upon, to evoke mutual affection. However, if this still does not result in a union, both parties come together and mutually reimburse the outlay of shell money. With this ceremony the matter is at an end.

If, however, the young couple are in agreement, then at their daily rendezvous the bridegroom brings the young girl presents, which she packs in her carrying basket, or he accompanies her to work in the gardens and works with her there. When this communication has gone on for several weeks and there is no danger that through unilateral or mutual aversion the projected union might come to nothing, the bridegroom begins to build a hut, helped by his relatives. When the house is ready, the relatives bring one or two fathoms of *tabu*, and hand them to the young couple. This ceremony is called *lake kinalatn;* that is, the house-warming.

In the evening the young couple go into the future dwelling for the first time, and the marriage is thereby completed. Further ceremonies no longer take place.

If the bride has been married before, the dissolution of the former marriage must be completed by repayment of the purchase price to the first husband or his relatives before she can undertake another marriage. The new suitor pays the stipulated price to the wife's relatives, a small feast takes place, and the wife follows the husband to his hut without further ceremonies.

Old people say that in former times on an appointed day all the marriage candidates had to gather at a certain place. Here they were seized quite roughly by the older people and thrown on the ground, one on top of the other. Those who lay underneath had to bear the weight of those above, and not infrequently they sustained considerable injuries. Finally, coils of *tabu* were brought out, and laid on the living heap, whereupon the weight was considerably increased, and quite often several of those lying beneath were crushed to death. After the elders had feasted their eyes on this sight for a while, they called on the young men to stand up, and the latter then set off to their concealment in their forest where, as described above, they had to spend some time.

Today this custom, as far as I have been able to ascertain, is no longer practised, and the milder form described is carried out universally, with a few small changes.

Polygamy is permitted, although not generally practised. As a rule it is only the wealthier people who can allow themselves the luxury of multiple wives. This situation is viewed more from the business side, since the outlay that is coupled with maintaining several wives is richly compensated, because they have to work for the husband in the cultivations and thereby provide him with a financial income. One of the women, however, remains the favourite, as it were, and her jealousy not infrequently succeeds in making life so miserable for the other wives and the lord husband that for better or worse he reverts to monogamy for the sake of domestic peace. The individual wives have separate huts; there is no difference between the children of the different wives.

We also find here a remnant of the totemism so widespread in Melanesia. It is not expressed by certain animals or other objects being used as totems; here one has the two designations *tavevet* and *tadiat*, which literally mean 'we' and 'they', and express membership or non-membership of a certain group. All those who are of the same lineage call themselves *tavevet* among themselves, and may be related to one another in the female or the male line; for them all others are *tadiat*. Relatives who are of the same lineage on the maternal side, may never marry each other.

As soon as a native enters a family as a son-in-law, there arise for both parties quite particular rules in the mutual relationships. A transgression of these strict rules would be regarded as a major break of tradition and punished accordingly. The son-in-law and parents-in-law address each other as *nimuan*; they never call each other by their usual names, and to do so is especially forbidden to them. This goes to the extent that if, for example, the father-in-law is called *tokapiaka* = to - breadfruit, or *tolama* = to - coconut, two not uncommon names, the *nimuan* henceforth does not designate the breadfruit as *kapiaka* nor the coconut as *lama*, but uses other names. The *nimuan* may indeed offer each other betel nuts and chew betel with each other; it is, however, strongly forbidden to them to eat or to see each other when one or other party, the parents-in-law or the son-in-law, is taking their meal. Likewise it is forbidden to the son-in-law to step into the dwelling of his in-laws. The daughter-in-law, after the marriage is completed, stands in exactly the same position with her in-laws.

Part of these rules also covers the brothers-in-law (*maku*). They may not address one another by name, nor sleep in the same house. On the other hand they can visit one another in their dwellings and take meals together. After the wedding the sister is no longer permitted to associate or speak with her brother, she never pronounces his name, but designates him by another word.

This institution can lead to quite peculiar situations for white people, who are not familiar with it. I recall a case where father-in-law and son-in-law were arraigned together; I was functioning in the capacity of assistant magistrate, and although I was aware that a native can never be induced to say his own name until another native has been called to say that name, the prohibition that existed in this case was unknown to me at the time. It was not possible, neither for the magistrate nor for the assistant magistrate, to establish the names of both delinquents. Moreover, both people were from Blanche Bay, and had no acquaintances on Kerawara in the Duke of York group, where the court was then in session. All entreaties and all threats were in vain; it only remained to send the bailiff by boat to Blanche Bay to collect several natives who were not prevented by usages and customs from naming both of them. From this situation I got to know the ramifications.

If the marriage, as previously mentioned, can, for some petty reason, be dissolved as simply as the wife's family returning the purchase price to the husband, there are, however, a large number of examples of marriages that are ended only through the death of one or other party. Many of these marriages can also be held up to our civilised concepts as ideal. The wife, who must lead an existence very full of burden during the marriage, remains faithful to her husband, raises the children, works in the gardens, carries heavy loads to the market, and makes a great effort continually, from morning to night, for the benefit for her husband. She is no less proud, when through her providing, the husband is in a position to lay by shell money, and the husband for his part shows his gratitude by handing over a small part of the earned shell money as hers. Indeed it can happen that before his death he may express his gratitude by giving her a larger quantity of his shell money as a present. The shell money acquired in this way does not go into the *tabu* house of the head of the family, who has nothing to do with it at all, but the wife stores it in the *tabu* house of her own family, and when she dies it goes to them or to her children. The husband also shows his gratitude to a good wife by drawing her into all consultations, and seldom undertaking anything without first obtaining her approval.

The birth of a child is always an important occasion. When the pregnant woman feels the first contractions, the female friends and particularly the older, more experienced women, are quickly summoned to assist at the birth. The pregnant woman kneels down and embraces one of the house posts, the older woman assisting takes her place behind her. With both hands she massages downwards on both sides, over the abdomen of the pregnant woman, thereby pressing the foetus downwards. Seldom does the delivery proceed unfavourably for the young mothers.

The birth of the first child, especially when the wife belongs to a chief or a wealthy man, does not go by without gifts of *tabu* and other solemnities. Some days before the birth, relatives and friends of the future father bring gifts of all kinds, in recent times especially items traded from the Europeans. When the wife feels that her delivery is near, the female relatives of the husband assemble in the dwelling; that is, those who are married and have children. The woman in labour lies in the open air on a coconut mat. In order that the birth goes smoothly and is not influenced by evil spirits and witchcraft, the sorcerer (*tena papait*) obviously dares not be absent, and practises his craft most earnestly, in a grave manner. From his little basket he takes a small pouch of burnt coral lime, murmurs his incantations over it and holds a little of the contents between thumb and forefinger, blowing it into the air in all directions. Evil spirits in the vicinity are scared away by this. The lime pouch is then handed over to the women who rub the body of the woman in labour with the blessed contents, whereby all possible magic bestowed by evil spirits to complicate the birth loses its power. However, since the enchanted lime alone has insufficient power to drive off all evil spirits, the sorcerer brandishes magical bunches of plants in all directions, among which the particularly potent green-yellow-red striped species of *Dracaena* (*pal akada*) should not be missing, nor the rapidly murmured incantations. All that the woman in labour eats or drinks is likewise enchanted before use.

After the birth of the child, it is handed over to one of the women of the husband's family; or if none is present, then the closest female relative of the young mother takes her place. Should the newborn be a boy, the assembled women intone the far-reaching cry 'Hüh! Hüh!'; if it's a girl they cry, 'Huh! Huh!'. This cry attracts all married women; young girls, however, must remain outside the enclosure and dare not enter the compound. Meanwhile the closest relative of the woman in childbirth has cut through the umbilical cord with a sharp shell or a sharp piece of bamboo, and smeared the wound with the leaf sap of *Erythrina indica*. After the birth the mother is carried into the hut by the women. The spouse then presents *tabu* to the women who have assisted at the delivery.

If the birth has taken place in the early morning or before noon, the relatives of the young mother hurry along, to hand over a gift of *tabu* to the father; it consists of a piece of *tabu* 1 to 5 metres long. If the birth occurred in the afternoon or evening, the gift-giving ensues the following day. The day after that, the spouse repays by distributing betel nuts and pepper among all the wife's relatives, and smaller pieces of *tabu*. The newborn child is now brought forth and admired on all sides. Meanwhile a little heap of fragrant and magical herbs has been piled up and set alight. Nearby lie, if the baby is a boy, all the tools that he will need in future life: a club (*aul kubar*), feathered spear, slingshot and stones, bamboo knife, digging stick, and so on; if the baby is a girl, a rain cape (*kukuwui*), a little basket with betel and areca nuts, a little piece of *tabu* and a bamboo knife are laid down. The heap of fragrant herbs is lit, and a woman swings the baby through the smoke and says, 'Grow strong! Earn a lot of *tabu*! Throw the spear and sling the stone!' Should the baby be a girl, the exhortation goes, 'Grow big, grow strong for work, so that you can till the fields!' A sorcerer must be there of course; he extends his hand in the smoke and takes a little ash between his fingers, then rubs the baby's eyes, ears, temples, nose and mouth with it, so that the infant is strongly charmed against evil spirits and witchcraft. On the same occasion the child is given a name. As a rule the father chooses the name of a relative or friend, and gives this person a piece of *tabu*. However, if he accedes to the special wish of a male or a female neighbour to name his offspring after him or her, then the latter gives a small gift of *tabu* to the child. They are not fastidious in the conferring of names: any object out of the three natural kingdoms is chosen, any deed that has already been undertaken, any event that coincides with the birth. All male names are prefixed by the masculine article *to*, all female names by the feminine article *ia*; a boy is called, for example, *to kaur* (the bamboo (m)), a girl *ia kaur* (the bamboo (f)); *to vinau* (the creeper (m)),

Fig. 11 Mother and child. Gazelle Peninsula

ia vinau (the creeper (f)), and so on. On about the tenth day, when the navel has healed, the baby's head is shaved and rubbed with lime. On this occasion those people who had given the baby's father a gift before the birth, assemble and receive reimbursement in the form of shell money. Betel is distributed and the newborn is admired.

The first born, be it a boy or a girl, is provided with all possible delicacies by the closest relatives of the father during the subsequent four to six months; the best taro and yams, the best fish, and the finest foods are brought as a gift to the suckling infant every day. But when this period has passed, the father pays for it with shell money and betel.

The described celebrations take place only at the birth of the first child, all other births are attended by smaller ceremonies.

Girls who become pregnant without being married, first of all attempt to expel the foetus. Should this not succeed, then at the time of delivery they take themselves off into the forest, where the birth takes place without any assistance. The newborn child is killed immediately after the birth and buried without ceremony.

Otherwise the young mother is quite proud of her infant. When she has recovered from the effects of the delivery, usually after a few days, she takes her newborn about everywhere with her. A square of bark cloth is folded together, laid over breast and shoulders, and knotted across the back. The infant is enveloped in the folds so that only part of the tiny head peeps out and a little leg or two dangles. Besides this burden, however, the mother, as usual, still carries the basket filled with heavy loads, by means of a carrying band around her head. In the gardens she prepares a spot for the little one under a shady bush, and folds a mat over the baby to protect it from flies and other insects. Cleanliness is not seen as essential; if the mother happens to come to the beach or to a spring, a few handfuls of water are poured over the child and the worst dirt washed off. Where water is hard to come by, a few drops from the drinking shell must suffice for the daily toilet.

The mother breastfeeds the child until it can walk. At the same time it must get used to other forms of food from very early on: taro, yams, bananas, and so on, are chewed by the mother, formed into tiny balls, and pushed into the baby's mouth. This diet agrees well with infants if they are particularly healthy, and they appear round and plump, to the great joy and happiness of the mother, who is very proud of this. The father does not have much to do with infants; outside the house the infant is always given over to the mother, in the dwelling the lord father condescends most graciously to carry his child about for a short time in his arms, but there is never a display of special love or affection. As the child grows, it follows its mother until about the sixth or eighth year, but a boy will follow his father more as he gets older. Then in most cases the boy will shift to his uncle's compound, if such is available, and from then on actually belongs to him. Girls stay with the mother up until their marriage; even as small children they must be helpful in the gardens, and at eight or ten years they already carry heavy loads on their back. The boys help the uncle in his gardens, practise the various dances, and are proud when they are first accepted into the *duk-duk* or *ingiet* societies. From youth onwards they take pains to imitate the older people in looks and gesture as well as in behaviour, and a childlike, happy disposition or childlike boisterousness is basically foreign to them. A fourteen- or fifteen-year-old boy is already adult in his total appearance and behaviour. At this age his upbringing and education, insofar as as one can call it such, is complete; what he has not learnt up till now, he will not learn later either, when all his thoughts and aspirations are directed towards the needs of daily life. It is not uncommon for boys who were distinguished as being bright at an earlier age, to become apparently dull as the years progress. In the missionary schools it is frequently observed that children up to the age of twelve or fourteen learn quickly and easily, but with the onset of puberty they suddenly fall away and absorb nothing further.

At the death of a native the solemnities are no less numerous, their extent is, however, in accordance with the position that the dead person occupied during his lifetime. Chiefs, or those who held a similar rank, receive on their death the highest respect that one is in a position to give, whereby an honoured position is assured for the spirit of the dead man in the next world. Women and children are buried with less ceremony.

In the following, I will describe the interment of an *a gala*, as I witnessed it a few years ago. The person in question was a very old man who had enjoyed great respect over a wide area. He had been ill for a long time, and as it eventually became clear that he had only a few days, perhaps only a few hours, left, the great wooden drum (*garamut*) was sounded, and the signal was passed from compound to compound. The relatives streamed in from all sides, and the compound was soon full of men. The closest relatives sat in the hut, around the dying man, held his hand, touched his body, and murmured soothing words. Outside the hut the gathering women set up a loud lamentation; the rest of those assembled squatted on the ground, chewed betel nut and conversed in undertones.

After this had gone on for several hours, death finally came, and this event was immediately announced to the neighbourhood by drum signals. The wailing of the women increased, and a number of men joined in. In the meantime, the corpse was laid out on coconut matting in the hut. The death had taken place in the afternoon, and it was decided to bury the body the following afternoon. The drums sounded without interruption throughout the night, as did the lamentation of the women.

Early the following morning a low, upright frame was set up in front of the hut and decorated with coconut palm leaves and bright foliage. The corpse was then brought outside and arranged in a sitting position with the back against the above-mentioned frame. Men and women, close relatives, came forward to adorn the corpse in the traditional manner. Face and body were painted black, red and white; the head was adorned with a large plume of white cockatoo feathers and a headband; a broad necklace of cuscus teeth was tied round the neck; armlets and other jewellery were put on the corpse and bright *Dracaena* leaves and other strongly fragrant herbs were strewn around. The thumbs of the outstretched arms and the big toes of the outstretched legs were then tied together with a fine cord.

While this was going on, a group of men, women and children destroyed the gardens of the dead man, tore out taro and yam plants, knocked down stands of bananas, and felled a number of young coconut palms.

Meanwhile the lamentations of the women continued to ring out. Each newly arriving group raised a heart-rending cry of grief and intoned a lamentation in which the dead man was invoked, his passing mourned, and his praises sung in all manner of keys. After the arriving mourners had fulfilled their duty, they sat down in the crowd, chewed betel nut and chatted in muffled tones.

The men had meanwhile brought out the great coils of *tabu* from the *tabu* house of the deceased,

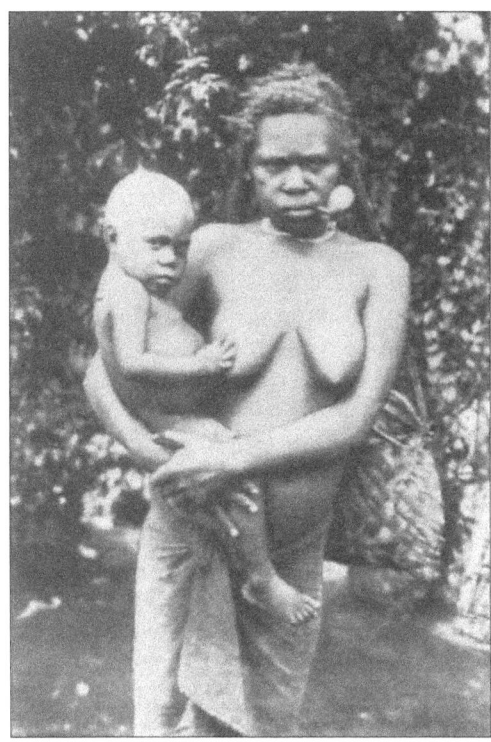

Fig. 12 Mother and child. Gazelle Peninsula

who was a very rich man, and arranged them beside the corpse and on the frame behind him, so that the dead man was once more surrounded by all the family treasure. Then the well-known, loud cry of the *tubuan*[4] sounded from the forest, a similar cry sounded from another direction – it was as if the forest were filled with it – and then a number of masked figures came leaping and springing from the bushes. A deep silence now reigned, the lamentation had ceased. With mighty leaps the *tubuan* danced round the corpse; with long-handled axes they hacked into the ground and into tree trunks round about, then suddenly they disappeared into the bush. Then the drum started up again and the lamentation began anew. Suddenly the call of the *tubuan* was heard again, and they came into view a second time, danced before the corpse to the accompaniment of the drums, and then sat down on the ground nearby.

The closest male relative then brought forward a coil of *tabu,* opened it, and laid it at the feet of the corpse. The *tubuan* then arose, performed another brief dance and placed themselves in a row opposite the corpse. A relative of the dead man then gathered up the open coil of *tabu* and distributed the shell money among the *tubuan*, who picked it up, danced again before the corpse and disappeared into the forest.

With this, the honouring of the dead man by the *tubuan* was concluded. However, there followed a further series of ceremonies which, in their way, were rather pathetic. It is the symbolic farewell from objects with which the dead man was occupied during his lifetime, or was in close connection with. The sea, on which he travelled so often during

4. More about the *tubuan* in Section VIII.

Fig. 13 Women in mourning. Gazelle Peninsula

his fishing trips, approached (that is, a man brought seawater in a bamboo tube and poured it onto the ground in front of the dead man); the field which he had tilled and planted said its farewell by a man emptying out a basket full of soil; the fruits of the field and forest took their departure by betel nut, taro and other fruits being laid down. Sometimes the dead man's canoe is brought out and the corpse placed in it briefly, in a sitting position; the paddle that the owner used during his life is placed alongside. Sometimes the canoe is used as a coffin and the body is buried in it. Years ago, in a village on the Varzinberg, I saw a body laid in state in a canoe, which was placed on a bamboo scaffold about 4 metres tall. In this case burial had been totally disregarded. This is, however, a rare event. The rule is burial in the ground.

During the previously described symbolic farewell ceremonies, the relatives have dug a grave. This is about 1.5 metres deep and corresponds with the body length of the dead man; it is dug either inside the hut of the dead man or in front of it.

The corpse is now fully decorated; that is, lime mixed with red earth is poured over it, lengths of *tabu* are bound round the neck, arms and legs, a larger quantity is laid alongside the corpse and buried with it. Then the dead man is wrapped in mats and tied in with lianas. Meanwhile an ear-splitting wail of lamentation is raised, in which all women especially join in at full volume. The men then lift the corpse and carry it to the grave, where two of them jump in to receive the body and position it in the cavity. There now arises a greater din than before; the men join with the women in a deafening wail, they lean over the grave apparently as if to follow the dead man into it; relatives drag them back, to prevent them from their intention; others scrape soil into the grave with their hands and feet, and only when the wild throng disentangles itself does one see that the grave has been filled in, in an incredibly short time.

After this paroxysm of grief, reaction sets in to some extent. Those assembled sit down round about, recuperate by chewing betel and then await, with the greatest peace of mind, the next honouring of the dead man, namely the distribution of shell money. This distribution can also take place before the burial of the corpse – no special rule appears to be observed. If the dead man is an *uviana* of great wealth, large amounts of shell money are distributed to those present. I have been present at burials where close on 2,000 fathoms of shell money were distributed. This too follows certain rules. The mourners usually sit in divisions, classified by sibs or families. The distinguished people, like the *a gala*, *uviana* and *luluai*, receive the greatest portion, often up to 5 fathoms. Then the remainder follow in descending order, so that several receive only a span length of *tabu*. The more who come to the distribution, the greater the fame of the dead man.

From the interment of the body in the grave until the following morning, the music of the great wooden drums continues unabated. This has the purpose of facilitating the entry of the spirit to *Tingenataberan*. *Tingenataberan* is a place that lies far to the east, where the departed souls go. As soon as the dead man is buried, the spirit, *tulungiana*, rises; however, it can only enter *Tingenataberan* at sunrise, and the drums must sound without interruption to support the wandering spirit on its way. This drum music is called *tulatulai*. At the rising of the sun all gaze intently towards the east; should a cloud stand before the rising heavenly body, this is a sign that the spirit is entering *Tingenataberan*. Here everything is in superabundance: *tabu*, bright-leafed *Dracaena*, loudly beating drums and continuous dancing and feasting. Before entry into *Tingenataberan*, the soul is asked by the spirit Tolumean, 'Where is your *tabu*, where are the armlets that were given to you in the grave? How much *tabu* was distributed at your death?' If the answer turns out to be satisfactory, nothing prevents the entry; if, however, it is not satisfactory, the soul is banished to *Jakupia*, after the spirit has ripped off its buttocks so that it becomes crippled and thereby identifiable. *Jakupia* is a wretched place, without festivities or dancing, without abundances of any sort.

Earlier on, the wealthy and distinguished were buried at sea in St George's Channel. The ceremonies both before and after the sea burial were the same as I have described previously. The body was laid, amidst weeping and wailing, in a canoe and towed out to sea to be sunk with the canoe. This custom has been given up, as a result of the influence of the Christian missions, or is at least fast dying out.

As a sign of mourning the body is painted with a mixture of soot and oil. Close relatives blacken their entire body and renew the mourning colour daily; the further removed the degree of kinship, the lesser is the display of mourning decoration. The length of the mourning period also varies. Close relatives mourn for a year or more, more distant relatives only for a few weeks or a few days. Women have a particular sign of mourning, in which they make themselves exceedingly ugly; they smear their head with a thick ointment of oil, soot and earth, and use it to shape the individual strands of hair into approximately 3-mark-sized, flat, filthy plates, which are arranged over one another like scales. Such a filth- and soot-covered old woman belongs among the most repulsive things imaginable.

For natives of low standing, and for women and children, burial occurs with less ceremony, nor is the grieving and lamentation so pronounced as for the death of a wealthy or mighty person.

It is quite difficult to ascertain whether these lamentations and mourning customs correspond with the true feelings of the natives, or whether they are only exhibitions which the event demands. In many cases the latter is indeed the case; one can often observe a wife, after heart-breaking lamentation and copious tears, chewing betel at greatest leisure with her friends, chatting with them over inconsequential things, or laughing and joking with them. On the other hand I also know cases where the grief was deep and real. Men, who are by nature reserved, consider it unseemly to display their grief;

Plate 6 Sinking fish baskets (*wup na tatakia*), Gazelle Peninsula

nevertheless I have witnessed old men letting the tears flow down their cheeks when I have shown them photographs of long-dead sons or wives. Women apply less restraint on their feelings, and one frequently finds them grieving in an out-of-the-way spot in the forest, or in the gardens shedding copious tears for their dead. Widows, with whom one happens to come into contact, pour forth silent tears at the mention of their dead husband, and when it became known that I had the photograph of one or other of the dead, I was frequently begged to show it to the weeping person.

After a year or so, a special mark of honour is prepared for distinguished people, in which the skull of the dead man is exhumed, painted red and white, adorned with a plume of feathers and placed on an expressly erected rack. The *tubuan* and the *duk-duk* play a prominent role in this; they perform dances and organise ceremonies, and on a certain day the neighbourhood streams in, to receive gifts from the relatives, partly in *tabu,* partly in pigs, hens or crops. On this occasion the tribal treasure of *tabu* is openly displayed on a decorated, bamboo scaffold. *Loloi* (money in a coil) is ranged alongside *loloi* in a long row and beside this are heaped the pigs, hens and field produce intended as gifts (Meyer and Parkinson, *Papua-Album*, vol. I, plates 16-18).

One might postulate ancestor worship here. However, the natives have no concept of such a thing. The dead, whether ancestors or not, enjoy no veneration of any kind, neither do parts of the skeleton. The exhumation and painting of the skull, which I have previously described, is not bound up with exorcism or magical charms; the skull is for a moment the visible sign of the presence of the dead man, in whose honour the festival is held. The fact that one pays no especial reverence to it, is demonstrated by my being able to buy this skull for a trifle, without any difficulty, after the completion of the celebration.

I might mention here that in earlier times, according to the comments of several old natives, it had been the custom to bury alive one or more slaves or several wives with the body of the dead chief. The custom had disappeared with the arrival of the first colonising settlers, a good thirty years ago now. However, several older people in various districts have assured me that in their youth they had been present at such burials. I have no grounds for doubting this information. In Bougainville today this custom is still practised, or at least one or more slaves are killed in honour of the dead man. The idea on which this is based is that the souls of those sacrificed follow the dead man in the beyond, and serve him there. On the Gazelle Peninsula, varying quantities of shell money, as well as items of jewellery and weapons are laid in the grave with the dead man for this purpose. The custom still practised at the filling in of the grave, of leaning out over it with the ostensible intention of letting oneself be buried with the corpse, alludes to an earlier, now fortunately no longer existing custom, whereby close relatives freely followed the dead man into the grave. A particular incident of this kind is known to me; it took place in the inland district of Viviran in 1884. At the burial of a dead chief, one of his nephews leapt into the grave, or, which does not seem improbable to me, was shoved. There then arose an indescribable, wild confusion; some of those present scraped earth into the grave without stopping, others tried to prevent this and won the upper hand insofar as they succeeded in bringing the already partially buried person back into the daylight, although as a corpse. In the entanglement of a wrestling crowd of men, two older men were crushed to death as well, and a few died a short time later as a result of wounds received. In these inland districts, still little influenced by the settlers, many things may still happen that are unknown to us. But on the whole, I think that this custom has died out today, and is only recognisable still in the wild tumult and the efforts of the mourners in pretending to throw themselves into the grave.

Today, wherever north-eastern Gazelle Peninsula people have settled, they use a sea snail shell as money; its upper curvature is cut through, so that the individual pieces can be lined up on strips of rattan. This money is called *tabu* on the Gazelle Peninsula and *diwarra* in the Duke of York group. The sea snail from which this money is prepared is of the genus *Nassa*. The *camelus* variety of *Nassa callosa* is the most frequently used. Use of this snail shell, both as currency and as jewellery, is universal in most parts of New Britain, but also extends over a large part of New Guinea, although as far as is known, exclusively for the preparation of articles of jewellery. On the south coast of New Britain, in the regions east and west of Möwehafen not far from the South Cape, the snail shell likewise finds use as currency; here, however, it is prepared a little differently, in that the upper curvature is almost completely removed, and only a thin slice is used. The inhabitants of the Gazelle Peninsula use this preparation of the snail shells not as money, but only as raw material for the manufacture of ornamental items, as discussed later. The south coast inhabitants too, thread these shells on strips of rattan, seldom in lengths over 1 metre, and tie these to one another in bundles of varying size. In Möwehafen the snails are used in this form as means of tender, and called *eddi*, but also on the other hand used as material for the production of many items of jewellery.

The *tabu* of the Gazelle Peninsula is surrounded with dark mystery for many of its owners, and even this has of course added much to enhance its value. In the Duke of Yorks where the *tabu* was introduced from the Gazelle Peninsula opposite, there is no knowledge of the origin of the money in the districts around St George's Channel and in the countryside around the Varzinberg; it is believed there that the money was brought to the people by spirits, and it is handled with a certain spiritual reverence.

Shrewd natives know how to exploit this in order to enrich themselves. I know of several such cases, which clearly illustrate this. A few years ago a rumour suddenly spread that a woman who lived in a village a few kilometres from my dwelling, possessed with the help of spirits the gift of quickly increasing *tabu* that had been handed over to her by the natives, so that the owners received it back doubled and tripled. Numerous natives, to whom this promised easy and effortless winnings, then deposited a wide range of sums with the wonder woman. Of course the spirit was not always in the mood for the task, it did not immediately increase the money paid in, but condescended only now and then to pay back the instalment with interest. Then too the depositor was given the most variable instructions, to make himself acceptable to the spirit, and when he did not observe these, repayment became very protracted. However, when patience was apparently at an end, first this one then that one was repaid their *tabu* with a handsome increase, and this then appeased the impatient ones and produced new clients. I warned in vain about the swindle, for I saw through it from the outset, and it was absolutely nothing other than a New Britain repetition of the Dachau bank swindle conducted by a local, Adele Spitzeder. For a long time my warnings were in vain, but finally those to whom the spirit had shown no blessing became impatient, and demanded in rage the repayment of their shell money. As Spitzeder refused, under all sorts of pretext, the administrative authorities had to mediate, and it then turned out that a considerable sum belonged to those swindled. But so firm was their faith, that even today very many natives do not want to believe the betrayal; indeed the cunning woman began the same manipulations soon thereafter in another district, with success; of course then to be severely punished by the authorities, upon which the helpful spirit made no further appearance.

On another occasion it was reported to me that on the plot of land belonging to a native whom I knew, there stood a tree from the top of which at certain times the spirits shook *tabu* onto the ground. Any person was allowed to gather this wonder-money, but beforehand he had to pay a certain sum of *tabu* to the owner of the tree, in this case a piece about a metre long. As a result of this information I went to the place, to see this wonder for myself. I could easily see that my presence was not very convenient for the owner, but nobody dared to turn me away. The wonder tree was a fairly large *Ficus*, and the ground round about was carefully cleaned. I found on the site not only the owner of the tree but also a number of natives who had taken their places early in the morning, and now intently awaited the *tabu* rain. On the day that I chose for my visit, the spirit had not been in a very free-giving mood. Now and then he had thrown individual snail shells from the top of the tree and those present had enough shells in total to produce a piece of *tabu* about 2 metres long. They were unprepared snails, such as are not found in this area, and this made it all the more mysterious. I remained there about an hour, and during this time about twenty snails fell to the ground here and there. It was quite clear that the snails had been put in the tree previously, but I could not immediately discover how it was made possible to allow them to fall individually, for in the transparent crown of the tree nobody was concealed, and in spite of the greatest scrutiny I could not discover any mechanisms. Several days later I discovered that the native in question, with several of his relatives, had bought a quantity of raw, unprepared snails from a white trader on the beach, who had brought them from Weberhafen, and they had paid a good price for them so as not to let news of the deal spread to other natives. The spirit was still active for some time, then he stopped dispensing his gifts completely; I also discovered that no really big benefit had been derived, the amount of *tabu* gathered up seldom equalling the admission fee. That the owner of the tree had a nice arrangement, I was certain. Then several months later I found out accidentally, through the talkativeness of one of the natives involved, how the affair had been set up. During the night the participants had tied individual leaves loosely together into little containers at the top of the easily climbed, many-branched tree, and laid a few snails in each one. As during the night there is very often total calm with no leaf stirring, the leaf containers retained their shape; however, as soon as the wind began to stir in the forenoon, the leaves sprang apart and their contents fell to the ground.

The natives on the north coast and Weberhafen of course never let themselves be caught by such a ruse. They know very well where the shell money comes from, even while telling their customers all kinds of fables about it. Each year, at the arrival of the southeast wind, these natives fit out canoes to undertake a journey of several months to the region at the foot of the volcanoes Father and South Son; often these voyages extend as far as the Willaumez Peninsula. Here they barter *Nassa* snails from the natives, indeed they themselves also fish in the shallow bays with muddy bottoms where the snails live. The Gazelle dwellers give this region the general name of Nakanai.

These Nakanai journeys are not exclusively for trading purposes; they frequently bear the character of raids, for when a native can take something from a weaker person without punishment or danger, he does so with relish. In Nakanai he knows that he is undisturbed, the imperial authority sits many kilometres away at Herbertshöhe and as a rule does not concern itself with matters that take place so far away. Also, no complaint reaches Herbertshöhe from Nakanai, and the native returning from his trading voyage is far too cunning to boast about how many gardens he has plundered during his absence, nor how many Nakanai people have been cannibalised. That the reciprocal commerce is not always friendly, is demonstrated by many spear wounds on the home-comers; it is equally certain that the 'fatalities' during the voyage indeed do not always have a natural cause.

I have had occasion to visit the Nakanai region several times, and the shy and fearful behaviour of the natives, combined with their constant preparedness with weapons, clearly shows that they do not exactly expect friendliness from visitors.

After the Nakanai voyagers have come home with the *tabu* obtained, the *Nassa* snails are prepared as previously described and threaded on rattan cords. This new money is inferior for a while, because it is not white. However, it gains a white shade over the course of time by scouring and bleaching.

When large quantities of *tabu* accumulate at a place, wheel-shaped coils of it are prepared, which can sometimes contain up to 500 fathoms or more of *tabu*. Such a coil is called *loloi*. As a rule it is covered with dry pandanus leaves and then wrapped round with a firm plaiting of strips of rattan. Such coils are opened only on very rare occasions and the contents distributed; they are, so to speak, the basic capital of the family to whom they belong.

Smaller sums are of course also kept as *loloi*, but these are opened and distributed at festivities, funerals and on other occasions. The old, wrapped *loloi* indeed also bear names, often the name of the *uviana* who put them aside long ago, or the occasion on which they were rolled up.

Shell money is not rolled up everywhere, but stored in baskets in the form of neat bundles laid together. This is the case in the St George's Channel region, for example, where the money is not always so plentiful as in the areas lying further to the west. These bundles are called *tutuqai*, and are decorated by all kinds of snail shell and shellfish appendages, brightly coloured strips of rattan and the like.

Smaller sums up to 50 fathoms are kept in baskets, some fully threaded, others in sections of varied length.

In daily business the husband or the wife carries a small supply of *tabu* with them according to their circumstances, pocket money so to speak. Running expenses are met from this, and it cannot be denied that the ever-practical native possesses in *tabu* a currency which allows him not only to make quite small payments and outlays very conveniently, but also to accumulate the smallest earnings in order to set aside gradually quite a decent little sum from these savings.

For fixed sums there are certain names. A single snail shell is *a vuana pal a tabu* or *palina*; up to the number 5, the word *palina* is added to the number in question; for example, 5 snails are called *a ilima palina*. From 6 onwards, the individual snail shells are always counted in pairs, and one pair is called *a tip*. Six snail shells are therefore 3 pairs or *a tip a nireit* (*a nireit* is the designation for 3 when items are counted); 8 snail shells are 4 pairs or *tip na ivat*. The odd numbers up to 9, like the values up to 5, are named by appending to the number in question; for example, *lavarua na palina* (7), and *lavuwat na palina* (9). All quantities up to 38 are designated by tip if in pairs; for example, *tip na arip* (10 pairs), *tip lavurua* (7 pairs), *tip na arip ma tip ilima* (10 pairs plus 5 pairs = 30); if unpaired the preceding pair is designated, plus one. For example:

11 = *tip ilima ma a vuana* = 5 pairs and a single

19 = *tip i lavuwat ma a vuana* = 9 pairs and a single

37 = *tip na arip ma tip na lavutul ma a vuana*; that is, 10 pairs + 8 pairs and a single.

Forty snail shells are *a waratuk* or *a dodo*. Two *waratuk* are 1 bal (Matupi: *a turu melmelikun*); 2 bal are 1 *papara*, that is, a side, so-called because the length of the piece is reckoned from the middle of the chest to the fingertips of the outstretched arm, thus in many places it is also called a *bogobogo*, that is, the chest (on Matupi *a leke*, the length from the armpit to the opposite fingertips). Two *papara* are a *pokono* or 1 fathom. On Matupi 2 fathoms are called *a vuna em-tabu*, in Ralum *a ura pokono*, and 3 fathoms are *utul a bal* which in Ralum would be called about 0.75 fathoms. Three fathoms are *a gaina*; 10 fathoms are *a tutuqu* or *arip*; 20 fathoms are *ura arip* or *ura tutuqu* (Matupi = *a kiga*).

A full fathom contains therefore 320 individual snail shells; that is, a *pokono* = 2 *papara* = 4 bal = 8 *waratuk* = 160 *tip*.

For paying out larger amounts, the counting of individual snail shells stops and it is numbered only according to *pokono* or fathoms. One therefore seeks to profit by the counter being a man with short arms, while the recipients select a very long-armed one.

In counting larger sums, or when *tabu* is distributed among those present at certain ceremonies, it is quite amusing to observe the unconcern with which the payers throw great quantities of the highly valued money to the recipients, and with what indifference the latter let it lie undisturbed for quite a while and scarcely touch it, as if it goes against the innermost heart to pick the thing up. However, all this is only hypocrisy, for there is nothing in the world more dear to the heart of the native than *tabu*.

In the Duke of York group where the designations for counting are different from those on the Gazelle Peninsula, shell money (*tabu* or *diwarra*) is also counted differently:

a tip are 4 individual shells; *takai nara* are 20 individuals;
tul a no tip are 30 individuals; *ru i nara* are 40 individuals;
ru i nara ma no tip = 50 individuals; *tul a vin nara* are 60 individuals or one *taben*;
wat na nara = 80 individuals; *lim na nara* are 100 individuals;
purutina nara = 120 individuals; *ina gava* are 200 individuals;
gagawa = 400 individuals.

There, greater lengths of *diwarra* are measured by the unit *taben* or 60; for example:

2 *taben* are *ru ara*
3 *taben* are *o i na gawa*
4 *taben* are *vat na ara*, and so on.

From the Duke of Yorks the *diwarra* has also found entry to parts of New Ireland opposite, but not in great quantities.

Tabu to the natives, then, represents our cash. In daily life it is the value standard for general trading, and in the markets one haggles and bargains over the value of goods on offer just as in our markets in Europe. If, for example, the supply of taro, yams, fish, and so on, is great, then the price drops; if there is short supply, the price rises. All payments in *tabu* are standard when it is a matter of financial reimbursement for goods supplied, or for a service rendered, or for an expression of respect; on the other hand again, the amount varies when it is a case of payments which bear the character of a fine or atonement. As it is written in our penal codes: 'Punishment is by a fine from... Marks, and not exceeding ... Marks etc.' so also with the natives the size of the payment of *tabu* is measured according to the degree of culpability.

A native does not willingly dispense *tabu* if he does not have the prospect of recovering it, with interest, by any way possible. The apparent free giving at certain festivities is based as a rule on careful calculation, and whoever has much money, has numerous means of increasing it. The purchase of young maidens as future wives for the young men, the liberal feasts and celebrations at the time of the *duk-duk* and *ingiet* ceremonies are all calculated to turn a financial profit.

In the Duke of York group even today a domestic type of money is prepared, known by the name of *pele*. In trading there it is not used as money, but is the medium by which *tabu*, called *diwarra* here, is bartered from the natives of the Gazelle Peninsula. On the Gazelle Peninsula itself the *pele* is never used as real money; it is used to some extent for the preparation of certain items of adornment; however, the greatest part goes from the Gazelle Peninsula to Nakanai, where *pele* is very highly treasured, and is used as a means of exchange in purchasing the *tabu* snail shell (*Nassa*), so highly valued on the Gazelle Peninsula. The *pele* consists of small, circular discs about 4 millimetres in diameter. These discs are made from various shellfish and marine snails. The manufacture is the task of the women. First of all, the snails or shellfish are broken up into suitable, small pieces. By means of a small stone these are prepared to the point where they approximate the desired disc shape. A small hole is then bored through the centre of the disc with a drill. Irregularities on both surfaces are removed by rubbing the small plate on a stone, with sand and water, and the disc is then threaded onto a loop of fibrous cord. In earlier times the rim of the little disc was again carefully ground off after threading, so that it was completely smooth. In recent times, where demand has grown, one is no longer so painstaking; the threaded discs are again worked with a stone chisel and prominent excrescences are removed where possible, but careful smoothing of the margins no longer occurs. Older strings therefore differ from the more recent in that they feel polished, whereas the more recent fabrications are mostly rough. Individual shell cords are usually knotted into bundles of ten and are traded in this form. Length of the cords varies; older cords were up to 25 centimetres long, more recent strings are seldom over 20 centimetres, usually less.

While threading the individual discs, care is taken to thread those of one shade together, and among the colours dark-violet strings are differentiated as *kalakalang*, whitish strings as *piir* or mui and reddish-orange coloured strings as *biga*. These latter, because they are less common, have a somewhat higher value; the white and the dark violet shell have the same value.

Although *pele* is prepared on all the islands of the small group, there exists, nevertheless a certain division of labour. On the main island of the Duke of Yorks the individual small plates are roughly prepared, to be drilled and fashioned into round discs on the smaller islands of Mioko, Mualim, Utuan, Kerawara and Kabokon. In earlier times, before the arrival of white people, certain families had the privilege of coming to the Duke of York group to exchange *pele* for *tabu*. The white *pele* went especially to areas on the St George's Channel, the bluish and dark *pele* on the other hand mainly to the north coast of the Gazelle Peninsula.

The preparation of this small disc money is, in any case, a skill that has been transplanted from New Ireland to the Duke of Yorks; the money still found today in New Ireland consists of similar small discs, which are prepared from different materials in the various regions.

From everything that has been said up till now about these natives, it is stressed that their total thoughts and endeavours are directed to the accumulation of *tabu* or shell money. No rendering of service, be it ever so small, remains unpaid for; when a native makes a gift, it indeed demonstrates his goodwill, but he definitely expects an equivalent return, preferably in the form of shell money. He accordingly devises various ways and means by which he can put himself in possession of the highly coveted *tabu*.

One of these is called *vuvue* or *vuvuei* and consists of goods being distributed that are then repaid at an organised feast appropriate for this. Only well-off natives can permit this, because not insignificant costs arise. The course of events is as follows. A native distributes all kinds of gifts to the people in his neighbourhood. Since the arrival of the white people these goods consist of merchandise like knives, spades, cotton material, belts, tobacco, pipes, and so on; in olden times foods of all kinds, garden produce, spears, clubs, decorative items, and so on, were distributed. The recipient in question then knew that in time he would have to make payment for this. When the general day for payment came, the donor erected a small, carefully made hut, upon which he had expended his utmost artistic ability. The ceiling of the hut consists of a painted arch called *popo*, hence the entire building is called *pal na popo* or *pal na vuvuei*. Its construction exhibits no small artistic ability. A bamboo frame the same size as the arch is thickly covered with bamboo battens about 2 centimetres wide, wound round with *mal* (bark material). This winding has the purpose of holding fast the lime mortar that is now put on. This lime mortar is carefully laid on and smoothed with a small piece of bamboo. When the mortar is dry, the white surface is painted with red and black colours, and the artist creates all kinds of designs to the best of his ability; for the most part he stylises human figures, concentric circles, zigzags and wavy lines. The house posts are often carved, often wound round with flowers; the sides of the little house are open. Between the supports a low trellis is attached, 30 to 50 centimetres high, and this too is painted and decorated with entwined flowers and carvings, mostly bird forms. Around it runs a border, about a metre wide, of bright leaves and buds, so that the hut rises as if from a flowerbed. The roof too is not forgotten; the edges are carefully supported and hung with garlands of white feather down; from the peak of the roof or its ends are raised long sticks decorated with feathers or flowers, and red hibiscus, multicoloured *Dracaena* and croton branches are placed among the roofing material. The whole small building makes a very fine, pleasing impression, especially when the flowers and garlands are fresh and blooming. On the floor of this hut banana fronds are laid, on which a sumptuous meal is spread, consisting of baked fish and hens, roasted and scraped taro tubers over which is sprinkled not only grated coconut, but also milk pressed out of the grated coconut kernel. On long, high frames beside the hut hang numerous bundles of bananas and at the foot of the frames are laid husked coconuts for drinking (*kulau*), and great heaps of sugar cane.

On the appointed day, advertised to the entire neighbourhood, men, women and children stream in in great numbers. Each one is festively decorated. By village or by family, dances are presented, firstly by the women then by the men; the festive atmosphere is not troubled by often five or six different groups dancing at the same time, accompanying their dance with loud singing, each group striving to drown out the others. The host of the feast stands to one side, as though he were totally indifferent to the whole thing. However, when the dance is completed, each group approaches him and and those who had previously received any item, lay their payment in the form of shell money at his feet, usually a little over the actual value. And so it goes on, until all have paid. The feast-giver observes closely that each one carries out his payment according to the gift, he also notes those who do not pay and later makes sure that his due is provided. It is quite astonishing how much acuteness of memory the natives apply to these events on the day. Although often several hundred have to make their payment, none is forgotten, no matter how small the individual item that was given previously, and which now must be paid for according to its greater or lesser value in *tabu*.

On completion of the payments, the titbits arranged for display in the *pal na popo* are distributed, and likewise the fruits hanging from the frames, and general feasting ensues.

The feast-giver usually makes a handsome profit, and in so doing increases his *tabu* wealth quite significantly. I know of one case in which the outlay was about 300 fathoms of *tabu* (monetary value about 750 Marks), the income 420 fathoms of *tabu* (about 1,050 Marks), a profit that must seem particularly high to a native.

Today things are much simpler. The *vuvuei* has remained the same in principle and the festivities still take place, but the painstaking building of the *pal na popo* or *pal na vuvuei* is already beginning to slip markedly into oblivion. For the most part they are now simple, undecorated huts, not to be compared with the really pretty and tastefully decorated little houses that were erected about twenty years ago for these events, and in which the organiser justifiably took great pride.

The dance presented on the occasion of a *vuvuei* is called *kulau*; it consists of set figures with precise body movements, and is danced only at this event.

It often happens that in time of difficulty, someone lends shell money to another. If a wealthy man borrows a certain amount of *tabu* from another of his equals, perhaps because he does not want to break a complete roll of *tabu*, or in order to complete one, the lender regards this as a favour and demands no interest. At the repayment the borrower puts on a small feast to express his appreciation for the kindness done. In all other cases the lender calculates interest, at quite a high level. For example, if a native, on the death of a relative, borrows *tabu* from his neighbour to distribute among those present, he must pay about 50 per cent for it: the natives calculate that for every ten lengths of *tabu* borrowed, fifteen lengths must be repaid to the lender. On other transactions as a rule 20 per cent is calculated; that is, for every five lengths of *tabu* the borrower must repay six. The time period plays no role; if the loan lasts one year or ten, the interest remains the same.

Another way of obtaining *tabu*, was by a game that was still evident at the time of my arrival in the archipelago in 1882, but which has not been practised for many years now. A framework was prepared from thin strips of bamboo, in the form of a large rooster that appeared quite lifelike when it was thickly oversewn with feathers (fig. 14). On the underside the framework had an opening wide enough to put over the upper body of a man. Three or four youths masked themselves in this way and then went from dwelling to dwelling presenting dances at each place, for which a piece of *tabu* was presented to them. However, since school attendance was neglected through such activities, the native mission teachers banned the game.

Fishing with traps plays a not insignificant role on the north coast of the Gazelle Peninsula. In Blanche Bay and at its entrance as well as eastwards and westwards from Cape Stephens, this method of capture is used. In individual spots in the Duke of Yorks as well, fish-trap fishing has become established, but not to the same extent as in Blanche Bay.

The traps either float on the surface, firmly anchored to the sea floor, or they are sunk to the bottom. The former, *a wup* and *a widam*, are used exclusively for catching a certain fish, *urop*, or with the article: *a urop* to be exact, which periodically appears in great schools on the surface, and is highly prized as a delicacy by the natives. It must not be missing from a feast; those who can, buy the

Fig. 14 Rooster mask. Gazelle Peninsula

fish as a particularly fancied food, and willingly pay a price that must be regarded as relatively high by natives, since for a full-grown specimen it generally amounts to 1 Mark. On the table of the settlers the *urop* is a welcome course.

In the sunken traps, considerably smaller in size than the former, and called *a wup na tatakia*, all kinds of reef fishes that live at the bottom of the sea or on the coral reefs are caught; the bright, varied contents of these smaller fish-traps are, as a rule, the delight of ichthyologists, and also supply the kitchen with many valuable contributions.

The *wup* in its completed form has the shape of a large balloon and is somewhat wider at one end than the other. The manufacture requires considerable skill, and great patience and time. First of all mature bamboo canes are cut in a suitable place in the forest, split into long strips about 4 to 5 millimetres wide and 2.5 to 3 metres long, and the edges and insides carefully scraped and smoothed. These lengthwise strips, which form the outer body of the fish-trap, are called *pal a wup* (pal = house); wider strips are similarly prepared for different use. From the outer, hard bark of a type of rattan, thin strips are cut, 2 to 3 millimetres wide, which are very supple and serve as bindings in the later stages of manufacture.

First of all the inner part of the trap is made. This consists of about ten to twenty bamboo strips, 1 to 1.5 centimetres wide and 2 to 2.5 metres long, according to the size of the fish-trap. These lengthwise strips, *pal a bul*, are attached at about two-thirds of their length to a small bamboo ring, about 15 to 25 centimetres in diameter, and the ring is closed with a net-like wickerwork of fine bamboo strips; this ring with its mesh is called *aubene*

(= net). The individual strips, *pal a bul*, are now attached at both ends to bamboo rings, one of which forms the upper end, through which the fish get into the trap; the lower end is of course similarly open, but serves less as an entrance to the trap. The upper end, about 50 to 60 centimetres in diameter, and the lower, about 40 centimetres in diameter, are now prepared particularly carefully. They are the same as each other in arrangement; the *pal a bul* are attached to the outermost ring, and there follows a thick, funnel-shaped wicker-work, *pal vavatur*, approximately 15 to 20 centimetres wide, consisting of bamboo strips about 1 centimetre wide, then a wicker-work of narrower strips, *pagal a tit*. The rest of the length of the *pal a bul* remains free and without mesh, and fish that enter through the openings easily succeed in reaching the interior by pushing aside the sticks, but cannot swim out again because the staves do not yield from the inside outwards; the wicker-work, *aubene*, prevents the fish from passing through the fish-trap along its length; once in the funnel-shaped corridor the fish for better or worse must pass into the interior of the fish-trap through the easily yielding staves, *pal a bul*. To strengthen the upper or trap end of the fish-trap, a round collar of rattan and bamboo strips, about 3 centimetres thick, is laid on the inner rim, and the entire wicker-work is tied fast onto this; the ring, *a pulpul bat*, also serves for fastening the plaited rattan cords, *a virvir* by which the fish-trap is attached to the float. To the lower end is fastened a long, thin rattan cord, lal, used in raising the fish-trap from the water into the canoe to remove the possible catch; this end is provided with a cross-form wicker-work, *kakatua*, by which the individual staves of the fish-trap achieve a firmer binding. The outer covering of the fish-trap is formed from bamboo strips, *pal a wup*, lying densely over one another, laid over rings of varying width that give the fish-trap its external form, and are firmly attached to them by means of narrow rattan strips, *pidikai*. These rings, made from bamboo strips, are of two types: broad rings, *loko*, to give the fish-trap greater firmness, and narrow rings, *piai*, which, secured with the *pal a wup*, form the real shell of the fish-trap.

Various accessories belong to such a net, namely the float or buoy, to which the fish-trap is attached, the anchor rope, and the anchor. The float or buoy, *babau*, consists either of a bundle of firmly tied bamboo canes about 4 to 5 metres long, or a wooden float usually made from the inner wood of the breadfruit tree, which is not attacked by the boring clam; in the latter case the 4 to 5 metre long wooden buoy has a deep, broad indentation at one end, *kala ta dokop*, to which the *wup* is attached by means of the *virvir*. In the middle, the buoy has a further indentation, *kokobot*, which serves to receive the anchor rope, *vinau*; the latter is wound round the buoy and secured to it in a particular manner, called *paraparik*.

The anchor rope, *vinau* is made from lengths of rattan; usually three to four of them are wound round one another and held in place by wrapping with fine strips of rattan about 10 centimetres apart; the wrapping is called *gogo*. The anchor ropes are often of great length, occasionally up to 300 metres long if the *wup* needs to be anchored in deep water; the anchor ropes for the *widam*, which resemble the *wup* in form but are less solidly constructed because they are laid in lesser depths, are correspondingly shorter.

The anchor, *vat* (= stone), is a conical rattan basket; the securing head, *kiki na vat*, about 75 centimetres in diameter, is thick cane wicker-work on which coral blocks are piled into a conical heap. Then the rattans radiating out from the anchor head are bent upwards and these *vatutia* are secured with rattan rings, *vat a lil*, running round and round, and a strong loop, *kol*, is formed at the upper end.

When all is ready, several bamboo floats, *goaka-ra*, are attached above, and to one another. On this are placed the anchor and the anchor ropes, the latter wound into great coils. The completed fish-trap is placed in a canoe, and the fisherman sets out, buoys in tow, to the place appointed for laying the fish-trap. The fisherman, by using familiar landmarks, can reach the exact spot, whose depth he knows. Having reached the spot, the anchor rope is secured to the ring of the anchor, which can be be carefully lowered. As soon as it has touched bottom, the upper end of the anchor rope is secured to the buoy and the fish-trap is joined on. In order to recognise the site of the fish-trap, a young sapling or a stick tied with brushwood is set up on the buoy. This sign, *au anai* is visible from afar, and every owner of a fish-trap recognises his property by this.

From land the owner maintains a good lookout, to note when fish go into the fish-trap; since the traps often lie 3 to 4 kilometres from the beach, a good eye is required to spot the fish gliding in.

The fish-traps which are sunk to the sea floor, *wup na tatakia*, are considerably smaller, about 1 metre long, and more cylindrical in shape. All kinds of bait are laid inside, and by diving they are set in position on the coral reef. A thin anchor rope, *kuika* made from interwoven lianas, extends from the fish-trap to the surface, and a small float attached to the upper end indicates the position of the fish-trap.

The completion of a deep-sea fish-trap, *wup*, with its accessories, is the occasion for a small feast. The women bring the necessary taro, yams, bananas and coconuts down to the beach and prepare them there, beyond the bounds of the fishing place. On this site, to which women are forbidden

Plate 7 New Guinea type of canoe on the 'Lieblichen Inseln'

entry, stand the spacious huts in which the fishing equipment and canoes are stored. On the whole, women are not allowed to have anything to do with the preparation of fishing equipment; but it is permissible for them to carry the heavy coils of rattan, from which the anchor ropes are prepared, from inland to the seashore. It is forbidden for women even to touch the completed fish-trap and its accessories, because this might bring about an unfavourable outcome, and every catch could be spoiled. During the preparation of fish-traps and accessories the men avoid the women and have no sexual relations with them. Before its immersion, the fish-trap and its accessories are the subject of all kinds of sorcery, which has the purpose of bringing about a good catch. To the accompaniment of the murmuring of magic spells, the fish-trap is painted with red ochre mixed to a pulp with the sap of a particularly magical tree. This is called *ramarama*. Besides this, magical herbs are placed in the fish-trap and during this procedure a man skilled in magic murmurs luck-inducing incantations over the sea and over all the fishing equipment, which will not only invoke an abundant catch but also plead for calmness of wind and sea, so that the anchor rope does not break and the fish-trap be carried off. On no account should an unclean pig approach the fishing site on the beach, and similarly, the preparers of the equipment must abstain from any contact with a pig, and from eating pork, since this would totally thwart the success of the fishing. This superstition is so strong that, for example, the offering of pork for sale in the vicinity of the fishing site is not permitted, nor the transport of a pig in a canoe. A fishing site is given up once and for all should an enemy malevolently throw pig offal, entrails, and so on, into it, an offence that, if discovered in earlier times, would have been punished by death.

Catching fish is carried out in many kinds of ways besides fish-traps, however. Methods vary with the different areas of the coast, and are dependent in many ways on local conditions. A quite widespread type of fishing is by means of *pakapakat* and *vinot* which is used along shallow stretches of shoreline to catch a particular fish, called *karua* by the natives. The *pakapakat* is a net about 1.5 metres deep, provided with floats on the upper edge and sinkers along the lower edge; the *vinot* consists of two, crossed-over bamboo canes that form a wide angle. Inside this angle a triangular net is spread. If a school of *karua* appears in the shallows, two men go into the water with the *pakapakat* and place it so that the fishes' way of retreat to the open sea is cut off. Those carrying the *vinot* then position themselves in knee-deep water, one *vinot* always abutting its neighbours, thus forming a broad arc. At a given signal, the men with the *pakapakat* make a noise and the terrified fish jump, describing broad arcs above the surface, into the *vinot* held before them.

For catching the fish *tatalai* which stays in great schools in shallow water close to the beach at certain times of the year, they use long baskets woven from coconut palm leaves. These are held just above the surface by men wading up to their waists and standing closely together. One or two men then scare the fish, which leap into the baskets. The method, like the baskets used, is called *watar*.

Net fishing is universal, and the natives show great dexterity in the making of the nets that are called by the general name *ubene* or, with the article, *a ubene*. The *ubene* are variously named according to the type. *Lal* are the big nets which as a rule belong to an entire village or community. They are up to 1.5 metres deep and are fitted at the lower edge with sinkers and at the upper edge with floats or buoys. Through the entire upper edge runs a rope as thick as a finger, with free ends, *tulu*. To use it, the *lal* is taken to sea in one or more canoes, depending on its length. They carefully try to cut the fish off from the open sea, and surround them with the net; once this has been achieved, the fishermen pull both ends to shore by means of the tulu, and, with the net, the enclosed fish. In earlier times they fished at the beach with a type **of** very fine-meshed net for a fish barely 3 centimetres long, that arrived from time to time, known as ainanga, and also prized as a delicacy by the settlers. Since the introduction of mosquito nets by the white people, these have been used for catching the small fish.

Small, funnel-like containers, *ungut*, usually the length of a hand, with an upper opening of 5 to 10 centimetres are prepared from the thorny branches of the rattan plant. The rows of thorns are positioned in such a way that their sharp barbs are directed inwards. A piece of bait is fastened on the floor of the funnel, and the apparatus is then placed between stones on the reef. Fish coming headfirst into the funnel are caught by the hooks and cannot get out.

The fish spear, *padik*, with two or more prongs, is recognised but not widely used, however. Hook-and-line fishing too is not significant. The earlier, native fishhook, *qeo*, has now totally disappeared; I recollect having seen it quite rarely in earlier years. Wherever line fishing is carried out today, European equipment is used. The original fishhooks were manufactured from the bones of a certain fish, and were very primitive; from the small significance of line fishing, the hook has never been developed or improved.

In some places great stretches of shallow water are enclosed with coconut palm fronds; at certain intervals wide openings are left, and are closed after a certain time. Fish which have entered at full tide are easily caught at low water.

Poisoning of fish, or more accurately stupefying them, is well-known in certain places; for example, on the island of Matupi. The technique is called *aniboko*. The roots of a certain liana, *wun*, are crushed, and poured into the stomach of smaller fish, caught previously. These are then sunk at short distances apart, and the big fish that swallow the bait fall into stupefaction, which brings them up to the surface, where they become an easy prey to the waiting fisherman in his canoe.

A type of prawn found in rivers, named *kidama* by the natives, is caught with fine-meshed nets.

All fishing is the men's work; women cannot be involved with catching fish, nor in the preparation of the various equipment. Modern times have, however, brought about a change, and one can now observe women knotting fishing nets.

Turtle fishing is carried out everywhere, yet nowhere so systematically as by the inhabitants of the north-east Gazelle Peninsula on the extreme western outposts, from the island of Urar to the islands of Masava and Masikonápuka. Although there are turtles year-round, the real fishing season is limited to the period of the south-east wind, because the sea is too stormy in the north-west season. Usually a great number of vessels all set off at once on the hunt, and the provisioning of these with food is the job of the women. They also provide each vessel with square pandanus mats, from which the men can quickly erect a protective roof when necessary. The men prepare the nets needed for the expedition; these are from 20 to 30 metres long and 1 to 1.5 metres deep. The lower edge is weighted with stones and shells as sinkers, and a thick rope is drawn through the top row of mesh. These wide-meshed nets made from thick fibres are obtained from the island of Uatom and from the villages on Cape Livuan. Turtle hunting begins as soon as they reach the vicinity of Cape Lambert; but the real hunting grounds lie much further southwards, where uninhabited sandy areas of beach extend for a great distance. According to long-standing custom the hunting ground is divided between the participants from the different districts. Capture is carried out in various ways, but always in relatively shallow water or on the reef, where the turtles cannot escape by diving. When they sight a turtle whose location requires capture by net, they lower this into the water and try to surround the creature as quietly as possible. If this is successful, the net is quickly pulled more and more tightly, and the natives standing in the water seize the prey and lift it into the vessel with the help of their comrades. By careful stalking they can also successfully surprise the creatures feeding in shallow water, pounce on them and secure them as previously described. Turtles encountered on the high seas are caught as a rule by a skilfully thrown spear. Capture of the creatures during the mating season is very easy; natives maintain that this takes place on the sea floor, and that afterwards both animals rise to the surface. It should be very easy to capture them in this situation; the fishermen simply swim up to them, take hold of them and throw them into the canoe. Very many turtles are also caught on the beach where they are surprised during egg-laying. The natives say that the turtles dig a hole about 40 centimetres deep and 15 centimetres wide in the sand with their front flippers, a few species also using their heads for this. When the hole is ready, the creature puts the rear portion of its body in it and in a short time lays a considerable number of eggs, 100 or more. After about ten days the young turtles break out of the eggs, dig their way through the covering of sand to the daylight, and seek the sea. Both species of *Chelonia* are caught as well as the leathery turtle (*Sphargis coriacea*). The flesh of the two former is very tasty, and the shell of *Chelona imbricata* is a valuable item of trade. The flesh of *Sphargis* is less favoured.

When a sufficient number of turtles has been harvested, the hunting party turns for home. During the expedition only the speared or otherwise killed animals are consumed; the living turtles are tied by their front and back flippers and brought home. On the men's arrival after weeks of absence, a great feast is put on, for which some of the harvested animals are provided for roasting. Small areas are fenced in shallow water for that part of the catch that will be slaughtered later, and the secured animals are placed inside.

Canoe building on the Gazelle Peninsula is to some extent a monopoly of the natives of the small island of Uatom (Man Island). Vessels obtained from there are recognisable by the prows fixed to both ends, and are designated by the name *kakala*. Vessels are also obtained from the Duke of York group but are inferior, however, and come in two types, recognised as *mut* and *pongpong*. The general name for a canoe is *waqa* or *uaqa*; usually the word is heard in combination with the article *a*. The actual body of the canoe is usually produced from the wood of the *iting* (with the article a *iting*), which is really soft and therefore easy to work with. However, in sea water it is quite durable and does not easily crack or fracture. Small imperfections in the wood, which let in water, are packed with the pounded kernel of the *tita*. An obliquely rising prow is fastened to both ends. In the *kakala* the prow is doubled, as in figure 15.

The long prow is called *bakabakan*, the lower one *bitonomarum*. The *mut* canoe obtained from the Duke of Yorks has only the longer prow, not the shorter point behind it. The prow of the *pongpong* is shorter and shaped like a hook, bending inwards (fig. 16). These three different types of canoe are therefore easily distinguished by the shape of their prow. Their size is naturally very different; there are small, single-person canoes, and all larger sizes up to twelve or sixteen people sitting one behind the other, for only in very rare cases is the width sufficient to allow two men to sit side by side.

The prow is carved from a single piece, yet in such a way that at its foot the wood divides at an acute angle, like wings, so that it can be attached to both sides of the boat; the angle thereby arising at both ends of the canoe is named *tabaran*. The spirit protecting the canoe would stay here; the inside of the canoe is called *waquwaqu*.

The outriggers with the float are always fastened to the left side of the canoe so that one end is always the cutwater, although in practice this front part of the canoe is not always directed forwards, but is frequently pointed in the opposite direction. However, a bow end, *luaina*, and a stern, *bit a uaqa*, are differentiated.

The outrigger boom, or more correctly outrigger booms, because there are always several, extend from gunwale to gunwale, and out over the gunwale on one side; the general term for these is *taraba*; the one in front is designated *taraba valval*, the one at the back *teitei* (*tei* = to steer) because the canoe steersman sits on this one, never on the one in front. The *taraba* are present in different numbers, according to the size of the canoe: the smallest number is two, one seldom sees more than six.

To give the *taraba* greater strength, they are fixed with several supports running at right angles to them; that is, parallel to the body of the canoe. These are called *aunuruk*. The *taraba* are forked at the outer end, so that they can be attached better and more firmly to the small pieces of wood serving as binders, which stick out of the float. The float, *aman* is a piece of soft wood about four-fifths of the length of the canoe. It varies in thickness according to the size of the canoe, but it is seldom more than 20 centimetres thick and usually cut square.

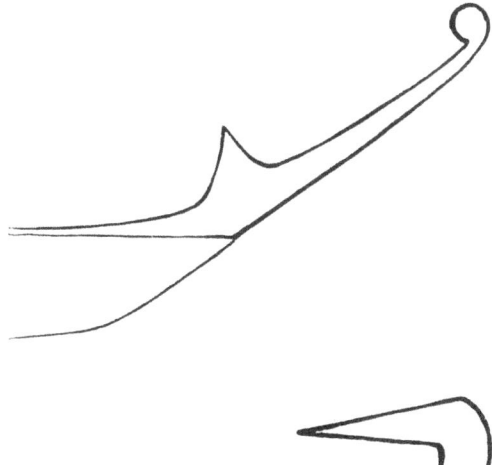

Fig. 15 Prow of the *kakala*

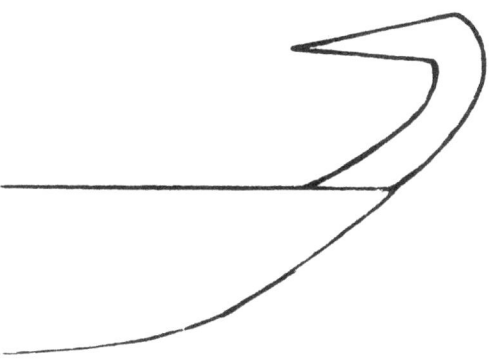

Fig. 16 Prow of the *pongpong*

Both ends are pointed and are called *bur na aman*; the *aman* is usually charred in the fire to make it stronger in the water. From the *aman* small flat boards rise in pairs at fixed distances according to the separation of the outriggers from one another. These are called *li*; they are tightly arranged, with their pointed ends driven perpendicularly into the wood of the float, *aman*, and the forked ends, *aur na kubau*, of the outrigger, *taraba*, firmly attached; as a rule they project somewhat beyond the forked ends, and are firmly bound to one another at their upper ends. The canoes obtained from Uatom are not secured to *li* by their front and rear outriggers, but to two small tree branches called *pererek*. These branches are not driven into the float like the *li*, but are inset by means of a right-angled projection, *pal a kau* or *patimur*, and bound on by cords; the forked ends project above the outrigger; canoes from the Duke of York islands do not have this embellishment.

A thick rattan cane is laid along the top of both gunwales from front to back, and is secured to the side walls of the canoe by thin strips of rattan. This fastening is named *paqul*. Small wooden boards are used as thwarts, a little wider than the width of the canoe. These thwarts, *pal ab* or *pal a qul*, are somewhat indented on the lower surface at each end, and these notches hook over both gunwales, thus giving greater strength to the whole canoe. The port side of the canoe, the outrigger side, is named *na man*; the starboard side is called *natalai*.

New canoes are often decorated with long white cords of down which are stretched from the canoe over the outrigger; this fastening, *qoqol na wub*, is also put on when the *tubuan* (see Section VIII) presents it to the water; on this occasion the ends of the *li* are also fastened with bunches of bright leaves.

The vessel makes demands on the owner. After each time it is used it is drawn up on the beach and either brought under a thick protective roof or covered with coconut matting to protect it from the sun's rays. Prior to this it is washed both inside and out with a thick lime slurry. In order that the damp bottom of the boat doesn't suffer damage, the canoe is raised on two or three forked supports, and the float is similarly treated.

Sails for propelling the vessel were previously unknown, and only came into use after acquaintance with the white settlers. In spite of this, for the most part propulsion today seems to be by means of shovel-shaped paddles, named *wo*.

An ostentatious canoe, *uaqa na pedik*, was customary in earlier years; today, however, like so many other things, it has already disappeared. This canoe was constructed just like any other, but at both ends between the soaring prows and the gunwales it had extremely fine, open-work carving, which was done by the most skilful carvers of this tribe. Bows, outriggers and float pegs were brightly painted and richly decorated with feather and down cords. It was prepared by wealthy natives and presented amidst great festivities; the curious, streaming past, paid, according to rank and fortune, a piece of *tabu* which was laid in the canoe. The designation *pedik* indicates that sorcery and belief in spirits were connected with this; the present generation, however, is not familiar with it, a further indication of how astonishingly quickly many old customs have totally disappeared under the influence of the new culture.

Medical knowledge among the natives of the Gazelle Peninsula is not insignificant. Even though it is now difficult to distinguish real remedies among the charms so often used, it is nevertheless an incontrovertible fact that for certain illnesses sundry more or less effective medications are known to them. These come almost exclusively from the plant kingdom. Medical knowledge itself does not have a high standing; on the other hand the possessor of it enjoys a special respect, and attains greater importance through the supposed inspiration by spirits. The natives' anatomical knowledge is quite remarkable. This is of course a consequence of cannibalism: knowledge of the structure of the human body and the importance of the various organs being gleaned from this. One might assert that their knowledge in this connection would far exceed that of the average, educated European. They can report accurately the position of the individual internal organs, and are able to judge whether liver, lungs, stomach, and so on, are implicated in the illness. Many years ago I was summoned by the natives to a wounded man who had been hit by a bullet in a battle with a neighbouring tribe. It was reported to me that the bullet had penetrated the left side, injuring lungs and stomach, and had lodged in the right wall of the body. When I wanted to examine the injured man more closely, they showed me the site on the right side where the projectile was lodged, and it would have been an easy matter to extract it. I did not attempt to carry out the operation, however, as the injured man lay at the point of death. Lungs and stomach were undoubtedly shot through, although my medical knowledge would scarcely have extended to establishing this. The natives, however, gave impressive reasons for their assertion, and I was in no position to contradict. The wounded man died about two hours after my visit, and the following day, at the burial, they showed me the bullet that had been removed before his death; the corpse displayed a cross-shaped incision, about an inch long, through which the bullet had been extracted.

The natives' surgical knowledge extends to the treatment of skull fractures originating from slingshot stones, undoubtedly their high point. Should

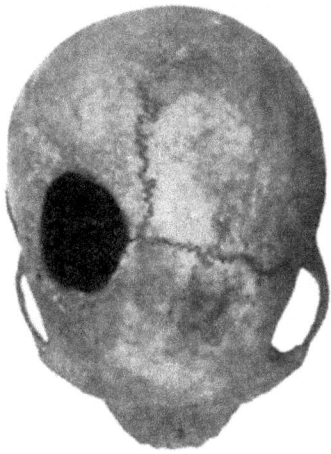
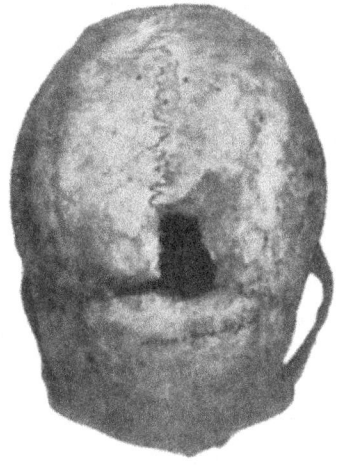

Fig. 17 Trepanned skulls from the Gazelle Peninsula

a native be knocked insensible by a slingshot stone in battle, he is immediately dragged unconscious from the battlefield and brought to the person entrusted with the treatment of such wounds. This man immediately assesses the nature of the wound. Should the stone have crushed the temple, then he immediately pronounces the wound as fatal and undertakes no operation. If on the other hand the frontal bone is crushed, he immediately proceeds to trepanation. His instruments are the most simple imaginable: an obsidian sliver, a sharp shark's tooth, or a sharpened seashell. Before the operation he washes his never very clean hands in water from a *cubica* (a coconut that is full of fluid but has not yet established a kernel); the wound is also carefully washed with the same water. Whether this fluid therefore has antiseptic properties I cannot say; the fact remains, though, that it is used. With one of the previously mentioned cutting instruments the surgeon now makes a long incision transversely across the contusion, to bone depth. Two assistants, aided by a thin strand of rattan attached to a lock of hair, slowly and carefully peel back the corner of scalp freed from the bone, until the surgeon has laid bare the entire damaged part of the skull. The next task involves removal of the bone splinters. The individual fragments are carefully removed with a sharpened piece of coconut shell, until the brain is visible. The surgeon now carefully observes it; should he find that the brain has a gentle, pulsating movement, he is very happy, and promises a rapid recovery; however, if he observes no movement, it is a sign to him that bone splinters have penetrated the brain, and he then assumes a serious demeanour. However, he does not give it all up for lost, but begins to search for concealed bone splinters. For this purpose he carefully parts the brain folds until he finds the bone splinters hidden between them and removes them; the instrument used is the coconut shell sliver mentioned earlier.

If all is crowned with success up to this point, the next stage of the operation begins. This consists of the surgeon smoothing the edges of the opening in the skull with a sharp object, a sliver of obsidian or a sharpened seashell, so that all sharp edges are removed until the hole is round or elliptical; great care is taken that fragments rubbed off don't fall into the cranial cavity. When this task is completed, the actual operation has ended, and the surgeon now takes the necessary steps to allow the wound to heal. He covers the hole in the skull with a small piece, *mal,* of inner bark from a certain tree, or

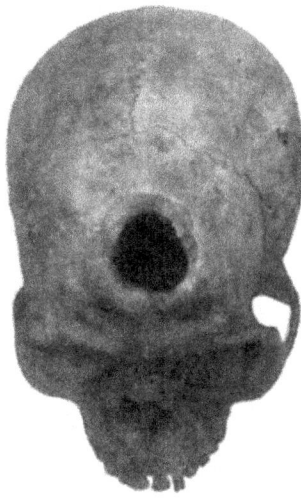
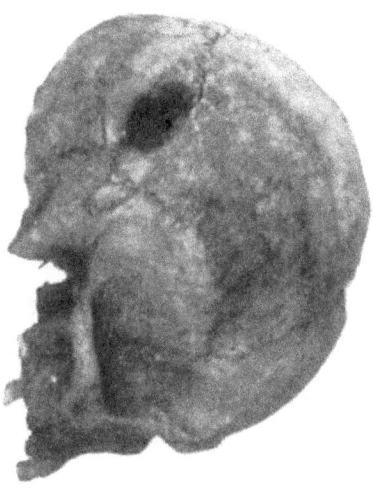

Fig. 18 Trepanned skulls from the Gazelle Peninsula

with a small piece of innermost leaf of a certain banana, which has previously been held for a few moments over a charcoal fire. Then the scalp flaps are slowly and carefully drawn over the skull and laid in their original positions. The hair around the wound is now cut off, and finally the whole area is carefully washed with water from a *cubica*. To hold the scalp flaps in position and thereby enable healing to take place, the upper part of the head is covered with a tight-fitting, wide-meshed network of strips of rattan, bearing the name *kalil*.

The surgeon ought now, by our standards, to be pleased with his work, but far from it; he now fastens on that which, in his opinion and in his clients' conviction, is the only effective means of producing real healing, namely various charms. In this case two particularly powerful healing charms, named *mailan* and *aurur*, are blown into the air, hung round the patient's neck, or else attached to some part of his body. Without this aid, the operation would not be complete, and in the opinion of the natives would have no favourable outcome in any case. Whether it be in consequence of the skill of the surgeon or as a consequence of the charms, this much is certain, that in almost all cases the operation is successful. Not only do I know of a great number of such patients, who today, many years after the operation, are still alive, but also my collection contains many skulls of natives who have lived a long time after the operation and many of whom I knew personally. All these skulls clearly show the smoothing of the edges and the ensuing scar tissue. In European collections, too, such skulls are certainly not a rarity. It can be marvelled that the always difficult operation is successful in so many cases, albeit with primitive instruments, even though they are used with the utmost care. The patient is usually unconscious during the course of the operation. The native doctors, *tena papait* (*tena* = one who is skilled; *papait* = charm), tell me that when a person regains consciousness during the operation, he loses consciousness again after a short time. An old native counted thirty-one cases in which he had undertaken the operation; of these, twenty-three were still alive; many of them had been brought before me. One of these had been trepanned twice, both times successfully; he is now an old man of about sixty. He received the first wound as a youth, the second about twenty-five years ago. It might happen that after the operation mental disorder appears, either permanently or episodically, but I know of no incidence of this occurring.

This operation is similarly known in the Duke of York Islands. The missionary, Mr Crump, tells me that a V- or Y-shaped incision is made there, and the wound is subsequently bound with dry strips of banana stalk. Moreover, on the Gazelle Peninsula the surgeons may have variations in technique, in such districts that are less familiar to me.

I must comment here that the operation is only undertaken when after removal of the scalp it is observed that the cranial bone is completely depressed and shattered. If the skull is depressed and individual pieces of bone still hang together, further intermixing is avoided; the skin flaps are carefully brought back into their correct position and the wound heals normally. Such depressed skulls are often brought to me; the skull wound had healed and formed a deep dent.

On the entire southern half of New Ireland and the offshore islands of Gerrit Denys and Caens, trepanation is also known. From the close relationship of the Gazelle Peninsula tribes with the tribes of southern New Ireland we should not be surprised. Here the operation is also carried out by men and, as far as I could ascertain, in the same way as on the Gazelle Peninsula. However, in medical practice they are even further advanced, in that trepanation is also resorted to there for certain illnesses, to give palliation to the patient, namely in the case of epilepsy, and for chronic severe headaches. In these cases an incision is made in the skin, and the frontal bone exposed. The latter is then pared with a sharp seashell until a furrow and finally a fissure is created in the frontal bone; the scalp is then again laid over it, medicinal plants laid on top, and after a short time, about ten days, the wound has healed. This has now led to trepanation of the skull by paring being regarded as a certain cure for various illnesses, and, in order to protect her children from headaches and epilepsy

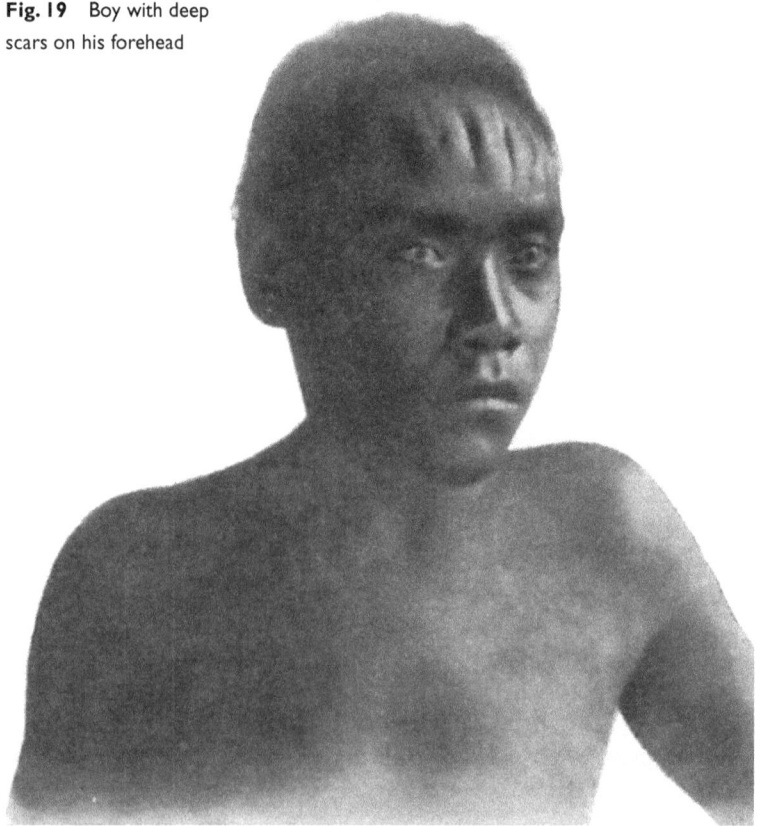

Fig. 19 Boy with deep scars on his forehead

during their entire life, a caring mother does not neglect opening the frontal bone of her children by scraping; in some districts this trepanation takes place only once, but in other districts, on the other hand, twice or three times. Years ago I tended to regard the scars resulting from the operation as 'decoration', although I could not explain how a palpable, deep furrow occurred in the skull bone. Several years ago, in the vicinity of Cape Santa Maria, I was attracted by the pitiable cries of a few children, who, with several women, formed a small group in the shallow water of a small stream. I was not a little astonished when I saw on my arrival that two, approximately three-year-old girls were being held fast by several women, while their mothers vigorously scraped the exposed frontal bone with a sharpened shell blade. The scraping in itself did not seem to cause great pain directly to the little ones, the cries were indeed more of a protest against the enforced restraint, for as soon as there was a pause in the latter, the cries also stopped. The operation continued until a fine fissure, about 1 centimetre long and 0.5 millimetres wide, was evident, then the wound was rinsed with the not very clean water from the stream, and crushed leaves were laid on it; the binding was a strip of old cotton. The children operated on seemed to be hale and hearty; after completion of the operation both left the place holding their mother's hand. This form of prophylactic trepanation only occurs in children, indeed only in the period between the second and fifth years. Fatalities must be very rare. The scars are very visible in later life and extend from the centre of the forehead right up to the hairline; when two or even three such operations are performed, the scars lie as a rule 2 to 2.5 centimetres vertically, side by side, and when a finger is traced over the frontal bone operated on, one can feel very clearly the deep furrows caused by the scraping. In the skulls of such natives that I have seen, the skilfully produced cleavage of the frontal bone had already completely healed (fig. 19).

In the case of bone fractures too the natives of the Gazelle Peninsula know how to help themselves. The *tena papait* is usually quite skilful in the management of arm and leg fractures, which he regularly treats. He fits the bone ends together and applies several bamboo saplings as splints. He also manages forearm fractures, and especially fractures of the tibia, surgically, by making a deep incision right to the broken bone and then exposing the fracture points as much as possible. Next he shaves a sliver about 6 centimetres long and 1 to 1.5 centimetres wide, from a certain type of bamboo. He forces the sliver down through the wound right to the bone, and draws the skin flaps over it, whereupon the broken limb is firmly wrapped round. After about two weeks he removes the bamboo sliver, and the wound heals like any other. I have seen a fracture of two right-side ribs treated in this way, and the patient recovered in a relatively short time in spite of the drastic cure.

On all the islands of the archipelago extraction of blood is a popular operation, practised by every native as a curative against any kind of pain. True venous blood-letting is indeed unknown, but blood is withdrawn from the body through numerous incisions. Forehead, back and chest, and frequently other parts of the body as well, are often covered with the scars of healed incisions. With truly stoical calmness, a Melanesian submits to this always quite painful operation, when not uncommonly fifty to 100 such incisions are made, 0.5 to 1 centimetre long and about 2 millimetres deep; the distance between the individual incisions varies, but usually amounts to 2 to 5 millimetres. Quite significant volumes of blood are thereby extracted occasionally, and entire pools of blood reveal the site of the operation. The efficacy of this blood-letting is not doubted by any native, and at the slightest pain he submits to it with the greatest forbearance. After sufficient blood has been drawn off, the wounds are rubbed with burnt coral lime, often also with a mixture of coral lime and certain crushed plants. Healing then ensues after a few days.

On the other hand, the only resource against internal illnesses is sorcery, and as a consequence of this the most basic rules of precaution, which in the initial stages of the illness might perhaps have led to a favourable outcome, are again most grossly neglected. Should the sorcery not help, then no other means would help anyway. Every year pulmonary illnesses claim numerous victims, although with appropriate care many a life might have been saved. In cases of epidemics, which are not infrequent, the mortality rate is frightful; especially so with dysentery, which claims countless victims. In vain can the white man take the most stringent measures and be on guard day and night; none the less the patient perishes, because he eats things that are, per se, not easily digestible, thereby undeniably causing aggravation of the illness, or death. Epidemics like smallpox, such as we experienced years ago in Kaiser Wilhelmsland and parts of New Britain, can completely decimate whole areas, and this is so well known to the natives that in many places they kill the sick at the appearance of the first symptoms, to prevent further spread of the epidemic.

The natives on the whole do not have much faith in the white man's cures; unless doses administered are high, or have drastic effect. Glauber's salt, castor oil, and so on, enjoy great popularity, as do all remedies that are distinguished by a horrible taste. There is little trust in medications administered in drops. On the other hand a native will undergo the most difficult and complicated operation by a white doctor with the greatest equanimity. He has absolute faith in the knife, and it often happens that a worker will go to his white employer with a request for surgical intervention for pain of any sort. The level of stoicism with which the natives undergo the most painful procedures without crying out in pain or pulling back a muscle is astonishing. In this regard they can be put forward as an example most worthy of emulation by the majority of white men, who lose courage at the mere sight of a knife.

One of the main questions we are faced with in establishing colonies, is to what extent should we raise and improve the sanitary conditions of the natives over time? The appointment of medical officers in individual districts is already a great step forward, but it is only the first step in a long series of measures that must necessarily follow if we want to assist in improving the sanitary standards of the natives. Vigorous education about cleanliness, not only of the person but also of the dwellings and their surroundings, is above all essential. The dwellings themselves cannot be considered unhealthy; in most cases they are appropriate to the circumstances of the natives, and might, with the exception of the sleeping places inside them, be regarded as suitable to their purpose. Where bare earth serves as a bed, often with a simple palm leaf mat as a groundsheet, it must be emphasised that raised, plank beds should be substituted, for which suitable material is easily obtained in abundance. I do not see the question of clothing as being so absolutely important, and I believe that by introducing cotton garments into areas where the people previously wore no clothing, we cause more illness than we might well imagine. Formerly the native seldom, or never, washed his loin cloth or whatever garment he wore, and within a short time these were thick with dirt and stains. Now he wears a few rags, whether they are dry or dripping wet, and it is apparent that he will often catch cold and frequent lung infections. However, all the changes can only be achieved with time, and it is pleasing to see that many of the plantation workers, who have come to recognise the need for hygiene and tidiness during their employment, continue to value the new experiences after their return home.

Furthermore, in particular cases where medical knowledge can be regarded as not unimportant, by and large in illnesses of which the cause is not obvious, wild superstition is revealed, expressed in different ways. Above all, there is a widespread superstition that when a person who has slept for several nights in a hut or in a compound with a sick person, goes off to another hut or another compound and sleeps there, the condition of the sick person consequently deteriorates. This is designated by the word *kubak*. In order to get round the problems arising from this, it is customary to isolate the sick man completely, with some of his friends, to give other family members more freedom of movement. These friends or nurses of the patient then serve him day and night, and must sleep near him, particularly at night. Should they leave the sick person for whatever reason, suspicion immediately falls on them that they are responsible for the deterioration in the illness, and the more frequent their absence the more the indisposition increases. The sick person will then indeed say: '*A kubak* (so and so)', indicating that the person named has aggravated his illness by his absence. Relatives of the sick person then turn on the person indicated and attempt to bring him back; should he refuse, it is regarded as an evil intention, having the aim of aggravating the condition of the sick person, or even causing his death. This leads to all kinds of hostilities which, according to the connection of the person concerned, can have dangerous consequences. No other superstition has such a hold as this one, and in cases of illness it is almost impossible to persuade an inhabitant of a compound where the sick person is, to leave the compound at night.

Should a sick person die, everyone is of the firm conviction that it is the result of sorcery, and although the sorcerers enjoy very high respect, it can happen, however, especially when the dead person had been a man of position with great connections, that the respect is lost and it causes the downfall of the sorcerer. The latter must now pull himself out of the invidious position as well as he can, usually by paying *tabu* to the relatives and followers of the dead man. If, however, he is successful in clearing himself in the eyes of the people they proceed to other measures. A few whiskers or head hairs, a piece of the ear or finger, and so on, are then cut from the corpse, and a man adept in this kind of sorcery murmurs his spells over them, summoning the various spirits to punish the evildoer. This sorcery, named *kom* or *komkom*, never fails in its purpose, and should someone die soon afterwards, it is believed that this is a result of the *kom*, and that the dead person has brought about the death of the sick person through sorcery.

The *kom* is also used to prevent the theft of poultry. A small piece of the fowl's claw is cut off, a magic spell cast over it, and the fragment is buried in the ground. When someone steals this enchanted hen he becomes quite decidedly ill or he dies.

On the north coast of the Gazelle Peninsula there is a frequently used spell, in which a person who wishes evil, throws a stone over the house of a sick person, at the same time pronouncing a certain incantation. This should bring about the death of the sick person and is the cause of numerous disputes. This behaviour is known as *varlili atanai*, and is taught in the *ingiet* societies.

As a rule it is essential to the effectiveness of the charm that it contains an article that forms a part of the one to be charmed; for example, his hair, a piece of his clothing, or something that has some kind of connection to him, such as his excrement, his food scraps, his saliva, his footprints, and so on. All such items can be used as *panait*; that is, as a medium for a *papait* or charm, consisting of an incantation or the murmuring of a certain spell combined with blowing hand-held burnt lime into the air. It is self-evident that the native clears away all such objects in conformity with these powers. This is the basis of the normal neatness of the compound, consisting of the earth floor being carefully swept each day, not for the needs of cleanliness and tidiness at all, but purely as an endeavour to remove everything that can serve as a spell to an evildoer. A native conceals or burns his shaved off locks of hair, or wipes the spat-out betel nut saliva off the floor just as carefully.

Another widespread superstition is that certain birds possess the power to announce the death of a man. Should such a messenger of death cry in the vicinity of a hut, it is hurriedly driven off by yelling and stone-throwing. The same omen is also conveyed by shooting stars, which in the natives' minds are spirits that journey down to the earth to collect a man whom they have chosen.

In epidemics, which take a heavy toll, it is not uncommon that in the evening old and young arm themselves with burning palm leaves and sprigs and rangee, raging and wailing, through the entire village and round it, with the thought of driving out the evil spirits bringing the sickness. Even though the epidemic is seldom averted by this, such a driving-out of spirits offers the beholder one of those many unforgettable, eerily beautiful pictures, of which the archipelago is so rich. The landscape lying in deep darkness is suddenly lit by single torches that dart along among the bushes. They are quickly joined by numerous other blazing torches in the glare of which the huts and foliage sparkle, and which light up the wildly behaving natives, who move through the bushes and round the village waving their torches and yelling and gesticulating as loudly as possible.

The native also protects himself against sorcery and illness by charmed cords, either quite simple strings or ones decorated by *tabu* snails or small leaves of *pele* at each end. These cords, called *kanubu* are blown over with lime by a sorcerer and given healing powers by spells. They are worn not only to prevent an illness but also to cure one. In the former case they are worn round the neck, in other cases bound round the affected part of the body. There are various kinds; the most important and most highly regarded are the *kunibu na ingiet* bestowed by the *ingiet* society, and the *kunibu talisabu* which is knotted round the ankle in a particular way.

One might now suppose that the native, given the chance, would gladly accept the services of a white doctor. However, this is not the case. A white doctor, be he ever so qualified, does not impress a native at all. The opinions of the latter on what is and what isn't beneficial to health, differ very widely from those of the whites. A laxative, a plaster for a wound or an ointment are acceptable to him, but he remains sceptical about operations of any sort. Should the doctor amputate his leg or arm in order to save his life, he can be certain that the amputee's family will interpret this act of kindness quite otherwise, and if only they could, they would prepare all unpleasantness possible for the doctor. When there is absolutely nothing else, they will indeed allow themselves to be treated by the white doctor, but they don't bestow particular faith on him, and moreover they make use of their sorcery as far as they can.

Quite frequently one encounters the opinion that the natives have become accustomed to living from day to day without a care of any sort. This is a very inaccurate view, because the native actually leads a life plagued by all kinds of anxieties. Among the greatest plagues of his life belongs his excessive superstition. He sees himself surrounded constantly by evil spirits and their influence. He trusts nobody, for who knows whether his nearest neighbour, his ostensibly best friend, is not trying by sorcery to bewitch him with calamities, illness and even death. Everywhere he perceives instances that he has been targeted; he suspects treachery and deceit everywhere. We cannot be surprised therefore that mistrust is a dominant feature in the character of the natives, not only the New Britain people but Melanesians generally. I would like to point out that for this reason it is much easier for a European to win the trust of a native, than for a native to trust a countryman from a distant region. Of course the native regards the white man as a being who is far superior to him in many things; the many evil spirits and the hurtful sorcery that surround the natives on all sides have no detectable influence on the European, therefore he is a white man from a land where there are other spirits and other charms, over which the local spirits and sorcerers have no power. To tell the natives that neither spirits nor sorcerers can harm them, is preaching to deaf ears; the feeling in the background is always: you have spoken well but we know better. So long as everything goes well, things are fine; this is usually regarded as the result of a spell or similar. But should the smallest calamity or the slightest failure occur, this can be ascribed without doubt to the influence of an evildoer, be this spirit or human agent. It was thus explained a short time ago by my gun-boy, who goes pigeon hunting for me; he would no longer go hunting with a certain native, for whenever he was in this person's company he frequently missed the pigeon at which he was aiming, whereas when he went alone he seldom missed. In the gun-boy's opinion, the companion had used some kind of magic so that he missed. On the whole natives judge things in this way, even though the situation may be explained very easily on natural grounds. The native is, once and for all, not susceptible to basic common sense; his only rationale is, and remains, sorcery on the part of evildoers or the influence of evil spirits. I have often listened with great amusement to the tales of the natives when they recounted how, in earlier times, they had brought the heaviest artillery in sorcery into battle against my wife and me, often at great expense, and with exceptional trouble, but always in vain. The lack of effect of the sorcery lay in native magic having no influence on whites, but nonetheless they are steadfast in the belief of its success against natives.

One of the most popular and simplest potions is the *malira*. This consists largely of objects from the plant kingdom – leaves, fruit, roots, resin, plant juices, and so on – that are secretly administered in various combinations: dry, fresh, in powdered or ground form, or by rubbing into the one to be bewitched. Usually one tries to mix it in with the food of the person to be bewitched, or with the powdered lime chewed with betel nuts; it is often sufficient for the person in question simply to be touched by the *malira*. The composition of this potion is very wide-ranging and diverse; new mixtures are continually being put into circulation and should be spirit-inspired, according to popular opinion. A new *malira* is given by the inventor to others, and obviously they have to pay for the favour. The price varies according to the reputation of a *malira*, corresponding both to the goal to be achieved and the effectiveness of the means. A *malira* of repute is therefore a good source of revenue for the inventor. Potions are used for the most varied purposes: they are believed to awaken love, or to encourage women to give ear to licentious proposals. Furthermore, they are believed to cause particular illnesses, or to prevent recovery from an illness, and much more. The potions that awaken love enjoy special demand. Although the *malira* itself is of a harmless nature, the native firmly believes in its excellent effects. Should these not occur, a reason is always to be found why the effect was not achieved, and other *malira* are sought.

The *malira* must not be confused with the *tarin* or *taring*. The latter is a poison and is used as such, to cause death. Of course there are different sorts of *taring*, that are probably none other than *malira* or potions, but the native markedly differentiates between them. The *taring* is likewise a great secret, although there are also several methods that are known to the great majority. I have investigated a number of such poisons as to their efficacy, by giving them to animals in their food. Several of them are undoubtedly fatal; others cause long-lasting and often fatal illnesses. A certain *taring* is obtained by drying individual portions of fish known to be poisonous, and rubbing them with burnt lime; several other media are dried-up plant juices that are prepared like *malira*. One medium that causes insidious, chronic illness is the thorny, fine, small hairs of the bamboo sprouts; these are scraped from the plant and mixed with food; they penetrate the gut wall and cause painful symptoms, and frequently death.

The potions that go under the name *malira*, are to a great extent used against women. But besides these, there are a very great number of media that men use among themselves, and which are grouped under the name *pepe*. Now one man of course can use a spell on another through *pepe*, to harm him. However, *pepe* is more frequently used in order to be inspired by the spirits. Both *pepe* and *malira* are media that are imparted from the spirits to humans.

The preparation of the *pepe* is a secret belonging to certain natives, to whom it has been communicated by spirits. It consist of parts of plants, that are crushed and, with betelnut and lime, formed into small packets wrapped in betel leaves. These packets are laid at the foot of the tree that the spirit in question has chosen as his dwelling. There are a great number of *pepe* spirits with different names. These are conceived as having an animal form but with a man's head; the body has the shape of a fish or a bird or a lizard, and so on. Each of these spirits prefers a particular tree, and each bestows on the *pepe* the ability to make a certain revelation to those whom the *pepe* adopts; for example, how one should decorate oneself for certain dances, which hair style or body painting should be used, how the bunches of bright leaves used in dances should be arranged, how the conical hat of the *duk-duk* should be decorated, how the little hut used for the *vuvue* celebrations should be adorned, and so on. The procedure is generally as follows. The owner of the *pepe* in question prepares the little bundles mentioned above, and then invites participants who build little huts or lean-tos under the tree. Every participant receives a little packet upon payment, and once they are all distributed, the whole thing is eaten. The effect initially is a state similar to drunkenness, followed by a deep sleep. Those sleeping are carried or led to the little huts. Here they are now inspired by the spirits, and it is expected that the inspiration should occur immediately after the first dose; if this is not the case, then the procedure is continued until the inspiration results in dreaming. The one inspired then imparts the inspiration of the spirit to the owner of the *pepe*, and the owner then sells this revelation to others for a certain sum, of which the one inspired receives a small portion.

Several years ago I personally experienced the effectiveness of a certain *pepe*. The mixture would not be placed among delicacies, it tasted sharp and aromatic, and after the onset of a feeling of dizziness I soon fell into a deep sleep. The *pepe* had proved its effect so far but the inspiration, which in this case should have disclosed the assembly of a hair decoration of feathers, did not occur; on the other hand on waking up there occurred the sensation of a mighty hangover, with the probably inspired resolve never to test the power of the *pepe* again. The partaking of areca nut with betel and lime can certainly evoke similar responses in people who are not accustomed to using this stimulant. However, since all natives are experienced betel chewers, the ingredients must have a strong narcotic effect in order to cause the deep sleep in them too.

The spirits who invoke the *pepe* inspiration dwell exclusively in trees, and indeed each individual spirit has a particular tree, regarded as its dwelling. As a rule individual parts of this tree, flowers, fruit, sap, bark, roots or leaves have more or less magical power and find their use in some form in the preparation of the *pepe*.

Short feuds and long wars belong to the order of things on the Gazelle Peninsula, as in the whole of the Bismarck Archipelago. In earlier times more so than now, as fortunately the influence of settlers and the imperial government is beginning to bring about a change for the better here and there. However, where this influence does not exist, the most trivial reason is enough to cause the natives to have recourse to weapons. Fortunately these wars, although beset with great uproar, are not very bloody. A few dead on both sides suffice to pave the way for negotiations of peace, and close friends are always willing to act as intermediaries, for as such they receive special incomes and fees that are quite acceptable, from both parties. Although these wars have lots of disadvantages for the parties as a consequence, I have come to the conclusion, after many years of observation, that it is incorrect for one to see in them the reason for the decline in population. Of course it cannot be denied that as a rule the slain enemies are men in the best years of their lives, but on the other hand I believe that war has a stimulating effect on the natives, sharpens their intellectual powers and also develops their physical characteristics. Without war and feuds a primitive people grows sluggish, becomes mentally as well as physically indolent and in the course of time disappears from the scene. We see this frequently on the small islands of the Pacific Ocean, where nature offers abundant means of sustenance that can be obtained without special physical effort. On all these islands where neither war nor labour requires exertion of mental or physical powers, the population regresses, in spite of an apparently strong constitution. Therefore when we forbid the natives to conduct war, we must carefully consider how to provide them with other means of stimulation, such as work. If the population of the archipelago could be urged into daily, regular work, the broad, uncultivated areas that are everywhere at the moment might soon disappear, and a stronger, healthier population might gradually grow. A native would never take to regular work on his own initiative, however, and it is the duty of the administration, the missions and the settlers to encourage the natives to work, by gentle pressure, to make useful members of the community out of them.

But back to the wars on the Gazelle Peninsula; the reasons that form a *casus belli* are known to everyone; women are most often the cause. The relatives of the offender immediately hasten to deliver the amount of *tabu* customary for that particular offence to the injured party through a neutral party. Acceptance of this prevents the outbreak of hostilities. But in order to be prepared for every eventuality, preparations are made for war. Sentries are posted to thwart a possible surprise attack, the rolls of *tabu* are sent with the women to friendly natives in the neighbourhood or, should there be danger in delay the treasure is hidden in pre-arranged places in the forest. The weaker party even vacates its dwelling site and sets out for the *kamare* or battleground, as a rule an open grassy space from where the enemy's approach can be observed.

Should the offered atonement money not be accepted, the real war, *winarubu* or *winarua*, begins. The parties stand facing each other, but are very much on their guard about coming to close quarters. Sham attacks are made, each party taunts the other, and after this has continued for a while, particularly with the intervention of darkness, the whole crowd withdraws, for night is no friend of any man, and one sleeps better in a hut than on the wide field of battle. The following day the affair breaks out again and only goes on until the intermediaries are in agreement with the offended party on a certain sum of atonement, and this has been paid over.

The case becomes more complicated if some particularly great heroes kill one of the opposing party in an ambush. This can only be atoned by vendetta, and the number of slain must be the same on both sides, before a peaceful resolution can be contemplated. In such an event, each party pays the other a certain sum in atonement for the slain, as well as a sum for the original offence and the case is thereby brought to a close.

If one or other party in such feuds succeeds in killing a man of standing, an *a gala* or *luluai* or similar, then the situation is even more complicated, for his death can only be avenged by the slaying of an adversary of equal rank. Relatives of the slain man bind small segments of *tabu* on their battle spears while murmuring magic spells, and then set out for the *kamare*. Here a particularly brave *luluai* steps from the ranks, dances and gesticulates in front of the enemy, hurls a stone at them, or throws the spear wrapped with *tabu,* a *rumu na tutuluai.* This is a challenge that indicates that the war cannot be ended before blood vengeance has taken place.

The slain enemies are eaten by the victors when the bodies can be removed successfully, and the proceeds in *tabu* fall to the victorious hero, to whom a certain amount of *tabu* is paid for each meal portion.

Very long, drawn-out wars are ended by great festivities at the conclusion of peace, and the diplomats who have negotiated the peace and brought it to fruition pocket payment from both parties, which is well-earned, as they not infrequently risk their lives in their efforts. In earlier years I frequently had to take on the role of negotiator in my neighbourhood, and I may boast that I have concluded more 'everlasting peace' than most of the diplomats in the civilised world. One of these conclusions of peace has remained particularly in my mind, because after all the preliminaries had been conducted and the compensation price for each individual killed had been determined after long bargaining, a stubborn, elderly *a gala* persisted that three loin cloths, about 5 metres of cotton and fifty sticks of tobacco about 1 kilogram in weight should be handed over to him by the opposing party. This exorbitant demand aroused general indignation, and since I did not want to see my hours of effort wasted, I had to send a special messenger to my house to bring back the things wished for. The outcome was thereupon satisfactory both ways, although for my part, as the gift made to me consisted of two of the scrawniest hens that could be produced, I did not recover my expenses. On another occasion it almost cost me my life. Some formality had not been fulfilled and I was regarded unjustly as the cause. The consequence was that when, accompanied by my wife, I arrived on the spot, I received a hostile reception and had to withdraw immediately. Only my accurate knowledge of the native trails saved our lives then, but for all that there was no pleasure in an endurance run of about 5 kilometres over grassy plains and through deep ravines, now and then sprayed with pellets from the pursuers armed with muskets. Yet it will always remain a satisfaction to me, that four years after my arrival, as a result of my negotiation and in spite of earlier long-lasting feuds, the tribes in my area had established a firm peace among themselves, that has not been interrupted up to the present day, although occasions have not been lacking when distant tribes often attempted to involve them in their wars and tribal unrest.

I come now to a description of the weapons used by the inhabitants of the north-east coast of the Gazelle Peninsula.

As a long-range weapon the sling, *wajen,* comes to mind immediately, and the stone, *lika,* catapulted by it. The sling consists of a cushion of several pandanus leaves folded together, and two cords, each about 1.25 metres long. The cushion is tied together at both ends and thus takes the form of an elongated, shallow pod to receive the stone. The cords are threaded through both the ends, which are tied together; one of them ending in a loop or eye that is stretched over the middle finger when in use; the other cord ends in a multiple knot that is held firmly between thumb and index finger. The operator holds both cords in the right hand in the described way, backwards over the right shoulder. The left hand with arm outstretched holds the sling-stone firmly in the cushion, at the same time stretching both cords. With a sudden jerk when the left hand lets go, the right hand swings the sling several times horizontally in a circle above the head, then suddenly releases the knots held between thumb and forefinger, and the stone flies with great force from the sling. Today this weapon has almost disappeared into oblivion, the younger generation has nowhere near the practice nor the precision that was encountered in earlier years. I have known old people who seldom missed their target, and broke the bones or shattered the skull of an enemy with a sling-stone at eighty or 100 paces. To use a sling, a free, open field is necessary, as offered by the broad, grassy plains of the Gazelle Peninsula. In dense forest the sling is useless, and here other weapons, namely the spear, *rumu,* and the club, *ram,* come into play.

Spears are found in various forms, but when they have to be used as weapons of warfare, they must first be dedicated by a special magic spell, *malira.* Such means of enchanting the spears are called *kulit.* In earlier times all the spears were stored in a special *malira* house from where they were brought in time of need, when they used the particular charm when polishing the spear while intoning the spell; and together these would impart a deadly effect to the spear.

The most frequently used war spear is the *vulu,* a long, thin spear with an extended sharp tip and a gradually tapering butt. Below the tip a piece of bark is always laid round the spear and painted white with lime. In battle this spear must always be gripped in the right hand and thrown from that; held in the left hand it loses its deadly characteristics.

Besides this there are a great number of other forms, among which those decorated with bright feathers immediately draw our attention. *Ulang,* or with the article, *a ulang,* is a common battle spear which is decorated at the butt with a very decorative, conical feather ornament of bright parrot feathers. This spear is indeed used in battle but finds more use as a gift to a participant at a feast, to whom respect is thereby shown. The *pulpulu* is a feathered spear of a simpler style; several long hen feathers and a few parrot feathers are attached at the butt, and for this attachment the wooden end of the spear is wrapped around with a dry leaf of the fan palm; the *vivinegap* is decorated at its extremity just like the *pulpulu*, and in addition a part of the shaft is wrapped round with short feathers, and two rows of yellow parrot feathers are placed along opposite sides, each feather slanted a little towards the rear.

Besides these feathered spears, the spears adorned with a bone at the butt end are worthy of note. They are recognised under the name *lauka*. These spears too serve usually as a gift for participants at a feast. In this case the bone is replaced by a wooden imitation named *kavar tukau*. Bones on the normal *lauka* are almost always the leg bones of the cassowary. However, human bones are also used from time to time, and the spear ornamented with one of these is called *pal a kaluka*. With this one there is a unique state of affairs. If a native is indeed slain, the relatives attempt to get possession of the victim's tibia. This bone is then used for ornamentation of the *pal a kaluka* and remains there until the spear has brought about the death of the murderer or until it has pierced the victim perhaps killed by another native, several times. These types of spear are consequently rare in collections, while the *pal a lauka* with the cassowary bones are common enough.

The spear in the hand of a native at close range is always a very dangerous weapon, for long practice allows him to throw it with great accuracy and strength, with the result that frequently the body is pierced right through. But this skill too is gradually being lost, and in ten years' time the spear will be a completely harmless weapon.

For close-quarters fighting the club is used, and there is a whole range of types with different designations. Many of these have become so rare over the course of years that today older people bring the young folk to me, to show them the old items stored in my collection and to explain their significance. Many valuable accounts and clarifications have been given to me through this.

I have gradually become convinced that all the clubs can be divided into two large main groups: those that have been there since time immemorial, that everyone knows how to make, and that consequently are not linked with sorcery and superstition; these weapons served then, and still serve today, as weapons for attack as well as for defence; however, besides these there are a number of clubs that, being introduced from distant regions, attracted attention through their rarity and their peculiar shape, and were therefore associated with sorcery.

To the former group belong clubs known under the names *bakul* or *pakul*, *palau bubo*, *biri birika*, *lalam kutu*, *gelewa* and *kulai*. Their shape is easily recognisable in plate 8.

To the second group belong the clubs *palau*, *tawa* or *talum*, *tiara* or *mapina kumu*, *mukmuk*, *bau*, *aul kubar* and *duk duk kavivi*.

Palau consists of a thickened rod at the lower end with a bored out stone head inverted on it. This club was originally imported from the Bainings, after which the manufacture of the stone head became gradually known in the Varzin districts through Baining slaves. I was able to observe the manufacture of the stone heads here years ago, and the method exactly matched that still used today in the Bainings.

Several specimens of *tava* or *talum* were available at Varzinberg, and according to local inhabitants' comments came there from the Taulil. In shape the club has great similarity with such weapons from the Sulka region, and it is not improbable that it was originally dispersed further northwards from there by the neighbouring Saktai or Southern Baining.

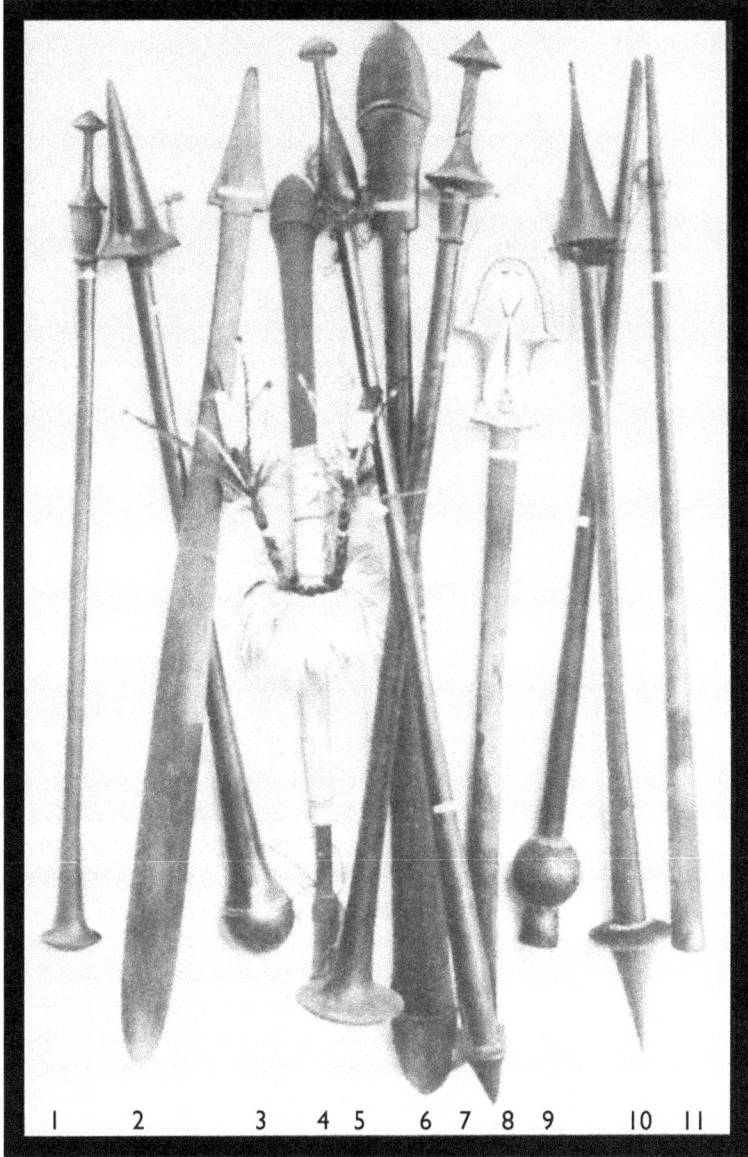

Plate 8 Clubs. Gazelle Peninsula

1. *mapina kumu*;
2. *palau bubu*;
3. *tawa* or *talum*;
4. *aul kubar*;
5. *tiara*;
6. *bakul*;
7. *bau*;
8. *boroï* or *pal a vat*;
9. *palau*;
10. *mukmuk*;
11. *biri birika*

Plate 9 Baining women bearing loads

Tiara, or after the linking charm, also named *mapina kumu*, was introduced from the region of Cape Strauch on the west coast of New Ireland. The club was regarded as somewhat rare and extraordinary by the natives.

Mukmuk is a club with a carved, conical upper as well as lower end piece. It had evidently been imported from southern New Ireland, where it is still common, to the opposite shore of St George's Channel, whence it was adopted into the neighbouring districts.

Bau is a universally used club, but I have not been successful in finding out anything about its origin.

Aul kubar is a *bakul* decorated with bright feathers and is certainly an indigenous invention, just like the *duk-duk kavivi* and the *boroï* or *pal a vat*, which originated after trading with the whites.

In the old days all these clubs were stored in the *malira* house, a hut expressly built for the storage of magic potions and all items connected with them. Today these types of houses no longer exist. Even on my arrival in the archipelago they belonged among the rarities, and I cannot recollect ever having seen one. In times of war these clubs were brought out after the usual incantations had been murmured over them in the hut and they had been polished with the *malira*, or this had been attached to them using the bright leaves of certain types of cordyline. The various *malira* had different designations, and each type was only used in conjunction with a particular type of club. The *tik a meme* was always used to enchant the *palau*; the *mapina kumu* and *bobo* were used in conjunction with the clubs *tava* and *tiara*; *mukmuk* was enchanted by the charm *kotkote*, and *bau* with the *malira* known as *au bukum*. *Aul kubar* which, as we have mentioned earlier, was also used in marriage ceremonies, likewise played a major role in war, with the *malira* unique to it; when an enemy was slain with it, the victor danced round the corpse, flourished the club in his hand, and tore down the feather ornament with his teeth.

All these different magic charms had the purpose of making the club deadly, so that a single blow would suffice to lay the enemy on the ground. Allegedly the charms were introduced here from far away, together with the clubs. The war hatchet *boroï* or *pal a vat* was a common weapon years ago. An earlier club of the same name with a wooden, sharp-edged head, similar to the *tiara*, had been improved by removing the wooden head and substituting an axe blade that came from the white traders. Ornamentation of the handle, a flat, broad, lancet-shaped arrangement, *ai lene*, was retained and carefully decorated. Today this weapon belongs among the rarities, and it is difficult to obtain a specimen, as by and large a great portion of the previously described types of club must have completely disappeared already.

Among the musical instruments the wooden drum *qaramut* or *garamut*, reigns supreme, extending throughout Melanesia. It consists of a wooden block, oval or pear-shaped in cross section; the interior of this trunk section is hollowed out through a long, narrow slit in the upper long side, a task that required great exertion in earlier times when iron tools were still unknown. Undecorated carved knobs serve as handles at both ends. Manufacture of a slit drum is permitted to every native, and such an instrument is found in almost every compound. It is essential that every head of a family owns a drum, because otherwise he would not be able to communicate with his neighbours by drum signals. Sound is created by gripping a thick rattan pole, about a metre long, between thumb and index finger of the right hand, and guiding the lower end through a ring formed by the thumb and index finger of the left hand, so that the pole strikes the wooden wall of the drum on one side somewhat below the slit. A far-sounding boom arises, somewhat like an empty barrel being treated in the same way. The beating of the drum is called *tintiding*; the pole *bua na qaramut*. As a rule the owner names his drum, either after the maker's name, or after a special event when the drum was used for the first time, or after its tonal quality.

By means of these drums the natives are in a position to send understandable signals to people living far away. Drum signals are differentiated as general signals and messages known to all natives and universally similar, and as private signals which are recognisable only to one district or to a certain group.

The following are known to me as common signals which are understandable from Cape Gazelle as far as Weberhafen, and are the same throughout.

The signal *tuktuk vaturia* means that an enemy has been captured and his body dismembered. To arouse the general attention of the neighbourhood, this signal, like all signals on the whole, is provided with an introduction, which is named *koai*. The *koai* consists of a series of rapid sounds in succession, not dissimilar to a drum roll; then follows the particular signal consisting of several slow hits, something like: 'ting; ting; ting; ting; tingting; ting; ting; ting; ting', and so on.

The signal sounds not only during the distribution and consumption of the corpse, but still several days after, as a rule with longer or shorter pauses during a period of five days and nights, as a propitiation as it were of the tribe whose member has been eaten. Scarcely has one party proclaimed its success by the *tuktuk vaturia*, than there sounds a signal called *pal a mia* from the opposing party, which has the purpose of calling together all men of the tribe capable of bearing arms. Each one who hears it yells a loud war cry twice, drops everything, grabs his weapons and runs without hesitation to the compound where the signal comes from. The head of the family has meanwhile divided *tabu* into small pieces 25 to 50 centimetres long, and each of those running up is given a piece, whereupon he breaks his spear, strikes the ground with his axe or club, and behaves in a warlike manner. This distribution of *tabu* is designated as *kukuau*. The signal sounds somewhat as follows: (*koai*): 'ting, ting, tingting; ting, ting, tingting; ting, ting, tingting; (*pal a mia*): ting; ting; ting; ting; ting; ting; ting', and so on. At each 'ting' those present yell their loud war cry.

When a man of importance has died, it is announced to the neighbourhood by a drum signal called *kukukur ta ra minat* from Weberhafen to Matupi, and *a lal tabu* from Blanche Bay to Cape Gazelle, but is the same throughout. It goes roughly: 'ting, ting, ting, tingting; ting, ting, ting, tingting', and so on. A generally similar-sounding signal is the *ibut ra bong* whose purpose is to indicate a particular day. Suppose, for example, that a chief has set down some celebration or other event for a certain day; now if it happens that for some reason the appointed time has to be postponed, this is announced to the surrounding area by the signal *ibut ra bong*. After the introductory signal has ended, the actual signal runs something like this: 'ting; tingtingting; ting;' the last somewhat louder and longer 'ting' indicates a day; should therefore the event be postponed for four days, the signal is repeated four times, on each occasion with an emphasis on the final 'ting'.

Besides these general signals, there are, as previously mentioned, private signals, *kulakula tiding*, whose meaning is known only to the members of a particular family or clan. Through these signals distant people can be summoned and small, important announcements made. These private signals are long-standing and unchanging, and it is incumbent upon the individual members of the family to commit these to memory, from youth.

As a consequence of this signal system it is possible for the natives to spread a message with great rapidity, and in the first years of my stay I was frequently not a little astonished when news of incidents in far districts was given to me perhaps scarcely an hour after the event; likewise the natives were always warned in time when I attempted to surprise them in their compounds.

After the *qaramut*, the *kudu* plays a significant role, as it is the musical accompaniment for all the dances. The *kudu* is a drum, shaped like an hour-glass and covered at one end with the skin of a monitor lizard, on which heavy blows are struck with four fingers of the hand. The walls of this kind of drum are not infrequently decorated and painted; a few of them have a handle in the middle, often in the shape of a frog or lizard, and so on; these ornaments have no special significance.

After both of these musical instruments I now come to a number of instruments that must also be included, but all of which, without exception, serve the purpose of making oneself acceptable to women. The sounds they bring forth serve as dance or singing accompaniment only in a few cases. The most widely spread of these is the *tutupele* or *tinbut*. This instrument consists of two wooden battens, about 1 metre long, 10 centimetres wide, and in cross-section a shallow ellipse whose shorter diameter is 2.5 to 3.5 centimetres. Both wooden battens are often provided with a shallow, trough-shaped hollow in the centre of the wood on one side. To use it, the player sits down and lays both pieces of wood across his legs, or lies them on two pieces of banana trunk, always making sure that a free space is left under the instrument, from where the emitted sound is amplified. The sound is created by striking with two small wooden clappers, about 3 centimetres thick, and is audible far off. A few players have developed particular skill, and understand how to strike regular drum rolls, interrupted by single blows, double blows and triples in quicker or slower tempo, by which extraordinarily great diversity can be brought to the playing. Especially on moonlit nights, the sound of the *tutupele* is heard far off in the villages; the lovelorn musician labours on his instrument with laudable patience for many hours, hidden, however, in the forest, for women cannot be present at the concert. Related to this instrument is the *tidir*, consisting of two dry, wooden rods that are held in the hands and struck against each other in a particular meter. It is not so far-reaching as the *tutupele* and serves as it were for more intimate transaction. According to its use the *tidir* has various designations. Thus it is called *tidir a malira* when the player gives a sign to his adored one that he intends to give her the love-inducing *malira*; the little rods are called *belequa* or *qaro* when a number of young men use them, squatting on the ground, singing their love songs; the designation covers both the music and the song.

The flutes, *kaur*, of which there are various kinds, belong here too. These flutes are produced from a certain thin-walled type of bamboo, about 40 to 55 centimetres long and about 2 centimetres in diameter. The upper, open end has a triangular notch, which is laid against the lower lip when playing; at the lower, closed end are a series of holes in pairs, 4 to 6 centimetres apart, that the player can close off with his fingers. The three tones created by the flute are repeated and combined in all possible modulations, and in the somewhat melancholy sounding melodies the lover expresses his yearning for his beloved. The *kaur* are either extremely simple bamboo tubes or they are decorated on the outside by the most varied burn patterns. In this decoration the maker lets his imagination run free, and if he is not lacking in patience the outside is provided with a confusion of ornamentation; human and animal figures are predominant but there are also concentric circles, zigzags, parallel lines, dots, and so on. These ornaments, however, bear no relation to the use of the instrument. Use is varied and is frequently connected with superstitious views. *Kaur na̦ pulu* is a flute prepared with evil intent; it is connected with the superstition that when another person, not the owner, plays it, he subsequently commits *pulu*; that is, unlawful, sexual intercourse with a member of his own clan, a crime regarded as incest and which in earlier times would have been punished almost without exception by death. Other types are the *kuvik na ka* that are played by young men in the gardens, the *kaur na tilik* and the *kaur na longlong* which are all connected with more or less powerful magic for evoking love in the hearts of the young native women.

Both the following instruments, *eiwok* and *dedede*, serve the same purpose. *Eiwok* consists of two roughly finger-thick little bamboo pipes of different length, lying side by side; and *dedede* is a regular pan flute of several bamboo tubes of varying length, fixed side by side, from which as many different tones can be made as there are pipes available.

Two further instruments likewise belong in this division, namely the *ŋgap* and the *baibai*. The former is an instrument closely related to the Jew's harp; it is made from a piece of bamboo of lancet-like shape, about 15 to 20 centimetres long, about 2.5 to 3 centimetres broad on the lower surface and running to a point. In the middle of this a long, narrow, thin leaf is peeled off; it sits with its base firmly attached to the broad end of the instrument, and runs sharply, just like the instrument, towards the pointed end. This sounding reed can vibrate freely in the cut-out slit. In use the instrument is held in the left hand, the pointed end with the reed is laid against the front teeth, and with the right hand the player gives a gentle tug by means of a thin cord attached to the base of the instrument. A vibrating movement arises, causing a low humming noise. The *baibai* is the nut of a type of *Cycas* (*baibai*); this nut is pierced by two pairs of opposing holes about 8 to 10 millimetres apart; a string is pulled through each pair of holes and fastened at the ends. In use, the ends of the strings are held in both hands and then the nut sitting in the middle is swung in a circle, upon which the double cords on each side of the nut become twisted; if this has gone on for long enough, the wound-up cord quickly unrolls with a gentle tug, twisting the nut around itself and thus creating a low humming or whistling sound; the rotating nut then rolls up the string to the other side, and a tug with the hand unrolls it again so that the whistling sound can be continued at will.

A woman's musical instrument is the *pangolo*, a musical bow serving only as a plaything, that is now only seldom seen. In the *Papua Album*, volume 2, plate 23, figure 2, a girl is depicted playing the *pangolo*. The instrument itself consists of a fire-hardened little wand in the shape of a bow, about 40 centimetres long. A thin cord is laid doubled around both ends, and in order to create sufficient tension, one of the cords is joined to the bow by means of an adjustable loop of cord. By adjusting the loop, the bow string stretches more or less tightly. The female player places one end of the bow against the front teeth and holds the other end in her left hand; in the right hand she holds a thin, small wand, usually the central rib of a coconut palm leaf and with it, by lifting and a quick rebound of the cord, sets the latter in an oscillating motion, thereby creating a low humming.

The bullroarer, which plays an exceptional secret role in Australia, New Guinea and the Solomon Islands, is also known on the Gazelle Peninsula, but only as a children's toy. On the other hand, on the western end of New Britain, at least along the coast west of Montague Harbour, as in Buka, Australia and New Guinea, the bullroarer is still a sacred instrument today, only used in particular celebrations, and not to come under the gaze of women.

Our Gazelle Peninsula native does not disdain decoration to beautify his body, he believes. Of course his views frequently run counter to ours, and we might count many of his means of beautification as disfigurements; on the other hand, we must further concede that in the presentation of items of adornment such as arm, neck and head bands he quite often demonstrates considerable taste, which frequently matches ours. For decking out his body, the native uses not only the most varied items of adornment, but also painting and the creation of artistic scars like tattooing.

I want to consider first of all painting, certainly the earliest form of decoration. It is designated by the universal name *wartumu*, but when it is put on for festivities of any kind it is called *minōng*, and when used for battle or war parties *wartūn*.

Application of the *minōng* is never just according to whim, however; each individual stroke, each dot, has its significance and its particular designation. The various types of *minōng* have different owners; for the most part they are in possession of them through inheritance, often also as a result of invention. Whoever wishes to use a *minōng* which belongs to somebody else must make a small payment to the owner.

I want to try to present a portion of the most practicable *minōng*. The colours used are: black, white and red; in a few cases green and yellow are also used; and, since the introduction of European goods, blue as well. The latter colour is scorned by conservative natives, however, and is only used by those progressives who have been infected with new ideas in the missions and in the service of whites.

Three strokes vertically down both cheeks, in the colours black, white and red, are called *lur* (= shedding tears).

A black stroke running from ear to ear across the cheeks and over upper and lower lip is *toboa*.

A red fleck on each cheek with a circle of white spots overlying it is called *dukaduka* (dotted).

If the entire forehead is painted white, this decoration is called *pulapulang*.

If powdered lime is painted by hand over one half of the face, the white design created is named *paparia* (*papar* = to deliver a blow, a box on the ears).

A streak along the bridge of the nose in a chosen colour is called *tongo na pap*.

A line in a chosen colour from the upper limit of the forehead right to the root of the nose is named *bioro*.

A line in one of the three colours from the inner angle of the eye over both eyelids as far as the ear is called *bingbat*.

A circle in any of the three colours, around the eye (in imitation of an owl's eye), is called *kurkur* (owlet).

A triple coloured, black-white-red line diagonally across the face is called *aukor*.

A triple coloured line from the inner angle of the eye in an arc over the cheeks as far as the temple is called *bebe* (butterfly). Women must wear this decoration in red only.

Upper and lower lip outlines in black, white or red are called *mulmul pap*. (This is a creature which the natives maintain is the size of a kitten but with a prominent snout. Only very few people claim to have seen it; it is said to gnaw young coconuts and to drink from them).

Like the face, the hair is also variously coloured, and hair dyes are named *warku*. When both sides are dyed red while the crown and neck are black, the adornment is named *vunvun*.

If the entire head of hair is dyed red, it is *warku nanami na la mar*; if it is powdered with yellow it is called *kobol* (see later under colour designations, page 144); dyed green it is called *limut* and black *utur*.

The teeth too undergo a peculiar process, in which they are dyed black. This coloration is created by manganese ore, which occurs here and there, and for which the native pays quite highly. The powdered manganese ore is crushed together with young shoots of the tali tree (*Terminalia litoralis*) that have been gently roasted over the fire, and the paste (*tawāl*) is kept for two days. Then the real staining of the teeth begins. The *tawāl* is mixed with the sap of a certain banana plant, *kalapua*, and put over the teeth; this is repeated for two consecutive days, and on the third day the *tawāl* is put on, mixed with the sap of a certain root. The teeth are already stained black by the fourth day, and are then polished with the juice of a plant (*Euphorbia*?)

to make the stain permanent. During the period of the staining the person concerned cannot chew anything; drinking water is poured into his open mouth and he is fed with chewed bananas. Sexual intercourse is strenuously forbidden to him during this time. Women stain their teeth only in particular districts; the procedure is the same.

I have been able to find no general term for body painting. However, here too each pattern has a different name.

Green, black, white and red stripes lengthwise from the shoulders to the ankle joints are called *mangingi*.

A black or white line from the shoulder down over the chest as far as the hips is called *baqal*.

A white line from the larynx to the navel is called *leva*.

A three-coloured line in the same position is *lalu*.

A similar line from the inner border of the knee diagonally across the upper part of the thigh to the upper margin of the hips is called *kawakawal*.

A triple-coloured line from the elbow across the upper arm to the shoulder and from there to the sternum, then doubling back along a parallel course is *limana virua*.

A triple-coloured line from the shoulder along the outer side of the arm to halfway along the upper arm is called *vauvd*.

If the upper arm is decorated with a triple-coloured transverse line just below the shoulder, it is called *kipakipa na lalai* (*lalai* = Trochus amulet).

A red or white cuff around the wrist is called *panau* (also an armband which is worn at marriage).

Two triple-coloured lines, running over shoulder, back, side, and chest, crossing over each other on back and chest, are named *veveuk*.

Two broad lines, one red and the other white, from collar bone to nipple are called *u*

The forms of body painting given in the preceding passage are encountered universally, but besides these there are still other local forms, that have a limited spread.

Painting as a sign of mourning is called *korkor* when put on the face, on the other hand it is *qiava* when worn on the other parts of the body.

Likewise, in war, body painting plays a major role, but here it is always a form of magic charm, *malira* and has a quite specific purpose.

Borqunai is a black spot surrounding the right eye and extending to the middle of the cheek. The colour is obtained from the soot of burned aleurite nuts mixed with oil.

If the right eye is coloured black while at the same time the left eye is red, this decoration is called *kotkot* (the black crow). If, on the other hand, the right eye is white and the left black, the designation is *kotkotz*.

A black-red line from shoulder to shoulder across the chest is called *ubu kum*. If the same line is exclusively white, it is named *minigulai* (a type of hawk).

A black line from the navel over the right breast and shoulder as far as halfway along the upper arm is called *ka meme* (*meme* = a flash, or red); it ensures that the warrior has a sure arm for spear throwing.

If the entire lower face is painted black, which is named *pap* (dog), it causes the one being chased to stumble in fear and fall to the ground when he hears the loud breathing of his pursuer like the loud panting of an extremely breathless dog.

The artistically made wig of human hair also belongs to war decoration, and is then called *warwoi* (wig) *a wardodo* or *ka ai wai*; it has the effect of its wearer being able to approach his victim secretly, unseen.

In the inland districts around Vunakokor the right half of the body is painted with black and red colours, while the left is yellow. This painting is called *malira baining* because it originates from the Baining people.

A red and a black line from the right shoulder across chest and back to the left shoulder is called *tur ma ra vi* (*vi* = a knife made of bamboo, with which the human body is dismembered).

I want to add a few comments here about the designations of the colours. There are no real names, the colours are always given by the object being compared with another, whose colour is to some extent accepted as the norm.

One will say, for example: it looks like, or it has the colour of the crow *kotkot*. Over the course of time it has become customary for the substantive to be used, unaltered, as an adjective. This will be clearly recognised in the following.

Black is named from the various objects from which it is produced, or a black object is named as a comparison. Thus, for example, the word *kotkot* is heard used as the designation for black. *Kotkot* is the indigenous black crow; all things black, especially shiny black objects, are so named. *Likutan* or *lukutan* is similarly called black, but more in the sense of the term 'dark-coloured'; *tuworo* is the black colour produced from the soot of the burned aleurite nut; *luluba* is the black morass in the mangrove swamps; *dep* is the black colour produced from the soot of the burned resin of the java almond tree; *utur* is produced from charred betel nut leaves mixed with oil. All these names are used to designate 'black', according to the blackness that one or other of the named items resembles.

Red is usually named *tar* or *tara*, which is the designation for the burned red ochre that is often used as a dye. Besides this, one often hears the designation *meme* – that is, lightning, especially when speaking of red cotton material – or *birau* – that is, fire flame – or *qap* blood, or *kubar*, which designates the red colour of the lips brought about by betel chewing.

White is *pua* or *pupua* (that is, the shining, sparkling, as, for example, the stars); *kabang* is likewise often used, and literally translated is 'burned coral lime dust'.

Green is often called *limut*; that is, moss, or green grass, or the green covering that forms on white objects through dampness. For pale green the word *qileqil* is used, that is a certain pale green type of parrot; *vok* is the darker green of the green *Eclectus* parrot.

Yellow, when used for pale yellow, is *leilei*; *pakar* is the yellow of the cockatoo crest feathers; *kobol* is a darker, or orange-tinted yellow.

For blue there is certainly the word *maremarumian*; this indicates a dark colour or an opaque colour, as, for example, the colour of the sea, which is apparently opaque. Other designations for blue are *bakut* (that is, the clouds, the heavens), or *vienau* the iridescent blue of a certain kingfisher, or *ioala* the blue of the common *Halcyon recurvirostris*.

A step further into the culture of the savage people, is of course the production of permanent body ornamentation, and the most simple form of this is that which we universally regard today as decorative scars. There are various designations for these, the most frequent are the words *buliran* and *vurvur*. The former indicates 'raised' scars, a common flat scar is called *manua* which also signifies 'ulcer'; the latter is called *bohren* and of course designates the production process, where wounds are produced by a charred, glowing wooden wand, and are rubbed with burnt lime and coconut milk to produce raised scars. For these scars the word *kotto* is also used; this is an obsidian flake, the instrument by which the wounds are caused.

A step further and we come to the widespread tattooing of the body. Tattooing in the Gazelle Peninsula natives is quite primitive; I have stated elsewhere[5] that I regard this tattooing as the remains of a regular patterning that was brought in by the original immigrants from southern New Ireland, where we still come across it today. On the dark-brown skin the slate-blue marking of the tattoo barely stands out, and this type of body decoration has therefore never achieved such a significance among the dark-coloured Melanesians as it has among the pale-coloured Polynesians. Tattooing is produced by making 3- to 4-millimetre-long parallel lines close to one another by really scratching the skin and rubbing the wounds with soot from aleurite nuts. The face in particular is tattooed. Three systems of lines over the cheeks, extending outwards from the lower eyelid, are called *lur*, meaning tears; a double line from the root of the nose around the eye is called *bebe* which is a butterfly. Therefore we find here the same designations as in face painting. Six rows of lines on each side of the chest from the nipple to the abdomen are called *tip* (that is, a small piece of shell money); all other tattoo forms are called *kotto*, the name of the instrument by which the wounds are made.

Decoration of the person by means of ornamental objects is particularly popular among males, but here too sorcery comes once more into evidence, in that many of the objects regarded by us as ornaments also possess allegedly powerful magical effects. I might almost say that there is no single object of adornment that is not connected with some kind of sorcery.

Hair ornaments are universal, worn not only at festivities but very often in daily life, and made particularly out of variously coloured bird feathers. I have mentioned elsewhere (page 123) that these items of hair decoration are described in a dream, by certain spirits that live in trees and whose intervention is brought about by partaking in a potion called *pepe*. These sorts of items of adornment vary therefore both in the assembly and the arrangement of the individual components. A few, however, are handed down from olden times, and are constant in form and arrangement. Among these are the most important ones, presented in the following.

Kangal, a bunch of bright parrot feathers, especially from the *malip* (*Lorius hypoenochrous*), with a white cock feather in the centre. This ornament is worn both in dancing and in war.

Lakua, a big bunch of white cockatoo feathers; worn both in dancing and in war, and also for decoration of the male corpse.

Totokoi is very similar to the *kangal*, however, small ornaments assembled from cuscus teeth (shell money from the Duke of York islands) and white shell discs are added on.

Wamein consists of the previously named feathers and those of a species of *Halcyon* with an outer rim of hog's bristles, the ends of which are dyed red.

Turlio is a bunch of yellow crest feathers of the cockatoo and *Halcyon* feathers; from this bunch there arises a human figure carved out of a sliver of wood, with outstretched arms bearing small bunches of a yellow-leafed plant. This ornament is a figurative representation of the *pepe* spirit *Turlio*, who is accepted as living in small bushes consisting of the *goragora* plant, the latter being represented by the bunch of feathers.

Beo is a crest of bright feathers going from the forehead to the neck; a carved bird (*beo*) is attached to the forehead side, and waggles from side to side with head movements.

Kawawar is a bunch of cassowary feathers falling from the crown of the head to the nape of the neck; small red feathers from the *malip* are fastened to its ends.

Bal a marit is the same ornament but pulled further towards the forehead, ending there with a short tuft of bright feathers. To both last-mentioned items of adornment belongs a bunch

5. Internationales Archiv für Ethnographie, vol. 5, 1892

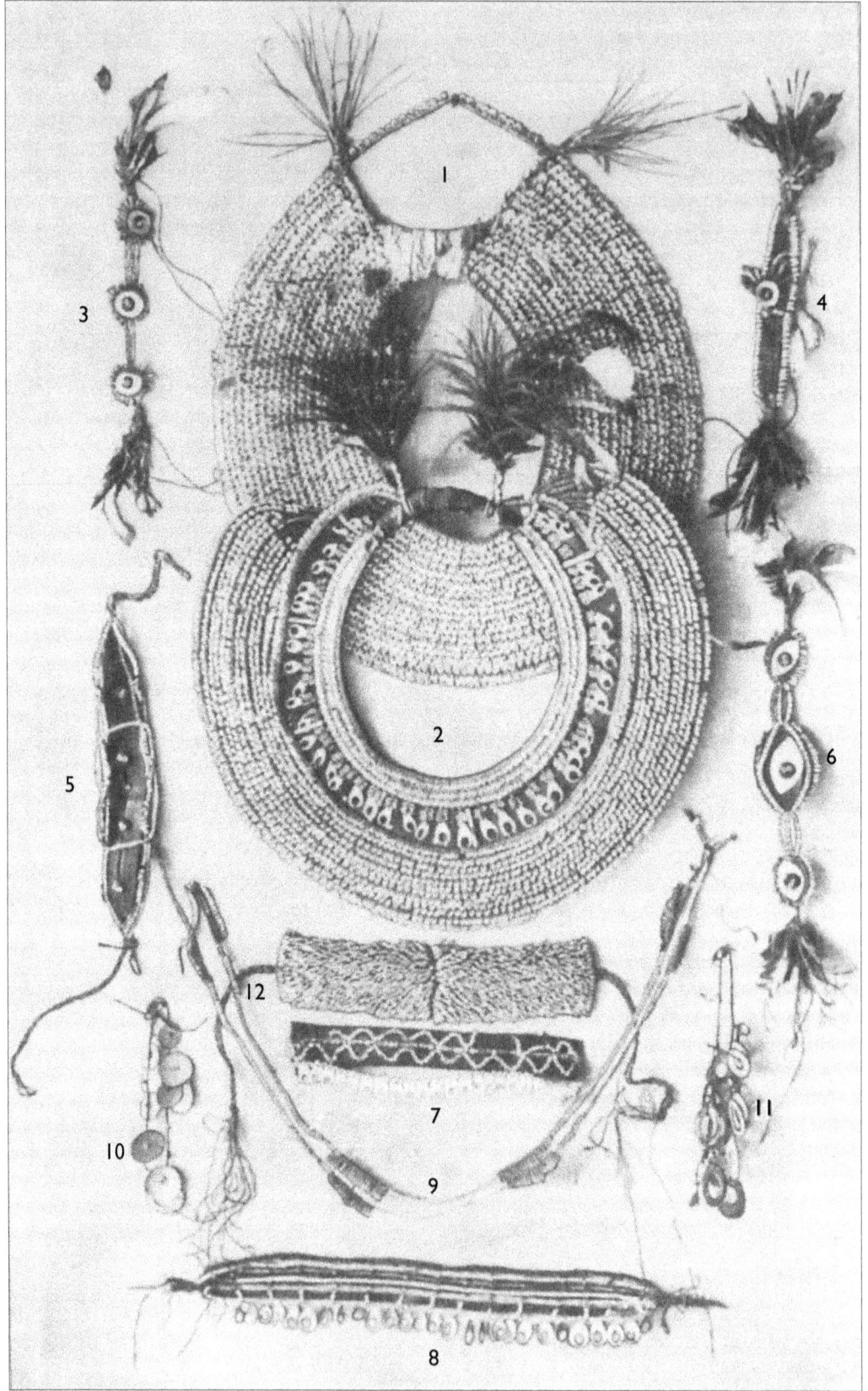

Fig. 20 Ornamental objects from the Gazelle Peninsula (see page 65).

1. and 2. collars *middi*; 3. to 8. headbands (3. and 6. *rără na babat*; 4. and 5. *rără na vinarua*; 7. and 8. *wamaing*); 9. girdle *wipit*; 10. and 11. hair ornaments *kalaqi na warqu*; 12. necklace *ngut*.

of ginger (*kawawar*) that hangs down the back, or is fixed through an arm ring.

Wamain a koto is a crest of plaited bracken fern, a hand's breadth wide, extending from forehead to neck. The foliage is coloured black. This is a particularly powerful magical ornament that is often used in the *ingiet* feasts and protects against the evil influence of the spirits.

The beard is removed so that only a thin crown of hair runs from ear to ear over cheeks and chin. The beard is rubbed with lime, partly to give it a red colouring, and partly also to make the individual hairs rigid. This peculiar style of beard serves exclusively as decoration and has nothing to do with sorcery.

The majority of the following ornaments, as we usually call them, do not exclusively serve this purpose, but are in their way more or less powerful charms to achieve this or that goal, namely the goodwill of women and courage or invincibility in battle.

Figure 20 contains a number of the most common of these items.

Items 3 to 8 are headbands that are used in the most diverse situations. They are given the general name *rărā*. Items 3 and 6 are more narrowly designated as *rărā na babat* (*babat* = antidote), because they have the property of keeping evil spirits or the influence of dangerous sorcery at bay. Items 4 and 5 are *rărā na vinarua* that not only protect against danger in battle, but also make the wearer strong and courageous. Items 10 and 11 are named *kalaqi na warqu* (*kalaqi* = pearl shell, *warqu* = to rub or smear), and consist of small round, or oval egg-shaped pieces of pearl shell which are lined up and knotted together in the hair after this has been smeared with dyed coconut oil. In the natives' opinion they are a strong charm for winning the love of the female sex. Items 7 and 8, named *wamaing*, are headbands that serve the same purpose. Item 9 is a girdle named *wipit* that has the same result; it is wrapped singly or in a number of up to ten or twelve around the waist, and consists of a row of Duke of York shell money interrupted by series of cuscus teeth, *ngut*, and *tabu* snail shells; the arrangement of this object varies and implies greater or lesser efficacy; whoever can afford it strings on a greater number in varying arrangements, in order to be quite certain of achieving his goal. Both collars depicted as items 1 and 2 are called *middi* or *niddi*. They are plate-like, broad structures made from *Nassa* shells that are especially prepared, and not valued as *tabu*. The individual little snail shells are sewn firmly side by side on thin strips of rattan, and the individual strips are then attached side by side, often up to twenty or more. The lower *middi* was common earlier in several inland districts, and has a series of small disks of Nautilus shell which are attached to several slivers of *pele* and laid on a red backing. This object was worn by the men in battle in former times, because special magical powers were attributed to it; today, however, it has completely disappeared, and only rarely does the collector succeed in obtaining an old, good piece for a very high price. The neckband represented as item 12 is named *ngut*, (*ngut* = cuscus tooth) after the material from which it is prepared. The individual teeth are bored through at the root, and each tooth is fastened to the others by thin cord. This type of standup collar is very valuable because the material is imported from New Ireland, and according to demand fifty to 100 teeth can be bought for a fathom of *tabu*. Since a few of these collars contain up to 2,000 teeth, then the price of the material alone can be 20 to 40 fathoms of *tabu* or, calculated in currency, 60 to 120 Marks without including the manufacturing costs, and therefore it is only rich people who can afford such a collar. Also, it is only an item for show and has no magical powers. The same is true of the wide, thin armrings that are worn here and there by old, rich people, and are named *kakala* (*kakala* = *Tridacna* clam). These armrings are shaped like a thin disc, with a sharp outer rim; the width varies from 2 to 5 centimetres; the greater the breadth, the greater the value. These armrings are very rare, and good pieces only come into the hands of the collector through a particularly favourable opportunity; they are inherited within families, or when no inheritor exists they are buried with the deceased owner. I know of one case where two such armrings were purchased from a native at a price of 150 fathoms of *tabu* (about 450 Marks); certainly they were two splendid pieces, 4.5 centimetres wide. One might think that the price should be considerably lower, since the raw material, the *Tridacna* clam, is plentiful on all the reefs. However, the high value is qualified in that it is not the common *Tridacna* shell of the reef that is used in manufacture, but a fossilised *Tridacna* shell found in isolated gorges beyond the Varzinberg. This species of *Tridacna* is certainly the same one that still lives on the coral reefs today, but by long deposition in the ground the shell has gained a particular alabaster-like structure, that is immediately noticeable to the expert.

The planning of the above-mentioned magical adornments is then not at all such a simple affair as the casual planning of a necklace or a bracelet in Europe. If the magical powers are inspired by the *pepe* spirit, then of course these powers are fixed into the particular article, and in its fashioning they are immediately transferred directly to the wearer; this is the case, for example, with the *wipit* and the *kalaqi*. However, the magical powers of the *rarā* for example, are a consequence of the sorcery of the *ingiet* and must be renewed each time, in order to be really effective; they are to some extent the external sign that the wearer is immunised by special *ingiet* sorcery. For example, in order to make a *rărā na babat* effective, the sorcerer prepares the following. Small, half-cooked pieces of taro, coconut and chicken flesh are wrapped in certain *Dracaena* leaves and little bundles are shaped; the following types of *Dracaena* are particularly powerful: *mette, tikua, mette karau, tokabangia,* and *rangiene.* The sorcerer then gives the prepared morsels to the person in question, and they have to be chewed and swallowed by the latter. This is in itself a small test of courage for this type of food is anything but tasty for tongue and palate, being harsh to the taste and with a quite abominable tang. After partaking, the man grasps his spear or his club and lays the *rărā* on his forehead; he is then immunised against all dangers of the battle.

The nose too must suffer in order to adopt a characteristic of *ingiet* sorcery. Of course these magical decorations are disappearing more and more, because not only do the settlers laugh about it, but the numerous workers who have come to the Gazelle Peninsula from all the other islands laugh as well. As a rule the native is very sensitive to ridicule, and the nasal decorations, however much they might possess strong sorcery and magical powers, do not have the power to resist ridicule. The most widespread are, or more accurately were, the nasal ornaments *ibut* and *bilibaqu*. *Ibut* are small, approximately 1 to 1.5 centimetres long wooden pins, three or four of which are inserted into each nostril, for which small holes are bored. *Bilibaqu* are the long, quill-like cassowary pinions, which are inserted through a hole in the nasal septum and are frequently decorated at both ends with *pele* shell disks. More rare are the *mu(m*, a small ornament of five or six cuscus teeth fixed alongside one another like a fan, secured into the side of the nose by a single tooth at right angles to them. All these are *ingiet* attributes and require a certain manipulation of sorcery to become effective.

Frequently the natives of the Gazelle Peninsula are seen decorated with flowers, bright leaves and fragrant plants, not only during festivities but also on apparently impromptu occasions. These bundles of foliage or flowers are in fact not so much a decoration as more importantly the bearer of certain magical powers, having this purpose or that. The bundles are given the common name *purpur*, according to the various combinations each purpur has a special name.

Lom, for example, is a necklace bundle of yellow-green, strongly scented leaves of a plant bearing the same name; it serves exclusively as a decoration and has no secret properties.

Pur kikil is a garland of various leaves and herbs worn around the neck and falling over the chest, shoulders and back; it contains a special, powerful spell to awaken the love of a woman.

Munuba (bracken) is a garland of hanging, black bracken leaves which gives special protection in battle.

Winna is a broken-off bunch of red *Dracaena* with a stem about 0.5 metres long. The fronds are knotted round the neck and the stem hangs down the back. This gives protection in battle against all kinds of wounds. Like all similar media it therefore belongs to the group of charms designated by the group name *mailan*. *Winna* is quite a detailed charm; not only can the wearers not be called by their proper names (they must address each other as *to malik*), but the women also accompany the brave warriors at a distance and continually sing a song in which they summon the *kalivuvur* (whirlwind) to protect their husbands.

One might now think that the natives would very rapidly become convinced of the uselessness of all these charms, since wounds and death occur in battle in spite of them, or the courted beauty remains cold in spite of all love spells. However, this is not the case. Should the desired effect not occur, it is not the fault of the sorcery or the charm, but the fault of other counter-spells, but for the most part the fault of the wearer himself, because he has not fulfilled the imposed conditions, or has done this or that which makes the spell ineffective. The inventor of the spell, who is well paid for each occasion on which it is used, is well aware, in the event of failure, of the need to provide some plausible reason which has frustrated success. Perhaps the person in question stepped off first with his right foot instead of his left in setting out; perhaps this or that spirit encountered him on the way; perhaps the chicken that he ate did not have the prescribed colouring, and so on, so that a new attempt and a corresponding new payment must be made. A few years ago when a virulent dysentery epidemic cut down many natives, the earnings of the sorcerers flourished, and since all was in vain, a great raid was arranged on the spirits. This consisted of old and young armed with coconut palm torches, enchanted bundles of plants, and spears and clubs, rampaging through the village and its surroundings with frenzied yells, and after several hours of strenuous effort returning home satisfied, in full assurance that they were now finally rid of the evil. However, when this too was shown to be a wasted effort, the explanation was found that one of the evil spirits had hidden himself behind a rock, or in a hollow tree trunk or some other cranny, persisting in his evil ways, and every objection against that was in vain.

Dancing, which plays such a major role with all the South Seas folk, both Melanesian and Polynesian, has great significance to the inhabitants of the Gazelle Peninsula as well. The natives, who are not otherwise particularly attracted to physical effort,

Plate 10 Sulka men in front of their huts; on the left is a rich harvest of taro tubers

display extraordinary staying power in the dance and do not notice when, after hours of effort, streaming with perspiration, they sink to the floor completely exhausted.

I would regard it an impossibility to describe the dances in detail. Cinematography and gramophone combined would be the only way to give a satisfactory impression of them. However, I shall attempt to give a general survey of the dances of our natives.

Dancing is always accompanied by song and music, and no opportunity is missed to put on a performance. Marriages, births, funeral feasts and all the preliminary ceremonies connected with them are suitable occasions; but besides these there are numerous other opportunities which are never overlooked. The completion of a dwelling house or the enclosure of the compound, the first use of a new canoe, the end of harvesting in the taro or yam fields, the killing of a pig, the completion of a larger community project, all provide the opportunity for a dance. Of course *duk-duk* meetings and those of the *ingiet* cannot be held without dancing and singing. By and large, dancing can be divided as follows: ceremonial dances such as those performed by the *duk-duk* members and the *ingiet* societies (see Section VIII), and profane dances which are common on all other occasions.

The ceremonial dances generally have a constant character. They are performed according to traditional rules, accompanied by songs that are often so old and venerable that their meaning has become completely lost to the singers. They consist in part of sounds strung together that in olden times were words, but have gradually been mutilated over the course of time so that they are no longer recognisable.

The profane dances and songs have undergone a far greater alteration. Here too of course there are traditional forms, but, on the other hand, new songs and new dances continually arise, which have a longer or shorter existence according to their popularity.

It is interesting that our natives have been ahead of the civilised countries of the Old and the New World for centuries, specifically in the protection of intellectual property. Native writers, composers, choreographers and designers have enjoyed this protection since time immemorial. The creator of a dance, the writer of a lyric or the composer of a melody is master of his creation to such an extent that nobody else would dare to reproduce this product without previous permission from the owner. Since permission must always be purchased with a certain amount of *tabu,* a small revenue always flows in for a popular dance creator or writer. This protection extends not only to the original writer or composer, but to his descendants after his death.

Almost all dances are line dances; circle dances are totally unknown. The men, like the women, always dance in separate groups; quite exceptionally, an esteemed elderly lady is permitted to dance with the men. In this case she then plays a dominant role in the presentation, in some way forming the centre in all the turns or dance movements. A man never takes part in a dance for women. On the other hand children are permitted to take part in dances, and both father and mother look on with great pride as their children imitate the various body movements, showing great skill among the rows of dancing men or women. In the compounds one can frequently observe father or mother giving their son or daughter the first dancing lesson, at a very early age when they have barely learned to stand. A bright flower (or a whole bunch) is placed in each of the little one's hands, and, while holding these in his hands, he must raise his arms alternately above his head, sideways or out in front, at the same time raising his little legs or bending his knees.

Wealthy or influential people have a specially constructed dance place. This consists of an avenue 20 to 40 metres long and 4 to 6 metres wide, bordered with brightly coloured bushes and often shaded by giant forest trees with thick foliage. The superficial humus layer is dug out to a depth of 0.5 to 1 metre as a rule, and is thrown up as a low wall on both sides, so that the site seems to resemble a long, shallow channel. This dancing place, *taman*, is always carefully cleaned and is the owner's pride and joy. However, people are not very fussy in choosing a dance place; if no *taman* is available, then any free site in front of the huts or in the forest is suitable.

If someone has invented a new dance and written and composed an accompanying song, he assembles his circle of acquaintances and rehearsal begins. According to the level of complexity of the individual movements, the rehearsal goes on for a longer or shorter period. Very complicated dances often require a daily rehearsal of several hours over a period of four to six months. During the rehearsal, the basic idea is explained to the participants, after which the various actions, arm, leg and hand movements are taught, all having the aim of presenting a particular event as a pantomime. The accompanying song does not always have a connection with the pantomime presentation, and it is difficult for an uninformed person to be any the wiser after the presentation. To the white spectator a dance appears as a double to quadruple line of dancers holding bunches of brightly coloured feathers or flowers in their hands, their bodies decorated with all kinds of patterns with heads and bodies adorned with all kinds of jewellery, accompanied by a loud, not quite so lovely sounding song which is sung in unison by all the dancers, performing all kinds of movements: stepping or skipping, now forwards, now backwards, now standing or crouching, performing particular movements with the feet, stretching hands and arms, now to the right, now to the left, swinging the bunches of feathers or flowers in prescribed movements. Apart from the varied body decorations the dances seem exceptionally monotonous and all the same to a foreigner, whereas they are actually a complex series of different body movements, precisely measured according to set rules and patterns, and presenting, in pantomime, a quite specific event. I have discussed the ceremonial dances of the *duk-duk* and the *ingiet* in detail elsewhere (Section VIII).

It is customary in the dances to adorn the body from head to foot, not only by painting but also by putting on items of jewellery, as discussed above. The head is especially worthy of attention, and the arrangement of bunches of bright feathers, coloured leaves and flowers, delicately shaped shell discs and tiny, carved figures representing animals or human forms often discloses very good taste, which might scarcely be expected in these natives.

b. The Baining

Now that I have described the inhabitants of the north-eastern Gazelle Peninsula comprehensively, I can turn to the Baining. A description of this tribe, their manners and customs will turn out to be far more brief, for although we are quite well informed by the investigations of Father Rascher,[6] especially about the North Baining, there is little over all that can be told about them, because in every aspect they are a totally primitive and simple people, such as I have encountered nowhere else in the South Seas.

In facial features the Baining has a pronounced similarity to his eastern neighbours. He has the same coarse features, the same tightly curled hair arranged in ringlets, the same skin shade. As he is a mountain-dweller, his physique has become significantly modified by his way of life, when we compare him with his neighbour. His body is more muscular, his chest broader and better formed, and his leg muscles in particular are strongly developed. He is therefore adapted to follow the steep paths of his mountain homeland up hill and down dale for long distances, even with the heaviest loads, without any apparent effort or sign of exhaustion; even small five- or six-year-old children are excellent mountain climbers, and inspire the involuntary admiration of the foreigner.

Men as well as women wear their hair cut short. Men often wear full beards, although they have learnt the plucking of beards from their neighbours, and have adopted it here and there. The body, especially chest and back, is usually hairy, and hair colour varies from reddish-brown to almost totally black. The same applies to head hair, which is never embrocated with lime, but is certainly bleached by sun, wind and rain.

Chiefs in the narrow sense of the word do not exist. The heads of the families hold weak sway

---

6. This worthy man and exceptional scholar of the Baining region, together with four missionaries and five sisters of the Sacred Heart Mission, was murdered on 13 August 1904 by the Baining, on whom he had devoted all his energy in a truly exemplary way.

Fig. 21 Village scene in the Baining territory

over their family members and through working in the fields several families are bound into a loose association. Permanent dwellings or hamlets are just as little in existence. The Baining are migratory agriculturalists. Wherever they have laid out their taro field they settle for a while; when the field is exhausted, they choose a new site, often quite a distance from the previous one, and then construct their primitive huts there. Through these wanderings they gain a precise knowledge of their mountain homeland, and, founded upon a well-developed sense of direction, they are able, to an astonishing degree, to find their way in the forested gorges and steep mountainsides even though an actual path does not exist. Over huge boulders, fallen tree trunks, and through old, abandoned gardens they find their way directly to their goal and never get lost. Features that are scarcely evident to another eye, such as a snapped bough, a broken twig or a slightly scratched tree trunk are unmistakable signposts for them. Also, land and soil do not belong to anyone, the site on which the garden is temporarily set up seems to be regarded as property only for a moment, but they do not recognise a lasting claim; an allocation through inheritance, purchase, gift or barter is equally unimportant.

Father Rascher has recently provided valuable information on the difficult language, and I attribute to him the concise section on Baining language that the reader will find in a later chapter.

The Baining believes that he and his descendants, like all men generally, derive from a man, Herini, and a woman, Sichi. These first people have come forth from the spathe of the *Areca* palm. Among themselves they are called *a chácat* (plural of *a chachracha*); all other people especially the eastern neighbours and shore-dwellers are designated as *a lba* (plural of *a lbacha*).

Their belief in human mortality has the following basis.

A long time ago the sun called all created objects together. Everything came quickly, only the human stayed away and did not obey the command. Then the sun bestowed immortality on those who had assembled; the human who was not present, however, did not share in this gift and must therefore die. Everything else lives for ever; the stone and the rock retain their form, the sea is always there, the sky with the stars arches continually over all. The snake does not die either, it sloughs its skin and then lives on. Had the human been obedient, he would have received this feature of the snake.

The spirits of the dead, *a ios* (plural of *a ioska*), it is true, continue to live after death. However, they have no fixed residence, they exist everywhere. It is worth noting that people regard these spirits as being without substance and have a unique word for this, *sasik*, which means as much as being present but not visible; a philosophy that is not encountered elsewhere in the archipelago, where the spirits of the dead are represented in this or that form. They also have no fear of these spirits and relate no superstitions to them.

The sole spirit that causes fear in the Baining is a mystical snake, *a chamki*. This slithers about and eats the excrement of people who must then die. *A chamki* has numerous children which live in gnarled trees, in knots and outgrowths, and which are just as dangerous to people.

Otherwise the Baining is free of all superstition, a feature that must be stressed, in contrast to all his neighbours. He does not appear to have a sufficiently strong intellect to ascend to comprehensive superstition. Should a friend or relative die suddenly, he ascribes this to his enemy the shore-dweller, but he does not meditate on the why or wherefore.

The shore-dweller (colonists of the northeastern Gazelle inhabitants) is his general enemy. He knew how to completely subjugate and enslave the mountain-dwellers. In earlier times the Baining were taken away in great numbers as slaves, and traded as such to remote regions of the Gazelle Peninsula. It was worse still when the unsuspecting Baining were enticed in great numbers to the beach and there mercilessly slain, for the sole purpose of serving as roast meat for the evildoers at their feasts. Thanks to the Catholic mission a change was finally brought about, and now the Baining at least enjoy a secure life, although the shore-dwellers still regard the produce of the industrious agriculturalists, especially the taro, as their property, and take as much as they please without compensation or reimbursement. But gradually a change is taking place here too. The instruction and example of the white missionaries have to a large extent done away with the earlier subservience and slavish obedience, and the younger generation, who enjoy instruction in the mission schools, do not want to know about the superiority and presumption of their neighbours.

The marriage of a Baining is a very simple story. If a maiden pleases a man, then he proposes to her, or asks through the parents whether she would like to be his wife. If she is willing, then the situation is good; if she does not want to, she declares this without hesitation and that is the end of it. Often the suitor lets the woman be abducted by a friend; the latter waits by the path until the woman comes along, takes her by the hand and leads her to the admirer's hut. She does not refuse, but follows willingly; however, when she nears the hut she makes her decision on the spot: remains there if it pleases her, or goes away again unmolested after she has declared her disinclination. However, if the affection is reciprocated the woman follows her husband, lives in his hut, helps in the taro field, and the union is seldom broken. No festivities, no feast, no ceremonies of any kind are customary. In spite of this, the Baining woman enjoys a significantly more independent situation than in the other tribes of the archipelago; she takes part in the men's speeches; both sexes eat together; she does not allow any excessive workload to be forced upon her, and she hands the care of the children over to the lord and master when she has to take her load of taro home or to market. In the latter case, one frequently sees the man, armed with a spear, carefully carrying his little child in his arms, or when bigger he lets it ride on his shoulders.

At a birth there are likewise no ceremonies arranged. Several older women assist the woman in labour, but often she looks after herself. The birth of a child does not disturb daily life at all; after two or three days the young mother is working in the mixed garden as before. The infant is laid on a pandanus mat, or on leaves in the shade of a tree and left to itself. There is no talk of child-raising as such, the boy or girl learns those tasks which will be required of them as grown-ups and as useful members of the family at a very early age, and since the sum of these is not very great, they soon achieve the desired mastery.

On the death of a Baining, be it man or woman, it is just as simple. The family assembles, as do neighbouring friends, and a brief wail of lamentation is intoned over the dead person. A simple meal of taro is prepared and all those present share it. After they have departed, a grave is dug and the corpse laid in it; in many villages the grave is filled in, elsewhere the corpse lies there freely exposed. Whether dogs or pigs use the dead body as food seems to make no difference to the survivors. Yet it is characteristic that after a death the atmosphere in the huts seems to be subdued or solemn. For a period of several days no loud talking or raised noise is heard, a sort of solemn stillness rests over the neighbourhood of the place of death.

Child murder is apparently practised only when the mother dies as a result of childbirth. The baby is then killed because there is nobody otherwise to take the child, suckle it and raise it. Child mortality is quite significant, however, as a result of primitive nursing, insufficient food, and the total unfamiliarity of the natives with illnesses, their causes and their cures. For this reason the Baining tribe is not very numerous, and the future will show whether the missionaries have succeeded in raising the natives to a higher level, so that they are better equipped to withstand the rigours of the climate. On the mission stations the children, for whom residence there is on the whole agreeable, are instructed not only in Christianity but also urged into cleanliness and orderliness. Under supervision from the missionaries they must build good, roomy houses for their own accommodation, carry out regular cultivation of various tropical produce, and since they are on average quick-witted and not untalented, it can be expected that the indefatigable activities of the missionaries will, over time, bear good fruit. The small settlement of the missionary Father Rascher in the Baining Mountains, with the pupils' little houses built in regular rows, erected from local materials and wood cut by the builder, might without exaggeration be called a model settlement, from which spiritual as well as physical benefit must come for the Baining.

That the Baining, in spite of his uniform daily life, also has a mind for great celebrations requiring extensive preparation and related expenditure of food, will be demonstrated in the discussion of the mask dances (Section VIII). But in other ways too he is a friend of festivities, in which pure enjoyment is always foremost. If the taro field has produced a rich harvest a great meal is prepared, the neighbours turn up, and people enjoy being there, while extraordinary quantities of baked tubers are consumed and group dances are performed. Other groups sit round about, chewing. Suddenly the dancers stop, those sitting round jump up just as quickly, grab stones, pieces of wood, food remains or rubbish, and with laughs and shouts pelt each other with the missiles for a short time and then sit down again; new dance groups form up and the previously described scene is repeated. Young men carry this sport as far as hurling human excrement; married and older people take no part in this.

Cannnibalism was common until not long ago, but disappeared under the influence of the Catholic missionaries. No characteristic customs took place. The victim was simply slain and prepared in exactly the same manner as if it had been a pig or a dog. The Baining presents himself today in his original state as an apparently quite harmless child of nature who possesses no predominantly good features, yet is not governed by particularly evil tendencies either. He has good talents but these do not develop; he cares about the maintenance of his daily life; all else is of secondary importance for him. He does not accumulate possessions, he is content with a primitive shelter that protects him against rain especially, but he sleeps on the bare ground and is apathetic towards everything that we would call dirt. His only wash is provided by the rain, which falls abundantly in his homeland, and it is amusing to see the care with which he crosses a shallow river, leaping from rock to rock in order to protect his naked, dirt-stained body from the cleansing influence of the water.

The main food source of the Baining consists, as already mentioned several times, of taro. Cultivation of this nutritious tuber is not without great difficulty and requires considerable expenditure of energy. Several families unite as a rule for communal establishment of a mixed garden. First of all the virgin forest must be felled, then the trunks and branches of the fallen trees chopped up and piled into bigger and smaller heaps. When these have dried out they are set alight and as much as possible of the felled wood is burnt; thick trunks that are not yet completely dry and offer resistance to the fire are left to lie where they have fallen. The cleared field is then surrounded by a strong, thick wooden fence for protection against wild pigs, and the native exhibits astonishing skill in erecting this, using solely a wooden cudgel. As soon as the enclosure is ready, they make a funnel-shaped hole in the ground with a stick sharpened to a point, *a hul* (plural *a huleichi*) and plant the taro slip in it. Soon the entire field is planted out with slips at regular intervals, and then the women's work begins, consisting of removing the weeds that grow in wild profusion between the taro plants. In the fertile soil the taro tubers grow to considerable size and when they are ripe after six or seven months, they are pulled out as needed, by the men, and the upper leaves and stem removed so that a stalk, 30 to 40 centimetres long, remains on the tuber. In the harvested sections of the field bananas are planted. Also, between the taro plants they plant a number of the most varied vegetables whose leaves are very popular as food, and which compete in flavour with several of our varieties of cabbage or spinach. In the fields a type of *Saccharum* is never absent, its unbudded flower heads providing a popular food.

After the taro harvest and the planting of the field with bananas, a new field, begun in the interim, is fully set up and planted out. The fields planted with banana enjoy no further care, the bananas are harvested when the bunches are ripe, but the fences are not renewed nor are the profuse weeds removed and they and the wild pigs soon destroy the remainder of the bananas. Meanwhile, however, a new field has been prepared, and want never occurs.

Since the Baining are no seafarers, have no canoes at all, and fishing in the rivers or on the beach yields little result, they seek their meat supply wherever they can find it. Pigs are numerous in a wild and semi-wild state, and the Baining hunts them with his dogs and kills the swine at bay with his spear. However, his hunting companion, the dog, is valued as a delicacy too, and is duly honoured at great festivities. An occasional wallaby or a cassowary are welcome changes to the menu. At the same time the Baining eats pretty well everything that he can catch, but an exception is made for all seabirds, which he calls *a lgieska*; that is, to be superior, to be strong, to be privileged.

The preparation of taro, like the roasting of pigs and dogs, is quite simple. Taro tubers are roasted on glowing coals, meat is wrapped in leaves and similarly prepared. The South Baining prepare their food with glowing hot stones, between which the food is laid, covered with leaves, and cooked. Food preparation by means of glowing stones indeed is also familiar to the North Baining; but they are then used in conjunction with an apparatus that is characteristic of the latter tribe, and to my knowledge is encountered nowhere else in the South

Plate 11 Group of Sulka men

Seas. This apparatus is called *a lus* (plural *a luski*) and consists of a tube of tree bark about 40 to 50 centimetres high and 20 to 30 centimetres in diameter. This tube is placed on the ground and a bed of glowing hot stones is laid inside; it is then covered with a banana leaf and a layer of vegetables is laid on it and once more covered with a banana leaf; then in the same order there follows a layer of hot stones, a layer of vegetables and so on, until the a lus is full; hot stones form the uppermost layer. After some time the vegetables are cooked, taken out, sprinkled with salt water and in this way provide a meal which under the circumstances must be described as very tasty and also agreeable to a European palate.

Betel serves the Baining as a stimulant and a luxury item. The North Baining uses it in the usual way, namely *Areca* nut with betel pepper and leaves, dipped in powdered lime. He burns the latter himself from shells or buys it from the shore-dwellers. The South Baining chew a certain aromatic tree bark, masoi bark of the Javanese, with lime and a type of betel leaf, but no fruit of the betel pepper.

On Baining house construction there is not much to say, it is the simplest imaginable. A primitive framework is covered with a foliage or grass roof, the sides filled in with sticks and pieces of trunk. They are so low that one can barely stand upright in them. Low openings lead to the interior, and this is devoid of any furniture; the whole family sleeps on the floor, often several families who live in a hut together; but pigs and dogs also find shelter in this dwelling and lie freely alongside their human masters. A flickering fire is usually lit, partly to keep insects away, and partly to provide warmth in cooler weather. In this space the Baining spends his night; during the day when he is not exactly busy in the garden he squats contentedly in front of his palace, devoting himself to his siesta and smokes a cigar, *suk* (singular *suiki*) of home-grown tobacco; when it burns out he rolls another; that is, he lays tobacco leaves together and wraps them in a green leaf, then places the whole thing into a cigar holder consisting of a thin bamboo tube. I can say nothing about the flavour for I have never been able to persuade myself to try it; however, the stench of the smoke provides a conclusion about the pleasant flavour of the plant.

His speech flows rapidly from his lips, sounding not unpleasant, and I must admit that I always enjoyed hearing Father Rascher's little pupils holding a conversation with him. Words followed one another in an uninterrupted stream of speech, accompanied by many gesticulations, of which the affirmative gesture particularly attracted me because it is so different from the usual one; namely in that one doesn't nod the head but shakes it energetically back and forth several times. Baining singing should by and large be considered melodic, although their songs seldom have an understandable content. Actually, predominant harmony is found in their loud yodelling, *snes*, that sounds out over a broad area from the mountains, and often when there are several voices, it can provide joy and pleasure to a European ear.

After this description of the daily life of the Baining I want briefly to put their skills under examination. Here too we are once more astonished to find that they demonstrate a not insignificant understanding of art, especially in the production of paintings on bark material, which I will discuss in more detail with their masks (Section VIII). These intricate, fine designs find a parallel nowhere else in the South Seas. Equally worthy of note are the nets, *a sangen neichi*, knotted out of brightly coloured cords, which when newly produced find use in dances but later are also used as carrying slings. Other nets or slings are produced from a fine liana and called *a gateichi*. All kinds of articles are carried in these. Taro are transported as a rule by the adhering stalks, and it is astonishing what loads the women can carry for long distances up hill and down dale. For this purpose they make use of a carrying band several metres long, woven out of tough bark material; with this the taro stalks are tied firmly to one another so that a loose loop is left free. This is laid over the forehead. To raise the load the woman sits in front of it with her back turned towards it; she adjusts the loop of the carry band around her forehead, bends her upper body as far forwards as possible, draws her legs under her and then rises slowly but surely to her feet with the load, often as much as 150 pounds. Indeed, this gymnastic feat seems quite easy – however, it is not to be performed by somebody unpractised. I have witnessed the attempt made by powerful Europeans with only half the load, always without success. The carrying band, *a garawacha*, accompanies the Baining woman everywhere and is her inseparable companion. Small girls must carry loads during childhood, and perform this quite remarkably, by our standards.

The preparation of bark material from breadfruit tree bark, and from the bark of another tree unknown to me, is the work of the men. The bark strips are beaten with a club on a stone in the riverbed until all the wood parts are removed by the beating and washing, and the pliable bark cloth remains.

By wicker-work the Baining produce bulbous, balloon-shaped baskets of great durability, from brown and black lianas. In the production of nets of all kinds they are just as skilful, and have fine and coarse, narrow-woven and wide-meshed nets according to their type of use.

With this the presentation of their accomplishments is largely exhausted – apart from the manufacture of their tiny articles of clothing and their weapons. With regard to the former there is not much to say; the men of the North Baining go completely naked, the women wear a narrow loin cloth of plant fibre, hanging down in front, suspended from a closely fitting girdle, while behind a long bundle of fibres dangles down like a tail, apparently without purpose. When sitting down, the woman gathers both dangling pieces with a swift, sure grip and clamps them between her legs. It is undoubtedly this artistic tail that has provided the motive for the assertion of the north-eastern inhabitants, that in the interior of the Gazelle Peninsula live men with tails. This girdle, *a niska* (plural *a nis*), is worn by all the Baining women. The men of the South Baining wear a girdle of bark cloth drawn between the legs; the girdle is frequently carefully ornamented by painting. We certainly wouldn't be wide of the mark if we infer that this girdle is borrowed from those tribes, Sulka, and so on, that live south of the isthmus and occasionally come into contact with the South Baining, known there as Saktai.

The weapons of the Baining consist of spears, clubs and slingshots. The spears are produced from the hard, outer wood of a certain type of palm easily split along its length, and are without any ornamentation. They are to a certain extent chiselled round, with one end chiselled to a point and hardened in a fire. In spite of the rough workmanship they are a dangerous weapon in the hands of the Baining, for from youth onwards they practise throwing, and over time attain astonishing dexterity and skill. The slingshot, *a vrika* (plural *a vri*), is absolutely identical to the slingshot of the north-eastern inhabitants of the Gazelle Peninsula; also, in throwing the sling-stone the Baining has had much practice, although this weapon finds use only in open country or on the shore, and by its nature cannot be used in forests and thickets. The club, *a machracha*, with the bored-through head is characteristic of the Baining. Its use has spread outwards from here as far as the inhabitants of the north-eastern peninsula, where it is known as *a palau*, and they also know how to make it. Previously, the most elaborate hypotheses had been put forward on the manner in which the boring out of the stone head had been carried out. The most simple explanation, as so often happens, had been overlooked. Professor Giglioli, in a comprehensive work on the stone clubs of the Baining several years ago, gave the correct explanation, which I made available to him from my observations. The native first of all searches for a suitable, already fairly round stone in a riverbed. He then takes it in his left hand and strikes it with another, somewhat pointed stone, always on a certain place on the future club head. A hollow gradually appears, and through continual hitting and removal of small stone fragments, it widens and deepens. A depression has now developed on one side; the same procedure is then undertaken on the other side, and the striking continues until the head is broken through and a hole formed. This is now gradually widened until it is big enough to push a rod through. This type of boring is customary among many other primitive peoples and is easily recognisable, since the opening is broader on the outer edges than in the centre. I was introduced to another type of stone drilling years ago at Berlinhafen in Kaiser Wilhelmsland. There the stone is drilled regularly by a bamboo tube with the help of moist sand, and this type of boring is easily recognisable because the bore walls are completely regular and of the same diameter throughout. The same type of drilling is also found among other peoples of nature; in the discussion on some areas of New Ireland I have pointed out, however, that very similar boring out could also be produced in other ways without a circular drill. The club heads of the Baining never have the flat, almost disc-like form that we recognise from particular areas of New Guinea. Strongly bevelled heads appear, but never with a sharp outer rim. The head is found in all stages, from strongly bevelled spheroid, to globular, to oval-shaped. The external shape is given to the head by rubbing on a hard stone; this type of grindstone with ground-in, trough-shaped depressions is found in all the watercourses and springs of the Bainings, and throughout Polynesia right to Europe, an indication that humans have universally carried on stone grinding in the same way. The club shaft is produced from hardwood, round, pointed at the upper end and thickened at the lower end. The drilled-out stone head is firmly fixed to this shaft, completely secured at the lower end by small wooden wedges firmly driven in, and the attachment site cemented with the crushed pulp of the parinaria nut. *Nassa* shells and red abrus beans are occasionally pressed into the cement as ornaments.

Besides this original club, the Baining has still other forms that have possibly been introduced from other areas. The flat club, about 120 centimetres long, about 8 to 10 centimetres broad at the lower end, narrower at the upper end and with a pointed triangular insert, might possibly be original; however, comparable specimens are also found on the north-eastern Gazelle Peninsula. In the Baining language this club is called *a virki*. On the other hand, the club called *a birichi* in the Baining language has undoubtedly been introduced; it has a similar shape to the *a virki*, but is circular, thicker below and carved into a conical wooden head at the upper end. The club which is called *saringeichi* in the Bainings has a pineapple-shaped head at the striking end, like the clubs that are familiar to us from the Sulka district, but is incomparably rough and more simple in presentation. A cudgel very similar to the stone-headed one almost certainly originates from there. However, it has a wooden head, almost globular in shape, gradually fused to the club shaft, instead of the stone head. I have also come across these types of clubs in the Varzin area, where, however, they belong among the great rarities.

Although sling shots and sling shot stones are customary throughout, the Baining, unlike his north-eastern neighbour, has not learned the art of trepanning. His medical knowledge extends to blood-letting by small incisions in the skin, and to staunch the blood flow he rubs burnt lime powder into the wound. He always binds wounds very carefully with all kinds of leaves, to which he ascribes healing properties, and which apparently have the desired effect.

The stone axe was his only work tool until a few years ago; today this has already disappeared, at least among the North Baining, and it is very difficult to obtain a complete specimen. Axe blades are still available here and there, however. Among the South Baining the stone axe is still frequently the only hand tool. Near Cape Buller on St George's Channel I saw this unique stone axe with the usual knee-shaped handle in the hands of men who had apparently just come from felling timber; however, to my great regret I could not obtain a single specimen, because the people were too fearful to await my approach. In the preceding I have given in summary a fairly thorough description of this interesting, primitive people.

c. The Taulil and Butam

It still remains for me to devote my attention to the small tribes of the Butam and Taulil.

If we proceed from Vunakokor (Varzinberg) in a south-westerly direction towards the Baining Mountains, then after we have left behind the inhabited districts at the foot of the mountain, we come upon no further human settlements for many hours. For a long period the path crosses the plain, overgrown with thick forest, until deep gorges traversed by silver-clear streams make the way difficult for us. One of these streams runs for a considerable time between two vertical walls, and in order to find a suitable way over it we have to go downstream for a while.

It was in this dangerous spot that some of the murderers of Mrs H. Wolff were surprised and killed by the Taulil in 1902, at the moment when, in great tranquility, they were catching crayfish. Having passed the gorge and scaled the hill we notice coconut palms. These indicate an earlier dwelling place of the Taulil, named Palakukur. Only after we have scrambled up still more gorges do we come across newly laid out gardens enclosed with quickset hedges and here and there miserable huts. The Taulil, who call themselves Tulil, live here. The history of this tribe is closely connected with that of the Butam. The Butam, who in earlier years were still fairly numerous, lived south-east of the Taulil, in the hills and on the plain south of the Warangoi (Karawat) River. To their backs lived the South Baining, who occupied the mountains of the interior. In 1883 to 1885 in the districts of Kambange and Londip on St George's Channel I frequently heard mention of the Butam, and the area of their habitation was pointed out to me, from the hills outwards. At that time this was already regarded as a tribe that was in the process of dying out, but it was a tribe with whom in those days one still came into contact from time to time on the shore, sometimes friendly, sometimes with hostility, according to the circumstances. The inhabitants around the Varzinberg always seem to have regarded the Butam as their enemies, and the chiefs of Wairiki at that time frequently recounted to me their raids against the Butam.

The Butam had a different language from the Taulil, but were friendly with them and occasionally fled to them when they were too fiercely oppressed by the Varzin people. Over the course of time, but still before the end of the 1880's, the entire Butam tribe was wiped out, and the few who survived sought protection by the Taulil and were adopted by this tribe. Yet here too they found no enduring peace, for after annihilating the Butam the Varzin inhabitants turned on the Taulil. It remains a mystery how the Taulil, besieged from all sides, could hold out up to today, but the impenetrable forest with its deep, steep gorges always offered a secure place of refuge to those attacked. That the Varzin-dwellers were the prime attackers is beyond doubt; their warlike raids had in part the aim of providing fresh human flesh for their festivities, and in part they were bent on seizing slaves. The custom of vendetta existing among the Taulil then led to reprisals against the attackers, and so there existed that bloody feud which has lasted until recent times.

The districts of Wairiki, Malakuna, Tingenavudu, Viviren south and east of Varzin, and the districts of Tamaneiriki, Vunadidir, Nau-mauma, Rebar and Rapitok west and north of Varzin, took part in these cannibal raids. Usually they succeeded in surprising the unsuspecting Taulil people in their gardens and then men and youths were speared; women, girls and boys, and even infants were dragged into slavery. The flesh of the slain was divided piece by piece among the participants in the raid. These hunts lasted for days and extended as far as the Karawat River, which one seldom dared to cross, for fear of the Baining who roamed those lands on the far side.

Yet the attack did not always turn out to the advantage of the attacker, and when such a raid did not succeed in surprising the Taulil it progressed to the disadvantage of the attackers, and the Taulil repelled them with high casualties. The previously mentioned village of Palakukur was the scene of many tenacious struggles. Here the Taulil had strongly barricaded themselves, and received their enemies with a hail of stones and spears, so that it was a long time before they were successfully driven out of this fortress.

Occasionally the Taulil also made an attack on the enemy region, and the districts next to them had to be continually secured against surprise attack. Several years ago the Taulil carried out an almost unbelievable act of bravery. One of their chiefs, Tokomet, had been killed and the need for revenge was paramount. They learned that the entire Viviren were holding an armed gathering in a certain compound. Several courageous Taulil made use of this situation; they crept into the compound and fell upon their enemies with such vehemence that the latter fell over one another in their wild flight, leaving behind three of the bravest leaders, dead.

The Taulil maintained a certain friendship with several of the neighbouring tribes between Blanche Bay and Weberhafen, and thus occasionally in recent years they have also come to my dwelling, so that I frequently have the opportunity of trading with them. Physically they are scarcely different

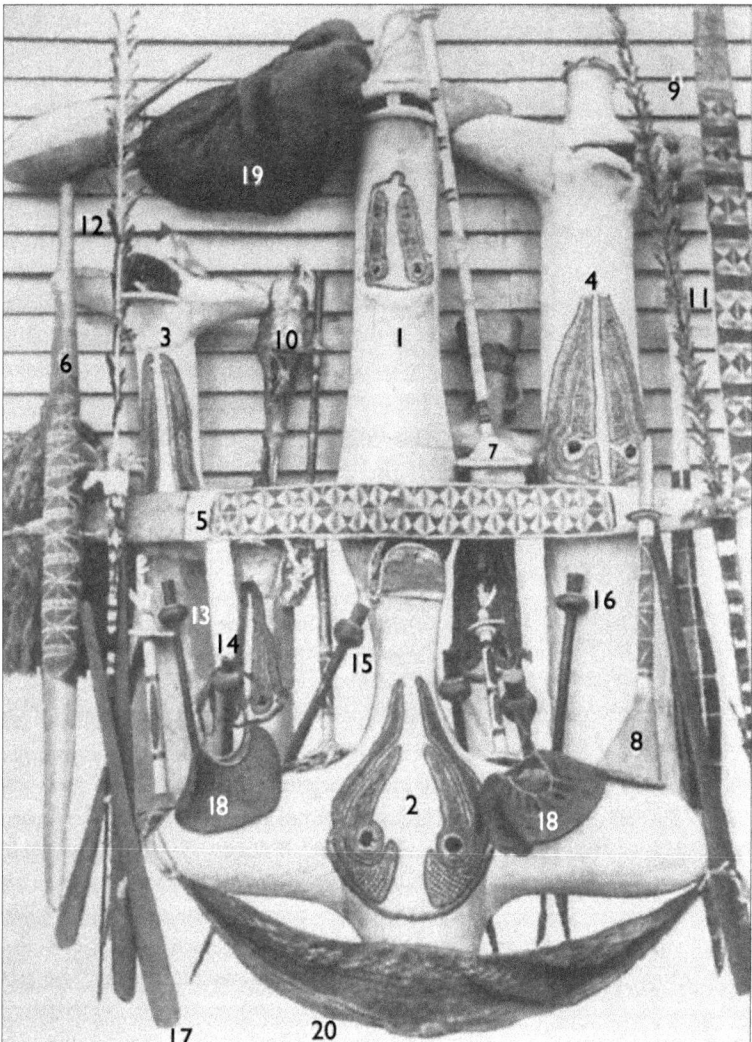

Fig. 22 Baining objects

1. to 12. dance items;
13. to 17. weapons;
18. to 20. nets and pouches

from the other inhabitants of north-eastern Gazelle Peninsula. They are somewhat swifter and more adroit in their movements, and their eyes betray a great degree of cunning. They are able to transport heavy loads with great endurance over long distances, but this is a characteristic they possess in common with all the inland inhabitants. They also visit individual tribes on St George's Channel with whom they stand on a peaceful footing. Many years ago I met a group of about twenty of them who were fishing in Rügenhafen, and on first sight threatened to become aggressive, until a native from Kambanga who was accompanying me gave them a sign of recognition, upon which friendly exchanges immediately developed. Father Eberlein sought them out in their present dwellings; he was indeed received somewhat mistrustfully; soon, however, after his friendly intentions had been understood, the mistrust gave way and food was placed before him with great hospitality. I am grateful to the Father for a large part of this information on the Taulil.

Although the Taulil are competent agriculturalists, they may, on the other hand, also be regarded as bold and persevering hunting people. The bulk of the work in the garden is the task of the women. The men roam in all directions in the forest and hunt wild pig, cassowaries and marsupials with spears; they fish with nets for many kinds of fish and crayfish in the numerous streams.

They have their own unique language, which is totally different from the language of north-eastern Gazelle Peninsula. The Butam too would have had a unique language. However, they are also familiar with the language of their northern neighbours with whom they currently converse, which indicates earlier, far more peaceful communication.

The Taulil language manages without any sibilants, just like that of the inhabitants of north-eastern Gazelle Peninsula. The affinity of both languages is striking, as with the Baining language. This is not surprising, since the Taulil tribe is wedged between both of these large tribes and has undoubtedly been combined first with one then with the other over many years, and has been influenced by both sides.

The population, which has melted away to about 300 people currently, has much in common with their north-eastern neighbours in terms of manners and customs. For example, they have the *ingiet* society in common, and thereby, also, the banning of consumption of pork by the male members.

Father Eberlein tells me that a second society exists as well, consisting of all the warrior men and youths; the members of this society cannot eat the flesh of the white cockatoo, nor that of the red and the green parrots; the pigeon, raven, a species of falcon, the flying fox, and particular species of fish and certain types of vegetables are likewise forbidden to them (*tambu*). The superstition exists that should they disobey this prohibition, they will lose their lives in the next battle.

d. The Tribes of the Central Part of New Britain

A number of linguistically different tribes dwell south of the isthmus which separates the Gazelle Peninsula from the rest of the main island, in the mountains bordered to the east by Wide Bay and Jacquinot Bay, and to the west by the high volcanoes of the Father group. However, as far as we can judge today they belong to a common ethnographic province.

Only in recent times has there been success in making contact with these tribes. A number of younger people have been recruited as plantation workers; several of these have been taken in hand by the Catholic mission, and here Brother Hermann Müller has not only studied the language with great diligence and endless patience, but also made numerous writings on manners and customs, demonstrating that we have before us a tribe significantly different from the tribes that live on the Gazelle Peninsula.

We owe the first more detailed account of this region to the Wesleyan missionary Brown who visited it in 1878. However, he did not go far beyond Henry Reid Bay and his description of this journey, given in the *Proceedings of the Royal Geographical Society*, justifies our assumption that he encountered the mountain tribe of the Gak*tei* who were then undertaking a military expedition against the Sulka who lived on the shore. The Gaktei tribe inhabits the mountain ridges between Open Bay and Wide Bay. It is probably identical with the Paleawe whom Father Rascher, while advancing inland from Open Bay, came across in the mountains; possibly it also inhabits part of the southern Gazelle Peninsula and is identical with the tribes encountered at Cape Bogengang and Cape Buller.

Suffice it to say that we still know very little about the Gaktei, and what we do know is based on the evidence of the Sulka. The Gaktei tribe seems to be in a state of constant feud with the Sulka tribe, and over the course of time the latter has been driven from the shore region in Henry Reid Bay, which it inhabited in earlier times, and pushed further southwards.

The Sulka distinguish two further neighbouring tribes, the Tumuip, a mountain folk, and the O Mengen, who occupy the shore in Jacquinot Bay and in Waterfall Bay as well as the mountains behind.

The communication between these three tribes is a peaceful one; they undertake trade by barter and enter into marriages with one another; on the borders of the various tribal territories there are villages where members of the different tribes dwell peacefully alongside one another.

The habitat of the tribes extends over the highlands interlaced with deep gorges and valleys which I have mentioned earlier. From the beaches to the mountain ridges and peaks, the eye perceives numerous, carefully laid out and maintained gardens, from which one might infer quite a substantial population. Several years ago, while aboard HIMS *Möwe* steaming close inshore looking for an anchorage, we were accompanied on the shore by a numerous swarm of people, and new crowds were seen hurrying from the mountains in wild haste over the steep paths down to the shore, probably attracted by the sight of a ship that was slowly approaching in such immediate proximity to the shore. Numerous rivers and streams furrow the valleys; the most significant are the Mävlu (Powell River) and the Vulvut (Henry Reid River), both emptying into Henry Reid Bay.

In the following passage I will discuss mainly the Sulka tribe; the descriptions are based on the writings of Brother Hermann Müller.

The Sulka, as already mentioned, oppressed by the Gaktei over the course of time, have had to retreat further towards Cape Orford; not long ago they also inhabited Brown Island not far from Cape Turner, and still visit this island in their canoes today to catch fish and turtles. They are safe here from their enemies, the Gaktei, since the latter have neither canoes nor can they swim.

The tribe falls into two divisions. Men of one division can choose only women from the other for marriage, and the offspring belong to the mother's division. Sexual congress between members of the same division is, as virtually throughout Melanesia, regarded as incest, and the guilty party is punished by death. Each division breaks down further into various families, *kha* (branch) or *ngausie* (vine). In each division nine such branches are recognised.

I Division: *o ngaurul, o letun, o tiling, o mamran, o masra, o keir, o luongan, o pamlikol, o kambuin.*

II Division: *o sos, o kemun, o kegen, o ngelmon, o sir, o pokan, o tigim, o mierlaut, o mugulpun.*

Among the Sulka the girl chooses her husband. She 'sets her heart on the man of her choice', as one says literally: '*T'el ka ngaung mang.*' As a rule she pours out her heart to her father or another close relative, and the latter says something like: 'Wait, we will invite him, in order to work on your behalf.' He then goes to the young man in question and puts the marriage proposition to him. If the latter is willing, he is conducted to the bride's compound where she has already prepared him a roasted taro which she hands, with a neck ornament, to him on his arrival. Acceptance of this gift is regarded as consent. The youth gives the neck ornament to his parents, upon which they pass a reciprocal gift to their son for his bride. The latter gives this in turn to her parents. The youth now remains in the compound of his future in-laws and assists his father-in-law in his work, especially in establishing a new garden for the young couple. After some time a day is decided upon for the bride's father to lead her to her intended, when numerous spectators turn up. The father takes his daughter by the hand, leads her to her bridegroom and hands her over to him. The latter takes the bride by the hand and together they take the path to his parents' compound; all the spectators follow. The youth hands the bride over to his mother and a pig is killed which, together with local dishes, is divided out among the spectators, who then go their separate ways.

The young bride, who henceforth until her wedding day is called *a mogäang*, now begins the life of a recluse, which often lasts for several months. In the rear of her in-laws' hut, a dwelling is prepared for her by means of a partition. She must stay here with another young girl, the bridegroom's sister or niece, who is called *a savlaure* during this time. During this period she is forbidden to touch taro that has been roasted between stones, meat, fish, and certain kinds of fruit, as food. Also, she must not drink water; she can quench her thirst by chewing cane sugar. Her food, consisting of certain fruits and taro that has been roasted in the fire, is prepared by the *savlaure*. The *mogäang* herself must touch nothing to make fire or to roast. The *savlaure* cuts the roasted taro tubers up into small pieces after she has thrown away the charred outer shell, for the *mogäang* must not touch this either. The latter then puts the pieces in her mouth by means of the rib of a coconut palm leaf, since handling them is forbidden. During this time an edible type of red earth is also given her to eat. The *mogäang* dare not be seen by any man; if she has to go out, she wears a long cloak of banana leaves extending from her shoulders to her feet, or covers her body with a mat; she must whistle also while en route, so that men become aware of her and promptly get out of her way. The women put designs on her breast, torso and back, partly by incision with obsidian knives, partly by branding with glowing ribs of coconut palm leaves. The bridegroom has to pay the women for this, with pork. During this time he is building his house.

This isolation of the bride has a great similarity with the isolation of young women in the Rossel Mountains of New Ireland.

When the period of isolation has expired, the wedding day is announced; pigs are slaughtered and food dishes prepared in quantity. The night before, the women come to the compound and spend the night singing with the mogäang; early in the morning they take her down to the water for a bath. After this they chew the aromatic *vankie* fruit, spit the chewed pulp over the bride and rub it in. She is then given a new loin cloth, and adorned with brightly coloured *Dracaena* leaves, and the necklaces and armbands given for this purpose by the bridegroom. This procedure is accompanied by the continuous singing of the women. Meanwhile the men in the compound are given gifts. When the bride is adorned according to local custom, she is led into the compound, where she is already awaited. Then the women present a dance and afterwards receive gifts. This brings the celebration to an end; the visitors gradually leave, and the newlyweds remain in their hut.

We now encounter the peculiar belief that man and woman, married and unmarried, are defiled by sexual intercourse. This contamination is called a sile, pronounced something like '*a sle*'. The married ones can cleanse themselves from this defilement by a process learned at their marriage – the men from the men, the women from the women. Unmarried ones afflicted with *sle* are avoided, and children are warned away from them by their parents. The contamination is supposedly detectable in their eyes. Nothing is accepted from them and particular care is taken to ensure that they do not approach the dance instruments (*o kol*). By their mere presence the painting on these instruments is sullied. One who is afflicted with *sle* will die of it, in the natives' opinion, unless a particular ceremony of purification is conducted on him. Therefore those who have transgressed must immediately confess and ask someone to cleanse them.

The purification ceremony for men proceeds publicly as follows. A certain quantity of coconut kernel is crushed and mixed with sea water and ginger, accompanied by the murmuring of magic spells. After the contaminated person has drunk this mixture, he is thrown into the sea and has to take with him the leaves from which he has taken the medicine, and place them under stones on the sea floor. After this bath he throws away his previous items of clothing and wraps a new loincloth round himself. While this is going on, the men sitting on the beach sing a certain song. Those who came across the two people during sexual intercourse are regarded as unclean as well, and require purification, which is, however, much simpler in this case.

When a woman gives birth, the consequence in the natives' eyes is that the men become cowardly, weapons lose their strength, and germination capacity is removed from taro slips destined for planting. To prevent this, the following ceremony is undertaken. As soon as it is known that a woman has given birth, the male inhabitants of the compound assemble in the men's house (*a ngaulu*), bringing branches of a strong-smelling type of tree; they break the twigs off and place the stripped leaves on the fire. All those present take twigs with young shoots in their hands. One of them pronounces certain words over ginger held in his hand, and then shares it among those present. The latter chew it and spit it onto the twigs, which are then held over the fire and later fixed onto the shields and weapons in the house, the taro slips, the roofs and over the house doors.

The newborn receives from the mother the name of one of her relatives.

The firstborn sons and daughters in most families are favoured more than the other children. Among poorer families this occurs less frequently, because the means for the required festivities are lacking. When the firstborn children have grown up, a feast is given in their honour, at which the boys become *o teivol* (that is, the favoured one, the sublime, the unapproachable), and the girls become *o kuhuingol* (with the same meaning). At these feasts, given by the parents with the other relatives also contributing, the child sits on a seat, with neck, arms, shoulders and loins decorated as much as possible. The hair of the head is cut all round and adapted so that it forms a garland around the head. The boys are naked, the girls wear normal clothing. Thus the honoured ones sit and are admired by the gathering throng. Now clothing of the boy takes place. A close relative steps up to him, rubs his hips with a new loin cloth, murmuring soft magic spells over him, and then dresses the child in the new loin cloth. From now on the boy must no longer go about unclothed. Then various masked people appear and perform a dance, after which all those present are given gifts. On this day the teip is also initiated into the secrets of the masks; he is led into the mask house where everything is shown to him, and it is impressed upon him most emphatically not to divulge anything about this to women. Before his eyes a volunteer is cudgelled soundly, and he is threatened with the same punishment should he ever disclose the secrets to women. The man who was beaten receives a new loin cloth as reward for his pains.

In order that a child swiftly learns to walk, his little legs are tapped with grass stalks while speaking the words:

A nhar volvol, a nhar volvol,
Ja volvol in kam sisir k'ol!

That is, 'Light foot, light foot, be nimble so that you walk and stand.'

In order that the child quickly learns to talk, his mouth is tapped while saying: '*Gu nere, gu nere! Ja muiiang i tit kar i nan! Ja muiiang i lenar!*' That is, 'Speak mouth, speak mouth! Affront your father and your mother; insult your friends!'

To wean a child, it is taken to a neighbouring compound so that it does not see its mother. As a substitute for maternal milk, cane sugar is chewed, the juice spat into the cupped hand, and fed to the child.

Plate 12 Group of women from the 'Liebliche Inseln'

The boys are soundly beaten by a masked man, *a mongan*, so that they develop strongly and become big.

When the boys have reached a certain age, about ten to fifteen years, they are circumcised. Occasionally the entire population of neighbouring villages gather for this ceremony. The operation takes place in the men's house; the instrument used is a sharp obsidian knife. After circumcision the sides of the boys' noses are pierced. Those circumcised must remain in the house until their wounds have healed. For eating and drinking they behave like the *mogäang*. If they go out, they wear a mantle as she does and the *kol* instruments are blown to warn the women to go out of their way. When their wounds have healed somewhat, they are led, over several successive days, to an isolated spot on the seashore. Coconut kernels are grated, laid on a taro leaf and sea water is poured over them. Then *Dracaena* leaves are steeped with another plant (*porkhe*). Someone murmurs an incantation over ginger roots, chews them, then adds the chewed mass to the mixture. Upon this, the boys are seized one by one, raised in the air and thrown into the sea. In order that each one tumbles in a somersault, the person involved in lifting the boy has to hold the boy's hair firmly between his teeth to align the boy in the proper position. After the bath they are given some of the grated coconut kernel to eat, and they have to smear their bodies with the mixture, using the *Dracaena* leaves. After use the latter are laid on young *holaut* saplings, because it is believed that one will then grow as rapidly as these saplings.

At the time of circumcision the boys are called *a vorongtuk* (that is, literally 'the noses'), and the men in attendance are called *o savlaure*.

When the wounds have fully healed, a great feast is presented. On the morning of the feast day the *vorongtuk* are bathed, smeared and adorned like the *mogäang* on her wedding day. They are then led to the compound where men and women dance. On this occasion various masked people also dance. The *vorongtuk* watch the dancing from a scaffolding erected for them, or from the roof of the house. In several villages the dancers take them on their shoulders and dance round with them. From now on they can be seen in public again, but persons of the opposite sex must still get out of their way, and above all must initially avoid any relationships with them.

The Sulka are of the opinion that circumcision is essential for procreative capacity, and for invigoration and strong growth of the youths. Those who have evaded the festive and public circumcision, probably to avoid the associated costs, are circumcised secretly.

An important ceremony in the life of a young Sulka is the blackening of the teeth. The black substance *a kät* traded from the Tumuip (probably a manganese-containing earth) is mixed with the grated bark of a tree, *girpil*; the mixture is then called *a mui*. From the moment when the blackening is carried out on the youths, they are called *o gitvungol* for the rest of their lives. Usually the ceremony is undertaken on several youths at the same time. The young men must lie in front of the fire, protecting their bodies from the heat with pieces of wood or banana trunks in front of them. When the blackening is spread on the teeth they must get them as close to the fire as possible, while the men assisting cover their eyes with their hands so that they suffer no damage from the heat. The operation naturally draws many inquisitive visitors into the compound again. Some of the men stay in the house, some outside; all the women sit in the open. A song is sung during the ceremony:

Kekät to ri vunginaie, e, e, e!
Kekät to ri vunginaie, e, e, e!
Pel mui ri vunginaie, e, e, e!
Pel mui ri vunginaie, e, e, e!
Vangei ka lo moge to, e, e, e!
Ka lo moge to e, e, e, and so on.

Should the blackening not stay on the teeth, it is the fault solely of the *gitvungol*. They say: 'they have something evil on their hearts', and first have to confess this. If they have acknowledged anything, one of the men assisting takes a piece of wood and spears it towards the fire while uttering certain words, according to the deed committed. Upon this, the black should stick fast.

As soon as the first coat is dry, they cry: *ōh! ūh! ēh!* and a second coat follows. Meanwhile the guests are entertained with pork, yams and taro. Soft food is pushed to the back of the mouths of the *gitvungol* so that they can swallow it directly without having to chew it. When they want to drink, water is trickled into their wide open mouths.

In order that the blackening remains firmly on the teeth, strings are bound onto the little fingers, the little toes, and the hair of the head, with incantations. Coconut palm fronds are plaited together and fixed in the house for the same purpose. When going out, an accompanist must rattle an instrument called *veren* to scare away certain birds and lizards, whose very glance is sufficient to cause the blackening to disappear from the teeth.

When it has been determined by the experts that the blackening has soaked in well and is fast, the *gitvungol* are led down to the water and bathed, while spells are again uttered over them. The attached magic strings are removed and bound on certain plants; the head hair is shorn round the head, while being retained in the middle; then they are smeared and painted, given a new loin cloth, and a new necklace and a new little bag, *a gol*, are hung round their shoulders. They are given a lime container in one hand, betel leaves in the other, then they return together to the compound where the guests are entertained to a celebratory meal.

Now in order to remove blackness that perhaps penetrated the body during the ceremonies and to prevent it causing harm, ginger roots hung in the house for precisely this purpose are taken to the sea several days later, crushed, and the expressed juice, mixed with sea water, is given to the gitvungol to drink. Then with grated coconut kernel in their mouths they are thrust into the sea, where they have to swim for a distance underwater. On emerging they have to eat up the grated coconut in their mouths and then they return to the compound.

In the days before this purification ceremony they must avoid contact with women, and are not allowed to drink water when they feel hot. If when overheated they go to the water to drink, they must keep the little toe or the little finger in the water long enough until they are cooled off. They declare that the *kät* might tempt them to consort with women during this time. Should they not resist the temptations, the *kät* leaves them; they are ridiculed and their teeth become white once more.

When a Sulka dies, all the natives from neighbouring compounds assemble round him to weep and wail. The dead person is stretched out on his bed and adorned; the interior of the house is also decorated. The dead person's garden is destroyed; edible fruits are shared out, young fruit trees uprooted, pigs killed and distributed, and the dead man's weapons are broken. On the death of wealthy and prominent men their wives are also slain. The guests remain by the corpse, which is buried the following day with much lamentation. A narrow, deep hole is dug inside the house and the dead person is fixed in a sitting position on a specially constructed crossbeam. The upper body rises above the hole, and over this a small tower-like structure is erected and well covered with banana leaves. The hole is lined with leaves in such a way that no soil touches the corpse. Stones are laid round the little tower and a fire kindled and kept alight. The relatives sleep for a time by the corpse, the men on one side and the women in the other half of the house.

After a time the driving out of the dead person's spirit takes place. The time appointed for this banishment is kept totally secret so that the spirit does not hear of it and perhaps prepare to resist. On the previous evening, many dry coconut leaves are dragged together, and very early the following morning, when the *kau*-bird sounds its first notes, the natives suddenly raise a great cry; they strike the walls of the house, shake and rattle it, light dry coconut leaves and leap in all directions with them and then throw them on the path. They believe that the spirit of the dead man, terrified by all this, will make himself safe elsewhere. Those who have slept by the grave are now thanked with pork and produce, and from then on sleep in their own houses again.

When the corpse's flesh has completely putrefied, the remains are taken from the grave and wrapped in leaves. The bundle containing the remains is hung up in the house. After several days a memorial feast takes place in the dead man's honour. The pork and produce for this are laid out in advance, in portions for the individual families. Then at the feast the son of the dead man puts the bundle of his father's remains on his shoulders and assigns each family their pork and produce, after which he takes the remains back into the house. At the feast, which lasts for three days, men and women dance, the latter with and without masks.

If someone builds a new hut, the remains are transferred from the old dwelling to the new.

Natives who have no relatives, or who have done evil in the locals' opinion, or who have been slain outside the compound, are not buried inside the house on their death. Their corpses are laid on rocks, on scaffolding in the forest, or buried where they were slain. Those who have died suddenly are not buried. A frame is made in the house, the body wrapped in leaves and left to putrefy on the frame inside the house. Fruits are laid before the closed door of the house and the compound is abandoned.

In order to protect their treasures, their necklaces, their armlets, their dog and possum teeth and the like from theft, many bury these things in the forest, in an old wooden drum covered with a stone. If somebody dies without having disclosed the hiding place of his treasure beforehand, his spirit remains with it in the form of a large mouse. So if the heir is looking for the treasure and frightens the mouse away, he need look no further. Then the spirit appears to the searcher in the night and says: 'You have hunted me from my treasure, go and collect it!' Next morning the lucky person goes to the place where he roused the mouse and digs up the treasure.

In mentioning festivities, pork is nominated as the mainstay of the meal. Nonetheless, among the Sulka there are both men and women who do not eat pork and who are called *o lapgiel*, to distinguish them from *o ngemsilang*, the pork-eaters. The mother decides whether her child will be *a lapgiel* or *a ngemsilang*. The *lapgiel* form no special secret society. While others are presented with pork at feasts, the *lapgiel* receive neither fish nor the flesh of other animals. The *lapgiel* who have been unfaithful have no special punishment to fear, and are only branded by being named *lapgiel peaik*.

When a child dies, the father must pay the maternal uncle a gift consisting of shell money, armlets, and so on, for the loss of a member of the family.

After death the person's soul comes to a place called Mlol. They have only unclear, blurred concepts about the life of the spirit at this place, which the Sulka imagine is situated 'within the earth'. Before the spirit gets to Mlol it encounters two rocks, Kilkil and Kovangal, where it is questioned about its life. If it is generous it may travel on further; but if it is miserly it must wander back to the south into the region of the O Mengen. There it is transformed into a rock, and must stand in the surf.

Spirits drink from the rivers Lonan and Lopo. Those who have been slain must drink the blood-stained water in which they have bathed.

During the night there reigns great fear of the spirits of the dead, because it is believed that they wander around at that time and feed on humans. One kind of spirit, *a kavengol*, shines by night like a glow-worm. In the minds of the Sulka shooting stars are souls that are tossed into the air to plunge into the sea. The tail moves because other souls have bound dry coconut leaves to it and set them alight. They then blaze during the flight through the air.

The *kot* is a higher being, hostile to humans. All violent, natural events like earthquakes, thunder and lightning also bear the name *kot*. The most feared of them all is lightning, the unfailing avenger of various transgressions. A *kot* is also believed to dwell in some waters. For example, a *kot* in the form of a snake lives in the Vleomem River, and in the Lerum River there is one in the form of an octopus. If a stranger comes and bathes in one of the designated rivers or drinks from them and laughs about it, the *kot* takes possession of him and creates stones and worms in his body, so that he becomes extremely ill and will die unless a sorcerer is successful in driving out the *kot*. This occurs by laying taro leaves and ginger on the chest and trunk of the victim and uttering spells. If the sorcerer is lucky and the operation is successful, amid universal astonishment the stones or worms come out of the victim's body onto the leaves and are burnt.

In the destruction of the village of Pahalum which was overwhelmed by a landslide, the Sulka perceive an act of vengeance by the *kot*. They recount it as follows: the inhabitants of Pahalum had laid a snake on the fire to roast it, without realising that a *kot* lived in this snake. After the snake appeared to be roasted sufficiently, they took it from the fire to cut it up. But to their astonishment they noticed that it was still completely raw and fresh blood flowed from it. Then while they were busy wrapping it up again to roast it once more, it suddenly became dark and a strong earthquake arose, but only around Pahalum; the deafening noise was, however, heard in all the surrounding villages. A mountain collapsed on Pahalum and buried it. One single person, a small girl called Lonelil, escaped with her life, although a falling rock crushed her leg. A stream, Sirar, bubbled forth from the ground on the unfortunate place, and now flows where the village previously stood.

In the waters and caves in the rock there are, according to Sulka, beings with bodies like humans, only more coarse and misshapen. These so-called *mokpelpel* or *vutangmem* live on certain plants and totally devour humans; hence the great fear of them. Oddly, the *mokpelpel* men are said to remain in their dwellings all the time and are seldom seen, while the women often go out. However, the latter can be heard from a great distance, because their extraordinarily long breasts make a clapping sound when they move. Thus if they hear a *mokpelpel* woman approaching, they hammer on a tree with a stone axe; then she will immediately turn back.

The existence of dwarfs is universally affirmed by the Sulka. These live in rock crevices and steal fruit from the gardens. Since they are very small in stature, they stand on one another's shoulders to reach the fruit, which they carefully break off so that they do not fall to the ground and make a noise. The fruit, which is passed down from hand to hand to the ground, is received by their headman.

In the village of Kolvagāt lives a man named *Kolol*, who keeps two stone figures sitting on the floor of a dark, specially constructed house. One is called *ngur pei* (our grandmother) and the other *ngur es* (our grandfather), and their names are uttered in ceremonies of the supernatural. They are brought produce as tribute, and this is left with them to rot. When *Kolol* positions the figures so that their faces are turned towards each other, the gardens should flourish. But should he place them with their backs towards each other, famine would arise and people receive a setback. An ancestor of *Kolol*, while digging at the foot of a mountain, is said to have come across these two figures and to have built a house for them at their request.

The mystical ceremonies used to effect a cure from illnesses, wounds and sores are called a peim. For this they take ginger, lime, betel nut and betel leaves, and these are chewed. The sick person is brought into contact with the mixture, and signs are made on his body while uttering certain magic words. If the desired effect does not occur, then this or that was incorrect during the ceremony. But in all cases the sorcerer must be compensated for his troubles.

In order to bring alleviation to a pregnant woman during the pain of labour, a man who has empathy with her pretends to be ill, lies down in the men's house and bends himself up as frequently as the pregnant woman's cries reach him. The men gather, and busy themselves as though they wanted to alleviate his pretended pain. This goes on until the birth has occurred.

The following sorcery is used to cause a girl to desire a particular person. The person takes *Dracaena*, murmurs magic words over ginger, chews it, then places it on the *Dracaena* leaves and rubs it in while uttering the name of the girl in question. The leaves are then hung in the house and a fire kindled below them; this takes place on the evening before a dance. On the day itself the person gets up early, pours chewed, enchanted ginger into a leaf funnel with sea water, and covers his chest and back with this mixture by means of the *Dracaena* leaves.

According to custom, the youth lays the bundle of leaves on a hut post and goes to the dance. When he sees the girl he ventures near her, and attempts to touch her with his back. Now when the girl sits down afterwards, she swoons, and in answer to those around says: 'So-and-so has enchanted me, I want to marry him. Ask him to come and cure me.' Then the young man enchants water and gives it to her. She drinks it and recovers. After the usual ceremonies the pair are then married.

If a young man develops a fancy for a girl, he can also use the following procedure to win her reciprocal love. He wraps certain types of plants in banana leaves, lies the bundle on a fire in an isolated place and sings a song in which the name of the girl in question is repeated over and over. He continues this for several days, until a dance takes place somewhere. On this occasion he rolls a type of cigar out of enchanted tobacco leaves and gives it to one of the girl's relatives, who has been let in on the secret, to smoke. The latter smokes part of it right in the girl's vicinity and blows the smoke in her face. He gives the rest back to the maker, who cuts it in two and places one part in the nest of a type of biting ant, and lays the other on the fire. During the night the girl suddenly experiences a strong affection for the young man. She will cry for him in public, take his hand, and beg him to marry her. Even if the youth repulses her apparently coldly, she will not give up pursuing him with pleas and cries. If she is restrained, then as soon as she is free again she runs to the young man and does not give up until he marries her.

If a wife runs out on her husband, the latter can avenge himself on her in the following way. He makes a noose out of twine, creeps carefully near the house where his wife is staying, and holds the open noose in readiness while he murmurs spells over it. As soon as the woman speaks he pulls the noose tight. Then he makes a fissure in a certain type of creeper and sticks the knotted twine in it. As soon as the first rain falls on the woman, her limbs will buckle, she will receive wounds, and generally become emaciated and die, unless a sorcerer succeeds in removing the spell. This procedure is called 'voice binding' or 'noise binding', and can also be used against men.

Another procedure is as follows: the husband attempts to obtain hair from the runaway wife, puts this in a hollowed-out fruit and carries it about with him for a while, waiting in hope that the wife returns. If this is not the case he throws the fruit with the hair into water where the kot lives. The latter is then reputed to enter the woman and gnaw away at her from within, so that she dies in great pain.

If the husband binds the hair to a certain type of swallow, the woman will then become fickle and run from one man to another.

If a cunning wife notices that her husband has

some of her hair, she goes back to him, acts as though she wants to stay with him, tries to get hold of the hair and then flees with it.

If a wife refuses to let herself be abused by a husband, the latter can avenge himself in the following way. If the woman is a *mogäang*, the husband watches in the vicinity of her house when the moon is in the first quarter. As soon as the woman goes out in the moonlight to relax from her captivity, the husband blows lime from his hand towards the moon and whispers the words: '*ivu, ivu, ivu, vuñ!*' This is supposed to cause her to bring monsters into the world or to become pregnant so frequently that she must soon die.

Still another behaviour is as follows: fruits are cut from three different trees, or a hole is bored in them, lime is sprinkled into the crevice or hole and certain spells uttered. The fruit is then crushed on paths that the woman must traverse, or buried. If the woman steps on the fruit or a piece of it, she becomes pregnant so often that she dies because of it. If a man has yearnings for a woman and she wants nothing to do with him, he can make her well-disposed towards him in the following way. He takes a coconut, murmurs spells over it and spits on the kernel. The nut is positioned where the girl or woman must eat it. When this happens, she loses her resistance against the man and willingly follows him.

To make the birth more difficult for pregnant women, the following method is used. The husband who wants to punish his wife in such a way pretends to be ill and must not speak. From time to time he moves his arms and legs convulsively, which is supposed to result in the foetus also making such movements, thereby causing the mother pain. When he believes that he has given the wife enough pain, or he fears that she will die, he pretends to be well again, and the wife will give birth without further difficulty.

A very widespread means of hurting people is *mumut*-sorcery. First of all they try to obtain food scraps, or the remains of a betel nut, or a betel leaf from the person to be harmed, and take this to the sorcerer. The latter divides this into two portions, and makes two little packets. He places one of these on the ground and kindles a fire over it; he ties the other to a rod by means of a cord, and sticks this near a pool in the ground so that the cord with the packet stretches into the water. He comes back after several days and now sees the spirit of the person who is to die sitting by the pool and staring in; he must approach very quietly so that he doesn't scare the spirit away. He then goes to the fire that he has made and kept alight over the other packet, and there sees the same spirit sitting warming itself. Then the person in question becomes ill, just from the smell of a roasted taro tuber, which indicates to his relatives that he has become the victim of *mumut*-sorcery. The bewitched person must die unless an antidote spell is used quickly. For this purpose, leaves are placed between the fingers and toes of the sick person, and likewise behind his ears. Then any kind of flying insect is caught, tied to a

Plate 13 Village scene at Nakanai

fine thread and sprinkled with lime on its abdomen. It is put into a bamboo tube and blown away so that it flies. It is now supposed to seek out the sorcerer and fly onto him; a crowd of spectators follows with shouts and cries; of course incantations are not lacking as well. On its flight the insect sprinkles lime onto the sorcerer and makes him recognisable to everybody. He is now beseeched to take the packets out of the fire and the water again; when he does this, the bewitched person becomes healthy once more. If the sorcerer cannot be moved by gifts amicably to withdraw the spell, then indeed force is used to compel him.

A drink of a grated, wild type of cucumber and the milk of a young coconut, well stirred with the bone of a flying fox should reduce the effects of the *mumut*-sorcery significantly.

Fruit trees are protected against thieves in the following way. Magical words are spoken over certain grasses which are laid on the tree trunks. Then if anyone approaches he becomes insane, eats tobacco leaves and raw taro tubers and does other nonsense. He runs round the compound with spears, clubs and stones, chasing everybody out; if anyone remains he throws something at him. One can save oneself from him by calling out the words, *o torhuk! o torhuk!* immediately he lets the upraised arm fall. He continues his disorderly behaviour until brave men catch him, throw him to the ground, and tie him up. After a short period he is set free again, secret words are murmured over a small taro, a banana and a type of yellow earth and these are given to him to eat, after which he becomes rational again.

Another method consists of the head of a certain type of bird being laid on the trunk of the fruit tree. Whoever approaches, behaves as though insane and attempts especially to imitate birds. Or else malat vines are stretched out in the mixed garden and other bewitched specimens of the same kind are buried in the ground beneath the former. If someone steps on the buried vines his upper thigh will swell and he will break his spine.

Above all, every item that must be protected against theft is invested with bewitched objects that inflict injury on a thief who carelessly approaches them.

In treading on *sma* seedlings the thief contracts severe diarrhoea. A *honpére* plants cause headaches; *ngitip* seedlings have the effect of breaking the thief's bones; coconut palms and betel palms are made safe from thieves by the bewitching of their own broad leaf-stalk ends, and tobacco plants are made safe by enchanted stones. Coming upon *mat* wood causes diarrhoea in the thief; whoever steps on *has* blossoms and dog excrement will lust to the point of madness and molest women in broad daylight, so that he must be slain.

Climbing up fruit trees that have been pelted with a bewitched stone will cause swelling of the testicles; treading on *kisong* seedlings causes a nasal ulcer, and on *mip* bark, ulcers in the armpit.

Even the murmuring of spells over fences will result in the thief who steals wood from the latter receiving a swollen head.

In addition, after the theft one can still reach the thief by sticking a human bone in the ground on the site of the stolen object; the thief will waste away and finally die.

For each of the evils that they incur by thieving, the thieves again have antidotes, except for the last-named, against which every means used proves insufficient.

A human lower jaw is wrapped with bark material, a layer of rattan is woven over it with gunhi bark and a piece of ginger tied on. The bone is exposed at both ends. It is worn into battle as a means of protection, on a string round the neck. If a weapon is raised against anyone who wears such a protection, he merely shows the bone to the attacker and the weapon falls from his hand so that he stands quite defenceless against the one attacked. However, against the Gaktei this protector is of no help, since they have similar ones that are much stronger than those of the Sulka and make the latter powerless. Also, a lower jaw gives no protection against common murder; only that the murderer of one who wears a lower jaw will die in the same way as the one whom he slew. Not everyone can create such a talisman, because only few know the necessary magic words, whose secrecy cannot be bought for anything in the world.

Using certain spells before immersion, one can be enabled to stay underwater for a long time. The same words also cure a chest infection. When the body of the sick person is rubbed with a taro leaf filled with water and wrapped with twine, while these words are uttered, the substance of the illness will go into the leaf with the water.

New canoes will be made swift by sprinkling with twigs during spells, and given protection against sinking. A new shield is brandished during incantations to make it light. By sorcery with ginger and words, catching nets will be made fruitful so that many pigs are enticed in. But should a bird's feather be substituted for ginger, the net will rip and the wild pigs get out again.

The forest can be bewitched so that an enemy's hunting remains a failure there; and there is another charm for a new house, to bring happy days to the inhabitants.

New drums, flutes and dance instruments must not be used before they are enchanted, to ensure marvelling and praise from the audience.

To make dogs aggressive so that they will attack wild pigs, a mixture of ground human bone, taro and buds of certain trees, enchanted with incantations, is thrust into the wide open mouth of the animal, whose upper and lower jaws are held apart by pieces of old loin cloth. As well as the above mixture, a ginger drink follows. Betel is chewed, and with certain incantations the dog's paws, ears and muzzle are touched with it. After this the dog is thrown over the roof of the house in such a way that he comes down on the other side. Early the following morning the animal is given warm taro to eat, his eyes are washed with a *vaul* leaf while more spells are uttered, and he is then taken on the hunt.

A young pig is made pregnant by being given coconut with milk to drink and charms murmured over it, or else the same ceremony is used as that for women. Spells also have the effect that pigs grow rapidly and become fat.

If a patch of forest has been set aside for a new garden, then the day before they begin to clear it, ginger is thrown on it and trampled in. When the patch of ground is clean and they begin to plant the enclosure, again ginger is laid on the first fence plants; thus the whole fence will serve well. Ginger and a certain type of sugar cane are also the first plants to be planted in the enclosed site, with incantations. If there is a suspicion that the site has been enchanted earlier, somebody leaps about with a *Dracaena* and a long, painted stone with ginger on it, crying öh! öh! öh! while the hewn forest is burned. The enemy's sorcery is thereby rendered ineffective. To promote the growth and prosperity of the taro and yams, one either leaps about with them, uttering spells, before they are planted, or chews betel and touches the slips to be planted out with spittle while again murmuring spells. Also, *honpére* twigs and ginger are stuck in the ground in their vicinity for the same purpose.

So that bananas and sugar cane flourish, ginger is planted nearby with incantations. Also for this purpose, many abstain from bathing in the sea, from the enjoyment of food for whose preparation sea water is used, and from taro which is well-cooked between hot stones.

When the coconut palms do not produce well, a Sulka kicks them with his feet in the very early morning as soon as the *kau* birds have sounded their calls, and utters spells at the same time.

While the gardens can be given advantage by sorcery, by use of other spells with the help of other media they can, on the other hand, be harmed, so that they fail.

There are also rainmakers among the Sulka. To enchant rain, stones are blackened with burned *vankie* fruit and laid beside certain plants and buds in the sun. After this, shrubs are laid in the water, the stones placed on them and then further shrubs on top, while a certain song is sung. Then a little house is built over the heap in the water and the rain will not be much longer in coming.

If it has rained long enough and they want it to stop again, stones are laid on the fire with incantations, and when glowing they are placed outside in the rain. The raindrops that fall on them burn themselves, and it stops raining. For the same purpose hot ash is flung in the air where, in the Sulka's opinion, the rain gets burnt.

When an enemy lays out a garden, the Sulka, with certain words, can cause the occurrence of a prolonged drought, in which the garden must of necessity perish.

Stormy seas causing ill-favoured people at sea to drown, are summoned up in the following way. A feather is enchanted by using lime and hung in a little house over a fire. When the feather begins to swing to and fro over the fire the sea becomes stormy. To restore calm to the sea, they take the feather away from the fire. Another method for the same purpose is as follows. The Sulka catch two birds, a *tongtong* and a *mursongik*, take a feather from each and let them fly away again. The sorcerer ties the feathers to a cord with a *kangi* leaf, and attaches the cord to a fishing rod which he sets into the sand on the beach, so that the feathers hang down close to the surface of the sea. As soon as he has said his incantations he hides, and then the sea adopts a stormy motion. In thunderstorms a spear is set in the ground in front of the hut entrance, with the point upwards. This will prevent a lightning strike because they believe that lightning is frightened that it might hurt itself on the spear tip. The people believe that they drive away earthquakes by sounding the shell horns and striking the big wooden drums.

If natives come visiting a village, on that day the hosts plant neither sugar cane nor *pit* because they believe that it would not then germinate. Had sugar cane or *pit* already been planted on the day when visitors came unexpectedly, the cuttings are pulled out again and laid aside. At night the digging stick is laid outside so that it gets cold. In the evening a firebrand is thrown onto the path to the garden with the cry: 'The day before yesterday warriors came (= the buds of the cuttings), today so-and-so has come with his warriors.'

Also, sleepiness overcomes the people on the occasion of a visit, so that they sleep in until broad daylight.

Anyone breaking the creeper *a kopurik*, or merely touching it, will have a sprained arm. If someone touches the fruit of the creeper *a lopakau* (which is bigger than a head), their head will swell as thick as the fruit.

If someone who is going fishing is bewitched – for example, with the words: 'Catch human bones! Catch your spirit! Catch so-and-so' (a dead person) – his labour is fruitless and he will not catch anything.

If the Sulka go to the Gaktei border and stop there, they do not name their enemies by name for otherwise these might come quickly and kill them. There they name the Gaktei *o lapsiek* (that is, rotten tree trunk), and believe that thus the limbs of their feared enemies will become clumsy.

By certain deeds the vengeance of the *kot* (see page 81) is provoked, so that the guilty person is struck by lightning or meets his death by some other natural event. Such actions are, for example, teasing a dog, forcing an animal to dance, killing a snake in the water, throwing live animals into the water, hanging a bird up by its feet, and so on. Also, whoever tells the old folktales in the daytime – this should only be done during the evening or at night – is struck by lightning.

When a boy eats the entrails or the foetus of a slain animal, his belly will be slit open in battle so that the entrails hang out. If a boy eats the flesh of a cassowary or a certain type of fish at the time his teeth are to be blackened, he will contract severe diarrhoea. If he eats the *guvin* fish, then at the appointed time when he has to hold his mouth over the fire he will develop a mouth as pointed as that of the fish.

A ring around the sun means that somewhere somebody has been slain. The ring encircling the sun is the blood of the slain person. A ring around the moon indicates that somewhere a great feast is going on. The phosphorescence of the sea is evoked by spirits, which bathe in the sea at night.

The children are forbidden to be too noisy and boisterous, because it is believed that their joy will cause a visit from native strangers.

If a person sneezes, the Sulka believe that somebody has mentioned his name.

The Sulka recount the following: several Luongan people (see tribal divisions) live apart from the others in separate villages. They prepare masks in the form of a great fish. When the mask is ready and deemed to be good, a man slides backwards inside it through the great throat. The mask is so big that he finds plenty of room inside. He takes lime and ginger with him to prevent the influx of sea water into the mask. The mask's inhabitant carries a long, sharp stone with him for cutting, and now swims around with the mask, named *lekal*, looking for people. For example, if he spots someone swimming, he approaches this victim and cuts him through in the chest region, then pulls the lower portion of the body into the throat of the mask while withdrawing towards the tail end. A child is not cut through but merely killed, and taken in one piece. The *lekal* then swims back to his home, and boasts to his people about the deed perpetrated: 'I have killed mine, now you go out and try it!' He then pulls the catch he made out of the mask; after this exhibition it is buried. In heavy seas the *lekal* cannot make headway. When he tires he goes ashore, crawls out of the mask which he puts on his shoulders, and goes further along the beach on foot. Lime and ginger make him invisible. From time to time he is heard by the Sulka when he imitates the sound of a pig.

Another tale goes as follows: a long time ago there lived a man who saw himself reflected in the water. When he saw that he was ugly he sprang into the sea and has lived there ever since. His wife, who sprang into the sea with him, bore him many children so that now the rul people have become very numerous. If taro are taken to sea in a canoe, the smell attracts the rul people, and as soon as they are seen the taro are thrown to them. The rul people seize the taro, and no longer follow the canoe, which they otherwise would surely have bored holes through.

Certain sorcerers, *o erīp*, understand the secret methods that bring about the death of people. These killing techniques are called *pur-mea* (= bewitching people). This belief of the Sulka has a great influence on their lives, and without a knowledge of this, many of their usages and customs might remain inexplicable.

Every death of a strong person, apart from those who have fallen in battle or died by suicide, is ascribed to *pur-mea* and vengeance is demanded. However, the *o erīp* sorcerers can only use this particular spell against a person who is alone when encountered. As soon as there are witnesses, the spell does not work; this also explains the unwillingness of the Sulka to go out alone. The sorcerer kills his victim either by striking, strangulation, biting through the jugular vein, pressure on various parts of the body which should cause an internal haemorrhage, or by a thrust with part of a spear or a sugar cane through the anus into the torso, and so on. He has previously enchanted the murder weapon. In order to catch the victim, he lays a snare or throws an enchanted stone at him, to cause him to fall; then he leaps on him and kills him in one of the ways described. When death has occurred, the sorcerer throws a handful of enchanted soil over the dead person, who then comes back to life and goes home. Having arrived there he feels ill and lies down, perhaps saying: 'I have been bewitched with *pur-mea*!' This confession can still save him, because an antidote spell is then used. Unfortunately many do not make this confession, because they are angry with their circle of acquaintances who let them go out alone. Death occurs in the manner that the sorcerer has arranged, after a short or long period. Sometimes the dying person names his murderer shortly before his death, and the relatives then take on the obligation of avenging the death.

After the interment one man tears a bean pod apart before the eyes of the dead man (before the little tower has been wrapped over the upper body of the corpse). When night has fallen, an eye of the dead man comes out of the grave. It is shining, and small to begin with, but grows ever larger, buzzing like a flying beetle and going up and down in the house. Those present take stalks of *pit*, rub them between their hands and cry: '*mā! mo'l! mo'l! preng! preng! preng!*' or whistle. The eye then goes out the door and takes the path to the murderer's dwelling. Rising and falling, it circles trees: the crowd follows, yelling and whistling, right to the murderer's house. The eye goes inside and circles the murderer until he knocks it to the ground and lights a fire on top of it, upon which it disappears with a loud crack. Thus the murderer is identified.

Other methods of identifying the murderer are equally irrational. For example, a tree (*Erythrina indica*) is cut down, decorated, bewitched and set in a hole in front of the dead man's house. Then, in response to questions, it will, by signs, give the identity of the murderer.

The obligation is on the dead man's relatives to avenge his death by murdering the identified sorcerer who can, however, with sufficient necklaces and armlets, still buy his freedom; otherwise he must die, even though perhaps innocent. To carry out the vengeance the relatives usually hire a skilled, strong man, who accomplishes the task with a few assistants. After the deed he stays for a while with the relatives, who in turn must protect him from the vengeance of his victim's relatives. Immediately the big drum is sounded, and a crowd of armed men comes to the house where the avenger is staying. The murdered one's group comes likewise armed, seeks the body and buries it. The following day both parties assemble in the avenger's yard. There is singing, the triton horn is blown, and the men perform war dances in which they throw their spears reciprocally into the shields. After all have received hospitality, a sham fight still takes place until finally gifts are distributed to the relatives of the murder victim, and peace is concluded. On a later day the murderer solemnly brings the murder weapon to the one who had hired him; the latter hangs it up in his hut and prepares a general feast as a fitting conclusion.

The depth of the belief in mystic murder, pur-mea, among the Sulka is demonstrated by the fact that the daily farewell greeting is an allusion to it. '*Nga pur in*' (= they kill you!) is called after somebody departing, and '*mur tugus*' (= all of us!) is his reply.

e. The Tribes of Western New Britain and the French Islands

The further westwards we go in New Britain, the less we know about the life of the inhabitants. From St George's Channel to Dampier Strait there is only one European settlement, and any observations are extremely inaccurate and incomplete due to ignorance of the language. The natives of various northern districts of the Gazelle Peninsula do trade actively with the Nakanai district, but what they tell us of the habits and customs of the Nakanai people rings patently unbelievable, and must be taken with a grain of salt. According to the stories of these Gazelle Peninsula argonauts, the Nakanai people are far beneath them in every aspect, and they relish this in portrayals whose object is to present themselves as better, more accomplished people. This is a characteristic of all natives; every conceivable wickedness is laid at the door of the esteemed neighbour, often without any justification, and we can be fairly certain that with closer investigation the reality will present itself quite otherwise.

We are already quite well informed about the Sulka tribe. Through Father W. Schmidt (*Globus*, vol. LXXXVI, no. 5), who had access to Father Bley's notes on the Sulka language, we know that these must be associated with the 'Papuan languages'; that is, languages which have no recognisable connections with the Asian mainland. This is in contrast to the Austronesian or Malayo-Polynesian languages (Polynesian, Malay, Indonesian) which point for their origin to southern Indochina and possibly even to northern peninsular India. The same goes for the Nakanai language and likewise for the Baining language, and we might well accept that the further west we go in New Britain the more predominant is the Papuan element. As far as the ethnography of these regions is known to us, Papuan features are demonstrably dominant, thereby corresponding with the spread of the language.

The designations Papuan and Melanesian have been used fairly arbitrarily up till now. Only after we have become more closely acquainted with the languages of the groups known till now as Papuans and Melanesians, do we reach a position of being able to delimit the boundaries of both groups more rigidly and precisely. Previously these designations were really only geographical concepts, so that under Papuan we understand everything belonging to the large island of New Guinea, and under Melanesian all that which extends north-westwards from Fiji and New Caledonia in numerous groups of islands: New Hebrides, Santa Cruz, Solomon Islands, Bismarck Archipelago, as far as the Admiralty Islands, and those small islets further west. Within this region it is only over time that it will become possible for us to determine which tribes are recognisable by their speech as pure Papuan or pure Melanesian. Ethnographically or anthropologically one will perhaps never succeed in establishing a sharp distinction.

In the Sulka tribe the physical resemblance to the inhabitants of Kaiser Wilhelmsland is already striking, and this similarity is greater still in the people of the opposite coast of Nakanai. There is nothing to indicate that a close, intimate trade with the tribes of the Gazelle Peninsula ever took place, which would have led to a strong intermingling of both groups. On superficial observation Baining and north-eastern Gazelle inhabitants might perhaps be regarded as members of one and the same tribe; on the other hand cursory knowledge is enough to distinguish, for example, Sulka and Nakanai people from the inhabitants of the Gazelle Peninsula. The broad nose and the coarse facial features of the latter are only present to a lesser degree in the western neighbours. In the latter a semitic cast continually appears in the face, particularly the shape of the nose, which is found almost universally in New Guinea. The further westwards we go, the more common this feature is. I remember a few years ago, during a voyage to the Willaumez Peninsula in HIMS *Möwe*, together with the then imperial governor, Herr von Bennigsen, and Herr Geheimrat Dr R. Koch and others, having seen an elderly chief at Hannamhafen whose Jewish features struck us all. This resemblance became absurdly humorous when the old gentleman, at his own request, fitted my pince-nez on his protruding organ of smell, and unconsciously called to mind the typical Jewish bankers, so well known to us from pamphlets. This characteristic facial shape, which occurs particularly strongly in men, is the sole physical difference between the western tribes and the inhabitants of the Gazelle Peninsula. In skin colour, hair growth and body height I was able to find no difference, at least no general one.

The Nakanai people are frequently distinguished by their tall stature; in general, however, body size does not go beyond average. Skin colour in western New Britain is on the whole somewhat paler than on the Gazelle Peninsula, but I believe this is due to local influences. In the plantations I have been able to observe that people from western New Britain seem paler on their arrival than the Gazelle inhabitants, probably because their homeland consists of shady forests. This paler shade had already disappeared one month later, when the people went about their daily work in the plantations.

One finds everywhere small nuances in skin colour within the individual tribes; and to use paler or darker skin as a characteristic feature, I regard as very misleading. Papuans and Melanesians have a brown basic colour, Polynesians a yellow-brown one; and within both of these groups extremes occur, on one side and the other, making it very difficult to recognise a basic shade. A very interesting example is instantly observable in the Bismarck Archipelago. Some time ago two Germans settled there, on a small island in the Duke of York group, sitting out in the sun naked for the entire day and maintaining a strongly vegetarian diet. Both people, who belonged to the very fair Germanic type have, after some time, as a result of this way of life, taken on the skin colour of the Samoans, and, were it not for the blond hair and beard, might be indistinguishable from the Samoan mission teachers, who are frequently active in the Duke of York Islands.

On a stretch of the south coast of New Britain, beginning about 15 nautical miles west of Cape Roebuck and extending as far as Cape Pedder, including the Arawa Islands offshore, we find a unique skull form produced by artificial deformation. In the entire protectorate I know of nothing similar or related. In the Solomon Islands this peculiar custom is also unknown; we come across it again only on the island of Malikolo (New Hebrides). The custom does not extend to the opposite, north coast of New Britain, although the inhabitants of both coasts are frequently engaged in peaceful trade along the land route. Deformation is practised by both sexes, but is not universal, for in each village a number of natural heads are also seen, as well as the deformed heads.

I have not been able to learn anything about the reason and purpose of this deformation; to my question: 'Why?' the answer was always given: 'The women say that it is beautiful!' I therefore tend to feel that we are dealing here with one of those widespread practices whose sole purpose is to enhance beauty. Thus skull deformation belongs with tattooing, scarring and wounding which the men of numerous native peoples undergo in order to appear more worthy to women.

Deformation is undertaken immediately after

Fig. 23 Group of women from the 'Liebliche Inseln'. (The children show the wrapping of the head)

the child's birth, by wrapping the head firmly with bark bandages, above the eyes. This wrapping is renewed daily and continues until the desired shape is obtained; that is, until the child is about 18 months old. Figure 10, on page 57, of a boy of about fourteen years old, is better than any description in demonstrating the peculiar shape of the deformed skull, for which these people have attracted the characteristic designation of 'pointed heads' from the local settlers. Apart from this artificial deformation of the upper head, the people are just like their neighbours both in their facial features and in other body form.

In each village there is a headman; if the villages are very large they often support several headmen. Nowhere does the headman seem to possess great power; he appears to be the central point around which the heads of the families or the oldest members of the families gather for advice. Both on the French Islands and Arawa I was able to observe that they threw out propositions of the so-called headman which differed occasionally from those of the older villagers, and that the same man submitted freely to the opinions of the majority. In all festivities the headman appears to be the leader, he is governor of the feast to some extent, and in battle too, if his age permits, he takes the position of a leader. At a celebration of peace between the natives of Arawa and a village opposite on the main island of New Britain, the festively decorated Arawa people travelled in their canoes to the village of their former adversaries. The Arawa headman delivered a speech to the mainland warriors assembled on the beach, which was replied to by one of the latter. Then betel nuts were offered by one group to the other and the Arawa people left their canoes and mingled among their former enemies. Pigs, dogs, produce of all kinds, fish, and so on, were then hauled out by both sides, and mutually distributed. However, according to people's assertions wars must be very common, and a minor offence can lead to feuds and blood-letting. As a consequence, on sites where fairly large villages were to be found earlier, no houses or people are present a few years later, since the inhabitants have sought a new dwelling site. On the islands the villages are more durable, probably because their sites are more secure and less exposed to rapacious attack.

Fortification of the villages can well be ascribed to this general uncertainty. This consists of a palisade wall with a narrow entrance. In Nakanai these palisades are even doubled in places, and it would prove difficult for an enemy to pass undetected through these. On a brief excursion inland from Möwehafen I encountered extensive gardens that had been established by the natives living on the islands around Möwehafen. The shelter huts erected in the gardens were likewise surrounded by a double, high palisade, and at our approach the entire group of men sought refuge in their fortress. Only after long entreaties did they open the barricaded entrance and allow us to enter. Apart from a primitive hut there was nothing noteworthy, except for a fairly roughly made, wooden, slit drum which was being beaten loudly on our arrival, probably to give the neighbours warning. On our departure the drum was beaten again, and when we reached a similar fortress about ten minutes later we found the people armed, but calmly standing in front of the entrance. One could conclude from this that these natives too know how to send intelligible drum signals to their neighbours.

Pitched battles are not undertaken. Each side endeavours to surprise the other, and whoever perceives themselves threatened with this, retreats as quickly as possible. Nevertheless these wars can occasionally have a very bloody outcome and cost the lives of a relatively large number of people. In the bay formed between the western side of Willaumez Peninsula and the main island (Stettiner Bucht on the maps) there are numerous villages, formerly heavily populated. I visited one of these years ago, and then journeyed on to the eastern side of the peninsula, before returning. On the return journey the ship anchored off the same village, but although barely a week separated the two visits, I found the village, which had consisted of about forty huts, completely destroyed. The houses were ashes, and a frightful smell of corpses drove us quickly from the devastated site. Inhabitants of neighbouring villages, who came alongside in their canoes, told us that inland tribes had surprised the village and slain all the inhabitants. Since the nearest neighbours are quite often the most bitter enemies, I did not place much trust in these tales; yet in this case I may have been told the truth, for in the neighbouring villages I discovered great unrest; women and children did not venture outside the enclosure, and these villages had been reinforced and modified to withstand an attack. Whoever may have carried out the attack, this much is certain: no less than 100 natives had lost their lives.

We should not be surprised that population numbers are not increasing under such conditions, the more so since many other circumstances are contributing to the decline. It has frequently been presented as fact that colonisation by whites, and the illnesses and vices brought with them, gave rise to the universal decay of the people of nature. More particularly, the dying out of the people of nature has been ascribed to spirits, in the form of common schnapps. There may indeed be areas where schnapps has this result, yet in Africa, where enjoyment of this product of material culture is flourishing, no great decline is noticeable. In the New Guinea protectorate, schnapps cannot be blamed, since its delivery to natives is banned, and its importation for sale to the natives has never occurred. There are totally different factors leading to the destruction of the South Seas people. To come back to New Britain, a smallpox epidemic tore enormous gaps in the western part of the island years ago. The epidemic had been introduced into Friedrich Wilhelmshafen from Java, and the inadequate protective regulations resulted in the illness infecting a large part of the coast of Kaiser Wilhelmsland and then, by trade,

Plate 14 Youth from Unea (French Islands)

leaping across Rook Island to New Britain, where it spread roughly as far as South Cape along the south coast and on the north coast as far as Nakanai. The result of this devastating epidemic, against which the natives were completely unprotected, can still be seen there in the significant decline of the previously quite numerous populations of the various districts, and one finds only mature adult men and women and the younger generation which was born after the epidemic. The population that was then in childhood and old age appears to have been totally annihilated. Not quite so devastating as epidemics, but nonetheless damaging, is the custom that on a native's death his wives are strangled. This custom is widespread in western New Britain, and nowhere in the archipelago does abortion and infanticide occur to such an extent as here.

No great care is taken in the construction of huts; the exceptions are those buildings that serve for certain celebrations and assemblies of the men, circumcision ceremonies in particular. In many places – for example, Nakanai and the Cape Merkus region – several families share one hut. These huts are long and low with several entrances; the interior is sometimes divided into different sections by mat walls, but just as often not. Here old and young dwell on the bare earth. In Nakanai men and women are often seen alongside the family pet, a fat pig, stretched out asleep, and it is self-evident that under such circumstances special attention is not paid to cleanliness. When the ground in the huts is sodden from heavy showers, dirty puddles appear and without further ado these are used as resting places for men and animals, so that it is often quite difficult to distinguish the pigs from the natives. On the French Islands when the terrain permits the huts are built in opposing rows, and I have observed this also on the Willaumez Peninsula; however, there is no general rule for group layout, for huts are found grouped around an open space or irregularly spread over it, with equal frequency. Towards the western end of New Britain we find reminders of the hut construction in Kaiser Wilhelmsland opposite, where as well as huts built on level ground there are also huts resting on poles, with a raised floor, below which is a free space for storage of all kinds of objects. In this area we also come across villages on poles, which differ only slightly from those in Kaiser Wilhelmsland. The open sea coast is never chosen for this; they prefer sheltered bays with shallow water, surrounded by mangrove swamps, which give the pole village inhabitants security against attacking enemies, partly as hiding places, and partly because they hinder the approach of an enemy, and in some places make it totally impossible.

Although the great majority of natives of western New Britain devote no great care of their dwellings, they are quite fastidious in their nourishment, and cultivate a fairly wide variety of foodstuffs. Tubers of taro and yams, especially the former, are planted in regular gardens, bananas are planted everywhere, and the coconut is not lacking either, even if not in great stands as in the northern half of New Ireland. We are largely unfamiliar with these tribes because of the low incidence of the coconut palm, since traders who establish themselves everywhere where there are products to barter, did not find a fertile field for trade anywhere here. The only exceptions were the French Islands, where large stands of coconut palms allow one to infer a previously significant population. Food is roasted over a charcoal fire, cooked between glowing stones, or cooked in bubbling hot springs as on the island of Naraga (French Islands). A more or less lively trade in earthenware cooking pots is carried out from the Tami Islands on the coast of Kaiser Wilhelmsland, especially along the south coast of New Britain as far as South Cape. This trade is less on the north-west coast and does not seem to extend beyond Cape Raoult. In those areas mentioned the familiar Tami pot is found occasionally, if only a few examples. People from Arawa advised me of the price of the pot, and even by native standards it is very high.

Pigs and dogs provide the natives with animal protein, and the various marsupials of the forest are also slain in great numbers for this purpose. Turtles are caught along the coast in great, wide-meshed nets. Similar nets, prepared from thicker cord and of enormous length, are used during forest hunting drives to surround great flat areas, into which the prey, mainly wild pigs, are driven.

I want to introduce here a peculiar, I might even say unique, industry, carried out in the region of Möwehafen – the harvesting of salt from the sea. Low huts are built with a simple roof to keep out the rain. Both side walls are open so that two light frames, one on either side, can be pulled out and pushed in again. These frames, about 75 centimetres wide, serve to support a large number of small troughs, made from pandanus leaves, side by side. The troughs contain sea water which vaporises when exposed to the sun. Through continued addition of sea water and the subsequent evaporation, a salt crust forms in the troughs; when this seems sufficiently thick, the leaf troughs are rolled together and tied in bundles, to be traded with inland neighbours. That salt harvesting did not extend far from here, even though salt water forms an almost universal trade item, is probably due to the great isolation of individual tribes one from another.

Eating utensils (and what can be regarded as such) are relatively extensive. Almost every adult male carries a spatula-like bone tool, used for breaking open betel nuts or removing the flesh from the coconut shell, on a cord round his neck or between arm and armring, or in the almost omnipresent shoulder bag. Sharp bamboo slivers and sharpened oyster shells both serve universally as knives for carving food. The coconut grater, a *Cardium* shell bound firmly to a little board, is never absent. Food is often served on fresh banana leaves; however, they also use plaited circular bowls or plates with or without a rim for this purpose, as well as oblong wooden dishes like those familiar on the Tami Islands. I have grounds for believing that many of the bowls that we encountered in the Tami Islands and around Finschhafen, were made on the south coast of New Britain, in the region between South Cape and Cape Merkus. Not only did the natives there mention that the Tami people have a predilection for bartering for the wooden bowls, but I also found bowls in widely varying stages of manufacture on the tiny inhabited islands round Möwehafen. The characteristic decoration which distinguishes one end of this type of wooden bowl, particularly the large specimen, was produced with care in every case, as was the smaller decoration on the side. This type of bowl is found from South Cape to the westernmost point, as well as on the Willaumez Peninsula and the French Islands. In both the latter regions, local manufacture is out of the question; the French Islands allude to the wooden bowls of the main island of New Britain opposite; and, on the Willaumez Peninsula, the interior of the main island is designated as the site of origin; probably the bowls pass along the trade route from one coast of the island to the other.

Cooking is universally a task for the women, although the men occasionally lend a hand, especially in roasting pig and dog. As with most Melanesians, the main meal takes place in the late afternoon, after the necessary material has been gathered during the day, from the gardens, in the forest, or on the sea. Any leftovers are packed in baskets and stored until the next mealtime; in this case when they get up in the morning they eat some of the food. Young coconuts provide drink only during festivities; usually cold water is drunk at mealtimes, and, almost without exception, empty coconut shells provide water containers, stopped with a leaf, sometimes singly and sometimes two or three wound with cords and tied together.

Fire lighting is achieved by friction, as throughout the Bismarck Archipelago.

Luxury items of the natives of this part of New Britain are the same everywhere, namely tobacco and betel with the necessary adjuncts. Tobacco, which was introduced not long ago on the Gazelle Peninsula and the rest of the archipelago by the white traders, has already been in use for a long time in western New Britain, and without doubt had been imported from Kaiser Wilhelmsland opposite. The domestic plant is evil-smelling and has an absolutely frightful taste, no doubt partly as a result of insufficient preparation; nevertheless smoking has spread everywhere, and young and old seem to be imbued with the greatest sense of well-being when they exhale the dense, stinking smoke into the air. The plant is rolled together between the hands and wrapped in a green leaf; after the smoker has taken a few powerful draws, the thick cigar passes to the next man, and so on until the last remnant has died out. For chewing betel the same ingredients are used as elsewhere: areca nuts, betel pepper or leaves, and burnt lime. The lime containers are frequently prepared with great care, sometimes out of a flask-like squash, sometimes from a piece of bamboo cane.

The close relationship of these tribes with the Papuans shows especially in their ornaments and items of decoration. On the French Islands and Willaumez we encounter the wing-like armbands bedecked with *Nassa* snail shells. We find these from Cape Cretin to Friedrich-Wilhelms-Hafen; besides this, boars' tusks and dog teeth stand in high regard, just as on the coast of Kaiser Wilhelmsland opposite. On the other hand forms are produced which have to be regarded as typical of certain regions. Figures 25 and 26 give an approximate idea of the richness of their jewellery, as well as of the resemblance to similar objects from New Guinea, and characteristic deviations of individual objects. Decoration is worn especially during dancing and festivities, although it is never entirely absent in everyday life. In Nakanai, in the region of Möwehafen, and on the Arawa Islands it is the men in particular who are distinguished by decoration; girls and women are less decorated and occasionally appear to borrow the men's items of adornment. At any rate, I have not been able to observe a characteristic item of female decoration anywhere.

Plaited rings, especially piled high, serve as head decoration, and are worn on certain occasions in Nakanai (fig. 26, nos 17, 18). These rings, six to ten in number, are 1 to 5 centimetres wide; that is, the lowermost ring is the narrowest, each succeeding one is gradually broader. The outer rim of the flat ring made of fine plaiting, is sewn with scale-like shell discs (*Nassa*) laid over one another. Usually the narrowest of the rings is laid first on top of the cloud-like, combed-up hair, then follows the second and gradually the remainder, so that the broadest ring forms the uppermost layer. Instead of rings they also wear plaited caps, consisting of a single piece in the shape of a truncated cone, on the outer surface of which the *Nassa* discs are then sewn in a ring, achieving the same effect as with the rings piled on top of one another. Over this ornament the hair is frizzed out in the form of a hemisphere and pierced with the small bright feathers of various parrots, a hairstyle that has to be described as very tasteful and original. Powell, in his book, *Wanderings in a Wild Country*, gives an illustration of this hair decoration; however, it

Fig. 24 Men of Möwehafen

is arranged incorrectly, as he shows the broadest ring below and the narrowest above, instead of the order being just the reverse. Everywhere the face is beautified by painting; in Nakanai it is anointed with red ochre, and white lines of powdered lime are added around the eyes and over cheeks and nose. The nasal septum is pierced, as on the Gazelle Peninsula, and a cassowary pinion, decorated at the ends with *Nassa* discs, is pushed through the hole. Earrings are found everywhere, in the most varied shapes. A generally more extensive earring consists of a ring-shaped disc of turtle shell, 3 to 6 centimetres in diameter, whose outer rim is sewn with small discs of *Nassa* (fig. 26, no. 9). These earrings (*sip* on South Cape) are worn individually or in bundles of six to ten in the markedly extended ear lobes. On the island of Mérite (Unea) the ear ornament has a marked resemblance to a similar ornament on Kaniet and Wuwulo, where admittedly it is only worn by women, while on Mérite it is a distinction of the men. The uncommonly extended ear lobe, which hangs as far as the shoulder, is adorned with a large number of turtle shell rings, about 15 millimetres in diameter. The number of rings varies, and ranges from fifty to more than 100; on the lower end is a plaited band about 4 centimetres wide and 12 centimetres long, closely decorated with four to six rows of *Nassa* discs, pushed through and bent over, so that the whole ornament does not weigh much less than 0.5 kilograms. In the Arawa Islands they wear only this plaited band decorated with *Nassa* snails, from the end of which one or several sea snails hang; in this form it is called *noknok*.

Headbands are favoured especially in the French Islands and Willaumez; however, they are also found in the same form on the south coast of New Britain opposite, where they are called *neningo*. These are about 20 centimetres long and consist of a lower band of two to three rows of scale-like *Nassa* diskettes laid over the top of one another. Over this is a quadruple row of dog canine teeth, arranged so that the rows of teeth are placed opposite each other; that is, the points of all teeth in the lower row are pointed to the right, those in the second row to the left, in the third to the right, and in the fourth to the left (fig. 25, no. 5).

For pinning up the hair they use various comb-like instruments, which are left sticking in the hair, partly to have them always at hand, partly also as ornament (fig. 25, nos 3 and 4). In the latter case the part of the pin or comb sticking out is sometimes decorated with bright bird feathers, and sometimes by being wrapped around with *Nassa* snail shells, coir seeds and so on. At Montague Bay the men wear huge wigs of cassowary feathers, attached to a hemispherical plaitwork covering the upper half of the head. On the crown is attached a bunch of red parrot feathers. I tend to regard this wig as a war decoration, possibly also a dance decoration; in any case I saw this head-covering only on my first visit, when through unfamiliarity with the whites, the people exhibited hostility; I

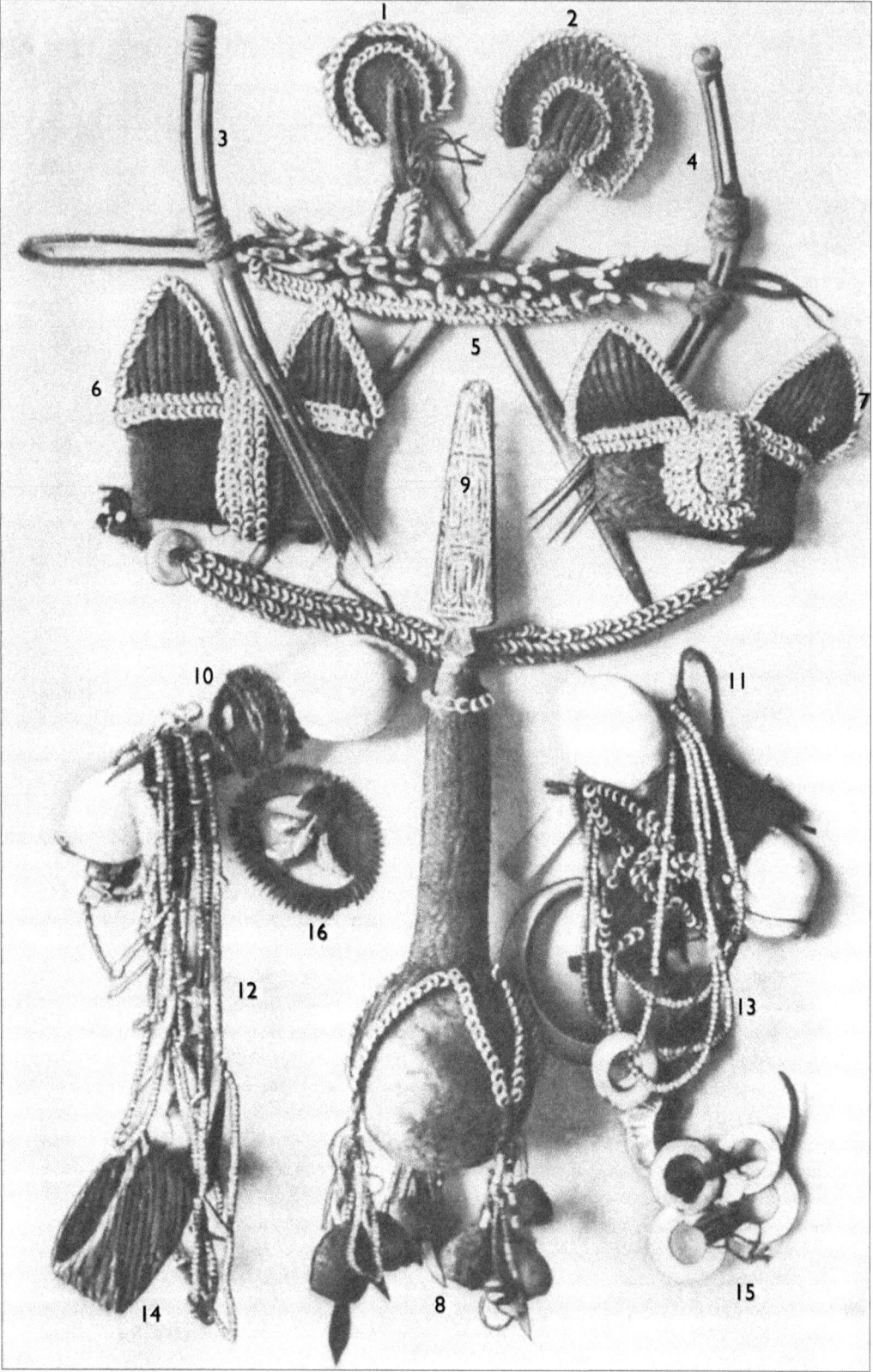

Fig. 25 Decorations and other items from the French Islands

1. and 2. lime spatula; 3. and 4. hair pin; 5. headband; 6. and 7. armbands; 8. lime container; 9. girdle; 10. and 11. chest ornament; 12. and 13. necklaces; 14. armband; 15. chest ornament; 16. hair ornament

did not see it later in use, although it was offered to me for sale.

The beard is removed, almost throughout the entire western part of New Britain and on the French Islands; partly by shaving with sharp obsidian slivers, and partly by plucking individual hairs of the beard. Various seashells are used for the latter purpose; the hairs are clasped between a pair of shells and removed with a sharp tug, or each individual hair is clasped between two thin cords that are twisted together. The hair is also twisted in with the cords and then pulled out.

Neck and chest ornaments are encountered abundantly in all tribes, and the closer one gets to the western end of New Britain, the more closely does this type of ornament resemble that of Kaiser Wilhelmsland, not only in form but also in production materials. *Nassa* snail shells and coir seeds are wound round the neck in various arrangements singly or in several strands as cords and bands, likewise strings of about 3-centimetre-long pieces of cassowary pinion, strung in such a way that the individual pieces are separated by two or three *Nassa* snail shells; coir kernels are also used instead of *Nassa* snail shells, but not as often. These types of strings are found both on the north and south coasts, and on the French Islands; they seem to be regarded everywhere as a form of currency; in any event they are stored in very large quantities, packed in baskets in the huts, so they are apparently not used exclusively as objects of adornment. For this purpose they are wound in numerous rows round the neck so that they hang down over the chest. Quite often the chest ornament hanging over the chest is attached to the neck ornament. The former, which also provides chest protection in many parts of Kaiser Wilhelmsland (which indeed is why we regard it as a battle ornament there), is exclusively an ornament here and is not in a position to protect the wearer against any kind of wound. On the northern side of New Britain and on the French Islands, we come across the familiar Ovula snail shells from Kaiser Wilhelmsland, attached in such a way that they abut one another on their long axes. Plaiting is attached at the joints, embroidered with *Nassa* shells or with coir seeds, and a triple-lobed network decorated with *Nassa* embroidery forms the lower part of the ornament (fig. 25, nos 10 and 11). On the south coast pig tusks seem to stand in higher regard than Ovula snail shells. As a rule they are arranged in pairs; the more closely they approach a complete ring shape, the greater their value. Smaller boar tusks which form only a half-circle, or are even smaller, are either attached in pairs or in several pairs to a 15- to 25-centimetre-long, rod-like plaiting that is decorated on the edges with *Nassa* snail shells; the attachment points are wound round with *Nassa* strings (fig. 27, nos 1-3). These types of chest or-nament are always worn on strings of *Nassa* snail shells, arranged in rows like the *tabu* of the Gazelle Peninsula, or else in bands plaited from fine fibre in characteristic ways.

Nassa snail shells, which find such abundant use here as items of decoration, do not seem to hold the position of money as they do on the Gazelle Peninsula. On the greater part of the south coast of New Britain they are known as *eddi*, a name that calls to mind the plate-shaped neckbands, *middi*, of the Gazelle Peninsula. I refer to the more detailed description of this ornament in the discussion of items of decoration from the Gazelle Peninsula.

Besides the items of decoration already discussed, we find large polished rings made from seashell, attached to one another in pairs like the boars' tusks, worn as chest ornaments, on both the north and south coasts. They are almost always produced from the thick end of a certain large species of *Conus* shell; I have never noticed *Tridacna* rings, probably because the art of boring is unknown.

Held in very high regard is a chest ornament of the large, golden-rimmed mother-of-pearl shell. The outside of the shell is ground clean and polished, and the closed end is completely removed so that only a half-moon-shaped piece of the shell remains. It is very difficult to get hold of these breast-plates, which are seemingly highly treasured.

Girdles are not worn everywhere but turn up occasionally. On Nakanai, strings of *Pele* discs from the Duke of York Islands, which have reached here by trading, are wrapped round the waist. On festive occasions men, especially, wear these strings in great numbers so that they form a thick pad. The Sulka and almost all the inhabitants of the south coast wear bark loincloths; these are up to 4 metres long and about 25 centimetres wide, and are often decorated with very tasteful designs.

Armlets are present in great abundance. On Nakanai they are prepared from turtle shell, and a great number, often as many as twenty, are laid on top of one another; they are then attached to one another by thin bast fibres. *Trochus* rings are everywhere, both those that are only slightly prepared, as well as those that are carefully ground and polished. On the north coast, west of the Willaumez Peninsula, the *Trochus* armlets are furnished with an engraved pattern and the indentations are filled with a black resin, so that a black and white design is produced, like that reproduced in figure 28. This type of decorated armlet is also found abundantly on the coast of New Guinea opposite, which it has reached through trading via the Rook Islands. Of far greater significance, however, are the plaited armlets, which display a very great diversity in form as well as in decoration, yet almost always show the greatest correspondence with similar objects from Kaiser Wilhelmsland (figs 25 and 26).

Complete armlets are plaited, and the plaiting

consists of thin fibres about 1 millimetre wide, which in part retain their natural grey or grey-brown shade, and are also stained red, yellow and black in part. The production is so painstaking that at first glance one believes that one is observing a dense, smooth tissue. Often the fibrous material is first plaited into cords 3 to 5 millimetres wide, which are then processed into armlets, by which the plaiting attains a rougher and coarser texture. In the French Islands, as on almost the entire north coast, but most frequently towards the west, they use a cord made of golden yellow fibre for such plaiting; this is identical to the cords that Dr Finsch illustrated in his Erfahrungen und Belegstücke, plate XXII (14), figure 3, from Finschhafen. These types of golden yellow cords cover a wide area; I have come across them both in Huon Bay and in Finschhafen, and also in Astrolabe Bay. They are prepared apparently as trade items, for west of the Willaumez Peninsula, as in Huon Bay, great hanks of this material were offered to me. Besides this plaited cord, a similarly prepared dark brown cord is found, especially west of Willaumez, and as a rule both are used together as material for armlets, in such a way that the golden yellow cords stand out as decoration against the dark brown background.

Seldom do the armrings consist of simple plaiting; in most cases they are sewn with *Nassa* shells. The edges are almost always embellished with a single or double row of closely abutting *Nassa* discs, often vertical rows of the same snail shell are laid transversely across the plaiting from edge to edge, or they form a zigzag line between the upper and lower edges. From Nakanai along the entire north coast and on the French Islands the armrings are not infrequently adorned on the upper edge with triangular single or double lobes, as we find so often in Kaiser Wilhelmsland.

These kinds of armrings from Willaumez can scarcely be distinguished from those of Finschhafen, although the industry is a local one in both places. Of course it is not impossible that these kinds of products also pass from hand to hand or from tribe to tribe along trade routes, or as gifts at festivities, as marriage gifts, and so on, and might occasionally be found far from their place of manufacture.

On the south coast armlets sewn with *Nassa* are worn less; here simple, closely plaited armbands 2 to 3 centimetres wide are more common. On South Cape, a bunch of white fibres or several long, bleached pandanus ribs are stuck in behind it.

On the Willaumez Peninsula and in the French Islands the wrist is encased in a cuff of densely packed plaiting. This cuff is not uncommonly plaited from variously coloured strips of fibre, so that bright patterns are created. In the same regions a very similar closely packed plaiting quite often also surrounds the ankle, and frequently extends 10 to 15 centimetres up the leg from the ankle joint.

Both items are plaited directly onto the body of the wearer, and can only be removed by cutting off. Anklets made of 5- to 7-millimetre-wide strips of rattan, roll-shaped and 5 to 7 millimetres broad, are worn both in the north and the south.

The universally occurring decorative scars, found both on men and women, have to be regarded as body decoration. Usually arms and chest are decorated with these scars, in some places the upper thigh as well. They are very arbitrary in design and never form a particular figure; the most common are circles, or rows of several juxtaposed transverse or longitudinal scars.

Tattooing is only encountered very occasionally, and is restricted to single broad lines, either above the eyes or across the cheeks. These bands consist of closely adjacent lines, about 3 millimetres long, scratched with a sharp sliver of obsidian and then rubbed with black colouring material – ash from charcoaled coconut shell as a rule. In Nakanai you come across this tattooing most often, and it has undoubtedly been introduced from the Gazelle Peninsula natives, because it has the same patterns as there.

Weapons used in the western part of New Britain are the same everywhere, namely slingshots, spears and clubs.

Shields are borne everywhere as protection against wounding, just as in Kaiser Wilhelmsland; on the other hand bows and arrows have never been observed. Around South Cape we find a weapon that, in its style forms an exception for the South Sea islands and also for New Guinea, namely the blowpipe, *a iu* or *lambu*, and the dart blown from it, *ingra*. The blowpipe is not used as a weapon of war, however. It is used exclusively in hunting birds; yet it is noteworthy that this Indonesian instrument is encountered here. The blowpipe is made of various thumb-thick pieces of a particular, thin-walled species of bamboo joined together. The single tubes are carefully pushed into one another; the sites of the joints are smeared with resin and tightly wrapped with cords of fine fibre. The whole instrument is 3 to 4 metres long. The darts consist of 1-metre-long, thin bamboo slivers; one end is cut to a long, needle-sharp point, the other end is tightly wrapped in a down-like plant material over a length of 10 to 15 centimetres. In hunting birds, the hunter creeps as close as possible to his prey and then aims the long blowpipe, in such a way that he has a tree branch or something for support. The dart is then blown full blast out of the pipe, and an experienced hunter almost always hits his target over a range of about 20 metres. In hunting four-footed animals, especially pigs and wallabies, a spear is used in conjunction with the previously mentioned, wide-meshed, set nets into which the wild animals are driven. Hunting spears are not different from war spears,

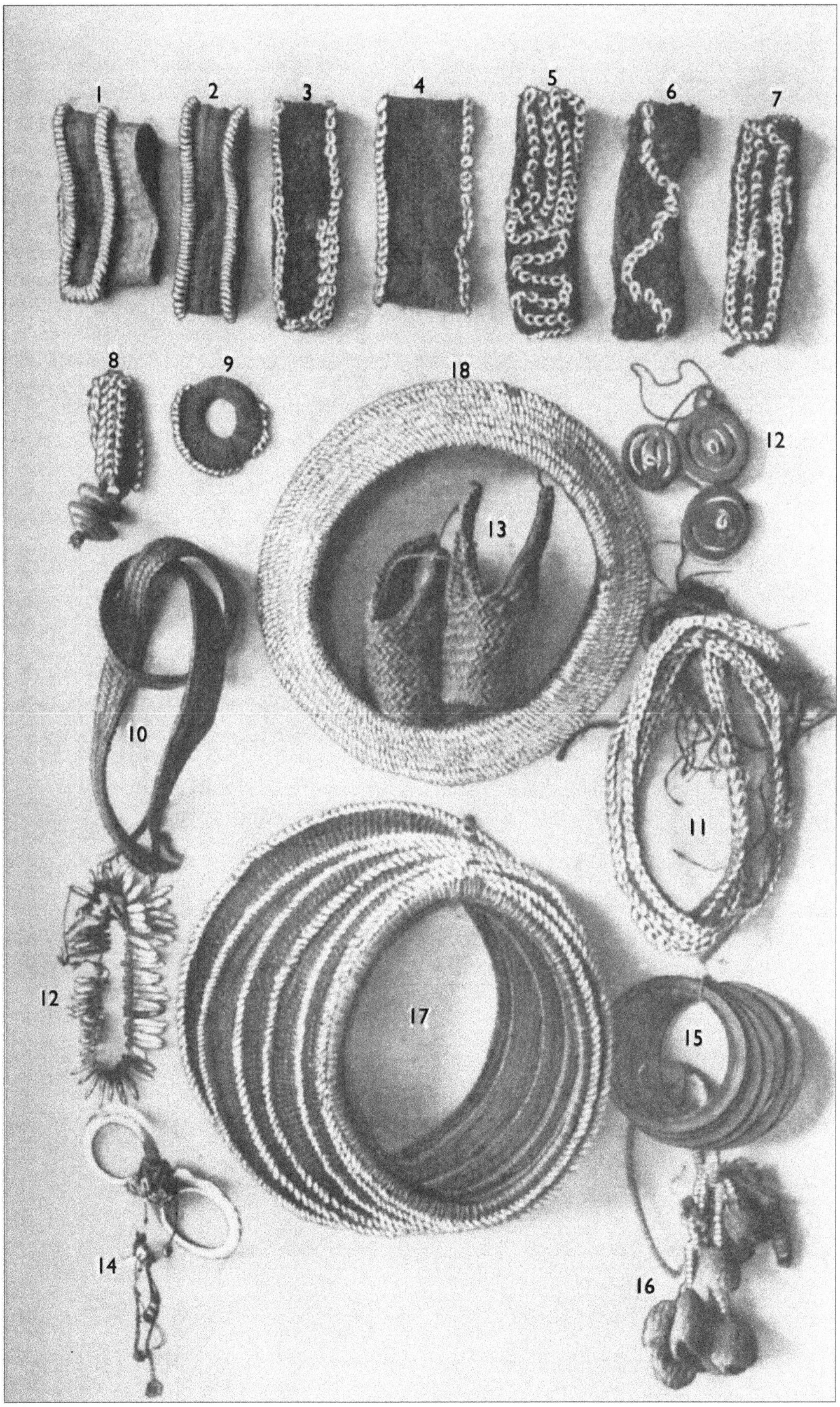

Fig. 26 Items of decoration from the Willaumez Peninsula and the adjacent coast

1. to 7., and 13. armlets; 8. and 9. earrings; 10. and 11. girdle; 12. necklaces; 14. chest ornament; 15. turtle shell arm rings; 16. girdle ornament (rattle); 17. and 18. head rings

although spears certainly differ in form in the various regions. In Nakanai, among the Sulka and the neighbouring tribes, the spear is made from a specific palm wood and is 3 to 4 metres long as a rule; the sharp end is very often armed with a cassowary claw, which remains fixed when the spear is withdrawn from the wound, giving rise to severe inflammation and pus discharge. A 4 to 5 metre lance is familiar on Nakanai although it is used only in rare cases as a weapon, and is much more a ceremonial spear which on special occasions is carried as a distinction by those who are entitled to it. The front end is armed with a cassowary claw and a cassowary leg bone is fastened on the rear end. About 25 centimetres above the bone the spear is wrapped in a layer of thin palm leaves, which serves as the base for a long band of *Nassa* shells joined flush edge to edge (fig. 30), in which the spear is tightly wrapped over a length of 1 to 1.5 metres.

Both the upper and the lower ends of the wrapping are surrounded with a cuff-like plaiting of bast fibres, besides which larger and smaller tassels of white cockatoo feathers are inserted into the wrapping. Ordinary war spears never have this decoration; they are completely smooth from one end to the other.

On the French Islands and on Willaumez, as well as west and east from there, we find spears with the front end adorned with two rows of barbs. These barbs consist of either strongly bent thorns of a certain species of plant, or more often of the bristly spikes with which various fish species are armed. These thorns are 5 to 15 millimetres long, very pointed and sharp, and are set in two opposing rows from 2.5 to 6 centimetres apart. The part of the spear armed in such a way is 75 centimetres to 1 metre long. Attachment of the thorns is highly characteristic. Each barb has a broad basal area that is used for attachment in an ingenious manner. First of all the end of the spear is tightly wrapped in a fibrous cord about 1 millimetre thick, and the barbs, in opposing pairs, are fastened into the binding by laying on strips of rattan about 5 millimetres wide. The strips, which cover the broad base of the barbs, secure these by being wrapped round the body of the spear. The entire reinforced part of the spear is then rubbed with *Parinarium* resin to give even greater security to the barbs, which become so closely bound to the shaft that they seem to be growing from it. A wide binding of red fibres and plaited cords completes it. At regular intervals between the barbs small tufts of red-dyed fibres and coir seeds are fastened, also tufts of coloured bird feathers. Another form of spear has a smooth tip with or without cassowary claw, and a cassowary bone on the rear end. About 20 centimetres below the bone the spear is wrapped in fibrous material up to a length of 30 to 35 centimetres. This binding consists of red fibrous material at both ends, about 8 to 10 centimetres long; in the middle there is plaiting of black, red and yellow fibre strips about 2 millimetres wide.

With good and careful manufacture of the plaiting, the individual, coloured woven strips are arranged in such a way that yellow, red and black rings and zigzags alternate with one another. The plaiting often recalls similar plaiting round spears on Bougainville, or clubs from the south-eastern Solomon Islands. Although preparation of the various war spears is universally familiar, material is not available everywhere. In the French Islands cassowary claws and bones are obtained from New Britain opposite via the trade route. As a rule cassowary bones are wrapped in bundles of ten, and often great numbers of such bundles are found stored in the huts on Mérite and Deslacs.

Towards the western end of New Britain these barbed spears are less common and the war spear as a rule is completely smooth and round with a

Fig. 27 Items of decoration from the south coast of New Britain

1. chest ornament; 2. and 3. chest ornament with necklace; 4. earrings; 5. money cord (also necklace).

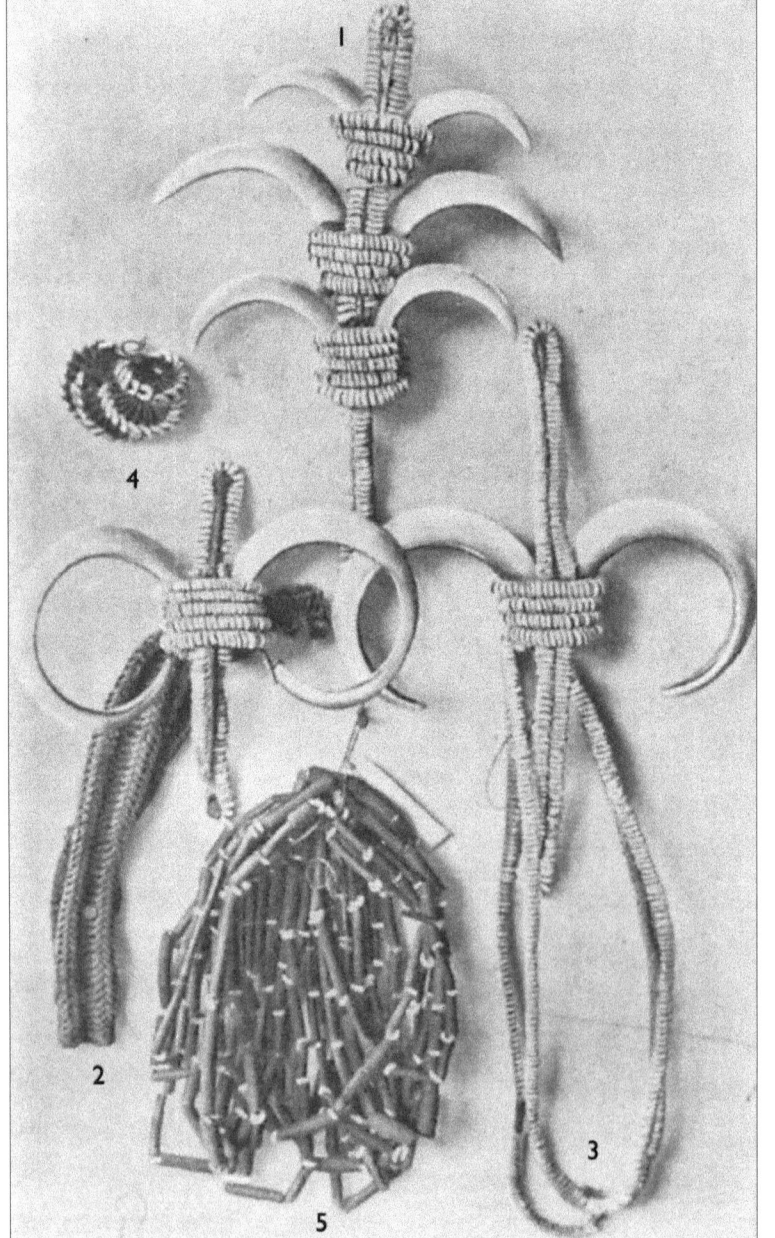

long tip; the butt end is especially thinned, and the thickest part of the spear is always its mid-section. At Cape Gloucester years ago I saw, quite sporadically, spears that were wrapped with possum skin somewhat below the point. Since such spears are common in Kaiser Wilhelmsland, but apparently seem to occur only occasionally on the western end of New Britain, it may be assumed that they arrived there through trading.

Among the distance weapons belongs the universally used slingshot. This, as on the Gazelle Peninsula, is produced from a bowl-like cushion of pandanus leaf with two long cords. In the French Islands and on the north coast of New Britain the cushion is produced from the fibrous plaiting which covers the base of the coconut leaves, and the two cords are carefully plaited from fine fibres. The cord, which is held in the hand when hurling the stone, is provided with a disc of turtle shell the size of a 2 Mark piece [about 27 mm diameter], to prevent the cord held between the middle and index fingers from slipping out of the hand. The second cord, which is released when firing, is held between the thumb and bent index finger; it is smooth on the upper end so that it can be released easily.

Slingshot stones are available in great numbers of suitable size and shape from riverbeds everywhere. In the French Islands, supplies are obtained from the main island of New Britain opposite, where small wide-meshed net pouches plaited from lianas, filled with the ammunition, can be seen in the markets.

Clubs are found particularly among the Sulka and their neighbours, and are of a characteristic shape and highest quality manufacture. Both figures depict the shapes of the principal clubs of these areas. All of these clubs have a larger or smaller cone-shaped knob on the grip end.

Club 1 in figure 32 is found often on the Nakanai coast, although it has without doubt been traded from the hill tribes. Among the Sulka this club is fairly widespread. The whole club is round and the striking end in cross-section is narrowly lancet-shaped, and reasonably tapering. Clubs 2, 3 and 8 are likewise fairly common among the Sulka and their neighbouring tribes; 2 strongly calls to mind the club named *virki* by the Baining, which is known also as *tawa* or *talum* on the north-east Gazelle Peninsula, where the head of the club does not, however, taper as in the Sulka version.

Numbers 3 and 8 are, to a certain extent, modifications of number 2; however, number 8 might have arisen from an attempt to copy a club with a stone head. Clubs 4, 5, 6 and 7 are from the same region, but they are mainly a product of the inland tribe, the Tumuip, or, as they are called by the Nakanai people, the Paleawe, which is why these clubs are found now and then in Nakanai, where

Fig. 28 Decoration of a *Trochus* armlet

Fig. 29 Men of Mérite (French Islands)

Plate 15 Village on the French Islands (Naraga)

they have arrived as battle trophies. They are carved into a pineapple shape at the striking end, with three to eight rows of knobs, arranged in such a way that one row of knobs is always situated in the intervals of the adjacent rows. Most of these clubs are distinguished by painstaking workmanship.

Figure 33 depicts a series of clubs from the region between Jacquinot Bay and Montague Bay that has only become familiar to us in recent times and that deviate markedly from other clubs in the protectorate, especially in form. Clubs 1 and 2 are of the same basic form; 2, however, deviates substantially from 1 in that the blade is distinguished by surface relief and by painting in various colours. The broad, blade-like striking end is thick and heavy, the lower side having a sharper edge. The carved decoration, like an eye on the blade of club 2, is found again on clubs 3 and 4, which are otherwise devoid of any further ornamentation. From our understanding they are a quite unwieldy weapon. Club 3 can be wielded with one hand, while 4, because of its weight, requires both hands.

The shape of 3 rather brings to mind the shape of a boomerang of the Australians, but is always used as a hand-held weapon.[7] Clubs 5 and 6 appear to be a wooden imitation of a long-lost stone instrument. The handle is clearly differentiated from the blade, the latter of course being prepared together with the handle out of a single piece of wood. The instrument is strongly reminiscent of the ceremonial stone axe from the Normanby Islands (British New Guinea), which, however, has a finely polished stone blade. Another similarity is that the reproduced blade, as evidenced particularly by number 6, is of lesser thickness, exactly like the stone blades of the Normanby axe. According to the comments of the natives, the Montague Bay axe is, however, a war weapon and not, as in the Normanby Islands, a state or ceremonial axe.

Further along western New Britain, clubs apparently lose importance; what has come into my view from these regions consist of fairly rough batten-shaped clubs with a simple tapering or a triangular-ending haft, a modification of the cone-shaped pommels of the neighbouring tribes.

Shields serve as defence against weapons of all kinds, throughout western New Britain. These are completely unknown on the Gazelle Peninsula: sufficient evidence that the peninsular tribes have never come into close contact with the western tribes nor even descend from them. As far as we know, three different types of shield are in use on western New Britain. The form in figure 35, which depicts a Sulka shield from the front as well as the reverse side, is very characteristic of this district. The decoration is of course varied but always revolves around the main motifs. The shape is always the same, an extended oval, the long diameter of which is about three times as great as the short one. The shields are made from a light white wood; the front surface is slightly curved and the edges hemmed with strips of rattan. At the midpoint of both

7. Howitt, on page 265 of his *Native Tribes of South East Australia*, portrays a number of clubs, of which No. 4 in particular, called *luiangel*, from western Australia, bears a great resemblance to this club.

diameters a projecting boss, matches a depression on the reverse side which contains the hand-hold running in the direction of the long axis. Above the boss on the outer surface run a number of rattan strips which cross at the highest point of the boss.

Both front and reverse sides of the Sulka shield are decorated with carved ornaments and these are accentuated by various types of painting. Again we find, as with the Baining ornaments, that the meanings which we Europeans give to these, are basically false. Both figures on the outer side to the right and the left of the central boss might well both signify human figures; the circular, or more accurately almost round designs on both the front and the reverse sides could represent eyes, and correspondingly from the swirls around them one might construct a human figure. It is unfortunate that the Sulka, who carve and paint these figures want to have absolutely nothing to do with such an interpretation, to the extent of laughing in one's face when such a meaning is implied. Anyway I am not in a position to give an explanation of the designs, since obtaining one was impossible; however, there is no doubt that the designs have a significance, but here, as in so many cases, we must have patience until closer acquaintance with the tribe provides us with information.

In the area both east and west of Montague Bay, along the entire Nakanai coast from Duportail Island to the Willaumez Peninsula and westwards across it, and on the French Islands as well, we find another form of shield which, although varying in individual details has the same basic shape and the same organisation of decoration. This is an indication that a relationship exists between the inhabitants of the north coast and those of the south coast, which manifests itself in other ways as well.

The basic shape of this shield is a long rectangle with severely rounded corners, the length being about five times the breadth. The borders are mostly edged, but they are often decorated with a string of white down feathers. In the centre there is usually a boss which on the reverse side contains the depression for the hand grip; this is densely plaited over cross-wise with red-dyed rattan strips; similarly both ends of the shield are decorated with strips of rattan laid crosswise over one another, or more accurately reinforced, to prevent splintering of the light wood. Here too, both reverse and front sides are decorated, and on the front surface the design also gives the impression of a face. It has not been possible for me to unravel the decoration of the reverse side (fig. 36).

These shields differ in decoration according to district. The shields of Montague Bay on the southern side are almost exactly the same as those of the Nakanai region on the northern side. The latter, however, are much more primitive and rougher in the whole presentation and decoration; painting is

Fig. 30 Cords of *Nassa* snail shells for wrapping the spear shaft

a. Upper surface;
b. Underside

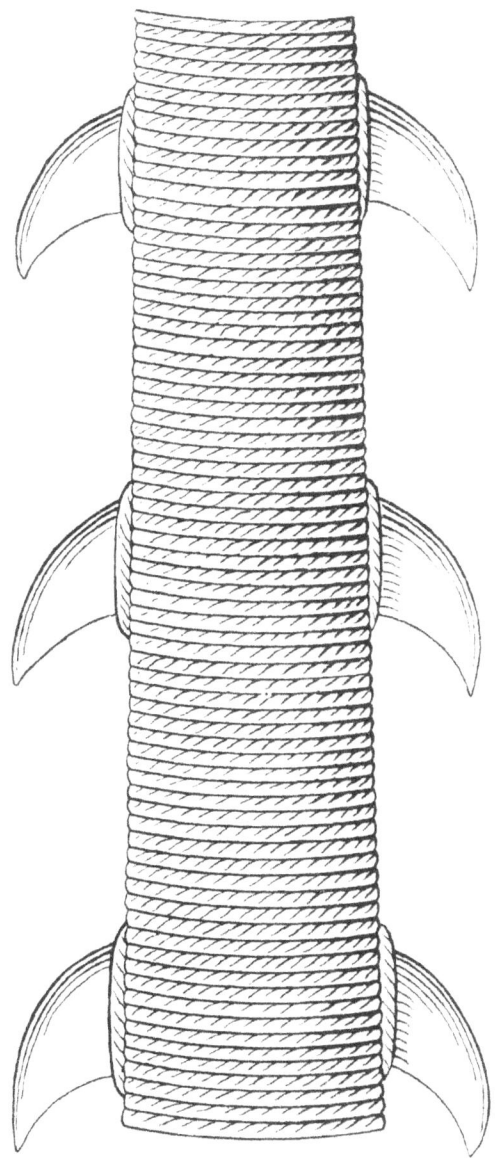

Fig. 31 Attachment of the barbs to the spear by binding

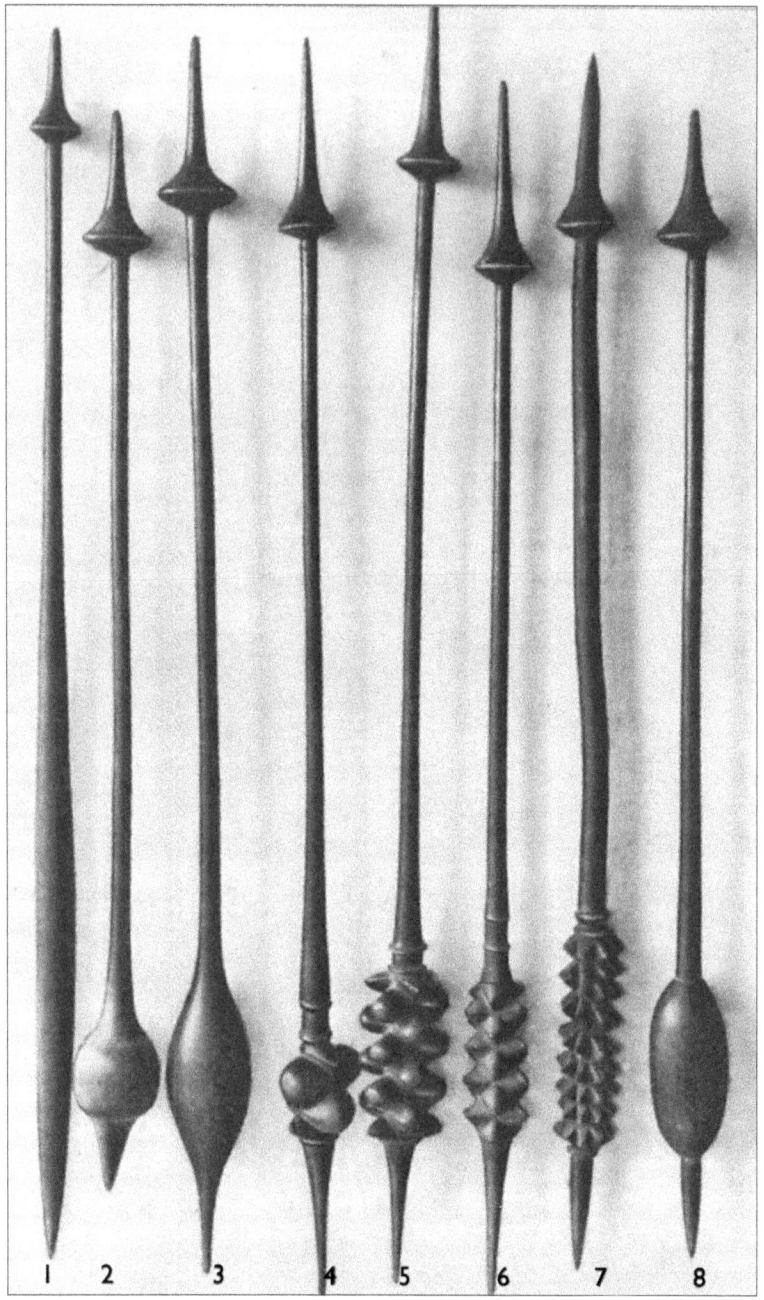

Fig. 32 Clubs of the Sulka and O Mengen

often only hinted at, likewise the carved pattern. Frequently the edging with strips of rattan is missing as well, and the crosswise binding of the shield. However, on Willaumez and the French Islands quite significant deviations occur, for there especially the shield is produced with far greater care. The shape is more slender and narrow than those of the Nakanai and Montague Bay tribes, and the length is about seven and a half times greater than the breadth. The decoration of the front side is the same as those of their neighbours and here too we can discern a face both on the upper and the lower surfaces of the front side. The boss of the front side is carved in the shape of a bird and painted, and the binding of the whole shield with wide, red-dyed bands of fibre is far more carefully done.

The entire rim of the shield is most neatly and carefully hemmed with a thick rattan plait, from which tassels of fibre or of bird feathers dangle at brief intervals. Decoration of the reverse side is just as carefully performed; the outlines of the design are easily carved into the soft wood, and painted in white, black and red. According to the natives these figures, always referring to two forms in particular, represent certain sea creatures (fig. 37).

The shields described above, in spite of all the differences, have many features in common, and can be regarded unquestionably as variations of one and the same basic form. Further to the west, around South Cape and beyond, there appears a totally different form. Here the shields consist of three convex battens, arranged in such a way that two more narrow battens lie alongside the broader central batten, bound together by strips of rattan and other fibrous bands (fig. 38). The breadth of the central batten is as great as the breadth of both lateral battens. By binding together, three roughly square panels are formed, with a right-angled panel at each end; the combined squares are adorned with smoothly inlaid decorations which are enhanced by painting. Decorations of the reverse side are more rarely carved, but in most cases are only painted on. I have not been able to obtain anything reliable on the significance of the individual decorations.

All of these shields are produced from a very light type of wood, and are held with the left hand in battle, to cover the body. Most specimens have been pierced by spears, and the natives have a great dexterity in intercepting spears. At Montague Bay I was able to observe how, during an attack, the shield was held in the left hand, with the arm slightly bent in front of the body, to catch the weapons of the opposing party; at the same time it was regarded as dexterous to present always the narrow side of the body to the enemy, and to use the shields fully in this position as much as possible.

Right at the western end of New Britain still other forms appear; however, these never came into my purview. At any event the shield depicted in figure 38 is very extensively used at the western end of New Britain.

The stone axe is never used as a true battle weapon; its prime importance is as a hand tool. Both the shape of the stone axe and the material for the blade are not always the same in the various districts. We find a very characteristic axe on the French Islands, the Willaumez Peninsula and on the opposite south coast of New Britain, around South Cape. The blade is not fastened into a wooden haft or a wooden sheath but, like several stone axes from the northern Solomon Islands, wound round with a piece of rattan. The blades (fig. 39) are of various sizes, produced from a hard, black type of stone, and carefully smoothed and polished over almost the entire upper surface. To retain the actual blade in position, small ledges are ground on both sides, about a third of the way from the edge; below these ledges the rattan cane forming the handle is bent round the blade and then tied together with thin strips of rattan and tightly plaited over. This plaiting extends about 8 to 10 centimetres down the haft from the blade. I have seen this type of axe used as a hand tool in the production of house posts. However, it is also used as a sago mallet for loosening the inner pith of the sago palm, and I have in my possession a specimen captured in Stettiner Bay on the eastern side of the Willaumez Peninsula, when the natives of this area were driven back during an attempt to raid the boat of a European. Thus, from time to time it does have use as a weapon.

West of the Willaumez Peninsula one frequently finds axes in use with blades produced from Tridacna shell. They have the shape of a hollow chisel and stick into a conical sheath consisting of two hollowed out halves. This sheath is placed at the rear end of the blade and then firmly tied on with strips of rattan. The hand grip consists of a knee-shaped wooden handle, the short end of which is pointed and stuck into the upper narrow opening of the wooden sheath.

The attachment of the stone axes from Nakanai is similar, although in this region the blade is not of Tridacna shell, but prepared from stone similar to lava. The shape is also not that of a hollow chisel, but a common axe with a straight, rounded-off cutting edge. The wooden sheath of the Nakanai axe is far thinner and more artistically worked, also proportionally longer than the sheaths east of Willaumez. For tying they use a thin cord twisted from strong fibres, with which the whole sheath is tightly strapped round from bottom to top.

Everywhere on the great western part of New Britain obsidian slivers play a major role as a cutting implement. The material is available everywhere, and slivers with hair-sharp cutting edges can easily be detached. All cutting work that we find in this area has been done with such obsidian slivers, and in places where the canoe ends are adorned with decoration in relief, or where wooden bowls are decorated with deep carving, these slivers lie around in great numbers. When such a knife becomes useless, it is thrown away without any attempt to resharpen the cutting edge, and a new sliver is broken off.

Mother-of-pearl shell is likewise used everywhere as a cutting implement, especially the black-rimmed mussel pearl not uncommon on the beaches.

The coastal tribes, more especially the islanders of the offshore islets, are seafarers, but to varying degrees. For some, sea voyages consist only of small trips along the beach from one friendly village to another, or fishing trips to uninhabited islands in the neighbourhood. Others, however, are seafarers in the true sense of the word, and do not fear making relatively long voyages across the open sea in their canoes. Naturally this has an influence on the construction and the outfitting of the canoes; the more extensive the voyages to be made in them, and the greater demands to be made on their seaworthiness, the better made they are.

In Nakanai, on South Cape and at many places on the western tip, the canoes are long single trees, prepared without artistry from a hollowed-out tree trunk, equipped with booms and a float on one side for better stability. Both ends are occasionally

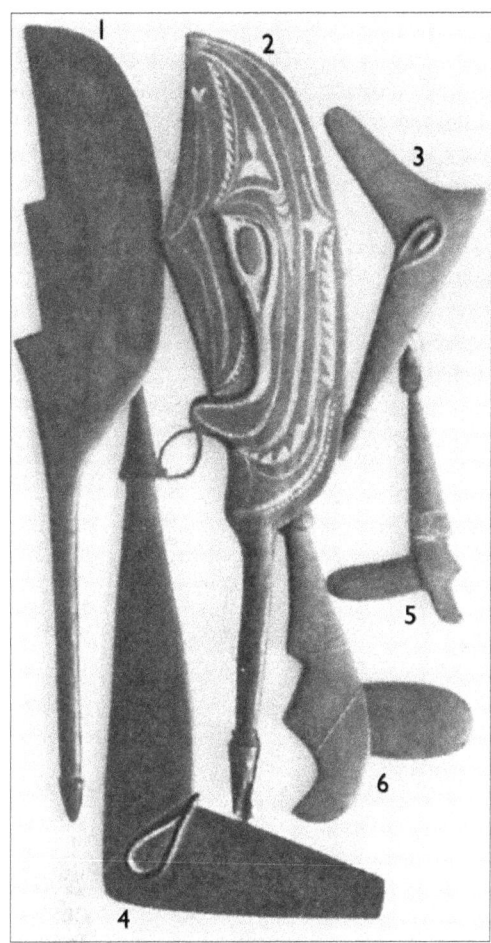

Fig. 33 Clubs from the region between Jacquinot Bay and Montague Bay

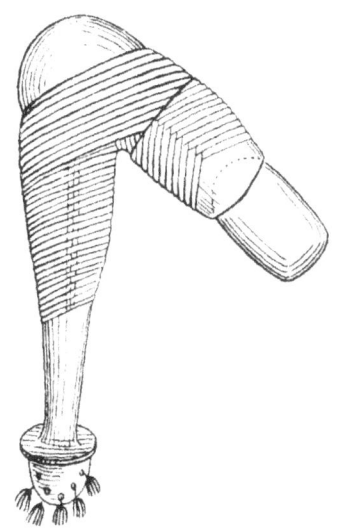

Fig. 34 Stone axe from the Normanby Islands

decorated with surface reliefs that are enhanced by painting; in most cases, however, no decoration is used. In Nakanai, according to usual custom, the outrigger is removed and the body of the canoe is pushed under the roof of the hut as protection against sun and weather. The Sulka take significantly greater care in production; their canoes are wider and more spacious, furnished with small superstructures at both ends, and both gunwales are raised by a long plank. Both prows and the gunwale planks are decorated by painting, and these figures frequently recall in a quite lively way, the modern European decoration which we designate by the words Art Nouveau, since generally all painting from this region has an extraordinarily characteristic pattern. Its uniqueness is increased still further in that, besides the common red, white and black tones, various green and yellow pigments are also used. On the French Islands and further towards the western end of the island of New Britain we find even better made canoes, the seaworthiness of which is significantly greater, and which are not powered exclusively by paddles but by sails as well; indeed these sails are of the form used, for example, on the Tami Islands.

Canoe size varies a lot; on the north coast and on the south coast I was able to observe long canoes that often carried twenty people. The canoes never carry such a load at sea; seldom are they seen on the open sea with more than six people aboard,

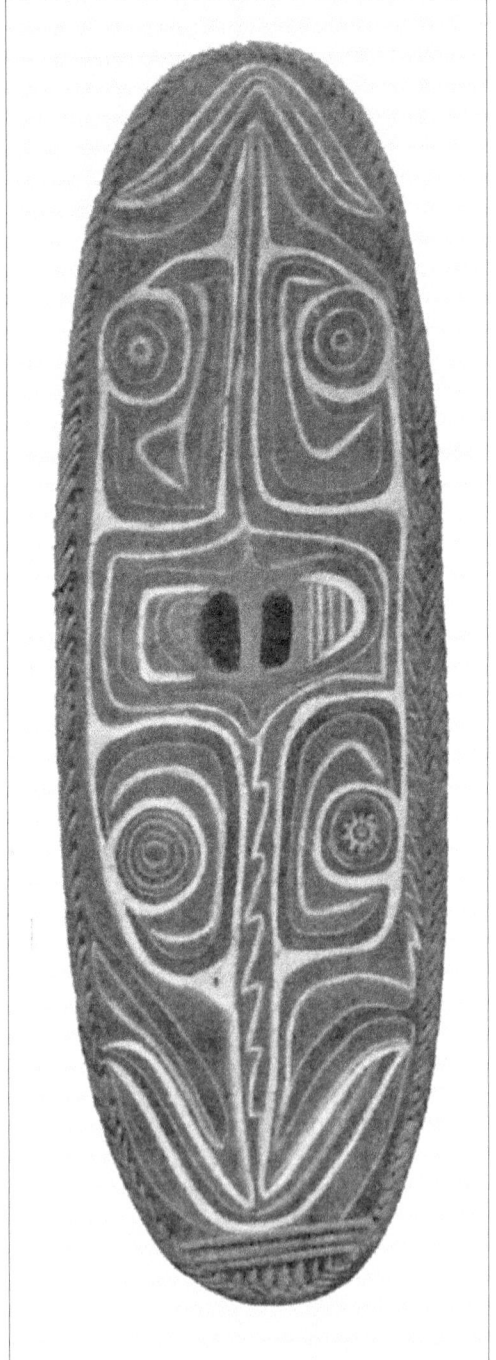

Fig. 35 Sulka shield [back (left) and front]

Fig. 36 O Mengen shield [front (left) and back]

although close inshore in calm water they frequently carry up to twenty natives. On the Arawa Islands and further west of there one often comes across the great two-masted sailing canoe which is so common in New Guinea. The natives say that they purchase these canoes in the west, from other natives. Eastwards beyond Cape Merkus I have not seen them.

I wish to mention here that natives are driven quite frequently from south-eastern New Guinea onto the south coast of New Britain particularly. Thus about fifteen years ago a number of natives were driven from the D'Entrecasteaux Archipelago onto South Cape, and at Cape Gloucester I met people from the Trobriand Islands who had been settled there for so long that they spoke the local native language and felt so contented that they declined transport home. According to comments by the natives on Arawa (Liebliche Inseln) different pale-skinned natives were driven there, but they had been slain because they resisted. However, today there are still two older women on the island who, by their paler skin and their facial features, indicate that they originated from the south-eastern New Guinea islands. This kind of immigration also explains why at Cape Roebuck, for example, objects were offered to me that had come without doubt from the Woodlark Islands. How far these shipwrecks really extend is demonstrated by the case that, years ago on Roissy Island, a shield from the Trobriands was offered to me, which although very old, still bore traces of the characteristic painting found nowhere else.

In pages 143 to 166 of his excellent book, *Unter den Papuas*, Dr Hagen has given us a comparison of the various theories on the origin of the crinkly haired races, and also developed his own views, which deviate somewhat from the others. Finally, however, having considered all such apparently acceptable answers to the question: Where do these people come from; to which 'race' do they belong? we still come back to Dr Hagen's answer: 'I don't know, nobody knows, not even the Papuans themselves!' I have already emphasised in various ways that the population is extraordinarily mixed throughout the entire region; nowhere have we succeeded in authenticating a pure race. Certain external features, especially the hair, have been put forward, quite justifiably, as distinguishing features. But between these two main groups, the crinkly haired and the smooth-haired, there are so extraordinarily many blends that when other characteristic features are placed alongside, we are often not in a position to say whether the peculiarities of one or the other group predominate.

With regard to the Bismarck Archipelago type, Dr Hagen holds the view that it is an independent form belonging to the Austral-Papuan region, which has developed here and is closely and intimately related to the Australian type. Both belong together and form a secondary principal variation of humankind. The author points out, with justification, the great similarity, for example, between the New Britain people and the Queenslanders, and this similarity has also struck observers like Dr Finsch.

From travellers' reports and other accounts, we now know that in Tasmania up until not long ago there was a tribe which showed even greater similarity with the then-living natives of New Britain. Above all, the Tasmanians had the crinkly hair of the archipelago inhabitants, whereas the present Australians as a rule have smooth, curly hair. If we now look at the accompanying map, which was taken from the work, *Island Life*, by Alfred Wallace, I believe that there is no difficulty in explaining the similarity of Tasmanians and the inhabitants of the archipelago. The map shows the probable shape of Australia at the beginning of the Tertiary Period. At that time that part of the world consisted of two large main sections, western and eastern Australia, separated by a broad arm of the sea. The northern-most tip of Australia was formed by the present-day Cape York. It is presumed that eastern Australia at that time was inhabited by a crinkly haired tribe which, if not completely identical, was still closely related to the inhabitants of New Guinea and the inhabitants of the Bismarck Archipelago. The inhabitants of western Australia belonged to a different tribe, which was probably very close to the Arafurans. At a later period, when, as a result of uplift, the sea separating both main islands gradually disappeared and a solid bridge connected the two islands, a migration of the tribes took place. In particular it was the smooth-haired western Australians who pushed eastwards along the new path, annihilated the crinkly haired eastern Australians and interbred with the survivors. In the south, the Tasmanians remained undisturbed by this immigration because, at a later period, Bass Strait separated their homeland from the rest of eastern Australia and set up an insurmountable obstacle

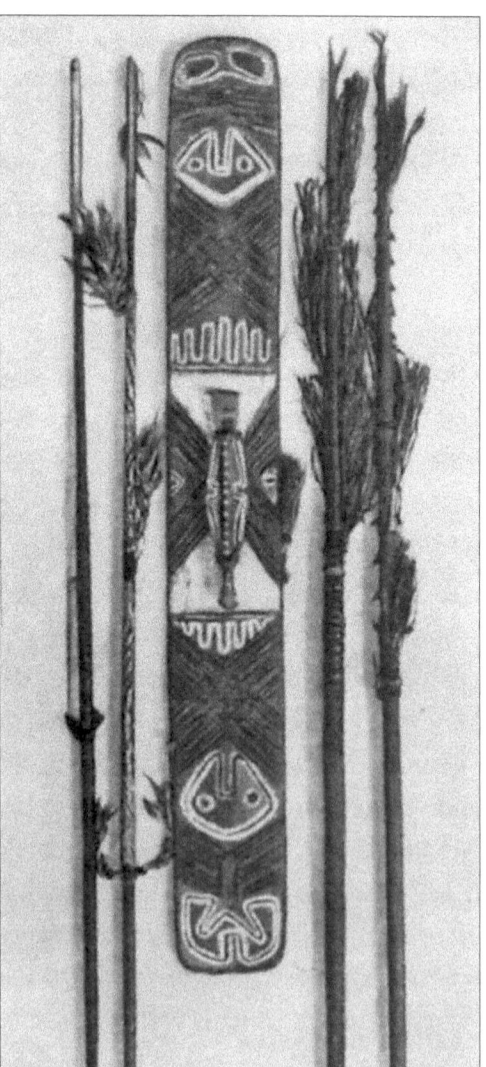

Fig. 37 Shield and spears from the French Islands

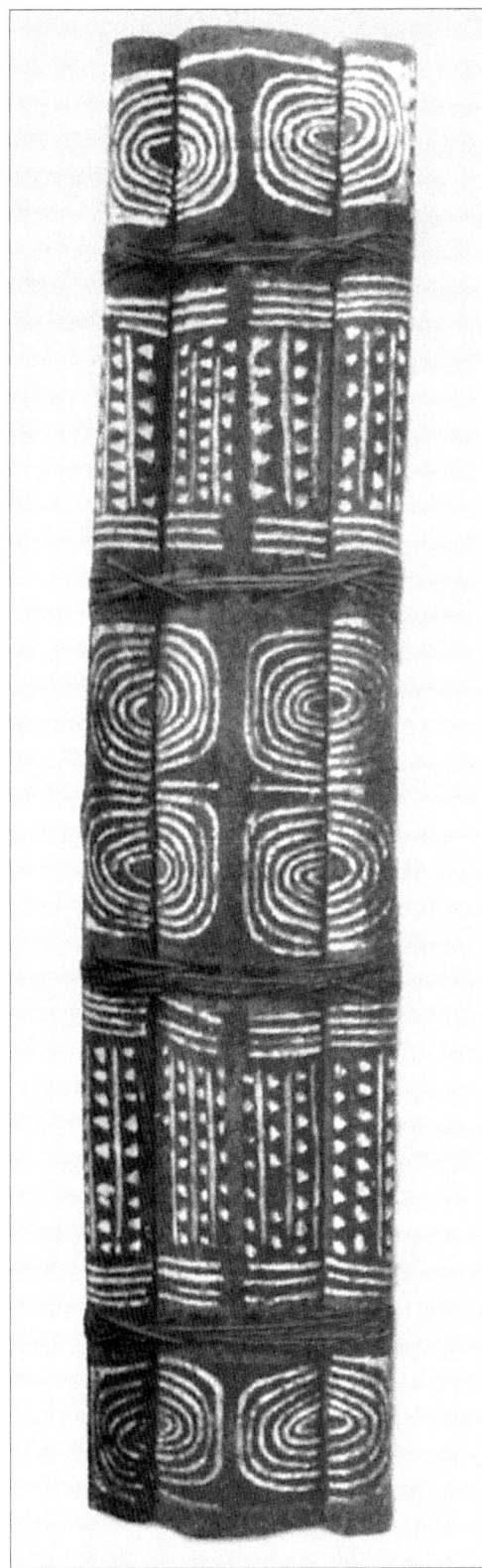

Fig. 38 Shield from South Cape [front (left) and back]

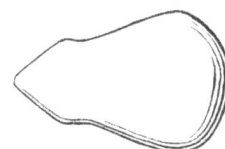

Fig. 39 Stone axe blade from Willaumez

against intruders into the south, just as the sea also forced a halt to their migrations in the north.

Between Cape York and the Bismarck Archipelago is inserted the high eastern end of New Guinea, whose population, as we knew up until a few years ago, had not much in common with the inhabitants of the Gazelle Peninsula or of southern New Ireland. However, since the Governor of British New Guinea, Sir William MacGregor, so highly renowned for exploration, traversed this part of the island in 1896, we know that in the ranges there dwells a tribe that is strikingly different from the coastal inhabitants and has a far greater similarity to the people of the north-eastern Gazelle Peninsula. A member of the expedition, on first seeing natives from the area around my dwelling several years later, was astonished at the great resemblance of the New Britain people to the natives he had

Plate 16 (Top) Village scene on the 'Liebliche Inseln'

Fig. 40 (Above) Village scene at Kombiuß ('Liebliche Inseln'). House of the Kaiser Wilhelmsland type

encountered years ago during the ascent of Mount Scratchley.

When in an earlier section I represented the population of the island of New Britain (with the exception of the Gazelle Peninsula tribes), as being closely related to the tribes of New Guinea, I was referring only to the shoreline population of both islands. Between South Cape and Cape Roebuck isolated tribes dwell in the mountains, differing remarkably from the shore-dwellers. I have become acquainted with only few representatives of the former, on the occasion of a journey along the coast.

They had astonished me by their great facial similarity to the Gazelle Peninsula people, and upon questioning it was explained to me that they were prisoners of war, and therefore slaves, from the mountains.

We are thus in a position to reconstruct the

entire sequence of a population which exhibits all the features of a closely connected and related tribe, from Van Diemen's Land to New Ireland.

Whether this tribe formed the original population, or whether another existed before it, is difficult to determine, as indeed nowhere else is there found such an interbreeding of different races as on the islands of the Pacific Ocean. It seems certain that all these islands were inhabited in primeval times by a dark-skinned race; whether this race stood close to the Negritos, the Arafurans or the Australians is hard to determine, the more so since all three groups, and others, apparently interbred frequently, partially through gradual immigration into new areas, made possible by bridging of the sea gap as a result of powerful upthrusts. Similarly, major sinkings would have broken up land complexes and divided the population onto numerous islands and island groups.

That the geological situation has in many ways been the decisive factor in the distribution of population over the Pacific Ocean, we must accept as certain. As a significant uplift is verifiable in the west, so too in central Polynesia or to the east an equally strong sinking is demonstrable, as has been shown, for example, by the drilling into Funafuti atoll, carried out in 1896 by Professor Sollas under commission from the Royal Society, London.

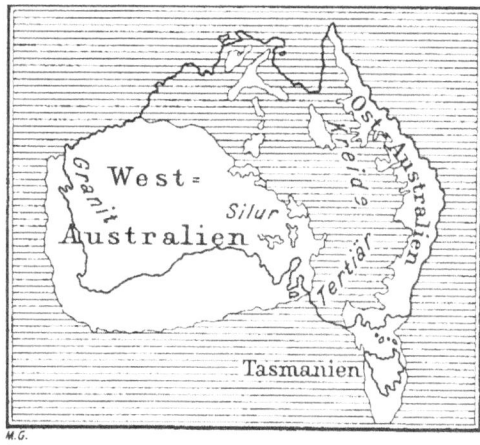

Fig. 41 Probable shape of Australia at the beginning of the Tertiary Period. (Present-day Australia is drawn in outline)

11 New Ireland and New Hanover and their Offshore Islands

1. The Land

The island of New Ireland (Carteret's 'Nova Hibernia') is long and narrow, separated in the south-west from the Gazelle Peninsula by St George's Channel.

The southern tip of the island, Cape St George, lies at 4°51'S, and 152°52'E. The mountains over 2,000 metres high, on the southern part of the island, are visible from a great distance. On closer approach, the eye perceives a seemingly unbroken forest from the beach up to the highest mountain peaks, interspersed here and there with green grassy meadows on the eastern side. Deep valleys divide various mountain chains stretching from south to north, of which the central chain, the Rossel Range, is the highest. Both to east and west the mountains extend almost directly into the sea; a narrow foreshore exists only here and there. Streams large and small pour into the sea from the numerous gorges; there are no navigable rivers. In the dry season these streams are to a large extent harmless rills; after heavy tropical rain, especially during the rainy season of north-westers, they suddenly transform into mountain torrents which float mighty forest trees into the sea and carry huge boulders and much rubble along with them. Especially on the eastern side, in the Siara district south of Cape Santa Maria, these watercourses are particularly large, and when one is sailing past the stream beds they appear as though they were broad causeways leading inland.

On the maps part of the island still bears the name *Tombara*, a designation that the natives do not know, and is derived from the word *tanbar* (south-east wind or south-easterly direction). It is high time for this name to disappear from the maps.

The high, southern part of the island stretches mainly from south to north, with a small mountainous projection pointing north-west. The greatest breadth of the island here reaches about 30 nautical miles, the north-south length about 60 nautical miles. The continuation of the highlands stretches a further 25 nautical miles north-west, and then drops off fairly steeply into a depression connecting this part of the island with the main part, which is traversed by the Schleinitz Range. This depression, between the villages of Kurumut in the west and Nabutu Bay in the Bo district to the east, is not much more than 5 nautical miles wide. Stretching to the north-west, the Schleinitz Range forms the backbone of the island and then gradually becomes lower to end finally on the flat North Cape.

The total length of the island from Cape St George to North Cape is about 200 nautical miles.

In the east a number of small islands lie offshore. Coming from the south we first encounter the small St John group (named Wuneram by the Solomon people, and Aneri by the inhabitants of the New Ireland coast opposite), consisting of a larger mountainous island and a smaller hilly one. As far as I could ascertain the larger island is called Ambitlé by its inhabitants, and the smaller Bábase. North-west of St John lies the small group of the Caen Islands. This consists of a southern island, Malenaput, off which the smaller islands of Malelif, Maletafa and Bit stretch out to the south-east, separated by narrow sea channels, and a northern island, Tanga, separated from the southern island by an arm of the sea about 6 nautical miles wide.

About 45 miles north-west of the Caen Islands is the bigger island of Gerrit Denys, Lir or Lihir, and then in a northerly direction the small islands, San Bruno (Mali), San Joseph (Massait), and San Francisco or Maur. About 30 nautical miles west of Gerrit Denys lie the two Gardner Islands, and separated from the northern one by an arm of the sea is Fischer Island or Simberi. I am still unclear as to the names of the two Gardner Islands. Although I visited them quite often and made various inquiries, I never succeeded in gaining satisfactory results. Other new names were always given me, so that I finally came to the conclusion that I was being given the names of individual districts. On current maps the strait that separates both Gardner Islands is depicted incorrectly; it lies rather further north, and separates the islands in such a way that the northern one is the smaller and the southern one the larger. On New Ireland opposite, both

Map 3 New Ireland

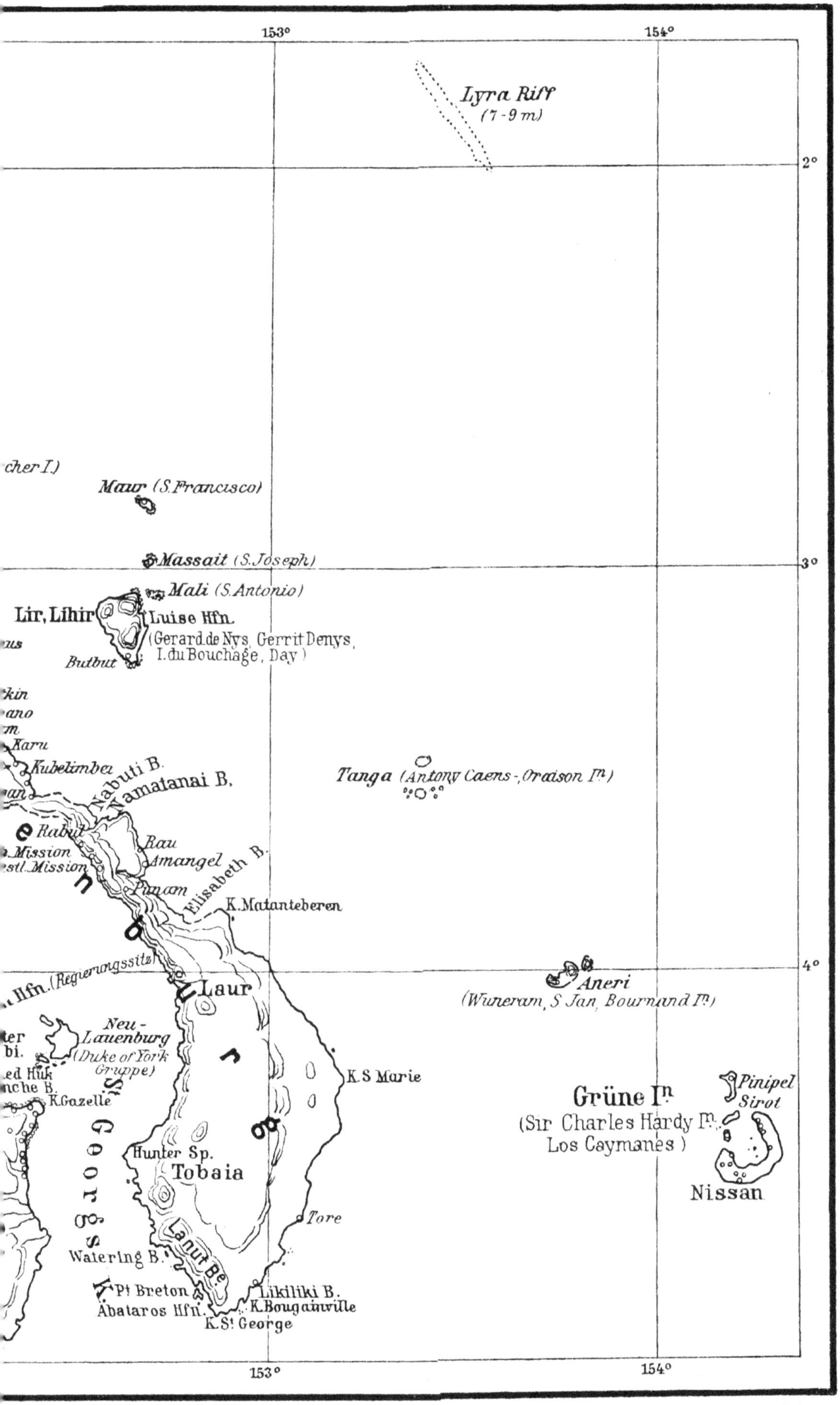

Beilage zu Parrkinson, Dreissig Jahre in der Südsee.

Gardner Islands are called Tabar.

All these islands are high and mountainous, and for the most part volcanic. On Gerrit Denys and St John numerous hot springs rise here and there from the ground, and the earlier craters are still clearly visible. Besides the volcanic rock, raised coral formations also occur, and island groups are more or less surrounded by coral reefs.

South of the north-western end of the island of New Ireland lies triangular Sandwich Island (Djaule) with a small island at the northern end. This island consists totally of raised coral banks.

Between New Ireland and New Hanover which is situated about 25 nautical miles further west, there are numerous large and small islands and islets which belong ethnographically partly to New Ireland and partly to New Hanover. Two straits navigable by the largest ships, Steffen Strait and Byron Strait, run through this maze of islands from north to south. All the islands consist of coral limestone.

The island of New Hanover itself measures about 25 nautical miles from east to west and about 20 nautical miles from north to south. In the north and north-east a few small raised coral islands lie on coral reefs, forming relatively good anchorages, with their reefs and the larger island opposite. About 4 nautical miles south-west of the westernmost point of New Hanover, Cape Queen Charlotte, lie the small, low Portland Islands on a common reef. The principal island, New Hanover, consists in part of raised coral formations; however, the higher part of the island reveals other rock, although a geological investigation has not yet established what it is.

The surface area of all the above-mentioned islands totals approximately 13,500 square kilometres, that is, about the size of the grand-duchy of Mecklenburg-Schwerin, and the extent of the islands from Cape St George in the south to Cape Queen Charlotte in the extreme north-west is 247 nautical miles or 470 kilometres.

I will now attempt to give a detailed description of New Ireland as I have come to know it from numerous journeys. The coasts are especially well-known; exploration of the interior has only been undertaken in most recent times. The southern highlands with the mighty Rossel Mountains make a great impression by the steepness of the mountains and the multitudinous transections of them by deep gorges and valleys through which the mountain streams seek to make their way, foaming and roaring, to the sea. The east coast drops steeply into the sea everywhere, and only in the northern part, south of Nabutu Bay, does the land flatten. The west coast has the same character, except that several small harbours, known to us since the time of Dampier and Carteret, lie a little north of Cape St George. The first of these harbours, Port Praslin, lies beyond the small island of Latau, between it and the main island; however, it is of minor importance as an anchorage. Somewhat better is the small harbour lying about 2 kilometres north, formed by the small island of Lambon (Wallis Island) and the main island. As a consequence of the high mountains of the main island and the equally impressive height of the island of Lambon, it is to some extent sheltered from the prevailing winds, but it will never be of importance as a harbour since the surrounding land is steep and rocky, and unsuitable either for building houses or for establishing plantations. It was here that the famed expedition of the Marquis de Ray eked out its existence for a while at the beginning of the 1880s. The harbour is named Port Breton on the maps. About 5 nautical miles further north, another harbour, Carteret Harbour, is formed by the small island of Lamassa (Coconut Island) and the main island. This, although somewhat more spacious than the previous two, is of little value for the same reason. The harbours would only be of value if mineral wealth of any kind were found in the interior of the island, and it could be transported overland to them. It is not improbable that the mountains of this part of the island contain minerals. Even by the end of the 1870s, Australian geological authorities had announced the possibility of finding minerals, after examination of rock samples submitted to them; recently coal has been found at one site, although indications are that it is of poor quality; but since only the most superficial layers have been examined, it is not impossible that further investigations of deeper layers will produce a better result. Neither on the east nor on the west coast of this part of the island is there a completely secure anchorage; the steep shoreline drops just as quickly below the surface into the depths, and depths of several hundred metres are found close inshore.

The Rossel Mountains extend a ridge about 1,000 metres high to the north-west, gradually lowering towards the village of Kure. Towards St George's Channel this extension of the mountain

Fig. 42 Northern tip of the island of Nusa. Raised coral reefs

range drops steeply away; to the east, from Cape Matantéberen to the inlet indicated on the maps as 'Grosse Bucht' [Deep Bay], the mountain is fronted by a not insignificant flat of excellent fertility, and east of the cape is an anchorage (Elizabeth Harbour), which is well protected at times. The plain is particularly well inhabited, and village follows after village. The opposite coast is quite heavily populated as well, as is the Siara district south of Cape Santa Maria on the east coast and the districts of Topaia and Laur on the west coast. Inland, in the valleys and on the mountain slopes, dwells a population which is usually on a war-footing with the shore dwellers. However, as far as we know, the mountains are on the whole only sparsely settled.

The previously described southern part of the island, to a certain extent, forms one main division of New Ireland, geologically differing from the part stretching further to the north-west.

Between Kure and Deep Bay (Nabutu Bay) is a depression that reaches no more than 200 metres tall and is about 5 nautical miles wide from shore to shore. The part of the island beyond, connected with the southern mountain region by this depression, is raised coral limestone throughout, forming a long ridge stretching to the north-west, the Schleinitz Mountains. Certainly in external appearance this mountain chain differs from the southern highlands. The mountains are broad, rounded domes, and the valleys are less steep and deep; the height too is less and barely reaches 1,000 metres. This part of the island has its greatest breadth, about 21 nautical miles or 40 kilometres, in the region opposite the Gardner Islands. The Schleinitz Mountains gradually flatten towards the north-west, and finally terminate in a gentle ridge which runs out into the north-west plain.

That this part of the island has been raised up at different periods of eruption is clearly evident on the north-eastern coast. The coast here often forms steep, coral limestone walls which stretch like a frequently interrupted embankment from the Gardner Islands to North Cape. Inland this wall does not fall steeply away, but passes gradually into a plain that is very swampy in places. This plain is of varying breadth, and is particularly prized by the natives because of its fertility. After traversing it one is suddenly confronted by the steeply falling coral limestone walls of the mountains, which still in places show the earlier shoreline clearly, where heavy, pounding swells have produced grottoes with broad, overhanging roofs. The swampy plain has undoubtedly been a lagoon in prehistoric times, bordered by a barrier reef which was interrupted by passes, and now forms the outer wall of the shore. This structure appears very clearly at Nusa Harbour on the north-western tip of the island. On the partially deforested former barrier reef, which drops quite steeply to the present shoreline, lie the administration centre of Kavieng and the houses of various traders. Beyond is an extensive lowland plain, the former lagoon, which is now covered to a great extent with coconut plantations and native settlements. The deep undercuts which now lie at least 10 metres above sea level demonstrate that this former barrier reef too has been subjected to repeated uplifting. A further example of this is given by the Dietertberg (220 metres) and above all by Mausoleum Island (Salapio) between Steffen and Byron straits, which have a pronounced terrace structure, and in which the various stages of uplift are clearly recognisable.

The entire archipelago filling the gap between New Ireland and New Hanover is a result of these uplifts.

Before I turn to an account of these islands, I want to describe the most recent part of the island of New Ireland in rather more detail. Both the north-eastern and the south-western coasts have no harbours; in places there is a shoreline reef, against which the sea breaks with great force; where the reef is absent, the ocean rolls its waves directly against the rocks onshore. The north-eastern coast is well populated as far as North Cape, where there are quite considerable stands of coconut palm whose produce is sold by the natives to the traders settled here and there. The south-west coast is less rich in coconut palm stands and settlements, but is nevertheless fairly well populated; here the villages lie at greater or lesser distances from the shore and the natives concentrate mainly on taro and sago for food. South of the north-western corner lies the small island of Djaule (Sandwich Island) which plays a major role in the mythology of the northern New Ireland people. It is somewhat triangular with a westerly directed baseline about 4.5 nautical miles long; the other sides are both about 7 and 6 nautical miles long. Both this island and Archway Island to the west, and small Angriffs Island offshore from the coast of New Ireland opposite, consist of raised coral formations. Mount Bendemann (200 metres) on Djaule is the highest uplifted feature. Between the islands off the north-western end of New Ireland there is good anchorage for ships; the most well-known is tiny Nusa Harbour, a little south of North Cape. Here ships up to medium size find a safe, spacious haven, bordered to the east by the main island, and to the west by the small islands of Nusa, Nusalik and Nago. As a consequence, the various agencies of the island trading firms are also located here, and it is also the site of the imperial administration for this part of the island.

Cultivations have been undertaken on New Ireland only recently. Several of the small islands on Steffen Strait have been planted out in coconut palms by whites, and the imperial administration has set up extensive coconut palm plantations at Nusa harbour near the Kavieng administration station. Trade with the natives has been going on since the beginning of the 1880s, when the firm of Hernsheim & Co. founded the first settlement on the small island of Nusa, and a second soon after on Kapsu, about 20 nautical miles south-east of North Cape. Both these settlements experienced a very precarious existence for a time; first they were attacked by the natives and the traders killed, then they were occupied once more by enterprising people who kept the business going. Today, when relations can be considered relatively under control, a large number of such trading stations have been established on the north-eastern coast.

Missionaries were in the field before the traders, for in 1875 the Wesleyan mission founded the first stations on the New Ireland coast opposite the Duke of York Islands. They have made good progress here and currently support a larger number of missions under the leadership of Samoan or Viti teachers who are under the control of a white missionary. Since 1902 the Catholic mission, which has its main base in New Britain, has also settled on this coast.

The archipelago between New Ireland and the island of New Hanover consists, as already mentioned, exclusively of raised coral banks and depositional islands, which over the course of time have become overgrown with luxuriant vegetation. They are separated by numerous straits and arms of the sea, navigable in some places by larger ships, and in other places not even passable by small boats. The most significant are the two passes leading from north to south, known as Steffen Strait and Byron Strait. Straits that are less deep, but still navigable by medium-sized ships, are Albatross Channel between Baudissen Island and the Kabien Peninsula on the main island, and Ysabel Strait between the east coast of New Hanover and the series of smaller islands offshore. Some of these islands are inhabited; the majority, however, are unpopulated, probably because, until quite recently, first the New Hanover people then the New Ireland people (depending on whether or not the island inhabitants were tribally related to them), attacked and killed them. Recently, with the development of more peaceful relations, settlements on the islands have increased, and enterprising whites have acquired a portion of them in order to transform them gradually into coconut plantations.

The island of New Hanover is mountainous and rugged in its south-western half; the mountains gradually flatten towards the north-east and form an extensive, fissured plain which is enclosed by a border of mangrove swamps on the shore. The mountain range is not yet sufficiently well known, but does not consist exclusively of raised coral banks, although these do exist on the coasts. The mountains are distinguished by their steepness and several of them, like the approximately 400-metre-high Stoschberg, bear the greatest similarity to a gigantic sugar loaf. The soil of New Hanover is extremely fertile, and since there are enough safe anchorages in the north and east, the entire north-eastern half of the island is eminently suitable for tropical plantations.

New Ireland is of lesser significance in this regard. True, there are larger and smaller stretches excellently suited to the cultivation of tropical products,

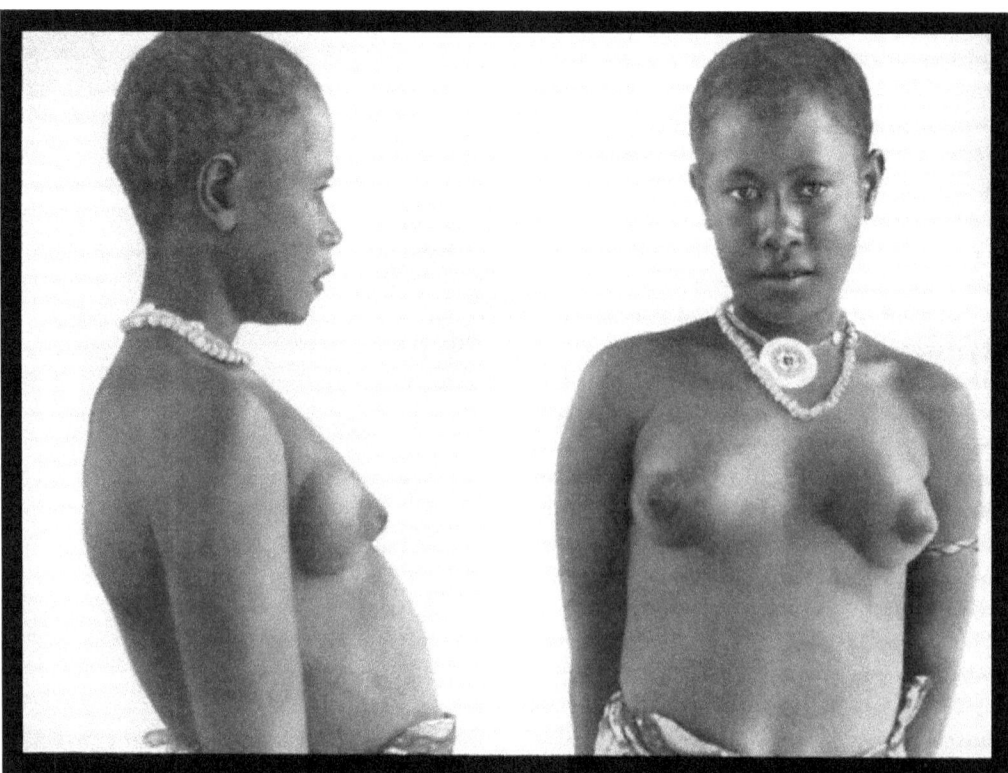

Plate 17 Girl from northern New Ireland

but rapid development of this island will always be hindered because of difficulties arising from sea transport due to the lack of good, safe anchorages. After setting up administration stations the imperial administration with great energy undertook road construction. Already, good roads lead from the northern end of New Ireland along both the east and west coasts, and with crossroads linking both coasts of the island in several places, this has improved into a road system that encourages trade.

2. The Natives

Now let us turn to the population: here, just as in New Britain, we can distinguish several main tribes spreading over the countryside from certain centres. Just as the mountainous southern part of the island is significantly different geologically from the less hilly north-western part, so too do the inhabitants of each part of the island differ significantly from each other in many aspects. The inhabitants of the southern part (as I have established in greater detail on New Britain), are closely related to the inhabitants of the Duke of York Islands and of the north-eastern Gazelle Peninsula. The population of the north-western part is very different in speech and in ethnography from their southern neighbours, although a blending and a gradual transition from one to the other is clearly recognisable. The original border between the two tribes was certainly the narrow tie between Kure and the east coast, where the last projections of the Rossel Range fall away to the north. The southern tribe, crossing this border, has mixed with the north-western tribe. Further settlement of the north-western part of the island appears to have taken place from New Hanover. Above all, on closer examination of the population we find strongly pronounced differences, which indicate that a mixing of very different elements has taken place. This is not quite so striking in the southern part of the island as in the north-western part. In the latter, besides dark-brown or black-brown people, who are barely distinguishable from someone from Buka or Bougainville, we find pale individuals whose skin colour is no darker than that of the Samoans or Tongans. The paler skin colour is particularly prevalent among the women, and many of them, in spite of the curly hair, surprisingly call to mind Polynesians. Some of the merchants who settled here married native girls, and the children born of such unions quite often have smooth, fair hair, and blue or grey eyes; in Europe they would not stand out in a pure-blooded crowd of children. I feel it would be an interesting proposition to study in more detail the various mixtures that are now encountered in such great numbers in the South Sea islands. Through this tribal cross-breeding there arise many strange forms that might be able to give us a hint about the origins of tribes that are today regarded as a uniform type, but which might possibly be the result of interbreeding of different races. I know, for example, a girl of about fourteen whose father is Chinese and whose mother is a full-blooded native of the Gazelle Peninsula. If one were to send the girl to Wuwulu or to Aua, one would without doubt regard her as a native of that place; skin colour, the lightly wavy hair, the characteristic, yet less slanted, mongoloid eyes: everything fits the traits on those islands perfectly.

In another case, where the mother is a native of New Ireland with pronounced Melanesian features and the father is a European of Semitic origin, the daughter has a darker coloured skin with strongly curly hair and a pronounced Semitic nose. Again, the child from the marriage of a fair-haired Norwegian and a pale New Ireland woman is of pronounced European, almost Nordic features; the child has smooth, flaxen, lightly wavy hair and skin colour which has only a quite imperceptible tinge of yellow. The daughter of a Frenchman from southern France and a New Ireland mother could be regarded in all her features as an Italian from the Rome region.

Mixes between New Ireland women and Solomon Island men, natives from Buka or Bougainville, have shown the paternal features most sharply as a rule; similarly, children of New Britain women and Solomon Island men show the type of the latter. The son of a Buka islander and a woman from Nauru has the dark skin colour of the father and the smooth, bristly hair of the mother. Children whose mother was a woman from New Hanover and whose father was a native of Buka with clear intermixing from a paler race, show traits that in some are closer to that of the father, and in others closer to that of the mother; the male children have a more pronounced Solomon Island character than the female children.

The people of the smaller offshore islands and island groups on the eastern side (which are, as already mentioned, of earlier, volcanic origin), have founded colonies on the main island whose members even today differ in habits, customs and speech from their neighbours. Tanga and Aneri founded a colony on the eastern side of southern New Ireland many years ago, in present-day Siara, beginning about 8 nautical miles south of Cape Santa Maria and including a number of quite well-populated villages along a coastal strip of about 10 nautical miles. Both island groups still conduct an active, friendly trade with Siara, while standing more or less on a war footing with all their neighbours. Furthermore Tanga and Aneri form the bridge across which there is a steady connection for commerce and trade with the Nissan group, and thereby with Buka and the Solomon Islands generally. In this way traits of one population have passed to the other, in part to be taken up as an exact copy, and partly to be more or less modified, without, however, disowning their origin completely. I will return to this in the ethnographical description.

Similarly, Tabar and Lihir have founded colonies on the main island of New Ireland opposite, with which they are still in friendly-neighbour communication. About twenty years ago there was no such friendly relationship between these colonies. This has changed a lot since then; in particular labour recruitment, which has introduced the people of different districts to one another, has torn down the barriers restricting communication; thus through power of authority the vestiges of enmity have been removed by the administration.

The character of the people in the north and in the south is very different. In the south we find a great similarity to the inhabitants of the Gazelle Peninsula. The people there have the same closed, almost sullen character, tending only a little toward communicativeness. This is also demonstrated in the layout of the villages, which almost universally consist of separate, enclosed compounds, within which the inhabitants are not exposed to the peering gaze of their neighbours. They have a dislike of strangers and foreigners, and where occasion arises this is expressed in raids and attacks. Since the founding of the missions and, through the influence of the imperial administration, hostilities against whites have diminished significantly, and traders can settle down anywhere unmolested.

The population of northern New Ireland is considerably more lively, and has on the whole a higher intelligence than that of the southerners. Dancing and singing and extensive festivities with great feasting are the order of the day here, and work is pushed aside to the best of their ability. Nevertheless the northern New Ireland person is a sought-after worker in the plantations, since as a result of his greater intellect he grasps things easily and, after a brief introduction, understands the work he is to do. When he knows that he is being watched he works to the best of his ability, but when one's back is turned he lays his hands in his lap and loafs about. On his own territory, circumstances permitting, he is quite importunate and insolent, when he knows that he can get away with it. However, he willingly submits to authority and after a short time becomes a useful subject. Since a human life is of not much value to him, in earlier years attacks on whites, and unfortunately murders, occurred quite frequently. However, since a police station has been set up in northern New Ireland this has stopped, and the earlier infamous coast today belongs among the safest regions of the archipelago. The natives have connected their villages by broad highways that are maintained in good order, they have bridged rivers and watercourses with solid bridges, and taken pride in carrying out the work carefully. From the northern point of New Ireland one can now undertake a journey of 200 kilometres along the east coast on good roads, equipped only with a stick and a little tobacco to give as reward to bearers or for well-performed courtesies. In northern New Ireland the missions still have no notable success to show, and only in the most recent times, after the imperial administration set up secure, ordered conditions, have individual stations begun to instruct the natives in Christianity.

Cannibalism was practised throughout New Ireland and New Hanover until not long ago. Through the influence of both the missions and the imperial administration this custom has been restricted at the present day to isolated parts. In the Rossel Mountains, for example, it is still flourishing, and in those areas where the European influence is felt it is often practised in secret.

As a rule it was the bodies of those slain in battle that were eaten by the opposing party, when they could get their hands on them. Yet not only in open warfare did one capture the highly prized roast meat, but rather more by cunning, sudden attacks. All who were slain were dragged away: men, women and children, both old and young. Often expeditions were undertaken to far distant regions to obtain human flesh. On such occasions several districts united for a communal raid. As a rule attacks took place at night, and they rubbed their bodies with black dye to disguise themselves. The captured corpses were removed as quickly as possible and taken to their destinations.

On the New Hanover coast years ago I surprised a number of such hunters, who were returning from a raid in four canoes, holding about fifty men. After a lively hunt we succeeded in cutting off one of the canoes from the shore; the crew sprang into the water with their weapons in order to reach the thick mangrove cover of the near shore, which they succeeded in doing. The captured canoe contained three corpses, two youths and a just-matured girl. All three had been killed by axe blows and pierced with spears; the lifeless bodies were tied fast to thick wooden stakes by lianas. I learned later that the canoes that escaped carried a similarly horrible cargo; sadly, we were not fortunate enough to chase the raiders from them. In the harbour about two hours distant we later met the remainder of the tribe that had been attacked, to whom we delivered the bodies.

Having arrived at their destination, the corpses are taken by the women with loud shrieks of joy, and preparation is begun immediately. This consists of first rubbing the body with sand at the beach and washing it. Butchery then takes place after the bodies have been laid out for several hours, and the neighbours have been summoned by drum signals to celebrate the tribe's triumph and incidentally to pick up part of the roast. Chiefs have the right to reserve the best morsels for themselves, but must, however, give precedence to the host, and pay him in shell money for the portion offered. Everyone tries to get a small piece, for by partaking they believe that they will gain greater bravery or strength or cunning. Indeed, over the course of time, cannibalism becomes a passion for many natives. Certain members of a tribe as well as the corpses of those who have the same totem sign, are not eaten. How one determines this in the latter case, has still not been made clear to me, because membership of a totem is not made recognisable by outward features; yet it is an indisputable fact that these corpses are not eaten. In isolated cases prisoners are tortured to death, just as on the Gazelle Peninsula in earlier times. On the island of Lir, or Lihir, an act of cruelty is still prevalent which will hopefully soon belong to the past. Should the chief have a craving for human flesh, he assembles his entire tribe including the slaves who have been acquired during raids, having previously shared the name of the sacrificial victim with a number of his trusted friends. All sit down in a broad circle on the open ground of the village. At a signal from the chief the chosen few fall upon the victim, hold him fast and poke a hole in his body behind the collar bone. Small, glowing-hot stones are crammed into his body through this hole, and the unfortunate person is then released. He staggers about in appalling agony until death releases him. This horrible custom is said to have been common earlier in the greater part of New Ireland, and it is also known in the Duke of York group, but only through hearsay as a consequence of trade with the New Ireland coast opposite. On St John's Island they are said to have scalded the still-living slaves in the hot springs there, a custom that several years ago appeared so abhorrent to a number of visiting natives from Nissan (Solomon Islands) that a serious skirmish almost broke out between them and their hosts. And yet the Nissan people are terrible anthropophagi also. Cannibalism and human torture do not always go together therefore, even though we have to acknowledge it for New Ireland and isolated parts of New Britain. In this connection I want to note that even though the consumption of human flesh is, or more correctly was, widespread among Melanesians, it cannot be said to be a universal practice. In many parts of New Britain we find the custom stigmatised as an atrocity which occurs only among the neighbours, who are despised as being on a lower level. Even in the Admiralty Islands, both among the Moánus and among the Matánkor, there are numerous individual tribes that abstain from the consumption of human flesh. It must indeed be a characteristic of humankind that one looks down on anthropophagi as on a lower, more degenerate and despicable level of the species. Nothing can appear more abhorrent to civilised people than cannibalism; however, if we observe that people look upon their cannibalistic neighbours with contempt, while they stand on the same level of development and share their views of right and wrong in all other things, we are forced to accept that even among the so-called savages there exists a feeling deep within their heart which shudders before these sorts of degenerate acts against their own people.

I want to mention here the behaviour of Melanesians towards murdered white people. In the course of many years here I have never been able to substantiate a case where slain whites were actually eaten by the Melanesians. The bodies of murder victims have certainly been dismembered from time to time and individual parts taken to remote districts, to some extent as evidence of the murder effected, yet nothing definite is known about consumption of these parts. It seems inconceivable that the cannibal who eats his own kind should spurn a white person. But remember the groundless superstitions of the Melanesian which, I believe, have also carried over into the consumption of human flesh where he expects a perfecting of himself from eating the body of the slain. It is therefore conceivable that he does not eat the body of a slain white person because in his opinion the spirit of the slain person would exert an influence over him that does not seem desirable. The late king Goroi in the Shortland Islands, on questioning and without guidance, gave me the same explanation, though with the not very flattering observation: 'Spirit belong all white men, no good!' Generally one receives the answer that the flesh of white people does not taste good! I regard this as an excuse behind which the crafty native hides his fear of the spirit of the slain. Corroboration of this comes from the fact that in some cases parts of the skeleton of slain whites are preserved by the natives because they ascribe special powers and characteristics to them. Thus the upper arm bone of a European slain at Kambaira on the Gazelle Peninsula was carried around in a little shoulder basket by a chief there, because he imagined that he was thereby procuring a part of the spiritual superiority of the murder victim.

The view that the presence of skulls or human jaw bones in a hut is a sure sign of the cannibalism of the inhabitant, is completely erroneous. In isolated incidences this is certainly the case; often, however, these skeletal parts are memorials to the dead: parents, relatives or friends, and have as little to do with cannibalism as the locks of hair that people in Europe keep as remembrances of the dead. As a consequence of this piety towards the dead, many a native has been the victim of ill-considered punitive expeditions, since the presence of these human remains has been regarded as proof beyond doubt of his guilt.

Equally erroneous is the notion that cannibalism is the main factor in the great decline in population numbers. Certainly in many areas the population of particular districts has been sharply decimated by headhunting, but overall the loss of human life as a result of cannibalism is proportionally barely greater than the enormous losses brought about by wars in civilised countries. In many peoples of the South Seas we find a rapid decline in population, in spite of their not subscribing to cannibalism. To count up or to discuss the individual factors in detail would take too long. It appears, however, that all the South Sea tribes possess a certain weariness of life that robs them of the energy essential for living and this had resulted in a general decline of population long before the arrival of the whites.

Marriage is significantly different in individual parts of the island. We find in the south, as on the Gazelle Peninsula, the purchase of women by the family elders, who then hand over the purchased girl to the younger members of the tribe. On New Hanover and in northern New Ireland this custom is also present in places, but not to the same degree as in the south. Young women there lead a far freer and unrestricted life until they finally choose a husband. In very many places it is not the young man who makes the first step but the young woman, who via female intermediaries makes known to the man in question that she wishes to favour him with her choice. If the chosen one agrees, they live together henceforth as man and wife. Gifts are exchanged and a festive meal is put on. But marriages are concluded exclusively between two individuals who have different totem or tribal signs. Marriages never take place within a totem group, and sexual intercourse between members of the same totem group is regarded as incest, and is punished by death.

In the north, the marriage is not one of great stability. Both parties may freely separate, and the woman then goes back to her clan, and any children born during the marriage go with her. Also, wife exchange frequently takes place, but only between members of the same totem group. Because of this very loose relationship the tribe and the population suffer to an especially great extent, for the women regard children as an inconvenient appendage and use the most varied methods of aborting the embryo, partly mechanical such as strong kneading of the abdomen, leaping from a high block of stone or a tree trunk, strongly binding the abdomen, and so on, and partly through medication, as represented by various familiar plants. Through this bad habit the women weaken themselves in such a way that they die early and do not contribute to an increase of the tribe, so that the latter always decreases in number. It can be accepted as a certainty that the number of women is half the number of men, and during the period of my stay in the archipelago the population of these regions has declined rapidly. Further decimation is brought about by the custom of entire villages or groups occasionally undertaking to have no children at all. I know two previously quite heavily populated districts which, as a result of such an agreement, have almost completely died out today. The motive for this practice is certainly in part the inborn indolence of the natives. A large family creates more work and increased effort, therefore they avoid this by destroying the offspring. Other grounds also contribute, particularly the essence of the totem which often makes the selection of a husband or a wife very difficult, because a large group is not in a position to obtain the necessary wives from a smaller group that has only a small number of marriageable girls at its disposal. The forbidden sexual intercourse within one's own sib then gains ground in secret, and with it the abortion of the foetus. Now if one considers that the girl has already yielded to sexual intercourse by the eleventh or twelfth year and undergone foetal abortion by all kinds of barbaric means, then it is clear that after continuous repetition of this procedure the body becomes weakened to such an extent that at an early age the woman is infertile anyway, and a later, true marriage will remain childless. Girls of sixteen or seventeen make no secret of the fact that they have brought about an abortion three or four times already. Still other customs, as yet unfamiliar to us, contribute as well. In one of the above-named districts female infertility was the result of a prohibition or a vow that had been most strictly implemented since the death of a chief known to me by name. Whether the dead man had imposed the prohibition before his death or whether the vow had been made in his honour after his death, I have never been able to clarify despite all my efforts. However, I tend towards the opinion that we are dealing here with one of those customs that are incomprehensible to us, but that occur here and there from time to time, and have the purpose of honouring a dead person. By way of example, years ago on the Gardner Islands after the death of an influential chief, the honouring consisted of the whole sib speaking not a word for months, and all sib members passed by one another as silent as a post. What it takes to comply with such an obligation can be judged only by those who know the merry, bright natives of that island; and to those who submit willingly to this obligation, adding a bar to marriage would not matter either, the more so since other supportive motives are contributing as well.

No order of the authorities can combat these customs, no threat and no admonition. Perhaps the Christian missions could bring about change, but the Christianity of the natives consists of outward appearance for the time being, the spirit of the people still clings to the past and is subject to old established practices.

Polygamy is universally permitted. From what has been said above, however, it is understandable that it is practised only in isolated cases. Married life is far from ideal; the wife is to a great extent the workhorse. For the most part she attends to the work in the garden, but still has much free time to relax, of which she also makes abundant use. Obedience to the spouse is a virtue that she does not know, or practises only to a limited extent, and marital discord is the order of the day. The lord and master, when finally his patience is exhausted, resorts to a stick or his fists and this results in the wife, if she can manage, rushing to her sib and enlisting the help of her relatives. Thus marital quarrels frequently lead to conflicts and bloody feuds of long duration.

The birth of the first child is always celebrated with great feasts. It is a curious practice that on this occasion mock battles occur between the men and the women. The former arm themselves with short, but quite solid sticks, the latter grab stones, clods of earth, hard fruit, and so on, and, apparently incensed, both parties fly at each other. After a short struggle in which quite effective blows can land, they separate amidst laughter and banter and sit down joyfully to the meal. Pigs must not be missing from these festivities on New Ireland. The greater the number of pigs and the bigger the specimens, the greater the renown earned by the host. At one feast in honour of a dead person in a village on the north-east coast, I counted thirty-seven pigs weighing 80 to 200 pounds; besides this, around 5,000 to 6,000 pounds of taro tubers were stacked next to them, about 300 bunches of bananas and a similar quantity of the round, cheese-shaped packets of sago. The feasting on such an occasion goes on for several days and the participants devour enormous quantities that would command the greatest astonishment from a European observer. An individual would, without apparent effort, devour portions of 4 to 5 pounds of pork, a similar amount of taro, several handfuls of banana and a number of sago cakes.

Special customs do not take place for the onset of puberty. The boy practises spear-throwing with his peers, and when he is bigger goes fishing with the older people. When he is big enough, he goes into battle with them. Girls stay with their mother, go with her to the garden, and are instructed in dancing at an early age. When they are bigger they enter into a love affair, secretly or openly, until they happen to get married and come under the hood. This is no metaphorical expression, since all married women, after their wedding put on a hood, *gogo*, made from pandanus leaves, which bears a distant resemblance to the old Prussian grenadier cap. This cap is always worn in the presence of men, and is taken off only when the woman knows that she is not observed. They are not very careful in the presence of boys and striplings, but etiquette requires that on the approach of an older, married man the *gogo* is immediately donned. This practice was introduced from New Hanover and has spread over a large part of northern New Ireland. In the wood carvings mentioned later, we find the female figures frequently wearing the *gogo*, a sign that that carving had been produced in honour of a dead wife.

With the exception of the *gogo* the woman does not bother very much with clothing. A bundle of fibrous material, sometimes in natural shade and sometimes dyed red, hangs front and back from a cord laid around the stomach. Young girls present themselves as God has created them, and likewise without exception the men go in Adamitic costume. In recent times both genders cover themselves with bright calico material; the men strut about in trousers, jacket and hat, and appear awkward in this civilised attire and often quite unclean. The unclothed brown figures of earlier times without doubt created a significantly more favourable impression on the foreign viewer.

The sight of these clothed men makes it quite clear to us that men's clothing came originally from the endeavour to decorate themselves; since dressing for protection against the effects of weather is not necessary anywhere in the Bismarck Archipelago. That is why one occasionally sees an islander proudly wrapped in an old winter overcoat, a present from some settler for whom keeping this moth-eaten thing is not worth the effort. That the native does not feel comfortable in the foreign feathers can be observed on many occasions, but the quest for imitation and the thought of now appearing significantly more elegant, in short fashionable, causes him to make a sacrifice. In many cases, I regard dressing in European materials as directly unfavourable to health. A naked native gets washed by rain and feels no ill effects from it; the clothed native does not take off the clinging cotton materials, wet through from the rain; they dry on his body and cause lung problems, to which he is particularly susceptible. We should not regard the nakedness of the natives as a cause of the (probably to our eyes) immoral lifestyle. Nakedness, of itself, evokes no sensual arousal in a native, and the prudishness of a totally naked New Ireland girl is just as great if not greater than that of the majority of our fashionable European ladies. To the European, the native in Adam's costume actually does not appear as naked; the brown skin in itself to some extent substitutes for a suit. I have frequently been able to observe how itinerant European women have, in a very short time, learnt to regard the appearance of a naked native as not offensive a sight, whereas a naked European would undoubtedly have aroused their disgust or their anger. Even for a white man who has lived for many years among the natives, a naked fellow countryman would not be a feast for the eyes; the native in the unclothed state appears less uncovered than a naked European who makes a helpless, angular and awkward impression when he sees himself deprived of his protective shell; he does not know whether he should go or stay, the whole freedom and ease of movement has become lost to him with the removal of his clothes, and he arouses a feeling of offence, whereas with the native the exact opposite is the case.

In places in southern New Ireland where, as on the Gazelle Peninsula, they practise marriage purchase, a peculiar practice predominates which has often been regarded as a traveller's tale, but which is, however, based on fact: namely the temporary barricading of the young girl before marriage. Inside a tightly enclosed hut they erect a smaller chamber made from several light poles covered with coconut matting (plate 18). The young girl settles down inside, and for a long time is seen only by the parents, who feed her very well with choice food, and escort her outside in the evening to answer the call of nature. According to comment by the natives, this seclusion lasts from twelve to twenty months. During this period the young woman attains a noticeable girth, and her skin is markedly bleached, so that after a basic wash one might imagine that one is confronted by a somewhat dark Samoan woman. Both the plump shape and the pallor of the skin are regarded as special marks of beauty. A fattened beauty of this kind came to my notice only once; she had been released from imprisonment just two days previously and been given a basic wash, which may well have been very necessary, since during the enclosure washing is regarded as unnecessary. She was apparently subjected to a public exhibition, for many people sat round about, marvelling; and I too was fetched specially in order to express my admiration.

The fattening had proceeded well in this case. The little one, who might have been about fourteen years old was in reality as 'fat as a pig', and the women sitting nearby caressed the fat arms and thighs with admiration or patted the thick cheeks in delight.

Burial customs in northern New Ireland have many peculiarities. When somebody dies, a bier is made out of spears, the decorated corpse is laid on it and then carried from house to house by the relatives. All those present begin a loud weeping and wailing: men as well as women and children. Relatives elsewhere are summoned immediately, and assemble in the house of mourning; friends and acquaintances of the dead person also hasten along.

On the second day a catafalque resting on four stakes is erected in front of the house and the corpse is laid on it. The greater the status of the dead person, or the greater the influence he had had, the higher are the posts of the structure, yet seldom more than 2 metres high. A wood funeral pyre is now set up beneath the structure. It consists of the usual wooden billets but also of carvings that have been used in earlier funerals; in recent times they also break up boxes and crates brought by workers and add the wood to the pyre. The carefully arranged wood pile is then set alight and at the same time a close male relative climbs onto the catafalque, holding a spear in his hand. From time to time he touches the head of the corpse with the spear while singing a monotonous song; this continues until the flames of the funeral pyre necessitate his leaving the structure. The fuel for the fire is constantly replenished until finally the flames have destroyed the structure and the corpse topples onto the glowing embers. The same man who had earlier stood on the structure now steps forward and removes the liver from the corpse with his spear; he shares it out in small pieces among the young men present, together with ginger root. After this ceremony more fuel is thrown onto the fire until the corpse is completely burnt to ashes, and when the embers have gone out a simple protective roof is erected over the site.

During the cremation there sounds a steady, deafening wail of grief, voiced by all present. After the cremation an opulent feast is partaken. That for the relatives is set up beside the funeral pyre; a similarly rich meal is prepared for the friends and acquaintances of the dead man, a short distance away.

Several weeks later the ashes at the cremation site are mixed with coconut milk, and the mourners smear themselves from head to foot with the paste. On this occasion a feast is set up again for all those assembled. For the present the funeral rites are at an end until they reach their conclusion with the annual *malengene*.

The actual mourning lasts from the day of death until the day on which the mourners sprinkle themselves with the ash (*karong*) of the funeral pyre. During the period of mourning the men are not permitted to rub powdered lime or lime paste into their hair.

On New Hanover the funeral procedure is similar; unfortunately, however, I have never had the opportunity of being present at a burial. If we go along the east coast of New Ireland the funeral customs gradually change as we go further south. Cremation is retained but the preceding ceremonies are different. For example, at several places the corpse lies in state in a hut, sitting in a small canoe; the whole body is sprinkled with a mixture of red ochre and burnt lime, and the hands of the corpse, in a sitting position on the bier, are pulled into the air by thin cords tied to both thumbs, so that the arms rise up with elbows bent and hands raised, as if in a position of supplication. In this position the corpse is then buried, or cremated on a funeral pyre.

In some areas the prevailing practice at cremation

Plate 18 The house in which a young girl is incarcerated before marriage

Above: The small hut where the girl spends her time is visible in the background

Below: Side wall of the hut removed

is the setting up of a figure to represent the deceased. The figure is life-sized and plaited from a certain liana, or more accurately the body, fashioned from foliage and grass, is plaited over with a thick liana. The face is represented by a wooden mask. These figures are displayed on a scaffolding during the mourning period and are, as a rule, burnt with the corpse at the conclusion of mourning.

In certain districts in the Rossel Mountains they have a quite characteristic burial or, more correctly, preparation of the body, although one which I have never had the opportunity to see personally, but which has been reported to me by one of the Methodist missionaries stationed there. The corpse is first placed in a sitting position, then it is not only rubbed with coral lime but is packed, in the true sense of the word, in powdered lime and the whole thing is then tied up in leaves. This bundle is placed on the cross beams under the hut roof and stored. My informant, Mr Pierson, tells me that he has seen such bundles that were only a few days old yet spread no cadaverous smell; he had seen them in multiples in the huts of the natives, among them some which had apparently already been stored for a number of years and were coated with a thick crust of dust and soot.

Often, however, the dead are interred in the normal way, although in the districts where this is practised, they bury bodies at sea as well. The choice of burial method is not left to the discretion of the bereaved; however, I have been unsuccessful in obtaining exact information on the nature and manner of regulating this decision. This much is sure: that certain people are buried exclusively at sea after their death, while others are buried in the ground. In any case the former method is the more fashionable, as it appears to be the privilege of chiefs; however, it is possible that totem customs are taken into account here, since the children of those women who have been buried in the ground after death, are interred in the same way, even when the husband and father had been buried at sea. Yet this is not an irreversible rule, for upon questioning, natives declared that after their death they would be buried as their fathers were. Perhaps we are dealing here, as is so often the case, with customs that have been introduced from other regions and been reserved by the immigrant generations, while being partially adopted by the original population and combined with previously existing customs, or modified by them. Doubt over the burial method does not exist and, at my instigation, those in the villages who would have their graves in the sea and those who would have theirs in the ground arranged themselves into two distinct groups without further ado.

In general, when I had the opportunity to observe interments of various kinds, the corpses were decorated with bunches of feathers and items of adornment, and in many places they were provided with shell money or weapons, betel nuts and eating utensils, as on the Gazelle Peninsula.

Dancing and singing are not fostered on any island in the archipelago as much as by the people of New Ireland, probably because the daily work leaves extensive free time for this pleasure. Nowhere else in the archipelago do we find such a variety of dances with such varied figures. Here too the dances are mimic presentations, and each individual movement is precisely deliberated and rehearsed, so that, in precision of movement, a group of experienced dancers could confidently be a match for a European ballet. To describe the individual dances in detail would be far too broad a task; it may suffice to introduce several of the main dances, which are divided into different groups. Dance presentations that I have witnessed can be divided into erotic dances, war and battle dances, pantomime representations of certain events, and dances that are dedicated to the totem or the tribal emblem. This division is valid only for the men's dances; in spite of all my efforts I have not been able to place the women's dances into a precise system.

Erotic dances are very popular, and are presented mainly at festivities to honour the dead. On this occasion the dancers wear the *tatanua* masks mentioned elsewhere (Section VIII), which make the wearer unrecognisable. Besides the mask the dancer wears a cloth of fern and other foliage round the waist, extending from the girdle to the knees. At the presentation the spectators form a circle within which the orchestra takes its place. The latter consists of wooden drums and boards and pieces of bamboo, which are beaten in rhythm. The band is supported by a choir which puts as much effort as possible into drowning out the droning drums. First the orchestra plays a kind of overture. Then from the side, usually from out of the bush, one sees a number of masked dancers approaching; slow, deliberate steps bring them closer to the dance place, now stopping, now looking about on every side, before finally uniting as a group at the predetermined spot. The group then presents, with orchestral accompaniment, a number of measured movements that can hardly be called a dance, since they consist of the masked people slowly circling one another as if one wants to ferret out who the other might be. This lasts for about ten minutes. Then suddenly there approaches, likewise from out of the bush, a single masked figure who moves toward the group in the manner previously described. As soon as the masks perceive this new mask, they apparently fly into great excitement, trot towards it with rapid steps, then draw back, while the newly arrived mask gradually closes with the group. Then begins a very comical presentation which depicts the approach of a man towards a woman, since it quickly becomes clear to the spectators that the recently arrived mask is a female, while the first masks represent men. The men now seek to make the woman receptive, by each endeavouring to supplant the others. Meanwhile the beautiful one remains apparently cold towards all love-suits, pushing one of the flatterers back firmly, turning her back on another, or demonstrating her displeasure through other unmistakable signs. But finally she declares that she has been conquered, and acknowledges one of the masked men as her lover. The latter is now full of joy, which he expresses by all manner of leaps around the beloved. The rejected suitors now withdraw to one side of the dance place, and hand the stage over to the two lovers who now portray an intimate approach, not without initial resistance from the beautiful one, who finally lends an ear to the declarations of love from her chosen one. Even though the representation does not lack earthy realism, especially in the final scene, it cannot be said that the dance is obscene. The comic and the grotesque are predominant in the production, and are even further elevated by the carved and painted *tatuana* masks with their dyed crests, which call to mind the old Bavarian helmets. I need not comment that the natives find nothing disgusting; old and young, men and women, boys as well as girls, gaze on the hustle and bustle quite calmly, and at the end acknowledge their appreciation to the participants with loud shouts.

Even though the native maintains a certain decency in the large, public gatherings, there are other dances in which he recognises absolutely no limits. However, these sorts of presentation take place on fenced-off, densely enclosed places where the gaze of the curious, to whom attendance at such dances is not permitted, cannot penetrate. These types of dances are not suitable for a detailed description.

War and battle dances are presented with the same musical accompaniment as the dances previously described. The dancers take care of the singing themselves. They assemble in a double row or in several rows, each man holding an ordinary battle spear in his hand. The whole body is in ceaseless movement from beginning to end of the dance; legs and feet make rapid trotting movements or bend at the knee, they are thrown to right and left, forwards and backwards, the arms flourish the spear, make feigned thrusts that stretch the enemy on the ground in pantomime, after which the spear is withdrawn with a solid tug. Meanwhile the head and trunk bend and sway in all directions, yet each movement is studied so precisely that even when a hundred dancers are performing the various complicated movements simultaneously, rapidly following one another, all perform in unison. The turns and figures of these dances vary to the greatest extent because first one then another finds a new figure, and when this finds appreciation it is practised by the dancers and is presented perfectly on the next occasion.

The pantomime dances that represent a particular event are equally abundant. They do not differ significantly from similar presentations on the Gazelle Peninsula; it may be that the northern New Ireland people are more outgoing in humour than the calmer, more self-contained Gazelle inhabitants, and accentuate the comical moments more in their dances.

Those dances that for want of a better description are called totem dances, are extremely characteristic. Here they portray the movements of that particular animal which serves a particular group as a tribal designation. In northern New Ireland, certain birds serve as totem signs. The performers are always the owners of the totem sign in question. Here is demonstrated what an acute observer the native is, how minutely he knows his totem bird and its habits, and can imitate them. By way of example I want to introduce the dance of the rhinoceros bird people, whose totem is the rhinoceros bird (*Rhytidoceros plicatus* Forst.). The dancers arrange themselves in pairs one behind the other in long rows. Each person holds a carved, painted rhinoceros bird's head in his mouth; hands are mostly folded behind the back. The rhinoceros bird is recognised as a very shy fellow that feeds in great tranquillity on suitable fruits in the treetops, while never dropping his guard, continually turning his head in all directions to reassure himself that no enemy is in the vicinity. Should one appear, he lets out a characteristic cry and flies off loudly beating his wings. All of this is given a very realistic interpretation by the dancers. Their heads turn to right and left, forwards and backwards; one eye is half closed, the other glances sharply in a particular direction; each movement is performed unhurriedly, in circumspect calm, just as the real bird does it. Finally the cry is sounded and the noisy wing-beats imitated.

In another dance of this sort the pigeon is represented as the totem bird, and is pursued by the snake; that is, the evil spirit that is the totem's enemy. The dancers arrange themselves in two long rows, one behind the other; the front pair represent two pigeons. First a communal dance is performed; then gradually the front pair assume a leading role, dancing individually or as a pair along the line of the other dancers until reaching the far end, then returning to the front. These movements represent the hopping of the pigeon from branch to branch in the treetops. Meanwhile the other dancers form a peculiar figure that represents the snake. This is done as follows. The back pair of dancers step back a little; one steps in front of the other; the one behind bends his left leg forwards somewhat and his right leg sideways; the second dancer then sits on the bent left leg of the first dancer, in turn placing both his legs in the same position; the other dancers gradually close up in the same way as this pair, so that there was finally a long line in which each dancer sat on the knee of the dancer behind. This line, awkward in its combined movement, represents the snake, which tries to encircle the pair of pigeons, which are meanwhile performing a lively dance. From time to time, when the snake's intention is noticed the pigeons fly off; that is, both dancers immediately separate, and then reunite for a combined dance. This goes on until all the dancers, especially those representing the snake are totally exhausted, since in the position described each dancer has to use his utmost strength to follow the combined movements without the connection being broken. This figure is seen in other dance productions as well, and then it has different meanings; in one instance it represents seagulls which alight on a floating tree trunk. The corresponding head and arm movements are different in this case.

Women's dances are of course different as well, but no pantomime presentations are found here; rather, the dancers endeavour to give expression to the daintiness and grace of the female body through strongly measured movements. The series of dancers, arranged in pairs, strike up a song in the highest soprano register. Their bodies are tastefully decorated, particularly with flowers and bright leaves, and each dancer holds a pretty, bright posy of flowers in her hands. Graceful and often very complicated movements are performed with hands and feet, and when such a dance is carried out by a number of young girls, it is actually a beautiful sight. The slender brown figures, in the adornment of youth, turn very gracefully in slow movements, take small steps forwards or backwards, treading as carefully and lightly as though they were treading on eggs, bend their hips, raise and lower their hands and arms, and now and then cast their gaze on the spectators as if asking: see how attractive I am? All obscenity is strenuously avoided.

After what has been said, it is obvious that these dances require lengthy practice. In the event, a lot of time is spent on practice and both boys and girls are instructed by their elders from early childhood. The mothers watch very proudly and happily as their barely two-year-old daughters attempt to imitate the movements of the dancers with greater or lesser skill.

The singing that accompanies the dance is provided in part by the dancers themselves and in part by the drummers, and is a continuous repetition of certain phrases which apparently have no connection with the dance and seem nonsense to a European listener. Incidentally, what I have said in discussing the songs of the Admiralty Islanders (Section IV) is valid for this part of the archipelago as well. While the songs sound nonsensical to an uninitiated person, they are understandable to the natives. They express the highpoints in a concise form by certain key words, whereby the full significance of the song becomes clear.

A part of the musical instruments has already been named in the preceding paragraph. Here too, the drum is a hollowed-out tree trunk with a narrow slit as a sound-hole; the widely audible tone is produced by hitting the side wall with a stick. The hour-glass-shaped striking drum so widespread on the island of New Britain was unknown anywhere on New Ireland until a few years ago. Recently, returning islanders who had been in the service of settlers in New Guinea and on the Gazelle Peninsula brought the instrument to their homeland, and it is now found here and there. Whoever is familiar with the decoration and shape of these drums can establish without difficulty whether a certain specimen has been imported from the Gazelle Peninsula or from Kaiser Wilhelmsland. A signal language as on the Gazelle Peninsula exists only in southern New Ireland, not in the north nor on New Hanover.

Very characteristic and typical of northern New Ireland, is the instrument depicted in figure 43, which must be ranked among the stringed instruments, although it bears not the remotest similarity to European instruments of this type. It consists of a wooden block 35 to 45 centimetres long, 20 to 25 centimetres wide and 13 to 17 centimetres thick. The upper side is formed into three separate tongues by narrow slits. Both central tongues are about 7 to 10 centimetres square and slightly convex. To use it, the native holds the instrument between his knees and strokes across the convex side of the wood with the flat of both hands, which have been previously lightly rubbed with the resin of the breadfruit tree.

The tone arising, or more accurately the three tones arising, bear a great similarity to the bray of a donkey. This characteristic instrument is called *nunut* by the natives, and the tone that it produces is regarded by the uninitiated as spirit voices.

A very widespread instrument, but especially common in northern New Ireland, is the pan flute, assembled from five to eight pipes about 5 to 6 millimetres in diameter, fixed side by side and gradually shortening. The instrument is not used with the dances; it is used by both young and old to establish their musical genius.

The weapons of the New Ireland people are not significantly different from those of the other inhabitants of the archipelago, and consist of clubs, spears, and slingshots with slingshot stones. Spears and slingshots are by far the most customary. Since the introduction of iron, the club has been joined by the axe as a weapon for close combat and, like everywhere else, has been provided with a very long handle when a weapon, as on the Gazelle Peninsula. The free handle end is more or less transformed into a broad, decorated blade. Firearms are very popular, but since the declaration of the German protectorate, providing them to the natives is forbidden. Very many of the earlier attacks and slayings of white people were caused by efforts to get hold of firearms, partly in order to act against the punitive sorties of the administration better

Fig. 43 Musical instrument from New Ireland

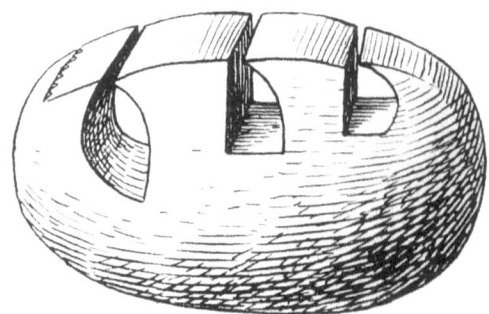

armed, but mainly to wrest any advantage from the less favourably placed neighbouring tribes by having superior weapons. On none of the islands of the archipelago have so many successful attacks on whites been recorded as on New Ireland, and from time to time it has taken great effort to bring the disturbers of the peace to order or to administer exemplary punishment. Today this situation is disappearing; the establishment of police stations and the development of a network of roads have broken the previously warlike, rapacious spirit. White visitors can now wander undisturbed from village to village on good roads, greeted in a friendly manner by young and old.

The club has spread from New Hanover to Cape George. In New Hanover two forms in particular are encountered: a round and a flat form; their length is from 80 to 130 centimetres. The round form has a diameter of about 4 centimetres at the striking end, while the flat form is about 7 centimetres broad at the striking end, tapered off to both sides. Both forms are decorated with carved and notched ornaments, very similar to the ornamentation of the spears. I will discuss in detail the significance of the ornamentation when I talk about the spears. The New Hanover clubs have spread as far as New Ireland, and occasionally they are found southwards as far as the coast opposite the Gardner Islands. In the southern half of New Ireland quite different forms occur, similar to the clubs of the Gazelle Peninsula. For example, we find the forms illustrated in figures 1 and 8 on plate 8 at Cape Strauch, and it is not improbable that they were introduced to the Gazelle Peninsula from there; the form in figure 10 is predominant in southern New Ireland, and was evidently transplanted from there to the Gazelle Peninsula. Then again, in the Rossel Mountains we meet another club, similar to the New Hanover flat form, whose extreme striking end is decorated with a characteristic eye ornament. According to comments from the older people, this represents the face of a spirit that gives strength and courage to the wielder of the weapon. In the villages inland from Cape Giori I was impressed by flat clubs with a characteristic form; they had no pronounced striking end, but both ends were expanded into a broad, fan-like blade, and in order to hold it in their hand they had to grasp it by the thin mid-section about 4 centimetres in diameter. This implement was difficult to use as a weapon and according to reports given to me it was used in dancing. For years I have tried in vain to get hold of these types of implements; however, like so many other things, they seem to be no longer used today. Indeed clubs were never used very much anyway, and today we would find more specimens in European museums than on the whole of New Ireland and New Hanover.

Slingshots and stones are still used everywhere in the southern half of New Ireland and also on the offshore islands. However, they had a far greater spread in earlier times, since during road construction in areas near the northern end of New Ireland, numerous carefully worked slingshot stones have been found, different in shape from the missiles that are still used in the south. During his voyage along the east coast of New Ireland, Dampier found slingshots in an area where they no longer exist today, which he named Slinger's Bay. The slingshot stones found are on average 5 centimetres long and 2.5 centimetres in diameter at their thickest part. The ends are tapered. Because of a lack of suitably shaped gravel, they worked a dense, almost crystalline coral stone into slingshot stones. In the south, stream beds and beach yield satisfactory, readily available material in the form of rounded stones, and these are used just as nature provided them, as is also the case on New Britain. The slingshot appears never to have been used on New Hanover.

Of far greater significance is the spear, both on New Hanover and New Ireland. From New Hanover two different forms of spear seem to have spread to the north of New Ireland, as well as to Sandwich Island. Both forms are the same in that they consist of two particular parts – a bamboo shaft and a spear blade or spear point of hard palm wood, which is tied firmly to the shaft by careful wrapping with fine, strong fibre. The most widespread form has a circular cross-section gradually tapering to a long, needle-sharp point. The second form has a flat, lancet-like, more expanded point; in older examples from New Hanover this frequently follows an intermediate section (between point and shaft), decorated with incised hooks and ornaments. This form often has no shaft end of bamboo and is frequently made from a single piece of wood. The fissures in the carved decoration, as well as the inside of the hooks, are as a rule filled with red ochre or burnt lime, so that the dark pattern of the carving is clearly enhanced (fig. 44). These spears are now a great rarity.

On the shafts there is almost always ornamentation, always of the same type. Professor von Luschan in his book *Beiträge zur Völkerkunde* has given a number of good illustrations of the unrolled decoration (plates 36 and 37), and is of the opinion that this is a case of the remnants of a stylised human figure. The natives admittedly have other ideas. Of course the majority have nothing to say about it. The sum total knowledge is: it belongs like that! or: it has always been made like that! However, several older men from New Hanover have advised me that the figure represents a snake or, more accurately, a spirit in the form of a snake, news that was apparently just as unfamiliar to the younger people sitting round as it was to me. On New Hanover the snake plays a major role as an

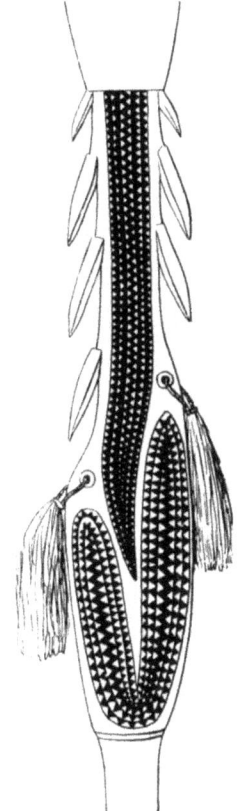

Fig. 44 Ornamented part of a spear from New Hanover

Fig. 45 Decoration of a club from New Ireland

evil spirit, just as on New Ireland, where we see it depicted in various ways as the enemy of the totem animal on the familiar carvings. As mentioned earlier we find the same stylised decoration on the clubs and, as on the spear shafts, in such a barely recognisable form that one can hardly talk about any interpretation. However, in my possession is a very old, carefully carved club with a flat striking end, one side of which is adorned with a figure in surface relief that is fairly clearly recognisable as the form of a snake. The fissures are filled with burnt lime and the decoration stands out clearly, as depicted in figure 45, as a dark carving on a white background.

On clubs of recent date the ornamentation is just as carelessly presented as on the spear shafts; however, one can almost always recognise a head, which is depicted in the same style as the heads and faces in von Luschan's reproductions. In recent years enterprising natives have resorted to manufacturing clubs for trade. These are recognisable by their enormous weight and their decoration with triangular notches in varying order, with the old, original, stylised decoration still recognisable even though it has attained a completely different character through altered technique.

Further to the south is found another type of spear, which can certainly be regarded as the original form for this area, until partially supplanted by the New Hanover spear. It is seldom more than 130 centimetres long, about 1.2 centimetres in diameter at its thickest point, and made from a single piece of wood. The point is about 30 centimetres long and sharpened; below this, at the thickest part of the spear, there is a wrapping of fine fibres, about 4 centimetres wide, and, as a rule, coated with lime. The shaft slowly tapers right up to the butt where it is about 6 millimetres thick, and is partially decorated by incised notches and longitudinal lines. This light spear is a very dangerous weapon in the hands of the natives; a high level of throwing ability is attained through repetitious practice, and I have seen life-threatening wounds imparted over 40 metres. Because of the lightness of this spear, it is possible for the natives to carry a large number of them, usually a bundle of ten to fifteen, whereas only two or three of the previously mentioned heavier spears could be carried, with the warrior running the risk of becoming unarmed after a short battle.

Further south on the island, in the area opposite the Gazelle Peninsula, we again find the forms of that peninsula, either as long, throwing spears circular in diameter with extended sharp tips and strongly tapering butt ends, or more powerful spears with a human humerus bone on the rear end of the shaft.

The stone axe has now completely disappeared, and it is difficult to obtain blades. On New Ireland we find axe blades of both *Tridacna* shell and of various dark, lava-like types of stone. The shape is almost universally the same as on the Gazelle Peninsula, and stone blades from both places assembled in a common collection might not be differentiated according to origin, even by the best authorities. I cannot say whether the fastening of the axe blade was different, for in spite of many enquiries I have never seen an axe complete with handle. I have been given to understand by older people that the blades at the short end of a knee-shaped wooden haft were fastened partly with thin rattan strips and partly with fibre; therefore very similar to the Gazelle Peninsula method. The *Internationale Archiv für Ethnographie* vol. III has an illustration in plate 15 of a hafted axe, allegedly from Kapsu, about 20 nautical miles south-east of the northern end of New Ireland. Professor Giglioli who described this axe which is in his possession, believes that it must be a ceremonial axe because the knee-shaped haft is decorated with the carving characteristic of New Ireland, depicting two human heads with the single head of a lizard on the reverse side. I have for a long time regarded this specimen as a plaything, since it certainly could not have been prepared as an exchange-trade item because it was made at a time when such articles were not yet traded; also, as I could see at a glance, the care taken in the presentation of the carving was too great for it to have been made as mass-produced merchandise. Sadly, in spite of all my efforts and inquiries in and around Kapsu, it was not possible to learn anything more detailed about this axe. Many years later by chance I found out in a village on the coast roughly opposite the Gardner Islands, that this type of axe was laid in the grave of certain men at their interment. This custom apparently vanished a long time ago, since young men gathered round to examine the illustration and were as full of questions as I was. The bird placed on the head of the upper figure represents the totem sign of the dead person; the lizard on the reverse side of the head is a representation of the evil spirit that, in this form, is following the totem (that is, the present bearer of the totem) – a motif that is repeated in the most widely varied forms in numerous carvings from New Ireland.

The stone axes from New Hanover are very different from those of New Ireland. They consist of a thick, almost fine-grained basalt stone, and always have the same shape, although in different sizes. I have blades of all sizes in my collection: from 7 centimetres long and 2.5 centimetres maximum diameter, up to 25 centimetres long and 4.5 centimetres in diameter. The shape is round, and the upper end is pointed into a cone with slightly convex sides; the cutting edge is formed in the lower, more club-shaped end by grinding off a segment, and the ground surface is slightly concave as in a gouge. The whole blade leaves the impression that it is a stone imitation of the *Terebra* shell axe common in many places; for example, on St Matthias.

The axe haft is the usual knee-shaped form, but the blade is not always bound firmly to it, but is stuck into a wooden case, enabling the blade to revolve, so that the cutting edge can be perpendicular or parallel to the handle as needed. A complete hafted axe might be just as difficult to obtain today on New Hanover as it is on New Ireland; the true stone age has totally disappeared here in the relatively short time of barely twenty years, and has had to yield to the iron of the Europeans.

Apart from the axe, the people of New Ireland possess only a few tools. For fine carvings the axe is used for the rough hewing of the wooden block, then further processing is carried out with sharply honed shells, and a paintbrush of coconut fibre or other fibrous material completes the careful, often very fine designs. The sharp front tooth of a marsupial is used mainly for cutting thin turtle-shell discs, as these are often used for jewellery, and a sharpened bone serves as an awl or borer. For polishing wooden carvings they still use certain types of coral and the rough skin of the shark.

Decoration is on the whole less common among the New Ireland people than in other inhabitants of the archipelago. Painting of the body with red, white or black colours is usual at festivities. On the other hand, feather decoration is almost totally lacking, it is only used here and there in southern New Ireland. Since the cassowary and the cockatoo are absent on the island, effective decoration with the feathers of these birds is totally absent. The exclusive raw material is furnished by species of *Eclectus* and other parrots as well as a few species of gull. Earlier the people paid far greater attention to hairstyle than they do today. On the *tatanua* masks these earlier decorations are still copied, and in the illustration given by Tasman in his journal we see that this hairstyle was still customary at that time. It has been assumed that this crested hairstyle is an imitation of Spanish helmets; however, this does not take into consideration the fact that the first Spanish seafarers did not wear crested helmets, but wore conical sheet-steel or sheet-iron caps with a protective projection and a neck guard when they went into battle. Today this hairstyle has totally disappeared. A slight vestige is still found where the youths let a low roll of hair grow above the forehead while shaving off their hair in a semicircle above the ears on both sides of the head and rubbing the bald patches white with lime. The older people take great care over their beards; this consists of a moustache and short, mutton-chop side whiskers which run down from the ears to the tips of the moustache; beards are not infrequently touched up here and there with lime paste. Nevertheless, beards are not the rule; alongside bearded men one sees just as many clean-shaven individuals. Full beards are not common; they are found here and there among older men.

Scarring is more or less common, and is performed on arms, shoulders and the chest without any rules on arrangement. Tattooing, which I will discuss later, is practised only in the district of Siara.

Necklaces existed earlier in widely varied arrangements; today they too are almost completely replaced by European glass pearls. In the south the necklaces consisted especially of strands of human teeth as well as cuscus teeth, which were wound round the neck in several rows. Individual seed kernels were used for the same purpose. Neck ruffles

Plate 19 Spears from St Matthias and Emirau

1. Fishing spear; 2. to 6.spear tips; 7. to 11.shaft ends.

Fig. 46 Chest ornament (*kapkap*)

1. to 7. older pieces from New Ireland; 8. to 9. from New Hanover; 10. to 14. from the Admiralty Islands

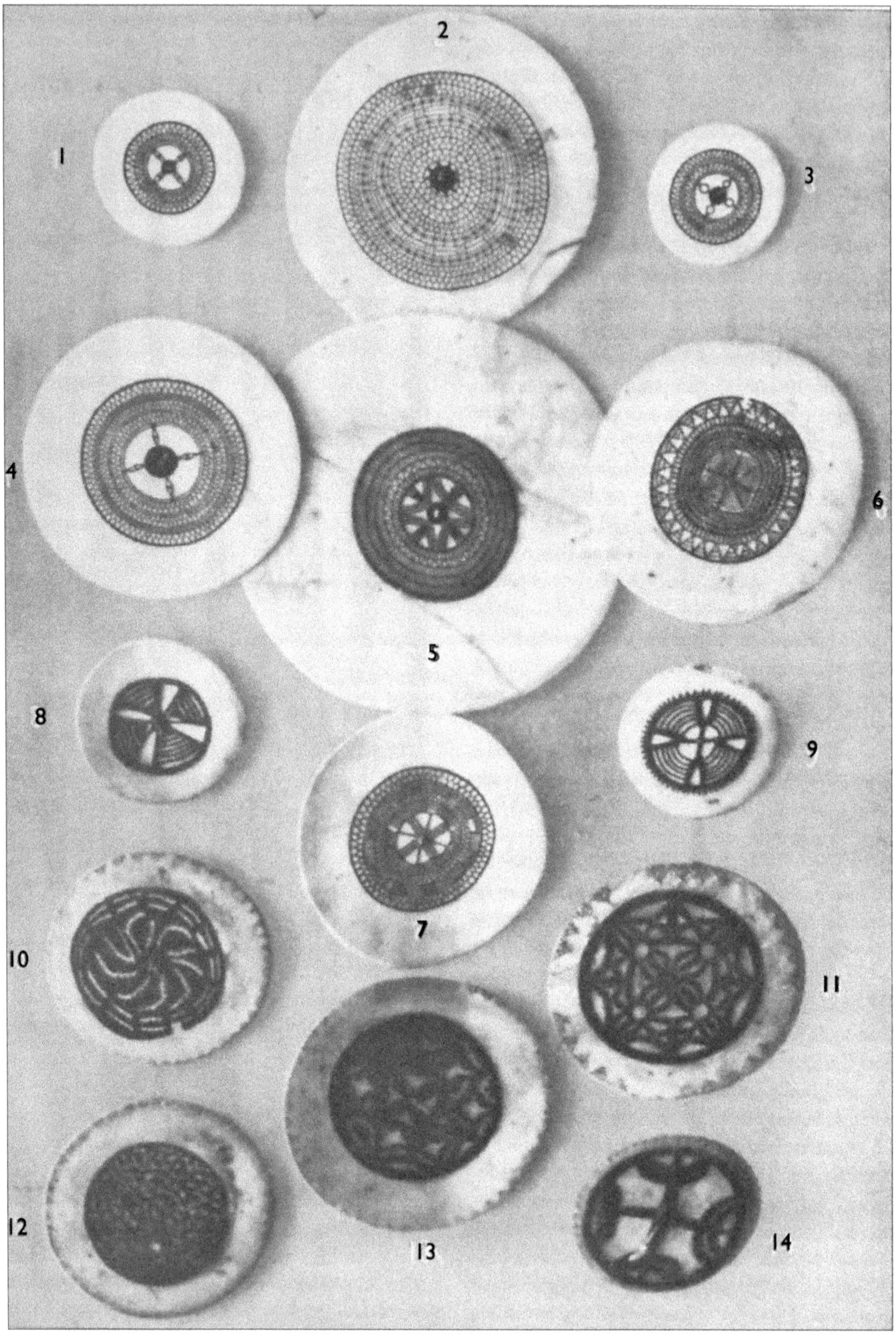

of fern leaves, usually dyed brown with sprinkled ochre, are worn still at dance feasts. An ornament that is still retained although gradually beginning to decline, is the breast ornament called *kapkap*. The *kapkap* consists of a round, white disc of 3 to 20 centimetres diameter, which is ground with great effort from the thick part of the *Tridacna* shell, and is not dissimilar to a thin alabaster plate. On this disc is laid a thin turtle-shell disc that, with the utmost care, has been carved into with an open-work pattern. The dark turtle-shell disc with its decorative design stands out effectively from the white surface beneath. Figure 46 shows older pieces that were produced before the introduction of iron tools; today, with better tools, they are produced with far less care. Specimens 1 to 7 come from New Ireland where, particularly on the Gardner and Fischer islands, the working was especially fine, as specimen number 2 demonstrates. Specimens 8 and 9 come from New Hanover and rank significantly below the examples from New Ireland in care of presentation. Specimens 10 to 14 come from the Admiralty Islands. In these likewise, the turtle-shell discs are less artistically worked, and the *Tridacna* disc is thicker and more clumsy, and shows the characteristic cross-hatching on the edges, which frequently appears as decoration in this island group. The *kapkap*, which is fastened to a thin cord around the neck, covers the upper chest if it is large, and is specifically a male ornament, although women and girls wear smaller pieces as well. The splendid, large pieces were always a rarity, and are only found extremely rarely today. Production of such large discs requires an extraordinarily large *Tridacna* specimen, and considerable effort in production.

On the southern half of New Ireland, particularly on the west coast, battle decoration is customary, and deserves more detailed description because nothing similar exists in the archipelago, with the exception of a few places on the north coast of New Britain and on the French Islands. In these areas battle decoration has been adopted from Kaiser Wilhelmsland, and is intended also as a piece of jewellery hanging in front of the chest. In New Ireland this purpose has been abolished, and the ornament, if one can call it that, is only seen on those natives who are engaged in a warlike undertaking. The ornament consists of a little wand 8 to 10 centimetres long, from the ends of which hangs a bunch of brown, spirally wound strands. Professor Buchner of Munich has made a detailed study of these strands, and found that they were made from the tissue of a particular species of butterfly. They are used as follows: the wearer grasps the little wand between his teeth so that both bunches hang from the corners of the mouth like a stiff beard, giving him a wild, fear-inducing appearance. As far as I could ascertain, this indeed was the purpose.

Armrings were far more common earlier than today; they have been partially replaced by ceramic imitations which were made in Germany and England. On New Hanover and throughout New Ireland armrings cut out of *Trochus* shell and polished smooth are very popular, and have migrated from southern New Ireland, across the Duke of York Islands, to the Gazelle Peninsula. In New Hanover their name is *mapa*, in New Ireland and on the Gazelle Peninsula *lai* or *lalai*. The ring is cut from the snail shell in such a manner that the partition wall of one revolution connects both the outer walls, thereby creating a projecting hook (fig. 47). The rings are 3 to 5 millimetres thick and wide, and of varying diameter according to arm thickness. They are seldom worn singly, but mostly as several, one above the other, forming a broad cuff. Several old items in my collection consist of about fifty individual rings, exactly matching one another, about 20 centimetres wide in all. In wearing them, one ring after another is placed upside down over the elbow and the projecting hooks are arranged precisely one above the other. Each ring links up exactly with the preceding one and as they are fairly forcefully ranged over the muscles of the upper arm, they retain their opposing position, and the indentation beneath the hook runs downwards across the armrings like a long groove.

On southern New Ireland and in the Rossel Mountains, armrings of another shape are customary. They are 2 to 3 centimetres wide and the outer surface is polished to a convex shape. The raw material is *Tridacna* shell. These rings have never been very common, and are exclusively the property of chiefs. Plaited armrings of thin cords bound together in various ways, often into bands up to 1 centimetre wide, and often into 5 to 6 centimetre rings, are still in use. They are almost always dyed with red ochre.

I must not forget to mention that boring through of the nasal septum and widening of the ear lobes is practised both on New Hanover and on New Ireland, especially in the northern half. In the hole through the nasal septum they insert a polished rod of *Tridacna* shell, 6 to 8 centimetres long. The ear lobes are enlarged by inserting rings of rolled-up palm leaves which are slightly springy, and gradually enlarge the hole. The latter ornament is worn by both men and women.

The other common adornment at the various celebrations consists of flowers and bright fragrant plants, with which head, neck, torso and limbs are decorated; the burning red hibiscus blooms are a preferred decoration, as indeed they are with all Melanesians, standing out effectively against the dark hair and the brown skin.

House construction may be described as most painstaking over the greater part of the island. On New Hanover, the hut is a long rectangle, the length about twice as great as the breadth. On the low side walls rests a slightly bowed roof frame of thin sticks, covered with the fronds of the sago palm or the coconut. The straight gable ends are clad with mats, which are carefully plaited in various diamond and zigzag patterns. As a rule the entrance is in one of the gable ends. Partly in order to protect the side walls from attack by thrown spears, and partly to have the essential fire material always at hand, they pile up split, chopped-up wood along under the overhanging roof. The New Hanover construction method extends to the northernmost part of New Ireland, although it is reminiscent of the housing further south, which is significantly advanced on the New Hanover houses in the care given to construction. A New Hanover house is depicted in plate 37 of the *Papua Album*, volume II; in plates 29, 31 and 35 the more carefully constructed houses of northern New Ireland

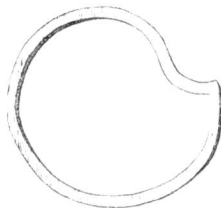

Fig. 47 Armring of *Trochus* shell

and the Fischer Islands are displayed. It can be seen clearly that these belong to a more advanced type. They are more spacious and have a projecting verandah on the long side, under which the doorway (always sited in the long wall), leads inside. Both gable ends are extended by sloping roofs and contain the sleeping area. The side walls are higher and permit entry to a fully grown person without stooping too much; overall the entire building is higher, and more spacious. In the interior of all these houses is the hearth on which food is prepared. It consists of a circular shallow hole, about 1 metre in diameter, in which are laid the cooking stones: fist-sized stone fragments that are made to glow before the food is laid on them for cooking. Other hot stones are then placed on top of the food and the whole thing is covered with a thick layer of leaves, which is only removed when the food is cooked. More recently, separate cooking houses have begun to be adopted, a practice that returning natives have brought with them from foreign parts.

House construction is more primitive further to the south on New Ireland. On the east coast huts are still built carefully, whereas on the west coast they are in part large beehive-type roofs with a low doorway through which one can only crawl. In many villages the floor has been excavated about 1 metre deep inside the huts, and a stay in these semi-underground holes is anything but pleasant.

Throughout southern New Ireland the dwellings are surrounded by stone walls, probably because intensive pig-breeding is carried out everywhere, and it is deemed essential to protect the houses against visits from these proboscidians. The natives are very fastidious, particularly in relation to the cleanliness of their living space, and the floor is always cleansed or covered with a thick layer of white beach sand where this is available.

Household utensils trouble the natives as little here as in the rest of the archipelago. The scanty possessions, spears and fishing equipment, lie on the cross-beams of the roof or hang from them. Eating utensils, stored in palm baskets, stand one on top of the other in the corner or hang from wooden hooks under the roof, should they need to be protected from attack by rats. The sleeping place is extremely basic and consists of a few coconut mats on the bare ground, or a low plank bed made either from five or six leaf stalks of sago or coconut palm laid side by side, or often from rough wooden spars as thick as an arm. On these narrow benches, seldom more than 30 to 40 centimetres wide, the native sleeps deeply and peacefully; a European would certainly fall off at the slightest movement. Yet the New Ireland person, like all the other inhabitants of the archipelago, enjoys a sound sleep throughout, even in old age. As a rule it requires a lot of effort to wake him up; strong shakes and far from gentle blows have the desired effect only after some time, and then quite an interval elapses before he has his five senses about him. However, it is worth mentioning that from time to time the native can go without sleep for a long period. In the gardens one can observe that the people, after having worked quite hard during the day, sing and dance on moonlit nights until well after midnight, or go night fishing in suitable weather, catching a couple of hours' sleep just before daybreak. They can continue thus for days on end without displaying signs of exhaustion.

The coastal inhabitants also take great care in the construction of their canoes. On New Hanover and in the far north of New Ireland they use a form which differs from the boats used further south. The canoe consists of a long, hollowed-out tree trunk, carefully smoothed both inside and out, with a long bow as well as stern. The bow is decorated with a stylised head, the stern with a hook-like figure. This dugout has no gunwale trimmings; from gunwale to gunwale and projecting over one side run the two or three outrigger booms to which the float is fastened by knee-shaped supports which are bound on by cords. These canoes are of various sizes and carry two to fifteen people. They are propelled rapidly by steering paddles; recently, however, sails have been introduced as well, and in the area round Nusa Harbour single and double-masted vessels are seen. In recent years a regular sailing port has built up here, and it is a pleasure to see the light vessels flying, in the true sense of the word, over the surface of the water in a good breeze, driven by the large, yet light, calico sail, navigated by a helmsman, with a companion managing the sail.

Further south, both on the Gardner and Fischer islands, the canoe takes another form. The lower part is made from a single tree trunk, but a plank the length of the canoe is firmly fastened to both sides so that the sides become higher and the canoe, which is always used on the open sea in these regions, cannot so easily be swamped by the waves. Booms and outrigger are attached by and large in the same way as in the previously discussed vessels. However, the two ends, to each of which a brightly painted carving is attached, are quite different. Both of these carvings represent protective spirits which are supposed to give protection against evil spirits of the sea, especially the shark, for which traps are enthusiastically laid everywhere in the region. In the frequently mentioned drawing in Tasman's journal, this figure is also sketched, although the illustrator has reproduced the carving fairly freely.

In southern New Ireland we again encounter the simple dugout with outrigger booms and float, but as well as this the great voyaging canoe without outrigger, which is a copy of the Buka vessels, transplanted via St John to the coast of the main island opposite, and from there to the west coast, and as far as the Duke of York Islands. This canoe has already been described on another occasion, and therefore I do not need to give a fresh description.

The dugout in itself only differs from that of the Gazelle Peninsula by the attached bow and stern pieces both bearing a flat, kidney-shaped leaf which is as a rule painted red (fig. 48). Since the region of the Gazelle Peninsula on St George's Channel south of Cape Gazelle is on a friendly trade footing with the coast of New Ireland opposite, from time to time this type of canoe prow is seen in the shoreline villages there.

Catching fish in New Ireland is carried out partly with the aid of spears, partly with line, and partly by means of sinking nets of various sizes. None of these methods differ markedly from those of the other inhabitants of the archipelago.

Characteristic of the northern half of New Ireland is shark-catching, carried out in this region by means of an unique apparatus that we encounter nowhere else in the archipelago and, to my knowledge, is known in no other area. The apparatus (fig. 49) consists of two separate main parts which are used together. The actual catching apparatus consists of a wooden float about 125 centimetres long. It is cut out of soft wood and comprises a round or square central piece about 15 centimetres either in diameter or square, with a round hole about 5 to 6 centimetres wide through it. From this central piece lancet-shaped wings go off to both sides, the greatest breadth being about 15 centimetres. These wings are bent slightly upwards and often placed a little obliquely to the long axis, so that they adopt the position of the slightly tilted vanes of a ship's propeller. Through the central hole the fishermen pull a long loop of plaited rattan of about a finger's thickness, and a knot at one end prevents the loop from slipping through the hole.

The support apparatus consists of a ring of rattan on which they arrange up to twelve half-coconut shells with holes through the centre. The whole thing is then used in the following way. The fishermen put to sea with the apparatus in their canoes, often going several kilometres offshore. Then they let the canoe drift, and one of the crew moves the ring with the coconut shells back and forth against the side of the canoe causing a clacking noise. This noise attracts the sharks, whose hearing must be quite extraordinarily acute, for although not a single shark might be seen beforehand, it is not long before they approach the clacking sound. When a shark is in sight the native prepares his catching apparatus by pushing the previously free-swinging end of the rattan cord through the hole in the middle, forming a noose beneath the apparatus. The shark, having circled the canoe several times, approaches the clacker close to the surface of the water and the native guides his apparatus so skilfully that the beast of prey puts his head in the noose. The moment a third of the shark has passed through the noose, this is tightened with a sharp tug, and secured. Now the shark cannot get out, and it is easy for the fishermen to wound it by spear thrusts, pull it in and finish it off by clubbing and spear thrusts.

Although Captain Keppel has described this method of shark capture fairly accurately in the description of his journey in the warship *Mäander* (vol. II, page 205), in the middle of last century, the reliability of his report had been doubted until most recently. The reason is, probably, that it is incredible that such a powerful carnivore as the shark would allow itself to be outwitted so easily. Yet whoever has witnessed shark-catching in one or other form will concede that the voracious robber knight of the seas discloses very little intellectual gift, and, as a rule, is very easy prey.

Tasman's journal contains a drawing that shows us that at the time of his voyage shark-catching in New Ireland was practised exactly as it is today. The drawing depicts a canoe with three passengers. From gunwale to gunwale lie several shark snares, whose significance has not been grasped by Tasman and he does not mention them in his journal. The snares appear to have been regarded as uniquely shaped seats.

Fishhooks have now been superseded almost everywhere by European iron fishhooks of varying

Fig. 48 Canoe prow from southern New Ireland

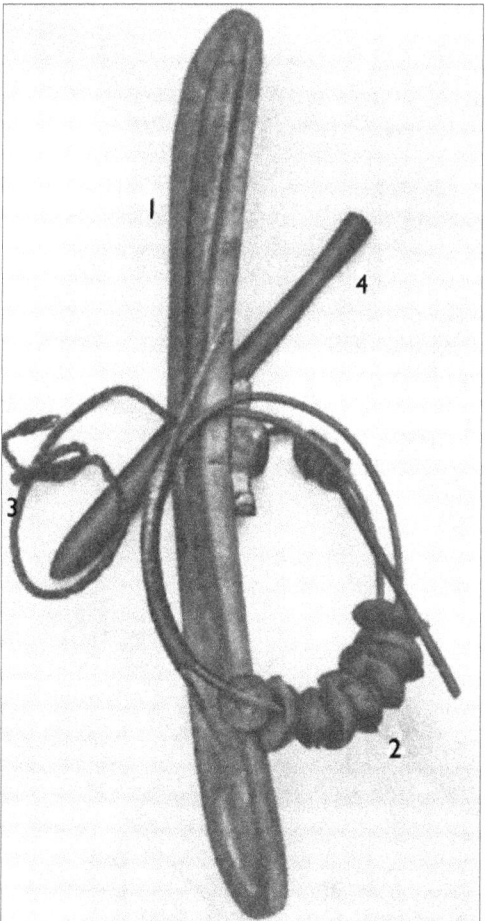

Fig. 49 Apparatus for shark-catching. New Ireland

1. float; 2. rattle; 3. noose; 4. club

sizes. In earlier years one could see the original item in use. In northern New Ireland the form was closely related to that of the Micronesian islands. The raw material was turtle shell; the shape of the hook was almost circular, and the pointed end was armed with a barb pointing outwards. In southern New Ireland the form was another, should I say more primitive, one. Here the hook consisted of a turtle-shell leaflet, 4 to 10 centimetres long and about 3 to 8 millimetres wide; one end was sharpened and bent round, forming a hook 1 to 3 centimetres long; on the other end was a small groove which enabled better fastening of the hook to the line.

Here and there on the east coast of New Ireland and on the offshore islands from time to time, one encounters the familiar Polynesian fishhooks, consisting of a longish piece of mussel shell with the pointed turtle-shell hook mounted on it.

Fish-traps are not found in these regions because the sea floor drops almost everywhere to such great depths, thereby making basket fishing impossible. To catch smaller fish in the inshore shallows and on the reefs, bigger or smaller enclosures are made out of coral stone. The fish swim in at high tide to become easy prey at low water when the enclosures are left partially dry. To catch very small fish, an unique apparatus is constructed at some places along the east coast. Long conical baskets are plaited out of coconut palm leaves, about 8 to 10 centimetres wide at the open end and 75 to 100 centimetres long. These baskets are secured side by side on a frame like a double-cross, fifteen to twenty as a rule, so that the openings all face the same way. The catching apparatus is now pushed along in the shallows by the fisherman, and the little fish get into the various conical baskets.

Sharks, dolphins and turtles are very popular everywhere, and the fisherman is paid a relatively high price for them. The custom on Tabar, Lihir and the opposite coast of the main island, of reserving turtle flesh for the chiefs, is reminiscent of Polynesia.

Different forms of currency, which are prepared by the natives themselves, are in use from New Hanover in the north as far as the extreme southern end of New Ireland. It is not very easy to ascertain the origin of the various types of currency. Several of them have local usage, and they are seldom found beyond the borders of the district within which they circulate; in this case it is easy to determine their actual origin. However, often, various forms of money circulate side by side and have differing values at different places, but in most cases they increase in value the more distant they are from their original homeland. It is then quite difficult to determine the origin, since most of the natives do not precisely know it, and only by chance does one find the site of production, often comprising only a few villages.

Highly prized on New Hanover and on almost the entire northern half of New Ireland is the money bearing the name *tapsoka*, which is produced on a few of the small New Hanover islands. It consists of small rose-red and white shell discs, 3.5 to 4 millimetres in diameter and about 0.5 to 0.75 millimetres thick, usually arranged in such a way that a number of white discs follows a number of red ones. These discs, arrayed on cords about 75 centimetres long, are put into circulation, their value being the equivalent of about 5 to 7 Marks. The natives obtain the raw material for making the discs from the coral reefs. A species of *Patella* yields the material for the red discs, while for the white discs they use various bivalves with white shells. The high value of *tapsoka* comes about because of the limited availability of the red discs. The individual discs are first cut roughly with a small stone and then bored through. The drill which is so widespread elsewhere in Melanesia is not used; but rather we see a device which is undoubtedly the forerunner of the drill: a very fine wooden bar about 60 centimetres long with the thickness of a coconut palm rib, about 2 millimetres thick at the lower end, and gradually tapering to a needle-sharp point. At the thick end a sharp sliver of quartz is fastened with bast thread. In drilling, the tip of the sliver is placed against the disc, and the bar is twirled back and forth between the palms of the hand. After the hole is made the discs are finely polished so that they appear completely flat and round.

Other types of currency are spread further southwards, corresponding with *tapsoka* in that they usually are made from shell discs, but from different species, which give a different appearance and a different value. The names of the types of currency are for the most part different in the districts in which they circulate. As already mentioned there are very many such strings of money. Several consist of small red discs about 2 millimetres wide, several of similar, white discs; others consist of alternate red and black discs arranged in a row, others again of pale brown and reddish-brown, rose-red or pale violet discs. Yet all have a different value and a different name, partly as a consequence of their shape, partly because of their colour and partly also through the order and arrangement of the discs. First and foremost, the so-called *birok* from the Laur district belongs among the collective forms of money. It consists of long strings of shells that, starting from a middle or central piece, hang alongside one another over many metres and are adorned with pig tusks at the end. They are used especially as means of barter for the large pigs which play such a prominent role in all festivities. Strings of money arranged side by side are used as girdles in many cases, and are then to some extent spectacular showpieces.

A unique division is formed in New Ireland by the Siara district on the east coast and the island groups of St John and Caen. The Siara people call the Caen Islands Tánga and St John Aneri, the latter name also being recognised by the groups' inhabitants, although both islands of the group are known there as Ambitlé (the larger) and Bábase. The Tánga people call St John Finni and Siara Baraff. The Nissan group is called Musson by the St John natives, and the inhabitants of Nissan designate St John as Wuneram.

The three districts interact freely with one another; that is, they undertake trading relations, and during these undertakings peace usually reigns.

Aneri buys pigs from Nissan, as well as bows and arrows, the latter, however, more as playthings, since they have never been adopted generally as weapons. As a means of payment they use a type of shell money from Siara, called *kémetas*. These are small shell discs about 2 millimetres in diameter that are called *kémetas kanontang* when they are a red colour and *kémetas mamang* when they are brownish; the former is the more valuable. Furthermore, on St John itself a reddish-brown shell money circulates, bartered from Siara and called *lolot*; in Siara, where it is made, it is called *jaben*.

Tánga buys pigs and red ochre on Aneri or Finni, and pays for them with armrings which, as a means of payment, are grouped under the common name *angfat*. There are two different types of *angfat*, namely *anoa ranguk*, armrings which have several parallel, shallow grooves running round the outside, and *tintol* with a single, deeply incised groove on the outside.

The *anoa ranguk* have different names and different values according to their breadth and the more or less careful production of the external grooves.

The narrow rings with shallow grooves are named *kisina witi*; broader rings with the same type of grooving are called *langkaukau*; the same sort with deeper grooves are called *aramat*; still broader rings with deep grooves are called *anmalmal*, and the very broad and most valuable are called *angfat na liman merivel*. The less valuable *kisina witi* are about 15 millimetres wide, while the very broad *angfat na liman merivel* are 80 to 90 millimetres wide and quite rare.

Production of these armrings is very laborious. A suitable piece is tapped out of a *Tridacna* shell and then drilling is begun. The process carried out in Berlinhafen, by means of a bamboo tube, is unknown; on the contrary they proceed like the Baining on the Gazelle Peninsula and tap on both opposing sides with a sharp stone until a hole is formed. These armrings have completely circular openings of exactly the same width on both sides, just like the drilled-out armrings at Berlinhafen. On Tánga the regular rounding is produced by further rubbing. As a rule they use a piece of wood and pumice dust; the latter is obtained from material washed ashore. Thus when we see stones cut through in that way we should not always draw the conclusion that they were drilled by a circular instrument. On the contrary, a breakthrough and further careful working can lead to the same result. To the experienced eye, the different production methods are evident without difficulty. Drilling as in Berlinhafen, with a circular instrument (bamboo tube), presents a completely round hole. A hole that is knocked through, even though it has had additional very careful work, always shows small variations in diameter. After completing the hole, the outside of the armring is rubbed on a stone until the desired shape is produced. Both the shallow grooves of the *anoa ranguk* and the single deep groove of the *tintol* are produced by a sharp stone sliver. It is not improbable that the Nissan people have learned this type of processing from their connections with the St John natives, since there they proceed precisely in the same way in the production of their *Tridacna* money, called *kuamanu*.

The inhabitants of these districts differ in many ways from the southern New Ireland people. They have an unique language and characteristic features in their traditions and customs that are absent in their neighbours, but on the other hand there are many things that point to an origin on northern New Ireland and in the Solomon Islands, although appearing in a modified form.

In their external features they show the greatest similarity to the southern New Ireland people, with the exception that here we find a characteristic facial tattooing (fig. 50), designated by the Polynesian word *tatau*, indicating fairly clearly whence this custom came to this area. Tattooing takes place exclusively among women after marriage and in women extends only over the face. The women are also the executive artists. The pattern consists of tattooed parallel strokes, which seen up close appear as a uniform, blue-black pattern.

First a double band of such strokes stretches from ear to ear across the forehead, a little above the eyebrows. From this double band a double zigzag line, usually five double peaks, stretches across the forehead, extending the double band right to the hairline. The women call this forehead pattern *taftaf*; it is designated as *am vatuat* (a species of large sea snail) by the men.

On the right cheek a leaf-like decoration is added, called *bantoang kamas* by the women and *bantoangkaka* by the men; it is an imitation of a bracken-fern leaf. The tattooing of the left cheek is quite different and consists of a double line running from the ear along the outer border of the lower jaw until roughly below the angle of the mouth; from here the double line runs upwards in an arc over the cheek and back to the ear, thereby surrounding

Plate 20 Dance sticks of the St Matthias women

tattooing pattern there as well. Certainly it is never found here in its entirety, but the isolated patterns still currently used are without doubt individual parts of the Siara pattern, which crossed St George's Channel from southern New Ireland with the original colonists (see p. 63).

Nothing is known yet about the language. However, quite often words occur that disclose a Polynesian origin, and the drifting ashore of Polynesians off course is actually no rarity on these islands nor on the entire eastern coast of New Ireland.

Otherwise, what we know of the traditions and customs of these districts is not a lot. Each village has a headman, who discusses all the more important matters with the older heads of the families. This village chief seems to exercise a not insignificant power, for nothing is undertaken without having heard his opinion or having received his permission.

Wives are bought. Payment consists of about 20 metres of *kémetas*, four to six armrings, one or two pigs, as well as taro tubers (*pas*) and coconuts (*kuen*), which both find use in a communal feast for the relatives of the young couple. The wife is the exclusive property of the man, and here, as, for example, on the north-eastern Gazelle Peninsula, the women are an ongoing cause of endless strife and family quarrels.

At the birth of a child, especially the firstborn, depending on the wealth of the parents a great feast is put on, called *én*. This consists of numerous pigs, fish and fruits of the field. If the father is a village chief then all villagers contribute to the feast, so that not infrequently thirty to forty pigs are supplied. When the boys are about twelve years old a big feast is put on again. For this celebration a separate, large house, *fél tabá*, is erected, and the provided pigs, fish and other foods laid inside. The boys take their place inside the *fél tabá* with the men and receive a new name by which they will be known from henceforth. Women may not enter these huts, although they may duly admire the dances of the men performed in the open. The feast is divided into special groups in which the sexes are separated.

At the death of a native the celebrations vary according to the esteem or the wealth of the dead person. With chiefs and rich people the expense is greatest, and culminates in a greater or lesser number of pigs being supplied. Occasionally up to fifty pigs are produced for a communal meal, not to mention a corresponding quantity of other food. The corpse is stretched out on a low scaffold in the hut immediately after death, and decorated with flowers and painted. Shell money and armrings are then piled up on the corpse; into one hand they press a lance and into the other a club or the long-handled war axe. Meanwhile mourners from the entire surrounding area gather, and the women set up the customary wail of grief. The pigs are now

the entire cheek. Inside this double line is found a cross-shaped pattern with one arm of the cross running from the ear to the corner of the mouth, the other from the upper part of the cheekbone to the middle of the lower jaw. The whole thing is designated as *anlis* (that is, *Canari* nut). Both patterns are joined by a double line running over the bridge of the nose, while the lower parts of both patterns are joined by a double line running across the chin. The chin is further decorated by a circle of dark dashes, and the tip of the nose by five fan-shaped dashes. A double zigzag running across the upper lip similarly connects both cheek patterns.

It is quite remarkable that although no contact exists between these natives and the inhabitants of the Gazelle Peninsula, at least not in the present day, it is nevertheless not difficult to detect the

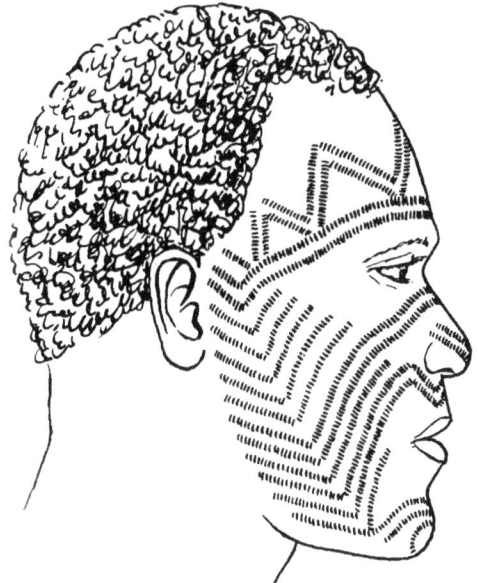
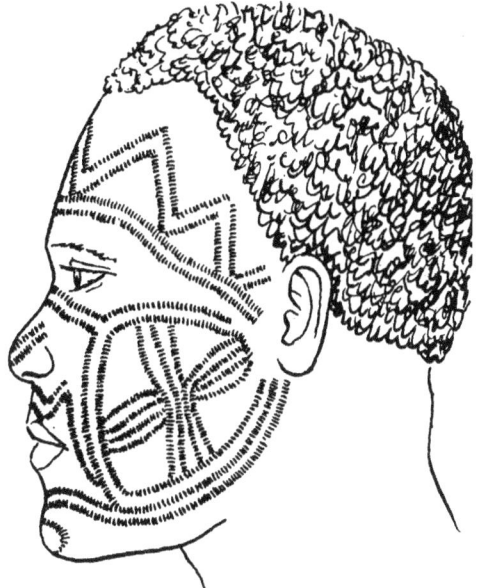

Fig. 50 Facial tattooing in Siara

killed and prepared with the other food. The young men, who are looking after the meal arrangements, work in the sweat of their brows. As soon as the meal is ready they proceed to share it out among those present, and after all have eaten their fill, the gathering breaks up, each going off to his home. The members of the immediate family remain by the body, and prepare the grave when the meal has ended. Not far from the hut a grave is dug, about chest deep, and the bottom covered with narrow battens from the hard outer wood of a certain species of palm. After the body has been lowered into the grave, they make a flat roof of the same battens, cover it with leaves, and close the grave. This type of burial is designated by the name *iläni* or *offo*. Natives of lower standing are put into the sea after death. The body is wrapped in coconut matting, weighted with stones and sunk in deep water beyond the reef. This type of burial is called *uli*.

After decomposition of the corpse buried in the ground, the skull is exhumed by the relatives of the dead man and carefully wrapped in leaves; likewise the upper arms bones are dug up. On this occasion a great meal is again put on, and the skull is set up at the feast place beside the food items put on display.

Here too the women raise their cry of grief, just as at the burial. When the feast has ended the skull is reburied and not exhumed again. The upper arm bones are used for the type of spear designated by the name *tuanére*. They are only used by relatives of the dead man and this is connected with the superstition that the spirit of the dead one will stand alongside the bearer of the *tuanére* in battle. The spirits of the dead (that is, of those who were buried in the ground) are designated as *tanguou* or *kenit*. They are invisible during the day; at night they appear to the survivors in the form of fire sparks or little flames. The spirits of dead men pursue the women, those of dead women creep closer to the men. All living people flee instantly at the appearance of spirits, for they bring sickness, lingering illness and death.

The spirits of those who have died in battle or suffered another violent death are designated as *fiu*. They all journey to Tanga and stay there in two great lumps of rock called *maleu*. These spirits, too, appear at night and fly around in the air alighting in preference on certain trees. The spirits of unborn children of mothers who have died in childbirth are known as *gesges*. They also go about during the day in the form of men and women adorned with special, very strong-smelling plants, and are thus recognisable from a great distance. They endeavour to entice living men and women and to seduce them. They pursue especially those who have had sexual intercourse with members of the same totem. The *gesges* live in holes in rocks and in stones. Other spirits live in the forest. During the day they take on the form of a dead tree stump, but during the night they pursue those who have offended against the totem. This spirit is called *tara*. They are black in colour and have bright, shining eyes. Among the Aneri it is believed that in hollow trees dwells the spirit *laulauvin*, who likes to chase young children and kill them. If they want to frighten children or make them hurry to their hut, they call out, '*Laulauvin* is coming!'

Snakes, including the black-and-white-banded sea snake, harbour evil spirits that punish especially desecration or disrespect of totem customs. Indeed in the Siara district they eat snakes, but when someone is pursuing such a snake he kills it only if it attempts to escape; if the snake stops, or coils itself or stretches its head towards the pursuer, the latter does not kill it but says instead, "Stop! This is a snake from Tanga or Aneri and not a Siara snake." On those islands named, the snake is not eaten.

Clubs (*marangas*), spears (*hiu*) and slingshots (*lo*)

are the common weapons, to which has been added the axe since trade with the white merchants. It is fitted with a particularly long handle for use in battle.

III St Matthias and the Neighbouring Islands

About 50 nautical miles north-west from the island of New Hanover lies the island of St Matthias, and west of it the small island of Kerué or Emirau, and Squally Island.

Since Dampier discovered the island, apparently nobody visited it until 1864 when work recruiters from Viti sought to establish connections with the islanders. The seemingly harmless people drew back at the landing of the boat, and both white men in charge of the boat settled down on the shore to await further developments. The natives seemed gradually to gain confidence, and approached timidly, but then suddenly fell upon the whites and speared them, and also attacked the crew seated in the boat. The latter succeeded in escaping after a brief struggle, with the loss of two further men.

Frightened by the event, other ships kept away until 1896. In that year a schooner from the New Guinea Company again attempted to establish contact. The natives came alongside in their canoes; bartering developed but led to hostilities after a short time, and the whites went for their guns. In 1898 the steamer *Johann Albrecht* of the same company attempted once more to make an approach, but with the same result. At the beginning of 1900 a small trading schooner again attempted friendly associations with the people, bartering was begun, but after a short stay things became alarming to the owner of the vessel; he weighed anchor and left, so as not be drawn into a quarrel with the natives.

In May 1900, I had the opportunity to visit the island. The then governor of the colony, Herr von Bennigsen, made a journey there in the imperial warship *Seeadler*, and the ship's captain, Lieutenant-Commander Schack, was kind enough to invite me as a participant. Our three-day stay was peaceful throughout; the natives were indeed very shy and always had their weapons in readiness, for which in view of the earlier events you could not blame them. The petty thefts that occurred, which had previously been the main cause for conflict, were allowed to pass over, especially as they concerned worthless small items, and we ourselves were for the most part guilty of their loss, because in our observations of the people and in our eagerness to trade we dropped our guard from our personal belongings, which represented desirable treasures in the eyes of the natives. Although we roamed often up to 10 nautical miles from the ship in the *Seeadler*'s boats, landing here and there, and were frequently surrounded by numerous natives, our interactions remained always peaceful and we came to the conclusion that a settlement of traders with a sufficiently strong troop of workers for exploiting the trepang on the reef would be possible. By taking the greatest care, drastic action against the islanders for paltry reasons might be avoided.

And so the Matupi-based firm of Hernsheim & Co. set up a fishery base on the small island of Kaléu in the same year.

Things went fairly well up until April 1901. The white traders were eager to establish friendly relations and the natives slowly got used to the presence of the foreigners. They began to fish for trepang and offer them for sale; in short it seemed as though future interaction would be peaceful. This situation was suddenly upset in an unforeseen way. The traveller Bruno Mencke had arrived in the Bismarck Archipelago. A steam yacht was at his disposal, fitted out to the degree of luxury of an imperial mail steamer, and with a very large crew of Europeans and coloureds. The intention of the owner was to carry out a scientific investigation of the numerous islands of the archipelago, and assistants appropriate to this purpose were on board the ship.

However, soon after their arrival in the Bismarck Archipelago, it became clear that science lay not so close to the heart of the owner of the ship as pleasure. Dedicated expeditions were not carried out. They visited particular areas of coast that had been well-known for years already, and then relaxed in the archipelago. Herr Mencke appeared to be weary of it already; malaria had almost totally banished the remaining interest in science, but nevertheless they decided on an undertaking in order to give at least relative justification to the proud name First German South Seas Expedition. The choice fell on the island of St Matthias, unquestionably one of the most interesting places in the protectorate. Ethnographically and anthropologically, many interesting things were anticipated here, also the zoological and botanical yields seemed very promising. However, virtually everyone not involved shook their heads sceptically after the goal of the expedition had become known, not because it was seen as unfeasible, but because they believed that none of the white men had the necessary attributes to lead such an expedition. The only one who could be considered so was the zoologist on board, Dr Heinroth, and that Herr Mencke would hand over the leadership to the latter was, as was generally known, out of the question.

Having arrived at the anchorage south of the main island, an expedition base was chosen at an apparently suitable site on the beach of the main island, and the workers began to set up camp. As soon as the undergrowth was thinned out and a limited space cleared, tents and huts were erected and food and trade goods were brought ashore. Meanwhile they had made the discovery that many essentials had been forgotten and the vessel *Eberhard* received the order to steam back to collect the missing items. Meanwhile, Herr Mencke, with his secretary, Herr Caro, and Dr Heinroth, as well as seaman Krebs and about forty well-armed natives, settled in to camp. Not much was seen of the natives of the island; a few dared to approach timidly, the majority kept a respectful distance, as was to be expected of such a 'faint-hearted band'.

In the first few days everything still went well, and they lay down to sleep quite peacefully. Whether watches had been placed seems doubtful. On one of the following mornings the order was given to take all the Mauser carbines apart and clean them. Dr Heinroth was already busy, Herr Mencke and Herr Caro were still asleep. Natives were observed creeping through the undergrowth not far from the camp, but since they were regarded as harmless they were left unchallenged. But suddenly a number of them fell upon the camp. Herr Mencke and Herr Caro were mortally speared straight away and Dr Heinroth was slightly wounded. Seaman Krebs stood in front of the tent with a loaded repeater and attempted to open fire, but found that the cartridges were spoiled and would not explode; he too was put out of action temporarily by a severe wound and fell senseless to the ground. Fortunately he regained consciousness fairly quickly, and was able to get the wounded Mencke into the boat in the general confusion. At first glance resistance was unthinkable, but soon several of the crew succeeded in getting their rifles ready and opening fire, upon which the attackers rapidly withdrew with several losses. The severely wounded Mencke was taken to the station on Kaléu where he eventually succumbed to his wounds. The body of Herr Caro had been taken away by the attackers. Upon the return of the yacht *Eberhard*, Dr Heinroth went aboard with his group and the First German South Seas Expedition was disbanded.

When the imperial governor of the protectorate again visited the island in September 1903, he found Mencke's grave opened and the bones removed. The only remains left of the unfortunate traveller was a piece of the upper jaw, recognisable by the gold fillings in the molar teeth.

After this outcome the natives became intrusive and killed several of the station workers, upon which the firm of Hernsheim & Co. dismantled their station and the natives were left to themselves once more.

A consequence of the renewed attacks on the part of the natives was that the imperial cruiser *Kormoran* was ordered to punish the islanders. A not insignificant number of St Matthias people were killed and several women and children as well as a teenage youth were taken to Herbertshöhe as prisoners.

I have dealt with the gradually developing interaction of the St Matthias inhabitants with the whites and the consequences rather extensively because the incidents on the whole give a genuine picture of the first approach of two races so basically different. Scarcely a single South Sea island can be named on which the same events have not taken place. However, we hope that the natives may be spared further nasty experiences. Trade does not lure any settlers to the islands in a hurry, for they are poor in profitable products, but the prisoners languishing in Herbertshöhe, who are enjoying humane and caring treatment will, on their return to their homeland, perhaps become the link to a peaceful approach. In the meantime, through the accounts of the three captive women it has become possible for the author to expand and correct his observations made in 1900 (*Globus*, vol. LXXIX, no. 15), although here, as everywhere else, there is still very much to learn.

The island of St Matthias lies about 1°37'S latitude and 149°40'E longitude and stretches from northwest to south-east over a length of 33 kilometres with an average breadth of about 11 kilometres. Off the southern side of the main island lie a number of raised, low coral islands, partially forming an atoll which is separated from the main island by a deep, navigable passage. In this strait ships find a secure anchorage.

The main island is mountainous and the widely visible high point, Mount Malakat, reaches approximately 520 metres. The shoreline is without exception steep, with a narrow offshore reef which expands up to 3 kilometres only on the south-western side. The north-eastern coast is flat and sandy on its southern half, and the mountains recede up to 1 kilometre from the beach. Here a number of

Fig. 51 Map of St Matthias

villages lie scattered among the palms. According to the natives the mountains are uninhabited. The low coral islands in the south are likewise inhabited, but not populous. The small islands, like the main island, show clear signs of uplift over long intervals. The limestone cliffs are deeply undermined almost everywhere by the sea swells, and also at places where today the sea does not reach. The central part of the island consists, as far as I had opportunity to observe, of volcanic rock.

The soil appears to have little goodness on the south-western side; the mountain slopes show broad grass fields and extensive jungle with many pandanus trees. The north-eastern side of the island appears to be more fertile; here the mountain slopes are partially covered with thick forest and coconut palms occur in greater stands as well. The small group is therefore of little agricultural importance for the time being.

The two main districts on the south-eastern end of the island seem to be called Elemakunaur and Roitan; north of these the very well populated districts of Itasidl and Etalat lie on the east coast. The names of the small islands on the reef on the south-western side are: Noanaur, Kaléu and Vangalu. The islands on the atoll to the south-west are Emusaun, Eiongane and Emanaus. A general designation for the entire island group or for the main island, does not seem to exist.

It has always been my greatest desire to encounter such a population as we find on St Matthias – such 'savage' people; people who have not the slightest semblance of a civilisation in our sense of the word. Here we find ourselves abruptly set down in a piece of antiquity, an antiquity that extends much further back than the beginnings of the civilisation known to us, or of that which we usually call 'history'. It was left up to modern times to come to realise that it was finally time to study the prehistory of humankind, and in museums and collections we find the creations of primitive people more or less totally lumped together, but the actual study of the children of nature themselves still contains great gaps. We investigate the depths of the sea, we attempt to reach the North or the South Pole and spend large sums of money for these purposes. Would that we could finally come to realise that for the foreseeable future the sea with its depths will be preserved for us in its present state, and likewise the North and South poles, but day by day the prehistory of our own kind is fading from the surface of the planet, and that we should make every effort to gather and preserve the remains of these primitive cultures, for modern civilisation, which is spreading further and further over the planet is acting like an eraser, irrevocably obliterating all the old signs and features.

St Matthias is one place where we are set down suddenly in the middle of a slice of human antiquity. Iron is totally unknown; knives and other iron tools are rejected in trade dealing. On the other hand they reach greedily for red beads or red scraps of material and at the sight of these treasures the thick lips draw back into a covetous grimace, so totally different from a real smile of satisfaction, which seems to light up the face from within in more sophisticated peoples.

The islanders are of medium height and dark brown skin shade. I was previously inclined to regard them as pure Melanesians, but having been able to observe at close hand the prisoners brought to Herbertshöhe, I have, however, modified this opinion, coming to the conclusion that they are Melanesians with a fairly strong Polynesian admixture, probably originating from the Micronesian islands. A number of natives have crinkly hair with small ringlets, as on New Ireland and the Gazelle Peninsula; however, there are numerous individuals as well who have curly or even completely straight hair. The crinkly haired islanders are always darker than the islanders with curly or straight hair. The prisoners in Herbertshöhe show the various transitions quite clearly; in particular, observation of a girl born of a woman there, whom my wife adopted after the mother's death, gives an indication that we are dealing with a mixed race, but one in which the Melanesian element is dominant. The hair on the child's head was almost completely straight in the first months after birth; with increasing age the hair became curly, although it did not combine into the characteristic, corkscrew, thickly spiralled tufts of pure Melanesian children of the same age. The numerous pure Melanesian children in my neighbourhood provided good comparative material. Also, the skin colour differed from the chocolate brown of my neighbourhood children, in that

Fig. 52 Men of St Matthias

she showed a tinge of grey that I have observed nowhere else.

The prisoners in Herbertshöhe have shown that they are not without intelligence. They very quickly learned the pidgin English used in the archipelago, showed great preference for ornaments and bright clothes, and would not put up with anything from the station workers, with whom they mixed, in spite of being the minority. I have come to the conclusion that they are quite highly endowed mentally, but are, unfortunately, irritable and hot-tempered.

The hairstyles of the islanders are nothing out of the ordinary. The women wear their hair cut short as a rule, the men let it grow somewhat longer, but not so long that it completely covers the neck.

Actual clothing for the men is out of the question. They are without exception circumcised and occasionally cover the glans with a *Cypraea ovula* just as in the Admiralty Islands. The local name of this snail is *bule* (in Samoa the same snail is called *pule*). Many of these shells whose internal windings are broken away, have a smooth, naturally white outer surface, others are decorated with a pattern of straight lines, triangles and zigzags, which are accentuated as black against the white background by layers of dirt.

The men wear large, carefully made combs (*zili*) of various shapes as head ornaments. These combs are made from ribs of small coconut palm fronds laid side by side, overlaid with a weave of threads like a dense fabric; they belong to the finest products of the islanders, and can be regarded as typical of St Matthias (fig. 55, nos 10 to 18). They do not serve as combs in the true sense of the word but as head ornaments; the densely packed teeth of the comb are pushed into the dense mass of hair, and serve simply as a means of fastening the character-

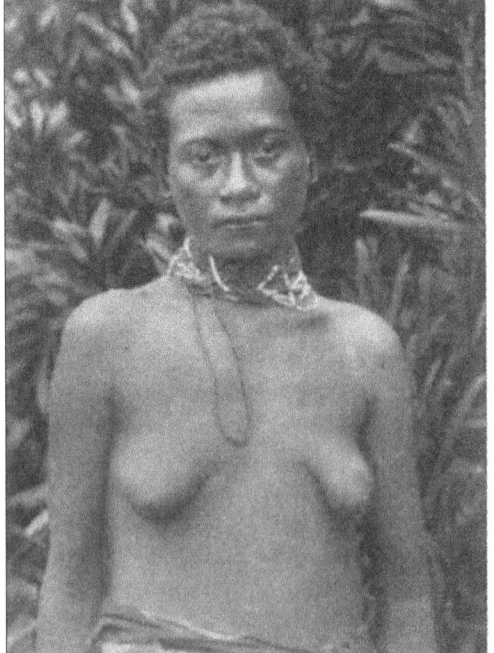

Figs 53 and 54 Women of St Matthias

Plate 21 Village scene on Squally Island

istic hair decoration; the upper, free section forms a rectangle painted white and russet with bigger and smaller rectangles, semi-circles and trapezes attached. These swing to and fro with every movement of the head. This head ornament is fixed behind the ear either on the left side or the right.

Furthermore, the men wear a loincloth (*aili*) about 2 centimetres wide, woven from black and golden-yellow strips of fibre so that alternating black and yellow triangles are formed; three or four of these girdles are often attached side by side, forming a broad-banded girdle (fig. 55, no. 3).

Around the neck both men and women wear long strings of circular shell discs named *wungoos*; the pale grey discs are interrupted at greater or lesser intervals by one or more black discs (fig. 55, no. 9).

Both this type of girdle and the string of shell discs are found also on the Admiralty Islands. On a walk I found the material from which the strings of shells are made: a small *Conus* snail about 1 centimetre long, from the thick upper end of which the discs are made. They are made from the same *Conus* snail on the Admiralty Islands.

The women wear rather more clothing. Two carefully made, quite fine mats are attached to a girdle in such a way that one of the mats hangs down in front and the other behind, extending from the waist to the knees. The local name for this item of clothing is *urungarang*. The girdle is about 5 to 6 centimetres wide and about 1 metre long. All girdles, *bais*, are produced from fine, yellow-grey, red and black woven fibres in such a way that red, white and black long strips appear in varying sequences of rows and breadths. At both ends the longitudinal fibres form a fringe about 8 to 10 centimetres long (fig. 55, nos. 4 and 5). These girdles bear an astonishing similarity to examples from Kusaie called *tol*; such girdles also occur on the Banks and Santa Cruz islands. In Kusaie the girdles are woven, likewise on Santa Cruz, where the loom has been introduced from the Carolines. I already had no doubt on my first visit that on St Matthias also, these girdles, like the previously mentioned mats of the women, were woven. However, I was not able to catch sight of a loom. Only on a second visit in 1905 did I succeed in establishing that a loom did exist, and that it did not differ significantly from that used on various Micronesian islands (see page 148 below).

Furthermore, both sexes wear fairly roughly polished armrings (*mare*) made from *Trochus*, as well as small turtle-shell rings (*puatil*) about 7 millimetres in diameter, in the nasal septum. The ear lobes are pierced and greatly enlarged, often decorated with numerous turtle-shell rings of the type previously described, just as on Ninigo, Aua and Wuwulu, where, however, the rings are significantly larger. As characteristic ear ornaments I also observed thin, circular discs of turtle shell about 2.5 to 3 centimetres in diameter; the surfaces were pierced by small, triangular openings forming a regular pattern. From the centre to the edge ran a slit, by means of which the disc was pinched onto the ear lobe.

The huts (*ale*, Samoan = *fale*) are very primitive and extremely dirty inside. A pandanus roof rests on low posts, just high enough to be able to stand upright beneath it. I did not notice sleeping places

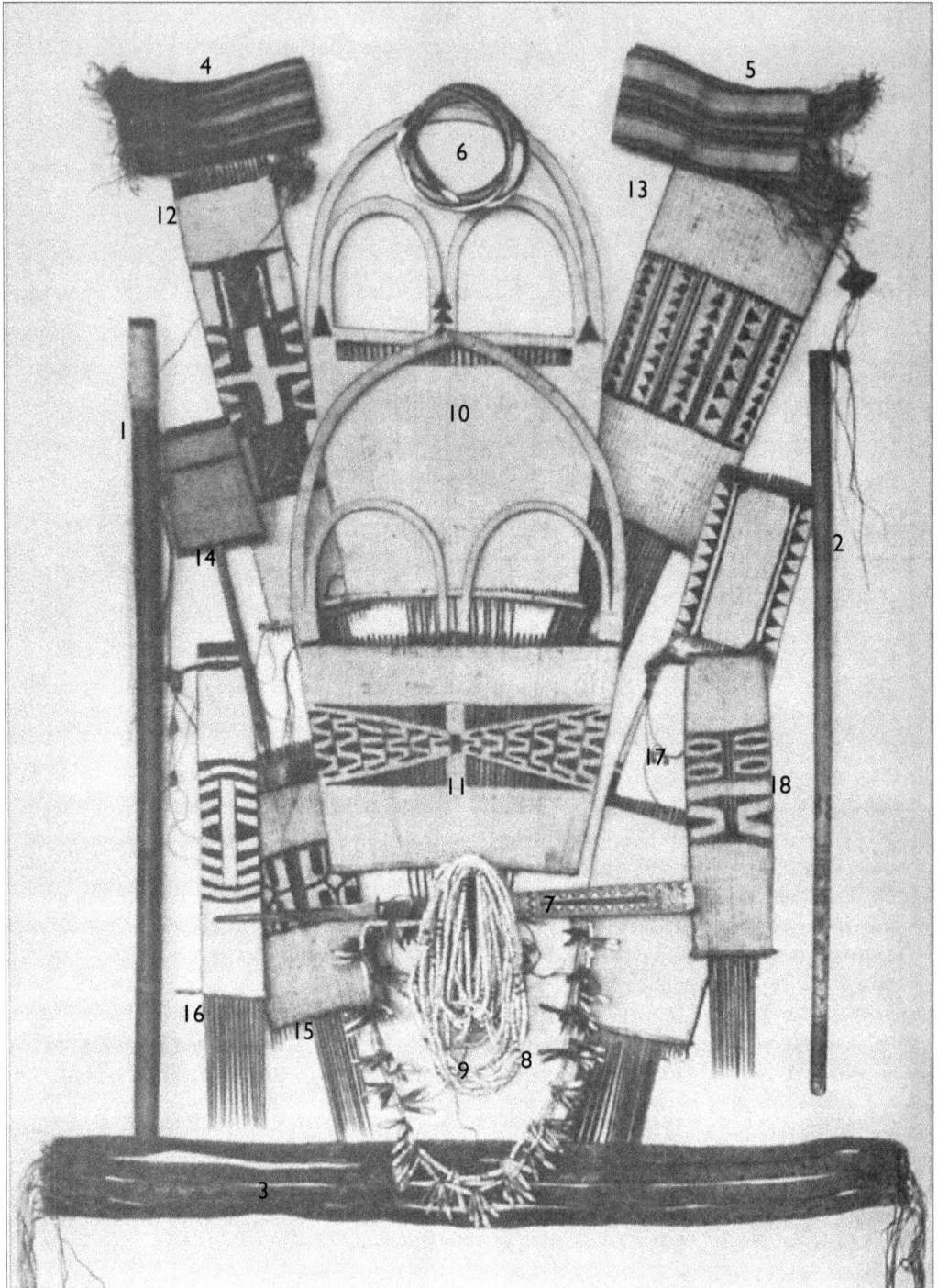

Fig. 55 Objects from St Matthias and Emirau

anywhere; the inhabitants appeared to sleep on the bare ground without anything to lie on. I found a fireplace in every hut and beside it a small heap of fist-sized stones which were obviously used in a glowing state for cooking food.

Household utensils were not available in a wide range nor in great numbers. Small wooden bowls 25 centimetres long and 12 centimetres wide were seen here and there, too small to be used for preparation or presentation of food; they were probably used for mixing ochre with oil, which both men and women rubbed into their hair and bodies.

Coconut shells (*teo*; the ripe coconut bears the Polynesian name *niu*) usually surrounded in a mesh net of fibrous cord and attached together in pairs, serve as water containers. Little baskets, closely woven and conical or elliptical in shape, were also used. They usually contained all kinds of small items, sharp pieces of shell, little bundles of leaves, sea snails and so on; the weave of these little baskets was the same as those similar objects that we know from the Admiralty Islands or from the Baining. Small net purses (*zeri*) with circular wooden rims, as well as small pouches (*tess*) prepared undoubtedly from woven material, were also used for storing small items.

Coconut scrapers (*aisamsap*) of a unique shape were found in the huts. A piece of thin trunk or tree branch was prepared in such a way that four lateral branches formed two front limbs and two hind limbs; a shell (*Cardium?*) was attached to the end, projecting somewhat over the front limbs, for scraping the coconut. To use this, the natives sat crosswise over the trunk section in order to give the necessary firmness to the instrument. This rough form of coconut scraper recalls the carefully prepared instrument of the Tauu islanders.

Among the less common household utensils belongs a short pounder of *Tridacna* shell; such pounders were about 12 centimetres high, and 7 centimetres in diameter at the lower, circular end, and 6 centimetres at the upper end. The lateral surfaces and the lower end were smoothed by polishing.

In and around the huts we also found fishing nets of various sizes. Several were very long – I estimated them to be about 100 metres long with a width of 1.5 metres; the lower edge was weighted with sinkers, sometimes stones and sometimes lumps of coral and sea snails. Small, pierced pieces of wood and the cork-like fruit of the Barringtonia served as floats. The big nets were called *ubén* (Samoan = *'upega*, pronounced *upenga*). Besides this, small hand nets, *kea*, were used on knee-shaped wooden frames. Fishing seems generally to be a principal source of food to the natives. Hand tools for the preparation of nets consisted of wooden needles with a slit at each end to take the thread. The net needles, *aisiel*, vary in length from 25 to 50 centimetres; both ends were bowed outwards like a lyre to take the thread. The shank itself was circular and the whole thing was polished smooth. To regulate the mesh size, they used a short, smooth little wooden board or a piece of turtle shell of varying width.

I was not able to acquire fishhooks, *uos*, on my visit; the iron fishhooks that we offered the natives were scornfully rejected. The prisoners at Herbertshöhe tell me, however, that fishhooks, some of shell material, others of turtle shell, are known.

Hand tools were present in the form of sharpened mother-of-pearl shell, used for cutting and scraping. In addition there were axes, *iama*, which I will describe in more detail. All specimens offered to us had a blade of *Terebra* shell, the thick end of which was ground obliquely to produce a semicircular cutting edge. Blades of stone or *Tridacna* were not seen. A knee-shaped piece of wood served as an axe handle and for holding the blade. Blade attachment is twofold; they are either firmly attached to the short arm of the knee-shaped wooden haft by means of rattan strips, or the blade is firmly stuck into a conical wooden sheath, which is bound to the haft in such a way that the blade can be turned in different directions.

The foodstuffs of the natives consisted, as far as we had opportunity to observe, of taro (*ási*), bananas (*uri*), breadfruit (*ulu*; Samoan *'ulu*) and several items from the plant kingdom unknown to us. Everywhere taro and bananas were cultivated beside the villages in quite extensive stands. Coconut palms were characteristically only sparse; extensive stands were not present on the small low islands. Small isolated stands occurred on the south-east side of the main island as well as on the northern end. Most frequently, however, the coconut palm appeared on the southern half of the north-eastern coast since there appeared to be a denser population, with whom we unfortunately did not come into contact. There are no dogs or chickens; a necklace of shell discs also contained a number of cuscus teeth, and this easily caught animal provided a food source here as on New Hanover and New Ireland. Pigs are not numerous on the small islands but should be present in great numbers on the main island. The coral reef and the sea seem to offer the natives a rich contribution to their nourishment; we saw canoes going out fishing every day, and fish (*koko*) were frequently offered to us for trade.

Areca nut (*búa*) together with betel pepper and burnt coral lime (*sangina*) serve as an enjoyment and a stimulant. The lime containers (*raba* or *gaba*) had the same shape as those on the Admiralty Islands, and were decorated on the outside with burned-on patterns which were also reminiscent of that island group in their design and shape. The lime spatulae (*rama*) were mostly simple, little sticks; however, odd, black hardwood ones, whose upper end was decorated with carved zigzags and parallel lines, were also bartered.

Triton snail shells (*kaúe*), with a circular hole bored through the side, serve as signal horns. Flutes of bamboo canes (*tukutaue*) with engraved burn patterns, and of the shape familiar on the Gazelle Peninsula, were offered as barter items. I did not see wooden drums during my visit, but the slit drums familiar everywhere in Melanesia ought to occur here as well.

As a result of the very primitive tools, canoe building is not at a high level. The canoes (*olimo*) consist of hollowed-out tree trunks with outriggers and float attached. The size varied; there were small specimens for one or at most two passengers, while others held eight to ten natives. No ornamentation, either in the form of painting or carving, was observed on the examples that we saw. The vessels were propelled by paddles (*hose*) with a broad, lance-like blade and a shaft about 1.5 metres long.

The islanders' weapons occupy a far higher level of accomplishment; the spear (*walau*) is one which by its entire finish belongs among the most superior products of Melanesia. Both the careful carving and the extraordinarily tasteful and rich decoration of both ends of the spear give this weapon of the St Matthias Islanders the right to be placed in the front rank of artistic carving from Melanesia. Therefore

Fig. 56 Decoration on spears and dance sticks

the spears certainly deserve to be described in detail.

The material consists either of palm wood or a tough, dark brown type of wood of medium weight. The length of the spear is about 2.5 metres on average. Two different types can be distinguished; those with their entire length produced from a single piece of wood, and those with a shaft consisting of an attached piece of bamboo tube. This piece of bamboo, about 0.5 metres long and about 10 centimetres in diameter at the thickest end, is pared very thin over a 10 centimetre length at one end; this pared end is split many times, and the shaft end of the spear is set into it. The lamellae of the pared cane are bound firmly to the shaft of the spear with fine, twisted fibrous cord, so that the spear and cane form a single tightly bound unit. This binding of the spear shaft to a bamboo cane is very reminiscent of similar binding of both parts on New Hanover and northern New Ireland.

The spears made from a single piece of wood are without decoration at the butt end. Those with shafts inserted into a section of bamboo are for the most part richly decorated at the end of the shaft, while the bamboo tube tied on is only rarely, or only very little, decorated with carvings. About 50 centimetres of the shaft, above the bamboo tube, are most carefully decorated in this type of spear, partly by carved parallel lines running round the shaft arranged in different ways, and partly by various ornaments in relief, which in my opinion are based mostly on leaf and flower motifs (figs. 56 and 57).

There follows a 50 to 70 centimetre portion of the shaft which is completely smooth, mostly circular in cross-section, and 2.5 to 3 centimetres thick. This part of the spear is held in the hand when the spear-thrower holds his weapon in readiness for battle; in old specimens it seems as though it is polished, as a result of use.

Following this smooth part comes the real tip of the spear, which is most carefully and richly decorated from the 70 to 80 centimetre mark to the very tip. The design of the decoration is similar to the shaft, but figures by far predominate and line motifs diminish.

The extreme point of the spear is smooth, circular in cross-section and about 15 to 18 centimetres long, then follows a row of barbs, on one side as a rule, although those with two opposing rows are not infrequently found. The barbs and their arrangement recall in many cases those from Wuwulu and Aua.

Individual spears have a number of notches, which may be regarded as a stunted form of barb, below the actual point with the sharply protruding barbs. This actual spear point is bordered by one or more bunches of fibrous material about 5 centimetres long. The subsequent portion up to the smooth middle section is beautifully decorated.

The spear points, and the inner side of the barbs in particular, are almost always painted red and black. By rubbing with burnt lime into the deepened grooves and surfaces, the surface relief decorations appear, and in the dark wood colour they stand out effectively against the white background. Around the bamboo tube, which is almost always painted white with lime, run narrower or wider lines in red or black at the shaft end.

As well as the previously described battle spears, the islanders use a multi-pronged spear for fishing. This is completely without decoration and consists of a thin pole about 3 metres long, to the end of which six to ten tips of hardwood are attached *en masse*.

At the time of my visit to St Matthias in 1900 we obtained a few sword-shaped objects of black-stained woods, about which it was not possible to ascertain precise details of their use. Through the punitive expedition of HIMS *Kormoran*, a larger number of these objects came to the Gazelle Peninsula, and the prisoners at Herbertshöhe said these objects were dance batons that the women held in their hands in certain dances. The local name for these dance batons is *rama*. They call to mind similar objects from the Rook group in the Carolines.

These batons are between 1 and 1.5 metres long. The lower end is sharply tapered like a spear, mostly circular in cross-section, but partly elliptical too. The upper third of the baton is broader, often widened up to 5 centimetres and strongly elliptical in cross-section; it terminates in a type of handle, often in the shape of a sword hilt from the Middle Ages. This entire upper part is most carefully decorated on both sides; the grooves and indentations are rubbed with lime, like the spears. Also, the decorations are on the whole the same that we see on the battle spears, but others occur as well, which find no place on the spears because of their shape.

After the preceding had already been written, in April 1905 I again had the opportunity of visiting the island and, in particular, of observing the people of the east coast of the main island. These, as might be expected, are completely identical with the population on the southern offshore islands, although somewhat more powerful, probably as a consequence of better nourishment. The huts of these villages are more roomy and are kept in a better and cleaner condition. In many cases they appear to be inhabited by several families together and have low plank beds for the inhabitants. However, besides this there are also bachelors' or men's houses which are never entered by women, and which are always recognisable by a great quantity of weapons. After the earlier events I did not expect a very friendly reception, but was pleasantly surprised to find that the natives were friendly and trusting everywhere and bore no ill-feeling. The rebuke given them may have had much to do with this; however, I believe that the friendly visits made by the imperial governor and the sojourn of several islanders in Herbertshöhe had far greater effect. I brought a few of them back to their home, and through them I was able to make myself understood to some extent to the islanders, via the frightful pidgin English, the *lingua franca* of the South Seas, which of necessity they had had to learn during their stay on New Britain.

I found that my earlier observations were confirmed, and had the opportunity of seeing the major part of the population. I have come to the conclusion that the total population amounts to not much more than 1,000. The men seem to be decidedly in the majority. The women, contrary to the Melanesian style, mixed unceremoniously among the men and were not at all shy or reticent. They showed fewer signs of hard work, and apparently enjoyed much more freedom than is customary among Melanesian tribes.

Although the islanders are not true seafarers and very rarely leave their coasts, on the eastern shore, there were large, carefully constructed canoes which I had not observed earlier. These stately barques are up to 24 metres long and are carefully carved and painted at both ends, not without artistry. The wooden uprights to which the outrigger is attached are carved and daubed with bright colours. The open-work carving vividly recalled similar productions found on the canoes on Kaniet, but particularly on both ends of the boat-shaped wooden bowls there. These large canoes are able to take thirty to forty full-grown passengers.

On the island of Emusaun I was shown a shattered Admiralty Island spear, thus proving that there is occasionally contact with the western neighbours. As far as I understood, they calculated five such visits, with the observation that the guests were not regarded well because they were warlike and quarrelsome. This matches the familiar attitude of the Admiralty Islanders. Also, even today they tell me at Papitálai on the Admiralty Islands that the now-dead chief Po Sing had been driven ashore on Emusaun years ago and stayed there for a short time but, because of the hostility shown towards him, travelled to New Hanover and returned home from there. It may not have gone so well for all visitors. This information is nevertheless interesting, as it shows that intermittent immigration took place from the west, and we can probably assume that the real settlement took place from there years ago, which is why even today there is great agreement in many ethnographic characteristics with the western neighbours. In Itasidl there are traditions of an immigration from the north, but this immigration must have been a long time ago, and furthermore it was not possible for me to ascertain where the immigrants came from, although the north was indicated with great assurance. However, that an immigration has also taken place from there seems beyond doubt to me and demonstrated especially by finding the Micronesian weaving loom on both St Matthias and Kerué (Emirau). This cannot have been imported from the Admiralty Islands, where it is unknown. The apparatus called *solo* or *solu*, is only somewhat smaller than the Micronesian weaving loom, so that one is unable to weave broad material. Weaving is the task of the women who, in a sitting position, keep the apparatus under tension by holding one stretching stick firmly with the feet, and the other by a girdle laid round the waist. Through weaving they make the narrow loincloth named *bais*, which is worn both by men and women, as well as clothing mats for the women. These are 20 to 25 centimetres wide and, like the girdles, are produced from naturally coloured and russet-dyed banana fibres. These mats were worn in various ways, either as aprons hanging down in front and at the back, or as three lengths sewn together and worn as a loincloth extending round the body.

About 17 nautical miles south-east of St Matthias, at 150°3'E longitude and 1°48'S latitude, lies the island, or more accurately the island group, of Kerué. Its main direction stretches from west to east, and consists of three individual islands, the middle or main island of Emirau and two small islets at the eastern and western ends, Elemusoa and Ealusau. The island is a raised coral reef, like the offshore islands of St Matthias, and is surrounded by reefs on all sides; the narrow arms of the sea which divide the smaller islands from the main island at eastern and western ends, are barely navigable to boats at low water. The entire length from east to west is about 8 nautical miles. The southern coast runs fairly regularly, and forms a small embayment only in the middle, with several islets on the reef; the northern side has a bigger indentation at the eastern end. The island is completely wooded and carries a fairly large number of coconut palms, particularly on the south coast and at the western end. Here dwells the population, which might not be more than 500 in all.

The population does not differ from that of the St Matthias group, although as a result of more abundant food resources they appear better nourished and more robust than the latter.

The language is exactly the same as on St Matthias and reciprocal trade exists, especially for the trading of spears, which are made in great numbers on Emirau.

On my visit I found the islanders friendly and forthcoming, although inclined to theft if they thought they could get away with it unnoticed; but in this regard they did not exceed the other South Sea islanders, and it was almost entertaining with what shrewdness they made all kinds of desirable

Fig. 57 Decorations on spears and dance sticks (plant motifs, derived especially from coconut palm leaves)

small items disappear. The houses, as on St Matthias, are better constructed and lie on the beach, grouped into several small villages. Each such village is governed by a headman, who was always the first introduced to me on my visit. This man seemed to exert a very significant influence on his village, and I could observe that his decisions were carried out without discussion. The women had, if possible, greater freedom than on St Matthias, and did not take much advice from the men.

As a unique peculiarity, I noticed here that besides the white *Cypraea* snail shell, the men also used a small yellow *Kürbis* species as a penis cover, but this is not bored through laterally as on Angriff Harbour in New Guinea, but provided with an opening in the end.

I had the opportunity of observing a festive gathering on the western end of the island. In front of a big, new hut a rectangular site was enclosed with brushwood and undergrowth; women apparently were not allowed to enter, although they were assembled in great numbers outside the place of festivity and were busy preparing food. About a dozen boys aged from six to ten years sat inside the house and I could assume with certainty that the people were in the process of celebrating a circumcision ceremony, although an evasive answer was given to my inquiry. The boys were adorned with girdles and necklaces and still uncircumcised; the feast was therefore probably a customary pre-celebration on such occasions. In the middle of the rectangular site sat a group of about thirty men and youths who intermittently intoned a loud song. This, heard at some distance, bore a great similarity to the fervent celebratory singing of a Catholic church service, and always ended in a drawn-out, gradually fading tone. They were in no way disturbed by my presence, which must have appeared the more noteworthy, since I was probably the first white person ever to have visited the island, and outside the place of celebration they gathered round and gazed at me in astonishment. Beyond the enclosure they were engaged in all kinds of pastimes; the women left their task and surrounded me, laughing and gesticulating, extremely pleased when I placed a few bright glass beads in their tiny outstretched hands. The men looked on laughing and for their part were just as happy when I handed over a fishhook, a scrap of red cloth or a 2-inch nail.

They were undoubtedly informed on the island of the earlier events on St Matthias, as the headmen were keen on signifying to me that the people of their island were good people, while on the other hand the people of St Matthias were bad. However, the St Matthias interpreters accompanying me laughed quite disbelievingly at this assertion, and recounted that the Emirau people began fights not infrequently during their visits to Elemakunaur and behaved in a very unruly way.

I was able to ascertain here that on both island groups various classes existed, which had certain totem signs and for whom marriage within the class was not permitted. Unfortunately my interpreters were not able to explain to me in greater detail. However, since I was successful in recruiting a large number of youths from both St Matthias and Emi-

Plate 22 Pole village of the Moánus on Ndruval

rau as workers, I will in time be able to obtain from them extensive accounts on customs and ways of life of these groups of people.

The land designated on the maps as Squally Island does not exist in this form. According to the co-ordinates the island lies at 150°38'E and 1°48'S, and is a small, raised coral island, no larger than 150 hectares; it is surrounded on all sides by reefs and covered in forest in which here and there a few coconut palms are visible. As we approached the small island, several small, very primitive canoes came towards us, but we were unable to persuade the people to come alongside. However, their greed allowed them to forget their fear, to the extent that they approached close enough to pass us a plaited basket on a long pole with the aim of receiving any gifts. Meanwhile their entire bodies were trembling and they seemed to want to conceal their fear by loud talking and shouting. Unfortunately we could not understand a word; neither could the St Matthias people nor the New Ireland and New Hanover natives on board understand a single syllable of the language. This was very rich in vowels, and almost every sentence ended in a long, drawn-out *ma* or *ha*, which seemed to be a source of great amusement to my native companions. We had to heave-to off the island during the night and could land only the following morning. Numerous torches on the offshore reef during the night revealed that the natives were keen fishermen. The following morning the canoes approached again; however, as I lowered both boats into the water and steered for the shore, they followed at a distance. The entire population had gathered on the beach, about 150 in all, and it was evident that they had hostile intentions. On the reef stood a whole line of especially battle-spirited heroes, who held long lances in their hands, ready to throw. The rest of the population had placed themselves behind, some armed with wooden clubs, others holding lumps of rock in their hands; even women and children were armed. Since it was up to me to avoid a hostile encounter at all costs, I applied myself first of all to talking. Now this is not an easy task when neither party has the slightest knowledge of the other's language, but a knife displayed, a bright string of beads, or a strip of red cotton material replaces language in such cases. This attempt at approach lasted for over an hour. Soon greed drove first one then another to my boat, and each time he went back with a gift, which aroused general amazement. Finally I was able to assume that they were convinced of our harmlessness, and allowed both boats to pass through the breakers to the beach.

Immediately we were surrounded and the greed of the individuals had to be gratified. This apparently pacified them; the bolder lance-bearers laid down their arms, I took the missiles from the stone-throwers, and gradually a state of armed neutrality developed. With an armed guard of four natives and one white man, I was now able to take a further venture. That morning I had observed that the natives all came from one direction, and anticipating the village there, I set about finding it. However, first of all I thought it advisable to

Fig. 58 Group of men from Squally Island

Fig. 59 Group of men from Squally Island

give the islanders a small firing demonstration, and I fired several shots at a tree trunk washed up on the beach. At each shot the entire population ducked, as if on command; the demonstration, however, was a success, since as I broke off for the village the whole crowd followed me at a respectful distance. After a walk of about ten minutes I reached the village. This lay behind a strip of bushes and trees right by the beach and formed a long street with the huts of the natives on both sides. The huts were very primitive, and consisted of leaf-covered roofs resting on the ground, with the owners' plank-beds fixed below. Besides these dwelling huts numerous smaller buildings were also present, serving as food storehouses. These were erected on four man-sized pandanus poles, about 2 to 3 metres long and 1 to 1.5 metres wide. The roofs consisted of pandanus mats. The poles were wrapped with pandanus leaves, whose smoothness prevented the island's numerous rats from visiting the storage space. Similar huts are known on Matty and Durour and on the Palau islands. A fair amount of fishing equipment, submersible nets, hand-nets and draw-nets were present in great quantity, otherwise the houses contained nothing of consequence. Having wandered through the village I set about taking a few photographs. The setting up of the camera was regarded with great mistrust each time, my guard covered my back and my revolver lay on the camera so that I was covered on all sides, and after distributing small gifts I was able to take a few useful photographs. The open, although not to the point of active, hostility of the natives persuaded me to cut my visit short. The firing of my gun had undoubtedly intimidated the people; however, I might assume that they did not know the deadly effect of firearms, and I knew from experience how easily, in this case, natives were led into undertaking an attack as soon as their initial shyness has dissipated. We therefore withdrew in good order back to the landing place, and I had already climbed into the boat when the natives who had followed us attacked the boatman, who still wanted to distribute a few beads on the beach, with clubs. One of my coloured men immediately fired a warning shot, which had the desired effect, as the crowd promptly dispersed. However, I had yet another unexpected delay as one of the St Matthias people accompanying me, armed with a spear, suddenly let out a loud war cry and in long bounds, brandishing his spear, set off after the islanders. The boatman and two of my people then had to be sent in pursuit to bring back the bold warrior. The latter had chased the whole crowd right to the village; however, here the natives made a stand, and a veritable hail of stones dampened the courage of the pursuer to such an extent that he promptly retreated. This again emboldened the islanders to a full-scale attack, and I was happy when I finally had all the people in the boats and could go back out through the breakers. Several shots held the attackers at a respectful distance; nevertheless a number of their missiles reached us, fortunately without causing injury. After we had passed through the breakers the whole crowd sat down peacefully on the shore and watched our re-embarkation on the schooner.

Although my stay on the island had lasted barely two hours, I was still able to get quite a good picture of the natives.

The type is without doubt pronounced Melanesian, but the relatively large number of individuals with curly, almost bristly hair reveals the Micronesian influence here too. The men are of medium size, dark brown and quite powerfully built. Circumcision was found in all of them, even in relatively small boys, so that the procedure must take place right in early childhood. The hair was worn medium length or short; the style of beard is characteristic, in that the men let the goatee beard grow long and arrange it in two to four long, twisted plaits which hang down as far as the navel. So that the long curls of the beard are not in the way when working, the ends are bound together with a cord and the latter is fastened round the neck so that the tips of the beard lie under the chin. Several old men had unkempt, bushy full beards, grey-brown in colour without curls, about which they seemed otherwise quite proud. Hair and beard, if not grey by virtue of age, is jet black in colour, and demonstrates that treatment with burnt lime does not occur. Likewise, the teeth were dazzling white; evidence that the enjoyment of betel is unknown to the people. All the men are completely naked, and the penis shell is also unknown. The women are smaller than the men and somewhat paler; the head hair was cut short in all of them; I saw young women who had scarcely outgrown childhood who were already mothers, and I believe that it might be subscribed to this circumstance that the entire female sex gave the impression of being aged excessively early. The women, according to Melanesian custom, wore a woven bark apron which extended round the lower body. I was successful in acquiring some parts of a weaving loom, unfortunately without any weaving started; sadly this find was lost in the later uproar. Such an apron is about 125 centimetres long and 50 centimetres wide and made from two pieces sewn together. They are very roughly prepared from naturally coloured pandanus leaf fibres, and resemble coarsely woven jute material. Moreover the aprons, after having been woven, are processed again by the women pushing thick fibre cords through the long threads with an awl, so that it appears as if the admixture consists of alternating thin, twisted threads and thicker untwisted strands. I was able to acquire such an apron clearly showing this further processing. Very young girls run around totally naked.

The islanders seem to have been cut off from all outside influences for a long time. I observed no ornamentation, and apart from a few elongated wooden bowls, no household equipment. As tools, there were roughly worked *Tridacna* axes with a barely usable cutting edge. The blades were fastened to a knee-shaped handle by means of a woven bark ring.

The spears, or more accurately lances, are 5 to 6 metres long, roughly made out of the hard wood of the coconut palm, scantily smoothed and of great weight, so that they most definitely would not be reckoned amongst the fear-invoking weapons. Because of their weight they were not thrown, but were used only as stabbing weapons in close combat. Each club being presented was on the other hand used as a weapon, and the coral rocks were above all the most effective means of defence. Both men and women knew how to throw fist-sized lumps with great precision over long distances, and I was heartily grateful, at the later attack, when we got out of range. Reminders of St Matthias were given by several of the lances having their lower ends pushed into a bamboo tube. The canoes are simple tree trunks, pointed both front and back and with the usual outrigger and float; most canoes were reckoned to be for two or three passengers; however, on the beach lay a large canoe which might have held ten men. At both pointed ends it was provided with a decoration consisting of a prominent knob, which bore a distant resemblance to a fish head with wide open mouth, although I do not want to assert that it should actually represent this.

Besides the previously mentioned fishing equipment there were also fishing rods about 3 metres long with a 5 to 6 metre line. For deep sea fishing they had an apparatus which I first took as an abnormal head ornament of the men in the canoes approaching us, as they had attached them to their locks in such a way that it hung down the back. However, I later found out that the apparatus was for fishing. It consisted of two bent canes fastened to each other in such a way that they formed an ellipse with fairly sharp ends. The longest diameter was about 50 centimetres, the shorter about 25 centimetres. The elliptical space between the canes was covered with a brown, paper-thin substance. The fishing cord was wrapped lengthwise around this apparatus. Neither on this apparatus nor on the fishing rods did I notice hooks; instead at the end of the cord two thin, sharpened little sticks were bound into a cross, probably replacing the fishhooks. They called to mind a similar apparatus in the Gilbert Islands which was used especially for catching flying fish.

That trade with whites probably occurred only quite rarely, mostly with passing ships, was revealed by the situation that no examples of modern industry were present. The only indicative item was an iron ship's nail which was fixed into an axe handle and fashioned into a narrow blade. The items that I distributed, such as plane iron, knives, beads, looking-glasses and armrings, aroused universal, long-lasting amazement.

Because of the total impossibility of oral understanding I did not succeed in learning the name of the island; the map designation Squally Island must be discarded unconditionally. This name, which originates from Dampier, refers probably to Emirau and not to this island which absolutely does not match Dampier's description. The sole discoverer is the Englishman Lieutenant King who, on his voyage from Sydney to Batavia in the ship *Supply*, sighted the island on 19 May 1790. His coordinates 150°31'E and 1°39'S are approximately correct. He named the island after Watkin Tench, the commander of the marines, and so all other names should disappear without further ado, and the name Tench Island be retained. From the individuals who came into view in their canoes, King gives a fairly good description of the islanders; on the other hand his assessment of the population, which he gives as 1,000 individuals, is much too high even for that time. The small island would not be in a position to sustain such a population, for coconut palms are only sparsely found and bear exceptionally small nuts; also the island is wooded, and the stands of trees show that large gardens have never existed. A few taro tubers no larger than a child's fist were present; however, as well as this the fruit of the pandanus tree and that of *Inocarpus edulis* appeared to form a main food source. In any case fishing is the principal source from which the islanders take their nourishment.

IV   The Admiralty Islands

This group forms to some extent the north-western end of that long, curved chain of islands and island groups which stretches roughly from south-east to north-west, and includes the New Hebrides, the Solomon Islands and New Ireland with New Hanover. The approximate position of the group is between 1°50' and 2°50'S, and between 146° and 148°E. It consists of a larger main island and numerous small islands and island groups. The former is about 50 nautical miles long and 10 to 15 nautical miles wide with a fairly mountainous surface whose highest points reach approximately 900 metres.

Just off the north coast of the island, on the offshore coral reef, lie a small number of islands. Far more numerous, however, are those situated off the south and south-east coasts, where they combine into several small groups situated in some instances at quite significant distances from the main island. The most important of these groups are San Gabriel and San Rafael to the east of the main island, the Jesus Maria group in the south-east, the groups St Andrew and St Patrick, Sugarloaf Island, Hayrick Island in the south, and even further south the Purdy Islands and the Elizabeth Islands, about 40 to 45 nautical miles from the main island.

The navigable waters between these islands are not without danger to shipping, because of the numerous coral reefs; the more so since the maps available are not very accurate. The main island offers quite good harbours and anchorages at various places, and also sheltered anchorages are available among the small islands of the offshore groups.

Because of its mountainous nature, the island does not seem to be of great significance for tropical agriculture. The total size, however, amounts to some 1,900 square kilometres (that is, the size of Saxe-Coburg and Gotha), but only a small part of this surface area would be suitable for cultivation. Possibly there are extensive valleys and plateaux in the interior of the island which would be suitable for agriculture, but for the moment we can only judge from the condition of the coast, as, up till now, no white man has ventured more than 3 nautical miles into the interior. The soil, so far as we can conclude from present tests, is of exceptional quality, The climate is humid, but not unhealthy, since malaria, which is widespread on the other islands of the archipelago, does not appear to be strong here.

Recently in the German press the usefulness of setting up a penal colony in these islands was discussed. It is to be hoped that this plan does not come to fruition. The experiences that England, France and other countries have had in this connection do not invite imitation. The system has proved to be costly everywhere, and the outcome, from their high hopes of making colonists out of the prisoners, remained far in arrear of the most widespread expectations.

The flora and fauna of the islands is essentially no different from that of the other islands of the Bismarck Archipelago. Pigs and dogs are present, the former even in a feral state. In the mangrove swamps the crocodile dwells in considerable numbers, a terror to the entire population; turtles, both *Chelone midas* and *C. imbricata*, are still quite numerous in places, and are eagerly hunted by the natives. The sea is rich in all kinds of fish and the dense forests ring with the continuous sound of

Fig. 60   Part of Lou Island

Plate 23   Men's house in the village of the Matánkor on Lou

numerous species of pigeon, of which *Carpophaga oceanica* is the most abundant.

The discoverers of the islands had hostile encounters with the natives in those early times, and communication with them has not changed significantly since then. Attacks on ships and the murder of their crews is unfortunately an all too frequent occurrence even today, and in spite of repeated serious punishment on the part of the imperial administration no change has been brought about. Merchants and trading settlements can be maintained only on the small isolated islands, where the white people dwell as if in a fortress. In recent years a not inconsiderable quantity of trepang and mother-of-pearl has been obtained from there by trade; however, more recently these trade sources seem to be gradually drying up. The copra trade is not significant, through a lack of large stands of coconut palms.

The population of these islands reminds us in many ways of the Papuans of New Guinea, with whom there are many external similarities. However, we are not dealing with a pure race here either.

Very many indicate admixture with a pale-skinned stock, although the Papuan characteristics are dominant. Communication with the islands on the New Guinea coast opposite still takes place today; whether this relationship is based on traditional knowledge of the location of these islands, or whether it was by chance, can still not be established with certainty. In 1897 I encountered two canoes from the Admiralty Islands on the small island of Jacquinot in the Schouten or Le Maire group. These vessels lay on the beach, carefully protected from the sun, and their crew were easily distinguishable from the Jacquinot people by their different hairstyle and their whole deportment. They were, as far as I could understand, from Sugarloaf Island, and on their journey had touched the Purdy Islands where they make frequent voyages, both to catch turtles and to collect oil from the stands of coconut palms there. They seemed to be on a friendly footing with the Jacquinot people, and gave me to understand that they had already been here for three months and contemplated making the return voyage only in a further three months. They occasionally stop over on New Hanover as well in order to regain their homeland at a favourable opportunity. In later discussion we will see how their influence is clearly recognisable on the western islands, such as Luf.

Their close relationship with the tribes on the New Guinea coast seems *inter alia* to be marked by the very frequent occurrence among them of the pronounced Semitic nose, which draws the attention of every visitor to this region of New Guinea, appearing again in the Bismarck Archipelago only on western New Britain, whose inhabitants are without doubt closely related to the Papuans of New Guinea. Otherwise they are well-proportioned and of medium height. The hair is frizzy but less thick than that of the Papuans; the spiral winding of the individual hairs which in New Britain (Gazelle Peninsula) and New Ireland, for example, produces the characteristic corkscrew tufts, is less prominent, and it is not uncommon to see islanders with curly, and even completely straight Polynesian hair. This feature, however, can probably be ascribed in great part to the customary piling up of the hair with a comb.

In some tribes the skin shade is paler than elsewhere in the Bismarck Archipelago; a lighter yellow is mixed in to some extent with the chocolate brown, sometimes dominating in such a way that the skin shade comes close to that of the pale Samoans. Such cases seem to allow a conclusion of immigration from Polynesia or Micronesia. However, the Moánus and Usiai have the colour of the Gazelle Peninsula inhabitants.

Intellectually the islanders seem to occupy a higher level than the other inhabitants of the Bismarck Archipelago. They are lively and highly excitable. They comprehend readily, and effortlessly learn a wide variety of accomplishments which seem an arduous task to other natives. Some of the boys who had spent time at the Catholic mission school learned to read and write with astonishing speed, and one of them on his return to his homeland wrote letters to the father who had taught him. When visiting a passing ship they examine everything most exhaustively and exchange observations among themselves with very great eloquence, supported by gesticulations with arms and hands. In contrast with the inhabitants of the Gazelle Peninsula or the Solomon Islands, for example, who observe everything with calm stoicism and without changing expression even though it may seem so amazing to them, the Moánus indulges in loud cries of astonishment; and if an object is not riveted or nailed down, you need to keep a sharp eye on him, for when he sees an opportunity he conjures away the marvellous, coveted item into his little baskets or into the canoe lying alongside, with great manual dexterity and the most astonishing coolness. This kleptomania often gets him into all kinds of trouble and strife, when he shows his courage by grasping his spear which is never far away and stubbornly defending the acquired loot. In this a further characteristic comes into view, which makes him very dangerous to the trader, namely his deceit and his hypocrisy. Surreptitiously holding his weapon ready he feigns the most charming expression, the most outgoing, friendly manner, in order to deliver a mortal blow to the unsuspecting person in an unguarded moment which he spots instantly and seizes without hesitation. Almost all attacks are put into operation with this system; first he succeeds in putting all suspicions to rest, which may often take days or weeks; the victim believes that he is surrounded by his best friends, until a blow on the head with a sharp axe causes him to realise his mistake, unfortunately too late. The great superiority and the big advantage of firearms, already long recognised, have motivated the islanders to acquire rifles, especially in the last five years. Since this was not possible by trading, they have attempted to meet their needs by the methods described above, on trading vessels calling in and at trading posts. With their success they have now become more dangerous than in earlier years, as they have shown themselves skilful with the acquired firearms and have put up strong resistance to punitive expeditions dispatched against them, so that these are generally unsuccessful.

The islanders divide themselves into three main tribes named Moánus, Matánkor and Usiai. The first of these live on the coast, build their villages on the shore or in shallow water on the reef, and their houses always stand on poles. The Usiai are inhabitants of the interior, and build their huts on level ground. The Matánkor form an intermediate group between the two; they are agriculturalists but also seafarers though not to the same extent as the Moánus. The Moánus designate with the word *Usiai* a native who stands in a certain state of dependency on them. From the beginning the Moánus have, through the possession of canoes, been rulers of the sea; they were superior to the inland dwellers by being more quick-witted and cunning, and indeed in many ways they still hold the power in their hands today, in that they compel the Usiai to grow food for them and to hand it over for very small payment or for no reimbursement at all, just as we find on the Gazelle Peninsula, for example, between the shore-dwellers and the Baining, or on Bougainville between the shore-dwellers and the inhabitants of the mountains.

In the ethnographic museums the products and implements of the natives are well represented, and the most striking among them are the spears with the razor-sharp obsidian tips (fig. 61). The latter come in all sizes up to a length of 25 centimetres.

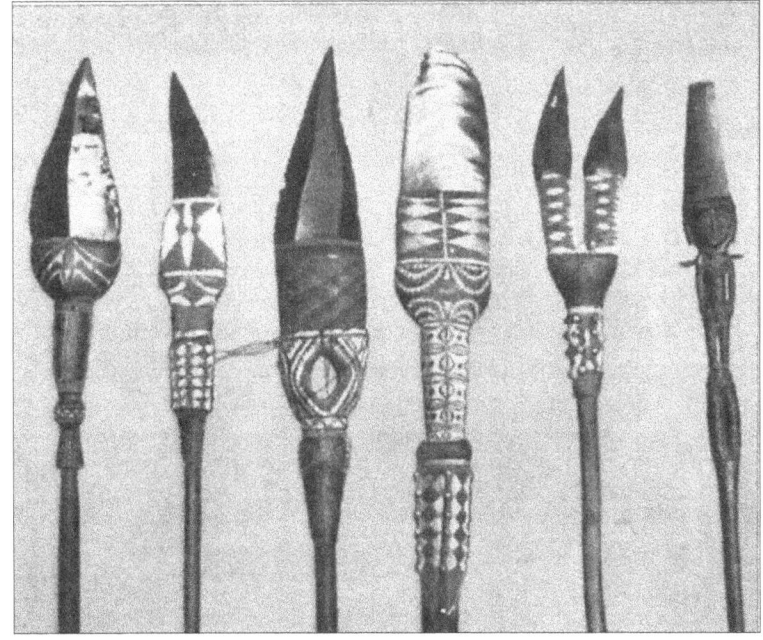

Fig. 61 Spears from the Admiralty Islands

The tips, which like both edges are produced by knocking off small splinters, have the sharpness of an excellent steel blade. The broad end of the blade is set into a wooden shaft, partly by wrapping round, and partly by puttying with crushed nuts. The shaft is occasionally carved and otherwise decorated; the carving frequently has the human figure as a motif, or that of a crocodile which we find universally represented in various forms in native carvings. They produce dagger tips in exactly the same way as the tips of the spears. To some extent they could be described as spears with broken-off wooden shafts. However, the daggers are used only in rare cases as weapons and more often represent our knives. Since the raw material for spear and dagger tips is not available everywhere, or supply is not able to meet demand, wooden-tipped spears are found as well as those with obsidian tips, and also spears with the long spines of a ray attached.

A type of battleaxe is found here and there, consisting of a carved, ornamented wooden shaft to which an obsidian blade is attached at right angles. However, I believe that we are dealing here with an item prepared by shipwrecked natives as a trade article. About twenty years ago these axes did not appear in the otherwise very extensive collections from there, and appeared on the scene only in more recent times. Dr Thilenius has reproduced such an axe on page 128 of volume II of his work and gives its origin as the island of Pidelo (more accurately Pitilu) on the northern coast of the main island, but he does not mention whether he had the opportunity of seeing this axe in use. In earlier years, on the island named Pitilu, I was able to observe a large number of armed natives, but none had such an axe as a weapon, and furthermore none was offered to me in spite of lively bartering in which anything and everything was offered.

Bows and arrows are found here and there, used exclusively for hunting; clubs are used in many places but always in very small numbers and of little significance in battle.

Stone axes were probably never used as weapons; today they are completely out of use; the collector rarely succeeds in acquiring blades without a holder. Two different axes were used; one was very primitively made – the blade produced from a hard, lava-like rock, simply being pushed into the thick end of a club-shaped piece of wood. It was, and still is, used by the Usiai. Another axe had the familiar knee-shaped wooden shaft to which the blade was firmly bound. These blades consisted sometimes of sharpened *Terebra* shells, sometimes of *Tridacna* shells, and sometimes again, of a grey-green stone. The form of this axe has still been retained, but the stone or shellfish blades have disappeared and given place to plane iron. The shafts are not infrequently carved and decorated. The Moánus and Matánkor possess this type of axe.

Tools are found in great numbers, in the most varied forms and serving the most varied purposes.

Pottery appears here also and is made over a considerable area, because the raw material is available almost everywhere. Yet here too, as in New Guinea, certain centres have built up where special care is bestowed on this art form, and consequently their products are more nearly perfect. The most common pot shape is spherical, the opening narrow or constricted and provided with a rim arching outward. However, there are also pots without rims, almost the shape of a deep bowl. Clay water jugs are used a great deal; they have two openings which are plugged by a stopper of banana leaves or a wooden stopper. Because of its porosity this type of water container is eminently suitable for keeping the contents cool. Pottery manufacture is the same as in the Solomon Islands and New Guinea. The women gather the clay, dry it, pulverise and knead it, and produce a mass of plastic material in the form of great lumps or balls. The working tool is a small, flat, trowel-like piece of wood. First the base is formed from a lump of clay, beaten flat. Rolls of the same material are laid on this base and beaten flat with the trowel, while the inner surface is supported with the left hand. Decoration of the pot is not customary; now and again one sees a few simple lines incised with a fingernail.

Extraordinarily characteristic are the large containers prepared for storage of coconut oil, frequently seen in the big canoes as transport containers for which, on account of their sturdiness, they are better suited than the transitory earthenware. A close weave of leaf ribs of a particular fern species forms the framework of these containers. Once the shape of the container is formed, it is coated inside and out with a layer of crushed *Parinarium* nut and then hung up to dry. After a few days the coat

Fig. 62 Wooden bowl from the Admiralty Islands

is dry and the container ready. Any kind of liquid can be stored in it. These pots serve especially as containers for coconut oil, which is used in many ways in food preparation. The indestructability of these containers gives them a great advantage over earthenware; empty containers are thrown roughly on top of one another in a corner without being damaged; they resist a rough blow without bursting, and if the *Parinarium* coat comes off the damage can easily be repaired. The shape of these containers varies a lot, as does the size. Some contain about 1 litre of oil, others on the other hand two to three bucketsful. The base is flat for standing on the ground. Often an outward-directed, broad rim is attached round the base; the bulbous shape of the container frequently ends in a narrow neck with a wide, sloping upper rim; others are broad below and narrow upwards; again others have the bulbous shape of the cooking pots. In order to hang the pots in the huts, the lower rim is surrounded with a rolled, thick ring of woven rattan in which the base of the vessel fits. Three or four rattan cords come off this ring, up around the sides and uniting in a loop above the opening.

The performance of the natives in the production of large and small wooden bowls is quite outstanding.

The most common form is circular, and the diameter varies from 15 to 125 centimetres. These bowls rest on four round feet carved out of the bulb, which are long or short depending on the curvature of the base. The upper rim is circular and carefully smoothed both inside and out. The outer rim is, as a rule, adorned with a band-like decoration; but the most carefully carved are the large handles protruding out over the rim, which are added to most of these bowls; they serve exclusively as ornaments, since by virtue of their attachment they are not suitable for lifting the often very heavy bowls (fig. 62).

Human, crocodile and bird figures serve as motifs for these handles, in conjunction with a decorative spiral. Other bowls resemble the shape of a bird (fig. 63) or a turtle, the head, tail and bowl-shaped body of which are carved from a single piece of wood. Shallow, oblong bowls frequently have fine, carved handles representing a crocodile; sometimes also an animal shape such as a pig or a dog in a realistic pose is shaped into a bowl, in which the body of the animal is hollowed out from the back (fig. 64).

Since these bowls are produced as a rule from hardwood, they demonstrate no small level of skill, the more so when the earlier hand tool could be regarded as the most imperfect of its kind. The acquisition of modern metal tools here as everywhere has not increased the old skill but led to a reduction in it.

The wooden bowls are used for the presentation and carriage of the most varied dishes. As a ladle,

when necessary, they use a decorated instrument made from a half-coconut with a finely carved handle. The many shapes of this ladle handle may be divided into three main groups. The first of these is a flat board, carved in open-work and decorated with grooves and small triangles; the shapes are angular and more or less square or rectangular; these handles always have the broad surface turned inwards toward the container. The second form has a shaft in which the spiral predominates; they are always at right angles to the spoon.

The third form shows various animal motifs in its decoration, also human figures in conjunction with the two previously described forms. The extremely great variety of decoration is characteristic (fig. 65). The power of imagination of the carver always introduces new forms.

A characteristic instrument, the significance of which was unrecognised for a long time, is a type of hook made from a club-shaped piece of wood about 20 centimetres long, into whose thick end a fairly long, curved boar's tusk is driven at right angles and wedged. For a long time it was regarded

Fig. 63 Wooden bowl in the shape of a bird. Admiralty Islands

Fig. 64 Wooden bowl in the form of a four-footed animal. Admiralty Islands

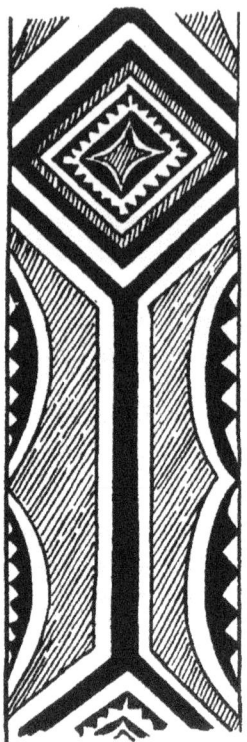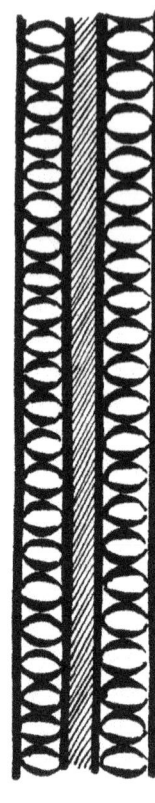

Fig. 65 Decorations of ladles, water containers, and so on, of the Admiralty Islanders

as a shark-hook because of its size, although by its shape it could scarcely serve as an instrument of capture. Further inquiries in later years revealed that this hook attached to a pole serves to bring certain fruit down from the trees.

Besides the previously described water pots, the natives also produce water flasks from the shells of coconuts. There are two kinds: one consists of a nut rubbed smooth, with a small opening, not infrequently decorated with raised ornaments by carving in relief. To the other a short neck is attached, made from a bamboo tube. Crushed *Parinarium* nut serves as a means of binding, and before the thick coating has dried all kinds of decoration are carved into it.

Obsidian flakes and sharply honed mother-of-pearl shell serve as knives, the latter particularly in food preparation, the former more in carving. The barb of a ray serves as an awl, used in various ways.

Hooks are used as fishing equipment; these were formerly made from *Trochus* shell, but these have been replaced by modern fishhooks. As well as these, they use a multi-pronged fishing spear, although not very often, while the main equipment is nets of various shapes and sizes, as well as draw-nets. The natives, especially the Usiai, even today, prepare the material for making the nets. This consists of a coarse or fine thread made from a fibrous plant, of great strength and durability. The individual fibres are intertwined, not woven. The plant that provides this material is the same as that used on the Gazelle Peninsula.

Both Moseley, from the Challenger Expedition, and Professor Thilenius have given comprehensive descriptions with detailed drawings of the islanders' canoes. They are seaworthy vessels, capable, as we have seen, of long voyages as far as New Hanover and the Schouten Islands. The body consists of a hollowed-out tree trunk; both sides are raised by a plank. Both ends are lengthened by stem and stern pieces which are built onto the body of the canoe. These pieces are frequently decorated, sometimes by carving in the form of a crocodile head, and sometimes by white *Ovula* shells which are fastened on with strong bindings. The outrigger bears a platform made from battens laid against one another, and another one is attached on the opposite side, rising somewhat obliquely in the air. The people crouch on these superstructures when sailing, or stow their spears or whatever items are being transported. A mast is erected on the bottom of the vessels, forward of the outrigger struts, and held in position by a pole fastened to the outrigger and by ropes stretched fore and aft. The mast has a fork at the upper end, through which runs the rope used for hauling aloft the four-sided matting sail; this sail is made fast between two poles. Large canoes often have double masts and sails. The paddles are of the usual form, with broad, lancet-like blades which are either carved with the shaft from one single stick, or else fastened to the shaft by strong bindings. No canoe lacks a bailer, with an inwardly curving handle. As with both ends of the vessel, so too the fork of the mast is decorated with carving, consisting of diamond-shaped grooves and stylised crocodile heads.

The village layout, as I have already mentioned, differs among the three tribes. However, there is little difference in house construction, although the houses of the Moánus are always erected on poles, while those of the Usiai and Matánkor stand on level ground. A further difference is that the Matánkor take greater care in construction, and the village site is cleaner and more tastefully laid out.

The houses of the Moánus are built in rows along the beach, and often out on the reef also, and the village lies completely free and open to the sea. The Matánkor build their villages in the forest, and if at all possible, on steep, near-inaccessible heights and ridges, for greater security. The solid fences surrounding the villages serve the same purpose. This is frequently a double fence constructed in such a way that the inner one surrounds the village proper and the site; the second fence, some distance from the first, encloses a belt densely planted with coconut and betel palms, and bananas. Here the natives' pigs roam about and they can as little bother the village as they can escape into the surrounding forest. Holes which do not extend to the ground enable entry. The normal dwellings are undecorated huts about 5 to 6 metres long, 3 to 4 metres wide, and seldom more than 3 metres high. The roof consists of sago palm leaves which are bent over rods about 2 metres long and pierced by a thin stick close to the rod to hold them in position. Woven coconut leaves also serve this purpose. The furnishings differ inside the huts depending on whether they serve as dwellings for the women or the men. Common to all are the low, table-like plank beds on four, often artistically carved legs that serve the inhabitants not only as beds but also act as a table. In the women's house the space is reduced by a frame taking up the entire central space, on which pots, water and oil containers, baskets of food, and all kinds of utensils are piled up, while the taro tubers gathered from the garden, and other kinds of food lie on the floor. The men's houses are somewhat more roomy because the previously mentioned frame is missing, but hanging shelves or a structure in the middle hold pouches, betel utensils and suchlike and, above all, a great number of spears.

Much greater care is taken in the construction of the bachelors' houses or, as they should more accurately be named, the men's assembly houses. The native carpenters have employed their greatest skill on posts, timberwork and roof frame, and individual parts are decorated with incised ornaments and the recurring crocodile head. Bird figures like grotesque, full-sized human shapes or human heads, also occur. These spacious houses, often 40 metres long, 12 metres wide and 8 metres high, up to the ridge beam, contain the trophies of past feasts in the form of lower jaws of pig or cuscus, as well as the finely carved plank beds and a great number of weapons. The property of the tribe is also set out on poles and trestles: bright, glass beads, ironware, looking-glasses, and so on.

It is understandable that the natives, who in their appearance wear so much frippery for show, also place high value on ornaments of all kinds. They vividly remind us of the inhabitants of New Guinea. By laying stress on cleanliness of the body they demonstrate that their outsides are not a matter of indifference to them. The most common decoration is daubing the body with red dye, or painting the face with red, black or white lines and dots over forehead, eyes, nose and cheeks. Necklaces of local white shell discs, replaced in recent times by multiple strings of white beads, are indispensable, as are carefully polished *Trochus* armrings with incised patterns on the outer side. The youth takes extraordinary care over his hairstyle. The crinkly hair is combed up and curled by a comb that is always close at hand, until it lies like a cloud over the entire head, sometimes carefully parted in the middle. These combs are made with great care. They consist of the ribs of coconut palm leaves laid side by side, their ends stuck into a network of fibres coated with *Parinarium* glue. This end section is decorated in various ways and brightly painted.

The pierced ear lobes are tightly wrapped with cords of white beads or decorated with discs of coconut; the nose too is not forgotten, for a cylindrical rod ground from *Tridacna* shell, 18 to 20 centimetres long, pointed below and with incised decoration, hangs from the pierced nasal septum on a string of beads. They also wear an almost complete ring of coconut shell, about 1 centimetre wide in the middle and tapering at both ends, stuck through the nasal septum. Also, the peculiar pattern of tartar on the upper front teeth is regarded as beautification of the face. This tartar deposit is sometimes so thick that it pushes the upper lip upwards and juts out beyond it. The deposit is carefully tended and given a regular shape by grinding and scraping. Chewing of betel seems to favour the formation of this peculiar ornamentation, which is, moreover, apparently a designation of chiefs and influential men.

Besides the already mentioned neckbands we find in conjunction with them a chest ornament, similar to those known on New Ireland in the form of the *kapkap*. As on New Ireland the ornament consists of a *Tridacna* disc, but seldom as thin; the rims are always decorated with a triangular ornamentation consisting of fine lines which, because of gathered dirt, stand out black against the white disc surface. The open-work turtle-shell plate that lies on the *Tridacna* disc is never as finely worked as on New Ireland. The pattern on the turtle-shell plate is occasionally completely irregular. Figure 46, which depicts a number of from both New Ireland

and the Admiralty Islands, clearly shows the great difference in presentation.

In his dancing the native reveals himself in his full splendour. Not only is the body painting very painstaking, but ornaments are displayed that are never seen in daily life. Particularly outstanding are the armrings, kneebands, girdles and aprons that deserve a more detailed description. Small discs 4 to 6 millimetres in diameter and about 1 millimetre thick, produced from the upper, thick end of a particular small *Conus* shell, serve as the principal material in the manufacture of these items. They are expert at processing these small discs into armrings and girdles which one has to admit are very tasteful. The aprons made from these discs are quite outstanding. Thousands of these discs are used in the production of such an apron, and consequently they have a not insignificant value in their homeland, so that only rich people or chiefs are able to afford such a luxury. The size of these dance aprons (fig. 66a) varies greatly. They range in width from 15 to 40 centimetres, and in length from 20 to 60 centimetres. The upper end consists firstly of a close bast weave which is in part decked out with bright, parrot feathers; upon this weaving the actual apron is aligned, consisting of rows of shell discs on which supplementary black shell discs, a particular species of coir seed, and various other seed kernels form patterns. Figure 66 will give an idea, better than any description, of the extraordinary care devoted to the manufacture, as well as showing the beauty of the work.

The women too wear an apron in dancing, far less carefully worked than the men's apron. The women's apron (fig. 66b), consists of a soft, pliable piece of bark to the upper surface of which tassels of shell discs, coir and other seed kernels and birds' feathers are sewn at short intervals.

The lower edge consists of a row of pendant shell discs with seed kernels on the end. In dancing, one of these aprons is worn in front and another behind, both being held on by a girdle. The young girls and women are expert at performing dainty body movements which set the embroidered apron in a swinging motion, and this seems actually to be the main purpose of the dance, for when the aprons sway gracefully and picturesquely after a particularly successful step, loud cheers break out.

Today this type of apron is rarely found, if not made with imported European material, especially glass beads and bright rags – I might say adulterated and thereby significantly diminished in beauty. The natives do not seem to understand that the blending of European articles reduces the value of their original decorative items; here, too, this preference for European industrial items has arisen from the feeling that all things new are to be preferred to the old, a situation that we can often observe among civilised nations as well.

Finally, the curious penis shell must also be reckoned among the decorative items; covering the glans of the male member in battle or in dancing. This shell is always a medium-sized *Ovula ovum*, with cross-hatched patterns incised on the outer, white surface. The internal spiral is partially excavated, and the glans and foreskin are squeezed into the fissure thereby formed. This shell is always carried in a small, woven pouch on a cord around the neck or under the arm, by the adult natives able to bear weapons, so that it is always in readiness. Analogous items of adornment are known to us only from St Matthias in the Bismarck Archipelago; on the other hand we find a similar penis covering in New Guinea, although made not from a shell but from a small species of gourd as in Angriff Harbour.

Probably the tufts of hair and other ornaments also belong among the decoration. These are worn on a cord around the neck during war expeditions so that they hang down the back. The tufts of hair are of varying length and have a loop above, through which the cord is pulled. The thick, hanging plait is wrapped round, and the wrapping is daubed with bright patterns; the lower end forms an almost fist-sized tuft of hair. Other neck ornaments are carved out of wood and represent stylised human figures, also crocodiles and crocodile heads, turtles and fish; but the most characteristic is the neck ornament of human upper arm bones or thigh bones, to which the trimmed wing feathers of the frigate bird are tightly bound to one another along the shaft, so that only the joint head of the bone shows. A replica of this ornament is made from a wooden batten similarly wrapped in frigate bird feathers with the protruding end, corresponding to the head of the joint, carved in the form of a human head. I know of neck ornaments that are similar, although in other shapes, only from

Fig. 66 Aprons from the Admiralty Islands

a. men's apron; b. women's apron

Plate 24 Moánus women from Lalobé with their children

the Solomon Islands, where they are regarded as amulets that protect the wearer against wounding in battle. Perhaps those from the Admiralty Islands are based on a similar idea as well.

Also, mention must be made of the implements used for chewing betel. The lime containers are made as a rule from a species of long pumpkin constricted in the middle, with dark, symmetrical drawings burned on to the yellow upper surface. However, besides these pumpkin flasks one also sees vessels made of bamboo cane, the sides of which are similarly decorated with burnt-on designs. Quite extraordinary care is exercised on the manufacture of the long wooden trowels with which the burnt lime is taken out of the lime containers. These trowels are made from a dark wood with the lower end flattened like a spatula, while the upper end is ornamented with a carefully carved decoration. Here we find the human figure and the crocodile head as the principal motif.

As a sign of mourning for the dead, the closest relatives, both men and women, wear a peculiar head covering, still rarely found among our collections. This head covering, called *la*, consists of a stiff yet pliable piece of tree bark with a shiny, black resinous coat on both sides. This rectangle is about 25 to 30 centimetres long and about 14 centimetres wide; at each end three black-lacquered, woven bands are attached, with cords at the ends bound together at the wearer's neck. This headband is frequently decorated on the black surfaces with beads and shell discs in various arrangements. I have come across this sign of mourning only in villages of the Matánkor, and I believe that it is unique to this tribe.

The Matánkor, or as they call themselves in their own language, the Marankol, are, particularly in the manufacture of ornaments of all kinds and in the production of all kinds of carpentry and carving, far superior to the Moánus and the Usiai. They are the people who decorate their huts with carved poles and roof frames, they prepare the large and small wooden spoons, indeed even canoe construction rests mainly in their hands.

The items described above stem in the largest part from the Moánus and Matánkor, particularly the latter, who hand over their articles to the former. We have as yet had little contact with the Usiai. Insofar as I have seen them, during a visit to the pole village of Lalobé, north of the island of Ndruval, where several of them were staying on a visit, they seemed little different in body form from the Moánus, although the physiognomy of a mountain people was strongly pronounced, particularly in the more powerful musculature of the legs and in the broader, more developed chest. In facial features they differed in no way from the Moánus, while their clothing was the same and consisted of a narrow loincloth drawn between their legs. However, this costume is not universal; the Moánus apparently take it off in their canoes, and are not always clothed in the villages either.

On the other hand the Matánkor always wear a girdle with a strip drawn between the legs to cover the genitals. Chiefs or people of high rank wear a strip of bark a hand's breadth wide both in front and at the back, extending from the girdle almost to the ground, a distinction that we also know from several of the Carolines (see, for example, *The Caroline Islands* page 136, the diagram of a chief from Rúl). In body form there is, at least as far as the Matánkor of the southern islands are concerned, a notable difference between them and the Moánus. Their skin colour is significantly paler, stature is smaller and more slender, the head hair is frequently vigorously curly, in the odd individual even totally straight, and the nose is less broad than in the Moánus and the Usiai. Indeed one also finds the pronounced Semitic nose among them. The Matánkor, who live on the northern islands of the group, are less pronounced in these bodily characteristics, and resemble the Moánus more closely, probably as a result of close intermixing through marriage with them and with the Usiai.

Women's clothing is basically the same in the Moánus and the Matánkor, and consists of a woven grass apron, *uo*, rough on the outside, or more accurately two such aprons that hang down in front and behind, and are held together by a girdle. For the Moánus these girdles are made from thin cords that are wound round and round the body, similar to those of the women on Ninigo. Among the Moánus the women's heads are shaved completely bald; among the Matánkor only partly so. Among the latter, one also finds women with short hair or with a hairstyle in the shape of a cloud, like the men.

The women everywhere are richly adorned with ornaments; their ears are full of the most varied earrings, wrists and ankles are covered by broad cuffs made earlier from discs of local shell, and today from red, blue and white glass beads. Neckbands and necklaces as well as strings laid crosswise over the chest appear to be particularly favoured by the fair sex. The women's figures are really dainty; the small, delicate hands, which show only slight traces of work, are quite striking. The skin tone is significantly paler than the men's, probably because the women stay in the huts a lot, while the men roam about in the sunshine at sea. It was not without great difficulty that I succeeded in photographing several groups of women, and for this I am grateful to the influence of my friend Max Thiel of Matupi, who used his full, charming amiability on the native women, aided by copious distribution of tobacco, in order to banish the earlier shyness and withdrawal. However, I am also indebted to the headmen who finally put an end to the resistance of several beauties by a command, although in a less charming manner than my friend Thiel.

Finally, I must describe in greater detail the large wooden drums (fig. 67), which are found in great numbers in the houses of the chiefs and in the men's houses. The size varies: one finds small drums 0.5 metres long and monstrous examples 3 to 3.5 metres long with corresponding circumferences. All consist of a single piece of wood, a complete section of a tree trunk which is hollowed out through a long, narrow slit on the upper side. To facilitate this work a circular hole is also made at both ends in the very big specimens, and the inside is hollowed out through these holes. When the hollowing is completed, both holes are closed up through tight-fitting wooden plugs. These drums are decorated, almost without exception, by dainty relief carving, both along the slit and on the side walls; however, characteristically a human figure is attached at both ends as an extension of the slit, in such a way that at one end the head and chest are visible and the legs at the other, while the body of the drum represents to some extent the abdomen of the figure. These figures are either those of a man or a woman. From the explanation given to me in the village of Punro on Lou Island I could gather only that the natives (Matánkor) actually regard the drum body as the belly of a man; unfortunately the sentence relating to this remained unintelligible to me. The tone of the drums, audible over a great distance, is not produced by blows with a stick against the side as in other parts of the archipelago, but by striking with a bent piece of wood about 40 centimetres long. The drummer holds such a stick in each hand, and beats the sides of the drum with great rapidity and skill just below the slit. A drum or signal language is known to the natives. These instruments are also used for dances, and when eight or ten drummers are using all their energy on such occasions, one needs strong nerves to put up with the deafening din.

Some of the photographs accompanying this section were taken in the villages of Punro and Sali on the island of Lou, the same villages visited also by Dr Thilenius. This island is known as the source of the best-quality obsidian (*bailo*) for the manufacture of spear points. Obsidian is also obtained from both the Poam Islands. It is obtained by mining, when

Fig. 67 Drum from the Admiralty Islands

deep shafts are dug and blocks are brought up to the surface, from where they are traded to other parts of the archipelago. Blade manufacture is a skill practised by only a few of the natives. On Poam there was only one man skilled in manufacture; in both the abovementioned villages on Lou there was nobody, and we were told that a certain man from a neighbouring village was acknowledged as the craftsman. The blade-maker on Poam gave us a demonstration of his art. After a small block of obsidian had been carefully selected, he gripped it in his left hand and knocked small slivers off one side with a stone weighing about half a pound in his right hand. Then he closed his hand firmly round the block so that the side rested against his palm while his fingers gripped both ends. He gave a sudden, gentle tap with the stone against the outside of the block, and immediately a long sliver sprang off the opposite, free side. With gentle taps this sliver was fashioned completely into a spear tip. Apparently obsidian has a definite fracture plane which the manufacturer knows how to find and to exploit in his work.

It was extremely interesting for me to see a growing kava plant (*Piper methysticum*), in the village of Lou. The natives appear to regard the plant, designated by the name *Ká*, as something quite special, and reported that the roots are crushed between stones and the expressed juice is drunk by the men. Thus preparation of the drink is exactly the same as, for example, on the island of Ponape in the Carolines.

With regard to the designations of the various tribes which will be characterised in greater detail in the following passage, I should point out that these are ascribable to the Moánus, who designate all members of their own tribe by this name. The significance of the name is not clear to me. On the other hand, the designation Usiai, which is used by both the Moánus and the Matánkor for the inhabitants of the interior of the large island, seems to be synonymous with 'tribe'; I draw this conclusion from a remark by the chief of Ndruval, who accompanied us in our boat, and, in response to a question about who might the fishermen be, who were fishing on the reef, answered that they were 'Usiai Lalobé' – men or tribe from Lalobé, a large Moánus village on the main island opposite. The word Matánkor means face of the land (*mata* = face, *nkor* = land) and might have arisen from this tribe inhabiting especially the islands offshore from the main island. So much is certain, that the Usiai are the original inhabitants, and that the Matánkor immigrated later, perhaps from New Guinea, but more probably from the north, from the Carolines. On the other hand I cannot accurately place the Moánus. In my opinion they are a later migration which, through their intelligence and their battle lust, rose to a dominant position, especially over the much earlier Usiai, while the Matánkor were for a large part in a position to preserve their independence. Then, through marriage and other kinds of intermingling over time, a partial blending took place, particularly of Matánkor and Moánus, although in many cases both have retained their original traditions and customs.

The preceding, as well as the following notes, may well contain a lot of new material. Yet it can give us only a very incomplete picture of one of the most interesting peoples of the archipelago. Only when mission stations have been established in the group and a basic knowledge of the various languages has been obtained, can we hope to make comprehensive conclusions about this part of the archipelago. However, there is no immediate prospect of this. The warlike attitude of the islanders and their hatred of all settlers, who are regarded as awkward intruders, and also the punitive expeditions that often have had to be mounted against the islanders in recent years, will still bear their evil fruit for a long time to come, so that even missionaries are not in a position to establish a firm foothold. A police station for the group is indeed planned, and would contribute much to the pacification of the islanders; however, the economic interests in the group are so small that other areas of the protectorate justifiably deserve preference in this regard.

When I write a description of the intellectual life of these islanders, I have to confess that I am entering quite an unknown area. On my brief visits it was not possible to make detailed studies, although I was successful in carrying out worthwhile observations here and there and gathering a wealth of material. There is always a lingering doubt whether what I recorded was not based on an error on my part, or whether they had not, as is not infrequent in such cases, parcelled up a fairytale to get rid of the troublesome questioner as quickly as possible.

A few years ago the then governor, Herr von Bennigsen made an expedition to the Admiralty Islands on the warship *Kormoran*, and brought back several of their youths, who were handed over to Father P.J. Meier. One of these youths, the chief's son Po Minis of the Moánus tribe, showed himself to be exceptionally quick-witted and intelligent. Through him the reverend father obtained very valuable information especially about the Moánus tribe. These reports, which were put at my disposal with the greatest willingness by the recorder, confirmed not only my own observations but offered a great wealth of new and previously unknown material. It is to be regretted that after about two years Po Minis was sent back to his homeland, where he soon relapsed into old habits and finally came back into the hands of the administration, who for punishment exiled him to the government station of Kavieng on New Ireland.

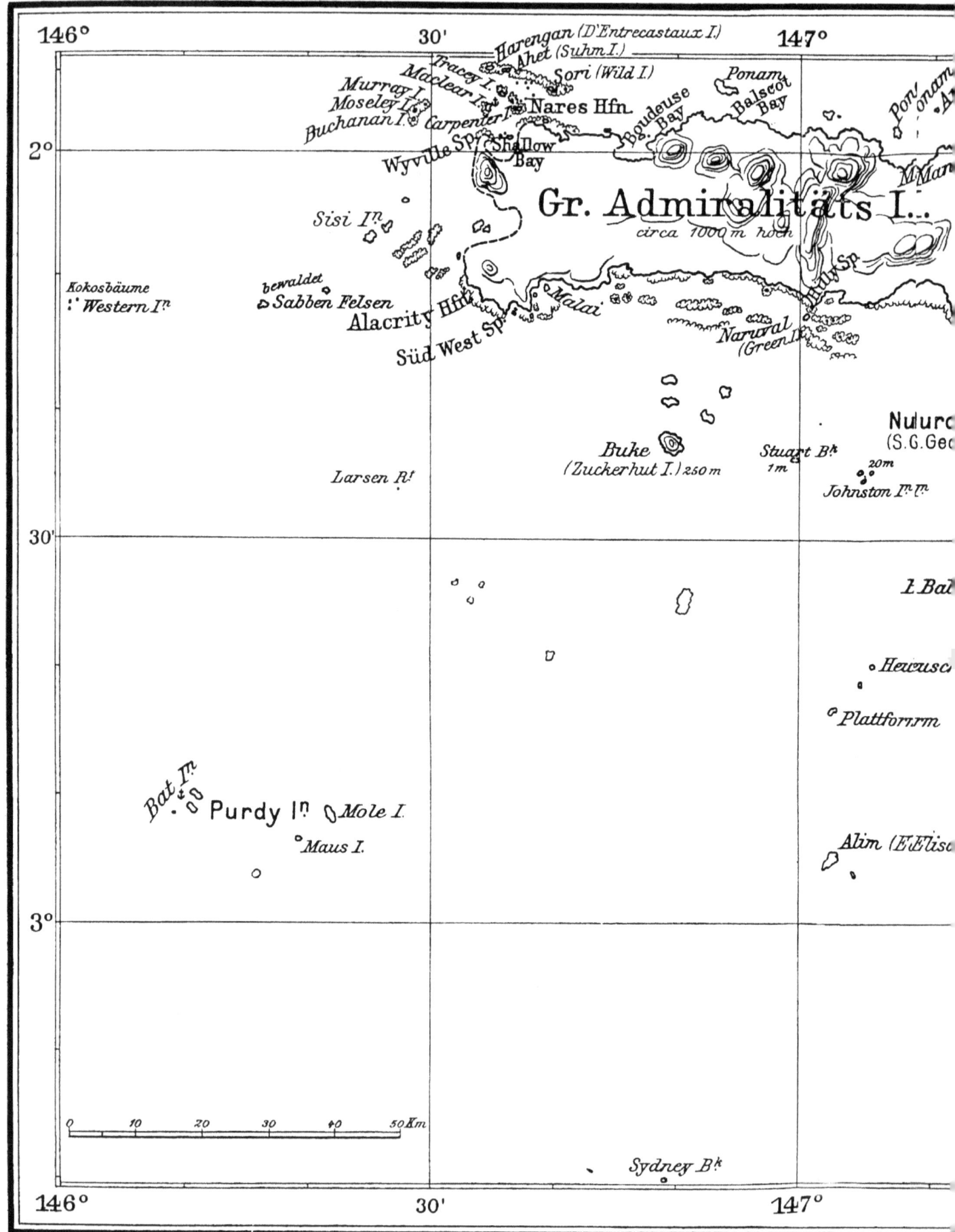

Map 4 The Admiralty Islands

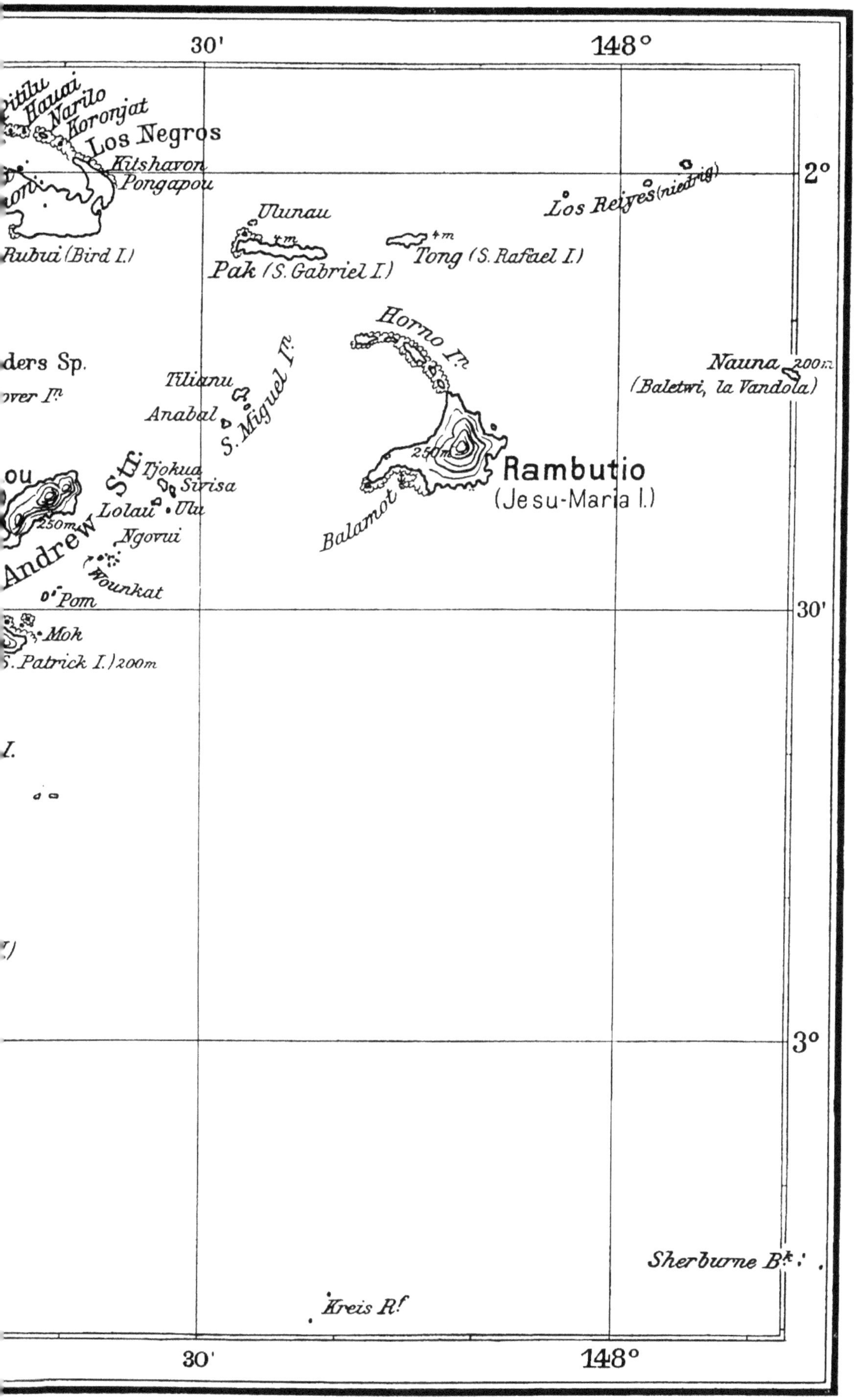

Beilage zu Parkinson, Dreissig Jahre in der Südsee.

I have been able to check parts of Po Minis's accounts on the spot, and to establish them as in accordance with the truth throughout, so that his collective reports can indeed be regarded as valid.

Po Minis characterised the individual tribes as follows (I present his accounts in word-for-word translation as well as in the original text):

The Moánus build their houses over the sea. The Moánus are expert in canoes, they are expert at paddling, they are expert at propelling the canoes forwards with poles, they are expert at swimming, they are expert with the wind, they are expert at sailing. They are expert with stars, they are expert with the moon. They are expert with the large fishing net. They are expert on spirits, they are expert at sorcery with the pepper leaf, they are expert at sorcery with lime. The expertness of the Moánus is great; their language is only one and the same.

(In the Moánus language this is: '*Ala Moanus ala asi um cala clati ndras. Ala Moanus ala pas e ndrol, ala pas e pos, ala pas e tone, ala pas e kauënai, ala pas e kanu, ala pas e paleï. Ala pas e piui, ala pas e mbul. Ala pas e kapet. Ala pas e palit, ala pas e kau, ala pas e nga. Ala Moanus pas eala, maudrean; augan eala ndro arai.*')

The Usiai live in the bush. The Usiai are not expert on the sea, they are not expert at paddling, they are not expert at propelling the canoes forwards with poles, they are not expert at swimming, they do not skilfully avoid obsidian spears in canoes. The Usiai are taro growers, they are sago scrapers. The Usiai are snake eaters, they are cannibals, they drink seawater. The Usiai's bodies are dirty, they have foul breath, their teeth are encrusted with dirt. Their language is different the whole time.

(In the Moánus language: '*Ala Usiai ala lati lonau. Ala Usiai ala kakau e ndras, ala kakau e pos, ala kakau e tone, ala kakau e kauënai, ala uetaraui pitilou uiau e ndrol poën. Ala Usiai ala mangasawu, ala taiauapi. Ala Usiai ala kauiamoat, ala kauiarawat, ala kauiaüati, ala kulumuandrus. Ala Usiai tjangiala pukaün, puaala porauin, popou i taui liaala. Augan wala ndre arai.*')

The houses of the Matánkor stand on the beach. The Matánkor are expert with the canoe, they are expert at sailing, they are expert at swimming, they are expert with the large fishing net. The knowledge of the Matánkor is not great. They do not know the stars, they do not know the moon, they do not know sorcery with the local pepper leaf, they do not know sorcery with lime dust.

(In the Moánus language: '*Ala Matankor um eala iti mat. Ala Matankor ala pas e ndrol, ala pas e paleï, ala pas e kauënai, ala pas e kapet. Ala Matankor pas eala maudreau poën. Ala ue pasani pitui poën, ala ue pasani mbul poën, ala ne pasanis kau poën, ala ne pasani nga poën.*')

I will add further explanatory comments to this characterisation of the individual tribes.

The Moánus. They navigate both on land and sea by the stars. Also, the time of the arrival of both predominant winds, the north-wester and the south-east wind, is recognised by star positions. When the Pleiades, *tjasa*, appears on the horizon at nightfall, this is a sign for the beginning of the north-west wind. On the other hand, when the Scorpion, *pei* (= stingray), and Altair, *peü* (= shark), rise into view at the beginning of twilight, this is an unerring sign for the imminent arrival of the south-east wind.

The headmen especially, are informed in star knowledge, by tradition.

The three stars which make up Orion's belt are called: *Ndril en kou* (= line fishing canoe), because they resemble the three men who are usually occupied with line fishing in a Moánus canoe. (The canoe used for fishing with the large nets is called *ndril en kapet*, and the war canoe is called *ndril en paün*.) When this star pattern disappears on the horizon in the evening, the south-east wind sets in strongly; this is also the case when the same star pattern is visible on the horizon in the morning. This time of the year bears the name *kup tjulan tjasa*. When the 'line fishing canoe' rises in the evening, the rainy season and the north-west wind are not far off. The star pattern of Canis major is called *manuai* (= bird). When this star pattern is aligned so that one wing points north while the opposite one is still not visible, the time has come when the turtles lay their eggs in the sand, and many natives set out for the Los Reyes group, three uninhabited islands that are particularly sought-after by turtles. The western island is called Towi, the centre one is named Mbutmanda, while the eastern one is Putuli.

The Milky Way is named *sauarang* (= daylight). The evening star is called *pitui an kilit* (= steering star). At sea they can navigate easily by this star.

The three stars of Aquila, with Altair in the centre, are called *pitui an kor* (= land star). The Corona is called *pitui an njam* (= mosquito star). When this star pattern is sinking, mosquitoes enter the houses in swarms. The two largest stars of the Sextant are called *pitui* and *papai*. When this star pattern is visible in the early morning, the time is favourable for catching the fish called *papai*.

Dorado is called *kailou* (= a species of fish); the Aurora Australis has the name *kapet* (= net).

The Moánus name the seasons of the year according to the position of the sun. If the sun is north of the equator, the season is called *morai im paün* (= war sun); war is conducted against enemies especially during this time. When the sun stands over the equator the period is called *morai im kauas* (= friendship sun); this is the time of peace and reciprocal visits. When the sun turns to the south the colder season begins, *morai im unonou*.

They observe the moon especially for catching fish, since at the arrival of the different phases of the moon particular fish species predominate, and they set about catching them.

Compass directions are known to the Moánus, and they differentiate *kup* (= east), *ai* (= west), *lan* (= south) and *tolau* (= north). It is astonishing to see the confidence with which they are able to orientate themselves at any time of the day; the sun serves as their reference point, and after observing it for a short time they give the various compass points precisely.

The above may be sufficient to demonstrate that the Moánus do not boast gratuitously: 'They are expert on stars, they are expert on the moon.'

But the Moánus also assert: 'They are expert at witchcraft!' They believe in numerous spirits and say that with their help they can do all kinds of things. A benevolent spirit plays a major role in the life of the Moánus, and he is called upon in all kinds of danger, distress at sea, during battle, in sickness and calamity. The following invocation at a time of war will serve as an example. The chief sticks a pole into the ground and takes up a position a short distance away, holding a sago loaf in his hand.

> *Papu! Abulukau coi ito! Ko njak kiene ndrita mbulukau oïo! Ko taui mbulukal eïo ki ta on e kei ito, konowa io, io u ta on e ala rawat! Mbulukal eïo i ne ta on e kei poën, ioia lau oio, ioia ne la ta on poën.*

Translation:

> Father! See here the sago loaf belonging to you. Come here to my sago loaf! Let it be that as my sago loaf strikes this pole, I, I will strike men in the same way! If my sago loaf does not strike this pole, then I and my people will not be struck either.

Sorcery, called *kau*, is practised before a battle, to ascertain whether an attack is in fact advisable. A betel leaf is rolled up, a piece bitten off and chewed with *Areca* nut. The spittle is allowed to flow in the roll, which is then opened. According to the path of the spittle they decide either for or against a battle. If the spittle flows over the middle of the leaf the battle takes place immediately; if it flows to the right it is also a favourable sign, only they must wait a while; should it flow to the left, this signifies a disastrous outcome.

Another means is the sniffing of a pinch of lime dust (*nga*). If this causes an urge to sneeze, battle commences; if not, the warlike undertaking is dropped.

The Moánus say that the Usiai are far superior to them in number, but they are without cohesion among themselves, compared with the Moánus, who unite at least in critical moments. Their fragmentation is the reason why they are always held in subservience to the Moánus. However, the state of war is not permanent but restricted, as we have seen earlier, to a certain time of the year. Outside this period they trade and visit reciprocally for dances. Both Moánus and Matánkor marry Usiai maidens, and this situation of relatedness has the effect that certain Usiai become permanent allies of the Moánus and Matánkor. The Usiai are skilled warriors, but they always fight from ambush, and do not love the open, front-on attack like the Moánus.

The war ends when either party has at least one dead and the defeated party offers gifts of friendship. Should the gifts be rejected this is a sign that revenge is sought, and the battle becomes prolonged. This situation lasts until either party runs short of food, for obviously the gardens cannot be cultivated during war.

Prisoners can buy their freedom; however, if they do not have the means, they are made slaves (*tapo*).

The Usiai live in isolated tribes, frequently in enmity among themselves. This fragmentation consequently gives rise to a great difference in Usiai languages.

In their gardens the Usiai cultivate taro, sugar cane, bananas and sago. Yams are grown by the Usiai only on Palual (St Patrick Island) and Rambutjo (Jesus Maria Island).

The Usiai make carrying baskets or pouches, girdles and armlets out of plant fibres, and trade them to the Moánus. They also prepare the large, unbreakable oil containers out of wickerwork, but do not know pottery, which is made only by the Moánus.

For currency all tribes use shell money made from small, round shell discs that are prepared particularly by the women on Sóri (Wild Island). Recently women have introduced the manufacture on Haréngan (D'Entrecasteaux Island) too, and on Papitálai.

The dances of the Usiai do not have great variety. The two principal ones are the following.

If an Usiai presents another with a pig, he takes ten lances, nine in the left hand and one in the right or should they be heavy, four in the left and one in the right. The dancer capers on the spot in an increasingly rapid rhythm, to the sound of the wooden drum and when he stops he hands over the lances to the presenter of the pig.

Besides this solo dance they also perform a group dance, in which many people take part. All trip round in a circle holding lances in their hands. In the centre stand two lead singers who accompany their song with drumbeats. When the dance has ended, all the lances are laid together as a gift for the organiser of the feast. The women hold mother-of-pearl shells in their hands instead of lances.

For the dance the Usiai twist their long hair together into a plait at the back, and decorate it with bright feathers. Like the Moánus, they also put on the penis shell.

The method of burial among the Usiai is, briefly,

as follows. The body is placed in a sitting position and decorated. When this is completed it is laid out in the hut until putrefaction occurs. About three days after death the body is buried inside the hut, and the women keep a vigil on the grave for months, wailing loudly for the dead person.

The Matánkor are, as we have seen in their characterisation, a link between the Moánus and Usiai. The word Matánkor means: face of the land, beginning of the land; the opposite is *kaleüiankor* – that is, tail of the land, land's end. Similar juxtapositions with *kor* (land, village), are found in *palankor*, head of the land, tongue of land; *kinkor*, receptacle of the land; *ndruankor*, back, reverse side of the land, which looks out on the open sea; *londriankor*, midland; *mburunkor*, end of the inhabited land, and so on. The Matánkor mainly inhabit the islands that are off the main island in the north, as well as several islands in the south. Their villages are situated sometimes on the beach, and sometimes on steep mountain slopes for security.

The Moánus inhabit the following islands and locations. A crown of Moánus villages extends along the southern side of the main island. Dr Schnee, in two papers entitled *Beitrag zur Kenntis der Sprachen im Bismarckarchipel* and *Über Ortsnamen im Bismarckarchipel*, has given valuable contributions to the knowledge of the land. It is excusable if minor errors, which can creep in all too easily, appear, especially in the case of language and place names. According to this the main island is called *Tschebamu* by the Moánus (that is, bush, forest); actually the word is *Tjawómu* and is the designation of a mountain ridge visible from a great distance (see later, in the stories and legends). In a Moánus song the main island is called Patánkor; that is, tribal land. The designation is pictorial, and indicates a tree trunk; the main island is regarded as the trunk of the tree and all the surrounding islands are accordingly called *ngaronkor* = root lands, roots of the land. Often the Matankor name the main island simply *kor*. The word *taui* is a misinterpreted Moánus word, and means: to lay down, to bring, to give, and is not a designation of the main island.

Moánus settlements on the south coast are:

Lómpoa (*lon*, interior, centre, *poa*, hollowed-out coral rock), not Lomba. The Lómpoa coast is occupied by mangroves and is not suitable for agriculture. There are no coconut palms there; the people live exclusively from fishing, and barter for their other necessities with fish.

Mbúnai or Ponai – that is, sea cucumber; similar to Lómpoa.

Tjawompitou = land source of the pitou (*Calophyllum*) which grows here in great numbers. The soil is better, and coconut palms occur.

Pére; that is, 'my brain'. The name is based on the inhabitants' custom of bringing home the heads of fallen enemies. They are smashed on stones and the brain removed. The Pére are a strong tribe and have numerous warriors.

Patúsi (solitary rock, *pat* = rock, *si* = one), not Pedussi. The name comes from a single, soaring rock. The coast is covered with mangroves, and the inhabitants obtain food by catching fish. Since fishing is almost the sole source of income for all these villages, this has led to a precise delimitation of the fishing grounds. Trespassing on neighbouring grounds not infrequently leads to hostilities.

Lótja (middle of the mangroves) a small tribe who likewise live by fishing.

Poauárei = mouth of the Uarei river (*poan* = its mouth, *uarei* = the name of the river; the word *uarei* is compounded from *uai* = water and *rei* = a freshwater fish). The designation Páure is based on misinterpretation.

Tjápale; that is, what kind of sail (*tja* = what, *pale* or *palei* = sail), not Tschábĕlĕ. The inhabitants of Mbúke have introduced pottery here and this, besides fishing, is the source of income for the inhabitants.

On the north coast of the main island are the following Moánus settlements:

Papitálai = sand of the eel (*papei* = sand, *talai* = eel). This was earlier a Matánkor settlement called Teng. The tribe was almost wiped out by war and sickness, and the Moánus from Mbunai finally bought the site and settled on it.

They intermingled with the survivors of the original inhabitants and the result is their somewhat different language. The Moánus cultivated the site, so that today it is fairly important and the chief, Po Sing, had a widespread influence until his death not long after. Papitálai's enemies are the Matánkor who live in Loniu, Lombœrun and Pitilu. Dr Schnee believes he has heard the name Kalobössen used for Papitálai. This might have arisen through misunderstanding; he probably means: Kor e Po Sing = village of Po Sing.

The islands inhabited by the Moánus are:

Siwisa (not Sepessa), the middle Fedarb island. It is rich in betel palms and also has stands of coconut; the inhabitants are disinclined to gardening, but catch fish and have a vocation as canoe builders. The uninhabited rocky island, Tjókua, with its few coconut palms and good fishing grounds also belongs to the Siwisa people.

Lólau = surreptitious, because the Moánus of

Fig. 68 Lalobé pole village of the Moánus tribe

Siwisa attacked the Matánkor there at night time, killed them and drove them out. The island has good stands of coconuts and the Siwisa exploit them.

Kéa = a species of tree; this is the fourth of the Fedarb islands and is separated from Lólau only by a reef. The four Fedarb islands have the group name Ulu = spring tide, in memory of one that inundated the islands years ago and caused many drownings.

Ngówui (Violet Island). The name is a pictorial representation of the word Mopui = citronel grass, which grows here in great abundance; otherwise the island is completely covered in coconut palms.

Paláia = landspit where people bathe, so named for a favourite bathing spot.

Ndréü = a shoreline tree; on this island (Berry Island) signs of the abovementioned flood are clearly visible because it destroyed almost the entire stand of coconut palms.

Uainkatou = water of Katou (*uai* = water; Katou was the name of the last chief of this island). The island is also called Polot, *lot* = ulcer; this is an abusive name for Po Katou, who was covered completely with sores.

Kumúli (Broadmead Island); the word is derived from *ku* = a fragrant ornamental plant, *mari* or *mali* = to spit. The plant in question is chewed and spat out for the purposes of sorcery.

Móuk = a species of tree; the designation Mokmandrian is a European invention.

Takúmal. The name Mok-lin is likewise an erroneous designation by Europeans. Both these islands are inhabited by a single tribe. The population is numerous, and there are a large number of children. The men of Móuk are skilful fishermen and warriors; they were the people who killed the trader Maetzge years ago. They conduct warfare with Siwisa, Ndriol, Polótjal and with Pálamot (the latter three are on Rambutjo (Jesus-Maria Island), and also with Lóu (St George Island) and Mbúke (Sugarloaf Island). Earlier, the island of Alim (Elizabeth Island) belonged to the Móuk people. This island was taken from them as punishment and given to trader Molde. It is densely covered in coconut palms.

On Rambútjo the Moánus have two colonies: Ndriol on the eastern side and Pálamot on the southern. Ndriol was earlier a large settlement but was heavily attacked by the people of Pak (San Gabriel) and lost many people; a remnant sought refuge on Patúam, the outermost of the Horne Islands, but were taken by surprise and killed there too. Pálamot, situated in a mangrove swamp like Ndriol, has a large population. Pálamot people settled years ago at Limondrol on Papitálai. Their chief Kámau was the instigator of the attack on the sailing ship *Nukumanu*, the crew of which was murdered. The Pálamot people are competent fishermen; the women are skilful at making canoe sails. The island of Tiliánu (San Miguel) also belongs to the Pálamot people.

The Moánus from Papitálai claim the three uninhabited Los Reyes Islands: Towi, Putúli and

Plate 25 Matánkor women of the island of Lou. A number have mourning bands round their heads

Mbutmanda.

Mbúke = Mbúkei = the *Tridacna* shellfish. Besides Móuk this is the most populous of the Moánus colonies. The island is rich in coconut palms and is named Sugarloaf Island by the whites, on account of the mountain which rises to a considerable height in the middle of the island. The mountain provides clay for pottery. Mbúke is on a war footing with Móuk, Ndrúwal and Haréngan (D'Entrecasteaux Island). The inhabitants of Sisi are their allies. In recent times, out of fear of the whites, many Mbúke people have settled at Malai Bay on the main island.

Ndrúwal = pole of the cousin (*ndru* = pole, *wal* or *walwal* = cousin, relative). Two cousins settled there and built their houses. Strife developed between them and in a rage one demolished the poles of the other's house. The island has few coconut palms, but on the other hand many pandanus, from which excellent canoe sails are produced. The name Rubal (Green Island) is incorrect. Alongside Ndrúwal, from which it is separated by a narrow strait, lies the island of Tjovondra, where a Moánus settlement also existed earlier.

Ndrówa = only rock (*ndro* = only, *wa* = *pat* = stone, rock); the Ndrówa people only catch fish, but they had to flee from the people of Pere and Pak to Mbúnai. On the map it is named Dover Island.

I now come to the dwelling places of the Usiai. They inhabit the whole interior of the main island. On the south side they live near the beach, and a sign is given to them by a canoe sail, upon which they hurry down to the shore. On the north side they are further inland, from where they are summoned by the *Triton* horn and the big drum. The land of the Usiai is the abode of spirits, and two places in particular are well known in this connection. One place is the uninhabited gorge Ndrótjun (*tjun* = a species of tree, *ndro* = only, exclusively) and lies inland from the island of Réta. The other site is called Latjeï and lies inland from Sanders Point. The Usiai also inhabit the large island of Palúal or Paluar (St Patrick's Island). They are known as yam cultivators and for the manufacture of hair combs. They are almost always at war among themselves but are on a trade footing with Móuk.

Rambútjo is also inhabited for the most part by Usiai who cultivate bananas and yams. In their district lies the spirit home Limbúndrel = end of the ladder (*lin* = his end, *mbundrel* = ladder), because steps hewn into the rock lead down into the gorge.

Ndrótjun, Látjei and Limbúndrel are therefore the three dwelling places of the spirits, to which is added Tjawórum in the vicinity of Lóniu where, however, only benevolent spirits stay.

The first three places are gruesome beyond imagination. They are situated in the mountain solitude – yawning abysses whose perpetual darkness cannot be penetrated by the sun. Here live the evil spirits. The foremost of these is called *kot*, distinguished from the other spirits, *ala palit*. It does not wander on the ground but flies through the air and spreads a fire glow around itself. The *kot* is eternal and unchanging; the only one of its kind. The *ala palit* are recruited from the spirits of dead Moánus, Usiai and Matánkor. Chiefs and rich men and all the bad people as well, come to these gruesome places after their death. The chiefs and rich men are taken by the evil spirits because they envy them their wealth. Now their revenge comes after death; they set before them only the excrement of men and pigs as food, and they must be happy with this if they do not want to be completely destroyed by the spirits.

The bad people, the liars and murderers, are taken by the spirits for punishment for their evil deeds.

If a chief becomes ill, it means that the *kot* or *palit* has kidnapped his spirit. In fantasy the *kot* is seen during the night, wrapped in firelight. They then summon the sorcerer, who has to bring the spirit of the sick man out of hiding; the fire in the house is put out and the spirit is attracted with gentle piping. The sorcerer now attempts to interrogate the kidnapper of the spirit, and if this succeeds the illness is cured. However, if the evil spirit has irretrievably kidnapped the spirit of the sick person so that even the sorcerer cannot bring it back, then the sick person is got rid of by the neighbours.

Whoever acquires the evil spirits has an uncertain chance of survival, for they can completely destroy him and eat him; or they may tolerate him. The Moánus experiences the latter when he hears the spirit of the dead person gently piping in the house of a relative, especially a son; the spirit is thereby proclaiming himself as a protective spirit of the son or relative, they too can rely on this protection should they be taken by evil spirits after death.

Whoever comes to the benevolent spirits in Tjawórum is not subjected to the danger of annihilation. The spirits in Tjawórum must claim the spirit of the dead man; if they do not come quickly enough, the evil spirits step in and eat up the spirit of the dead man. Thus, during an illness a rivalry develops between good and evil spirits; a relative of the sick person strikes the wooden drum and summons the benevolent spirits.

When the *kot* flies through the air laden with the souls of men he is heard clearly when he hurls them into the ravines, for a noise like thunder arises. When many souls are thrown down, the noise lasts a long time.

The dwelling places of the Matánkor on the main island are:

Teng, merged into one with Papitálai, but built on the shore while Papitálai stands on the reef.

Lóniu = middle of the coconut palms. The Lóniu call their site Bárakou; the population is very large and they own many coconut palms, besides being keen gardeners. Polygamy is in their blood, and the number of children is great. The name *Kaloboubou* is an incorrect interpretation and should be called *Kore e Po Pau* (Po Pau is the local chief). The island of Potomo (Bird Island) in the Matánkor language, or Popapu in the Moánus language, belongs to Lóniu. In the bay lie several small, uninhabited islands visited when catching fish; they are called Ndrúwiu and Tjuándral.

Pongópou, in the Moánus language Pongopong, a species of sea grass. The number of inhabitants is small; agriculture is their main occupation. The people are connected with Papitálai. In Pongópou is found a grove of the forest spirits, *kasi*. They live in trees, and are not well-intentioned towards men, entering their bellies to eat the entrails. The site Kintjáwon belongs to this settlement.

The Los Negros Islands belong, with one exception, to the Matánkor. They inhabit the following islands:

Korónjat = land of the njat tree (*kor* = land, *njat* = an apple-like fruit).

Ndrilo = noise, produced by coconut palm leaves being dragged through the water.

Háuai in the Moánus language, Hóneï in the Matánkor language. A few years ago the population retreated to Pitilu, driven out by the people from Hus, who had recruited assistance from Sisi and Haréngan. At this time the stands of coconut were for the most part destroyed.

Pitilu in the Moánus language, Pitjilu in the Matánkor language. The population is large but is split into two warring factions. The people from Lúhuan (the western part) and Poekálas (in the centre) fight with both the eastern sites of Pahakáreng and Ndrel; they only come together during the time of dances. Fishing is the main occupation and they barter for their other needs from the Usiai with both fresh and smoked fish. Shark-catching is a specialty of the Pitilu people. The period of shark-catching is called *morai im peü* = time of the shark, or *morai in kup* = sun in the east, sunrise. The wind is then strong, and tree trunks that had come ashore in the north-west wind, are driven back into the sea. Many small fish gather round these rotting tree trunks, a dainty morsel for the sharks, which swim close to the surface following these drifting tree trunks. Numerous canoes then set off on the hunt. The smaller sharks are simply caught by hand, the larger ones on a hook. Like the Pitilu people, the people of Hus, Andra, Ponam and Sori also catch sharks.

The Pitilu are recognisable because they paddle noisily; that is they strike the paddle against the side when dipping it into the water. The Moánus paddle noiselessly, dipping their paddles into the water without touching the canoe.

Burial is roughly as follows. The body is buried the day after death has occurred. The corpse's forehead is painted red, and a red stripe runs across the cheeks; the hair is powdered red. Armrings decorate the arms and shell money is laid on both sides of the corpse, to be distributed among those present at the burial. Then the body is wrapped in pandanus mats and buried in the hut.

The Moánus are the middlemen for the Pitilu, and procure canoes for them as necessary, particularly from Polótjal on Rambútjo. Similarly they procure blocks of obsidian from Lóu. As a separate product the Moánus sell their earthenware pots to the Pitilu. The Moánus buy nothing from the Pitilu, nor do they buy any wives who do not have the greatest reputation; on the other hand, Pitilu and Usiai intermarry. On the whole the Moánus look down on the Pitilu with a certain contempt. They throw at them their everlasting bartering and lazy lifestyle which does not lead to establishing gardens. They also make fun of them because of their cannibalism. The Pitilu retort that they do not regard the flesh of the Moánus as succulent, and taunt them that they have bald heads, whose hair has been burnt by the sun and that they are lovers of the cadaverous smell.

The following islands belong to the Pitilu:

Mándrindr = a species of tree with edible fruit; the island is uninhabited and is avoided by the Moánus because of its many snakes.

Réta = Moreta, in the Moánus language the betel pepper leaf. The island is very rich in betel pepper and also in wild pigeons.

Mbutjoruo (*mbutjo* = small, uninhabited island; *ruo* = two), two small mangrove islands that are used as fishing grounds.

Hanita is the island between Pitilu and Hus. It is uninhabited and belongs to the latter.

Hus has a dense population of fisherfolk. The inhabitants are also potters, and collect their clay requirements from the main island. Their trade with the Usiai is very active.

Andra is also heavily populated. They fish and make shell money. The small island of Papimbutj to the east, which is covered with casuarinas, also belongs to Andra.

Pónam in the Moánus language and Poném in the Matánkor language; this is the dwelling place of a kind of forest spirit named *ngam*, which are very similar to the *kasi*, and behave towards men in the same way as the latter. The Pónam, Hus and Andra people are deeply involved in *ngam* sorcery. In the centre of Pónam stands a large house from the roof of which hangs a big wooden basin and with *Dracaena* bushes around. If the Pónam want a stranger slain, they lead him into this house and entertain him, but surreptitiously add *ngam* potion to the meal. On his return to his home territory, death ensues. The *ngam* usually live in trees, and are only called into the house occasionally, when the sorcerer wants to use them.

Sori (Wild Island) in the Moánus language, Sóhi in the Matánkor language, is well populated. Here, in particular, manufacture of shell money is carried out, a principal task of the women. The Moánus trade the shell money for the following items:

1. Ready-made obsidian spears. They pay 3 fathoms of shell money for ten spears.
2. Coconut oil. A large container of coconut oil costs 30.5 fathoms.
3. Blocks of obsidian. About twenty lance points are produced from a large block. Two obsidian blocks cost 10 fathoms.
4. Strings of beads made from glass beads, length for length.
5. Manganese ore for colouring the body black. The ore is dug up by the Moánus on the main island. A small parcel costs 3 fathoms of shell money.

Dog's teeth necklaces. A necklace of 100 dog's teeth is worth a girdle of thirty strands of shell.

Sori is divided into three warring chiefdoms:-

Ahet (Suhm Island) is uninhabited. It belongs to the Haréngan, who fish there.

Haréngan (D'Entrecasteaux Island) is well populated and the inhabitants have a well-nourished appearance. They only fish, and barter for all their food needs from the Usiai.

West of the main island lies the coconut-rich island of Sisi. Pak (San Gabriel) lies eastward; the four districts comprise Tjawókil in the west, Liröu in the centre, Poantólau to the north and Hárai in the east. The Pak people are the most disreputable of the entire group; they are constantly at war with one another, they are known as thieves and violators of the usages of hospitality, and their villages and yards are distinguished by a great lack of cleanliness. They are not only gardeners, but also fishermen, and catch turtles. As their island has great stands of coconut palms, they also prepare a lot of oil which they trade to all districts. The people on Pak are cannibals; they bury their own dead in the ground.

North of Pak lies the small island of Hulungau where two white traders were murdered years ago.

Tong (San Rafael) has only a small population. The inhabitants are fishermen but also gardeners. A lot of oil is prepared on this coconut-rich island.

On Rambútjo the Matánkor colony of Polotjal can still be distinguished. The inhabitants are the most skilful canoe builders of the entire group; they also carry out comprehensive gardening. As warriors they have a reputation for great cowardice.

Naúna (La Vandola) is inhabited by a few gardeners, who are also fishermen. On the island live spirits called *kapou*, which are visible from time to time. In the early morning they can be seen warming their bodies in the sun's rays. They are completely covered in hair, and the hair on their head is snow white. They live in a gorge, *Mbuli an kapou*.

On Naúna they are expert at calming a rough sea by magic; likewise they are expert at rainmaking, and causing a continual downpour to stop. The inhabitants of this island were attacked recently by the people of Rambútjo. A large proportion was slain while the rest fled to Pak. Today the island is completely uninhabited.

Lóu (St George Island) is well known throughout the group as the major source of obsidian. The obsidian is recovered from shafts which go deep into the ground. The island's surface is covered with numerous shafts. The Lóu are also gardeners and own a lot of coconut palms. The individual districts are, like Pak, gripped in almost uninterrupted warfare. Only recently have they taken up sea voyaging, and thus they are not yet good at paddling.

Póam a ruo, or Póam aru kor, are two of the Maitland Islands; the third is uninhabited. Obsidian is obtained here as well, but the inhabitants are best known for raising pigs, and as such they carry on a spirited trade with other islands.

We are a little more extensively informed on the traditions and customs of the Moánus.

We again encounter the totem system in all the tribes of the Admiralty Islands, as in the greater part of Melanesia – the system in which certain animals serve as the totem sign of a particular group of blood relations. In the Admiralty Islands we find the following groups:

1. The group of the Kol. This has five different signs: Kanas, a fish species; Pou, the pig; Lauat, the cuscus; Mbuai, the crocodile, and Kemendra, a large species of fish. The Kol are especially strong on Papitálai.
2. The group Poëndrileï, a species of fish; predominant on Siwisa.
3. The group Pal, pigeon; it is especially strong on the island of Pak.
4. The group Pëu, shark.
5. The group Kobat, crab.
6. The group Tjunjak, a species of oyster, and Sawol, mother-of-pearl shell.
7. The group Tjauka (*Philemon coquerelli*) and Pongopong, a fruit.
8. The group Uri, pigfish.
9. The group Kareng, parrot, and Karaat, turtle.
10. The group Karipou, a species of heron.
11. The group Tjilim, a species of starling, and Tjihir, parrot.
12. The group Ngong, tern, and Palimat, flying fox.
13. The group Kata, frigate bird, and Kanaui, tropic bird.
14. The group Kanau, tern species.

The group insignia, *patandrusu*, is inherited by the child from the mother. Members of a group sign must not intermarry; recently, however, this has become less strict. If the totem animal is edible, the bearer abstains from consuming it.

Here too we could not obtain any information about where this custom came from or how it arose. The people of Pak claim copyright. People of the same totem who are opposed in battle do not attack each other. Shipwreck victims and enemies of the same sign are treated as friends, and one does not steal the property of the same totem group.

No visible sign is present, not on the body, the houses nor the canoes.

The greatest shame for a Moánus is to enter into a marriage with a member of the same totem group. This is seen as incest. The Usiai and Matánkor do not observe it so strictly and have quite a bad reputation in the observances of the code of good behaviour.

Polygamy is customary, and the chiefs in particular enjoy a large number of 'better halves'. Furthermore, the rule is that nobody personally buys a wife for himself; this must always be done by somebody else, often, however, with the suitor's shell money. Although, as we have seen above, maternal right is the fundamental law, it is still often broken, and the father has the right to claim the child, but only with the agreement of the maternal relatives.

The maternal uncle usually buys the first wife for his nephew, but should the father claim rights over his son, then he arranges the purchase. However, any relative can buy a wife for the youth. Neighbours who want to ingratiate themselves for any reason can give a wife to a youth as a gift. However, these wives are not obligated and they frequently return to the giver. A woman captured in war is never retained by the chief, otherwise people would say, 'He has no shell money and must steal a wife.' Girls are sold only when they have reached maturity, although a sale can be arranged beforehand. Purchased girls help the mother-in-law until the actual wedding, and the future husband must not see her; when she approaches he has to hide.

Polygamy causes much strife and quarrels, often leading to bloody fights among the wives. The price of a girl is usually 100 fathoms of shell money. If the shell money does not amount to this, it is supplemented by dog's teeth, pigs, containers of coconut oil, and so on.

Chiefs lay the rib of a coconut palm leaf for each of their wives, in a basket unique for this purpose.

In buying a wife no attention is paid to tribal membership, whether Usiai or Matánkor, but notice is certainly taken of the totem or tribal sign, which are supposed to be the same in all three tribes.

On the actual day of the wedding the father or uncle of the young husband distributes his entire stock of shell money to those present; the money is refunded at a meal given by the relatives of the bride.

All cooking utensils, drinking vessels, pandanus umbrellas and bast clothing which the wife brings into the marriage become common possessions, while her shell money, if she has any, remains with her relatives. However, should the need arise she places it at the disposal of her husband, who regards it as a loan. From the day of the wedding the wife has control of all the household items and supervision of the shell money stored in baskets. Nets, boats and their equipment, and weapons are under the husband's control. The wife can certainly own a garden, but no land.

The woman's tasks extend to preparation of food, drawing water, keeping the house and yard clean, working in the garden, catching smaller fish, and weaving mats and sails.

If the wife dies, the goods brought into the house at the time of the marriage go to the husband, but he must make a small gift to the relatives.

Marriage does not bring the wife totally under the husband's power; at any time she can withdraw and seek protection from her relatives. It seldom happens that a husband kills his wife as this would incur the revenge of the relatives.

Just as little does the father have unlimited rights over the children. The abundance of children is generally not great among the Moánus. Móuk and Mbúte are exceptions. In the following circumstances sexual abstinence is practised:

1. Two to three days before the outbreak of war, so that the husband will not be weak.
2. Five days before fishing with the large nets.
3. Two days before attendance at the sequestering of the youths in the men's houses. The youths are divided off in isolation there; should a non-abstinent, married man enter, the youths might become weak. However, if the married men visit the youths then the latter can pay a return visit and talk with the women on this occasion; in all other cases it is customary that the youths keep out of the women's way.
4. Ten days during the *kalou* ceremonies described later.

At the wedding the men make sure the bride is pure. Should she be violated before the wedding, the shamed bridegroom exacts a bloody revenge on the perpetrator or his relatives. Men who have intercourse with an unmarried girl therefore have an interest in keeping her quiet, and not infrequently kill her. Girls know how to have an abortion; usually this is done by jumping from a high place.

Miscarriages are caused by evil spirits, and so no woman stays overnight in the forest or on the sea for fear of coming under the spell of the evil spirits.

The Moánus have various ways and means of seducing a woman; first through sorcery by means of manganese ore or red ochre. Any contact is sufficient to make the potion effective. It can also be done by signals, such as poking out the tongue, winking and blinking, making a smacking noise with the lips; and they also make marks on the bark of trees or throw small pebbles or little bits of wood at the woman.

Common women are kept; as a rule these are women captured during war. They are lodged in the men's houses. On the completion of a house the chief often places one or two women at the disposal of his people.

Adultery is not punished by death, but probably by a traditional thrashing. The adulterer must pay shell money by way of atonement or duel with the husband. If a child is born, the husband raises it without compensation.

Widows may remarry two months after the death of their husband. Any children from the first marriage do not go with her into the second marriage, but remain with their father's relatives.

Chiefdom is more prominent here than, for example, on the Gazelle Peninsula. Each village has its headman, often two or several, each with his own following. If these headmen are brothers or are closely related, the relationship is as a rule peaceful; otherwise there are as many hostile situations as there are headmen.

The followers of a headman consist firstly of his close relatives; and besides these, according to his wealth, there are recruited servants or mercenaries for whom he pays 20 to 30 fathoms of shell money. He can also add to his following the youths and boys captured in battle, but these are unreliable and run away at the first available opportunity. I have already reported the fate of the women captured. However, after one or two years, as a rule, they are released from captivity.

The unmarried people of a chief dwell in separate houses: the men in the men's houses, the girls with the chief's wives in the women's houses. Married people have their own houses. The followers of a headman have a certain independence; individual members can establish gardens, own boats and make shell money and other items. But normally the work of their master takes precedence. They must help with fishing; they cultivate the gardens, erect houses and build boats on the order of their master. When war breaks out they must of course take part. For these services the chief provides his people with everything necessary for living, distributes part of the war trophies and organises dances and celebrations.

A further task of the servants is to protect the master's gardens against theft, watch over the piggery enclosure and apply themselves to raising dogs. Dogs are money, partly on account of their canine teeth and partly because of their use in packs for hunting wild pigs, a sport that is only engaged in by headmen.

The power of the headman over the servants is otherwise not great, and they sort out their quarrels among themselves without their master's intervention.

If the servant has unpermitted intercourse with the women, he fights it out with the master; the wives attempt to help the insulted husband. Peacemakers are almost always on hand to take the spears away from the opponents, but not to prevent them from effectively bruising each other with their fists. Then both parties chew betel, and peace is established once more. Theft and false accusations are settled in the same way.

If two women quarrel and beat each other bloody, peace can be re-established only when both brothers, or both nearest male relatives, have thrashed each other.

If a headman happens to pass by, he can settle the quarrel by demanding shell money from the transgressor; however, the quarrelling parties never turn to him.

If a servant shows cowardice in battle or does his work badly, or the master loses property through his fault, then the master grabs a stick and gives him a thorough thrashing. Capital punishment is administered only in rare cases, as a rule only as a right of retaliation; a murderer therefore immediately flees far away. However, if he flees to a chief who is friendly with his master, the former represents his friend by taking revenge.

At a marriage the master is helpful to his servant; in many cases he finances it exclusively; often he helps by a grant of shell money. The servants' wives help the chief's wives in their work.

An estate is dealt with as follows: when a headman dies then his son or the number one wife distributes the movable property and shell money to all who have attended the funeral. Seldom is a small part of the money withheld. The successor must now accumulate his own treasures; this occurs either by trading or through gifts given to him during his visits to neighbouring districts.

Plots of land, boats and equipment, and lances, remain with the male heirs.

The same is done at the death of a servant, except that the headman takes the lion's share for himself. If the servant owns gardens or boats, the chief arranges with the heirs who will receive what.

The Moánus has a clear concept of property. Cooking utensils and pigs are identified as his property by signs. He claims everything that he has prepared personally or has had made, and what he has raised. His plots of land and real estate are not marked out, and one often tries to cheat the other by claiming fruit trees that his forefathers did not plant or by wilfully increasing the boundaries of the fishing grounds, or by attempting to appropriate another person's dogs or pigs. This leads to all kinds of fights and scraps, in which the right of the stronger is the distinguishing feature.

If a pregnant woman feels her time approaching, she remains in the hut and eats only fish and sago.

She does not eat yam roots so that the child will not be long and thin; she rejects taro tubers lest the child be short and fat; she does not touch pork lest the child have bristles instead of hair.

An experienced midwife assists her at the birth. Immediately after the birth the baby is washed and the mother remains in the hut with it for twenty days. During this time admission is forbidden to men, including the father. Women look after both mother and child, and at the end of the twenty days the woman bathes, and a feast is put on in her honour.

The child is given a name on the day of the birth. Neither father nor mother take part in this as the giving of the name is the task of the relatives. The name usually contains an allusion to some particular event. A child may therefore have a whole series of names, from which one develops over time into a principal name.

When the child grows and the hair of its head becomes long enough to bind into a top knot, the sorcerer shaves the head completely bald while uttering spells that wish the child well in its future life. The hair is never cut again. Until marriage it is worn loose, either hanging down or piled up high, but then it is wound together into a top knot. At the hair-cutting a solemn feast is organised, and the participants receive paddles, umbrellas, clothing, carrying baskets; lances, pottery and so on, from the parents.

Among the Lóniu, Pak and Tong, circumcision of the boys is combined with this ceremony.

Soon after this celebration another ceremony is undertaken by the boys, called *kalou*. The purpose is to encourage growth and success of the boys, so that they become big and strong. For this purpose all the men withdraw into a house constructed for the ceremony. On the first day the sorcerer hands coconuts to the boy and says, 'Eat the coconuts so that you will not die! Be courageous in battle and strong against evil spirits! May you marry many wives!' The isolation lasts for nine days, during which the boys eat fish for food.

When the young fellow first grows a beard, he may put a comb in his hair. When menarche occurs for the girls, a big feast is organised. If she is already engaged, the parents of the bridegroom must provide the pigs, cuscus and fish; the girl's relatives provide taro, yams, sugar cane, sago, coconut oil and coconuts. If the girl is still unsold her parents pay for the meal themselves.

The ceremony of piercing the ear lobes and the nasal septum is imperative. It is undertaken only on older boys and girls. Whoever withdraws from this ceremony becomes the victim of continual scorn. The nasal septum is pierced with a thorn, and the instrument is left in the wound. Slitting of the ear lobes is done by means of a sliver of obsidian, and a leaf roll is inserted into the opening to enlarge the wound. The blood is carefully collected in a coconut shell and then buried, so that the wound will heal quickly.

After this operation the boy is confined for twenty days and the girl for six months. If they have to leave the house for any reason during this confinement, they cover themselves right to the top of the head in a type of sack made of pandanus leaves. During the isolation the boys and girls may not cook; all food is brought to them by others.

After the confinement a big feast is organised. The man who has performed the operation receives 20 fathoms of shell money, the one who collected the blood receives 10 fathoms. The women who attended to needs during the confinement receive gifts of shell money and household utensils. Both girls and boys are decorated festively for their reappearance. The hair is coloured red with ochre, the face painted, armbands and legbands are worn, as well as a girdle of shell money, and the little basket of betel nuts is under the arm.

Probably nowhere else is the state of war so permanent as among the Moánus, and as a consequence the tribe that otherwise unites internally in all situations in order to increase and flourish, is vanishingly small. The Moánus are never lacking in excuses for war, as is already evident from the preceding, but they also go to war without any reason but out of the love of fighting. The death of an enemy is the main thing; taking over of territory is of minor importance, but it does occur when the enemy is totally annihilated and driven from his dwellings. War trophies, consisting of boats and equipment, shell money and other property, are not spurned; houses are burned and cooking utensils smashed. Any living human, falling into the hands of the victors, is taken away as a slave. Whoever does not flee is slain, be they man or woman, young or old. The most gruesome cruelty is practised, and people are not infrequently tortured to death. If there is time, they also take the corpses of the fallen and sell them to the Usiai.

Sea battles in canoes are not infrequent. Both parties approach and, when in audible range, heap scorn and insults on each other. Then both canoes of the sons of the warring chiefs move forward a little and both sons engage in a combat in which three lances have to be thrown. When this single combat is over, an attack takes place from both sides simultaneously. The strategy is to kill the steersman of the canoe and then to prevent another taking his place. The canoe is then tipped over and the crewmen speared in the water.

If the wounds made by the obsidian points are not directly fatal, they know how to heal them with great skill. If slivers are in the wound, they are carefully removed and *Dracaena* leaves are laid inside so that the wound heals from inside out.

The boys practise throwing lances from childhood, and when they are older their fathers give them

Plate 26 Matánkor village on Lou

regular training. When this is completed they go into battle, and the war lasts until all newly created warriors have killed an enemy or at least wounded one.

At the end of this war a feast is organised in honour of the young warriors. All the warriors stand in two rows, with an old warrior on the wing. He chews betel and ginger and holds a bunch of *Dracaena* in his hand. Waving this in the air he says, 'Spirit come down on my sons! May they be as strong as a man! May they never tremble! May fear never overcome them! May they never laugh when women direct a word at them! May they equal me in strength! We fathers preceded them, we were always brave, may they equal us in strength and bravery!' Sometimes the individual young warriors are addressed similarly. Then follows a great feast and a dance.

Peace is invited by sending a bunch of betel nuts. Women are usually the intermediaries and pass unhindered between the two warring parties.

With the warlike nature of the Moánus, deceitful betrayal is not a rarity, and the natives recount numerous such incidents which by our standard would not give honour to them, but which they regard as heroic and worthy of imitation. However, a certain bravery is attached to such attacks, since the person concerned puts his life at risk and is summarily killed if he is caught in the act.

In the preceding pages, sorcery in various forms has already been frequently discussed. To deal with this subject exhaustively, we have until now been lacking in close contact with the natives, without which extensive reports cannot be obtained. However, sorcery plays such a major role that one cannot possibly overlook it.

The sorcerer is always a servant of the headman. The latter is concerned only with the sorcery that is used in war; he leaves all other potions to his subordinate. He is no different from other people in outward appearance; at the most he is recognised by the contents of the little basket on his arm – red ochre, manganese ore, ginger, all kinds of dried plants and tree bark, and so on, that to some extent form his tools of trade. He is very much feared by the women; they forbid their children from going too close to him. They avoid him and flee when they are alone.

The magic spells are as a rule secrets which the father passes on to his son. Some spells can be given to other people through purchase. There are likewise sorceresses who are especially devoted to the exorcising of spirits.

In the sorcerer's house there is always a great quantity of items that he requires for his handiwork – the various kinds of soil, the various plants, bark and flowers, bones and so on. They hang under the roof in ordered little bunches or are piled on frames. In his equipment there is also a wooden bowl in which the sorcerer lays food for the spirits each day. Other people take great care not to go too close to this bowl and certainly do not steal the contents.

The sorcerer has the reputation of consorting with the evil spirits and being able to summon them at will, for the Moánus have a rock-solid belief in spirits and allege having seen one or more of them at some time.

It seems self-evident that the sorcerer is a doctor

at the same time, since the Moánus regard all illnesses as the result of sorcery and believe that one spell can only be driven out by another.

Sorcery in illness consists of the following: touching the site of sickness with a *Dracaena* bush, by which the illness should be driven out; the spitting on chest, back, temples and forehead with chewed ginger; spitting all over the body with chewed, enchanted betel; chewing charmed betel beside the patient; painting with ochre or manganese ore; washing the whole body with charmed coconut milk; hanging a painted bone from the forearm (if the right side twitches the spirit will make him well; if the left side twitches he will die). They heal wounds by applying certain species of leaf. If a chief becomes ill, well-known sorcerers are summoned from near and far.

I have already given a few examples of the spells of the chiefs. Another spell consists of the headman stirring a bowl of water in front of him with a stick, and murmuring magic spells or pronouncing magic words over the talisman made from a human bone and frigate bird feathers (see page 162 ff.)

The charms for attracting women are known to all men.

Even in death the corpse is not safe from the art of the sorcerer. He spits on the corpse with chewed ginger so that the spirit will not harm the living, and lays ginger roots beside the dead person.

Moreover, on each and every occasion where they do not know how to help themselves, magic is performed. The thief tries to ascertain whether his contemplated theft will succeed or not. For a festivity to be successful it is imperative that the organiser dance over the festive site with a *Dracaena* bush, murmur spells and chew ginger. At fishing time, the sorcerer spits chewed ginger over the fishing nets; otherwise no fish will enter them.

Obviously the professional sorcerers are paid for their efforts. They usually receive 1 to 2 fathoms of shell money, and under some circumstances can amass great fortunes.

Burial is celebrated as follows by the Moánus: a certain death cult exists among their customs and burial is carried out under its direction.

When a Moánus dies, the corpse is laid out in the house until putrefaction is complete. The local environment has probably given cause for this custom; the houses are built on poles out over the sea, and the coastline as a rule is low and swampy and thus little suited as a burial site. Of course it is also possible that this custom has been introduced from other areas; for example, from New Guinea, where we also find it. In any case this custom also predominates among those Moánus whose village location would certainly allow them to choose suitable grave sites. General mourning around a dead person lasts for twenty days; the women watch throughout beside the body. This is laid out in the women's house so that the head lies towards the sea and the legs inland. Decaying body parts are put into baskets by the women and taken to the sea or buried in many places. When only the skeleton remains, this is carefully washed with sea water by the older women. Vertebrae, upper arm bones, thigh bones and fibulae are laid in a basket. This basket and its contents are buried anywhere. The skull, ribs and forearm bones are placed in another basket, which is sunk into the sea for a time to clean the bones completely and bleach them. They lay the bleached bones in a wooden bowl on fragrant plants and place this in the house where the dead man lived during his lifetime. The teeth were extracted previously from the skull, and the sister of the deceased makes herself a necklace of these. Then after some time the ribs are distributed by the son. The principal surviving wife receives two, and the nearest relatives one each. The ribs are then placed under the armrings as a memento of the deceased – a custom very reminiscent of New Guinea; for example, Berlinhafen. A big feast is put on at the same time as the distribution of the ribs, *kan e kasan* (meal at [the distribution of] the ribs); however, some time later there is an even bigger celebration, *kan kutan palapapu* (ceremony in honour of the skull of my father). Preparations for this feast have been made long before. All who were present at the first laying-out received a gift of shell money, and this is an implicit invitation to take part in the skull celebration.

The guests who wish to appear send jugs of coconut oil beforehand; a certain number of jugs is requisite according to the worth of the deceased. The number of guests can then be calculated from the number of jugs delivered. At the skull ceremony for great chiefs up to 2,000 jugs are assembled. A closed season is declared on betel and coconut palms, for the feast requires enormous stocks of these fruits. The host of the feast has a supporting frame made out of a tree trunk for the skull. The full artistry of the woodcarver is called on to decorate the frame with the forms of turtles, birds and other figures; a dog keeps watch at each end. On this scaffold rests the skull.

When the great day of the ceremony arrives, the sorcerer must strengthen the host through his magic, so that he is not afraid in front of the crowd. He sits down on the shoulders of the kneeling host and takes hold of his topknot, which he tugs vigorously to and fro. If hairs cling to the sorcerer's hands this is regarded as the bashfulness of the host; if his hands remain clean, the words will flow undaunted from the mouth of the host. Then the sorcerer places the skull on the previously mentioned scaffold, *tjinal*. This is situated in a north-south orientation; a jug of oil is placed on the northern end, and a container of water on the southern end.

The drums brought from the whole region now raise a mighty din, and the host steps forward and delivers his oration. This is, as a rule, a eulogy of the deceased as well as of those present and an abuse of absent enemies. The host does not miss the opportunity of sounding his own praise, which consists of his having put on this great feast. Then the drums come in with their far-reaching, booming noise.

Next the sorcerer steps forward and takes the skull in his hand. The host of the feast steps up to him, takes a bunch of *Dracaena*, dips it in the jug of oil, hits the skull with it and says, '*Papu oi!*' (You are my father); then loud drumbeats. He hits the skull a second time and says, '*ko tangise kan eoi!*' (Accept the food prepared in your honour!) again, loud drumbeats. He strikes a third time and says, '*ka sapui io!*' (Protect me!). Further supplications follow: Protect my people! Protect my children! all followed by loud drumbeats. Then the real feast begins, with which the ceremony is concluded. The skull is then carefully stored away.

To conclude, here are a few examples of Moánus songs. Not that these are of themselves any more interesting than other songs of the Melanesians; on the contrary, to us they seem a stringing together of single sentences without apparent connection and without meaning. However, a native has given an explanation of these songs, from which it transpires that they are not so meaningless as they appear. They are based on events that are known in detail by the audience, and these need only to be hinted at to be understood without further ado. To the European, on the other hand, they must appear disconnected and unintelligible. Undoubtedly all the other numerous songs of the inhabitants of the Bismarck Archipelago are put together under this system, and what we have regarded until now as a jumbled series of words, develops on close acquaintance into a coherent story.

1. Song of the Chief Po Sing of Papitálai (Papitálai dialect)

Ahää – E. Mo en Pitilu, kono ngou!
E njuni io ila pel. Ac – O. Me te net i menuai.
Wa: ani io akeïs? E njuni io ila pel. Ae - E. Me
  te net i menuai.
Wa: ani io akeïs? E njuni io ila pel. Ae – Ae.
Tjatjeman pel eoi. Taui pelile poam. Ac –

In common speech this song would go as follows:

Mo en Pitilu, oi kone ngou! Oi a njuni io ila pel. Angan eoi i me teio. Io nat i manuai. Io u wa: oi ani io akeïs? Oi a tjetjemani pel eoi. Io ku taui pel kile poam.

Translation:

Pitilu, you are drunk! You call me taro pulp. Your speech comes (to my ear) to me. I am the son of the bird. I reply: When do you eat me? You brag about your taro pulp. I will stuff taro pulp into your mouth.

The words on which this song is based originate from the chief Po Sing (now deceased) from Papitálai.

Po Sing wanted to make peace with the neighbouring Pitilu people. When he assembled them around him in Papitálai it turned out that they were not inclined to do this.

The peace proposals of Po Sing were met with abuse, and one of these was that they would eat Po Sing like taro pulp. He wanted to distribute lime, they on the other hand would cut off his arms in order to buy burnt lime; he wanted to feast them with coconuts, but they would cut off his legs in order to teach him to climb coconut palms; he wanted to give them gifts of shell money, but they would tear out his entrails and buy so much shell money with them since the intestines would be long; he wanted to set betel before them, they would cut off his head and buy betel nuts and pepper with it.

They parted, empty-handed, and a few days later the Pitilu people attacked the people of Papitálai and killed one of them. Po Sing was now out for revenge, and as the Pitilu were paddling to market several days later to trade with the Usiai he ambushed a canoe carrying ten men and one woman. All were captured, and after Po Sing had directed the above words at them they were ruthlessly murdered. The corpses were sold in pieces to the Usiai in the manner with which they had threatened Po Sing.

With the words, 'I am the son of the bird!' Po Sing was indicating his membership of a clan which had a bird as totem. Many Moánus do not eat human flesh but sell the captured enemy corpses to the Usiai.

2. Song of the crocodile (Papitálai dialect)

Ehee – E. Io mbuai – E. Io mbuai – Ho.
        Io mbuai – E. Io mbuai – Ho.
        Io mbuai i Lolu.
        Io u sa kau ita – Ho.
        Pa ki an amo ramat. – Ho.

Translation:

Ehee – E. I am the crocodile – E. I am the
        crocodile – Ho.
        I am the crocodile – E. I am the
        crocodile – Ho.
        I am the crocodile of Lolu.
        I have come swimming – Ho.
        He (the crocodile) wants to eat a
        man
        – Ho.

The syllables Ehee – E and Ho are exclamations that are often added at the beginning or the end of a sentence in songs.

Lolu is another name for Papitálai, and the people regarded themselves as children of a mythical crocodile named *Málai* which would stay there and is described as completely tame, so that it always ate only enemies of the Papitálai and brought back stolen pigs to this tribe. On war expeditions the tribe identified itself with the friendly-disposed crocodile.

They tell each other that it lives in the water surrounding the rocks on which the men's tribal parents, Nimai and Niwong, first settled. This rock is hollow, and you can climb up through it from below. However, you always murmur the following speech, '*Rrr – katjako, tjupüko*' which means, 'I am a native, my navel stems from this land' (*katjo* = my navel; *ko* = land); 'my paternal uncle stems from this land' (*tjupo* = my paternal uncle; *ko* = land).

The song is sung after a successful war expedition.

3. Song of the woman Hi Pak from Keritje (Fedarb dialect)
Io u se ndrua Tjokele.
Io u taui kalo.
Io u tou kalo i ewoën.
Io limo i kine ngong.
Pale u lau i kine kanuu.
Kamal eïo kóun.
Io u se ndrua Tjawokil.
Io u taui po.
Io u taui po i ewoën.
Io kapase i kine ngong.
Momote paleï i kine kanuu.
Kamal eïo kamau.

Translation:

I stood on the beach of Tjokéle.
I waved.
I stopped waving.
My hand was tired.
The sails going southwards had disappeared.
My husband is Kóun.
I stood on the beach of Tjawókil.
I cried out.
I stopped crying out.
My jawbone was heavy.
The sails had disappeared at the spot where they are hauled ashore.
My husband is Kámau.

On the island of Pak, a great feast took place at which Po Sing from Papitálai and his neighbour, Kámau or Kóun (the left-handed one), from Limóndrol appeared. Hi Pak offered her love to Po Sing but he rejected her. However, Kámau offered her betel, a sign of his acceptance, but departed in the afternoon without taking Hi Pak. She hurried to the beach of Tjokéle and waved her hand, but nobody noticed her; she then ran to Tjawókil and cried out her love but without success.

The above songs are several examples of countless ones of similar type, which continually appear, celebrate some particular event, and go from island to island, from district to district, until they are succeeded by a new song.

V The Western Islands

Under the designation 'western islands' I am including the little islets and island groups which lie west of the Admiralty Islands. Starting from the west they are as follows: Matty or Wuwulu, Durour or Aua, the l'Echiquier Islands or Ninigo, the Hermit Islands or Luf, also called Agomes, and the Anchorite Islands or Kaniet.

We begin with a description of the first two islands, which belong together geographically and ethnographically.

1. Wuwulu and Aua

Both these islands lie about 40 nautical miles apart, the first at 1°43.5'S latitude and 142°50'E longitude, the second at 1°26'S latitude and 143°10'E longitude. Both are low coral islands rising only a little above sea level but covered with fairly rich vegetation. Apart from the undemanding coconut palm which is present in significant stands, we find the characteristic beach flora of the South Sea islands and also the breadfruit tree and banana, as well as taro plants. As a result of this rich plant growth, a deep humus layer has built up over the years on the coral banks, so that the inhabitants are in a position to cultivate a sufficient number of food plants. Thus they are not, as on numerous other coral islands, totally dependent on the coconut palm and fishing. However, from time to time a noticeable lack of food occurs so that the daily rations have to be reduced to a minimum.

Neither island offers an anchorage; from the edge of the fringing coral reef the undersea walls of the island fall steeply into the depths, and just a few boat lengths from the reef no bottom is to be found at 200 metres.

Until several years ago the inhabitants of the islands were totally unknown to us. Since their discovery by Carteret they had only been visited occasionally by passing ships, and these left us no reports about contact. In the mid-1890s the steamer *Ysabel* called at the island, and the horticulturalist Kärnbach, who was on board, gathered a number of weapons and implements that were offered for sale, and these reached the Museum für Völkerkunde in Berlin. Professor von Luschan recognised immediately the uniqueness of the acquired items and drew attention to them for the first time in the *International Archiv für Ethnographie*. Consequently the island was visited more frequently and the firm Hernsheim & Co. set up a trading station on Matty in 1897. However, the trader posted there was killed after a short time. The reason for this is still not clear; however, one might only suspect that he had sealed his own fate.

In June 1899, I had the opportunity of visiting both islands for a few days and was able not only to make a number of observations on the spot, but also to take a series of photographs, some of which were published in *Globus* (vol. LXXVIII) and others in the *Papua Album*, volume II.

Since that time our knowledge has had no significant increase, in spite of the firm having stationed a trader on Matty again in 1901. From an approximately fourteen-year-old boy from Wuwulu who came to the Bismarck Archipelago in 1902, I was able to find out the names of the various ethnographical articles as well as obtaining more detailed information on their use. Other accounts of the items in question must be taken with circumspection on account of the lack of knowledge of the language by both parties.[1]

Before the decimation of the natives mentioned in the footnote, both islands were fairly densely populated. Aua had about 2,000 inhabitants, and Wuwulu about 1,500. Although contact took place between both islands, for the most part this was said to be hostile. The Aua people, because of their greater numbers, seemed to be a threat to the inhabitants of Wuwulu, whom they not infrequently attacked, especially when, on their own island, food supplies were fast becoming exhausted. Since the establishment of a trading station, the natives of Wuwulu have enjoyed greater security, because the Durour people have discontinued their raids for fear of the white trader. The natives of Ninigo, about 75 nautical miles to the east, communicate occasionally with both islands. The Ninigo people are very

---

1. Since this was written the firm Hernsheim & Co. revisited both islands in 1903 in the person of Herr Hellwig, to plunder the field with regard to ethnographic items to such an extent that the beautiful old objects are no longer available. What they make there now is of poor quality compared with their earlier items. As far as I could gather from Herr Hellwig he was unsuccessful in gathering many new items; on the other hand he had made comprehensive, detailed studies on the use of the items and their manufacture, which he hoped to publish. He also found out several things about traditions and customs; however, as is easily understandable, there are many gaps in this.

The noticeable reduction in population numbers since 1902 is very unfortunate. Currently the population on Matty has been halved, and when Herr Hellwig left Durour at the end of 1903, the mortality rate was abnormally high. Malaria is said to be the cause. Whether malaria

Plate 27 Men of the Moánus tribe from the village of Lalobé

reigned there before the arrival of the whites is difficult to say. It has been established that the islands are teeming with *Anopheles*, and since this species of mosquito is known to transmit malaria to humans, one could assume that the illness was introduced there by infected traders or their workers, and then transmitted by the *Anopheles* to the less resistant islanders. Islanders who were taken to Agomes as workers quickly went down. It might be hoped that the administration would take prompt steps to combat the malaria and thereby save such an interesting little tribal group from dying out. If this does not happen, similar to the Matty islanders in many ways. Between Ninigo and Durour there is a smaller island, named Allison Island on the maps, which has been settled by a colony of Ninigo people.

The inhabitants of Aua are without doubt the stronger and healthier. On Wuwulu one is already aware of signs of an incipient tribal decay. Elephantiasis is quite common here, and also skin rashes and unpleasant wounds, especially on the face and the lower extremities. While painstaking cleanliness predominates on Aua, on Wuwulu they do not seem to value cleanliness particularly, neither with regard to their bodies nor their dwellings and surroundings.

Otherwise the population of both islands is probably one and the same. Bodily appearance, language, traditions and customs, dwellings, weapons and implements are the same, although, with regard to the latter, minor differences exist. In all that the islanders manufacture they show an extraordinarily well-developed technique; one must involuntarily be astonished at the very precise shapes of all items there, and at first glance be inclined to assume that their working tools must be highly developed. Yet this is not the case, as I shall point out later when describing them. Sadly there occurs here too, as everywhere else where the natives come into contact with the whites, a rapid decline in artistry. Already on Wuwulu, for example, items are being made which are only rough imitations of the earlier, accurately produced objects. They have sold the old things, the white man brings new and practical implements, and soon these replace all that was characteristic. The beautiful objects which are now the decorations of our domestic museums, will within a few years belong to the rarities and antiquities in their own homeland.

I would not be wrong if I present the population of both islands as a branch of the Malayo-Polynesian tree spread so widely over the South Seas, and standing right next to that division that we give the general designation 'Micronesian'. The skin colour is that of the Samoans, a pale brown; the hair is smooth or wavy and curly; the facial features are agreeable, and in numerous individuals regularly formed and matching the claims of our European idea of beauty. The men are slenderly built and of medium size; the women as everywhere else are somewhat smaller but universally have, especially in their youth, elegant, well-rounded forms, well-built limbs and extraordinarily delicate hands and feet. In facial features a slight prominence of the cheekbone is noticeable, as well as slanting of the eyes. Several natives have these characteristic features strongly developed, to such an extent that one could quite easily mistake them for Malayans.

The eyes are lively and intelligent, and the whole attitude of the people indicates a high level of intellectual capacity. Their movements are quick and lively, and their speech is accompanied by gesticulations with hands and arms.

How long these islanders have occupied their present location is difficult to determine. We might certainly assume that they have emigrated from the Indonesian islands. Of course the New Guinea coast is only 87 nautical miles away, but the first glance by the most superficial observer shows that our islanders have not the slightest thing in common with the Papuans. Several weapons, especially the long, broadsword or halberd-like striking weapon recalls in a surprising way, as Herr von Luschan maintains, an old, Chinese, iron weapon. Possibly these forms are imitations of iron weapons that arrived here through shipwrecked Chinese seafarers; possibly they are copies of earlier weapons which were common in their original homeland, but because of a lack of the necessary material in the new land they were copied in wood. Imitations of modern axes and long knives are now very common since the islanders became familiar with these objects a few years ago, and they are copied so skilfully that even at a short distance they would deceive the most careful observer. Perhaps on closer acquaintance we will succeed in drawing a conclusion on the origin of this interesting little group of people, from legends perhaps, and on the basis of comparative language studies.

During the visit to both islands the carefully constructed houses of the natives (plate 29) stood out from a long way off. On Aua the entire population is settled in a large settlement which bears the same name as the island. On Wuwulu the houses are gathered into several separate villages. The dwelling houses, *walœa*, are rectangular wooden structures of varying size; the smallest are about 4 metres long and 2 metres wide, the larger 7 metres long by 3 to 3.5 metres wide. They are built directly onto the ground without an underframe or foundations. Construction is as follows. The four corners consist of four upright, cleanly cut and smoothed rectangular posts. The walls are built from wooden boards prepared with the stone axe to be about 20 to 30 centimetres wide and 5 to 6 centimetres thick. The walls are pushed into the grooves made in the corner posts, and are fashioned so precisely that the edges tightly abut one another. Hard wooden pegs serve for further fastening, connecting the ends of the wallboards to the corner posts. The walls are 2 to 2.5 metres high; the gable ends are raised further vertically in the same way as the side walls. The roof consists of plaited coconut palm leaves or *Pandanus* leaves, and rests on a framework of thin sticks. The roofing material is firmly attached to these sticks by coconut fibre cords. The hut entrance is at the gable end as a rule; it is a rectangular opening 50 to 70 centimetres square, just big enough to let a man through, and is closed by a board door carefully fitted to the opening. The door can be closed from the inside. This door hangs at the upper end by means of strong fibrous cords passing into two holes bored in projections on the inner edge of the gable plank. The interior of these dwelling houses

Fig. 69 Youths from Wuwulu

is kept very clean; the floor is covered with a thick layer of snow-white coral sand. In the middle stands a rectangular hearth surrounded by thick, wooden planks with an under-layer of broken coral fragments, on which the fire is lit for cooking food.

In addition, the dwelling house has one or more beds for sleeping, made of smoothed boards neatly put together; and a frame for storing wooden bowls and other utensils.

Under the roof they stow weapons and other effects. Both the inside and outside of the dwelling houses are always whitewashed clean with lime.

Besides these dwelling houses there are numerous small houses which are of the same construction as the dwelling house, but rest on four thin, round supports and have a plank floor. These little houses are far smaller than the dwelling houses although just as carefully constructed. I am not yet completely clear about their use. These always contained food items and their erection on four supports could have the purpose of protecting the food from rats and mice. However, they could also be little houses dedicated to the gods, similar to the dainty little houses on the *Palau* islands; the foods which they contain might then well be regarded as a sacrificial offering. These little houses are named *lea*. Huts of plaited coconut palm leaves erected without great care serve apparently only as resting places for the sick. I did not notice houses

then these islanders will go the same way as their neighbours on Agomes and Kaniet.

The quite extensive oral material gathered by Herr Hellwig will, after study by a linguist, probably give us significant conclusions on the position of the Matty islanders in the colourful mixture of peoples of the South Seas.

In 1904 the already greatly reduced population on Durour was further decimated. In the spring of that year the local natives murdered a merchant settler and two Chinese. In fear of vengeance on the arrival of a trading schooner, numerous for meetings or discussions; although there are plank-covered seating frames raised on posts and covered over by a protective roof, but these seemed to be a favourite spot for young and old, men and women. Besides the previously mentioned buildings the canoe sheds (*pale uá*; fig. 69, right rear) should be described. They are simple sheds of two sloping, somewhat arched roof surfaces extending right to the ground, open at either end. They are built without special care or decoration, and are 5 to 20 metres long, according to the length of the canoe stored inside. These canoe sheds lie close together along the beach, the gable ends facing the sea, in many cases concealing the dwelling houses sheltering further behind them.

No particular plan seems to predominate in the layout of the villages. In fact, several dwelling houses form short streets, which are, however, just as often blocked by houses built across them. The house surroundings are kept scrupulously clean, and the spaces between are spread with fine sand and broken pieces of coral.

As careful as they are in construction of their houses, the islanders are just as careful in the building of their canoes, *uá* (figs 69 and 74, in the background). It is astonishing how splendid and carefully made canoes can be produced by people without iron tools. The typical canoe consists of a hollowed-out tree trunk, and tapers at both ends into a long, straight prow like the prolonged jaw of a swordfish. The upper edge of the ends of the canoe body is formed by a carefully added piece of wood, which tapers rapidly into an upwardly directed spike; these points are suitably lengthened by accurately fitting, long and very thinly worked extensions, *na úna*, which in turn are often decorated with bunches of human hair. When many canoes lie side by side, the two vertical extensions are removed as a rule and stored in the canoe, to avoid being broken off in the event of collision. The outrigger, *tamáne*, is attached to the body of the canoe in the usual way. The size of the canoes varies considerably. There are canoes 18 metres long which hold twenty men, and small ones 3.5 metres long which take one man; in between these are all possible sizes. The island of Durour in particular has a number of very large canoes, probably for their occasional raids on Wuwulu; on the latter island medium and small canoes dominate.

On both islands the canoes are treated with great care. This is shown not only in the workmanship but also by their habit of hauling the canoes over the reef and putting them under cover in the sheds immediately they return from sea, and whitewashing them inside and out with lime after every use.

The canoes are propelled with paddles, *póre*. These have a broad blade tapering to a point that, with the handle, is often made from a single piece of wood; frequently, however, the blade is attached to the handle by cords. In such a case, handle and blade are attached to each other so skilfully and accurately that it is hard to find the join. For bailing out water they use wooden bailing spoons, *ázu*, with an inward-curving grip, carved from a single piece of wood. Mat sails do not appear on the islands.

The weapons (fig. 70) of the islanders are, like everything they make, beautifully and neatly worked. At first glance one would be tempted to assume that they were made in a workshop equipped with modern tools. Everything is neatly rounded and smoothed; the individual parts are so carefully fitted together that the join can hardly be seen; the barbs of the spears are so symmetrical that their production would cause great trouble even to a practiced European woodworker.

The weapons can be divided into several main groups, namely wooden spears with or without barbs, close-quarter weapons whose ends are armed with sharks' teeth or with sharpened turtle bones, clubs and wooden swords. Included among the weapons is the multi-pronged fishing spear which on suitable occasions is also used against men.

The wooden spears, both the completely smooth ones with a simple point (fig. 70, no. 10), and those armed with barbs (nos 6 to 9) have the group designation *ogióge*. The length varies between 2.5 and 4 metres. The shaft is carefully smoothed; the simple point is long, drawn-out and very fine and sharp. The barbs are either arranged in a simple row on one side, or are symmetrically opposed in two rows; besides these there are spears whose barbs are attached around the spear tip like overlapping scales.

The close-quarter weapons with sharks' teeth are called *paiwa* – both the small, hand weapons with a short handgrip and a double row of three to five sharks' teeth, and the long-shafted, lance-like weapons which have a shaft 1 to 2 metres long and are armed at the end with two opposing long rows of sharks' teeth (fig. 70, no. 5). Both types are strongly reminiscent of similar weapons from the Gilbert Islands. The shaft ends of the long *paiwa* frequently end in a neatly carved crescent-shaped knob. To this group also belong the long weapons, one end of which is armed with a carefully sharpened piece of turtle bone (fig. 70, no. 11); this form is named *au i á ue*. The bone blade has the shape of a half crescent moon; the downward-curved point and the concave side are feathered off. They are used in pursuing the enemy, when the sharp, concave side of the blade is used as a hook, partly to cause severe wounds and partly to cause the enemy to fall. They have similar weapons, to which small barbs of turtle bones are attached in two opposing rows; these form a transition between the weapons just described and the shark-tooth spears. This type is designated *au i á ue* also.

Clubs are given the group name *puleta*. The basic

natives fled in their canoes. Shortly after their escape stormy weather set in; not suited to high seas most of the canoes went down, and their crews with them. In June of that year the imperial governor was able to determine that on that occasion approximately 500 islanders found their graves beneath the waves.

The information and accounts given above relate to the time before this catastrophe.

form is a round baton with a sharp-edged, broad pommel (fig. 70, no. 1). The lower end of the club is slightly broadened and is oval in cross-section. However, there are characteristic variations in the shape of the pommel, which should not go unmentioned here. A simple knob is the general rule; there are, however, double knobs, and multiples placed one above the other in such a way that the adjacent knob which is connected with the one below by a thin shaft, is always made somewhat smaller (fig. 70, no. 2). These types of knobs are nothing but decoration. However, it is different when the knob ends in a long drawn-out point that can be either round and smooth or armed with barbs like the *ogióge*; the club can then be used occasionally as a spear. I have come across a similar connection between club and spear in Bougainville.

Quite unusual is the weapon that has the shape of a mighty, double-edged sword with a straight handle or that of a long-handled carving knife (fig. 70, nos 3 and 4). Both types have the name *awuáwu*. Herr von Luschan has already suggested earlier that these weapons are probably imitations of old Chinese iron weapons. Wherever the original example of this weapon may have had its origin, it is certain that the *awuáwu* are imitations of iron weapons. This is confirmed not only by the form of the blade but by many details of the shape, which although totally irrelevant, the natives have to some extent retained. Thus from time to time we find the iron or brass ring (which in the original weapon was attached at the point where the iron blade was inserted into the handle to prevent the latter from splitting), faithfully carved in wood; likewise small heads on both sides of the handle in imitation of the rivets or bolts whereby the blade of the original was attached to the handle. Several shafts have ornamented ends often in the shape of a crescent, as in the long-handled *páiwa*, but frequently in a totally different form. I possess a specimen in which the shaft end has a wooden ring carved out in one piece, which stands freely as a loop, and is without doubt the imitation of an iron ring.

I will follow with a description of the fishing spear *nawa*, because this is not only used for fishing but is also used as a weapon in battle. All these fishing spears have four prongs. The shaft is thickened at the end and contains four carefully made grooves into which the ends of the individual prongs fit exactly.

For inserting the prongs they use as glue a substance which bears great similarity to our gum arabic. The prongs, which rise a little obliquely from the spear shaft, are wrapped around and fastened to one another with cords for better stability. Only a few *nawa* have smooth points; by far the greatest number have barbs which follow one another more or less closely in a row. On Aua I saw fishing spears in which prongs and spear shaft were carved out of a single piece of wood; here the prongs were circular and smooth.

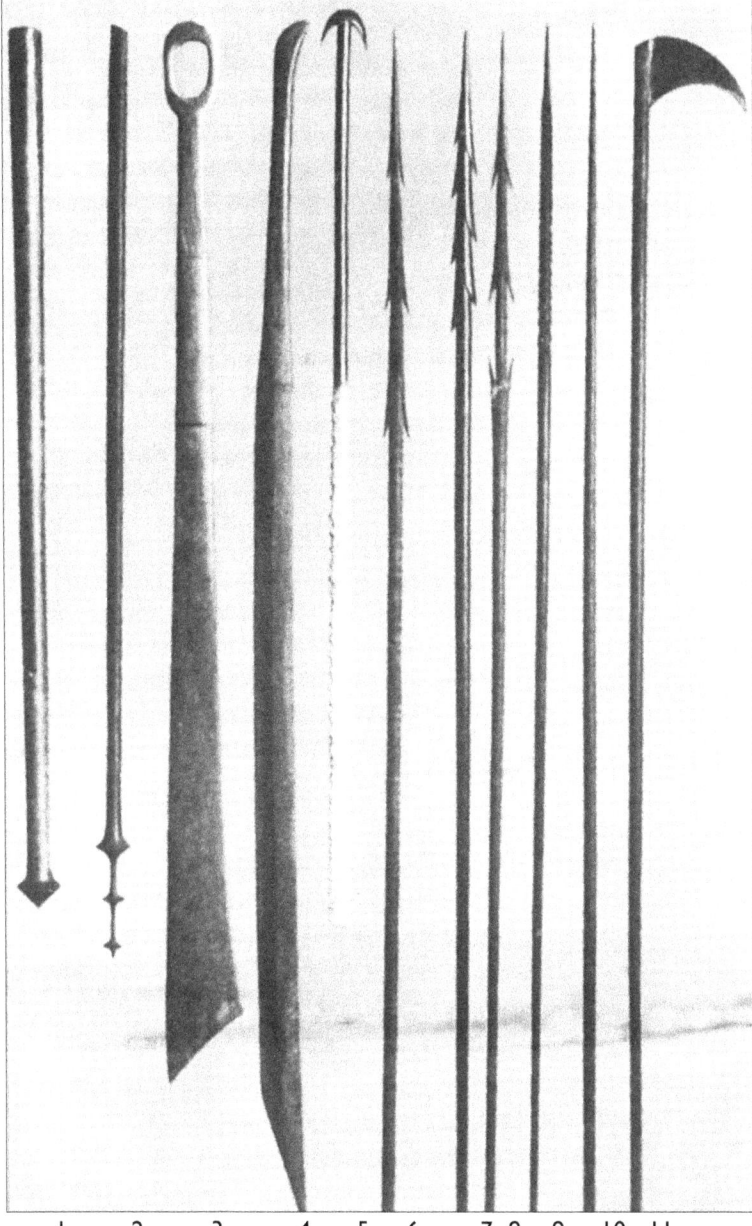

Fig. 70 Weapons fom Wuwulu and Aua

Before I leave the weapons I want to mention that Dr Karutz of Lübeck, in *Globus* 1903, volume 2, has attempted to demonstrate the relationship of a few Wuwulu weapons with weapons from the island of Engano, western Sumatra. The short, hand weapons from Engano have a surprising similarity with the short *páiwa*; and the relationship of the long weapons with two rows of bone blades (often replaced in recent times by brass handles), with similar weapons from Wuwulu and Aua, leaps out at us. A further proof is that foreign influences have made themselves felt on these remote islands, and these influences did not originate from the New Guinea coast opposite but have their origin far to the west. Perhaps the wooden swords have immigrated along the same path.

The axe blades, *poa*, produced from *Tridacna*

shell are distinguished by careful workmanship. Both the shape and type of attachment vary. We mainly find the widespread attachment where the blade is tied firmly with a knee-shaped hand grip, so that the cutting edge of the axe is at right angles to the handle. A second form has a straight handle and a hollow wooden intermediate piece into which the blade is pushed. The handle is up to 80 centimetres long, the outer end is somewhat thicker and has an elliptical hole bored through it which is about 35 millimetres long and 15 millimetres wide, and somewhat oblique to the long axis of the handle. The handle is wrapped with fibrous cord both above and below the hole, to prevent splitting. The intermediate piece is pushed into this opening. This is often one piece, but frequently also of two exactly fitting halves pushed together. One tapering end of the casing is pushed into the hole in the handle. The axe blade is bedded into the other, broad end, and the rim of the casing is woven over with cords or strips of fibre as reinforcement. At the outer edge the wooden case has a small, hook-like projection which serves to fix the position of a bast loop which passes round this hook and on to a projection on the axe handle somewhat beyond the hole, in order to hold the case and handle together better and more firmly.

The *Tridacna* blades are of different sorts; several have a regular triangular shape, and a straight cutting edge ground off one side running parallel with the axe handle; in such axes the casing usually has two hooks, so that the blade can be turned round as required; then the ground surface of the cutting edge lies to right or to left as is most convenient to the worker. Another type of blade is very long, up to 35 centimetres, and equally broad along the entire length. These are ground in such a way that the long sides are rotated a little towards the long axis, giving a tilted position to the cutting edge. The blade of these axes is semicircular and the faces of the sharpened blade are somewhat concave. The wooden casing has only one hook and therefore cannot be reversed. Thus one finds this axe form with the concave faces both to right and to left, so that the carpenter can preferentially select the most suitable axe according to whether the surface being worked on lies to his left or his right. This latter type of axe is used especially for hollowing out canoes; while with the first-described axe the side walls of the canoe and also the posts and planks in house construction are cut out and smoothed.

Domestic utensils are present in fair numbers and in the most varied form. To begin with, the great quantity of daintily worked wooden bowls is astonishing. The finest, uniquely shaped, are the rectangular dishes with an arched bottom and curved sides (fig. 72). This is called *apia*. As well as these, there are oblong bowls with rounded ends, hollow-shaped bowls with two small rectangular projections as handles, and also small, very fine double bowls with round ends, *táli*, and with pointed ends, *tábe*. Small, bucket-shaped containers holding one or two buckets are also found. For pounding taro tubers, *patilo*, and breadfruit, *mamá*, they use a wooden pounder, *pane*. These pounders, like all the other items of the islanders, are very neatly made: quadrangular or triangular in shape with stained decoration. The pounded fruit pulp is divided up with axe-shaped spatulas, *tigo* (fig. 73); for some time these were regarded as a type of axe. There are also wooden spatulas without handles, with a straight edge, called *tutuene piapia*. It is self-evident that they do not lack an implement for scraping coconuts, *águ*. This coconut scraper, *á-i*, consists of a quadrangular little board with an obliquely protruding blade-like attachment; at the end of this attachment is a *Cardium* shell as a scraper. To use it the worker kneels with one knee on the board, which gives the implement the necessary stability.

Included among the domestic utensils are woven baskets, *raba*, of coconut palm leaves. These baskets are frequently fixed to a cord, and these in turn to a broad hook, *tauia raba*, which is clasped round the neck or the shoulders for carrying the basket. Also included are the large chests constructed from wooden planks, with tight-fitting lids, frequently found hanging from cords in the huts. These chests are 50 to 70 centimetres long, wide and equally high. These serve as storage for all kinds of domestic implements.

As a stimulant the islanders have betel nuts, *tawuai*, which, as everywhere else, are enjoyed with betel pepper and burnt lime. Lime calabashes, *pulele*, are made from an oblong, gourd-like fruit constricted in the middle; brown decorations are branded onto the yellow surface, most commonly fish and fishhooks.

That such a bright and lively people as the islanders are given over to dancing and amusement comes

Fig. 71 Women from Aua

as no surprise. During my visit, one needed only to make the gestures of dancing for everyone there to start dance steps and leaps. As far as I was able to see these did not differ significantly from the dances of most Micronesians. Unfortunately the singing remained incomprehensible to me. I observed a long spear, split above into two or three rounded tips about 75 centimetres long, being used as a special dance accessory. These dance spears, which I can best describe by the term 'spear-rattle' are held in the women's hands in certain dances; the rhythmic thumps or shaking of these spear-rattles, *ko*, creates a rattling noise.

As an accompaniment to the dancing they use hour-glass-shaped drums, *aiwai* or *aipa*, which use the stretched skin of a large species of lizard, *uaki*, which runs about the island in a tame state. These sorts of drums come in various sizes. I have seen small ones about 20 centimetres high; the largest measured approximately 1.5 metres, with all possible sizes in between. At the intermediate constriction a small wooden loop is fashioned, through which the cord that fastens the drum skin is pulled.

It is quite interesting that the same form of drum reappears on the island of Ponape. The governor, Dr Hahl, told me that such drums are used at special large celebrations on Kitti. F.W. Christian says in his book, *The Caroline Islands*, page 138: 'The local drum is named *aip* ... I saw one in Palik, now in the British Museum, which was about 5 feet high.' This reports makes it probable that a relationship exists between Wuwulu and Aua on the one hand and Ponape on the other. Also, the names point this out: *aiwa* or *aipa* on Wuwulu and *aip* on Ponape are undoubtedly the same word.

There are still other points of connection, which lead us as far as the Polynesian islands. Here belongs a smooth spear-like stick about 1 metre long, made from tough, hard wood. One end is finely pointed, the other end is about 1 centimetre in diameter and carefully rounded. From butt to tip the stick is painstakingly polished. This stick, *punéne*, is a plaything for the male population, used by young and old. In using it, different groups are formed; each individual member takes hold of a *punéne* and flings it with the thick end forwards in such a way that it touches the ground about ten paces away and then shoots further in a broad, flat arc. Whoever throws furthest has won. Long, constant practice and great skill are attached to this stick throwing. In *Samoa* and Tonga we find exactly the same game, here named *tanga-tia*, except that they do not use such carefully made staves, but simple straight sticks, *tia*, from a particular wood whose bark is removed. We find the same game on Rotuma, where the staves are of a soft, white wood, and a rather egg-shaped piece of wood about 7 centimetres long and 2.5 centimetres in diameter is firmly attached to the throwing end. Wooden

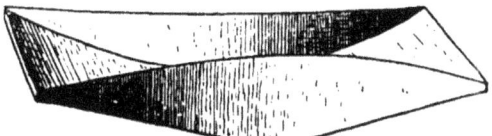

Fig. 72 Wooden bowl from Wuwulu

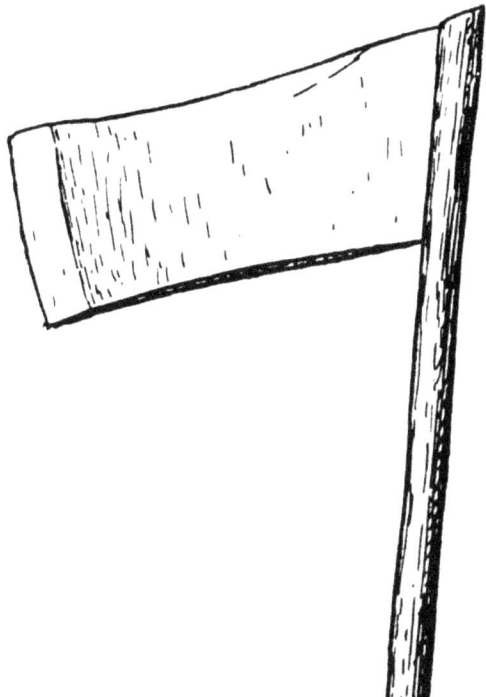

Fig. 73 (left) Axe-shaped spatula, Wuwulu

Fig. 74 (below) Men of Wuwulu are sitting on logs today

tops, *puélo*, which they spin in a bowl, seem to be a favourite plaything.

Fishing equipment is the usual kind. I have already described the multi-pronged fishing spear, *nawa*. On Aua they use long spears, up to 8 metres long, with smooth points for catching those sea creatures that live in deeper water at the edge of the reef. Otherwise they use fishhooks, *áwui*, ground from shell, and also nets of different kinds – the large sunken nets with sinkers and floats, smaller hand nets stretched on a wooden frame, and drawnets with a long wooden handle.

As far as the islanders' clothing goes, there is not much to speak of. The men go about completely naked; at most they cover their heads with an artistically fashioned hat, *tao*, made out of *Pandanus* leaves or with a wrap-round of green banana leaves. These hats which were made from bleached *Pandanus* leaves and decorated with characteristic wing-like extensions, seemed rare even during my visit; today they will have totally disappeared. The women wear a thin cord round their abdomen with a single green leaf attached in front to cover the genitalia, and a short bunch of coconut palm leaves behind. Most young girls go about completely naked. From strips of *Pandanus* leaves sewn together they made large squares of 1.5 metres. These were called *rauada*, and served partly as protection against rain or sunburn, and partly for wrapping up smaller items. In the huts the plank beds were covered with these as underlay.

I observed only a small amount of jewellery. There were roughly worked armrings of *Trochus*, *Pandanus* leaves with long, free-swinging ends were attached to the upper arm or below the knee. Occasionally I observed a woven armband with natural-coloured and black-stained *Pandanus* leaf strips. The women's ear lobes were pierced and enlarged to an enormous size so that they hung down as far as the shoulders. These pendulous ear lobes were adorned with round, turtle-shell discs, *alia*, so that disc lies on disc. To round it, a rib of a coconut palm leaf is laid along the ear lobe. The same ear decoration occurs on Ninigo and Kaniet, and also on St Matthias where the rings are smaller, however. Both men and women now and again wear simple necklaces of small *Oliva* snail shells about 1.5 centimetres long, strung together.

Boys and small girls wear their hair about 3 to 4 centimetres long. Youths and adults as a rule have it arranged in long locks, rubbed with a white paste; in some islanders these locks hang down the back as far as the waist; older men often wear their hair cut short. Youths plait long narrow strips of *Pandanus* leaf into their locks, and these flutter in the wind when running or paddling. As a head ornament they use, in many cases, a bleached strip of *Pandanus* leaf which is laid round the forehead and knotted at the back in such a way that two long tails hang down the back. The women appear to look after their hair carefully; dirty hair was not seen. The hairstyles were carefully piled up; I did not observe combs. In many cases the hair was parted in the middle and fell over the ears down to the neck. Hair colour is a deep, dark brown. The hair of the albinos, who seemed relatively common, was flaxen. A few albinos had a pale red skin over their whole body, others were patchy pale red and brown, and made an unfavourable impression with their squinting eyes surrounded by flaxen eyelids and brows.

I did not observe tattooing and decorative scars although I looked carefully.

As food they use coconuts (ripe = *águ*, unripe = *up*), which are sometimes eaten without further preparation, and are sometimes grated and mixed with other foodstuffs. Then there is taro, *patilo*, and a species of *Alocasia*, and breadfruit, *mamáa*, and to a small extent bananas, *parawu*. Taro and breadfruit are roasted between glowing stones and ash, and sometimes eaten in this state or sometimes crushed and mixed with grated coconut. The pulp is then baked again and is quite tasty. In specially arranged plant pits, as on Nuguria, Tauu and Nukumanu and also on many of the low, coral islands of the South Seas, they grow a species of *Alocasia*, whose rhizome is edible, like the taro tuber. Here it is called *fula*, on Nuguria and Nukumanu *paluka*, in *Samoa pula*. Fish, *nia*, serve in great measure as a foodstuff, the more so since there are no dogs, pigs or domestic fowls available on the islands. The large, well-nourished species of monitor lizard which runs around among the houses in a tame state, is not eaten. Drinking water, *rano*, is available in shallow, dug wells; salt water from the sea is called *ári*.

The language is the same on both islands. Although only little is known of it, it seems from the small amount of information yielded that we are dealing with a Malayo-Polynesian language. Of the few words that are known to us, they very much have the greatest similarity to central-Polynesian words.

Breadfruit is called *mama'a* on Wuwulu; in *Samoa* a certain species of breadfruit is called *ulu ma'a* (*ulu* = common name for breadfruit). Fish is called *nia*; in Samoan *i'a*. Ear is *ali'a*; in Samoan *talinga*. Tooth is *liwo*; in Samoan *nifo*. Woman is *piwine*; in Samoan *fafine*. Fire is *avi*; in Samoan *afi*. Canoe house is called *pale uá*, a combination of the words *pale* (Samoan *fale* = house) and *uá*, Samoan *va'a* = canoe). The flying fox is *bea*; Samoan *pea*. The tree *Terminalia catappa* is called *alie*; Samoan *talie*. This is an extract from a small list of about fifty words, about 20 per cent.

The word structure by its richness in vowels also appears to indicate a central Polynesian relationship.

From this we could perhaps conclude that the Wuwulu and Aua islanders are a branch of the great

Plate 28 Natives of the Matánkor tribe on the island of Lou

Malayo-Polynesian tree which, originating from the west, spread over the South Seas. Since settlement on both islands, foreign tribes have occasionally settled there in passing, or have at least made temporary contact with the islanders, and from these visitors new implements have been adopted, such as the sword-like *awuáwu* which is certainly an imitation of iron weapons. The similarity of several weapons from Engano could indicate where the Wuwulu people originally migrated from; the occurrence of the large, hour-glass-shaped drums on Ponape might perhaps give us a hint which route the migrants chose.

I was not able to observe any Melanesian influences during my visit, although the islands lie only about 87 nautical miles from the coast of New Guinea. Yet, according to Hellwig's reports, many Melanesian references should be found in the language.

2. Ninigo, Luf and Kaniet

Between the Matty group and the Admiralty Islands lie several island groups and isolated islets; firstly the small coral island of Manus (Allison Island) about 20 nautical miles east of Aua, and settled from Ninigo. The latter group, called l'Echiquier or Chessboard Islands by its discoverers, whose outliers are about 40 nautical miles east of Manus, consist of about forty or fifty rubble islands. Almost all lie within sight of one another, with the exception of several of the northernmost islets. The approximate spread of the whole group from south-west to north-east is about 35 nautical miles. Seven nautical miles south of the southern limit of the group, several smaller, uninhabited islands lie on an isolated reef, as does the small island of Ufe or Liot, which lies about 15 miles east of the eastern limit. These small islands were settled from Ninigo; however, the population is not permanent, but appears to visit only occasionally.

About 40 nautical miles east of Ninigo lies the small Luf group which consists of a coral reef on which a number of larger and smaller rubble islands have formed. The reef is roughly oval with a longer diameter of about 15 nautical miles from east to west, and a shorter north-south diameter of about 10 nautical miles. Several passes lead through the reef into a deeper basin which is intersected in part by coral banks; however, in the middle a number of higher islands rise up, formed partly from basalt rock. These in turn are surrounded by shoreline reefs and are dry at low tide. The largest of these central islands is Luf, a name which has been extended to the entire group, probably incorrectly. On the maps the group carries the name Hermit Islands. The designation of Agomes for this group is based on an error. The natives do not recognise the name, either as a common designation for the whole group or as the name of one of the individual islands. The name is a distortion of the name 'Hermit' which in the mouth of the natives becomes 'Aramis' or 'Agomis' and had been incorrectly understood by Europeans. Accordingly, the name should be removed from the maps. A general designation for the whole group is not known to the natives. The highest peak on the central islands is about 160 metres. Recently the group passed into the ownership of a European who settled on one of the smaller central islands, Maron, and attempted to make the rubble islands and the central islands, as far as they were not already covered in coconut palms, profitable from new plantings. The vegetation of the islands is relatively luxuriant, and bananas, taro and yams, apart from undemanding coconut palms, grow excellently, so that the inhabitants need suffer no lack of food resources.

Forty-five nautical miles north-east of Luf lies the small group of Kaniët or the Anchorite Islands. It consists of several rubble islands situated on a common coral reef. The largest of these islands is Suf, the easternmost of the group; the other five small islands are of lesser importance. Kubary, who visited these islands years ago, gives the presumed origin of the name Kaniet, which according to him is a designation of the Luf people, with which they describe the ugly, enlarged, pierced ear lobes of the women there. *Kahenien* (ear) and *heis* (ugly) is combined into *Kachiniesi* and abbreviated to *Kaeniesi* (*Kaniet?*) by the natives of the group. The islands are low, the vegetation poor, and the population in the process of dying out. About 18 miles north-west lies the small atoll of Sae or Commerson Island. It is uninhabited and is visited by the merchant stationed on Kaniet for the purpose of exploiting the stands of coconut there. Sixty nautical miles north-east below the equator lies the small group of Utan, two islands on the map; they should be well populated, but I do not know whether they have ever been visited by Europeans.

On all the above islands the population is rapidly dying out. On Kaniet there are still about sixty natives, and on Luf about eighty. The Ninigo group comprises 400 natives but a significant decline is occurring here too. Elephantiasis, syphilis, yaws, and so on, are the main causes of the decline. In earlier years, numerous workers were taken to the Carolines from here, for harvesting trepang, but only few ever returned.

We are grateful to Herr Kubary for quite an extensive sketch of the ethnographic situation on Kaniet, which is the more interesting since in his time the population was still numerous, and possessed many characteristics which have totally disappeared today.[2]

The present population is quite harmless. However, it is not long since they were still insidious and treacherous in their dealings with white people. In 1883 the imperial corvette *Carola* had to undertake a punitive expedition against Luf, because the natives there had murdered Hernsheim's traders and boatmen. The Ninigo population is still the most enterprising; they maintain southern connections with Aua and Wuwulu and to the east and north-east with Luf and Kaniet, although the presence of traders on the latter islands has gradually scared away the visitors.

Both Kubary and Thilenius agree that there is an interbred population on the islands, showing Polynesian and Micronesian characteristics but also Melanesian, the latter alluding particularly to the Admiralty Islands. Besides this, influences are evident which could be designated as Malayan and are probably of more recent date. This should not puzzle us, for where in the entire South Seas do we find an island where we can assert that the population is not the end result of multiple interbreeding and admixture of different races? In predominantly Melanesian populations we find many traces of a Polynesian admixture, and vice versa in predominantly Polynesian populations, as in the New Zealanders, the Samoans, and so on, clear traces of a dark, frizzy-haired race which could possibly be Melanesian.

In the following description of traditions and customs, weapons and implements, and so on, I am following the accounts of Messrs Kubary and Thilenius.

At the birth of a child, on Kaniet the baby was laid in a wooden dish (*finola*) and bathed with fresh water; after the bath all the hair was singed off the head with a glowing stick of wood and the little body was rubbed with coconut oil. Then the women brought their good wishes, and at the feast following in the evening the newborn baby was shown around, clad in a girdle of coconut fibre and a little chest ornament of turtle shell.

The child belonged to the father. Daughters remained indoors even after weaning, learned weaving while growing up, and helped in the preparation of meals, and household tasks. Sons were almost always passed over to another family for raising, and learned to fish, how to set up a garden, and so on.

As the time of sexual maturity approached, both the boys and the girls had to undergo a series of preparations and ceremonies.

After completion of the ceremonies the boys entered the company of the adult islanders. During these they were '*tabún*'; that is, totally excluded from society.

The headman determined the onset time of the *tabún*, when his son or those of his dependants reached the age of about ten to twelve years. On the reef far from land, or in the uninhabited *tabún*-covered region of the island of Suf a large house was built. The boys were brought here under the supervision of an old man, who bore the title '*úta*', and a limited number of male relatives. From the instant of entering the *amahei tabún* (*amahei* = house) the boys were *tabún*, and ate certain meals prepared specially for them, which their companions were not allowed to eat. The food was prepared by the natives in the villages and sent by the head-

---

2. Recently Professor G. Thilenius visited the islands, and published an interesting survey of his observations in the *Abh. der Kaiserl. Leop.-Carol. Deutschen Akademie der Naturforscher*, vol. LXXX, no. 2, entitled, *Ethnographische Ergebnisse aus Melanesien*, Part II.

man. As long as the boys still wore their hair *upa upá* – that is, hanging down loosely – they dared not eat any food cooked on hot stones, but only taro cooked on the open fire; they were likewise restricted from enjoying fresh breadfruit, coconut milk or old nuts with a spongy kernel; fish was only in dried or smoked form. Only when the hair had reached a length when it could be designated as *faosi*, did they dare touch food cooked with hot stones; however, they still did not dare to chew betel. Besides this there were still other stipulations of the *tabún* to be observed. It was forbidden for a boy to wet his hair with salt water, to catch any fish, look upon a woman, nor show himself to his father who might in an exception come to the *amahei tabún*. Should the father or headman come there, the residents hid in their sleeping area and stayed there until the others had departed. During their seclusion the boys learned the traditions and customs of their people from the *úta*, and also decorated the house for the moment of their release, and gathered in supplies for the feast to take place then. These supplies consisted of smoked taro which were cultivated in their own gardens. Under the supervision of the older men the boys went to the taro gardens in the early morning, taking a path stipulated by the *úta*, which was situated in such a location that they ran no danger of encountering the island inhabitants, especially the women, on the way. Yet, should the latter appear, the boys had to run away and hide immediately. The ripe taro were taken to the house, peeled, and arranged on long sticks to dry in the smoke; prepared in this way they could last for years. Decoration of the house consisted of festooning the interior with long, coloured coconut palm leaves, which were packed so closely together that you had to force your way through using your arms. If the hair had already reached such a length that the *úta* could to some extent calculate the precise point when a worthy hairstyle can be fashioned from it, then preparations began for the actual initiation. Banana plantations were set up and when after a while the fruit was ripe they were brought to the house which was then hung with bananas. When this had been done, the boys gave the village dwellers a sign, by singing and noise, that the time of the initiation had now come. The following day the fathers went to the house to see their boys now grown into youths, and displayed great joy at the reunion. The bananas were given to the headman, who distributed them among the other fathers. From then on the boys wore their hair bound up, and the *tabún* was lifted with regard to food.

Then follows a repeated complete isolation of the youths until the hair has become so long that the real men's hairstyle, *lubún*, can be produced from it. When this time is reached the boys are collected by their relatives, together with all their gathered supplies, and a general great feast is prepared; however, in the evening the novitiates always turn back to their house.

When all the preparations are complete, each youth receives a *patakom* – that is, a heart-shaped, bound wooden frame of sticks – the end of which, the free ends of the bent stick, are crammed down into his belt, while his head hair, separated out as far as possible, is attached to the upper end. The whole frame has a height of about 2 metres; the greater the surface covered with hair, the more respected is the wearer.

With this load, and in the head position this entails, the youth goes around his home island and under no circumstances dares support or hold the *patakom* with his hand. The headman's house meanwhile has been densely festooned with coconut palm fronds and banana leaves, and towards evening the youth enters with the *patakom* which has not been allowed to be set aside; all the relatives and a few friends are present. As soon as the youths have entered, a designated man reports by singing accompanied by drums, what has happened during the confinement. A festive meal takes place and the youth may chew betel for the first time. The headman then plaits the hair of the initiates. They now become his subordinates and go about with one another in a firm friendship.

From that time on, the man's head is sacred and no woman's hand dare touch it. It is therefore also no wonder that the islanders take great care of their hair; it should not be wet with salt water and is washed only infrequently with fresh water but is richly oiled with coconut oil so that it appears shiny black. The hairstyle called *lubún* consists of the shock of hair tied off over the shoulder, being laid forwards and bound crosswise one to seven times. Hibiscus and other blooms, red beans, and small turtle-shell rings are used for decorating the hair. Also the turtle-shell nose ornament is often stuck forwards in the hair, or long pieces of turtle shell hang down the back.

Naturally these preparations for the acceptance of youths into the society of the adults take a long time, often up to two years. Before that time the hair of the boy's head is *uku diáko* – that is, no hair – and women may touch it; only at the time of the *tabún-e uk* (*úku* = head hair, *tabuni* = sacred, forbidden) – that is, immediately the initial preparations for the initiation have started – does the state of sacredness of the hair come into force. At the onset of menstruation the girls are likewise taken to the isolated house and are then *tabún*. After a stay from one and a half to two years they leave; richly adorned they walk round the island and, depending on the capacity of the parents, a larger or smaller feast ensues.

During their childhood, somewhere between the fourth and sixth year, they must, however, undergo a very painful operation, slitting the ears, *apiteni kahinien fifen*. First of all, the evening before the operation, *tabún* is imposed on the girl; that is, the house where the women and the girl are staying cannot be entered by a man.

The small girl's right hand, corresponding to the first ear to be operated on, is wrapped in a *lágu-lágu* to promote the rapid healing of the wound made. The *lágu-lágu* consists of a loop from the vein of a small coconut palm which is fastened to the wrist with two long feathers from the frigate bird. The women stay awake all night and begin the operation in the early morning. The mother holds the child in her lap and other women stretch the pinna of the ear. The woman operating makes an incision with a sharp sliver of obsidian on the floor of the scaphoid fossa from mid-length first downwards to the level of the antitragus then with the child in another position, upwards to the triangular fossa. A roll of dried *Pandanus* leaves is inserted into the incision, the wound is washed with salt water and the divided border of the helix is protected with small *Pandanus* leaves. Two days later the binding is removed, and if the wound seems satisfactory the *lágu-lágu* is taken off thereby lifting the *tabún*, which also included a prohibition on the family from eating fresh fish or food baked between hot stones. About two months later the left ear is treated in exactly the same way. As soon as the ears have completely healed, the separated margins are densely garnished with turtle-shell rings, and elastic, springy veins of coconut palm are pulled through the rings, so that the separated edge stands out stiff and circular. The ear loop is still further enlarged by these springy leaf veins, and sometimes extend to the chest, which is regarded as a particular accomplishment by the woman.

The boring of the nasal septum is undertaken at an earlier or later age, and without special ceremony. For this process they use a sharpened piece of hardwood.

Upon completion of the celebration of attaining maturity, the young men and women take part in all the tasks of the adults, and especially from now on they are regarded as the equals of the latter in all things.

After death the corpse is either laid in a canoe, taken to sea and sunk, or buried in a shallow grave not far from the house, with face and chest downwards. All movable possessions of the deceased are laid on the grave and burned after about three weeks. Soon thereafter the skull is exhumed, at which time a funeral feast takes place; the skull is placed in a basket, hung up in the house and smoked. Bunches of leaves are fastened to the zygomatic arch; the orbital part of the frontal bone is bored through from near the zygomatic process to the orbit of the eye, and into both holes they push a bunch of leaves or small sticks, the latter bearing bunches of white feathers on the ends jutting over the forehead. The skull prepared in this way is not only a memorial, it is also used in numerous invocations to turn away the spirits (*pafe*) of the dead, which in general bring everything nasty and horrible, from their evil intent.

On Luf, ceremonies like those described on Kaniet are no longer mentioned. No records of them exist from earlier years; therefore we cannot judge whether similar customs were ever known there. Newborn babies are washed in the sea, and the afterbirth is buried in the forest. Any form of ceremony for the arrival of maturity is unknown today. The body of a man is interred in the canoe shed; that of somebody who died as a result of illness is buried in the forest. All movable possessions are laid on the grave, as on Kaniet. Here, too, the belief is firmly rooted that the spirits of the dead roam about and attract illnesses and all misfortune. They are supposed to roam about particularly at night, and food is left out for them so that they will leave the residents in peace.

We do not know much more about Ninigo than we do about Luf. The treatment of newborn babies

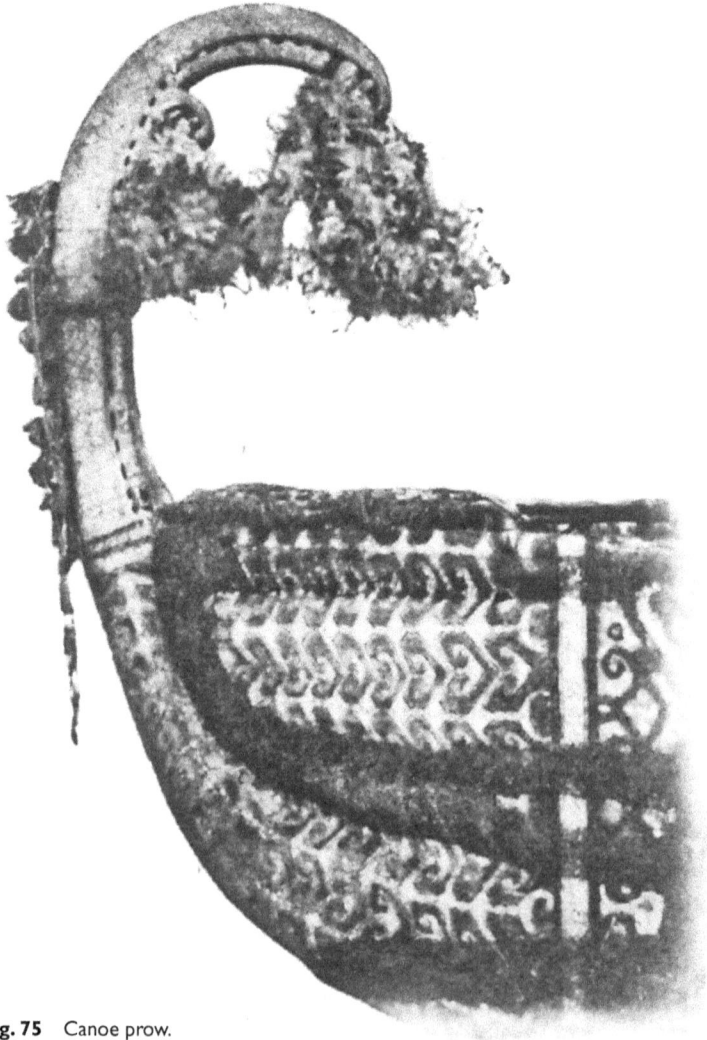

Fig. 75 Canoe prow. Hermit Islands

is the same; the burial is the same as on Kaniet. The souls (*amal*) of the dead also roam about, live in trees, practise all kinds of mischief and are banished by invocation.

It is obvious that in a population in decline, social behaviour will also show signs of the decline. What we see here is not to be regarded as the standard of what existed previously, when the population was flourishing. There are of course still headmen today; they seem to have been originally, according to their rank, leaders in battle; possibly they were also people who, because of their wealth, exercised a dominant influence.

The position of women is a subordinate one. On Ninigo monogamy prevails, the husband buys the woman from her father; it is the same on Kaniet, and on Luf it was the same in earlier days. However, on the last-named island, with the population decline and because of the scarcity of women, the custom has arisen in recent times of a married man giving his wife to another as a gift or surrendering her from time to time. The wife is, to a certain extent, the common property of all men.

A fairly active trade existed earlier between the various islands; in addition the Ninigo people traded with both Wuwulu and Aua. Even though peaceful conditions reigned for the time being, qualified by bartering from island to island, hostile encounters were also not infrequent, on account of the custom of taking natives of one island as slaves to the others. Whether the natives extended their voyages as far as the Admiralty Islands, about 100 nautical miles further east, is not established; on the other hand, it is certain that not infrequently boats arrived here from the Admiralty Islands.

Great care is taken in the construction of canoes. Dr Thilenius gives true-to-life illustrations of the Kaniet canoe in plates 19 and 20 and a detailed description. Since no suitably strong trees grow on the island, they resorted to driftwood. The size of the trunks driven ashore determines whether they will build a fishing canoe, *oai*, or a voyaging canoe, *muaij*. The *oai* is decorated at both ends by a projecting prow, which carries the same decoration as the wooden bowls called *finola*. Both sides of the canoe are raised as necessary by narrow planks, which are lashed to the edges of the single tree trunk by coconut fibre cords. To prevent the canoe tipping, outriggers and floats are attached to one side of the boat. The float is about two-thirds the length of the canoe, and is made from a light wood. The outriggers, four to five in number, are fixed to battens which are firmly driven into the body of the float. On the upper surface of the outrigger, beginning at the gunwale and covering half the outriggers, staves are laid side by side and firmly tied to the outriggers. They form a platform on which all kinds of equipment are loaded while fishing or during a voyage, since in the canoe itself there is little room. The mast is erected in the bottom of the vessel and is held in place by one of the long mouldings which run fore and aft, and by two hawsers which stretch from the masthead to the front and rear outriggers. The quadrangular mat sail is fixed between two spars; the lower spar bears a fork which is placed against the lower part of the mast; at about a third of the distance from the end of the upper spar is a hawser, which is placed over the fork-shaped upper end of the mast. By means of this hawser the sail is pulled high up the mast. Several guide hawsers then serve for further positioning of the sail.

On Luf the shape, on the whole, is similar, although the attachment of the outriggers to the battens driven into the float is somewhat different. Dr Thilenius mentions a large voyaging canoe that he saw lying on the beach during his visit to Luf but was unfortunately not able to examine closely because of a lack of time. Herr Thiel on Matupi, at great effort and cost, had this splendid item transported to his main station in the Bismarck Archipelago, at which site I was able to take a number of photographs of this rare piece – the last of its kind still in existence.[3] The substructure of this canoe, forming to some extent the base, is a single giant trunk. Both sides are raised by several planks and the ends of the canoe are made of special pieces. A superstructure is added to the strong outriggers, which bring to mind similar ones from Berlinhafen in New Guinea. On the opposite gunwale are smaller, steeply rising platforms which serve for stowing loads. Characteristic of these large voyaging canoes is the extension attached at each end, by which the prows obtain an increase in height. This is curved upwards and inwards, and is completely decorated with a carved diamond-shaped pattern. Shorter bunches of coconut fibres and knotted cords decorate both outer prow sides, and the curved ends of the prow are decorated with two gigantic bunches of feathers. The entire outer body from gunwale to keel is extremely carefully painted with several rows of regular figures in russet and white. The canoe has two masts with quadrangular sails.

However, better than the most detailed description, the accompanying plates 30 and 31 and figure 75 will give the reader an idea of this unique vessel, which could carry up to fifty people. One cannot doubt the seaworthiness of this mighty canoe, the less so when one remembers with what small, fragile vessels the Polynesians used to undertake long voyages.

On Ninigo the shape of the canoe is somewhat different. Here as well there are single tree trunks with outriggers and floats, masts and mat sails, but whereas on Luf and Kaniet the round form of the single trunk, corresponding to the natural shape of the tree, was observed, on Ninigo trimming of

3. Since then, this canoe has been housed in the *Museum für Völkerkunde* in Berlin.

Plate 29 Village scene on Aua

the tree trunk gave its specific shape.

The bottom is flat and the bulwarks stand outwards a little steeply, and have flat, hewn outer walls. A long prow of separate pieces is fixed at both ends, deviating not far from the horizontal and tending only slightly upwards. The canoe, although it shows no similarity in form with the Aua or Wuwulu vessels, nevertheless gives the impression that in its production the neat carpentry of the Aua people has found an imitation, although of course in a deviant form.

House construction has been dealt with in detail by Dr Thilenius in his work. In this regard great artistic skill does not appear on the islands. All the huts are low; on Kaniet the lateral surfaces of the roof are flat; on the other islands they are curved and reach almost to the ground. Young people's houses or meeting houses are not present, and are substituted by the canoe sheds, where these exist. Weapons consist of spears. On Ninigo a surprising similarity to the weapons of Wuwula and Aua is noticeable; on the other islands similar forms are present in a less complete presentation. They are long, thin wooden spears provided at one end with a more or less finely tapering point and a number of barbs arranged in rows. A special production technique is not noticeable; they give much more the impression of the rough and superficial, no doubt a consequence of the gradual decline of the islanders.

Betel chewing is common on all the islands. In older times on Kaniet and Luf they used an egg-shaped species of gourd as a lime container; however, today this has been replaced by a species of gourd introduced from the Admiralty Islands, constricted in the middle and decorated with black designs as in its homeland. Originally these had been a simple imitation of the ornamentation there, but, over time, differences have developed, to some extent creating an unique style. The lime spatulas from Luf are of special interest. Herr Grabowsky has dealt with these extensively, as more recently Dr Thilenius and Edge Partington. Originally these were decorated at the upper end with a pattern on one side, which goes back to the human figure. Years ago, as a consequence of the artistic skill of a single islander, a particular spatula shape developed, in the decoration of which the spiral played the main role. The decorated part in these implements is flat and done very splendidly in fine open-work. These spatulas are now found only in museums; they are no longer available on the islands themselves, because the artist died several years ago and had no successor to continue the developed style. On Kaniet the human figure is also used to decorate the lime spatula, but here the arrangement of the decoration is in double rows. Very rarely is the whole male figure produced; as a rule the decoration consists of a double row of heads one above the other.

The traditional costume on Kaniet differs in both sexes. The men wear a girdle of coconut cords which are wound numerous times round the waist; the women wear a broad girdle wound several times round the abdomen, and made from bleached strips of *Pandanus* leaf lined on the inside with bark from *Ficus indica*. These girdles are sometimes decorated on the outside with strips of bark and *Pandanus* leaves. The usual women's clothing is a broad piece of bark that is hung over the hips and extends as far as the knees. Another costume, which is only worn at celebrations, consists of an apron, or more accurately a double apron, the two parts of which are worn in front and behind. The front apron consists of a firm woven sheet about 20 centimetres long and 25 centimetres wide whose lower edge has rows of fringe-like strips of leaves in many layers. The rear piece consists similarly of a woven sheet which is, however, more narrow and up to 50 centimetres long; the fringe addition is likewise considerably longer. The sheets are patterned by interwoven bright fibres in diamond shapes. To hold both these pieces firmly, after they have been placed in the proper position, the body is wound round with long cords of coconut fibres, forming a thick girdle. The woven sheets project beyond the tied girdle both in front and behind; the leaf fringes cover the genitalia and the buttocks. On Luf a similar costume prevails, allegedly introduced from Kaniet, but here the fringed apron is decorated with bright feathers and down. On Ninigo the dress is the same, but according to comments from the natives it was only fairly recently imported from Kaniet and Luf. Originally both men and women went around naked, as the inhabitants of Aua and Wuwulu still do today.

Items of jewellery are scarce. On Kaniet we find the previously mentioned turtle-shell earrings and the nasal stick; the latter is made from either turtle shell or *Tridacna* shell. The comb, carved from soft wood, with an ornamented plate, should be included here. Leaves, coloured fruits, and white feathers in various arrangements also serve as further body decorations. On Luf even fewer ornaments exist. As ear ornaments they wear small turtle-shell discs, besides which they push little sticks of wood or shell through the perforated nasal septum and through the ear lobes. On Ninigo we find somewhat more characteristic ornaments. Worthy of particular note is a quite beautiful neckband of vertebrae from a small shark, to which are added at certain intervals sticks of polished red shell. Besides these, one sees simple turtle-shell rings as ear ornaments, and armrings of plaited fibres of a yellow-grey colour patterned with a dotted design of black fibres.

The wooden hair comb is not lacking here either; the long teeth extend from a carved blade, the decoration of which sometimes represents a human figure and sometimes an open-work zigzag design in various patterns.

A particular ornament of men, especially headmen and prominent people, probably an imitation of the usage on the Admiralty Islands, is the artistic design of dental tartar on the anterior teeth of the upper jaw. From the closed mouth a broad black strip projects between the lips and covers a part of the lower lip.

Wooden bowls are prominent among the less numerous household utensils. On Kaniet a characteristic wooden bowl is customary. This is carried round by the men and serves for storing all kinds of small items. These bowls, *finola*, are neatly and regularly made, bulbous in the middle, and sharply tapering at the ends into open-work carving. Coconut fibre cords stretching from end to end and wound round one another serve partly as handles and partly to prevent small items from falling out. On Ninigo they use pouches woven from strips of *Pandanus* for the same purpose, made in such a way that one is pushed inside the other like our cigar pouches; from Ninigo these have reached the other islands. On Kaniet, where they are expert at producing a flexible product from the bark of various species of *Ficus*, they use a pounder for this purpose, about 30 centimetres long, club-shaped and inlaid on one side of the club-shaped end with a piece of shark jaw. On the same island a wooden drum is used, but not of the customary hour-glass shape. The upper end is approximately double the width of the lower end and the sides are not constricted. A monitor skin is stretched over the wider opening.

Fishing equipment consists of larger and smaller throwing- and sinking nets as well as fishhooks of *Trochus* shell which are reminiscent of the shape on Aua.

Stone axes no longer exist today. The axe from Kaniet calls to mind a similar instrument from the Admiralty Islands; the blade was inserted into a club-shaped piece of wood so that the cutting edge was parallel to the handgrip.

VI   The German Solomon Islands, together with Nissan and the Carteret Islands

Both of the northernmost islands of the Solomon group belong in the German region. The larger of these is Bougainville, to the north of which lies the much smaller island of Buka. Still further northwards lie the two small isolated groups of Nissan (Sir Charles Hardy Islands) and the Carteret Islands, which I include here because they are inhabited by Solomon Islanders.

Bougainville's principal axis stretches from south-south-east to north-north-west. The southernmost tip of the island, Moila Point, lies approximately 6°53'S, and the northernmost point, King Albert Strait is about 5°24'S. A straight line between those points would measure roughly 266 kilometres. The average breadth is not more than 60 kilometres. The surface area of the entire island, together with the smaller offshore islands, is approximately 10,000 square kilometres, about the size of the grand-duchies of Oldenburg and Saxen-Weimar combined.

Although the coastline may be described as familiar, the interior remains as good as closed-off to us. Years ago I made a two-day excursion into the interior from Ernst-Gunther-Hafen (*Mitteilungen der Geographischen Gesellschaft in Hamburg*, 1887–1888, vol. III) without noteworthy result. Traders from the Shortland Islands have made short trips from the south coast to the villages inland but similarly without real success. Recently the Catholic Marist mission has settled on the east coast of Bougainville not far from Toboroi, and has already attempted to make inroads into the interior. We can hope to obtain interesting information from this source quite soon. I need to mention here that the route into Bougainville of about 20 kilometres sketched out on a map by Herr Hugo Zoller, in his book *Deutsche Neuguinea* is a fantasy. The journey undertaken by him, in which I too took part, did not extend 1 kilometre inland.

During the night of 24 to 25 August 1767, the English navigator Carteret sighted the Carteret and the Nissan groups. Then early on the morning of the 25th, he observed the island of Buka, which he named Winchelsea Island. We owe to the Frenchman Bougainville the discovery of the large island named after him.

Bougainville mentions the high mountains that traverse the island from north to south; however, he gave no accurate report on their height, because the mountain peaks were covered in cloud. Only in 1875 did the expedition on the German warship *Gazelle*, under the command of Herr von Schleinitz, give more detailed information about this gigantic massif, which belongs among the highest in the South Seas.

From whichever direction you approach the island, from far off you can see the mighty mountain peaks rising above the horizon. As you approach the island you can easily distinguish the northern Emperor Range with the 3,100 metre high Mount Balbi, from the southern, somewhat lower, Crown Prince Range.

The Emperor Range occupies the whole northern half of the island; on the western side it approaches the shore, and from the region of Fois onwards small coastal flats appear only intermittently. The mountains rise rapidly to significant heights, transected by deep valleys that form clefts in the mountain in every direction. Over the steep mountain slopes, covered right up to the peaks with a rich, evergreen vegetation, waterfalls leap into the depths, several of them over 100 metres high, rising from the sea like shining silver strips between the dark green of the mountain walls. On the eastern side the Emperor Range falls away less steeply; here it forms many gently rising mountain slopes with steep cross-valleys and numerous streams. Along the shore there is a narrow plain, scarcely 2 kilometres wide in places, although at other places (for example, from Nehuss Point south to about Cape le Cras) it is 5 to 10 kilometres wide. Also falling gently away is the northern margin of the Emperor Range, which sends out a high, steep projection right to the shore only at Banniu, while forming splendid, gently rising slopes east and west of there. Such gently rising slopes are noticeable especially east of the grass-covered Cape Banniu, continuing to beyond the totally flat Cape l'Averdie.

Fig. 76 Banniu harbour. North coast of Bougainville

From the high Mount Balbi the Emperor Range sinks rapidly west to Cape Moltke and then runs southwards constantly flattening, apparently separated by a deep valley from the Crown Prince Range, the high northern spurs of which push themselves like coulisses in front of the flat southern spurs of the Emperor Range.

The Crown Prince Range, although not as high as the Emperor Range – the highest point is approximately 2,360 metres – with its multiple clefts, its numerous peaks and serrations and its bare, smoking volcanic cones, offers a far more interesting view than the Emperor Range. It stretches like a crescent moon, one horn turned to the north, the other to the east. In the centre of the crescent is the approximately 1,285-metre-tall volcano, Guinot.

The northern slopes of the Crown Prince Range to the Bay of Arava [sic], as well as the entire western and southern slopes from Empress Augusta Bay in the west, to Cape Friendship in the south-east, and north of the latter, are eminently suitable for establishing tropical plantations. This also applies to the abovementioned slopes of the Emperor Range, and one could say without exaggeration that on the island of Bougainville are to be found such extensive, fertile stretches of land as on none of the islands of the Bismarck Archipelago; at best, in this regard Kaiser Wilhelmsland is superior to the island of Bougainville. However, the latter offers advantages which are not available in Kaiser Wilhelmsland, namely the relative ease of accessibility of the coast, which not only provides good anchorages everywhere, but also has a number of splendid harbours protected in all directions from wind.

With the exception of the Marists nobody has attempted to settle permanently on Bougainville. Hopefully it will not be too long before we see the thick forests of the island making way for the light, flourishing plantations. At the end of 1905 the imperial administration established a police station on the eastern side of Bougainville, opposite the Martin Islands.

To get to know the coasts of the island better I want to make a round journey with the reader, setting out from the southern tip of the island, Moila Point (incorrectly named Komaileai Point on the maps). The entire southern end of the island is a plain, then the ground gradually ascends to the gently rising foothills of the Crown Prince Range. Out of the coastal plain rise several small isolated cones, apparently extinct volcanoes. Above the treetops a plume of smoke rises here and there, a sign that natives have their villages and gardens there. About 40 kilometres inland soars the highest point of the Crown Prince Range where it turns eastward. About 22 kilometres east of Moila Point there opens before us the approximately 10-kilometre-deep cul-de-sac, Tonolaihafen. The shores of the harbour, particularly the eastern one, which seem to consist of a raised coral reef, are fairly high and enclosed by a wreath of mangroves, above which we see the broad tops of the virgin forest rising a short distance inland. Along the beach run coral reefs which seem here and there to make an end to further advance; but deep blue passes always open between them, and we are able to proceed right into the inner corner of the harbour, where ships find good anchorage in shallower water. We are now surrounded on all sides by high forested shores and could scarcely find a better harbour, for the high shores would also keep off the most severe storms. We see no settlement anywhere; the nearest natives live several kilometres inland and come to the harbour only occasionally to fish. In our mind we see the beautiful harbour occupied by numerous ships which from the storehouses erected on shore are taking on cargoes of all kinds of tropical items, produced on the German plantations stretching inland. Close at hand, however, we hear not the roar of mighty steamers but only the flapping wings of numerous rhinoceros birds which, startled by our visit, fly over the mirror-like water; we hear not the cries of industrious, working men but the loud call of the flocks of pigeons which still live in the tops of the forest giants, undisturbed.

About 13 kilometres north of the entrance into Tonolaihafen lies Cape Friendship. The entire stretch of coast is rocky and steep; the sea crashes and foams against the coral rocks and in the work of many thousands of years it has wrought them into fantastic grottoes and chasms. A little north of Cape Friendship a bare, steep, rocky island named Rautan not far from shore, lies surrounded by coral reefs. A narrow, yet navigable channel passes between it and the main island. Sailing ships need to be particularly watchful here, for a strong current runs through the narrow strait, and during unfavourable wind and weather conditions it can prove disastrous.

With the narrow pass behind us we observe a flat, sandy coast which stretches to the north-north-west.

Far out, about 15 to 18 kilometres, we see the foaming white crests of mighty breakers, a sign that there are extensive coral reefs. Actually, a mighty barrier reef stretches from Cape Friendship north as far as the Martin Islands, interrupted by several passes. Between the coast and the barrier reef the water is deep enough for larger ships. However, extreme care is advised when navigating this stretch, as precise soundings have not yet been made.

A few kilometres north of Rautan Strait is a fairly wide river, the mouth of which is blocked by a sandbar over which a heavy swell is usually breaking. Natives from the Shortland Islands maintain that this river is the outlet of a lake not far inland, which is fed by a number of mountain streams; both river and lake should be navigable by small vessels and large boats. The coast from here on consists of a 26-kilometre stretch of the same nature; it is flat and sandy and rises gently inland. On the barrier reef lies a small isolated coral island, Stalio Island (Otua), opposite the mouth of a fairly large river, blocked by a sandbar. However, with a good surf boat this can be crossed without difficulty and you find yourself in a fairly deep river that, for several kilometres upstream, is never less than 3 metres deep. The banks are flat at first and then gradually rise, and we make the observation that they consist of a deep layer of loam, rich in humus and intermixed with sand. Small canoes, which lie lonely and abandoned on the bank, indicate that natives are in the vicinity; we come to the same conclusion from the gardens along both banks. I followed this interesting river for about 10 kilometres, but did not have time to explore it further. But I would most urgently recommend later visitors to Bougainville to investigate this river. At its mouth you usually find numerous natives, armed of course with the inevitable bow and barbed arrows, but not as dangerous as they appear to foreigners. They usually come here to catch fish, but their home is somewhat further north in the Kaianu region.

North of the river mouth the spurs of the Crown Prince Range come closer to the shore and at the same time become steeper and more rugged. Beyond Kaianu they come right down to the shore. The huts of the villages are beneath palms on the slopes; we observe plumes of smoke rising far inland, and on the mountain sides there are cleared patches of forest, prepared for gardens.

Following the Kaianu district is the Koromira region. It is reasonably populated, and according to the natives the hinterland is also well populated although, as they maintain, by very bad fellows against whom the shore-dwellers have to defend themselves. This is a customary assertion of all shore-dwellers when questioned on the character of their inland neighbours.

From Koromira northwards the coast maintains the same steep mountainous character; in places small shore plains have formed, wedged between rugged promontories. On the outer reef we see two small uninhabited islets, the Zeune Islands (Kobaiai and Baikai), and, further north, in the lagoon the small island of Sovie. As soon as we have passed the rocky corner opposite the island of Sovie, we notice a larger settlement under palms on the flat shore. This is the village of Toboroi.

The people of Toboroi are peaceful; a large proportion of them come from the Shortland Islands, and at the time when King Goroi was extending his domain from there out over the southern half of Bougainville, they formed the northernmost outpost.

North of Toboroi lies a group of smaller, forested islands, designated on the maps as the Martin Islands. Between the largest of them, called Batamma by the natives, and Bougainville passes a deep strait, navigable by larger ships. The landscape of the pass is one of great beauty; tall, steep, forested mountains, rent by deep gorges, rise on both sides. The Marist Catholic mission has had a station here since 1902 – the first such settlement on Bougainville.

Leaving the small island of Arrove in the west, we pass round a steep point, where there is now a police station, and there opens before us a bay, broad and deep, with several adjacent bays, forming splendid harbours. On the southern and southwestern sides of the bay are excellent, fertile, well-watered stretches. Behind, the Crown Prince Range rises steeply, and when it is not enveloped in cloud we notice a peculiar geological formation. This consists of many sugar-loaf cones appearing to rise from a single base; the walls are almost vertical and often without vegetation; the peaks are covered in a thick green. The cones resemble gigantic termite mounds. When the cloud parts shortly after sunrise and the peaks of the cone become visible, while the mist still lies in the gorges and valleys like a white haze, the view of this peculiar mountain formation is particularly fine. The rock which forms these mountains appears to be a type of basalt.

If we come ashore in this bay at the right time, we can see played out before our eyes a fragment of native life that is already a rarity in the South Sea islands. From time to time, either for fishing or attracted by the arrival of a ship, the mountain-dwellers hurry to the beach. They do not come individually but in great crowds with the whole family, probably for mutual protection, and perhaps also because nobody wants to stay home in the village when the men are away, since the neighbouring tribes are not to be trusted. Completely naked, their black bodies painted with red or white stripes, holding bows and arrows as well as spears, the seemingly wild band with loud cries makes a dash at the visitors. The latter soon find that the people are on the whole quite harmless, and that the wild cries and incessant gesturing are a consequence of surprise and astonishment; for these mountain-dwellers have until now had little opportunity to see white people. Everything arouses their astonishment, their wonder: be it a bright length of cotton, sparkling glass beads, a looking-glass, knife, axe, fishhooks, and so on. They hand over their polished weapons as trade for a trinket, and behave like children when a long-hoped-for toy is given to them. Soon the women also lose their initial shyness, and throng around us to receive their share of the beautiful things. Among the young girls we see many slender, powerfully built forms with agreeable facial features from which the dazzling white teeth shine like ivory pearls; on the other hand the old women with wrinkled skin and deeply furrowed faces are the purest forms of the most ghastly Brocken-mountain witch. In recent years a certain number of these mountain-dwellers have been recruited successfully as workers in the plantations of the Bismarck Archipelago and, as a result of their hiring, it is expected that through them, once their time of service has expired, a greater number of their people will be persuaded to go overseas as well.

However, we want to look further round the bay. We soon find that the north-eastern part is pervaded by numerous coral reefs; however, there is deep water between them; and also the northern half of the bay has good anchorages. Outside the bay, between the Martin Islands and Cape le Cras lie the two small Dieterici Islands, uninhabited and surrounded by coral banks. Several similar small islets rise from the middle of the bay. The shores are flat with numerous rivers running into the bay. However, the land is swampy to a large extent, and is beset with flooding during the rainy season.

The promontory dominating the bay in the north-east is Cape le Cras (Mabirri). The land at the cape is flat, and gently rises inland; it has the same characteristics further north as well. From the cape the reef stretches further northwards once more, like a barrier; and about 14 kilometres north of Mabirri, a broad, deep pass bounded on right and left by jagged coral reefs leads into a quite spacious and completely safe harbour. Even the largest ships have space here. On the maps this place is designated as Numanuma; not quite an accurate name since the village of Numanuma lies to the north, outside the harbour. On a prominent point on the shore lies the village of Bagovegove which apparently has an exposed position, for I found in 1886 that it had just been rebuilt after the inhabitants had been driven out by enemy mountain tribes several years earlier. In 1889 it had disappeared again; the mountain tribes had destroyed it once more, but in 1894 it had again blossomed, only to be turned into a heap of ashes by the old enemy in 1895. Since 1898 it has arisen anew; this time the village inhabitants have been reinforced by a new influx from northern Bougainville and eastern Buka. On my visit in 1902 I counted 18 large war canoes and more than fifty ordinary vessels, which give the impression of a large population; it actually swarmed with men, women and children among the huts on the beach. In 1889, about 1 kilometre south of Bagovegove there was a small village called Sapiu. This too was destroyed by the mountain people.

The harbour surroundings are less interesting. Beyond Bagovegove lies a swampy depression that is impassable. South of the former village of Sapiu marshes extend far inland. The local people do not have a good reputation; they are inveterate cannibals, living in a constant state of enmity and war with their neighbours, and seeking to capture people both in open attack and by stealthy ambush. Whether the mountain-dwellers or the shoreline people are the aggressors I cannot say. However, I tend towards the opinion that the inhabitants of the coastal villages, mixed together from every district, are the real perpetrators, who settled here purely for love of fighting and plundering, and it serves them right when the mountain people frequently exact bloody vengeance.

The natives at Numanumahafen have had brief hostile encounters with whites as well. In the 1870s the small steamer *Ripple* was surprised by the natives. Captain Ferguson and several of his crew were killed, the rest were more or less seriously wounded. However, the few survivors succeeded in freeing the anchor cable and getting the steamer under way, which in view of the situation was a task bordering on the miraculous. Vengeance was not long in coming. The then mighty king Goroi on the Shortland Islands was a friend of Captain Ferguson. He assembled his warriors and launched a vendetta which lasted for several months during which the entire population of the Numanuma settlement was wiped out. Since that time the people have become more peaceable, but they are still the least trustworthy on Bougainville.

Almost due west of the harbour rises the mighty Mount Balbi (Toiupu), which caused such terrible disappointment for Herr Hugo Zöller because, 'after long observation and precise measurement', he found that it was only 6,000 to 8,000 English feet high. The 'precise' measurements by Herr Zöller allow, as we see, a range of at least 2,000 feet. I tend to give more credence to the older, 'imprecise' measurements.

It is not often that one beholds Mount Balbi with its entire surroundings clear and distinct; often it is concealed by clouds for days or weeks on end. At sunrise it is occasionally visible for one or two hours, then the mist rising from the valleys and gorges gradually closes round the peak and finally hides it completely.

The view from Numanuma when the mountain

is cloudless at sunset, is incomparable. Scarcely has the sun sunk behind the giant peak, concealing the entire eastern slope in deep shadows, than the highest peaks and the rims of the still active volcano Mologoviu, not far from the Balbi peak, shine as if surrounded by a silver halo. The sun's rays penetrate the crater and illuminate the yellow sulphur deposits so that the whole thing shines like a giant golden shell from which a plume of smoke rises which, illuminated by sunlight, passes gradually from deepest brown to dark yellow, then into a shining sulphur yellow, and finally spreads out high above the peak as a silver-white cloud which is slowly driven away by the wind. Such a view is a rarity, but whoever has enjoyed it once never forgets it during his lifetime.

A narrow strait close to Bagovegove between reef and shore, and suitable only for smaller vessels of shallow draught, leads back out to sea. The coast, stretching northwards, has a narrow coastal plain behind which the Emperor Range rises, with its splendid wooded slopes and valleys grooved by mountain torrents. Many small embayments with flat sandy beaches seem eminently suitable as sites for native settlements; actually, up until 1888 there were a number of villages here, of which the only evidence of their existence is the coconut palms planted by the villagers. The further north we go, the broader is the coastal flat and at Nehuss Point it is quite extensive. The barrier reef stops above Numanuma harbour and from there to Nehuss Point there are only shoreline reefs. Then a barrier reef reappears extending, with gaps, almost as far as the north-east corner of Bougainville.

North of Nehuss Point the beach recedes so that even the biggest ships can find safe anchorage between it and the barrier reef. On the reef are two small islands, the southern one named Hohn and the northern Tekareu. They are named Torututa and Torubea by other natives. A navigable passage between Hohn and Nehuss Point leads into the harbour beyond. The opening in the reef between the islands of Hohn and Tekareu, however, offers a wider opening, better in every respect. The coastal flat narrows here and the mountains rise fairly steeply from it. The population gradually becomes more dense; high above on the mountain slopes and ridges we see the carefully constructed huts, side by side in rows after the local custom. Beyond Cape l'Averdie the coastal flat widens and the outcrops of the mountain range are less steep. Numerous canoes filled with the almost black natives are nearly always seen here, some going fishing, others negotiating trade with neighbouring tribes.

The point designated by Bougainville as Cape l'Averdie is not precisely established. He sailed past at a fair distance from shore and could not distinguish that several small islands lay off the north-eastern end of the island. Once past these small islands we observe that the coastline bends to the west almost at right angles, and that on the corner that we indicate as Cape l'Averdie there is quite a good harbour, formed by the main island, the two small offshore islands, and the coral reef.

Plate 30 Sailing canoe from the Hermit Islands

The outer, uninhabited island is called Teworran, and the larger inhabited one closer inshore is Keaop. The entrance into the harbour is broad and deep, and marked on both sides by reefs. The outer harbour is very deep but the inner, which is protected by a reef running out from the main island, is a very good anchorage. Separated from the inner harbour and close to Keaop is a second reef harbour, which is excellent for smaller ships. A great advantage is that a stream, full throughout the year, opens into the inner harbour.

Since the people of Keaop are almost constantly in conflict with the mountain-dwellers, the stretches of shore opposite the island are uninhabited. The first inland villages are fairly far away from the beach. The inhabitants are industrious agriculturalists, and usually bring great quantities of produce, especially taro, to the shore. On the other hand, they are also extremely warlike, and only rarely does one see an unarmed male. I have sought them out at various times in their mountain villages and always found them to be friendly and forthcoming. Great friendship does not appear to exist between the neighbours, since in every village spears, bows and arrows lean against every hut, to be instantly at hand should anything arouse suspicion. Thus, should a visitor arrive in the village unannounced, he must not regard it as a sign of hostile intent when everyone immediately goes for their weapons and he suddenly finds himself opposed by a crowd of natives waving spears or armed with bows; after recognition the general joy is so much greater. Eventual exploration expeditions would scarcely meet with greater difficulties, and conduct would generally require much calm and tact; a domineering approach, unjust treatment, or straight-out violence would very quickly transform friendship into hostility, and frustrate further initiatives. The harbour at Cape l'Averdie, also named Ernst-Gunther-Hafen, will in the future be a suitable starting point for the opening up of the surrounding land. Great tracts of land could be cultivated here without causing even the slightest disturbance to the natives. I believe that organised plantations with strict work divisions for the natives would be welcomed throughout Bougainville, because these would contribute to pacification among the tribes and would create new markets for the surplus produce, especially food items.

About 4 kilometres west of Ernst-Gunther-Hafen lies another small harbour with good anchorage. It is named Tinputs, after the local village. A further 12 kilometres west lies small, safe Lauá harbour, on the eastern slope of the Banniu foothills. The entire stretch of shore between the two harbours is uninhabited, and only far inland do we encounter the first settlements. The land rises gently, and is intersected by numerous watercourses; many thousands of hectares of excellent generally fertile soil are available. In the north of Bougainville there is no other excellent agricultural area that is so extensive. All the advantages unite here to favour setting up plantations on a grand scale: splendid harbours, numerous watercourses that never dry up, regular rainfall, fertile soil, and no natives to be disturbed in their dwellings. Besides, in the interior and in neighbouring districts, there is quite a dense population, which for many years has been accustomed to sending their young people abroad as plantation workers.

On the western slope of the Banniu Range a deep pocket stretches inland, usually known as the harbour of Banniu. However, it is of less value as a harbour, partly because of its high shores and mountainous hinterland, and partly also because due to the north wind the sea drives in strongly, and does not allow ships to anchor. During southerly winds Banniu harbour is an excellent anchorage.

It is not improbable that the high Banniu Range is the same headland as that designated as Cape l'Averdie by Bougainville. He sailed with his ships far offshore and would barely have been able to see the low point that today we call Cape l'Averdie. The tall, thrusting Banniu Range, overgrown with pale-green grass, is visible from a fairly great distance offshore, and then appears to be the north-eastern tip of the island. Further description of the coast by Bougainville also corroborates our suggestion.

Beyond Banniu Bay the shore is high and steep, but from time to time small bays open out with flat sandy beaches. Here we generally find big settlements with quite large populations. Fleets of twenty to thirty canoes, each with twenty to thirty crew, can be encountered quite often as there is regular contact with Buka from here. We see large villages not only on the shore, but also on the heights the brown roofs peep out of the green foliage. For years the coast has been a principal recruiting spot for plantation workers, and so the people are less shy than elsewhere, and one can communicate with them through pidgin English.

We now approach the southern tip of Buka, sailing along the steep coast of Bougainville, now in the narrow, yet deep, King Albert Strait, which separates the two islands. I was the first white person to navigate this strait, in 1886. Since that time it has been frequently used by steamers as well as sailing ships. Of course an accurate knowledge of local conditions is essential for navigating the strait; in particular, the navigator must have a precise knowledge of the tide conditions, which change every six hours. Inside the strait itself lies the small island of Sohanna, dividing it into two arms, one going to the west, passing north of Sohanna, while the other passes the east coast of Sohanna, going south. Both are navigable, but the arm going southwards is preferable because the tide race is less strong.

When we have finally passed the strait fringed

by coral reefs, we find ourselves in a broad basin, bordered in the east by the island of Bougainville, in the north by the island of Buka and its offshore reefs, in the west by the mountainous islands of Matehes, Toioch, and Katitj, and in the south by a number of small islands. Also, on the side towards Bougainville there lie a number of small uninhabited islands. The current maps, which are drawn up mainly from Hugo Zöller's sketches, give a completely false picture of this area; for example, the large island indicated south of Sohanna does not exist. The broad basin forms an excellent harbour; ships have it in their power to choose the most favourable anchorage according to the prevailing wind direction.

The basin cuts deeply into the main island towards the south-west, thus forming a fairly long peninsula at the north-western end. This is steep and high to seaward, but towards the south sinks gradually down to the shore, and is enclosed here by a sometimes wider, sometimes more narrow border of mangrove swamp. If we come through the strait by ship and anchor in the large basin, we are met by the same natives whom we have greeted outside the entrance. This time they visit us not in their large war or ocean-going canoes but in small dugouts with outriggers, often also on simple rafts of thin wooden battens lashed together. They have come across the peninsula, which is not very wide, and are now in the vessels used for fishing in calm water. The entire peninsula is cultivated by the natives; the paths lead through large banana plantations and fields of taro.

The western coast of Bougainville is, first of all, a narrow coastal flat which widens significantly at the southern corner of the basin. The Emperor Range rises from the coastal flat firstly as a gently rising mountain slope, but soon loses this character and forms steep, almost vertical walls. The small islands in the basin are agriculturally of little value; but on the other hand, the coast and the hinterland of Bougainville, which border this splendid harbour, will gain dominant significance over time, because the soil is generally good, and numerous streams from the mountains ensure sufficient irrigation.

The further we follow the western coast southwards, the more the mighty Emperor Range unfolds before our eyes. As a rule its spurs come right to the beach, and enclose valleys that would be suitable for small plantations. In the valley floors, copious streams hurry to the sea; however, none of them is navigable. The range is well populated here, but the population does not have a very good reputation. Beyond Cape Moltke, the mountains become lower and the slopes more gentle, and the coastline forms a broad flat indentation with a well-watered coastal flat of fairly large extent. This is the Empress Augusta Bay, with the small Gazelle Harbour in the southern corner. HIMS *Gazelle* anchored here in 1875 during her circumnavigation of the world. During the south-easterly season the little harbour, protected to seawards by the flat Cape Hüsker, offers quite a good anchorage; on the other hand, during the time of the north-westers it cannot be used.

In earlier years, at the time of uncontrolled recruiting for plantations in Australia and Viti, Empress Augusta Bay was a region of bad repute. Recruiting boats were attacked from time to time by the natives, and their entire crews were slain. Since that time a lot has changed; the mountain-dwellers have vigorously oppressed the coastal villages while these were numerically weakened by population outflow; today in previously heavily populated districts we find barely one-quarter of the original number of inhabitants; several large villages have completely disappeared. The natives, so grossly vilified in earlier times, are in any case less hostile today. On several occasions I have visited the villages still in existence, and always found a friendly welcome; traders from the Shortland Islands come here in their boats to buy produce, and no attacks on white people have occurred for years.

From Cape Hüsker the coast stretches in a south-easterly direction to where we started, Moila Point. Several fairly large rivers draining the high Crown Prince Range enter the sea along this stretch; they are impeded to seaward by a sandbar, but are navigable to larger vessels for a fair distance inland. The land is flat and rises gently towards the range, forming part of that great plain that I mentioned at the start of our circumnavigation.

Finally, with sorrow, we cast a glance towards the Shortland and Fauro islands emerging in the south. Until quite recently the German flag waved there also, and the little groups took part in trade with their fellow German islands of Choiseul and Ysabel. Today these islands are under English sovereignty, and the blossoming trade established by German firms in the Bismarck Archipelago has turned towards the Australian colonies.

It still remains for us to become acquainted with the northernmost of the Solomon Islands, the island of Buka. It has already been mentioned that it is separated from Bougainville by the King Albert Strait. It is significantly smaller than Bougainville, its length from north to south being about 55 kilometres.

The southern half is mountainous; the highest point around 350 metres. The islanders call both this mountainous part and its natives Zolloss. These heights drop away fairly steeply to the north, and the northern part of the island consists of a plain, gently sloping from east to west. The whole island consists of coral limestone and repeated random uplifting is clearly recognisable here as in so many places in the Bismarck Archipelago. The entire eastern side of the island falls away steeply to the sea, and has an insignificant beach front only at the southern end. The western side is flat, partially bordered with extensive mangrove cover; the island's few insignificant watercourses all empty out on this side.

On the western coast, a series of coral reefs topped by islands stretches from Dungenun Point southwards, almost parallel with the coast. A lagoon is thus formed between reef and island, offering excellent anchorages.

The northernmost corner of the lagoon, Carola Harbour, is absolutely splendid. It is formed by the island in the north and east, and the coral reef topped by the three islands, Malulu (Entrance Island), Hetau and Parroran in the west. A wide, deep entrance leads into Carola Harbour from the west, between Malulu and Dungenun Point. Other entrances exist between Malulu and Hetau, as well as south of Parroran, between it and the island of Yaming. This latter island and the island of Betaz lie on the same reef; south of it, a pass leads into the lagoon, and to good anchorages behind Betaz, between it and Buka. On the reef stretching further south lie the islands of Matzungan and Sal, both similarly separated by passes. The island of Sal was uninhabited until a short time ago; the reason given by the natives was that on the surrounding reef a gigantic octopus dragged fishermen into the depths; even canoes and their occupants were attacked. Consequently the earlier inhabitants moved to Matzungan. However, the sea monster has not made its presence felt for several years. Many islanders staunchly declare that they have seen the beast in earlier years; one man still living on Matzungan saved his life by swimming, while his companions were seized by the tentacles and dragged into the depths.

Beyond Sal a series of small uninhabited islands extends in a southerly direction, to some extent a continuation of the previously described series. The gaps steadily increase and the chain ends with the small Phoon group south of Emperor Island. The high islands Matehe, Toioch and Katitj (both the latter are designated on maps as one island, Emperor Island) form to some extent a continuation of the mountainous south of the island of Buka.

At the southern end of Buka a small safe harbour must be mentioned, cutting into the southern part of the island and protected against all wind directions. A pass leads into the harbour from the west, between the southern point of Buka and the island of Matehe; a second runs through King Albert Strait between Buka and the southern offshore reefs with their small islands.

The western side of Buka, like the southern end, has a number of splendid harbours and anchorages; while on the steep east coast, with its great depths of water directly off the fringing reef, they are totally absent.

The island of Buka is densely populated, and for that reason alone might not be suitable for plantations to any great extent. The inhabitants belong to the same tribe that inhabits the island of Bougainville, and have for many years been accustomed to hiring themselves out as workers.

Both Bougainville and Buka yield little in products. The ships arriving to recruit workers as a rule take part in the small trade. The southern end of Bougainville is favourably placed, but trade there is drawn to the English Shortland Islands, and little benefit comes to the German settlers.

About 60 kilometres north-west of the north cape of Buka lies the Nissan group, or Sir Charles Hardy Islands. It is an atoll running east to west and surrounds a fairly large and spacious lagoon. The eastern walls are up to 15 metres high in places and drop away steeply. The island is interrupted by several passes at the north-western end; the southernmost of these, 4.5 metres wide, allows passage for smaller vessels into the lagoon, which forms a totally safe haven. In the middle of the lagoon, the inner rim of which is almost completely covered by mangroves, lies the small island of Lehon. As well as the passes mentioned, two others lead into the lagoon. These are navigable by boats only, and separate the two smaller islands of Varahun and Sirot from the main island.

North of the group and separated by a strait about 3 kilometres long, lies a smaller group, the island of Pinepil with the smaller island of Esow. This group too is a raised coral atoll, lying east to west with a pass at the northern edge leading into a small lagoon and navigable only by smaller ships.

On current maps the Nissan group is shown too large; actually it is about 15 kilometres long from north to south and about 10 kilometres wide from east to west.

The inhabitants of the island are emigrated Buka islanders, who still undertake annual journeys there. However, on the Pinepil group a strong admixture of paler Melanesians is noticeable, which is accounted for by a long-term, regular annual interchange between Pinepil and *wun*eram (St John). Both island groups are therefore most interesting because they form the bridge between the black Melanesians of the Solomon Islands and the paler Melanesians of the Bismarck Archipelago.

Finally, the Carteret Islands consist of an almost circular atoll on which are scattered the seven islands comprising the group. In the west and south, passes lead into the lagoon. Beginning from the southern pass, and proceeding through east to north the sequence of islets is as follows: Yelaule (uninhabited), Epiül, Ehánu, Ehüene (uninhabited), Yolása, Yésele and Yangaine (on the extreme western border of the atoll). The group is inhabited by about 250 natives, immigrants from Buka, who were driven out of the Hanahan district years ago. Their tradition teaches that the group was inhabited at that time by pale-skinned people who were gradually subjugated, and who left behind as isolated traces polished axe blades of *Tridacna* shell which are occasionally found in the ground today, and which match similar items from Mortlock and Ongtong Java. The population might probably, therefore, have been a tribe of Polynesians, since they occupy the abovementioned neighbouring islands even today.

Both groups, Nissan and Carteret, yield about 120 tons of copra and a small amount of trepang annually. The small Carteret Islands with their relatively dense population are of no agricultural significance. The bulk of export falls on the Nissan group and could be increased significantly if the natives would work the land and plant coconut palms, which would do extremely well here. Because of the great laziness of the natives, whose needs are abundantly met, this cannot be expected. The firm of Forsayth in the Bismarck Archipelago, which has maintained a station here for twenty years, has recently begun cutting down trees on the island and planting coconut palms.

The population[1] from time immemorial had the reputation of being savage and bloodthirsty. The earliest discoverers reported bloody conflicts, and this was still by and large the general rule until not many years ago. Not behind the back and by indirect means but openly and courageously do the Solomon Islanders attack white visitors. Although frequently driven back with bloodied heads by superior weapons, they always renewed their attack. It is difficult to determine who caused these hostile encounters first. The seafarers of old in their dealings with the natives were probably not always at pains to respect the peculiarities of the natives; they may often unwittingly have caused offence and thus, given the warlike and contentious spirit of the natives, who moreover could not communicate with the foreigners, a confrontation was unavoidable.

About the middle of the 19th century, a further element came into consideration which had not contributed to pacification of the natives anywhere in the South Seas, at least where, as on the Solomon Islands, a brave and warlike population lived. This element was the whalers, sandalwood harvesters and work recruiters. For the Solomon Islands only the whalers and recruiters came into consideration. At that time, the former found a lucrative field both west and east of the islands, and thus frequently came into contact with the Solomon Islanders. They soon realised that the latter could in a short period of time be trained into competent seamen, and that they were useful in other ways on board ship during the voyages. Many were compelled to take part in the long voyages, often being finally put ashore on a foreign island with foreign people. Such an experience would have caused bad blood; whalers, even had they not intended to augment their crew in the usual way, but landed after a long voyage to replenish their stores, were regarded as enemies in those regions, and were treated as such.

Worker recruitment was even worse. Whalers had always stolen only a small number of natives, and as the whales had soon almost totally disappeared from these regions, the hunters moved on to new hunting grounds. Work recruiters were far more intent on filling their quotas. They went from place to place, scouring the entire coast with their boats and, for good or evil, had to come into conflict with the natives, with whom they were not able to communicate, and who, from experience or from hearsay about the ways and means of recruiting, knew and regarded them as kidnappers. Sadly, it cannot be disputed that worker recruitment was for many years very often done by no other means, until the European administration succeeded in putting an end to this disgraceful conduct. But basically it was only cleared up when the authorities had annexed the islands, and they became governed by administrators. We should not be surprised that in those times murders of white people were recorded every year. These may have been brought about through their own fault or, as was sadly also the case, it may have been revenge for previous encroachments by other recruiters. At that time every white person was regarded as an enemy, whether he was a recruiter, trader, traveller, or missionary; the crime of the one has frequently been the cause of the death of another, completely harmless, friendly man.

Today worker recruitment is supervised by the authorities, and transgression on the part of white people belongs among the exceptions; consequently hostile encounters and attacks by the natives have become less frequent year by year. Recruiting has, over the course of time, become an institution known by all natives; they know that they will be taken to a foreign place, have to work there, and after a certain time transported back home, enriched by the sum paid to them. Many hundreds of their people before them have been taken to foreign parts and returned well looked after. They have learnt from the latter what goes on, and not only the attractive earnings but also a type of yearning to get to know this distant land with the wonderful things that those returned talk about, encourages them to go. Over the course of time, the natives have become familiar with the various work sites and, according to whether their reputation is favourable or unfavourable, the recruiter's task is made easier or more difficult. The good reputation of a place depends on several factors. First, the prevailing health conditions come into consideration; if only a few natives return, and report the death of many of their people, then the good reputation of a place is lost once and for

1. Those who want further information on the inhabitants of the islands mentioned, are referred to my more extensive publication: *Zur Ethnographie der nordwestlichen Salomoninseln* which appeared in 1899 in the *Abhandlungen des Königlichen Zoologischen usw. Museums zu Dresden*. The following is an extract from the contents of that publication which I have endeavoured to complete by adding a number of illustrations for better comprehension.

all; neither the most humanitarian treatment, the most extensive care, nor the richest payment can persuade the natives to go there. Inhumane treatment, especially insufficient or unacceptable food and payment, are secondary as far as the reputation of a work site is concerned. If a bad reputation precedes a place, it becomes very difficult to recruit labourers for it; if the opposite is true, then the recruiter has a full ship in a short time.

Of course many other factors are involved in influencing the success of recruitment. Perhaps a major feast is in progress or is planned in the district; in this case success can hardly be counted on. To leave a feast in the lurch cannot cross the mind of a native; the recruiting ship will come again, and the opportunity will be offered often enough to go abroad. Or if the village is at war with the neighbouring tribe, as is not infrequently the case; then the young men are needed for the defence of their homeland, and even though they want so much to go away, they are held back by the elders and the family heads by power and persuasion. In such cases it is advisable to leave the natives to themselves; for the departure of one or other of them not infrequently arouses bad blood in those staying home and causes conflict and enmity.

Worker recruitment of the present day should therefore not be confused with the atrocities of earlier times. One can maintain with complete justification that the increased contact between natives and white people which is caused by recruiting, exercises a not insignificant civilising influence on the former. They have learnt to recognise that the white man is not to be regarded absolutely as an enemy whom one must guard against, and whom at best one attacks with spear and club without further preliminaries; they have experienced that attacks on whites are punished in the same way as their initial attack; and although no great friendship has developed, a certain trust has arisen over the course of time.

In communal contact on the plantations and other work sites, the natives have let many old tribal prejudices drop, and the labour recruiting has undoubtedly effected forgiveness in the minds of the natives. Natives who earlier opposed one another as mortal enemies, interact in a friendly way after recruiting. Meanwhile they get to know one another; the old enmity, the traditional tribal hatred pass away while abroad, and when they return to their own villages when their time of service is completed, they mediate the initial approaches and frequently a lasting peace. On my numerous excursions to the various islands I have often had the opportunity of observing the gradually expanding peaceful contact of the natives with each other, and the benefits arising from this are also useful to the white visitor.

I have discussed labour recruiting here because many incorrect views prevail even today, brought about by people who know nothing about the whole business, or who know only the old recruiting methods and believe that nothing has changed since that time. Many years ago I fought with the pen about the then evil situation; today I would not actually know how one could make a reproach against the current recruiting situation.

The inhabitants of the German Solomon Islands belong to the great Melanesian stock. Nowhere else do we find this stock more pure and unmixed, probably purest on the large island of Bougainville, although here and there especially in the coastal villages, traces of a foreign interbreeding make themselves noticed, probably a result of immigration of pale-skinned Polynesians. The reason for the racial purity is probably found in the warlike ways of the inhabitants, in their hostility to everything foreign and the therefore inhospitable reception of all newcomers. By their location the northern Solomon Islands were not so heavily exposed to immigration from the east as were the other islands, further south-east. On the southern Solomon Islands, the New Hebrides, New Caledonia, and Fiji the Polynesian influence is obvious; on the other hand, on both our German Solomon Islands, Bougainville and Buka, it is concealed, and is only detected after careful observation. Natives from the small island groups of Sikaiana, Ongtong Java, Tasman, Marqueen and Abgarris in the north and east were occasionally shipwrecked on Buka and Bougainville; also the Gilbert Islands left their contribution, and demonstrably a few of the Carolines.

The mountain-dwellers on the island of Bougainville have a dull black skin shade and generally have crinkled hair, although not a small number of natives were sighted who, besides the black skin shade had straight, or less wavy hair. On the coasts but especially on Buka, Carteret and Nissan as well as the dull black natives, some who must be called dark brown are also encountered. Occasional light brown individuals are found here and there among the coastal-dwellers. They are interbred, with the Polynesian element predominant.

On the plantations in New Britain I have often had the opportunity of observing the interbreeding of various Melanesians, as well as with light Polynesians. A fixed rule for the appearance of the offspring of these marriages can hardly be established; in some cases the mother's characteristics were dominant, in others those of the father, while occasionally characteristic features of both parents appeared unmistakably side by side in the offspring. It is understandable that on the islands of Buka and Bougainville, where at least the influx of Polynesians must be regarded as smaller, the Polynesian characteristics are gradually almost totally blended in. However, the occurrence of such interbreeding is verified by a case that was brought before me years ago on Buka. I met a pale brown woman with curly hair and Polynesian facial features who, according to the villagers was the daughter of a Buka couple. Her parents were no longer living, but I was able to establish that the mother had been paler than a Buka woman should have been. She had therefore probably been interbred, the offspring of a relationship between a Buka man and a pale-skinned Polynesian woman.

Among the numerous mountain-dwellers that I have seen, I have never come across such a light skin shade. The dull black is by far the dominant one; besides this, an intensive dark brown also occurs, probably a result of interbreeding with the coastal tribes. The appearance of straight or slightly wavy hair here would hardly have occurred through interbreeding with straight-haired Polynesians. I was told at Arawa Bay on the east coast of Bougainville, and it was affirmed by the mountain-dwellers, that in the interior live a few tribes in whom straight hair is predominant and whose body size is smaller. I could not tell whether this is one of the many fables that the natives love to tell when asked about the inland tribes.

The language of the northern Solomon Islanders is not uniform. On Nissan and Carteret, which were originally settled from Buka, they speak the same language as on the latter island. The Buka language is also spoken along the whole north coast of Bougainville, and it is understood along the coast about as far as Cape Moltke on the western side and Numanuma on the east coast. The inhabitants of the Emperor Range have an unique language, as do the inhabitants of the Crown Prince Range, whose language is different again from that of the neighbouring coastal tribes. On the Shortland Islands south of Bougainville the Polynesian element is already clearly evident in the language. I give the numerals from one to ten as an example (Table 1).

The villages are each governed by one chief; however, powerful and enterprising chiefs exert influence over weaker neighbours so that the latter conclude defensive and offensive alliances with them. Such alliances are not uncommon, and unite whole districts near and far under one nominal overlord. The position of chief is inherited, the successor is named by the father, and is not always the eldest son. But if the chief makes himself unpopular within the tribe it can happen that he is relieved of his position, slain or driven out. Thus the chief Zikan of Lundis on the west coast of Buka was driven out by his people and found refuge with the chief Takis in Hanahan on the east coast of the island, where he remains at present. The Lundis people chose another person from their midst as leader.

The individual districts are in an almost constant state of war among themselves, although, in more recent times as I have already mentioned, through the communal labour of members of the different tribes, a more peaceful contact has got under way, expanding from year to year. This is the case especially in the coastal districts; the shore-dwellers are still on a war footing with the mountain-dwellers almost everywhere, and when the latter make their way down to the shore it is always in large numbers, for security against hostile attack. This goes so far that, even when the mountain-dwellers are trading with the shore-dwellers, mutual security is always established by a certain display of power. In 1902 I was an eyewitness to such an event on Bougainville. About 6 kilometres south of Keaop (Cape l'Averdie) the local natives met the mountain-dwellers, to trade. As a rule the mountain-dwellers obtain fish in exchange for taro tubers. The Keaop people, mostly women with their loads of fresh and baked fish, arrived; some in canoes, others on foot along the beach. Armed men formed a sort of advance guard. Soon after, the mountain-dwellers arrived; first the armed men, then the women with their loads of taro. Both groups settled down about 500 metres from each other on the beach and began loud singing. Meanwhile a group of men separated from both groups; an older man from each group stepped forward, holding a bamboo cane of water in his hand, and about a dozen armed warriors followed him. As both groups approached each other, the two old men met, exchanged a few words, and then sprinkled the water out of the container in all directions. Their followers then joined them, and

Table 1

	Buka	Emperor Range	Crown Prince Range	Shortland Islands
1	atoa	paäs	monumoi	kala
2	a huel	bák	kikako	elua
3	topisa	kukán	páigami	epissa
4	tohazi	tánan	korégami	efati
5	tolima	tónim	uvugami	lima
6	monom	tunom	tugigami	onómo
7	tohetu	towut	paigamituo	fitu
8	towali	towal	kitakotuo	álu
9	tosíe	tosie	kámburo	ul'a
10	maloto	sawun	kuvúro	láfulu

both parties exchanged betel nuts and ate them. Immediately the women recommenced their song, which lasted only briefly this time. After their singing, the women came up with their loads of taro, laid them in small heaps and then retreated. In turn the Keaop women brought up their fish, laid them beside the taro heaps and then stood aside while both old men looked over the trade goods, probably to check whether anyone had been cheated. Once the examination was completed, the Keaop women gathered up the taro tubers, and then the women of the mountain people gathered up their fish. Then, a further short song followed, and the women departed with the exchanged items. The men chatted for a little while then moved off after their women.

The whole business ran so calmly and in such an orderly fashion, without haggling, and without unnecessary gossip that one might believe that the greatest harmony reigned between both parties; yet the old people assured me that both parties in everyday life regarded each other as bitter enemies, but that the trading of foodstuffs produced a momentary peace. The purpose of this peace is not only the unimpeded exchange of foodstuffs but also the security of the women. As soon as the latter have left, it ends often enough in a battle between the men when one or other party finds itself in a majority.

The entire population divides into several totem groups, which have various bird species as their signs. On Buka the hen (*kereu*) and the frigate bird (*manu*) are the signs; not to mention the pigeon (*báolo*), the rhinoceros hornbill (*popo*), the cockatoo (*ána*), and several other birds on southern Bougainville. Male and female natives who have the same bird as a tribal sign cannot marry. Marriages can only be entered into when both parties have different signs; children from the marriage always have the sign of the mother.

Women are sold in most cases by their relatives, but it can also happen that captured women may be taken as wives if the tribal sign permits. The various types of shell and tooth money in circulation there serve especially for buying wives.

Payment of the usual bride price makes the woman the property of the purchaser, and as a rule no further formalities take place; at most a small feast which is given by the relatives in honour of the married couple, and is repeated in the same way a few days later by the new pair. At the marriage of chiefs there is somewhat more celebration. Dances are presented, and on these occasions brightly painted, carved clubs (*kaisa*) of soft wood are used. Polygamy is universal; whoever can afford it, has several wives; I know several chiefs who have more than fifty. It follows that there are numerous young men who have no wives, or at most one; the older a native becomes and the more wealth and esteem he accumulates, the number of his wives increases proportionately. On the whole the latter lead a quite bearable existence; they must work of course

Plate 31 Outrigger of a canoe. Hermit Islands

but the men also take part in this, and in the village they conduct important discussions, join in during the discussion and business of the men without taking a back seat, and not infrequently convince them to accept their points of view. It is therefore always a good policy during a visit to the villages to make friends with the old women first; once these have been won over, the men do not resist for very long. On the small island of Saposá I know an old, quite influential chief whom I visit regularly on my excursions. He is the fortunate possessor of about fifteen wives, among them two old women whom I have made special friends. During one such visit I discovered in the chief's hut an extraordinarily finely carved club that had probably smashed many skulls, which he did not want to sell me in spite of a tempting price. Suddenly one of my gracious lady friends got up, grasped the club, hobbled to my boat with it and in silence placed the expensive item in it. Neither the owner nor anyone else raised the slightest protest, and the club is still in my collection to this day. The old chief had a sullen expression but was delighted when I later paid him the original price offered.

Celebrations do not take place for the birth of children. On southern Bougainville, during pregnancy, a feast (*marromarro*) is held in which only the women participate. If a son is born to a chief, both mother and child must remain in the hut for one and a half to two years and only then are they allowed to show themselves publicly, when dancing and feasting take place. On Buka such cloistering does not occur and a feast as described takes place only when the boy is seven to eight years old.

Child murder does indeed occur on the German islands but much less than in the south-eastern group. In the villages one is able to see numerous children of all ages, and I know families with five or six children, apart from the chief's families where, according to the number of wives, offspring are found which would cause many headaches for a European father.

The population of the German Solomon Islands is therefore not in the process of dying out as are so many other South Seas populations. Even though they are not increasing particularly, at least there is no decline. Since their seizure by Germany, nothing has been done for them at all, even though they are the most fruitful area for labour recruitment; one might calmly assert that if in the Bismarck Archipelago we had to dispense with the islands of Buka and Bougainville as recruiting grounds, the plantation structure on the Gazelle Peninsula would be very questionable. Hopefully the German administration will soon find ways and means to create an orderly situation there, and of suppressing successfully the ongoing wars and feuds among the population. The powerful islanders would then multiply rapidly and the islands would be counted among the most eminent of Germany's possessions.

The islands would achieve the greatest yields if the extensive fertile stretches of land, which lie totally unused at present, were transformed into plantations by capital-rich undertakings. On the Gazelle Peninsula in New Britain the establishment of plantations, has in large measure, contributed quite considerably to the pacification of the natives and thereby advanced the development of the population. The same would be the case if similar establishments were brought to fruition on Bougainville; the conditions are so favourable there that, as I have already mentioned in the geographical description of the island, this island could be transformed into one of the most flourishing and productive of all Germany's South Seas possessions.

The death of a native gives occasion for many feasts. In the north – that is, on Nissan, Carteret, Buka and northern Bougainville – two methods of burial are known: burial in the ground (*ha zérokere deakui*) and burial at sea (*ahäree kuerre*); the latter method is the one most frequently used. Feasts and dances take place, and the mourners paint their faces with a type of white clay.[2] In southern Bougainville, as well as the previously described methods, there is a third, cremation (*kasivei*). Cremation is a privilege of prominent people, chiefs and the wealthy. The funeral pyre is set up between four poles, often carved and painted on the upper ends; the corpse is laid on top and burned during howls and wails of grief. The remains are gathered up and placed in an earthenware pot, then a grave is dug between the four poles (*kakalo*), and the pot is buried in it. During the entire ceremony, loud lamentations sound, only ending when the meal that has meanwhile been prepared is presented. About one month later, there is a second feast, which concludes the real solemnisation. The burial site is, as a rule, surrounded by a carved and painted board fence[3] and decorated with plants with bright leaves. On the death of a prominent person a slave is killed; the corpse remains unburied but is not eaten.

On our German Solomon Islands we find, as virtually throughout the islands of Melanesia, the institution of men's secret societies, connected with masking the face and concealing the body. On Nissan and Buka we find head masks that are not dissimilar to those on New Ireland; on Bougainville masking seems to be less essential, but, on the other hand, secret societies are in full flourish there. In the section on secret societies (Section VIII), the Buka and Bougainville connections will be discussed in detail.

The idea that the Solomon Islanders are, without exception, cannibals is generally widespread. On Nissan, cannibalism is universal; on Carteret, this frightful custom does not prevail, probably because on the small islands the small population is many times more closely related. On Buka and

2. See my photograph in Hugo Zoller's *Deutsche Neuguinea*, page 52. The women standing in the middle ground are wearing the white grief paint.

3. Guppy, *The Solomon Islands*, page 51. The picture represents a grave between the four *kakalo* which are still upright.

Fig. 77 Cremation of a corpse in Kieta on Bougainville

on northern Bougainville cannibalism is universal, while it is totally absent on the southern half of Bougainville, whose inhabitants look on their northern neighbours with disgust. If a line is drawn across Bougainville roughly from Arawa Bay in the east to Empress Augusta Bay in the west, this approximately forms the southern border of anthropophagy. In my opinion the coastal-dwellers are the worst cannibals, uniting in communal manhunts, especially to surprise the inland people in their villages and gardens.

On my travels in the Solomon Islands I have encountered various such expeditions, whose participants assert, of course, that they are going to a feast or are returning from one. The feast was without doubt a cannibal feast. In a few villages on the eastern coast of Bougainville I know for certain that regular manhunts into the interior are undertaken, and the proceeds that are brought home, both dead and alive, are sold to distant regions.

On the small island of Pinepil, north of Nissan, the head is separated from the torso, and after the roasted meat has been gnawed off, an artistic face is fashioned on the facial bones from the crushed kernels of *Parinarium laurinum*. Such skulls are stored in the huts as trophies. On Buka and Bougainville the lower jaw of the victim is kept as a trophy. In the chiefs' huts one not infrequently sees whole rows of these trophies stacked side by side on one of the rafters. Almost every chief has an unique feasting place for these frightful meals, not far from his dwelling. Bone remains and fractured skulls in great numbers show only too clearly that the feasts are not a rare event. Women and children eat their portion just like the men; however, it is forbidden for them to enter the area where the bodies are dismembered.

Cannibalism here, as little as in other regions of the world, has its origins in the absence of other animal food. Religious concepts are just as little the reason among the Solomon Islanders. I have frequently heard the cry used by islanders who had flown into a dispute, 'I have eaten your father (mother, brother, sister)!' This 'compliment' always led to a renewed violent outbreak of the quarrel, because the assertion contained an expression of the deepest contempt. Therefore, originally, eating the slain enemy was probably regarded as an expression of the most abusive humiliation that could have been rendered to him or to his entire sib. However, the old saying, 'Appetite comes with the meal!' does not prove to be so well founded anywhere else as here, since, for many, human flesh forms a much sought-after delicacy, and the slain, from far afield, unknown people with whom there has been no contact, either peaceful or hostile, are bought for flesh and eaten.

European influences have so far not been able to achieve anything against the cannibalism of the Solomon Islanders. I have known cases where youths who had served three years as diligent and reliable workers on the plantations in New Britain, had already arranged prior to their return home to undertake an expedition for the purpose of obtaining this long-missed luxury food. Years ago I interrupted a cannibal feast in a village on the Gazelle Peninsula. The natives had fled at my approach; the Buka people accompanying me scented the roast meat and were highly indignant when I would not allow them to eat the delicacies on the spot, but made them wrap them in coconut palm leaves and bury them out of the way in the forest. I am firmly convinced that they never understood this unnecessary waste, and have never entirely forgiven me.

Cannibalism is understandably one of the main causes of the continual reciprocal hostilities; white settlements would quickly bring about a change for the better, as has actually been going on for years already on a large part of the Gazelle Peninsula.

On southern Bougainville one or more skulls are stored in the public meeting houses. These are skulls of slain enemies and a remembrance of a victory won, not of a cannibal feast. The bodies of slain enemies are brought to the village in triumph, publicly displayed for several days and then buried.

A tattoo would leave no visible trace on the black or brown-black skin of the Solomon Islanders; they have therefore developed the custom of scarring the skin – that is, the skin is ripped with a sharp instrument, so that upon healing there are visible scars, forming various patterns. Boys are scarred between the ages of seven to eleven, and the pattern stretches across the face, neck and shoulder blades (Meyer and Parkinson, *Album von Papuatypen*, vol. 1, plates 26 and 27). Scarring in women stretches over the entire back as well, across parts of the breast, stomach and loins. The procedure is carried out with a sharp shell and must be very painful. The scarring of the wounds not infrequently proceeds irregularly; suppuration occurs, destroying the pattern, so that after healing unsightly bulges and irregular scars are produced. A well-healed scarring which shows the lines of the pattern clearly and distinctly is the greatest adornment of both men and women; the latter increase in value according to the beauty of the pattern. In plate 10 in the album of Philippino types by A.B. Meyer there are depicted two scarred negritos from Casiguran in east Luzon. The admittedly not very distinct scarring of the woman resembles surprisingly that of the Buka women.

Music, singing, and dancing of the Solomon Islanders belong in part to the characteristics encountered in this type of Melanesian. In comparison with the performances of other South Seas folk, the music must be set apart on a higher level; on the other hand, in many cases singing and dancing are very primitive, although one also finds performances which show a significant musical talent, and demonstrate a developed ear for rhythm and beat. First, I will briefly describe the musical instruments; they consist of drums of the usual type; that is, hollowed-out sections of tree trunk with a slit on the upper side. The sound is produced by light or heavy blows against the side, somewhat below the slit, by means of one or more rattan sticks tied together into a bundle. This drum, *tui*, produces a booming sound that carries a long way and, as in other districts, serves for signalling. The hourglass-shaped drum with a monitor skin stretched over one end, so widespread in other parts of Melanesia, does not occur here. Pan flutes, *kohe*, of bamboo cane, are used as well as drums. A pan flute concert can be regarded as a fairly high musical achievement for a primitive people. The flutes are not only tuned in octaves but have a tonal range from four to six completely tuned tones. (Meyer and Parkinson, *Papuatypen*, vol. 1, plate 29, presents such a choir.)

I will mention elsewhere the instruments used in the secret societies and regarded as sacred (Section VIII).

As well as very finely vocalised melodic songs which have a particular text as their basis, there are also favourite songs of the people; I could almost regard them as national songs: musical productions which, since they are not based on articulated words, might best be designated as a type of melodic howl. A melody cannot be recognised, and certain multi-voiced harmonies recur, but I doubt whether it would be possible to reproduce the whole thing in our musical notation. It is just the same with the dances: besides those with an excellent rhythm and a fixed beat from which every movement is measured, there are also those which consist basically only of a series of eccentric irregular leaps without a beat. This dance, and the corresponding howling song, have something so indescribably wild that often goose pimples are felt by the spectator; especially when it is seen, presented in the natives' homeland, possibly as the sole white spectator.

Imagine an open village square, surrounded by the low huts of the natives, the darkness enhanced by palms and other mighty, leafy trees. Naked forms crouch and lie in a wide circle, lit up by the flickering glow of a fire. Without a sound four or five older men, armed with spears, bows and arrows, walk into the centre; then the younger men join them, lining up in rows radiating out from the centre formed by the older men, and the youths arrange themselves on the outer periphery. Then the old ones in the centre begin a monotonous howl, and gradually the young men and boys join in, in harmony, and at the same time the entire group slowly begins to move round the centre point. Soon the tempo quickens, and the dancers on the outer rim have to make giant leaps to keep up. Right in the midst, shrill whistles sound, the dancers clatter their weapons, spring high in the air, and the excitement gradually rises to a point where odd dancers, bathed in perspiration, pitch out of the dense mass of dancers and throw themselves round in wild ecstasy on the ground.

The dance grows still more wild when the pan flutes and wooden drums take part. The musicians, with the deep-toned flutes over a metre long, form the centre round which the dancers are grouped, as previously described, some with smaller pan flutes in their hands. Then the flute music joins in with the ear-splitting howl, then a drum joins in, then several, and the noise rapidly rises to an indescribable din of the wildest kind.

Years ago I was witness to such a night-time dance on one of the small, densely populated islands in Carola Harbour, and the impression will ever remain, unforgotten. With tautened nerves and breath held I enjoyed the wild spectacle, and at the conclusion of the presentation my nerves gradually calmed with long, deep breaths. During long years' sojourn on the various South Sea islands, I have had the opportunity of observing the most varied dances, but none of them had anything even approximately as wild and spine-chilling as this Solomons dance.

I can be brief about house construction. On northern Bougainville and the smaller islands, the huts stand on level ground; they are 3 to 4 metres wide and correspondingly three to four times as long. The walls are about 1 metre high and above them curves the slightly arched roof made from the leaves of a species of palm (*Phytelephas*) or from coconut palm fronds (plate 34). The interior is partitioned off by two or more cross-walls. In southern Bougainville, the usual type of construction on the coast was probably adopted from the islands further south. Here the huts stand on high poles which between them leave an open space below. Besides this, the so-called *tabu* houses also occur on this part of Bougainville (illustration by Hugo Zöller, *Deutsche Neuguinea*, page 368, after a photograph taken by me). These *tabu* houses are assembly places for men; here visitors are received, here celebrations and feasts take place from which the women are excluded, as entering these houses is expressly forbidden them. The houses do not guard any kinds of secrets; they have probably developed from the need to keep the often quite burdensome female society at a distance. These assembly houses are constructed with great care; in particular the pillars which carry the roof, and the crossbeams, are frequently carved and painted. In places where there are no *tabu* houses, the great canoe sheds serve the same purpose.

One can scarcely speak of a costume; in the shoreline villages today one sees the loincloths introduced by whites, but they are by no means universal. The inland-dwellers all go totally naked, and we might wonder how they can, in this state, endure the low temperature, which is bitterly cold, particularly at night, in their huts often 1,500 metres above sea level.

The young men often wear a girdle woven out of brightly coloured fibres, which encloses the waist so tightly that it seems bewildering that they can endure such a constriction. Strips of rattan dyed red, long cords of threaded circular shell discs, or black and white strips of interwoven *Pandanus* leaves serve the same purpose. The young girls, when they are not completely naked, wear a thin cord round the hips from which a bright, usually red, *Dracaena* leaf hangs down in front to cover the genitalia. Married women wear a loincloth of fibrous material which extends to the knees; the apron is fastened by a girdle about a hand's width broad, which is frequently woven from bright fibrous materials and decorated with elegant designs. As protection against sun and rain the woman wear an item of clothing made from *Pandanus* leaves; it is a square of 1 metre, folded in the middle and sewn together at one end. It forms a cape which is placed over the head, and the wider lower end protects the back (plate 33). Married women put the cape on as soon as a stranger approaches. These capes are often produced from red-dyed and natural coloured strips of *Pandanus* leaves and embroidered with red, black and yellow *Pandanus* fibres, so that elegant, regular patterns are formed. On southern Bougainville, both men and women, especially the latter, carry a large dried leaf of a species of fan-palm, whose edges are embroidered with decorative patterns. This leaf is carried in the hand or under the arm and thus covers particular parts of the body according to wish.

The inhabitants of the German Solomon Islands are not so lavishly ornamented as in other parts of Melanesia. Red hibiscus blooms are a universal favourite as decoration for the crinkly hair, and one can scarcely think of a more effective decoration. When the warrior goes into battle he hangs a bundle of leaf strips, dyed red and yellow, round his neck so that the bundle hangs down the back. This ornament (*kehala*) is at the same time a talisman which protects the wearer. Also, a bunch of white cockatoo feathers is fixed in the hair as a battle ornament.

In the pierced nasal septum most men wear a 10- to 13-centimetre-long *Tridacna* stake (*huin*), sharpened at both ends. Earrings or ear pendants are not common. They are seen here and there, and are apparently a men's ornament.

Chest ornaments are worn in two different forms by the men, although not especially often. Circular *Tridacna* discs, overlaid with a bored-out turtle-shell disc, were earlier imported from New Ireland via Nissan; now, they are traded by the plantation workers and brought home. They are copied at their destination, in which case the turtle-shell discs never show the excellent workmanship of the specimens imported from New Ireland. Other circular and often oblong *Tridacna* discs are decorated with an engraved, stylised frigate bird; those discs (*kini*) prepared on Buka and on Bougainville itself stand in high regard, and are produced by only a few artists (Meyer and Parkinson, *Papua Album*, vol. II, plate 45).

Another extremely rare and extraordinarily expensive chest ornament named *kiá*, of which the deceased chief Koroi on the Shortland Islands owned several specimens, consists of a rectangle about 15 centimetres long put together from different coloured shell discs, from the lower end of which long strings of similar shell discs hang. On the opposite side of the rectangle similar cords form a ring through which the wearer puts his head. The ornament does not seem to be indigenous to the northern Solomons, but was introduced, probably by trade from the south (fig. 78).

Armrings of *Tridacna* shell appear in two forms: those circular in cross-section were introduced from the south via the Shortland Islands; the broad, thick armbands with a deeply incised groove on the outside were imported via Pinepil and Nissan, and produced on the island of Tanga in particular.

Fairly rough, superficially polished *Trochus* armrings are also worn. However, more highly prized are the plaited armbands (*basbas*) with bright patterns in red and gold sewn on. Also worth noting are the finely plaited armbands. Their preparation is noteworthy insofar as they form to some extent a transition between plaiting and weaving, if they are not to be regarded as a remnant of an earlier familiar weaving art.[4] This art is practised in northern Bougainville, Buka and Nissan. The apparatus used is called *paggo*.

The men, especially the youths, take great care in their hairstyle; the crinkly hair is pinned up with a pointed stick and the hair tips are carefully supported, so that a symmetrical spherical hairstyle emerges. This is occasionally dyed completely or partially green or red. Lime is never used for rubbing into the hair. The women style their hair only in their youth; when older the head is mostly shorn bald or the hair is formed into broad flat tufts with brown- or black-coloured clay.

Painting the face and ears with red or white colours is common everywhere. Young 'dandies' with a piled-up, spherical hairstyle often paint a narrow red or white stripe from ear to ear across the forehead at the hairline; as simple as this decoration appears, it is highly effective against the dark skin.

We find money in various forms on Bougainville and on the smaller islands. In the north, two types of string money are current, both made from teeth (*reki* and *baiu*). *Reki* consists of the teeth of the flying fox, *baiu* of dolphin teeth. The teeth are bored through at the root, strung at short distances apart on a strong cord, and then arranged in such a way by longitudinal cords and wrapping with fine fibres that they are directed to one side like a comb. Besides this, a type of currency is in use, imported particularly from the Carteret Islands, called *biruan*. This very highly treasured money consists of russet, white and bluish-white shell discs. For boring these discs, a primitive drill is used on Carteret. In the south of Bougainville a similar currency is found, made from russet shell discs (*mismis*), and a further sort (*áputa*) is in circulation in the Crown Prince Range, consisting of a string of small *Conus* shells with their ends cut off. The *mismis* was introduced from the islanders further away to the south-east, via the Shortland Islands; the *áputa* is made on the Shortland Islands.

On the island of Nissan, a type of money is used in local trade, deviating quite a bit from the previously described sorts (plate 35). It consists of pieces of *Tridacna* shell twice the size of a fist, which are bored through the centre and carefully smoothed and polished on the outside. Von Luschan, in *Beiträge zur Völkerkunde der Deutschen Schutzgebiete*, pages 74 and 75, mentions these pierced *Tridacna* pieces, and is apparently of the opinion that they are armrings in a certain stage of production. This is not, however, the case; in this particular form they are used exclusively as currency (*kuamanu*) and never prepared any further. The piercing of these pieces is characteristic. After a *kuamanu* has been roughly hewn out of the thick end of a *Tridacna* shell, the piece is ground by rubbing with sand and water on a hard coral block to give it a spherical shape. Drilling is carried out on both flattened ends in such a way that, with a hard stone or a sliver of *Tridacna*, a depression is produced as

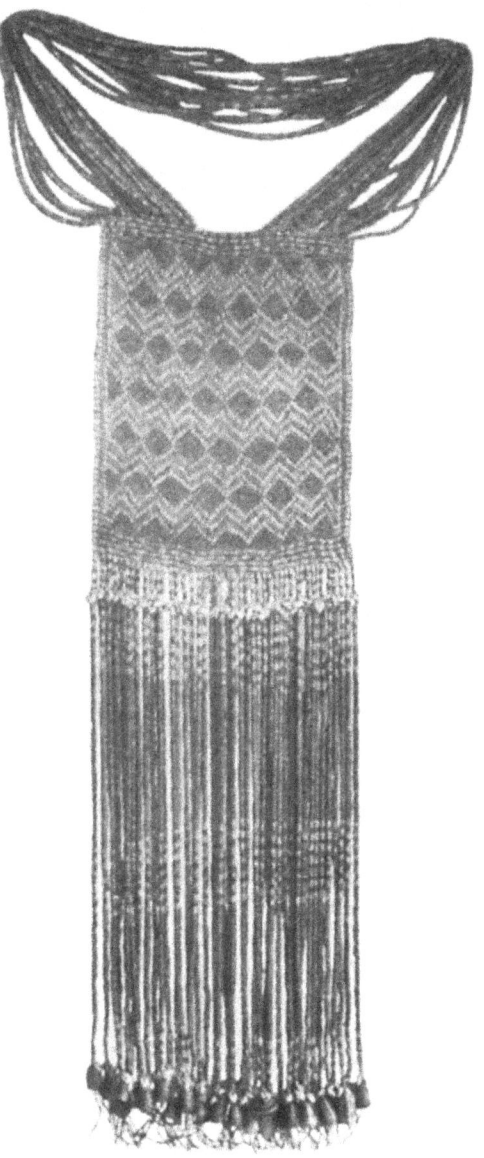

Fig. 78 Very rare chief's ornament of small shell discs

deeply as possible. Then drilling is continued with a piece of pumice jammed into a length of bamboo cane. By continual rotation of the cane the hole is gradually deepened from both sides until the stone is pierced. The pieces of pumice are washed up by the sea and carefully collected; many pieces are required, and rather a lot of time, before a smooth continuous hole is produced; but time is of no particular value to the natives. A complete drilled-out and polished *kuamanu* therefore represents a considerable expenditure of time and effort, which is scarcely proportionate to the imagined value of the piece. On celebratory occasions the money is displayed, to some extent as a reflection of the owner's reputation.

In dealings by the natives among themselves, the abovementioned items substitute the money of civilised people. A string of tooth money has a definite fixed value, just as the shell money and the *Tridacna* money. However, besides this, any property of the natives serves as means of bartering

4. See the discussion by Dr Danneil in *Internationales Archiv für Ethnographie*, vol. XIV.

and payment. Armrings, bows and arrows, spears, pottery, in short everything that a native owns, serves as an item of trade, even human beings. Thus, for example, a few years ago two young girls from Nissan moved to Buka in exchange for a large war canoe.

Household utensils in our sense of the word trouble the Solomon Islander only to a small degree. He does not have chairs and tables, nor likewise cupboards and trunks to store his treasures. A bed is unfamiliar; in most cases he sleeps on the bare ground or on a coconut mat. If he lives in luxury he builds a sleeping platform from bamboo canes laid side by side, or old canoe planks, and sleeps on them as peacefully as a spoilt European on an eiderdown pillow. If for any reason he is forced to shift, then the most valuable items are tied into bundles in less than no time and carried away by the women.

Let us look at the property of a native, to familiarise ourselves with his household utensils. These consist almost exclusively of objects for preparing food. First and foremost, the pottery claims our attention. Pottery making is the women's task. They gather suitable clay, dry it and pound it and remove all small pebbles. Next the pulverised clay is moistened with water, worked between stones and kneaded until a completely homogeneous mass is produced, and then the work starts. The hand tools are very simple; they consist of a wooden spatula and a round, or oval, smooth fist-sized stone. A lump of clay is beaten into a small disc with the moist spatula, then further lumps of clay are laid on top and beaten flat: one hand holding the round stone pressed firmly against the inside to provide resistance against the spatula. In this way the bottom and walls of the pot are gradually built up, and smoothed both inside and out with both instruments. As a rule the potter works on several pots at once, so that one processed piece is drying out a little, while another piece is being worked on. A few years ago photographs of potsherds were sent to me, clearly showing the imprint of fingernails on the inside. These sherds were found in Swiss pile buildings, and the imprint of fingernails had probably come about from the potter forming the vessel over the closed fist without using the stone like the potters of the Solomon Islands.

When the vessel is fully formed, it is dried out slowly in the shade, and finally hardened in a fire. For this purpose a small fire is built on the ground and the vessel placed on it. Burning logs are placed round it, and a fairly good fire is kept going for several hours. The pot remains there until it is completely cool. It has then been baked hard and is ready for use. They do not know how to produce a glaze for pots.

The shape of the pot differs in northern and southern Bougainville. In the north it is conical, with the side walls gently bulging outwards; the opening is wide and without a turn-out. In the south the vessels are spherical, the opening nar-

Plate 32 Village scene at Ernst-Gunther-Hafen, northern Bougainville

row and fitted with a broad rim curving outwards.

In recent times the Solomon Islanders have started making clay tobacco pipes. About fifteen years ago these were still very primitive: the bowl of the pipe was well formed, but they had difficulty producing a sufficiently long stem. The old specimens were therefore basically only clay pipe bowls with an appendage to which a thin tube of bamboo was fixed for use. Today, however, they make one-piece clay pipes with a 10- to 14-centimetre stem, and decorate the bowl with indented zigzag lines.

For crushing cooked taro tubers they use a deep wooden mortar with a peg-like extension on the lower end, to fix the implement firmly upright in the ground. A thick stick serves as a crusher. The outside of the mortar (*mamoro*) is often painted, and provided with shallow indented decoration.

In order to crack the hard shell of the *Canari* nuts so highly prized by all Melanesians, they use a heavy stone pestle (*kukono*; fig. 79). This is not infrequently carefully polished smooth, with the handgrip having an equally carefully made pommel. The nuts are laid on a flat circular board (*mamara*) and crushed with the *kukono*.

In southern Bougainville, beyond the village of Toboroi, plaited dishes and baskets of various shapes are used for serving the meal; there are shallow bowls (*dara*), with a steep narrow rim, deep bowls with a high rim (*doado*), and superb little oval baskets with a handle (*koko*).

Also, everywhere on the islands, they use baskets of various sizes plaited from coconut palm leaves. The natives show an astonishing virtuosity in their production.

Barely twenty-five years ago, the natives lived totally in the Stone Age, especially on the big island of Bougainville. Since then, they have steadily and unceasingly completed the transition into the Iron Age. Certainly no native will be found anywhere, not even in the most distant mountain villages, who does not know iron and iron implements. Throughout the shoreline and coastal villages the old stone tools have totally disappeared; already the younger generation barely realises that their ancestors used stone tools instead of the iron axe and the long bush knives and that they did their work just as finely and carefully as is done today with the far more perfect tools.

The stone blades of the axes were earlier produced exclusively on Bougainville, reaching Buka, Nissan, and Carteret via the trade route.

In the north two different blades are used. One sort, which I might call the Buka form, has a length of 21.5 centimetres; the rounded cutting edge is 7 centimetres long, and in the middle the blade is 9 centimetres wide and 5 centimetres thick. Somewhat above the middle of the blade, a 2.5 to 3 millimetre deep groove is incised. These blades are found especially on the north-western corner

of Bougainville and on Buka, Nissan, and Carteret. The second blade form, which predominates in the villages of the Emperor Range and in the north-east and east of Bougainville, is about 28 centimetres long; the cutting edge is about 5.5 centimetres long while the opposite end is about 1 centimetre wider. In the middle the width is 7.5 centimetres, and the thickness 6 centimetres. The corners of both the cutting edge and the head project a little, and are slightly curved on the sides. The whole blade is extremely carefully polished, and belongs among the most extraordinary accomplishments of all the Melanesians.

The attachment of both blades to the axe handles is characteristic. The handle does not consist especially of a knee-shaped piece of wood, as is otherwise usual in these implements, but of a piece of rattan which is wrapped twice round the blade and firmly fastened to it, while both free ends are bound to a handle about 21 centimetres long, at right angles to the blade (fig. 81).

Fig. 79 Stone tools from the Solomon Islands (pestles)

Fig. 80 Stone tools from the Solomon Islands (axe blades)

In southern Bougainville, a further two blades are used. One also has a rattan attachment, but differs, however, in form. The blade is about 19 centimetres long, the cutting edge about 9.5 centimetres wide and fairly strongly curved, while the butt end is about 1.75 centimetres wide with a groove about 3 millimetres deep for the rattan tie. However, the most widespread is a blade that is attached to a knee-shaped handle by means of two rings plaited from strips of rattan. These blades too are of particularly careful workmanship, and vary significantly in size. I have specimens that are 34 centimetres long with a semicircular cutting edge 5.5 centimetres wide. The side facing outwards when attached, is polished more convexly than the surface turned towards the handle. The blade gradually tapers backward, ending in a conical blunted point. In the shoreline villages, similar blades are found made from *Tridacna* shell.

Various sharpened shells serve, or more accurately served, as knives and scrapers, especially oyster and mother-of-pearl shells, as well as the shells of a particular species of *Cyprina*. I have seen curved boars' tusks, sharpened on the concave side, used as scrapers, especially for smoothing wooden objects. Various types of coral serve as rasps. Grindstones for sharpening stone axe blades are found in villages everywhere. They are large or small blocks of stone in which deep trough-shaped hollows have developed from long years of use, and have often been imported from distant areas. Otherwise, small, hand-sized grindstones of a hard fine-grained sandstone are in use, for polishing and sharpening of smaller objects.

I have seen drills both on Carteret and Buka, and they probably also occur on Bougainville. They consist of a piece of wood, about 35 centimetres long, the thickness of a pencil. A piece of quartz is pushed onto the lower end and fastened with strips of rattan. At about a quarter of the length from the lower end, a second piece of wood, about 20 centimetres long, is fastened on, crosswise. This is set in motion in such a way that a cord, about 50 centimetres long, attached at both ends to a stick about 20 centimetres long, is laid over a groove on the upper end of the drill, so that equal lengths of cord are on both sides of the drill. With a slow rotation of the drill, the cord is wrapped round it, then the right hand presses downwards on the stick, while the left hand holds the apparatus in place. Thus, the drill acquires a rotating motion, the cord runs out, and by the continued rotary movement, is wrapped round the other side. The drill tip turns, now right, now left, while the cross-stick acts, to some extent, as a spring gauge.

Today the previously mentioned tools have to a large extent been replaced by modern iron implements. In the coastal villages the present generation scarcely knows the hand tools of their ancestors; in the mountain villages many are still in use but within a few years here, too, all the original ones will have been replaced.

It is natural that such a warlike people as the Solomon Islanders take extraordinary care in the manufacture of their weapons. It is peculiar that they are not made everywhere; quite distinct areas produce bows and arrows, while others produce spears, and these articles find their way to far distant regions by barter along the trade route. As far as the German Solomon Islands are concerned bows and arrows are produced almost exclusively in the mountain villages of Bougainville; all that type of weapon seen in the coastal districts of the large island are made by the mountain-dwellers.

Buka obtains all its needs from Bougainville, and trades a portion with the Carteret Islands and Nissan. Since contact with the latter group is neither regular nor frequent, it can occasionally happen that the stock of arrows gets very low there. On Nissan this has led to the manufacture of unique arrows which differ from those of Bougainville particularly in the material for the barbs and the painting of the arrow tips.

The situation is similar with spears (fig. 82). In the villages of the Crown Prince Range a quite distinctive spear is produced in great numbers and finds its way north as far as Buka and Nissan, and south as far as the island of Guadalcanar. The spears made in the villages of the Emperor Range are far more varied in form and easily distinguished from the spears of the Crown Prince Range; they

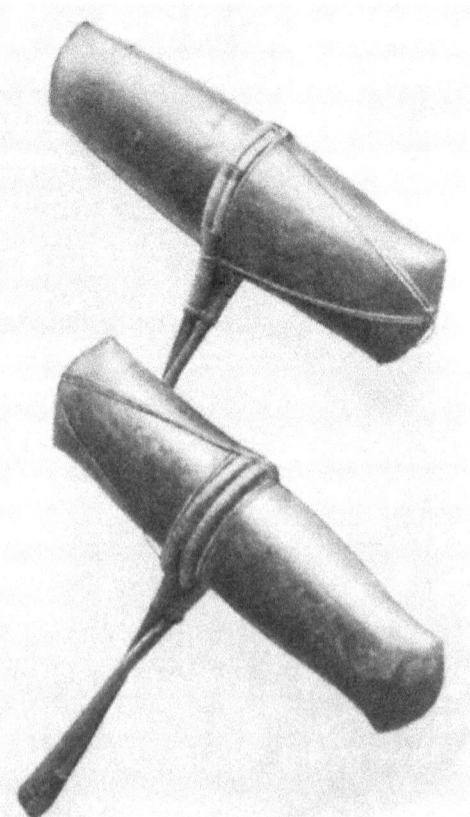

Fig. 81 Stone tools from the Solomon Islands (stone axes with handles)

are not so widespread.

The spear of the Crown Prince Range is about 340 centimetres long; of which 60 centimetres are the decorated tip. The spear is made from a hard, palm wood, and is about 2.5 centimetres in diameter at its thickest point; the butt end tapers to about 0.5 centimetres in diameter at the lower end. The inland inhabitants call this spear *kugu*. The various parts of the tip have their own names. First the outermost, approximately 1.5-centimetre-long tip is carefully wrapped with a yellow fibrous material; then follow six rows of barbs, arranged in fours so that those nearest the tip are the shortest. This group of six (sometimes five) rows of barbs is called *iruä*. Then follow two rows of four barbs each, markedly longer than the barbs of the *iruä*. These two rows are called *itina* and *itina takanne*, while the individual barbs are called *masinke* and *mámongke*. The barbs (*masinke*) of the row next to the *iruä* are about 6 centimetres long, and those of the next row (*mámongke*) are about 8 centimetres long. Following these two rows is a ring of four barbs about 10 centimetres long, called *puúgu*. Between the four *puúgu* are five rings each of four barbs about 0.5 centimetres long, called *sisika*. They are fastened to the shaft of the spear by fine fibrous strips and painted over with a type of white clay, *moruvassi*. The previously described parts together form the actual spear tip. The individual barbs are made from the wing bones of a species of *Pteropus*; the outward-turned end of each hook is sharpened, the inner end is inset into the shaft, bound with fibrous cord, and fixed in place with the pulp of *Parinarium laurinum* (*osio*) nut. A brown type of soil, *ugura*, and a white clay, *moruvassi*, are used to paint this part of the spear tip and the barbs.

Following the armed part of the spear is a decorated section, which is never totally absent even when occasionally not completely finished. This part consists of four sections: following the final row of barbs (*sisika*) is a carefully made binding of 1-millimetre-wide red and yellow plant fibres, called *rutta* and *rakagassi*. This plaiting forms a series of alternating red and yellow zigzag lines running round the spear shaft. The plaiting itself is called *tuu*. Following this plaiting there is a carving running round the shaft, and when unwound it reveals two human figures. This part is called *kägoi*, and should never be missing from a completed spear, nor should the subsequent pommel, *uiru*. The *uiru* is a knob, 3.5 centimetres in diameter, of red and yellow leaf fibres pressed closely together. The yellow fibres form a central ring about 3 millimetres wide, bordered above and below by a red hemisphere. Following this knob there is a further decoration of red and yellow fibres, but these zigzag lines do not run round the shaft of the spear but along it. Occasionally spears are to be seen with the entire remaining shaft wrapped in this red and yellow plaiting, but these are quite rare. They are used on special festive occasions.

The carved ornament *kägoi* and the subsequent sphere *uiru* have a particular significance. *Kägoi* is a spirit, and the carving certainly symbolises the spirit that gives the spear its deadly power. The sphere, *uiru*, is the spirit's dwelling. The same ornament often recurs on the shafts of arrows, although not always to its full extent.

In Professor von Luschan's *Beiträge zur Völkerkunde*, plate 38, figures 1 to 30 give a series of these *kägoi* figures in various stylisations.

The spears of the Emperor Range are extremely diverse in form, although they are inferior in the care of manufacture to those of the Crown Prince Range. We can divide them into four main groups:

Group I: Smooth spears without barbs;
Group II: Spears with barbs made out of the body of the spear;
Group III: Spears with inset barbs made from material different from that of the spear shaft;
Group IV: Multi-pronged spears.

In all these spears, ornamentation is extremely diverse, through painting, carving and the addition of plaiting or wrapping in dyed fibre bands. As a rule the spear shaft itself is round, but often also quadrangular, and the entire length wrapped in *Pandanus* leaves. Whereas there is a firmly established pattern of production in the Crown Prince Range, each manufacturer seems to follow his own style in the Emperor Range.

However, the principal weapon in the German Solomons is the bow and arrow. Everywhere in the villages they are kept close at hand, and one can scarcely imagine a man from Buka or Bougainville without this weapon in his hand. Even though the weapon is not immediately visible, only the slightest pretext is needed for the cherished weapon to be conjured up, ready to protect, within a few seconds.

A detailed description of all the different Bougainville arrows would be an extensive task. The forms are so diverse and differ so much from one another that a systematic division must suffice here. The following three groups encompass all the different types of arrow:

Group I: Arrows with a smooth tip:
a) with a round point;
b) with a sharp point.
Group II: Arrows whose tips are provided with barbs
a) with barbs caved out of the arrow tip;
b) with barbs made from a different material than the arrow point – that is, from bones, fishbones, spines, and so on – and artificially bound to the arrow tip by wrapping and cementing
Group III: arrows with several points, used in part for catching fish

The arrow always consists of two parts, the arrow

tip and the shaft. The wooden arrow tip varies in length from 30 to 50 centimetres. It is inserted about 3 to 4 centimetres into the tubular shaft and bound firmly in place by wrapping with fine bast fibres. Painting over the site of attachment with the crushed pulp of *Parinarium* gives further reinforcement.

Poisoned arrows are not found anywhere in the northern Solomons; the yellow fibre wrapping the arrows at the extreme tip is not poisonous, and serves only to support the otherwise easily damaged fine tip.

The shaft is 1 metre long on average. It is frequently wrapped at the bottom with fine bast fibres, and smeared with crushed *Parinarium* nut to prevent cracking of the shaft. The end is slightly grooved as a rule to maintain a more secure support for the arrow against the bowstring.

Most arrow shafts show an etched, black pattern over the individual knots on the tube. This pattern, *korokoroto*, is not simply ornament but rather a type of trademark. The arrow-makers on Bougainville put these marks on the arrow shafts to show their origin. The beach-dwellers frequently recognise which districts the arrows come from by the carved *korokoroto*.

The bow is made from the outer hard wood of a species of palm. It is 2 metres long as a rule, up to 4 centimetres wide in the middle and tapers gradually towards both ends. The outer side is flat and almost always stained dark brown or black. The side towards the bowstring is convex and mostly polished; along the middle runs a single or double black line. The best bows come from the Emperor Range.

The bowstring is twisted out of strong plant fibres and frequently wrapped in the repeatedly mentioned yellow fibre, partly as decoration and partly to stop the string from unravelling. The bowstring is permanently attached to one end of the bow, the other end is detachable, so that one can stretch it more tightly or more loosely as one chooses. The archer places the bow in front of him, holding the lower end with the big toe of the left foot; he then grasps the upper end in his left hand, bends the bow gently and with his right hand he releases the bowstring, which he shortens or lengthens depending on the degree of tension he wants from the bow.

When using it, the archer holds the bow in his left hand together with a supply of arrows. The index finger of his left hand is extended and presses the arrow lightly against the bow. His right hand grips the arrow between thumb and bent index finger, pressing the notch against the bowstring which he draws back at the same time. In shooting, the bow is always held in such a way that the arrow is level with the eye of the archer; according to preference, the bow is vertical or horizontal, or sloping either to right or to left. The previously mentioned black line on the inner side of the bow serves to some extent as a sight; the bowman always brings the bowstring and that line to such a position that they cover each other. The skill of some archers is astonishing, and they rarely miss their target. From youth onwards boys practise the use of this weapon, using smaller bows of bamboo cane and arrows made from the central rib of coconut palm leaves.

To protect the left arm against impact and rebound from the bowstring, they use a ten- or twelve-row spiral of bark, *haveloso*, which wraps round the forearm from wrist to elbow.

Of far lesser significance than the former weapons are the clubs, made of hard palm wood (plate 36, nos 1 to 3). Their average length is 130 centimetres. The striking end is most often lance-shaped, forming half the total length. The greatest breadth of the striking end is about 7.5 centimetres. Along the middle of the lance-shaped blade a prominent central ridge runs right to the tip; as a rule the blade is provided with a carved decoration on one side. The haft is about 4 to 4.5 centimetres wide and pointed at the end, frequently wrapped with

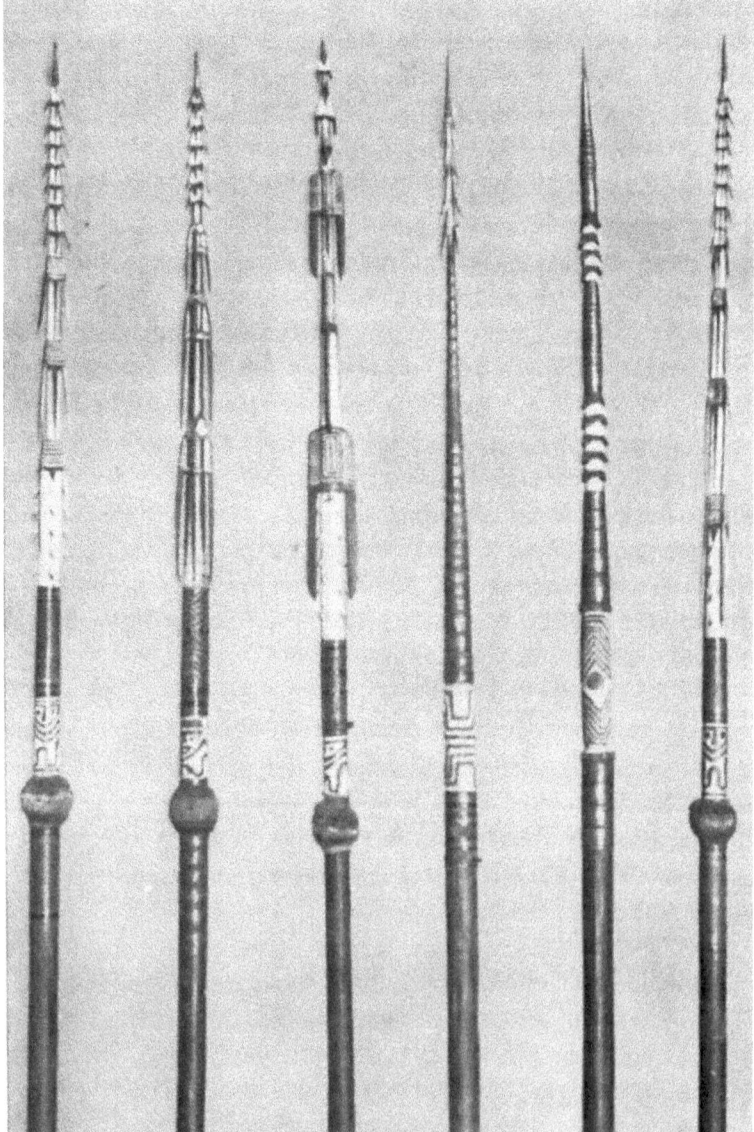

Fig. 82 Spears from the Solomon Islands

alternating red and pale-brown strips of rattan. On northern Bougainville at various times I obtained clubs differing from the previously described form insofar as the upper end was provided with a spear-shaped, barbed process, so that this weapon could be used both for slashing and for stabbing. Some clubs are provided with a carefully carved relief, the background grooves of which are filled with powdered lime. Now and then these clubs are seen in the hands of chiefs, and they are highly treasured. Some of these clubs have received a fine polish from years of handling; and they are carried by their owners as a form of status or display weapon, although there is no doubt that they also serve a very practical purpose as well.

The islanders conjure up great skill in the manufacture of their canoes. Floats consisting of four or five tree trunks lashed together serve for smaller trips and fishing on the reef, as well as simple boats with outriggers. The latter are made from a single tree trunk, taper at both ends and, according to their length, have two or three side outriggers to which floats are attached. On the island of Nissan these single trunks are especially narrow so that the hollowed-out section is just sufficient to put one leg in front of the other. These Nissan boats often have outriggers and floats on both sides. Larger examples of these vessels as a rule have a platform on the outriggers, consisting of staves lashed together. On this is placed, from time to time, a four-sided basket-like container for holding fish and other sea creatures. Less care is used on these vessels; some are completely undecorated, others have black and red geometrical figures on the prow and stern post, others have a bird or the grotesque human figure that we often encounter in the ornamentation there. On the Carteret Islands a triangular mat sail is used in sea voyaging. This is not an innovation but was mentioned by Carteret in 1767 as a characteristic of the islanders. Today light cotton sails, cut and styled after the European pattern, are being introduced gradually on all the islands.

The greatest care is used in the construction of the big canoes, which are made from planks laid alongside one another. Individual planks are first hewn by axe from a fallen tree trunk, and smoothed as carefully as possible. To make the not very hard wood more resistant to water, the edges are slightly charcoaled over a fire. Two long planks joined together form the bottom of the boat, the seam forming the keel line. The side planks are joined edgewise to the bottom boards; three to four rows of planks, more rarely five, suffice for constructing the sides. Bow and stern posts are produced as long prows running steeply upwards, each from two narrow planks. These prows are carefully decorated in relief and painted so that the decoration takes up both sides of the prow and projects up to 1 to 2 metres along the upper plank of the vessel. This decoration either takes the form of a broad multicurved band, or consists of a combination of the grotesque human figures so characteristic of the northern Solomons. The painting is almost always in red and black on a white background. From the tip of the prow right to the waterline, both bow and stern posts are decorated by a 40 centimetre fringe, *kehakehala*, consisting of dried strips of the leaf of a species of fan palm dyed red. The seams of the boat are made watertight by smearing with pulped *Parinarium* kernels. Inside, wooden frames give the boat greater sturdiness and resistance. These frames, *mapou*, are formed in such a way that they fit the internal shape of the boat precisely, and closely fit the sides of the boat, to which they are fastened. Thwarts run from gunwale to gunwale, and are indented at the ends so that the edges of the planks are inset into the groove. In this way they act as reinforcement for the entire body of the boat, by preventing the sides from bulging outwards or inwards. Although these boats have no outriggers, it is astonishing how skilfully the crew balances the pitching craft, even in the highest seas. According to its size, such a vessel can carry from ten to forty people. Chiefs' boats have a platform in the middle, on which the owner stands upright as a sign of his rank.

The boats are propelled by paddles. The paddle, *hose*, with a 1- to 1.5-metre shaft, has a wide, lance-like blade tapering to a point, and is often ornamented with the customary decoration in relief and painted red and black. In the small canoes one paddler sits behind the other; in the large vessels the paddlers sit in pairs on the thwarts, often twenty paddlers to a side. It is therefore possible to propel the light vessels with great speed; in a high sea the slender boats literally fly over the waves, so that sometimes over a third of the body of the long canoe is floating completely freely in the air. The crew fire one another up with calls and songs, so that occasionally there may be up to sixty paddle strokes a minute. Obviously such a tempo cannot be maintained for long; as a rule there are twenty powerful strokes per minute, and this still very rapid tempo can be maintained without exertion by the islanders for a long time. The women are practiced paddlers as well, and not infrequently a large canoe paddled by women is seen racing against the men.

Fishing is keenly undertaken on all the islands. Of course, on the larger islands it is only the coastal-dwellers who go fishing; the inland people get their requirements by trading with the coastal-dwellers, and pay quite high prices. Therefore fishing is a profitable business for the coastal group.

Among their fishing equipment are long submersible nets up to 300 metres long and 2 metres wide. These big nets are the common property of a family or a village. Besides these, individual islanders own smaller throw-nets, up to 10 metres long and 0.5 metres deep, which

Plate 33
Buka women

are skilfully thrown from the hand over small schools of fish in shallow water. Also, they use a net of varying size stretched over a knee-shaped wooden frame. The larger of these, often 3 to 4 metres long, are used in such a way that a number of fishermen surround the fish in shallow water, with net adjoining net. The circle is gradually drawn tighter and fishermen with small hand-nets catch the enclosed fish with little effort. On the southern half of Bougainville they erect high pole scaffolds in shallow water and attach a four-sided net between the poles, often stretched by two bamboo canes bound in the form of a cross. This net is sunk into the water by means of ropes from the scaffold; the fishermen sitting on the scaffold watch for fish swimming over the net, and catch them by quickly raising the net out of the water.

Fishing is also carried out by means of a kite on Bougainville and Buka. The kite is made of light dried palm leaves; the light cord to which it is attached is bound fast to the canoe. Another cord, from the lower end of which the lure and catching apparatus hang, extends from the kite to the surface of the water. The canoe is slowly paddled into the wind, and, when a fish strikes, the kite sinks as a result of the resistance, and the fisherman recovers his catch.

On the open sea bonito and other large deep sea fish are caught by means of hooks. For this they use the large canoes which can be propelled rapidly in any chosen direction by many paddlers. A long angling rod of bamboo is fastened on both right and left, pointing steeply upwards, and the fishhooks hang from the 30-metre-long line. These hooks are made from a piece of *Tridacna* shell as long as your finger, about 0.5 centimetres thick with a long oval cross-section. A notch is cut at one end to secure the fishing line more firmly; a 4-centimetre-long, curved, very sharp hook made from turtle shell is attached to the other end. The fishermen's skill is to propel the canoe so rapidly that the hooks travel on the surface of the water. The fish is attracted by the light colour of the hook, follows it and swallows the bait, thereby capturing itself. Modern steel fishhooks have not yet been able to displace these original fishhooks of the natives.

On the reef, fish are caught by means of multi-pronged spears and with arrows. In addition, the inhabitants of Buka and northern Bougainville fish with skilfully made fish-traps. The traps, *iwou*, are made from the ribs of a species of palm. They are about 1.5 metres tall and conical in shape; the broad lower opening is up to 1 metre in diameter. The closely aligned leaf ribs are fastened firmly together at crisscross intervals of 10 centimetres. To use it, they push a small ring of tough wood or rattan, about 20 centimetres in diameter, into the upper end. On the upper side of the ring is a thin handgrip, while the ring itself is for stretching the fish-trap. The fisherman holds the handle and the upper end of the trap in one hand, and when he spots a fish he puts the open lower end quickly over his prey. The Solomon Islanders know from experience to avoid the not infrequently poisonous species of fish; however, wounds from disturbing poisonous fish are not uncommon, especially during night fishing, often leading to a swift death.

Hunting too is vigorously pursued, especially on Bougainville; the principal wild animal is the pig, but wild dogs, or dogs that have run wild, all species of *Pteropus*, and the various species of cuscus, as well as birds, are diligently hunted and killed by spears or arrows.

VII The Eastern Islands (Nuguria, Tauu and Nukumanu)

East of the large Melanesian islands extends a long chain of small islands, mostly raised coral reefs or atolls, belonging geographically to Melanesia, but occupying a quite special position ethnographically.

Three of these small atolls, Nuguria, Tauu and Nukumanu, have been annexed by the German protectorate. A fourth group, Liueniua or Ongtong Java, by far the most significant, was German for a time but then by treaty passed into English hands.

Although the three German groups are of no great interest commercially and probably never will be, ethnographically they are of no small importance because in spite of being in a Melanesian neighbourhood, they are inhabited by Polynesians.

In volumes X and XI of the *Internationales Archiv für Ethnographie* I have reported extensively on these islands. Later, in the *Abhandlungen der Kaiserl. Leop.-Carol. Deutschen Akademie der Naturforscher*, Dr Thilenius, based to some extent on my earlier work, examined the entire island chain and discussed the origin of its inhabitants in greater detail.

Nuguria (Abgarris or Fead Islands) consists of two atolls divided by a deep arm of the sea. The southern one is the real Nuguria while the northern is called Malum. Both atolls stretch more than about 25 nautical miles along a main northwest - south-east axis. The maximum breadth of the atoll is about 6 nautical miles. The islands on the coral reef, of which the main island, Nuguria, is by far the largest, together encompass about 1,000 hectares. The group lies fairly distant from the larger islands – about 120 nautical miles from New Ireland and about 100 nautical miles from the northern end of the Solomon Islands. According to the map the position of the main island is about 154°50'E longitude, and 3°30'S latitude. The islands are provided with coconut palms and the firm E.E. Forsayth is carrying out a regular plantation business here. The company has planted out entire islands with coconut palms and can expect a significant income in a few years' time.

For years the population has been in the process of dying out. The current number is about fifteen. In 1902 alone, sixteen died, particularly as a result of influenza. The natives' physical resistance seems to be very low, and it will not be many more years before none of the present population exists. In 1885 when I first visited this small group I estimated the population to be at least 160 people.

Tauu, pronounced Tau'u'u (Mortlock or Marqueen Islands; Dr Thilenius names it incorrectly as Taguu), is likewise an atoll structure. It lies at approximately 157°E longitude and 4°50'S latitude, and the total land area of the islands is no greater than 200 hectares. The distance from Nuguria is about 150 nautical miles. The nearest point in the Solomon Islands, Cape le Cras, is about 120 nautical miles away. The island, like Nuguria, was taken over by a European planter, who is exploiting the stands of coconut and is bringing the previously unplanted areas into cultivation.

The population is in rapid decline and currently consists of about twenty people. In 1885 there were about fifty. Had the European owner of the island not looked after the small population, they might have already disappeared from the scene.

The Nukumanu atoll (Tasman Islands) lies at approximately 159°30'E longitude and 4°35'S latitude, about 135 nautical miles east of Tauu and only about 25 nautical miles north of the large atoll of Liueniua (Ongtong Java).

The surface area of all the islands amounts to 250 hectares. Here also the main product is coconut, but not much is exported because in proportion to size the population is fairly significant, actually around 300 according to a census that I took in 1900. That the mortality rate is less high here and the population more resistant is probably because new additions from the quite heavily populated Liueniua from time to time bring about a regeneration, which does not occur on the other islands because of their isolated positions.

All these islands are populated by Polynesians with a perceptible, though small, admixture of Melanesian blood. Now, all Polynesians have, to a

Fig. 83 Girls of Nukumanu (Tasman Islands)

Fig. 84 Boys of Nukumanu (Tasman Islands)

great extent, the habit of preserving old traditions, and as it is recognised that almost without exception these have an historical basis, it is of great interest to gather the remnants of these traditions and draw further conclusions from them. In the case of Nuguria and Nukumanu, the latter of which shows great correspondence with Liueniua, a whole number of such traditions is available. For Tauu the material is most inadequate; the population in their steady decline has apparently lost all interest in earlier times, and from several old songs I was able to determine only that the names Sawaii (one of the Samoan Islands) and Tikopia were familiar to them. One of the *aitu* or godlike revered ancestors is called Lotuma. One of the islands on the reef bears the same name, a name that is without doubt identical to that of the island of Rotuma. The name Tauu also reflects Samoa. We could therefore assume that the present remainder of the population is a remnant of an immigrant tribe from Polynesia, probably from Samoa, which used the islands of Rotuma and Tikopia as intermediate stages. While we have quite extensive information from the other islands about religion, the names of the gods and their functions, the numerous spirits that inhabit reef, sea and air, Tauu lets us down. The current high priest, a Nukumanu native shipwrecked here, is not totally reliable about the old, original beliefs; in his accounts I have often been able to observe that he has not been able to free himself from the impressions of his youth. Nevertheless, I was able to monitor his information sufficiently from the stories from Nukumanu and Liueniua. However, to him too the old legends about immigration and origin have remained unknown, or if he has heard them they have long since disappeared from his memory.

Before I go further, I want to give a brief account of the legends of the various islands.

On Nuguria I was told:

In the beginning two gods came over the ocean in a canoe with three women. They came from Nukuoro and Taraua. The names of the gods were Katiariki and Haraparapa; the three women were called Lopi, Tefuai and Tupulelei. When the canoe reached the reef, Katiariki struck the water with his staff and from the deep arose a bubble that burst on reaching the surface and from it sprang a third god, named Loatu. At the same time a sandbank rose above the ocean surface, beneath the feet of the three gods. Katiariki and Haraparapa were great friends and took Loatu into their band as well. However, when they observed that the island was desolate and undeveloped, Katiariki and Haraparapa decided to make a journey to seek food; Loatu was delegated to guard the island. During the absence of the former two gods, another god appeared, named Tepu. He came from Nukumanu, drove out Loatu and took possession of the island. Meanwhile Katiariki and Haraparapa returned with food, and when they saw that Tepu had taken their possession they were incensed, and in their anger they threw away the food that they had brought with them. This is why a certain edible sea snail and the yam plant occur only on the Malum group and not on the Nuguria group. Katiariki and Haraparapa summoned the evicted Loatu and all settled on Nuguria. Tepu lived on the small hill Mauga (mountain) and right to the present day this is hallowed ground and soil, dedicated exclusively to the gods and their worship. Katiariki and Haraparapa settled to the right and Loatu to the left of the hill, Mauga, and today they are all still regarded as higher beings.

Dr Thilenius quotes the following accounts given to him, according to which eight different immigrations are named:

- Katiariki, Haraparapa and Haurua from Nukuoro (450 nautical miles northward);
- Loatu from Sikaiana (590 nautical miles south-eastwards);
- Tepu, Apua, Akati from Tarawa (1,110 nautical miles eastwards);
- Nuguria, Mahuike from Sikaiana;
- Arapi, Tupulelei (female), Tefuai (female) from Tarawa;
- Ranatau, Lopi (female) from Nukufetau (1,440 nautical miles eastwards);
- Hooti, Aitu, Arei, Atipu from Nukumanu (300 nautical miles south-eastwards).

Finally, at the time of Tepu, Pakewa arrived from the high seas in the form of a fish.

No traditions are known to us from Tauu; however, in the holy house there an *aitu* is revered, bearing the name Loatu, a higher being that we also encounter on Nuguria, and on Nukumanu and Liueniua as well. Today in the *hare aiku* the following ancestors are venerated:

Loatu (from Sawaii?), Teporo and Lutuma, as well as the women Pukena, Tetuai and Hinepua.

In order to understand the legends from Nukumanu, we need to mention those from the neighbouring Ongtong Java. It was recounted to me in Liueniua:

Lolo lived on the sea floor and built up the coral reefs. When these had not yet climbed above the surface of the sea, a canoe came from afar with Siva in it. He saw Lolo's head rising out of the sand and gripped it by the hair which was being moved to and fro by the waves, and pulled. Lolo called to him to pull very hard, and Siva succeeded in pulling him right out into the open. Lolo, however, indicated to Siva to go away again, for his island was not yet ready, and also it was for his own use and not for outsiders; upon which Siva went further on. Lolo now built busily and made the reef so high above the water that waves were unable to wash over it. He then began to cover the rock with grass and plants, then with bushes and undergrowth, and finally with large trees.

During this period another canoe arrived, with four people, three men and a woman. Lolo, with whom two comrades, Keui and Puapua, had previously been associated, did not want the strangers to land, and ordered them to remain on the beach with their canoe. But the new arrivals begged and pleaded, and promised Lolo that they would teach him many new things that would offer great advantages to him and his island, so that finally Lolo relented, and gave them permission to set foot on his island. The men who had come in the canoe were called Ame le Iago, Sapu and Kau, the woman was called Keruahine. Their homeland was Makarama.

The new arrivals kept their promise. Kau taught how to make fire by rubbing two sticks together, which was previously unknown; he also showed how to prepare food with the aid of fire, which was not previously known either. Sapu brought coconuts out of the canoe, and planted them on the island, thus laying the ground for the present stands of coconut palms. Ame le Iago had brought taro plants, and with Keruahine he established the first taro crops. Keruahine introduced tattooing; Lolo stretched out on a mat and was tattooed by her with the still-used patterns. Tattooing was thus universal, and to the present day it is a women's task. Ame le Iago also showed the people how to make mats on a weaving loom for clothing men and women, and consequently weaving is still done by men; only the highest chief and his relatives do not practise weaving.

After a while Lolo chose Keruahine as his wife, but in so doing incensed both his comrades, Keui and Puapua, who also had their eyes on Keruahine, and Puapua was so angry that he left the island group completely and settled on the neighbouring Kikumanu (Nukumanu, Tasman Islands), where today he is still venerated in the *hare aiku*. (On Nukumanu he is called Pau-Pau.) Keui remained on the island but moved to the uninhabited part on the far side of the Keave burial site, where he built a house on the site of Kelahu.

In Keruahine's time Kapu lau lagi came from Nuguria in a canoe. Only after prolonged negotiations was he permitted to land, on condition that he remained living alone.

Lolo and Keruahine's children were Poho uru moro, a daughter who died while a child (*ulu mole mole* is called 'bald head' in Samoan), and a son, Kemagia.

Dr Thilenius's accounts begin first with Loatu, who, according to the accounts given to me, immigrated much later. According to Thilenius, Loatu and Laurumore and the woman Niua came in a boat from far across the high seas. They settled on Liueniua, but after some time had passed Loatu became jealous of Laurumore and caused the latter's hair to fall out. He was thus harmless to women and actually had no offspring. All chiefs originated from Loatu. The people stemmed from Uila, who came from heaven with five wives.

The north-western end of the Ongtong Java group is named Pelau after the main island. The Pelau people, significantly smaller in number, and under an individual headman, maintain a certain independence from the headman on Liueniua. They likewise venerate their legendary ancestors as *aitu*. Tradition there has it that Kepu was the creator of the island of Pelau and its first inhabitant. Later, Apio, Loaku, and Waikahi arrived, and the women Ogäi, Kehä and Keania. These are still venerated as *aitu* today and have their own *hare aiku*.

The significance of these traditions is without doubt that immigrants from the earliest times enjoyed divine veneration by their successors, but that they were men of flesh and blood who, for whatever reason, landed on the tiny islands, whether on journeys to unknown regions, or because they were driven from their homeland by wind and wave, and after long meandering finally found haven. The traditions from time to time give the original homeland precisely; for example, Samoa, the Ellice group, Rotuma, Sikaiana, Tikopia, the Kingsmill Islands, and several islands of the Carolines. Thus we are justified in concluding that the population of all these islands has arisen from an intermingling of the most varied Polynesian tribes. We are still more justified in such a conclusion because even today, from time to time new arrivals appear on the islands, having been driven from their homelands by unfavourable weather conditions. In the previously mentioned works of the author, as in those by Dr Thilenius, there are numerous examples of such journeys.

Furthermore the great similarity of language and the general appearance of the islanders support their belonging to the Polynesians. Again, the specific racial features of the Polynesians, the characteristic blue-grey spot as large as a hand, that is seen on the upper margin of the buttocks (called *ila* in Samoa) of all pure Polynesian infants until about five months old, is found here in most cases. I say in most cases because children are also born without this feature. The absence of the *ila* reveals intermingling with another race. Offspring of Samoan women and white men do not have this feature, and it is also missing in cross-breeding between Polynesians and Melanesians, even when the latter, as, for example, in the New Hebrides or in the southern Solomon Islands, have a high content of Polynesian blood. On Liueniua there are very few exceptions. On Pelau and Nukumanu they are already somewhat more frequent. On Tauu I was able to observe only a single infant, and in this one the blue mark was clearly visible. On Nuguria island in an observation in 1888, there were two out of six infants, in 1893 three out of four, and in 1900 not one out of four without the mark. Absence of the mark, which moreover does not occur without exception in either *Samoa* or Tonga, seems to indicate that an intermingling with another, impure Polynesian group has occurred. In *Samoa* and Tonga this is explainable by mixing with the Viti islanders, partly also with Europeans and members of other races. In Nukumanu, Tauu and Nuguria and on Ongtong Java we must similarly explain the lack of the spot by interracial breeding, and indeed we can, with justification, draw a conclusion on the greater or lesser purity of the race from the regularity or irregularity of occurrence of this mark. Thus the population on Liueniua is the most purely preserved, probably because this island was settled by pure Polynesian migrants. On Nukumanu and Nuguria, especially the latter, interbreeding with a foreign race is the most noticeable, and this can be explained if we consider their proximity to the Melanesian island groups of the Bismarck Archipelago and the Solomon Islands. Liueniua, by virtue of its larger population, was able to resist Melanesian immigration. The smaller groups were less fortunately placed. Thus on all of them we hear of immigration by Melanesians who sometimes moved on again after a long time, or sometimes settled there. The Carteret Islands have only in relatively recent times been settled by Buka people, and the latter encountered a pale people, whom they completely wiped out, and the sole trace of them is in the form of *Tridacna* axe blades found in the ground.

If we look more closely at the islanders, we become convinced that their outward appearance matches the Polynesians. The men are of medium build, although on Nukumanu and especially on Tauu tall men are quite common. On my first visit to Tauu I was quite astonished at the extraordinary height of the old men who received me at that time. On Nuguria a shorter type lives, probably because the principal immigration from the north came from the Caroline Islands, and the Caroline people, in spite of their close relationship with the central Polynesians, did not attain their height.

The skin shade may be regarded as pale brown. Darker and paler shades occur here as in Samoa, partly as a result of occupation, because some natives are more at the mercy of the sun's rays than others. Fishermen and outdoor workers are therefore darker than, for example, the headman who for the most part remains in his hut, and the women, who do not come out into the open often either.

Sometimes the hair is completely straight, sometimes in ringlets or wavy. On Nuguria I have seen hair that one would call almost frizzy, even though the characteristic small curls in the shape of a closely wound corkscrew, so characteristic of Melanesians, do not appear. Beards on the whole are sparse, although quite heavy beards are seen on Liueniua and on Tauu; I do not remember ever having seen a single heavy full beard on Nukumanu, nor on Nuguria.

In older age the women especially are uncommonly fat and portly, and, in this regard, what I had occasion to observe during my first visit to Tauu exceeded everything that I had seen, for example, in *Samoa* and Tonga. Several of the old Tauu women at that time were so stout that they were not able to move round, and had not only to be carefully carried from place to place by their less stout compatriots but also fed as well. In this regard Nuguria takes second place to the other islands probably because of the poor health of the population; however, well-nourished and stout women are of the greatest beauty in the eyes of the islanders.

I have already mentioned that the languages of these islands show a great similarity, and moreover are very closely related to the central Polynesian languages. Samoan is immediately and without great difficulty understood on the islands; however, closer investigation elicits the fact that many words originate from the north, particularly from the Carolines, proving once more that immigration occurred from there as well. Particularly on Nuguria immigration from the north, from all those islands that we recognise under the group name Micronesia, seems to be strongly represented.

Religious ideas are basically the same everywhere. Although the central Polynesian element is predominant, we find, however, only slight traces of the knowledge of a supreme god, which we certainly find elsewhere in Polynesia. The Polynesian gods Tagaloa and Maui seem to have passed into total oblivion. On Nukumanu they know higher spirits that live in Ba e lagi. Ba e lagi is an indefinite concept; it signifies both the residence of the spirit and the spirit itself. Ba e lagi has two children, namely Koko e lagi and Keagiva (the Milky Way). Koko e lagi is the guardian of the place Ba e lagi which the souls of the dead strive to reach, without sufficient protection from Keruahine, driven back under thunder and lightning onto the reef Muli a au. Keagiva sends the rainbow (*umaka*) and, if he is angry, the hurricane (*sisio*). The *makua* (see page 230) have the privilege of calling upon Keagiva, who then sends shooting stars (*kagaloa*) to cause disaster. Kagaloa is undoubtedly identical with the central Polynesian Tagaloa, but has gradually sunk from the idea of a supreme being into a subordinate position.

Spirits also dwell in the moon; the moon spirit, Makaga is clearly seen sitting in the moon twisting cords of coconut fibre.

Magu (on Nuguria *te taro*) lives in the evening star and makes wind and bad weather; Kauha (on Nuguria Atea) has his position in the morning star and makes the sunshine and good weather.

On Tauu they also know a dwelling place above the stars, where a higher spirit lives. His name is Taroa, which could be a distortion of the name Tagaloa.

On Nuguria they know a higher being, named i Luna te lagi, to whom all the living and lifeless are subject, also the ancestral godheads.

They do not make images of any of these higher beings for public veneration.

The whole religious cult is based on veneration of those first colonists, which are all revered as *aitu* or *aiku*. The cult of these ancestral gods is totally to the fore. Special dwellings, *hare aiku*, are erected for them, and many are built in all kinds of shapes.

On Nukumanu we find the god Pau-Pau (Pua-Pua from Liueniua) (fig. 85.) It is a roughly carved wooden figure about 5 metres tall and almost an exact replica of the images of Lolo and Keruahine

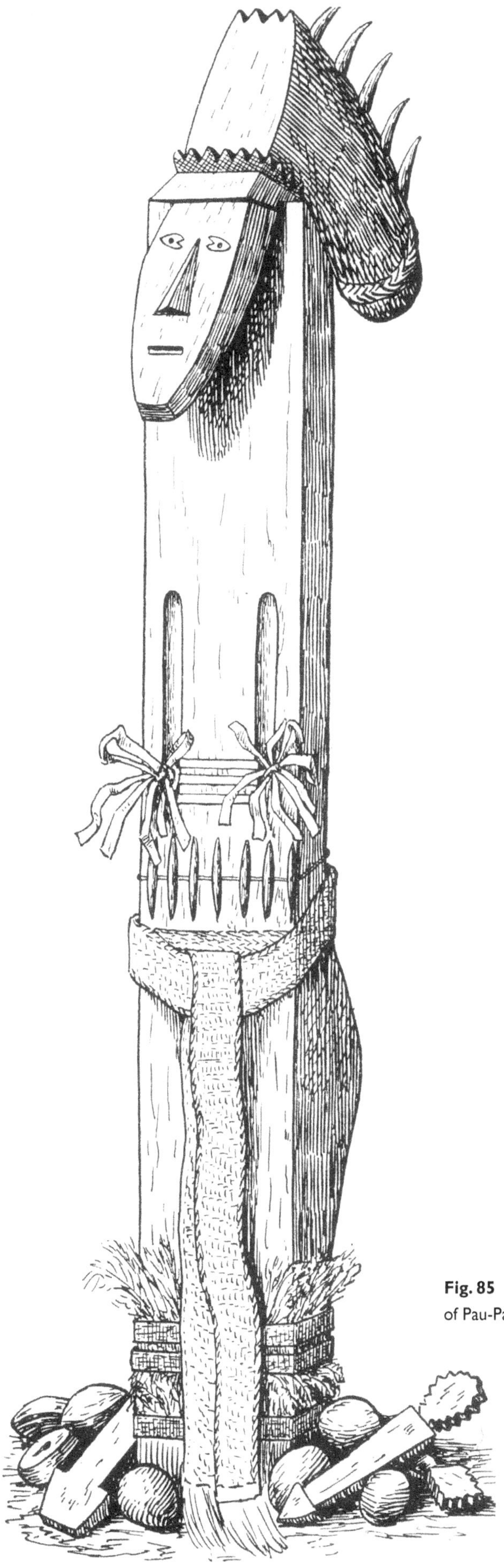

Fig. 85 Ancestral image of Pau-Pau. Nukumanu

set up in the *hare aiku* on Liueniua.

In their shape, the faces of these ancestral images strongly recall the large wooden masks from the Lukunor group (Museum Godeffroy, plate 29, fig. 1), which are called *topánu* there.

On Tauu the ancestors Loatu, Teporo and Hinepua are venerated in a *hare aiku*. The ancestral image of Loatu was a carved spear, of which the lower part of the shaft was broken off and set into a new piece of wood. The spear (fig. 86) could quite probably have been the personal property of the immigrant Loatu. I succeeded in acquiring this old item, and since that time a simple stick has been set up as a memorial to Loatu. Teporo's memorial is a black piece of wood about 4 metres long and about 15 centimetres in diameter at the thickest end, painted red at one end; it appears to be a washed-up fragment of a ship's spar. Hinepua's memorial is a simple rough wooden block without carving.

On Nuguria the memorial to Tepu consists of a rock. The hut erected over it was burned down a few years ago at the time of a punitive expedition, and as far as I know has not been replaced. Tepu's memorial by its nature avoided destruction; but according to comments by the natives there were other wooden memorials which were destroyed by the fire.

Over the years the ancestors have taken on godlike functions, and are venerated and called upon on all occasions. As intermediaries between the *aitu* and the people, a special class of priests or sorcerers developed over time, and enjoys a special reputation. Some of these priests provide the service of a particular *aitu*; others combine in themselves the ability to conjure up all *aitu*. Some are created temporarily, others remain priests their whole life. In the latter the occupation is passed as a rule from father to son. A special jewel of these priests is two large ornaments of turtle shell that hang from the nostrils. A fan and a folded mat also belong among their attributes.

The sorcerers or priests also fulfill the role of healers and doctors. They do not seem to know real medications; all illnesses are banished by murmuring special spells, rubbing with oil, sprinkling with salt water, wrapping with special sacred mats, waving certain green twigs to and fro, and fanning with the priest's fan. The evil spirits that cause all illnesses must then yield to the sorcerer; otherwise the illness is brought about by the anger of some *aitu* or other, and it must then be appeased by sacrifice and supplication until it changes its mind, whereupon recovery results; in the opposite situation death ensues.

As well as the ancestral gods, there is a large series of spirits which we can designate as spirits of nature, bearing the name *tipoa* (Nuguria), or *kipua* (Nukumanu). They inhabit the coral reef, the sea, the air, odd trees or certain rocky outcrops. They tease humans, cause illness and injury, and can be appeased by the mediation of certain priests or sorcerers. Their number is very great, and the designation of individual ones varies from island to island. Some of them have the property of becoming visible to the islanders at night; this always results in an illness or misfortune. Widely varying forms of sacrifice are brought to the *tipoa* or *kipua* just as to the *aitu* or *aiku*, to keep them on favourable terms.

The islanders split into several classes, which are the same everywhere. The chiefs and their male relatives form the highest class. On Liueniua and Nukumanu this class is called *tu'u*; but on Tauu, on the other hand, it is *tui*. (This is a still current Samoan word that is used for the highest chief or king, as, for example, Tui Aana, the highest chief of Aana, Tui Atua, the highest chief of Atua, and so on.) Following this class, in order, is the class of the *makua* or *matua* (in Samoa, *matua* = parents, the elders), with whom the priests rank equal. Then on the lowest rank follow the common people. The *tu'u* are the successors of the legendary ancestors; after death their souls remain on the island, sometimes in special houses, in the neighbourhood of the *aitu*, their ancestors. The souls of the *makua* or *matua* go after death to the legendary home that lies beyond the stars, when they have the necessary escort of the *aiku*. After death, the souls of the common folk go as a rule to a certain place on the coral reef.

The members of the highest class never marry women of their own class, but always from the lowest class. The women of this class must therefore always marry men of lower class. If, after marriage, men of a lower class had illicit intercourse with upper-class women, this would be punished by death in earlier times. It is possible that this custom still exists but is kept secret from fear of the whites. Women of an upper class, who, while not being married, have illegal intercourse with men from a lower class, were punished by female relatives biting off their noses and ears. I have seen such a mutilated person on Nukumanu and another on Liueniua.

Incidentally, before marriage the young women of all classes are quite unfettered in their way of life, but wisely remain within the confines of their own class.

The wives of deceased members of the highest class can never remarry. Widows or divorcees of the other two classes can seek a new husband.

Special marriage customs do not exist. The men of the upper class simply send their retinue to the house of the girl whom they desire and she calmly follows them. In the other two classes it is essential that the suitor brings the father of the girl a gift of mats, turtle shell and turmeric. Acceptance of this gift is tantamount to acceptance of the proposal, and without further ado the girl follows the suitor

Fig. 86 Memorial of Loatu, Tauu

Plate 34 Village scene on Nissan

to his hut. Divorces occur, but not often, and are mostly the result of scenes of jealousy. Suicide by the wife also occurs for the same reason; it is more rare in the husbands.

Birth celebrations and customs are likewise not of great significance. A type of feast is put on for the pregnant woman in the fifth month. The relatives bring food and a public meal is prepared; the sorcerer pronounces his charm over the pregnant woman. As a rule the child's grandmother performs the midwife duties. If the pregnant woman is married to a native of either of the upper classes the birth takes place in the house of the family head of this class. The women of the lowest class give birth in their husband's house.

The newborn baby is cared for by the grandmother; she shapes the infant's head by gentle pressure and then bathes it in the sea. Then the child is wrapped in mats, and for the following two days the grandmother (*kepuga*) holds it by the fire so that it is kept quite warm. Then it is handed over into the mother's care. After about four weeks the relatives bring coconuts and food and there is feasting again.

When the young boys are about ten to twelve years old the septum and wings of the nostrils are bored through, and clothing mats are donned. The ear lobes of girls of the same age are bored through, and at the same time they are dressed in clothing mats and tattooing is gradually carried out, from waist to knees. When this is complete the girls are ready for marriage. Boys are tattooed only after marriage. On Nuguria and Tauu, where tattooing is not customary, dressing in mats is regarded as a sign of readiness.

Funeral customs vary according to the class of the deceased. A dead person from the highest class is wrapped in mats and laid out on mats in the hut. A general wail of mourning begins, and continues uninterrupted for two days and nights. Then the corpse is buried in the burial ground set aside for the highest class, and the wailing continues for several more days, this time in the house where, in the people's opinion, the souls of the members of this class remain. At the same time a great feast is prepared. The priests of the *aitu* have nothing to do here because the spirits of the dead return directly to their ancestors, the *aitu*, and need no intermediaries.

If a *makua* or someone of equal rank dies, the corpse is laid out on a scaffold about 2.5 metres tall and rubbed copiously with oil and turmeric; the relatives then cover the corpse with woven mats. The priest then approaches, beseeches the *aitu*, and ignites dry flower cases of the coconut palm, which he lays under the scaffold. For each individual case he names an ancestor of the deceased. Every male *makua* approaches the corpse and has to recite the responses to a particular song that those round about begin to sing. Two days later, the corpse is brought to the *hare aiku*, where the *aitu* are implored to guide the soul of the deceased to the home above the stars. Then the corpse is fastened to a wooden frame, wrapped in mats, and interred at the burial site of the *makua*. A coral block is erected

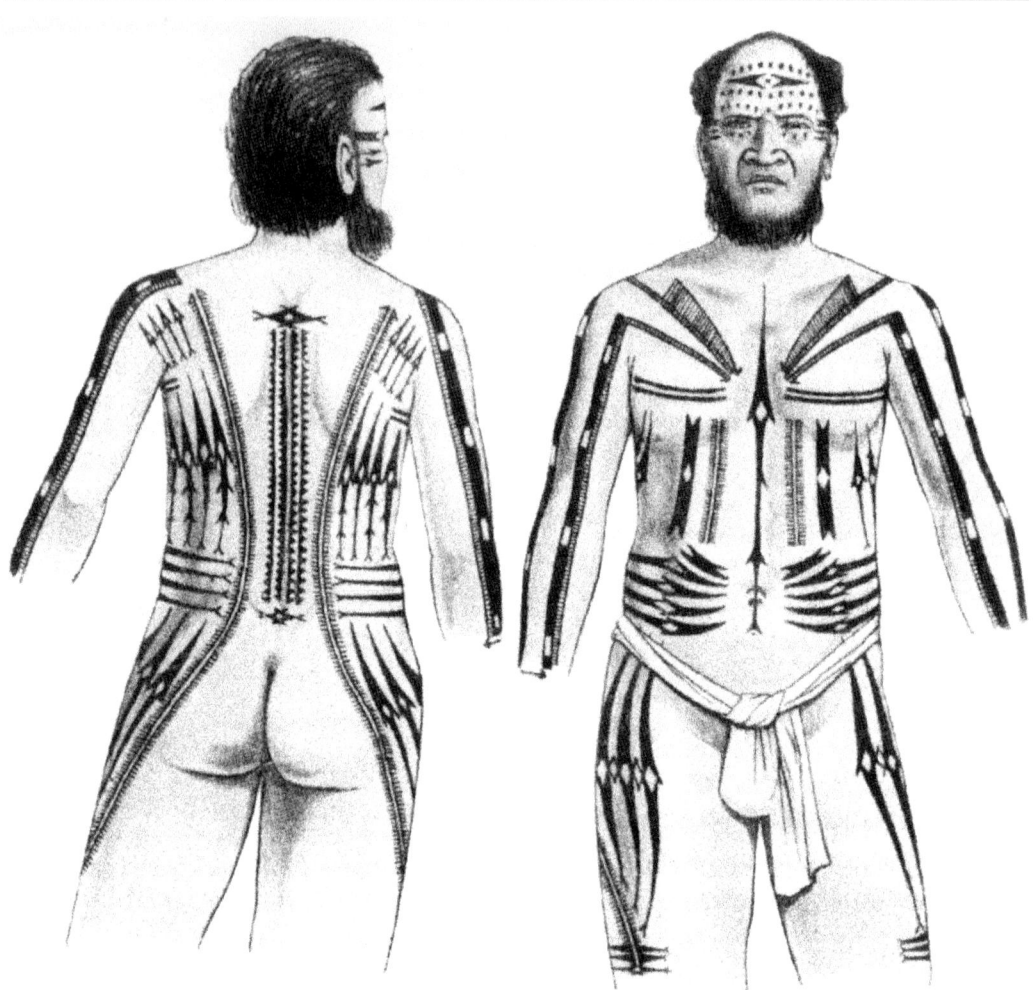

Fig. 87 Tattooing on Nukumanu. (Man, posterior and anterior aspects)

at the head of the grave, anointed with oil and wrapped round with consecrated *Pandanus* leaves. The widows of the *makua* cover their heads with plaited coconut palm leaves and wander around, lost, on the beach or in the forest for days. Those chancing upon them hide at their approach.

The lowest classes, after a short wail of grief by the relatives, are buried without further ceremonial. The same applies for all dead women.

Annually, around March, there is a general feast in honour of the *aitu*, which continues for four to six weeks depending on the availability of a greater or lesser food supply. At these festivities the clothing of boys and girls in mats takes place; the images of the ancestors are carried into the open, crowned, and adorned with mats. Children and adults form a procession with loud singing in honour of the ancestors, and the young folk in particular lead an unfettered and unrestrained life.

Tattooing (*tatau*) of the body is common, especially on Nukumanu. The predominant design matches the Liueniua pattern completely. Both men and women are tattooed, and the procedure for the latter especially is very comprehensive and time-consuming, for almost the entire body is covered with tattooed designs. Dr Thilenius has explained clearly the significance of the individual designs, which represent stylised fish, sea creatures, caterpillars, birds and birds' beaks, nets and replicas of occasionally washed-up decorated parts of canoes, and in no way come from any religious motives. The same tattooing had been fleetingly introduced into Nuguria, but had again passed into oblivion. On Tauu I certainly observed the same tattooing, but it transpired that the wearers of the tattoo had been shipwrecked from Nuguria and Liueniua. The Tauu people tell me that a long time ago tattooing was also customary on their island, and followed a completely different design.

Markings of a Samoan design brought contradictory comments, but I was able to conclude that they were similar, for they were all in agreement that the ancestors, not like on Nukumanu, covered the face, the arms and the chest with designs. The tattooing instruments were also known on Tauu, and I succeeded in acquiring several very old specimens.

The tattooing instruments are little wooden sticks about 15 centimetres long, into one end of which are stuck 2-centimetre-long fine-toothed blades of bone scraped thin, at right angles to the handle.

These blades are 2 to 6 millimetres wide. To use it, the instrument is held firmly in the left hand and, by gentle blows with a little baton held in the right hand, the fine points are driven through the outer

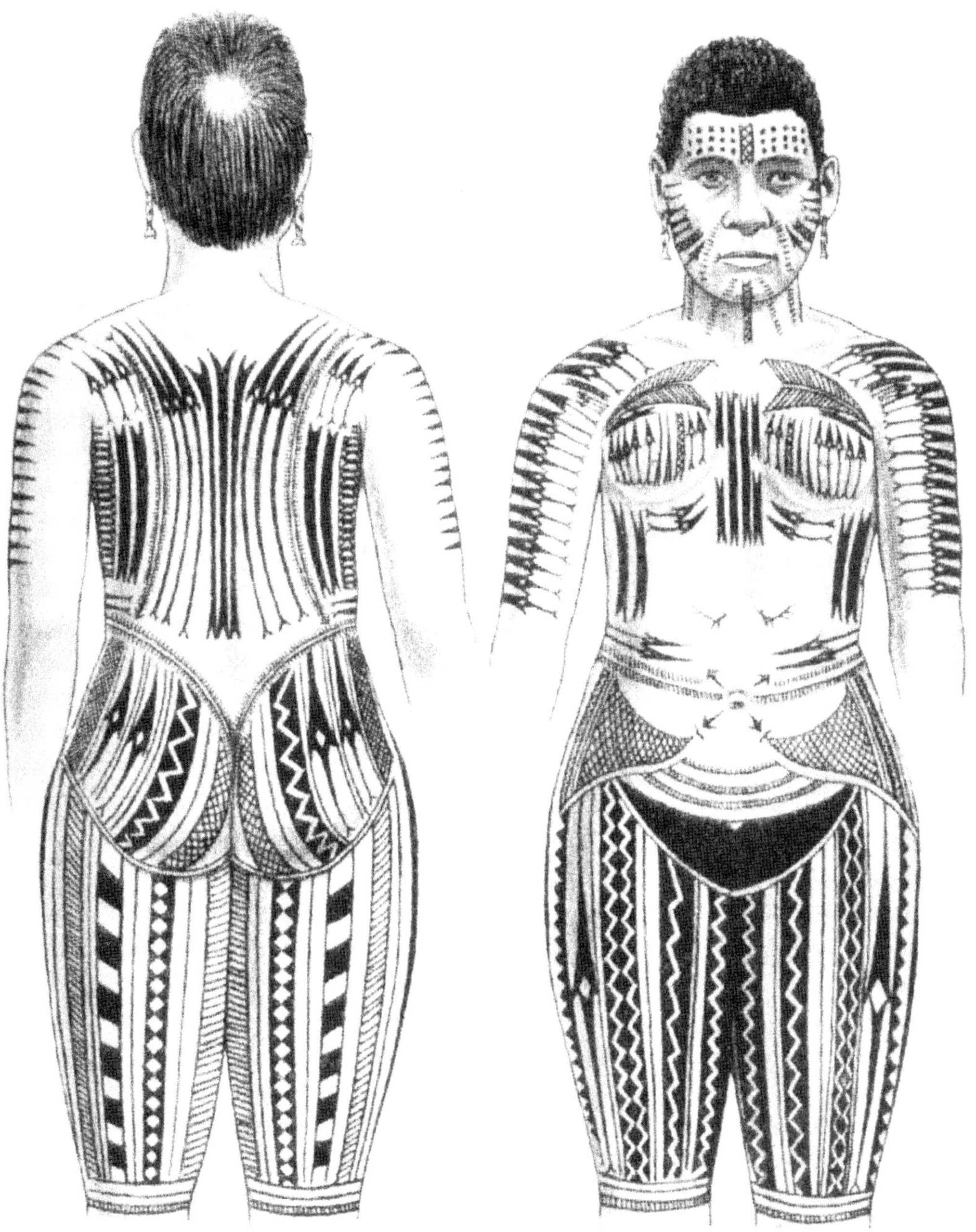

Fig. 88 Tattooing on Nukumanu. (Woman, posterior and anterior aspects)

surface of the skin, after the instrument has been moistened with black dye. Tattooing is exclusively a task of the women, who are recompensed with mats, turmeric, and so on.

The name of the tattooing instrument with which the design, *tatau*, is made, is *matau* on Nukumanu and Liueniua; on Tauu the instrument is designated as *taau*; in *Samoa* it is called *le au*, and on Nukuoro *te au*. The similarity is so striking that a conclusion can well be drawn on the homogeneity of the islanders.

In earlier times the natives were not so peaceable as they are today. One can quite justifiably blame them by and large for falsehood and cunning, even though today out of fear of punishment they suppress these characteristics more than previously. On Tauu in the middle of the previous century, the entire crew of a whaling ship was slain and the vessel destroyed. In the 1880s and 1890s, the Nuguria people killed peaceful traders and concealed the fact for a long time by a show of apparent friendship. Surprise attacks and slayings of ships' crews have taken place on Liueniua too. Even today they are not so particular about the truth, and the concept of yours and mine is not strongly developed. On the whole they are not very industrious and work only as much as is necessary to stay alive. Only the headmen accumulate property, at the expense of their subjects. In general one has to designate the islanders very much as having no wants. With fish and coconuts and the very small and poor-quality species of *Arum* that grow on the island, they satisfy their needs year in and year out. Recently the whites have introduced rice, which has very rapidly earned the general favour of the people.

The headmen rule their people fairly autocratically. On Tauu the headman's family has totally died out. On Nuguria and Nukumanu the ruling chiefs can produce a long family tree of their ancestors, extending as far back as the fabled first settlers, or *aitu*. The headman's office is inherited; however, the post passes first to the brother of the dead headman, if one is available, and only second to the son.

Although supremacy in all things belongs to the chief, he is not the sole possessor of land and soil. Of course, a certain not inconsiderable portion of this belongs in his possession, but by far the largest portion belongs to the *matua* class who have parcelled out the land among themselves. By gift or purchase, land and soil and all growing on it passes into the ownership of another *matua*. The third class of people have no ownership of land; they attach themselves to members of both upper classes, perform all types of service and form the following of the person in question, who thereby gives them a portion of his coconuts and other fruits, and allows them to fish on the reef and in the lagoon.

On the whole, the women lead quite a comfortable life and work outside only occasionally. The headman's wives lead a distinctly lazy life, lie on mats most of the time, allowing themselves to be pampered and waited on. They are always rubbed copiously with oil and turmeric, and spend much time on this toileting. They go only seldom into the open air, in order not to be burned by the sun, for a pale skin colour, which allows the tattoo design to appear sharply and strongly, is regarded as a particular beauty. If they travel from one island to another, a special shelter from the sun's rays is built for them in the canoe. At home they have a lot to say, and the husbands, right up to the highest chief, fear their malicious tongue which now and again leads to marital disputes where the husband exercises his authority with the stick. If a wife pushes the quarrel too strongly, this is sufficient grounds for divorce.

Wars do not occur among the small groups, although on the other hand there are disputes now and again, in which the individual families take part. These disputes can degenerate into brawls in which the women also take part. A few years ago on Nukumanu the then chief received a fatal stab wound on such an occasion.

Fishing forms the main occupation of the islanders. To a far lesser degree they take up farming, if it can be called that.

Everything that lives in the sea or on the reef is hunted; the islanders do not easily let go of anything edible. Single- and multi-pronged spears are common everywhere, and are used on the reef and in shallow water in the lagoon. Besides this they use smaller draw-nets, throw-nets and longer sinking nets, the latter being the common property of the whole population or of individual families. Small, cunningly constructed nets, fastened on cords between two cross-bound sticks, are set up in such a way that in diving the fish pulls the net over itself. These are used here as on the island of Apolima in Samoa. They fish also with hooks, some of which resemble those of central Polynesia, while others resemble hooks from the Micronesian islands. The material is mother-of-pearl, turtle shell and pieces of *Trochus* shell as well as a certain species of *Pinna*. The most interesting is a large hook made of wood, generally known as a shark-hook, although not used to capture this marauding creature but for catching a species of *Ruvettus* that is found outside the reef. This *Ruvettus* is spread far across the South Seas; it is caught here with exactly the same hooks as on the Gilbert and Ellice islands where the fish is called *ika na peke*. In several of the Carolines the fish and the hooks are not unfamiliar, and on Liueniua and Nukumanu we find the hooks in general use. On Tauu I found the hooks but the catching is no longer carried out; on Nuguria the hooks are likewise present, but *Ruvettus* fishing is dying out. The *Ruvettus* lives in deep water outside the reef and never comes into the lagoon. They fish for it only on dark nights and must go out on the high seas in their canoes for this purpose. These *Ruvettus* fishing expeditions are often the reason why canoes and their crews lose the island from sight in sudden squalls, and are shipwrecked in other regions. The *Ruvettus* hook or *auu* is made of hardwood, the longer shank is 20 to 30 centimetres long, the shorter 15 to 25 centimetres. At the upper end of the short shank the hook is fastened by coconut fibre cords at an angle of 45° to 50° in such a way that the tip of the longer shank is only 1 centimetre away. The long shank has a projection at the end for better fastening of the cord. This consists of a number of thin cords wrapped round with another, similar, one so that they form a fat rope 7 to 10 centimetres long which hangs from a 45- to 55-centimetre-long bar. From the end of the stick rises an open loop. Use of this hook is depicted in figure 89: a. is the line with which the hook is sunk; b. is a heavy coral block which pulls the end of the bar under water, so that the end of the stick is horizontal in the water and the attached hook swims freely.

Ruvettus fishing is a very popular sport since it requires not only the utmost skill in sailing and steering but also includes many dangers. It is a sign of maturity when the boy is permitted to join these night-time fishing expeditions.

The fish itself is an universal favourite food and a real delicacy, although the pleasure has strongly purgative effects, which is why in other places it is called *ika na peke*, the purging fish. On the small islands mentioned here it is known by the name *lavenga*.

The raw material for nets and ropes is supplied by the coconut palm in the form of coconut fibres, and a species of hibiscus with fibres that give a strong, long-lasting twine when twisted together. The coconut fibre cords are not twisted but plaited.

When fishing on the reef the people protect the soles of the feet, and more particularly the balls of the feet, by wearing firm sandals, *kaa*, plaited from coconut fibre.

One cannot talk of farming on a small coral island. Everywhere the coconut palms grow luxuriantly and require no special care; the smaller islands are almost exclusively occupied by this useful tree. The larger islands are forested in the interior; among the trees are the type of breadfruit with the big kernel, and on the seaward side of the islands a circlet of *Pandanus* trees, the fruits of which are enjoyed by the islanders as a source of nourishment. In the middle of the islands, protected against onshore winds by a dense stand of trees, the people conduct small-scale agriculture, which is characteristic of these islands. The islanders have dug flat pits out of the upper surface of the coral reef for probably hundreds of years. These are up to 2 metres deep and 100 to 500 square metres in area. In the bottom of the pit over the course of time they have built up a scanty layer of humus by throwing in all kinds of plant material, and here they grow a small species of taro and a considerably robust species of *Alocasia*, the latter cultivated in preference since the yield is more abundant and the cultivation less difficult. Bananas have been introduced only in recent times, but are still regarded as a luxury item.

The canoes of the islanders are hollowed-out tree trunks with an outrigger. Driftwood is frequently, I would almost say usually, used since the trees growing on the island yield a wood too hard and difficult for this purpose. They are very skilled at improving damaged sections of the trunks floating ashore by inlaying pieces of wood.

Years ago, on my first visit to Tauu, I saw big canoes lying in separate huts on the beach. Even at that time they could no longer be used by the diminished population because they were too heavy to be launched into the water, even with the combined strength of all the men. These canoes were up to 14 metres long and 1.5 metres deep, and were built from the keel upwards from planks laid side by side. Both fore and aft they had long steeply rising end pieces, carefully carved, and also at both ends a canopy which depicted roughly carved relief figures. Unfortunately, on this first visit I did not have enough time to take a photograph, but I was able to throw together rapidly the following drawing of one of the end pieces (fig. 90). When I paid a visit to Tauu several years later wind and weather had destroyed the canoes to such an extent that only small fragments remained. The natives said to

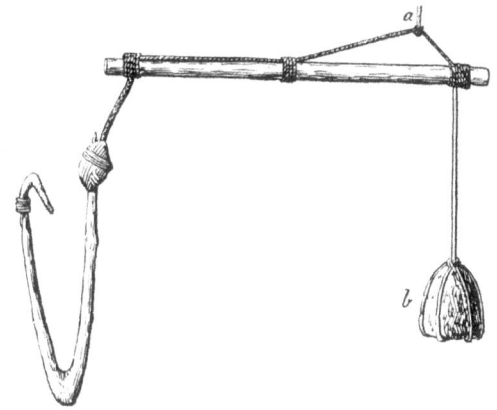

Fig. 89 *Ruvettus* hook from Nukumanu

me that earlier, people had sailed in these vessels far out to sea to catch *lavenga* (*Ruvettus*), and that large triangular mat sails were used. The drawing shows an oval plate at the upper end, hollowed out a little, like a dish; this served as a seat according to the headman.

In our small island groups the population lives on the main island of the atoll; the smaller islands are inhabited only temporarily during fishing expeditions or coconut harvesting; it may be that the headman exiled this one or that one who had made themselves unpopular in the village, to one of the islands.

The villages are laid out according to a particular system; wider streets run between the huts, and where the population is still numerous, as, for example, on Nukumanu, they take care that the streets are always swept clean and strewn with sand. On Nuguria, and especially on Tauu, this is not the case, because of the reduced population, and the latter island shows a sad decline.

The huts are constructed universally according to the same plan, about 6 to 8 metres long and 3 to 4 metres wide. The side walls are 1.5 to 2 metres tall; the roof rests on two to three posts about 6 metres tall, and projects about 1.5 metres beyond the vertical walls at the gable ends. Roof and side walls are, as a rule, covered with woven coconut palm leaves. The longer-lasting *Pandanus* are also used as roof cladding. The floor is pounded earth covered with coral sand. A shallow circular pit serves as a hearth. Implements hang on the side walls; on one end wall an open cupboard is often attached, mainly for storing coconuts. For sleeping or sitting down, they spread out woven *Pandanus* mats on the floor. The dwelling house, *hare* or *hale*, is far less carefully constructed than the houses of the ancestors, the *hare aiku* or *hale aiku* (or *aitu*). These are

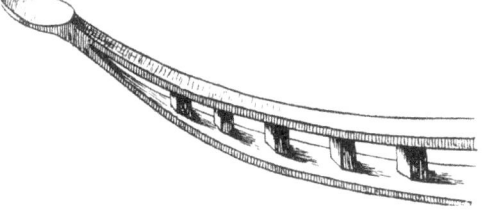

Fig. 90 Canoe prow from Tauu

Fig. 91 Wooden vessels. Eastern islands

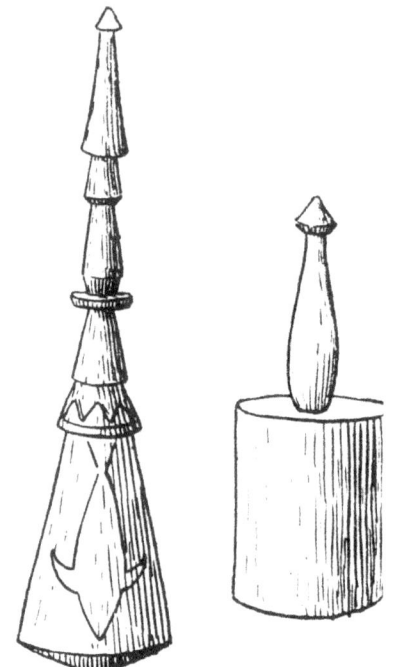

Fig. 92 Pounders. Eastern islands

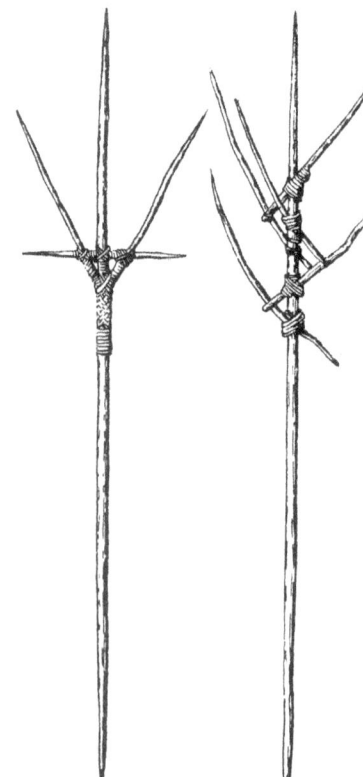

Fig. 93 Multi-pronged spears from Nukumanu

considerably larger, and the roof construction in particular is carried out with much care. The floor of the ancestor house or temple is always covered with coconut mats and is only walked upon by the priests, the other people sit along the walls.

The open space by the *hare aiku* is called *marae* (Samoan: *malae*); around which are the open huts that are regarded as dwellings of the spirits of the dead chiefs. Not far from the *hare aitu* is the sorcerer's dwelling, likewise a more carefully constructed house than the ordinary dwellings.

Every village has several wells; that is, deep holes dug into the coral base, where water gathers, especially when it rains. At the time of prolonged drought the water available, for the most part sea water seepage, is very brackish and undrinkable to Europeans; the natives, however, seem to relish it.

Above all, it is characteristic of these islanders that they are also able to quench their thirst with salt water without experiencing any after effects. This is a circumstance that must be considered when we hear of week-long wanderings of those adrift from their island. Europeans would succumb after a few days because of a lack of drinking water.

Not far from the village is a common burial ground. The individual graves are marked by headstones, and are always kept clean and tidy. Very often villagers are seen here, pulling up weeds, sprinkling a grave with fresh white coral sand, or garlanding the upright headstones or sprinkling them with oil.

Since the population of these islands consists of a mixture of many surrounding, mainly Polynesian groups, most of the ethnographic items bear a relationship with items from their homeland.

Domestic utensils are sparse. But everywhere we find one-piece carved wooden seats, *aluna* or *nahoa*, wooden bowls, *kumate*, *haufa* or *umette* (fig. 91), and coconut bowls plaited round with a network of fibrous cord, for storing oil or drinking water.

Wooden pounders, *kuhi* or *tuki* (fig. 92), of various shapes for pounding different foodstuffs, and coconut scrapers, *tutuai*, are found in all the huts. Coconut scrapers from Tauu are prepared particularly carefully; on the other islands they consist of a simple board or stick to which a shell scraper is attached. Baskets, both of coconut palms leaves and strips of *Pandanus* leaves, serve widely varying purposes.

As well as these household utensils, variously shaped scrapers and knives are found in the huts, some made of turtle shell, some of turtle bones, and also bone needles for sewing mat sails, but year by year they become more rare, and are in places already no longer in use, replaced by European items.

It is even more so with old weapons and implements. On Nuguria the principal weapon was a club about a metre long, made of mangrove wood; we find it on the other islands as well. Long smooth spears were also present, but seldom used. On Nukumanu we find spears used that in their multi-pronged shape resemble the lances of the Gilbert Islands; these occur also on Liueniua from where they were probably introduced (fig. 93).

As a close-quarters weapon in hand-to-hand combat they use a club-shaped piece of whalebone, called *paramoa* on Nukumanu (fig. 94). I have not seen this on Tauu and Nuguria. Axes and other instruments have totally disappeared today. At most they still have the blades. I have a few blades from Tauu and Nuguria (still in the original binding), which I was able to obtain years ago as last remnants. The raw material is mostly *Tridacna* shell; on Tauu there occurs a blade made from the *Terebra* snail shell as well. All blades are attached in the same way, namely to a knee-shaped piece of wood by means of firm wrapping with fibre. The *Tridacna* blades from Tauu stand out through their extraordinary length and their careful manufacture (see the illustration in *Internationales Archiv für Ethnographie*, vol. X, page 144).

I also obtained a very old wooden club from Tauu. The striking end is broad, thicker in the middle, tapering towards both edges; the handgrip carries an incised pommel at the upper end. From the same island I have several quadrangular blades with sharp cutting edges, and with two circular holes at the opposite end; the raw material is turtle bone. Fastening is achieved by fibrous cords; the edge of the blade is inset into the handgrip. The object very much resembles the spatula from Matty, used in food preparation (see fig. 73).

On Nuguria in earlier times a shovel was used, especially for preparing taro beds, and was not found on the other islands. The implement, called *kapa*, is no longer used (fig. 95).

On Nukumanu a characteristic weapon is still found, called *gipugipu*. It is a throwing weapon, made from a heavy piece of mangrove wood. Short conical sharp knobs are carved in, towards both ends of the actual body of the weapon which is about twice as big as a fist. When thrown by a powerful arm the instument would be capable of inflicting serious injury.

Ornaments are found only to a slight degree. In ordinary life they are not used as a rule; they appear at festivities, but one cannot say that they are an everyday item. Massaging with oil which is dyed intensively yellow by grated turmeric, is the main decoration. Its use is so extensive at celebrations that the people are literally dripping oil; the women especially seem to prefer such massaging, for it gives the skin a paler shade, a sign of beauty in the eyes of the men. The sorcerers or priests of the ancestors wear a characteristic turtle-shell ornament in both wings of the nose, consisting of two discs which hang down over the mouth. The priests never remove this item of jewellery; the old men wear it only at the annually recurring festivities.

Ear ornaments in the form of rings pushed into one another, and fish-like turtle-shell or marine-shell discs are not infrequent; plaited armbands are seen here and there, but all these items are now superseded by introduced glass beads.

An early, very special ornament on Nukumanu, probably introduced from Liueniua, was a series of worked whale teeth. These did not occur on Tauu and Nuguria.

At festivities women wear a wide belt to fasten the mat skirt, *moso* on Nuguria, *moro* on Nukumanu. This belt consists of about ten rows of about 65-centimetre-long cords of beads. The individual beads are made out of coconut shells about 5 millimetres in diameter and 1.5 to 3 millimetres thick; the outer rim is polished. The black coconut beads are interrupted at intervals from about 8 to 10 centimetres by one or two small white shell discs. This belt strongly resembles similar items from several of the Carolines. On Tauu this belt consists of two to four adjacent rows of white snail shells, each as large as a small hazel nut; these snail shells are firmly sewn onto a strong binding of plaited fibre.

On Nukumanu money cords are still made, called *kua*, common earlier also on Tauu and Nuguria. They consist of small discs of coconut shell, 7 to

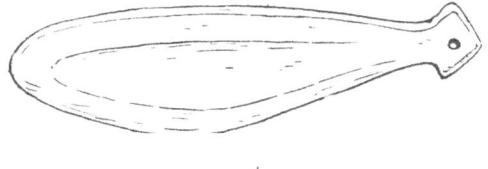

Fig. 94 Whalebone club from Nukumanu

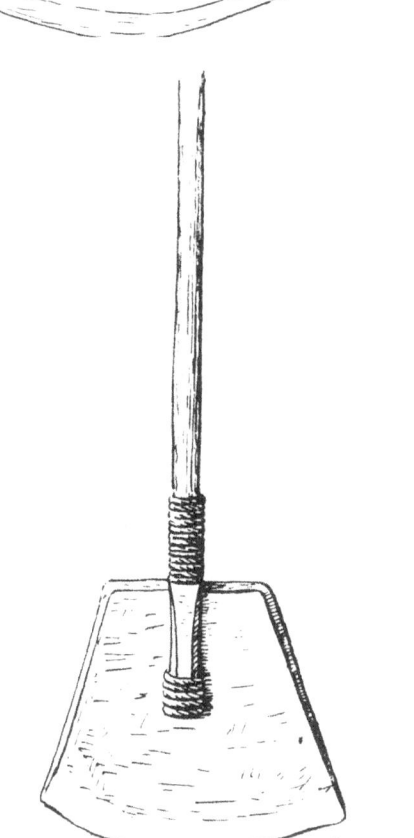

Fig. 95 Shovel from Nuguria

8 millimetres in diameter, the centre of which is bored out with the drill, *fao*. These discs are strung onto cords about 1 metre long, and five of these cords comprise a whole item. The manufacture is the women's task. We find the same cords again on the Gilbert Islands.

Clothing consists of woven mats, made from the fibres of a species of *Hibiscus*. Besides this, on Nuguria a finer weave is produced from banana fibres. The women's mat, *marau* or *mehau*, is about 175 centimetres long and 80 centimetres wide, and after manufacture it is dyed dark brown with a brown dye and oil. The men's mat is only about 22 centimetres wide, folded together and wrapped round the waist with one end passing between the legs and fastened behind.

Preparation of these mats forms a characteristic industry, which I will consider somewhat more closely because a weaving apparatus is used, enabling us to draw a conclusion on the origin of the population of these islands.

The weaving looms from Nuguria, Tauu and Nukumanu show no difference from the Liueniua and Sikaiana apparatus of which I hold examples. According to a description that I have, the loom on Tikopia ought to correspond with those from the previously mentioned islands. In his album (page 160), Edge Partington depicts a Santa Cruz weaving loom that is not significantly different. To my knowledge, the island is the southernmost point for finding a weaving loom. North of our islands we come across the apparatus again in the same form on Kapingamarangi or Pikiram. Further north, we find it on almost all of the Carolines, on Nukuor, Lukunor, Kuschaie, Ponape (now totally unused), Ruk, and further remnants on Yap, Sonsol and Mafia. When we see the apparatus that the weaving shepherdess from Milam in the Himalayan region (depicted in K. Boeck, *Indische Gletscherfahrten*, and reproduced in Lampert's *Völker der Erde*, vol. I, page 221) has spread out before her, then one might be tempted to regard it as an implement from Nukumanu that has ended up in the Himalayas, so closely do the individual parts match, and also the manner of using the apparatus. On Celebes Island we find it again, albeit improved upon, and in its main features it revisits not only the African continent and Madagascar, but also America. Ratzel, in his *Völkerkunde*, volume I, page 668, depicts a loom of the Bakuba (Congo region) as an example that 'where the older African cultural possession points outside, it points eastwards', and with regard to the loom he adds: 'The loom is significantly the same on both sides of the Indian Ocean.'

With regard to America, I refer to a diagram in the *Annual Report of Field Columb. Museum*, Chicago 1897-98. In plate 18 the typical home of a Hopi Indian family is depicted, and on the wall to the right we see a loom which, although not clearly visible, appears to have the main features of the Polynesian loom.

The old Egyptian pictures of the loom correspond reasonably with the apparatus that is used today on Nuguria and Nukumanu, and on page 248 of E.B. Tylor's *Anthropologie*, based on an Aztec picture, a Mexican weaver is depicted holding her apparatus exactly as they do today on the previously mentioned islands, although from the picture it emerges that the Aztecs did not know about the weaver's shuttle, but pushed the weft-yarn between the lengthwise fibres by means of a little rod.

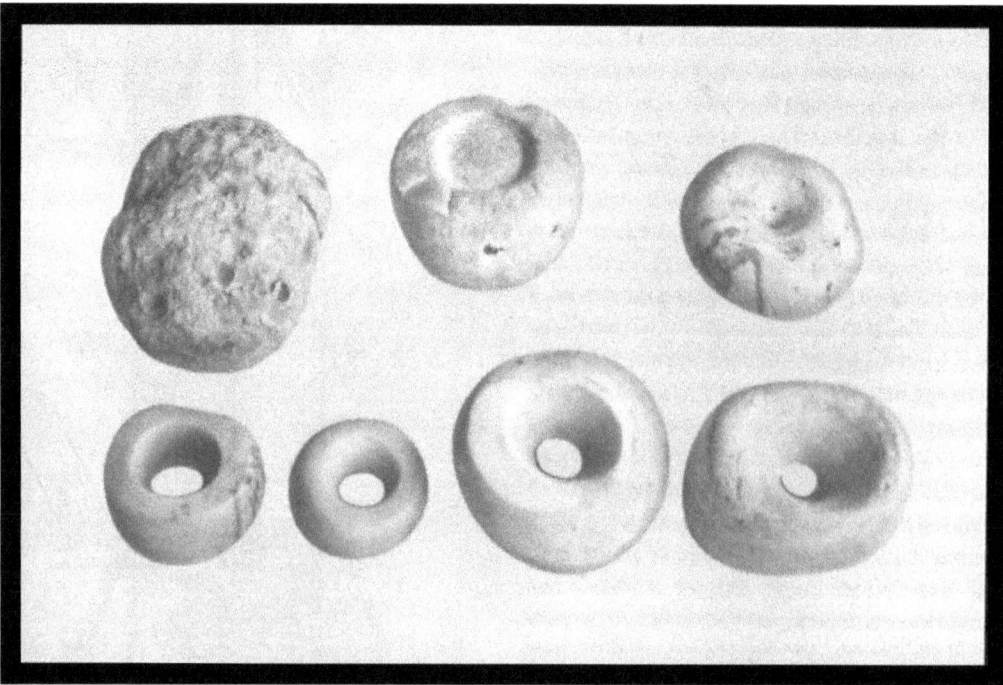

Plate 35 Shell money (*kuamanu*) from the island of Nissan. Various stages of preparation

There can be little doubt that this loom has its homeland in Asia and spread from there to all parts of the world, with the exception of Australia.

Its spread across Oceania extends through the Carolines as far as the island of Kuschaie; we do not find it further eastwards in the Marshall Islands, and there is no evidence that it has ever been there. South of the Marshall group, in the Gilbert Islands, and on the isolated islands of Paanopa and Nauru settled from the Gilberts, it is similarly unknown; and also on the Ellice Islands, *Samoa* and Tonga.

If we go westward from here we likewise do not find the loom in the Viti group inhabited by Melanesians, nor in New Caledonia, and this does not surprise us because the apparatus is a Malayo-Polynesian device, not a Melanesian one. On Santa Cruz where a strong Malayo-Polynesian immigration has made itself felt, the loom reappears, but we do not find it anywhere in the Solomon group. Thus it may be that the primitive apparatus which we encounter on Bougainville, Buka and Nissan, and which Dr Danneil has described in the *Internationales Archiv für Ethnographie*, volume 14, and drawn on plate 19, is not an initial stage of weaving, or to some extent a transition between plaiting and weaving as the author believes, but an atrophied form of the loom. In the Bismarck Archipelago and on the western islands south of the equator, the apparatus is also unknown. Recently, from the island of St Matthias north-west of New Ireland, belts and mats have become familiar; these are undoubtedly woven (see pages 143 and 148).

However, we find in places where the loom and woven material existed earlier, that the apparatus is no longer in existence. On Pelau, Kubary maintains that the art of weaving existed in ancient times. On the small islands of Mafia and Sonsol the art has vanished into oblivion, although remains of the apparatus and descriptions of the individual parts are familiar. It is the same on Yap, and on Ponape they still remember that 'in olden times' the art of weaving was practised. However, in 1901 I could not find an islander who knew the names of the individual parts.

The fact that the art of weaving has been maintained for a long time on the small islands like Nuguria, Tauu and Nukumanu is probably because new disruptive elements which wiped out traditions, did not occur. While it is unquestioned that these islands were populated in part from central Polynesia, to a large extent by involuntary immigration, these migrations were never in a position to replace the predominant north Polynesian element which had emigrated from those islands of Micronesia north of the equator, the Carolines. Although current traditions treat the immigrations from central Polynesia as the more important, this may well be because the central Polynesians retain far more the tradition of their roots than is the case with the Micronesians. Also, it is not improbable that the immigrated central Polynesians, as a consequence of their greater intellectual gift, acquired a dominant position in the social life of the small islands without damaging the traditional industry.

Outside central Polynesia the art of weaving is not known anywhere; and at the time of first discovery we find no mention of it. The Malayo-Polynesian group, which settled in central Polynesia undoubtedly never knew the art of weaving, and we can probably assume that this art was also unknown in the Asiatic homeland at the time of the emigration. Only later people who expanded out of Asia across the east Asiatic island groups, brought the skill with them. A section of these people poured over the Carolines, and from there southwards as a weaker stream, still carrying the loom with them and introducing it into Melanesian regions, where they were sufficiently strong in numbers to maintain their own customs and avoid absorption by the greater numbers of the Melanesian population.

If we look at the fabrics produced from the looms, we observe that the central Polynesian influence intruded in the bestowing of names. On Nuguria, for example, they weave great lengths of material of wider-meshed texture than the weaving used for clothing, and sew several of these widths together to make a protective net against mosquitoes. Here as on Tauu it is called *tainamu*. *Tainamu* is the Samoan designation for the tent-

Fig. 96 Women of the Greenwich Islands

Fig. 97 Weaver at work

shaped device produced from tapa, which is never absent from any house, and is spread out in the evenings to protect the sleepers from mosquitoes. The central Polynesians arriving on the islands did not find the customary material in their new homeland for making the *tainamu*, but found woven mats from which they could make them, and the old term was retained. On Nukumanu we find the designation *tainamu* for a completely different mat. Here a *tainamu* is a narrow, very long, roughly woven mat which is laid on the ancestral image *Pau-Pau* (fig. 85) as a belt, and in which sick people are wrapped amidst all kinds of incantations by the sorcerer. The woven material on Nuguria and Tauu which is used as *tainamu* (mosquito netting) is about three times as long as the clothing mats. If the same name is used on Nukumanu for other mats, it is possible that there they learned to weave long mats, weaving with long chains, from the islands to the west, and that the name given there to the item made by this weaving, was transferred to the style of weaving.

In the summary given on the opposite page, I have listed in table form the names of the parts of the loom on the individual islands, as far as I know them.

The wanderings of the Polynesians from their Asiatic homeland to the east form, on the whole, a still very dim chapter in the history of this people spread so far across the South Seas. Just as we are unable to show the location of their homeland with anything approaching certainty, we cannot indicate with any accuracy the intermediate stops which the wanderers made on their way to the east. If we look at the map of the Pacific Ocean, there are two main routes of migration. The southern route passes via the Sunda Islands, New Guinea, the Bismarck Archipelago, Solomon Islands, New Hebrides, New Caledonia and Fiji; the northern via the Pelau Islands or the Marianas to the Carolines, the Marshall and the Gilbert islands and on from there.

The further we go on the former route from west to east, the more the signs of Polynesian influence accumulate. On the eastern end of New Guinea, in the Bismarck Archipelago, on the Solomon Islands (particularly the southern islands of the group), in the New Hebrides and in Fiji, the Polynesian influence is universally noticeable. It is expressed not only in language but also in the institutions, in the life and customs of the islanders, indeed even in their physical characteristics.

It might, after all, have been possible that a portion of the Polynesians took this route from west to east. They would first have gone along the inhospitable coast of New Guinea, but everywhere they would have found not only a hostile reception from the warlike Papuans, but also a climate that would not have agreed with them because of the prevalent malaria. Both of these factors would have urged them on further, until they finally settled on the island groups to the east of New Guinea, while the majority finally found a permanent home on the islands that are to this day called, in the narrower sense, the central Polynesian islands.

However, I do not believe that this was the route the migrants took. The Polynesian elements that we find today on most of the Melanesian islands are the result of later Polynesian migrations, after they had already firmly established themselves in Polynesia; migrations which, favoured by wind and tide, went mainly from east to west.

These migrations were in part voluntary and conscious expeditions to legendary regions, and Polynesian tradition can tell much about them even today. However, in part, they were involuntary and by chance, when Polynesian seafarers were driven far from their homeland by wind and current, and finally landed on Melanesian islands. This explains why the Melanesian island groups adjacent to the central Polynesian islands, like Fiji, the New Hebrides and the southern Solomon Islands show the most Polynesian influences. These migrations took place since the time of settlement in central Polynesia and extended over a time span of several centuries, since they lasted until recent times; for not a year passes that a Polynesian is not washed ashore on Melanesian islands.

I believe that by the following observation I can demonstrate that the Polynesians came into little if any contact with the Papuans on their migrations from west to east.

It is known that the central Polynesians are a talented folk, very advanced in development. We can assume that the present culture, or more precisely the culture that was found by the European discoverers, was the remnant of an earlier higher culture that had sunk progressively lower during a century of wandering, under countless tribulations and privations and influenced by inferior tribes. The

Table 2: Comparative summary of the names of individual parts of the loom on different islands

(The numbers at the head of the columns refer to the numbers on the diagram)

Island	1 Tensioning	2 Tensioning strap	3	4 Shed rod	5 Heddle stick	6 Heddles stick	7 Sword	8 Shuttle fibres	9 Warp fibres	10 Weft	11 The fabric	12 Awl
Liueniua	ku'u	o	api	purugu	ka'o	u'a	langa	si'i'a	hau	ongo si'i'a	—	—
Nukumanu	to'o	atu	api	poronu	ta'o	u'a	langa	siha	hongo-himaro	hongo siha	mehau	—
Tauu or Marqueen	fa'o	atu	kabi	poronu	ta'o	tounga a maro	lama	sika	songo hau	popó	fa	—
Nuguria	tu'u	katu	kapi	pulene	ta'o	—	papa	hika	kano-mehau	kano hika	hau	—
Nukuoro	setun	atu und	kapi papa	tapa-nulu	toro	—	raune	sika	burata	rano sika	rohau maro	panule
Lukunor or Mortlock	anoy	pa'ap	kabi	ullut	nun	—	apin	asáp	—	*	—	—
Ruk	—	pa'ap	atir	anan	auzuru	—	opop	—	—	—	—	—
Yap	abáb	—	—	—	—	—	aviéw	—	—	—	—	—
Mogemok	tal	ülüt	a viw	tapang	ngung	ngung	aupop	sap	ther	ivach	a ther	—
Sonsol	tau	páp	tibád	tápan	ningir	—	aupoup	kadápi	mur	ifák	—	—
Mafia	yar	bäp	—	—	—	—	kobab	—	—	—	—	—

* *kaleman lap, lizop, palpal, longlong* are various types of mats. On Ponape the name for loom is *tantar* and on Kuschaie *puos*.

intellectual abilities had, however, remained, and so we see with astonishment how Polynesians with careful education quickly reveal themselves to be the equal of the whites. During their wanderings these talented people would undoubtedly have adopted such arrangements as afforded obvious advantages. I want to present two of them here, which the Polynesians must have grasped as advantageous novelties during their wanderings along the coast of New Guinea, in the event that they took this route.

The first is pottery. Along the entire previously described southern route the Polynesians would have encountered people who were expert at pottery and who used the clay vessels for their food preparation. I want to mention also that such a migratory journey originally would probably have consisted predominantly of men, and that during their wanderings they would often have taken native (that is, Papuan) women as wives or slaves. It is known that in New Guinea and on several Melanesian islands the manufacture of pottery is a task of the women. On their wanderings the latter would certainly have continued to practise their skills, the more so since the raw material was found everywhere and the preparation of food in earthen cooking vessels is far quicker than the Polynesian style of cooking with glowing stones. Nevertheless pottery has remained totally foreign to the central Polynesians; nor did the earliest discoverers report anything about this art. We must therefore assume that the central Polynesians did not know pottery in their original homeland, nor did they come into contact with people who were familiar with this craft. It seems beyond doubt that on grounds of expediency the Polynesians would have adopted cooking in earthenware containers had this method

Fig. 98 Loom from Nukumanu. (The numbers refer to Table 2, above)

been shown to them. Their wanderings were not overland but by sea in more or less seaworthy canoes. Now, it is obvious that the cooking of food in pots on extended sea voyages would have afforded significant advantages over the original method with hot stones. Firstly, they would not need to weigh the canoes down by transporting stones, and they would need far smaller quantities of flammable material, two items that would need to be taken into great consideration on long voyages in small canoes. Even today on the New Guinea coast we see small mud fireplaces on the vessels, serving as hearths for the cooking pots; how enlightening would the advantage of such an arrangement have been to the ancient Polynesians, had they had the opportunity of becoming acquainted with it. On these grounds I conclude that they did not take the southern route via New Guinea and the Melanesian islands.

A second point, which would have been adopted as an important innovation by such a talented and also warlike people as the Polynesians, is the use of bows and arrows as weapons. On the journey along the New Guinea coast and further eastwards, the Polynesians would have been dealing almost continually with tribes who used bows and arrows as weapons. Since contact between the travellers and the local population was as a rule hostile, one can regard this as certain. In my opinion the Polynesians would very quickly have grasped the advantage of the bows and arrows over the club and the spear, and adopted the better weapon. However, we can produce no case among the central Polynesians where bow and arrows are used as weapons. They have stuck to the weapons of their original homeland, the spear and the club, because on their wanderings they have not encountered peoples from whom they could have learned the use of a more consummate weapon.[1]

In my opinion, only the northern route remains as a path of migration, via the Carolines, the Marshall and Gilbert islands, and the available facts corroborate this route.

However, I want to premise here that I set the immigration of the Polynesians into the South Seas in two completely separate periods, which I differentiate as the immigration of the original Polynesians whose remnants are the central Polynesians of today, and the far later immigration of a closely related tribe, who expanded through the Carolines, the Marshall and Gilbert islands, and then in later centuries were succeeded by a new invasion with central Polynesian elements.

The migration of the central Polynesians most probably took place much further back in time than one usually believes, although there is no possibility of fixing the time precisely. Percy Smith, in his book *Hawaiki, the Original Home of the Maori*, specifies a genealogical tree of the rulers of Rarotonga that extends back to 450 BC. However, such traditions are to be treated with caution and should not be regarded as absolute historical documents.

We can hardly err if we assume that the migrations did not begin suddenly, like a downpour, and then stop. They probably extended over longer periods; the tribes set out on their migration to the east at a favourable time each year, and gradually reached the place where they finally settled in present-day central Polynesia.

On the other hand, somebody will introduce the direction of the ocean currents and the prevailing wind as evidence that the original Polynesians would not have been able to take this route. I must object to this, for after many years in the South Seas and supported by numerous observations, neither currents nor wind would have been an obstacle. Admittedly the direction of both these factors is predominantly east-west, but there are times of the year when both are not only very weak but even take the opposite direction. On many occasions between the equator and the Carolines I have encountered currents setting from north-west to south-east, and many sea captains have had the same experience, whereas handbooks give an east-west direction. Knowledge of the oceanography of the Pacific Ocean is still far from precise; so much is certain, that the currents in particular do not repeat constantly, from year to year. Where one encountered an easterly flow one year, the following year at the same time one often rode into a strong westerly current. A people who were skilful seafarers, certainly found no difficulty in pushing on from east Asia towards the east, especially when they were driven by boundless expectations of the beauties and bounties that the east seemed to promise.

Of course the journeys scarcely ran precisely along the same route. Storms occurred, adverse currents set and the travellers wandered here and there. Many would have been sacrificed, paying for their daring with their lives, and finding their death in the depths of the ocean.

In spite of all the difficulties, we see that the wanderers finally attained a goal and settled on the islands that they still inhabit today. Even today, through numerous small traits and habits of the central Polynesians, the remnants of characteristics that were adopted during the years of migration are revealed to the observer. Having, for the most part, to rely on the sea, the wanderers became superb fishermen; but when driven by hunger they also learned to value all other sea and reef inhabitants as food as well as the tastier fish; and in Samoa, for example, we still find today that scarcely a creature exists in the sea or on the coral reef, that does not serve wholly or in part as a source of food, no matter how unappetising the outward form might be. The far inferior Melanesians still look today with disgust and shuddering at how the Samoans, for example, consume with great relish reef animals that they themselves would only touch reluctantly, let alone use as food, although they otherwise enjoy their food.

The inconstancy in the character of most Polynesians, their restlessness and the little-developed sense for steady methodical work, is, in my opinion, a consequence of long years of wandering. Accumulating property, sacrificing oneself for one's neighbours, were hardly possible on their journeying. Everyone looked after themselves, provided for the current day; it was uncertain what tomorrow might bring. Whoever

---

1. Peschel in his *Völkerkunde* asserts that in earlier times the Polynesians knew about bows and arrows and that their use as a child's toy is a throwback to that time. He expresses the opinion that bows and arrows must have disappeared wherever hunting no longer served as a means of obtaining food, or where no hunting is available. As one travels east, north and south-east of New Guinea, hunting ceases. To me both these grounds seem untenable. On their journeyings, the Polynesians may possibly have become superficially acquainted with bows and arrows and copied them as playthings, while they never grasped their great advantage as weapons of war. Today the war weapon of New Guinea is and remains the bow and arrow. Their use in hunting is very small. On the great kangaroo hunts in parts of British New Guinea, and in pig-hunting universally, the spear plays a major role but not the arrow, because, above all, the Papuans of New Guinea can scarcely be called a hunting folk but are much more, and primarily an agricultural people who in part harvest the great wild stands of sago, but for the most part obtain the fruits of the field essential to support them, by regular farming. Besides, in New Guinea there are also vast districts that do not know bows and arrows but only

had something, shared it with his friends as far as it would go. If there was a surplus it was indulged to the utmost squandering, even when one could expect the most severe want the following day. We still find all of these characteristics in many central Polynesians.

After the arrival of the central Polynesians at their present home, a second, much later, great stream of migration from the west poured over the equatorial islands, the Carolines, the Gilbert Islands, and so on. These migrants mingled with the earlier arrivals and from this mixture arose the group recognised today as Micronesians. This later migration brought to the east a people who were far more closely related to the present Malayans and Tagals than to the original Polynesians. Even today on many of the Carolines we are astounded to find almost pure Tagalish or Malayan types. Natives of Amboina and natives of the Ruk Islands, for example, are similar to the point that they are very easily mistaken. This migration stretched eastwards but not beyond the Gilbert Islands; to the south, one branch found its way to the Greenwich Islands (Kapingamarangi), Nuguria, Tauu, Nukumanu, Lieniua, Sikaiana, as far as the New Hebrides. This branch brought the loom with it and the art of weaving.

This southern migration also reached the coast of the current New Ireland[2] as well as the outer islands offshore, and the many traces of Micronesian elements that we still find there today can therefore be explained. Of course the wanderers encountered a very large Papuan population on these large islands, on whom they were unable to impose their characteristics to such a great degree as on the small islands; for the most part they lost their characteristic features and attributes in the gradual intermingling, and adopted the characteristics of the people in their new homeland. On the small islands further to the west, Luf, Kaniet, Ninigo, Wuwulu and Aua, they remained closer to the original state. On Wuwulu and Aua we find the group maintained in its purest form, but on the other islands strong Melanesian influences have, over time, become important. That a continued migration southwards was not able to leave significant traces, I ascribe above all to the climate. Further southwards lay New Guinea, New Britain, the Solomon Islands, all areas where malaria is endemic, and since even today a Caroline Islander who goes to this region is quickly laid low by malaria, the same would certainly occur in that distant past.

On their wanderings to the south-east this Polynesian group was held up by the centra or original Polynesians, who had decamped once more, from their barely chosen homeland, and undertaken new migrations. The reason for these new migrations is unknown to us. Possibly they were a consequence of the inbuilt wanderlust of the central Polynesians. However, it is not impossible that natural events of extraordinary extent, especially volcanic eruptions, had caused the migrations. Even today on the Gilbert Islands there are legendary traditions[3] which establish that an initial immigration took place from Samoa, and that these immigrants maintained connections with their home island until a mighty volcanic catastrophe lead to settlement of all the Gilbert Islands. Likewise on Ponape they have traditions of invasions by central Polynesian people who followed a route via the Gilbert Islands and overthrew the old dynasty on Ponape, established new rulers and brought in new customs and institutions.

This latter, intentional emigration of the original Polynesians, sending its waves as far as Ponape, probably coincides with the emigrations that found their goal in New Zealand.

That powerful volcanic eruptions of relatively recent date have taken place in the Samoan Islands, are witnessed by the mighty, bare lava flows on the island of Sawaii, stretching from the centre of the island, as far as the north coast. Many years ago, not without great effort, I traversed this huge lava flow to its source; during a strenuous excursion taking several days. Everywhere one strides over a field of solid lava, which gives the impression that it had only just assumed a solid form. Numerous large and small craters, just as bald and naked as the laval fields, indicated the source of the latter. In many places I could clearly trace, for long stretches, the parallel lava flows of individual craters. The small eruption on the island of Sawaii in 1902 demonstrated that the volcanic activity has still not been extinguished.

Many things previously unclear to us, can in my opinion be explained by the preceding hypothesis. Let us reach back, for example, to the genesis of the mighty stone structures at Matalanim on Ponape.

It is beyond doubt that these came from a highly sophisticated people. Such a people were the first Polynesian settlers. Ponape was one of the first larger oceanic islands that they encountered on their migration, and we can probably assume that a main settlement was founded here. The mighty structures whose extent and magnificence have to be personally witnessed for their full significance to be appreciated, would most likely have served for religious purposes. They served the same function until the introduction of Christianity, and, in secret, are still used for this purpose today. However, the additional purpose that they had in later years, namely as a burial site for the high chiefs of Matalanim, would hardly have been the original one. The island of Ponape offers so much of interest today, that it would probably be rewarding to undertake more detailed investigations there, especially excavations.

Huge stone structures are also found on several clubs and spears, as on New Caledonia. I tend to maintain that the Polynesians, at least in earlier times, were a far more warlike folk than the Papuans have ever been, and would certainly not have suffered from a lack of practice in the use of bow and arrow. Use of the spear requires just as much practice, if not more, than archery, together with an adroitness and rapidity in body movements only acquired through extensive use. On Buka and Bougainville where we find bows and arrows in use today, they are also the principal weapons of warfare. There are few wild animals for hunting, mainly pigs, which are hunted as in New Guinea by means of dogs, which hold the pig at bay; only occasionally does the hunter use an arrow to kill the animal, in most cases he uses a spear. Bows and arrows are certainly used in New Guinea to kill the bird of paradise but this is only incidental.

2. More direct evidence of migration from the Indonesian islands seems to me to stem from several discoveries made recently at the northern end of New Ireland.

Several years ago I was given a stone sphere (fig. 100) with a broken handle, that had been found during clearing of a site at Nusahafen in Kavieng. In 1904, during an excursion on the small island of Nusa opposite, I found a fragment of a worked

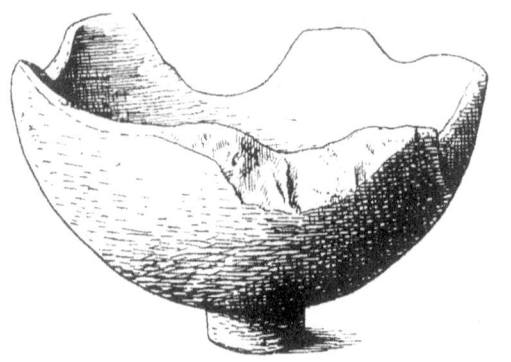
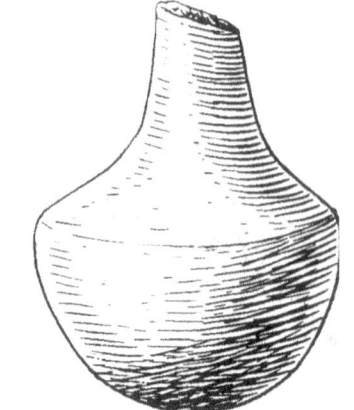
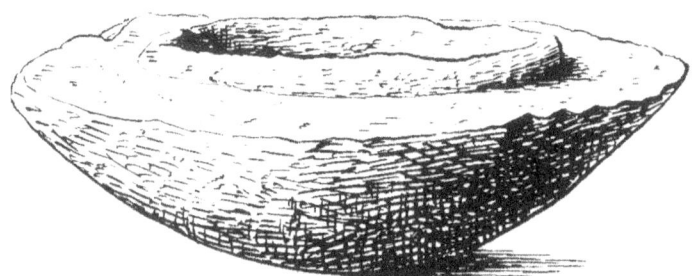

Fig. 99 (Top left) Stone bowl found on Mount Varzin, Gazelle Peninsula (about one-quarter actual size)
Fig. 100 (Top right) Stone pestle, found on Uatom (one-third actual size)
Fig. 101 (Bottom left) Stone bowl found on Nusa (one-third actual size)
Fig. 102 (Bottom right) Stone vessel found on Nusa (about one-eighth actual size)

stone utensil, and I was eventually able to find several further fragments that all matched one another so that the original shape of the object was easily recognizable, namely a stone bowl about 29 centimetres in diameter and 18 centimetres high (fig 99). The shape was roughly hemispherical; more conical at the lower end and ending in a peg that was unfortunately broken off. The bowl-shaped hollow was 6.5 centimetres deep and the stone knob found years before fitted exactly into the hollow, so that I had to assume that both pieces belonged together and were separated only by accident, so that one piece, the bowl, got to the island of Nusa, while the other, the spherical central Polynesian islands, structures about which the existing traditions give no clues. Thus great well-designed streets run through the island of Sawaii, and in parts of Upolu as well; these could be opened up to modern traffic without great difficulty were the vegetation covering to be removed. On Sawaii these structures are particularly large; like the Roman roads of southern Europe they lead over mountain ridges and along steep slopes, deep valleys have been bridged by pouring in huge lava rocks, and on the plains the remains of stone walls are seen, enclosing the sides of the road.

The present Samoans trace these roads back to the time of the Tongan invasion and call them *ala toga*; that is, Tonga road. It is hard to believe that the Tongans built these roads; if road construction had been carried out by subjugated Samoans, one would certainly hear something about it in the traditions, but this is not the case.

That the Tongans made strategic use of this road network at the time of their invasion seems more plausible, and the name may be based on this. However, the mighty structures were already in existence at that time and the history of their establishment lay so far back in time that nobody now knew anything about it. These roads were evidently already present when the previously mentioned great volcanic eruption occurred on Sawaii, as the lava flow has broken through a large section of one such road and destroyed it; at one place it can still be traced right to the edge of the lava flow, where it is suddenly interrupted by the latter but without much difficulty it can be found again on the other side.

However, these are not the only remains of a previous era about which nothing is known today. In 1877 the plantation of Mulifanua on Upolu was extended inland; the forest was felled and the fallen trunks and brushwood burnt. It was discovered that great stretches of ground were covered with layered stone walls. These formed small rectangles of a few square metres, surrounded by a system of roads that were also enclosed by stone walls. Centuries had not enabled the outlines of these structures to be totally destroyed, although only here and there did a few metre-long sections of wall remain in relatively good condition. The expanse of rubble attracted my attention, and I enquired from old Samoans who were acquainted with the legends and traditions, whether anyone perhaps knew anything of the purpose of these structures. However, nobody could give me an explanation. One old man from Manono, a descendant of a *faitaulanga* (heathen priest) did know that the mountain Afolau, not far from the ruins, had, in

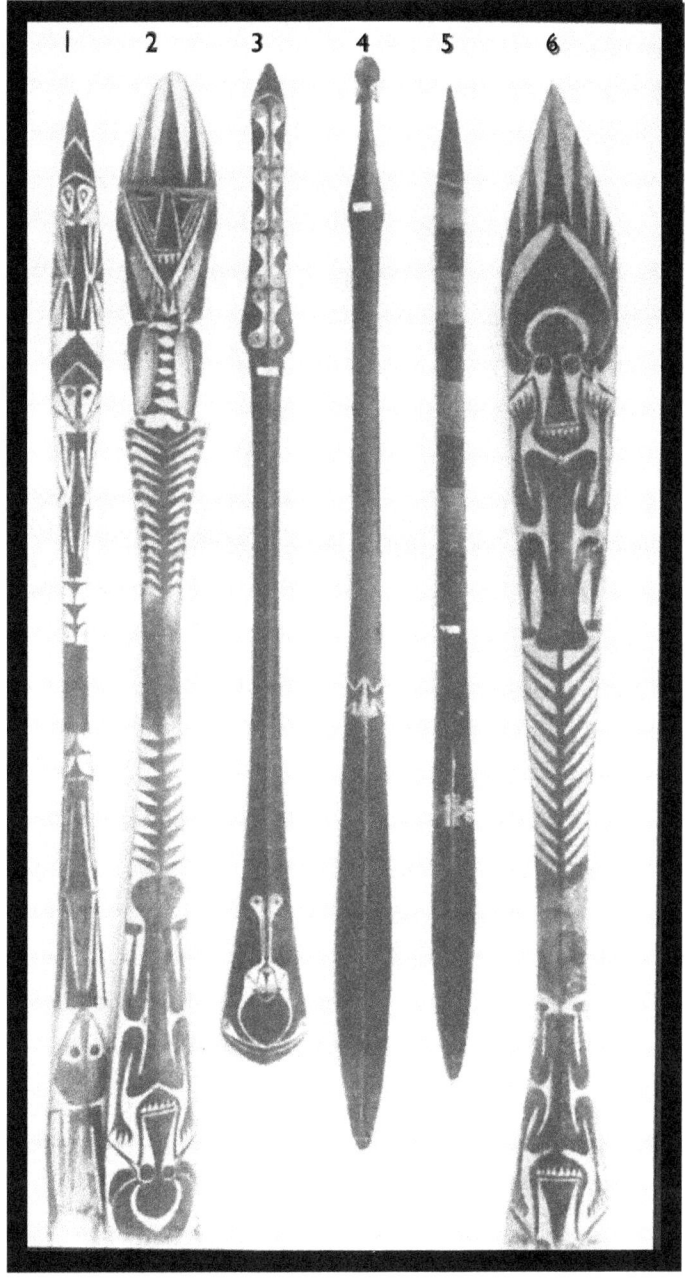

Plate 36 Clubs from Buka and Bougainville

1. to 3. old chief's clubs;
4. to 6. dance clubs

long forgotten times, been the dwelling of a god (probably a special cult). He also alluded to an old stone wall that even today bears the name *pasa* (holy wall), and, running inland from the beach, between the villages of Tifitifi and Satapuala, had gone from one side of the island to the other, but neither he nor other old people who were asked knew anything about this old cultural site. Yet a busy life must have predominated here in times past, as indicated by the numerous stone axes found here by the plantation workers. Unfortunately an extensive investigation was not possible for me. Soon the large field was planted out in cotton and within a short time the luxuriant shrubs shooting upwards made any surveys impossible. Today one might still successfully search there, as the cotton bushes have been gone for a long time and have been replaced by coconut palms which, being planted wide distances apart, allow a better view.

In the whole arrangement of the stone walls, which I regard as the foundations of the old structures, there is an astonishing similarity to the stone buildings at Matalanim on Ponape. On the latter island the basalt columns offered a suitable material for building structures, but in *Samoa* they had to be satisfied with lava blocks of irregular form lying about in great quantities, probably in combination with wooden structures which understandably have long since disappeared, so that today we are confronted with only the very rudimentary remains of the old structures.

It is not my intention to give an extensive presentation of my hypothesis on the migrations of the Polynesians, supported by numerous observations over the years. The preceding was given with the sole intention of clarifying the occurrence of pounder, was carried off to Kavieng opposite. Not long after, from a district of New Ireland somewhat far removed, I was able to obtain two other similar objects which were somewhat different in shape but undoubtedly had served the same purpose. One of these objects was a stone bowl (fig. 101) in the shape of a segment of a sphere without a peg at the lower end; the other was a columnar stone block somewhat tapering downwards, with a bowl made from the same stone block (fig. 102). The natives do not know where these objects came from, and have no use for them. Such items are unknown both in New Guinea and in the Melanesian islands; they were brought in probably from Indonesia, and, as the block depicted in figure 102 weighs over 20 kilograms the canoe that transported it could not have been too small or flimsy. [Figs 99 to 102 are drawn from pieces that are in the *Berlin Museum für Völkerkunde* and are just the same as the specimens described by Herr Parkinson, although the provenances might not be the same throughout. The items in figs 101 and 102 come from Nusa; the bowl depicted in fig. 99 is from the Varzinberg area on the Gazelle Peninsula; and the stone hemisphere, fig. 100, is from the island of Uatom. Editor's note.]

3. See 'Beiträge zur Ethnologie der Gilbertinsulaner' by R. Parkinson, *Internationales Archiv für Ethnographie* vol. II.

Polynesian similarities in Melanesia, not only in those areas where we see today a strong Polynesian element remaining undisturbed or more or less intermingled with Papuan components, but also in those areas where externally the Polynesian element has been completely absorbed by the Papuan, but has left behind unmistakable traces in the speech and in many traditions and customs.

Already by the time the original Polynesians were leaving their east Asian homeland, they undoubtedly formed a mixed race. A further dilution occurred on the migration, probably with a people who were very close to the present Arafurans. In support of an interbreeding, and quite a considerable one at that, with a Mongoloid people, there is, for example, the blue birthmark of the Polynesians, which Dr Bälz has demonstrated also in the Mongols, as well as the more or less strongly occurring Mongoloid crease in the upper eyelid, which we encounter, for example, frequently in Samoa, occasionally in the Carolines, and also on Wuwulu and Aua. The remnants of the dark people reveal themselves in the hair and the skin shade, and in many cases in the broad nose. Then there are those slight features that indicate a people like the one settled in the Mediterranean area today, and which stand out especially in the New Zealanders, but less so in Tongans and Samoans.

In conclusion I quote an assertion by Kubary in discussing the custom of the artistic moulding of infants' skulls by four flat stones, practised earlier in Samoa.

What is generally the actual reason for the Samoan, respectively Polynesian, shaping of the skull? Why was the ideal found in a round brachycephalic skull and not in an *ulu toi* (*ulu* = head; *to'i* = stone axe; *ulu toi* therefore = *axe-shaped head*) that we have already discovered in the neighbours, the Viti, like the Melanesians in general? The former Polynesians were certainly short-skulls who, in comparison with a long skull, found their skulls more handsomely formed and wanted to retain them. But if the Polynesians were a pure people they need not expect any long skulls among their descendants if they did not interbreed with a long-skulled people. But from the great eagerness that the Samoans displayed for the retention of their head form, which must have been very pronounced at that time since it communicated itself to all other groups of Polynesians deriving from Samoa, one can conclude that the then Polynesians or rather the original Samoans often found long skulls among their descendants and, clinging to their original homeland form, sought to suppress them.

VIII Secret Societies, Totemism, Masks and Mask Dances

It is typical of almost all Melanesians that they form societies and cloak them with secrets which are withheld from non-members and especially women. We know of such secret societies in New Guinea, New Caledonia and the New Hebrides, and we find it again, in the most varied forms, on the islands of the Solomon group and the Bismarck Archipelago.

It is difficult to establish the reason for these institutions. I regard it as fruitless to discover the origin from the natives themselves, when the institution goes back a number of generations. Here as in so many other cases the only response you would get would be: 'Our forefathers did it this way, and since we have learnt it from them we do it too.'

We have a quite significant number of more or less ingenious speculations about the origin of these customs. However, they all suffer from the authors all giving their fantasies too much free rein, fastening onto single events that apparently support their theories and suppressing others because they stand in contradiction. Futhermore, it is common to all these fantastic imaginings, that they revolve around a train of thought that is so far removed from a people of nature as the philosophical system of a Kant or Schopenhauer is from the comprehension of a budding sexton.

To put oneself into the train of thought of a Melanesian is not easy. Intellectually, he is at a low level; logical thought is in most cases an impossibility for him. What he does not grasp directly through observation by his senses, is witchcraft and magical art, about which further laborious investigation is a completely useless task. Most probably the explanation of many secret societies and the institutions connected with them lies in customs that have their origins in sorcery, either to prevent the evil consequences of magic or to help produce more favourable living conditions for the participants.

Not infrequently, ancestor worship and totemic notions are broadly or narrowly connected with the secret societies, but here too the reason can probably be found in sorcery and belief in the supernatural, and it is therefore little wonder that the natives gather together all customs founded on these sources, and over the course of time build up a certain system of practising them.

It is not my intention to examine the spiritual core of the secret societies as far back as their origin; I will endeavour in the following to describe individual connections of this nature in the Bismarck Archipelago and the German Solomon Islands, as they present themselves to the observer today. Many customs have, in spite of apparently diverse external form, arisen nonetheless from basically the same universal concepts, although having become so modified over the course of time in different regions and under different circumstances that the original basic idea and the original form can only be recognised with difficulty today. Also, it does not seem impossible either that, once in a while, a direct transposition took place in such a way that the institution was transplanted to other districts and, by virtue of the universal reliance of all Melanesians on mystery, found fertile soil. Otherwise it might not satisfactorily explain how in districts far apart small details in the ceremonies or external features of the masking correspond perfectly.

When I use the words 'secret society' here, I must add at the outset that I do not want to imply the associations of the natives in the sense that we use the word in Europe. A 'secret society' in the civilised world is an association of individuals known to one another, often only in restricted numbers, but always remaining unknown to all non-members of the society; indeed often the very existence of such a society is a deep secret. The secret societies of the natives can evoke this name only in so far as their customs and aims are known only to the members of the society; the members themselves are known to the community, and this circumstance in itself gives them an advantage over non-members in their daily life, and provides impetus to the latter to gain the privileges from being in this society.

Thus, on the Gazelle Peninsula, for example, every wife and every non-initiate knows who belongs to the society of the *duk-duk*; and in northern Bougainville every villager knows who is a *matasesén* and thereby initiated into the secrets of the *ruk-ruk* or *burru*; but the uninitiated have not the slightest knowledge of the ceremonies connected with them, partaken on rigorously separated sites; at the most they are told stories about ghostly apparitions and about sinister actions and behaviour.

Also, the customs of the secret society are not always a secret to the uninitiated. As soon as the secret society members deem it appropriate to present themselves publicly for any particular purpose that serves their society, they do it, although preserving secrecy by the active members appearing masked. Thus on the Gazelle Peninsula the *tubuan* and the *duk-duk* display themselves to the non-members, wandering from village to village in their characteristic masks. We find the same on Buka, where the *kokorra* present themselves masked in public. But always the real ceremonial site or assembly place remains strictly isolated from the uninitiated, and encroachment on it is punished with a heavy fine, often loss of life.

The initiated keep strictly quiet about the secrets of the society with regard to the uninitiated, and it is also very difficult for Europeans to penetrate the secrecy. First, one has to win the trust of the natives before one can contemplate talking on this theme or posing questions about it. Even then, one can be fairly certain that the most wondrous things will be told to the questioner and lies will be told; only numerous conversations with a wide variety of members, chance comments by individuals, or a fortunately chosen glance allow the wheat to be differentiated from the chaff.

Visiting the assembly places, or more accurately the ceremonial sites, is not difficult for the European after closer acquaintance with the natives; but he seldom sees very much that can give him clarification on the purpose or customs of the society. Either he is presented with an improvised hocus-pocus, or something completely irrelevant that bears little connection to what the society emphasises as the main element.

We find secret societies on the various islands of the Bismarck Archipelago: on New Hanover and New Ireland where they are partially connected with ancestor worship; on the north-eastern part of the Gazelle Peninsula in the form of the *duk-duk*; on the islands of Nissan and Buka in the form of the *kokorra*; on Bougainville as the association of *matasesén*. We find quite similar societies also, further to the south and south-east, throughout the German part of the Solomon Islands: the *matambala* on the island of Florida, the *tamate* on the Banks Islands, the *qatu* in the northern New Hebrides. We find them still further on New Caledonia and also in the Fiji Islands, although in reduced form and of lesser importance. Furthermore, in German New Guinea at Asa on Astrolabe Bay and in the societies that hold their assemblies at Parak (on the coast in the east and west of Berlinhafen), we recognise a related institution; it is the same with the mask dances on isolated islands of the Torres Strait and on the coast of British New Guinea opposite. On the continent of Australia, too, there are secret societies of various types, and in Dutch New Guinea and on the neighbouring islands at least vestiges are known to us.

From what we know of the secret societies today we still cannot form a totally clear picture of their aims and purposes; we are, I believe, tending too much to look for higher significance or a deeper meaning, and draw parallels and conclusions that are hardly sustainable. Over the years I have slowly come to the conclusion that basically every deeper significance is missing in all these secret societies, and that they simply serve the totally materialistic purpose of creating a higher standing of the members above women and non-members, that membership accords not only certain social advantages but also material pleasures, better food, the opportunity for laziness, for unfettered relations with the female sex, as well as the possibility of acquiring property at the expense of non-members. In some places, the secret societies even replace the organising and jurisdictive headman, when one is missing, and look after the maintenance of order within the tribe and the sustaining of the usual customs, while of course having their own interests and well-being foremost in their eyes.

In almost all cases, the uninitiated are told a number of horror stories of apparitions and relations with spirits, and all manner of strange noises are produced as further proof, ostensibly the voices of the feared spirits; however, introduction into the secret society consists of a longer or shorter isolation of the candidates, an admission fee payment to members of the society, and participation in certain ceremonies and feasts. Nothing really new is learnt by the initiate; the advantages that membership offers are bestowed on him from henceforth, and in his turn he regales the uninitiated with the same horror stories that were told to him earlier; he runs with the pack and enjoys the luxury of membership. Whether any of the initiates ever feel that they have been deluded in their expectation, of having relations with spirits or seeing spirits appear, is hard to say; however, I do not believe that this is the case. As a rule a native is not plagued with great thirst for knowledge; dealing with ghosts is a tricky business in his opinion. In any case it is better to keep out of their way. When perhaps in fear and trembling he makes the apparently fateful step and allows himself to be admitted to the society, he secretly rejoices that the frightful spirits and apparitions do not exist in reality.

Modern times have brought many enemies to the secret societies. The first of them is the white settler; he does not fear spirits and ghostly voices, he does not care about the traditions and customs of the natives, he does not respect the secret assembly places, and the more the native cloaks himself in secret affairs and silence, the more he sees it as his mission to solve the mystery. Many times evil befalls him through this; for example, I knew a trader who secretly took a *duk-duk* mask years ago. His somewhat airy home, a hut made from bamboo canes and coconut matting, was, however, not a suitable hiding place; the natives discovered the mask, broke into the house, pulled out the *duk-duk* and only my fortuitous intervention saved the trader from a sound thrashing, if not worse. Since this affair the natives avoided the place and took their products to neighbouring traders. Entering ceremonial sites and attending ceremonies is often permitted to white people, but the natives regard themselves as recompensed by the visitor's falling for the most outrageous stories and subsequently passing them on to the world as guaranteed truth, reported by an eyewitness, and causing the utmost confusion.

Most especially, the Christian missionary is an enemy of secret societies; he suspects the devil's work and is jealous of the influence of the members on society in general, an influence that he often erroneously regards as hostile to his efforts. A few missionaries have succeeded in restricting the power of the secret societies in the vicinity of their dwellings, or totally destroying them. However, among the missionaries there are also those who tolerate the secret societies, after they have recognised their significance and convinced themselves that they are basically of a harmless nature.

Also, the worldly authorities occasionally come into conflict with the secret societies when the latter inflict punishments and penances that do not always coincide with the clauses of the Penal Code; such proceedings are then forbidden and the reputation of the society falls.

I believe that both the Christian missionaries and the administration could, for their own purposes, mould and use these secret societies to the greatest advantage. So many a non-Christian institution had been skilfully adapted by the heathen converts of the previous centuries to fit the purposes of Christianity, at a time when many of the prospective converts certainly were no higher spiritually than many of the present South Sea tribes. The Protestant mission in particular shows how very intolerant it is of the customs of the natives. It seems to be inspired by the view that all the trappings of the natives, all their traditions and customs, have to be uprooted completely to give place to true Christianity, and extending out of this view they forbid anything and everything, unfortunately without giving the natives anything better, or any replacement whatsoever.

The consequence often is that slackness and indolence appear in place of the earlier daily life interrupted by celebrations and joyful gatherings, and lead to lip-service and hypocrisy, coupled with all manner of vices perpetrated in secret, which stand in far greater conflict with true Christianity than the original unchristian trappings. Of course there are also missionaries who, with a true understanding of the essence of Christianity, respect the harmless customs of the natives where these are not in direct conflict to Christian teaching, and this then leads to the peculiar spectacle that Christian natives in one district are still in possession of their old secret societies and their old customs still exist, while these are regarded as works of the devil in the neighbouring district. In the Duke of York group missionaries have succeeded in totally suppressing the *duk-duk* in many districts, while in Blanche Bay the teachers brought in from Samoa, Tonga and Fiji not only tolerate the *duk-duk* but also take part in ceremonies connected with it. Indeed I know of several cases where the teachers allowed themselves to join the *duk-duk* society and participated with their society brothers in the inherent advantages. A native from Makada in the Duke of Yorks, who for many years has been a keen and, as I believe, also quite an upright adherent of Christianity but is not permitted to belong to the *duk-duk* society there, has for long years taken part in all the ceremonies of the society in a district not far from my dwelling. When I occasionally made pretence of rebuking him, he explained that the customs of the society contained nothing that contravened the teachings of the Holy Scripture that he had read, and he therefore did not regard it as a sin to belong to the society and to take part in its ceremonies.

The *duk-duk* society of the north-eastern Gazelle Peninsula belongs among the most well-known secret societies of the Bismarck Archipelago. We come across it at St George's Channel, from Blanche Bay to Kambair (Weberhafen), and inland as far as the tribes of Vunakokor. Men exclusively belong to the *duk-duk* society, but several old women (*tubuan*) are occasionally permitted to join the society, in so far as they are allowed to participate in its dances outside the *taraiu*.

Fig. 103 The *duk-duk* assembled for a public dance

Fig. 104 The *duk-duk* on the *taraiu*

As a rule the ceremonial sites, *taraiu*, are entered only by members; however, an exception is always made for foreigners, especially whites; even my wife was finally permitted entry, not without murmurs from several old mystery-mongers. The location of a *taraiu* is known to all non-initiates, and they take great care not to set foot there because there is a heavy penalty. Should uninitiated relatives of a member intentionally or unwittingly have entered the *taraiu* the member must, for good or evil, pay the usual recompense to the society; how he recoups his outlay is his business. I remember such a case that occurred a few years ago. A man from Raluana, west of my home, had an understanding with a woman from Karawia; she left her relatives and met her lover on the beach at night to go with him to his home compound. However, the flight was noticed; the relatives rushed after them, and to get his prize to safety quickly the native had to cross the *taraiu*. The second transgression was far greater than the elopement in the eyes of the pursuers. They broke off the pursuit that was in any case only a type of formality, and the following day they reported what they had seen.

For the man, who belonged to the *duk-duk* society himself, there remained nothing but to pay the society the usual penance, in this case 30 fathoms of *tabu*.

A second case went as follows. A wealthy native had put on a *duk-duk* ceremony (Meyer and Parkinson, *Papua Album*, vol. I, plate 16 shows the ceremonial site for this occasion) to honour dead relatives at Raluana, during which there was dancing and feasting day and night on the *taraiu*, and members streamed in from all sides. The organiser of the ceremony, through forgetfulness, allowed a not yet fully initiated boy to enter the *taraiu*, for which he had to pay out 20 fathoms of *tabu* to the society; the boy came out of it with a sound thrashing.

Understandably on these grounds the uninitiated avoid the *taraiu* and the members impress the ban on them even further, since it is they, as a rule, who have to pay for a native the always very high penance in *tabu* on behalf of the transgressor. In earlier times it has happened that women who entered the *taraiu* were killed by the members of the *duk-duk*. I recollect two such instances during the first years of my stay. Today, the offence is no longer so severely punished, out of fear of the punishing hand of the administration.

The *taraiu* is situated in such a way that activities on it are not visible to any non-initiate; it is situated in the forest under tall trees and bordered by bushes and shrubs with dense foliage. At the time of ceremonies it is fenced in, where necessary for further protection from curious glances, by a high fence of coconut matting. On the site there are either one or two huts which serve as a hideout for the members and also probably as a storage for the masks and leaf costumes of the *duk-duk*. Since numerous *duk-duk* masks from neighbouring districts often come together on a *taraiu* and the erected huts are not able to accommodate everything, posts, *tagor*, about 1 metre high are dug into the ground as well. On these they hang the rings of leaves that form the costumes, and the characteristic headdresses. The *taraiu* is kept clean and tidy by the members; also, at those times when there are no ceremonies, the old men gather here, to take a little nap undisturbed, or to discuss the events of the day.

The *taraiu* is the official assembly point for the members of the society. On the other hand, whenever dances and ceremonies are organised outside the *taraiu* by the society, an enclosed space is set up on the temporary ceremonial site to enable the masked members to transfer their costume from one wearer to another, unseen by the crowd. Usually the isolated site is densely enclosed with coconut palm leaves so that those sitting in front cannot see what is going on behind it. These temporary places of refuge are erected only for special purposes and bear the significance of the *taraiu* only for a moment. They are also given a special name, *manamanaung*.

All preparations for a *duk-duk* ceremony are undertaken on the *taraiu* by the members; in particular the manufacture of mask costumes takes place here. These consist of two parts, a leaf wrapping for the upper body and a conical hat which, completely covering the head, rests on the shoulders. The masks produced are of two types depending on whether they represent a *tubuan* or a *duk-duk*. They differ in that the former's head-mask forms a short cone crowned with a large bunch of cockatoo feathers, while that of the latter is long and tapers to a point often to a height of 2 metres, decorated with small brightly painted wooden carvings, crowns of feathers and bunches of brightly coloured plant fibres and the like. Figure 103 shows four *tubuan* on the left, followed by a *duk-duk*, then two more *tubuan*, two *duk-duk*, and so on. In figure 104 two *duk-duk* stand in the middle, and a *duk-duk* mask stands on the ground at right.

The basic framework of all the masks is a conical shape of thin strips of bamboo (*aur*). Over this

Plate 37 Village scene on Nukumanu

they prepare a covering (*pakara*) out of dyed plant fibres, bast and similar material, which covers the entire head of the wearer of the mask while having extensive, wide holes to allow the wearer to see through, but sufficiently narrow on the outer side to avoid the wearer's face being recognised. A broad leafy or fibrous crown is attached to the lower edge of the conical hat, completely covering the shoulders. The leafy costume (*bongtagul*) is made from the leaves of a certain species of rattan (*bua*). The broad, lance-shaped leaves (*magu*) are entwined into wreaths (*qaqaina*) so that the leaves hang outwards; a number of such wreaths wide enough for the upper body of an adult to pass through are attached above one another, and two shoulder bands (*taltal*) of twisted foliage are attached so that the wearer carries the leafy wrap on both shoulders; further wreaths are put on over the structure just described and completely cover the rest of the upper body and the arms. The mask (*lor*) with the attached leaf or fibrous crown, for its part covers the head, neck and shoulders.

The full costume, especially in a fresh condition, is heavy and uncomfortable. The wearers swap from time to time or slip into the bush to take the mask off; in such a case they are always guarded by other members to prevent the approach of non-members. During the *duk-duk* ceremony one often sees natives with severely flayed hips or shoulders, wounds caused by the weight of the heavy mask costume.

The low conical hat of the *tubuan* is always distinguished by two large eyes (*kiok*). The long, drawn-out tip (*taukane*) of the *duk-duk* mask is decorated in the most fantastic manner; each person tries to outdo the other, and the arrangement of the feather wreaths (*pono*) or the tiny wooden figures (*tabataba*) show endless variation.

All members of the *duk-duk* are called *a umana lele* as opposed to the non-members, *a umana mane*; the initiation candidates may be young or old. During their novitiate they are known as *a umana kalamana*.

The *tubuan*, allegedly a female spirit, is the highest rank in the society. Only quite special natives who, through family inheritance, or through having attained the right of displaying a *tubuan* through purchase, own one. Every *tubuan* has its own special female name; for example:

the *tubuan* of the native Taibuk = *ja livuan*
the *tubuan* of the native Tokinkin = *ja vaga-buabua*
the *tubuan* of the native Toreget = *ja muruna*
the *tubuan* of the native Tomararang = *ja takin*
the *tubuan* of the native Tangi = *ja påk*
the *tubuan* of the native Tendin = *ja valval*,
and so on.

The owners of the *tubuan* are the wealthiest members of the society in influence and in shell money. Even today the owners of a *tubuan* can sell the right to other natives who do not yet have one. However, the sale of a *tubuan* is only possible to a rich man, since not only is the purchase price high but the celebrations connected with the transfer of the *tubuan* require large quantities of *tabu*, and it can happen that the buyer comes to recognise that the *tubuan* does not enrich him as he had hoped but has on the contrary cost him a lot of money. Whoever becomes the owner of a *tubuan* has taken on the duty of making it appear in a manner befitting its rank, and his neighbours watch that this happens. Should he neglect his duty then it can happen that his right is taken away from him.

In the Blanche Bay district as far as Cape Gazelle and the countryside inland, the *tubuan* and *duk-duk* institution is still not very old. In the area around Ralum, Tobata, who died a few years ago, first introduced the *tubuan*, having bought it from the native Tobavaliliu at Talvat on the slopes of South Daughter mountain. The latter in turn had acquired it in the Duke of York group. At Raluana and thereabouts the *tubuan* was bought at the same time from the island of Kerawara (Duke of York). At Kininigunan, and in the Cape Gazelle region, the *tubuan* had been introduced from the inland district of Kadakadai. In the Duke of York Islands the *tubuan* had been obtained from Birara; there, Birara was understood to be the settled region of the Gazelle Peninsula at St George's Channel. A native named Tarok, from the Virien district on the small island of Mioko, bought the *tubuan* from the native Taltalut in the coastal village of Landip on St George's Channel. From Virien on Mioko the *duk-duk* society has spread rapidly to the remaining islands and, as we have seen previously, from there to those parts of the Gazelle Peninsula which had contact with this group.

The introduction of the *duk-duk* to Virien on Mioko must have taken place in the first half of the 19th century. On Mioko there is an old man still alive, who, when a boy, knew the native Tarok who had introduced it there. The native Topile, on Kerawara, who died in 1901, told me that his grandfather had bought the *tubuan* from Tarok in Virien. Other old Duke of York people say, that when they were small boys, the institution was still regarded as a novelty. I can therefore assume with some justification that the *duk-duk* was introduced to the Duke of Yorks in 1820 to 1830 at the earliest, and from there in 1840 to 1850 to the Mother peninsula and the villages in and around the neighbourhood of Blanche Bay.

The original *tubuan* of Tarok from Virien was called *ja marinair* and is still called this today, as far as I know.

The society had also been transplanted from Virien to Laur. The Duke of York natives understood that to be the coast of New Ireland on the far side of St George's Channel. In this district today they still have the *tubuan* and *duk-duk*. The institution seems to occur there only in a very limited district, since only two *tubuan* are known, bearing the names *ja kabange* and *ja pitlaka*.

The Landip natives acquired the *duk-duk* secrets originally from a place called Kottokotto. Primarily, the region inland from Kabange and Landip appears to be the place of origin of the society; certainly all my acounts from the tribes at the foot of the Varzin and in the Kadakadai region indicate this area. Natives there say that the institution of the *tubuan* is very old, but make the reservation that there was a time during which their ancestors did not know the secret society. The origin does not appear to lie more than five generations back.

South of the villages on Kabange Bay and south of the Landip district as far as the northern shore of the Warangoi River (Karawat) there is a totally uninhabited region. Also south of the river there is at present no settled population; this is first encountered in the mountains, where we come across the resident south-east Baining. The inhabitants north of the river have no connection with these people. The society therefore can hardly have arisen from direct influence from the southern neighbours.

It is, moreover, hardly acceptable that the society arose within the village communities along the channel without impetus from outside; and I have no doubt that this took place, even if it is not possible for me to prove it at this time. The correspondence of many customs of the *duk-duk* society with the customs of the secret societies on the Solomon Islands, as well as with the customs of the secret societies of the rest of New Britain, indicates that the initial stimulus came from one or other place. Natives were often driven involuntarily in their canoes by strong winds and currents to other areas, and it would be erroneous to assume that in every case they were slain on arrival in the new land. Such shipwreck victims from other regions may have introduced the secret society, partly to gain status, and partly through the need to preserve their customs. The new institution met with approval and, over the course of time, was then padded out with new additions, new ceremonies and celebrations that corresponded with the new surroundings.

The *tubuan* is still called *turadawai* (treetop) by a few old people; likewise one often hears the *duk-duk* designated as *beo* (bird). It has not been possible for me to find out anything about the origin and the real meaning of both these designations. Perhaps they are rudiments from a distant region where the *duk-duk* originally came from. Perhaps also they are only designations of the *duk-duk* and the *tubuan* that are used in the presence of non-members, since, for everything connected with the two masks, the society members have various names, the significance of which is unknown to outsiders. This naming occurs particularly in the songs which the *duk-duk* members sing at the masked dance ceremonies when they appear in public. Here words are rendered unrecognisable by special endings, the usual designations of items of daily use being replaced by others, and to the listener, who does not know all of this, the whole thing sounds quite foreign and horrible. Moreover, in these songs I have been unable to find any deeper meaning. Like all other songs, they are simply a stringing together of sentences seldom having any interconnection. In Raluana they have two songs that I will reproduce here in translation as examples of the *duk-duk* poetry. One goes:

> Why don't you stop digging *pea* (a type of soil)!
> Chase away the *dimai* (a bird); the *dimai* is ashamed!

This is an old song originating from the time of introduction to Raluana. The following one is of more recent date; it had been bought from a writer in Kininigunan and enjoys great popularity.

> Behold the *kalangar* (parrot)! I admire his head.
> Javual (woman's name, *vual* = the mist) there on the sea, go away!
> Jaquria (woman's name, *quria* = earthquake) must shake!
> Janatatar (woman's name, *natatar* = a particular type of painting of the *duk-duk* hat), go to the sea!
> A storm is drawing near! The bird (*beo*, used here to designate the *duk-duk*) with the yellow tuft of feathers.
> We want to dance; we want to weep out on the path. Stop! Both of you will hear it again.
> The *kalangar* gets the headband, and all will sit down on the path!

These examples should suffice. All the other *duk-duk* songs are of the same style and just as unintelligible. When the song reaches the end they begin it over again and the same monotonous singing continues uninterrupted for many hours.

Normally in everyday life singing is *kakaile*, but the *duk-duk* society has a special name, *tapialai*, for its songs.

The initiation ceremonies in the Duke of York Islands and on the Gazelle Peninsula are generally the same. Here and there they have developed slight variations, according to whether the members of the society or the owner of the *tubuan* had more or less of a sense of the miraculous. In the districts round my dwelling the introduction proceeds as follows:

Should a male child, a boy or a youth, be accepted into the society, the father or the uncle of the person in question announces this to the owner of a *tubuan*. Usually the latter lets some time pass before announcing that the *tubuan* will appear at such and such a time; this appears to be out of regard for the members of the society who are planning to take in a novitiate, to give them sufficient time to make the necessary arrangements.

When the day of the appearance of the *tubuan* arrives, its loud calls on the *taraiu* are heard, and this is the sign to bring the novitiates. On the *taraiu* they lie down in a circle; the *tubuan* armed with a light stick dances in the middle of the circle yelling and gesticulating and strikes the novitiates with the stick; the members standing outside the circle do this too. They are very considerate in the distribution of blows; children and small boys receive gentle blows, bigger boys and youths, however, receive a rougher beating, which seems very similar to a severe thrashing, and this ceremony (*bakatia*) therefore seldom ends without yells of pain from the novices. The mother and female relatives sit at home in their huts during the proceedings, uttering cries of suffering.

After the *bakatia*, the sponsors, father or uncle, share small amounts of *tabu* about a span long among those present; obviously the *tubuan* receives a greater length, but never more than a metre long. Then the novices are given a meal specially prepared for this occasion (*rang davai*), consisting of fish, baked taro and the like.

When the meal is ended, the novices must again sit in a circle on the *taraiu*, and the *tubuan* steps into the centre, removes his conical head covering, then one of the wrapping rings of foliage, then another, and so on until he stands there totally bare. Pointing to the costume he then calls out: 'What do you want to do with it? Put it on, put it on!' But he has previously removed the straps of foliage, *taltal*, which pass over the shoulders holding the leafy wrap fast, so that the novitiates come to the conclusion that the entire costume, *bongtagul*, hangs from the body as a result of spiritual influence, without any other support.

After this small comedy, the men dance on the *taraiu* and the novitiates are taught how to make the leaps and steps of the *duk-duk*. The whole ceremony is called *palatutane*.

In the meantime it is impressed upon the newcomers that they are to say nothing about what happens on the *taraiu*, and the threatened punishment for violation is put before them. Then a sumptuous feast, *aingir*, prepared by the relatives of the novitiates, is consumed by all those present on the *taraiu*.

The initiation is then actually completed, although a series of further ceremonies follows. If the newcomers are still small boys, they must wait a number of years until they receive their own *duk-duk*, but if they are about twelve years old they obtain one immediately and go through all the ceremonies at the same time.

The conferring of a *duk-duk* ensues the day after the new birth by the *tubuan*. On the day of the actual birth of the *duk-duk*, *väkua*, the fathers or uncles bring the *duk-duk* costume, prepared meanwhile in secret, to the *taraiu*, from where the *tubuan* gives his loud cry, *i puongo*, accompanied by the loud din of the wooden drums, *kuddu*, announcing the birth, *kinavai*, of the *duk-duk*. The novitiates too gather at the *taraiu* where they remain throughout the night.

On the early morning of the following day, the *tubuan* with his newborn children, the *duk-duk*, presents himself to the public. If the *taraiu* is on the beach or close by, the *tubuan* and the *duk-duk* get into festively decorated canoes, and they are

Fig. 105 The *duk-duk* presents itself on the water

paddled along the beach by unmasked members, dancing and singing, accompanied by drumbeats. This is the *matamatam* (fig. 105). The appearance of the *tubuan* with his newborns is called *a bung na kinavai*, or *tubuan i kakawa*. Now and then it happens that the canoes in which the masked people have been paddled along the beach are wrecked. As soon as the masked people have left their canoes the *duk-duk* members pounce on these, smash them up and scatter the fragments in all directions.

At such celebrations there is always only one birthing *tubuan* present; however, several of them are always seen at the feast. With the exception of the one, the others are mere participants in the feast, from neighbouring districts.

When this *duk-duk* performance is completed, all the feast participants – that is, the old members as well as those newly accepted – go onto the *taraiu*; from here the procession, consisting of all those wearing masks and all other members, sets out to the feast place of the owner of the *tubuan*. At the very front those *tubuan* present march and leap, then the *duk-duk* follow, usually in pairs. The whole crowd of members follows behind and alongside, yelling, singing, drumming and throwing burnt coral lime into the air with both hands. Dances are performed on the feast place by the masked people, and members and non-members, women, girls and young children, who have come from throughout the district, lie around watching the leaps.

After the dances, there again follows a small comedy to give the non-members an idea of the power and strict rules of the *duk-duk* within the society.

The *tubuan* present grip fairly thick banana trunks, and the unmasked members leap around, to receive a hefty loud-sounding blow on the back, *a virua na pedik*. This is not so dangerous as it seems, for the juicy banana stem cracks very loudly on the bare skin and the blow may be quite painful for an instant, but goes away in a few minutes leaving neither swellings nor skin grazes. Those struck hide the pain, laugh and make jokes, also grabbing the banana stems and dishing out friendly, neighbourly blows that are always reciprocated, everything giving the impression that they are immune to pain and make nothing of such small things. The wives and female dependants of the victims screech out loudly during this scene and for a while the din is deafening.

After this small comedy has ended, all the *tubuan* and *duk-duk* arrange themselves in a broad circle, and the owners of the active *tubuan* stand in the centre of the circle. Immediately, there is an absolute hush (*Papua Album*, vol. I, plate 15). *Tabu* is now brought out and handed to those standing in the centre. Immediately, the masked men sit down on the ground, and 3 to 4 metres of *tabu* are handed out to each of the newborn *duk-duk*. This is also a comedy piece for the benefit of the spectators, to show how advantageous it is to be a member of the society. This public display is called *navolo* or *naolo*. Afterwards everyone, including the new members, goes back to the *taraiu*, the masked men remove their costumes and, after the day's activities, everyone fortifies himself with food that has been brought earlier by the relatives of the new members.

The following day the *duk-duk* begin the gathering of *tabu*, *ivane na dok-dok*. The new member accompanies the *duk-duk*, together with several friends and relations, who must all be members, probably to monitor the income; if the bearer becomes tired he slips into the bush, rapidly removes the costume, and another immediately puts it on to continue leaping and to announce his arrival by his loud barking call. During this period the new member does not put the mask on, although he always accompanies his *duk-duk* and sleeps in his company at night on the *taraiu*. Day by day the various compounds in the neighbourhood are visited and everywhere a large or small gift of *tabu* is collected. As a rule this lasts for about a month, but under certain circumstances this can be twice as long.

Often a wealthy native provides a special feast on the *taraiu* for the *duk-duk*, then he leads them to his hut and hands them the usual gift of *tabu*, *a tabu na duk-duk* (in contrast to the *tabu* that has to be paid to the *tubuan* and is called *a tabu na tubuan*).

During this collecting time a good attendance predominates on the *taraiu*; the members are always here in great numbers, and the father, uncle and relatives of the new entrants must therefore ensure that there is always enough food available. Supposedly, this is destined solely for the *tubuan* and must consist of special morsels, fish, chickens, baked taro tubers over which grated coconut has been squeezed, all kinds of vegetables, and so on. This festive food is called *kirip*.

After the *tabu* collecting has gone on for one or two months, the owner of the *tubuan* announces the end of the festival. All members, both masked and unmasked then gather on the feast place of the owner of the *tubuan* where after a short dance they sit down on the ground. The father, the uncle and the other male relatives of the new members bring them, or more accurately their *duk-duk*, gifts of *tabu*. Father and uncle pay 1 to 2 metres of *tabu*, more distant relatives a shorter length, which is laid in front of the *duk-duk*, tied to a bright *Dracaena* branch. The women send great bundles of prepared morsels which are all taken to the *taraiu* later. This day is called *a bung dok varvaki*. After the distribution of presents, all go to the *taraiu* again; and then the *duk-duk* is dead. The *tubuan* on the other hand never dies, he is always there; he appears now and again on appropriate occasions where he has direct involvement; he is immortal.

On the *taraiu* the masks are now dismantled. Everything that has value in the eyes of the natives, such as bright feathers, wood carvings, and so on, is stored; the rest, particularly the leaves of the costume, the framework of the conical hat, and so on, is stacked in the huts under the rafters and elsewhere.

After the death of the *duk-duk* everyone goes home, but the event is not ended by a long way, for, several days later, there follows the actual settling up. On the third day after the death of the *duk-duk* all those who have assisted in the ceremonies gather in the home compound of the newly admitted member. Each person receives a gift, whose value depends on how much *tabu* the *duk-duk* collected. The costume-maker receives a piece of *tabu* 2 to 3 metres long; the people who have worn the masks during the assemblies receive a similar amount. This distribution is called *war ma momoi*. It goes without saying that a sumptuous feast, *dodoroko*, is also provided for.

The following day all the members assemble on the *taraiu*; both this day and the celebration taking place are called *tar kulau*. The celebration consists of the father or uncle of the newly initiated going up to him and handing him a certain number of young coconuts, *kulau*; each nut represents 10 fathoms of *tabu*. Therefore, if the uncle hands his nephew three nuts, it means that the latter has to reimburse him 30 fathoms of *tabu* for his outlay. Often the father or uncle takes one or more nuts back and silently drinks it; this signifies that the newcomer must indeed hand over the requisite number of fathoms of *tabu*, but the drinker will contribute as many times 10 fathoms as the nuts he has drunk. The more *tabu* the new member must pay, the higher his rank. On

the settlement day, wealthy people present up to 100 fathoms of *tabu*; however, this is only boastfulness, for the shell money eventually goes back to them. The *duk-duks*, purchased for a large sum, are called *kabin e rak-rak*. They sit beside the *tubuan* at the feasting places and receive the best morsels of the feast. The rest, who deposit the usual payment of 20 to 30 fathoms, are called *a ni koro*.

As a rule, the new entrants have not gathered sufficient *tabu* to cover all the expenses of their sponsors. In this case they must then work to accumulate the necessary sum. If father or uncle have no money to afford a contribution, perhaps have even borrowed funds from wealthier natives, it may be two or three years before the person in question has gathered the full sum; he must therefore establish gardens, go fishing; in short he must gain money by any means. When, finally, after a lot of effort, he is the happy owner of the whole sum, there comes the great day of settlement, *a bung anidok*. Father or uncles prepare a great feast, which is brought to the *taraiu*. Here the members gather, and the full sum of *tabu*, bound together with a bright *Dracaena* leaf, is handed over by the entrant in question to his father or uncle. As mentioned above, father or uncle, to enhance the standing of the new entrant, often gives a large part of the *abu*, but accepts the whole amount for himself and stores it as *tabu na duk-duk* of the newcomer.

The feast on this occasion is so sumptuous that they can often eat for eight to ten days on the *taraiu*. During this period the *tubuan* also appears on the *taraiu*, gives his loud bellowing cry and receives a gift of a piece of *tabu* 1 to 2 fathoms long from each of the new entrants. The remains of the *duk-duk* masks, stored up till now in the huts, are then burned, *va pulung* or *pulpulung*, and the newcomer is now a fully fledged member of the society.

Now that we have learned about the full initiation customs in the preceding passage, many aspects of native behaviour that had earlier seemed unreasonable and unfair become clear to us. We now understand why the uncle or father hires out his nephew or son to strangers and later takes his pay; we also understand why the young people are not allowed to choose to go off here or there to

Fig. 106 The *duk-duk* lands on the beach

avoid their duties; all this is to guarantee that the relatives recoup their outlay. The person accepted into the society can never be tossed out of it; he enjoys all the advantages of the society throughout his life, namely participation in numerous ceremonies that, with the obligatory feasting, would otherwise have been inaccessible to him. Also, in the event of need the *tubuan* and the whole band stand behind him, taking him under its powerful protection should the need arise. It cannot be overlooked that the society exercises a significant educative influence by compelling the young people to silence, obedience and work. In my opinion, this situation could be further expanded and valued by a prudent authority or by the missionary societies as an educational factor.

The position of a *duk-duk* in the society is clear from the preceding passage: he is a subordinate member to whom the membership accords certain prominence. His superior, to some extent the guiding principal in the society is, however, the *tubuan*. It remains for us to define more precisely the position and the significance of the *tubuan*s to own a *tubuan*, then the owners must gain significant benefits, although they distribute *tabu* with apparent liberality and take other expenses upon themselves. Given the covetous nature of the natives, they would not do this if they did not have a view not only to covering their outlay but also to making a fine profit. The apparent largesse is based on the spender knowing full well that he will recoup the outlay with interest. During the initiation ceremonies as we have already seen, many pieces of *tabu* fall to the *tubuan* in respect of this ownership, but this amassing alone would not recoup the massive outlay. However, besides this, the *tubuan* has many ways and means of not only regaining his costs but of drawing pecuniary profit from the power bestowed on him by public opinion.

First, the *tubuan* has the right to exact punishment, which as a rule consists of the payment of *tabu*, collected by him in person. Should someone speak improperly about the *tubuan* or about members of the society, the *tubuan* is immediately on hand to collect *tabu*. In particular, women and non-members frequently feel his heavy hand. But members, too, who have transgressed in any way against the rules of the society are called to account and submit tacitly, as we have seen demonstrated, for behind the *tubuan* stand the *duk-duk*, forming a solid structure, to some extent representing public opinion, against which the influence of an individual is powerless.

In a district like, for example, the north-eastern corner of the Gazelle Peninsula, where no actual chief is recognised, the *tubuan* represents the principle of social order and conventional justice and looks after the maintenance of this. Now the native concepts of law and order are often very indeterminate, and are in many cases overcome by the feeling and consciousness of power and might, so that indeed nowhere else is the principle: 'might is right!' so conscientiously followed than in the exercise of the rights befitting the *tubuan*. This makes him feared, but everyone complies with his orders because resistance to the *tubuan* would lead to even more powerful repression, possibly even to loss of life. If the owner of a *tubuan* is a liberal man (that is, a native who is less covetous than his neighbours), then the rule of the *tubuan* is relatively mild. An acquisitive *tubuan* on the other hand conducts things terribly, and it can happen that the members themselves grumble about the heavy pressure brought to bear even on them, and finally *tubuan* from the neighbouring districts bring the situation back to normal. By and large, however, one could maintain that excesses by a *tubuan* are a rarity; the most recent was over 20 years ago. The influence of settlers, missionaries, and the administration has moderated the *tubuan*, and his activities must now be designated as very mild. Our concepts of right and wrong are so totally different from those of the natives that we often regard a punishment imposed by natives against natives as hard and unjust. In spite of this we hear no grumbles on the part of the one punished, because according to his concepts of justice he regards the punishment meted out to him as just and fair. In reverse, European justice appears to the native quite often as a shocking injustice, and he bows to it only because he knows that power is on the side of the magistrate. Thus, in most cases, the government of the natives is a covetous and hard-hearted *tubuan* against which nothing can prevail: at the end is open rebellion, and when it gets to this point the situation must be far gone.

To some extent, as the highest instance of jurisdiction, the *tubuan* has ways and means of protecting property. He guards taro, yam and banana plantations, protects individual trees and large stands of palms, and achieves all this merely by setting up a simple sign, consisting of a bundle of grass, a plaited coconut frond, several brightly painted coconut shells, and so on, on the item to be protected. This sign is the *tabu* sign of the *tubuan* and is rigorously respected out of fear of his vengeance. The owner of the item under protection pays the *tubuan* a certain sum of shell money for his efforts.

On the death of wealthy natives (plate 43) or at ceremonies to honour the ancestors (*Papua Album*, vol. I, plate 16) the *tubuan* can never be missed out; he exalts the ceremony or celebration with his dances, his mysterious disappearances and appearances evoke wonder and fear, but he makes sure that he is well paid for his efforts.

Although the *tubuan* primarily rakes in money for his owner, he still does not forget his children, the *duk-duk*; for the principle holds: 'Live and

Plate 38 Women on Nukumanu

let live!' and, in addition to the feasts and dance entertainments, many remnants of shell money fall to the *duk-duk*, most especially in the initiation of new members, but also in the collecting of fines.

Previously, violent acts would also have occurred against women and girls. Such a case never came to my knowledge, and old members also deny it. Today, certainly such behaviour no longer occurs, although, in the districts round Vunakokor, the *tubuan* still appears domineering and violent, and the administrative authorities do not make much difference.

From the preceding paragraphs it is evident that in reality the *duk-duk* society does not impart secrets or extraordinary knowledge to the new members. It may be that the initiates have now come to the conclusion that all that happens on the *taraiu* and under the jurisdiction of the *tubuan* and *duk-duk* masks is not the work of spirits but of quite ordinary men, a revelation which of itself may appear astonishing enough to the newly initiated.

A peculiarity of the Gazelle Peninsula are the skull masks, about which a lot has been written in the ethnographic literature, related to hypotheses with which I cannot agree.

Because the masks are made of individual pieces of a human skull, and because the skulls of the dead play a special role among peoples of nature (and here and there among the Melanesians), these skull masks signify something absolutely special. Although the natives, the makers of these skull masks, know nothing of these kinds of deep meanings, they do not want this to be recognised, and support this by saying: 'The present natives know nothing at all about the deeper meanings, but this is because, over the course of time, they have been forgotten!'

In volume X of the *Publikationen aus dem Ethnographischen Museum zu Dresden*, I have attempted to remove the enhanced significance of these masks, especially to disprove their connection with ancestor worship and honouring of the dead. However, new theories always emerge, finding apparent confirmation in some observation by a traveller or a missionary, who could have considered the matter only quite superficially. In volume XI of the *Internationales Archiv für Ethnographie*, Herr L. Frobenius maintains the deeper significance. In volume XIII of the *Dresdener Publikationen*, Herr W. Foy introduces a comment by by Father Fromm, probably with the intention of connecting the skull masks to ancestor worship. Father Fromm says in a letter published in the *Marien Monatsheften* 1899 that a skull mask was shown to him by natives going to a dance, with the words, 'Here, this is his father', pointing to a young man who stood nearby; several were also offered for him to buy. It is quite possible that the mask in question was made out of the bony skull of the father of that young man. The natives have, I have observed on countless occasions, so little respect for the remains of their fathers and relatives that it is entirely possible that the young man himself or someone else among his compatriots had

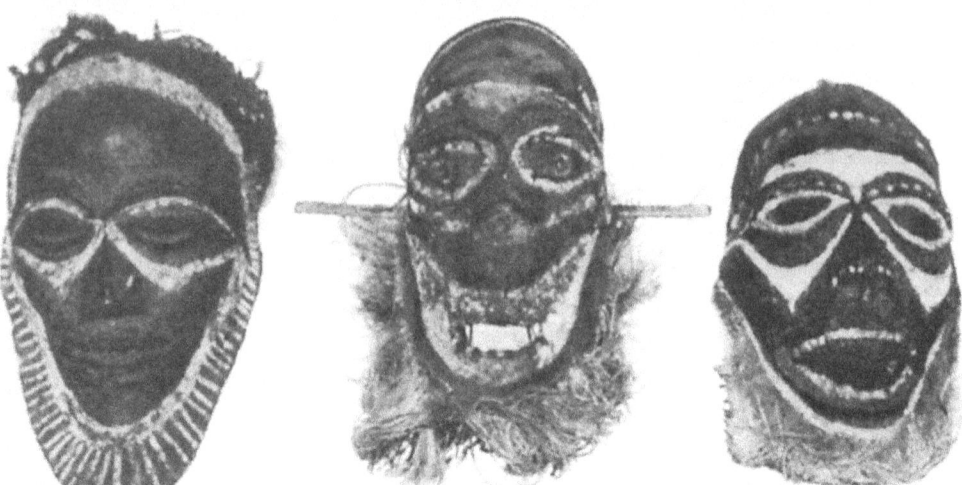

Fig. 107 Skull masks from the Gazelle Peninsula

uplifted the skull and made a mask from it. I have obtained numerous skulls from natives and know that fathers sold the skulls of their sons, and sons the skulls of their fathers, laughing, for a pittance. The son scarcely regards his father as a relative, and would never store his skull as something special.

Certainly a kind of skull cult is known on the Gazelle Peninsula. Skulls of wealthy people who have left a lot of *tabu*, are exhumed after a certain time, placed on a frame and ceremonies take place. However, this has absolutely nothing to do with the skull masks. These are the products of a very specific district, and I have succeeded in localising it precisely.

The skull masks (fig. 107) are made from the frontal and facial bones and mandible of a human skull. In order to achieve the greatest possible similarity with the face of a living man, the outer surface is coated with the crushed pulp of the *Parinarium laurinum* nut and then painted. Often the face is framed with a beard either formed from *Parinarium* pulp and then represented by painting, or made from actual human hair; and frequently also from pig bristles or stiff plant fibres. The same applies to the hair of the head, either made from real human hair or from plant fibres. Occasionally a piece of bark material extends from the upper edge of the mask covering the wearer's head. The mask is either held in one hand in front of the face, or a wooden cross-brace is fixed to the reverse side and gripped by the wearer's teeth (see the middle mask in fig. 107). The older masks look very realistic and are difficult to obtain today. The more recent masks are prepared far more crudely. I am, to some extent, of the opinion that the masks are still used today. When I arrived here in 1882 I made inquiries, and found that the skull masks were already dying out. High prices of *tabu* brought me several beautiful old specimens, and, enticed by this, they resorted once more to manufacture in order to sell the product to warships and other visitors.

The modern work is easily distinguished by an experienced person from the old genuine articles.

Use is manifold. When the shell money (*tabu*) is distributed at weddings the distributor holds the mask (*lor*) in front of his face during the distribution. After the distribution he puts it aside again. A further usage is that during feasts certain people, holding such a mask in front of their faces, make their way onto the feasting place and receive a portion of the food as a gift, to which, unmasked, they would not be entitled.

Earlier they are said to have worn the masks in dances; in spite of repeated assurances, this was not clear to me for a long time, for the natives always sing when dancing, and gesticulate with hands and arms, so that they would hardly be able to hold a mask in their teeth or keep it in position with their hand. Dancing with masks has been described to me by reliable sources as a slow, silent wandering round by the wearer while another part presented the usual noisy dance.

The home territory of the skull masks encompass the districts on the high plateau between Weberhafen and Blanche Bay, and the custom is restricted to this area. It is certainly not excluded that, in earlier times, the skull masks had been connected with a certain type of ancestor worship, but what one reads about this in various works is based exclusively on hypotheses that find no confirmation in statements by the natives. There is no item about which I have enquired more extensively over the last twenty years than these masks; and it would be incomprehensible if during this whole period not a single fact came to my ears indicating a higher significance, if one actually existed. Again and again from the most diverse quarters I heard the same details confirmed, and I believe that one can finally withdraw the skull masks from their attributed high significance without any damage to ethnology.

As well as the *duk-duk* masks and the skull masks,

face masks are also familiar on the Gazelle Peninsula, all given the name *lor*, that is, skull. They are, as a rule, very simple, consisting of a curved board in the shape of a face with a carved nose, a slit for the mouth and round eye holes. The background painting is white, and black and red stripes mark the individual parts of the face. They are, as a rule, provided with a helmet-like frame densely covered with fibres, representing hair; the form strongly reminiscent of the helmet masks of New Ireland. Without doubt these masks are a remnant of earlier, now gradually disappearing, customs. Today they are used only for dances that are designated as *malangene taberan* (that is, spirit dances), but nobody now knows which spirits they represent. However, these dances also have the character of all other vulgar dances; they are presented publicly for the amusement of those present, be they men or women, and no special regard is given to the masks themselves. A carry-over from old times, which likewise points to New Ireland, is that the dancers cover themselves with a loincloth or skirt of ferns, extending from the waist to the knees, just as we see during dances to honour the dead on New Ireland. This last circumstance is, for me, overwhelming evidence that we have before us the rudiments of a very old custom, which the original immigrants brought with them from their homeland on the far side of St George Channel. In all other dances, the inhabitants of the Gazelle Peninsula, from the Duke of York Islands to New Ireland, are completely naked, with the exception of the bunch of bright leaves and flowers that serves as a headdress. In the great dances to honour the dead on New Ireland the dancer wraps himself in such a leaf garment. This custom has been retained as a peculiarity on the Gazelle Peninsula where otherwise the total nudity of both sexes was customary only a few years ago, although the significance of the dance and of the masks has passed a long time ago into oblivion.

They have another kind of mask in Kadakadai, an inland district of the Gazelle Peninsula. These are similar in construction to the previously described masks, but with the difference that the face has a grotesque appearance from a dense plastering of lime with bulges of vegetable resin laid on top. Crooked noses and oblique mouth or eye apertures, enormous eyebrows of plant fibre, fantastic beards and the like are characteristic of these masks. They are actually helmet masks, covering the entire head, and bearing a fibrous trim on the lower edge, falling over neck and shoulders. This mask too represents a spirit, but nobody today has more detailed information. It is not impossible that this mask is the forerunner of a *tubuan* mask with which it shows many similarities. Also Kadakadai is a district adjoining the region from which the *tubuan* and *duk-duk* seem originally to have come. A certain interdependence between these masks and the *tubuan* seems to have existed until not long ago, according to comments by several old natives, in that at the appearance of the *tubuan* such masks came running a short distance in front of him, with a lot of noise, announcing his arrival so that women, children and non-members could quickly take flight.

Masks from that area, of which about twenty years ago I caught a glimpse, were real masterpieces as caricatures of a man's face. No two were alike; each one had a different aspect and small disfigurements or weaknesses were reproduced in such grotesque form and with such a sure feeling for the ridiculous and the exaggerated that it would be difficult, even for the most earnest, to look at them without smiling. The dances of the natives are, as a rule, quite monotonous and boring, but a dance by the Kadakadai people with these masks belongs among the most delightful that I can recall during the many years of my stay in the South Seas. What is made today is amateurish compared with the earlier items, and is at a much lower level both in presentation and in interpretation.

Of far greater significance to the population of the north-east of the Gazelle Peninsula than the *duk-duk* institution is the men's secret society designated by the name *marawot*, or *ingiet*. The *duk-duk* society could be removed without any difficulty by an administration ban, although no small disturbance might arise in all the native social institutions based on, and connected to it, but in time these would subside and be overcome. *Marawot* and *ingiet*, however, are so deeply ingrained in the whole spiritual life of the natives that no official order by the administration and no persuasive powers of the Christian missionaries would manage to root out the institution. Like so many old heathen customs still flourishing in secret in Christian lands despite centuries of persecution and combat, the *ingiet* institution too would continue in New Britain and only cloak itself in even greater secrecy than is the case today.

Marawot and *ingiet* have nothing in common with the *duk-duk* and, while the first-mentioned is of fairly recent date, the second institution extends far back into the people's past.

Marawot, in many places *moramora* as well, is the name of the site where the men gather; the site on which the dances, also called *marawot*, are performed is called *balana marawot* (*balana* = stomach, midpoint). *Ingiet*, or in other writings *iniet* or *ingiat*, is both the name for the dance of the initiated and, above all, for the society.

By far the largest number of male natives belong to the *marawot* or *ingiet* and call themselves *ingiet*. Boys are taken into the society even during childhood although they only learn and take part in the actual dances later.

The initiation seems to be without special ceremony; it is sufficient that the father or uncle of the native, who is in possession of the *ingiet* secrets, makes a small payment of *tabu*. The amount varies from a metre-long section to several fathoms. During the dance presentation the initiates squat in a hut where they are hosted by the older members. The real ceremonial place, the *balana marawot*, with the hut on it, is surrounded by a dense, high fence so that the uninitiated women and children cannot see the events going on there.

Only very special people can share the secrets of the *ingiet*. Each of these persons has their special *ingiet* which they own. Initiation into an *ingiet* permits entrance to all other *ingiet* societies. The dance, with slight variations, is virtually the same everywhere; on the other hand, the words of the accompanying song vary. It requires long intensive practice to dance the *marawot* correctly, and to learn the precision of the measured arm and body movements and the simultaneous stamping on the ground.

It is quite difficult to obtain reliable information about the institution but, by and large, one can characterise the society as one which gives the initiates the right to associate with the men, but more particularly introduces them to all kinds of sorcery, and acquaints them with numerous spells, including those which have the purpose of bestowing domestic happiness, family success, protection against illness, of conjuring up evil spirits, or of invoking sickness, death and ruin on neighbours.

The natives also distinguish several main types of *ingiet*, namely *ingiet warawaququ* (*ququ* = to be joyful, to be happy), or the spell to make happy and joyful, also known as *moramora*; and in contrast *ingiet na matmat* (*mat* = dead), or the death-bringing spell, also called *winerang*. Each of these main types has special gradations with corresponding names. A native who is initiated into all the different *ingiet* and has knowledge of all the magic formulae stands in high regard.

I have been present at numerous *ingiet* gatherings, and in the following section I want to describe several features in greater detail.

One such gathering was an *ingiet warawaququ*. A tall, dense fence of coconut and other palm leaves was erected in a clearing; the completely empty rectangular space within measured about 30 metres long by 10 metres wide. An open hut of the usual local construction stood at one end. The narrower end of the fence, opposite the hut, was neatly made from woven coconut matting; the mats were decorated with black, red and white paintings. These represented male figures with the characteristic legs bent at the knees and bent arms pointing upwards. Both longer walls were decorated with all kinds of bright leaf material, flowers and garlands of feathers, all producing quite a pleasant impression. Outside this enclosure, *balana marawot*, had gathered a large number of natives from the surrounding districts: ceremonially decorated men, youths and boys, as well as numerous women, who had brought large bundles of prepared food wrapped in banana leaves.

From the *balana marawot* there sounded a loud unintelligible song in the highest falsetto and the men and boys standing outside immediately went through the narrow entrance onto the site, which was soon filled to overflowing. The boys being admitted took their places with their male relatives in the little hut. Opposite the hut with their faces turned towards it, the decorated men gradually arranged themselves into several rows side by side, and on a given signal the dance began, with the wooden drums and a song providing the beat for the dancers. All the dancers joined in the song in the highest falsetto, which would have made great demands on the vocal chords. It ended suddenly, for the time being, and a single native then recited a number of sentences, also in a falsetto and with astonishing volubility, after which singing and dancing resumed as before. By and large, the dance did not differ from the other public dances, with the exception that from time to time all the dancers stamped their foot *a tempo* very hard on the ground several times, giving rise to a far-reaching droning sound. After each footstep a deep guttural sound was expressed in unison. This stamping was given the name *rurua*. The other movements and figures of the dance, *warawaqira*, the bending of the trunk, and the arm and hand movements were presented with astounding precision which indicated extensive practice, and could not have been executed better by a trained *corps de ballet*.

Another characteristic of the dance was that from time to time it showed a tendency toward obscenity, although this never degenerated but was always only hinted at; perhaps only in order not to arouse the displeasure of the European present.

After a dance had ended, the dancers, streaming perspiration, walked off the arena, and new ones walked on. This went on for several hours until all the groups assembled had presented their songs and dances to the best of their ability. Then the new members came out of the hut with their relatives and laid down the novitiates' entrance fee, *lili*, at the opposite end of the enclosure. Several of the earlier dancers then approached those newly admitted, holding a carved wooden board, *tabataba*, in each hand; they made a movement with this as if they wanted to bore through the boys, while saying: *jau tung tamam* (*jau* = I, *tung* = to make a hole, *tamam* = your child). Others brought spears, little bunches of bright feathers, necklaces and headbands, which they handed over to the new members, with a view to receiving the usual sum for these items in shell money later, by way of a reciprocal gift from the parents or uncles. On the ceremonial site human figures are occasionally erected, also bearing the name *tabataba*. They can hardly be called idols, since nobody pays homage or worships them. They are figurative representations of the spirits of highly regarded members of the society intended to be honoured after death, and always have only transitory significance for special ceremonies. Previously they made grotesque figures out of a soft tufa for the same purpose, and several of these came into my possession. The present generation does not recognise such figures, and only a few old men were able to impart the actual significance of the figures to me.

The women gathered outside were meanwhile conducting a lively trade with the morsels they had brought, which the dancers made short work of, once their task was done.

These ceremonies often last for several days on end.

The new members are henceforth *ingiet* and cannot eat pork for the rest of their lives, since an evil spirit lives in the pig and is summoned for the purposes of sorcery at other *ingiet* gatherings. At later assemblies they learn the dance and various songs, and are at the same time initiated into the mysteries of certain magic spells.

In the instance previously described, the magic spell is of the utmost simplicity. It consists of the words: '*A bul i manamana jau!*' It is a spell by which all evil spirits are supposed to be driven from the compounds and dwellings and, most importantly, from the family. It is performed by the person in question taking a branch of the *Karongon* bush in his hand and waving it to and fro with outstretched arm over the place to be protected, and touching it on the people and items to be protected while rapidly reciting the spell and repeating it many times.

Besides the previously described *ingiet warawaququ* there are a great number of similar spells for averting the influence of evil spirits and attracting favourable and gratifying living conditions. It is up to each person how many of these magic spells he wants to learn; after the initial introduction he has the right to take part in all other *marawot* and learn the special incantations and accompanying hocus-pocus there, paying the owner of the spell, of course.

All of these *marawot* or *ingiet* have different names; for example, *balu* (pigeon), *qelep* (species of palm), *tagir* (fruit of the *Eugenia malaccensis*), *varpidak* (the name of a certain native), *läkeläke* (to pass over something or to progress), and so on. It is not always obvious how these names are connected with the *ingiet*. In one case, *varpidak* is the name of the discoverer of a certain spell, and also its name. *Läkeläke*, to pass over something on the path, is a designation that is evoked by the way in which the charm works; the charm is laid on the path while murmuring the spell, and becomes effective as soon as the person to be charmed steps over it. I have never fully understood names like *balu* = pigeon, *qelep* = species of palm; it seems to me that they are words that the initiated men use to designate something special which is unknown to the women in the vicinity.

It was far more difficult for me to gain admission to the places where *ingiet na matmat*, the death-bringing spell, is taught.

Admission here is exactly the same as for the *ingiet warawaququ* or *moramora*, with the exception that women are kept strictly far away, and the participants, as well as the new members, must fast from early morning, and can take betel nut or food only after the conclusion of the *marawot*.

I was led by a member to a place in the forest, far away from villages and compounds. The site was set up temporarily for these special purposes; the paths leading there were barely recognisable. From far off we heard the high falsetto singing intermingled with the dull stamping of the men, repeated from time to time.

On the assembly place one is confronted first of all with the usual picture, the presence of numerous ceremonially decorated participants who performed their dance closely crowded together. All kinds of figures were carved into the bark of the trees round about, some easily recognisable as sharks, snakes, stingrays, lizards, and so on, but several required explanation before one understood that they represented ravens, dolphins, wallabies, and so on. These tree carvings were made to stand out more clearly with black, red and white paint.

In the middle of the site stood a tree trunk, which was buried with the stump end in the ground so that the roots with all their branchings and fibres soared about 2 metres above ground. The tree used for this is called *kua*. Decorated men, dancing and singing, moved in a circle around the tree stump, holding a small bundle of leaves that they laid on the ground around the upside down *kua* stump at the end of the dance. Then they chewed betel.

The assembly was, as I found out, a very special secret, and took place in such an isolated spot because a spell was taught which had the aim of killing an enemy at will by enchantment.

For this purpose the sorcerer must get possession of the *puta* of the person to be enchanted. *Puta* is anything that is or was connected with his body; a portion of his saliva, his excrement, his food, his hair or beard, even the earth in which his footsteps have left visible impressions. It is therefore no wonder that the natives conceal or destroy these items most carefully, or smudge any traces of them. After he has obtained the *puta*, the one who wishes evil wraps it in various leaves, the scraped bark of certain trees, soil, and so on, inside a betel leaf.

He then steps out in the line of dancers on the assembly place, holding the little bundle in one hand, and a carved and painted little board, the *tabataba na kaiya* in the other. All of those wooden figures depicted, for example, in the *Dresdener Publikationen*, volume X, plate 15, figure 3; plate 16, figures 1, 3 to 11; plate 18, figures 1, 3 to 5; volume XII, plate 7, figures 1 and 4, are *tabataba*. A *tabataba na kaiya* is a little wooden board on which the evil spirit *kaiya* is depicted either by painting or carving.

The little bundle with the *puta* is swung to and fro during the dance, and the *tabataba na kaiya* likewise. At the same time the name of the person to be charmed is uttered, and the whole series of evil spirits summoned, upon which the desired method of death is pronounced with the words: *u na wirua pit na nga* (may you die on the path)! or: *u na wirua ra na ta* (may you die at sea)! or: *u na bura* (may you crash down)! and so on.

The number of evil spirits summoned is very great for, according to the native's concept, there is scarcely any object that is not pervaded by an evil spirit. Evil spirits dwell in the snake (*wi*), the iguana (*palai*), the crocodile (*pukpuk*), the shark (*mong*), the pig (*boroi*), the crow (*kotkot*), the brown hen-harrier (*miniqulai*), the stingray (*wara*), the dolphin (*tokalama*), the wallaby (*dek*), and in numerous other animals.

In the middle, between the *moramora* and the *winerang*, is a whole series of other *ingiet* that can be learned by the initiated members if they wish. A native who is initiated in all the *ingiet* and who knows how to administer them very effectively, is called a *tena ingiet* (*tena* = one who is skilful). As a result of his thorough knowledge he is able to perform many things that are impossible to the only superficially initiated. Thus, for example, he can transform himself into a *wawina tabatabaran* (spirit woman); that is, he can take on the form of any woman at will. The *tena ingiet* is paid a certain amount of *tabu* to entice a given man, an intended victim of evil, in the form of a particular woman. When this man falls victim to the temptations of the *wawina tabatabaran*, he dies from a bleeding penis.

The *tena ingiet* can also cause death or illness in a man by pricking the footsteps of a person with the spine of a stingray, in a certain way. This spell is called *aqaqar*, or *raprapu*, and the one performing the spell is also designated as *tena aqaqar*.

It is understandable that the native, who sees himself surrounded by evil magic at every step, is prudent enough to have counter-magic available. Many *marawot* and *ingiet* societies therefore have the aim of teaching such antidote spells and magic incantations. These consist of a certain word or a certain phrase being rapidly repeated, thus listing the evil spirits in order one by one, to persuade them to go away. At the same time burnt lime is held in the palm of the hand and the incantation is murmured over it. Betel is chewed at the same time, and from time to time the chewed-up mass is vigorously spat from the lips over the object or person to break the spell.

I had occasion to observe such a *marawot* and I want to describe it, because it differs a little from the one previously described. On the carefully tidied place in the forest stood two parallel rows of upturned *kua* trunks, the roots uppermost, about 1 metre apart, and between each one a brightly leafed bunch of *Dracaena* forming a path about 2 metres wide. The decorated men stood in a row on each side of the path. Singing and dancing were the same as always, except that the individual turns were somewhat different. In the first turn, the front person, after several body contortions on the spot, danced along the outside of his fellow dancers and took up a position at the back; the new front person repeated this, and so it continued until the original front man had regained his position. Then a familiar *tena ingiet* stepped forward and with great lingual dexterity uttered a spell in a falsetto before stepping back. The dance began again, but with the difference that the two front dancers now danced along the inside of the path and took their position at the end of the row, just as before. While dancing through, each dancer deposited several *tabu* snails at the foot of the upturned little trees, probably as payment to the teacher of the magic spell. In this case the spell went as follows:

> *O qumqumele! O qumqumele! O qumqumele! O qumqumele!*
> *I na marue na pukpuk!* (*marue* = to spit out, to vomit; *pukpuk* = crocodile).
> *I na marue ra qalang!* (*qalang* = rat). *I na marue ra aele* (toad)!
> *I na marue ra qap* (blood)! *In na marue ra kumqumai* (offal)!
> *I na marue ra laqulaqu* (bunch of plants that hangs over the neck)!
> *I na marue ra timak! I na marue ra ingiet* (sorcery)!
> *I n a marue ra tabataba* (magic image)! *I na marue ra tava longo!*

This special *marawot* bears the name *pal na bata*. On the day of presentation, all the participants must fast until the end of the dance and the ceremony.

Somewhat isolated in the forest, about 100 metres from the dance place, was the actual *pal na bata*. It is the only building of its kind that I have seen; today they no longer go to the trouble of erecting such a building. It was surrounded on all sides by thick brushwood with a narrow path through it, so low that one could only get through by stooping. On a cleaned area stood a small hut with its roof decorated with feathers and flowers. All the posts were carved and painted, and represented various *tabataba*. Around the entire building, forming a courtyard, stood man-sized *tabataba* with bright body paint. They represented the spirits of famous *ingiet* members, and the new members gave a gift of *tabu* to all of them. When the youths had been introduced here they received a new name.

I want to mention here an *ingiet* ceremony that is no longer conducted, and is gradually disappearing into oblivion.

During my stay in the Bismarck Archipelago I have had the opportunity of observing it in two places: in 1888 on Matupi and shortly after at Nanuk, beyond Ralum. The ceremonial building that had been erected on Matupi on that occasion was depicted by Hugo Zöller on page 97 of his book *Deutsch Neuguinea* as a 'great dance festival on Matupi', from a photograph that I had taken. First I shall describe the building, which is called *pal na pedik* (*pal* = house, *pedik* = secret). The basic frame of this house is a high tree with the small branches stripped from the top so that only several main branches soar in various directions. Around this tree they erect a tower-like scaffold of bamboo canes, about 6 to 8 metres long and 4 to 5 metres wide, gradually tapering upwards. The branches of the tree serve as support for this scaffold. On the top of the 20- to 25-metre-tall structure a frame in the shape of a small boat is attached. The outside of the entire building is clad with foliage. At the foot of the tower stand a number of carved wooden figures called *tabalara* representing spirits, dead *tena ingiet* as a rule. A small opening at ground level leads into the building, and the people climb up bamboo ladders to the highest point of the tower.

Erection of such a building causes considerable expense and takes up quite a lot of time. Meanwhile the news spreads in all directions to the most distant of regions. A certain day is fixed for the opening of the festival. On that morning, a native noted as a *tena ingiet* performs a solo dance on the top of the tower and, to some extent, consecrates the building by loudly crying out incantations; such a dance is called *kakakä*. When he has climbed down, eight to ten people climb the structure and perform a dance up there, accompanied by loud singing. This presentation is called *pukur pal*. The participants who have come along to the celebration bring their young boys too, and they are introduced with special ceremony. The owner stands near the entrance, and the boys, festively adorned with bright foliage, feather decorations, and so on, approach him, holding several fathoms of *tabu* in their hands. He then asks them: 'What is your name?' They give their names and receive permission to enter the building. Inside they lay their *tabu* at the feet of the *tabalara* and, when they step outside, the owner hands them a brightly leafed *Dracaena* which they have to take in their hands. They are then given a new name, which they bear from then on at the celebration of the various *ingiet* customs and ceremonies. The festivities last for several days, depending on the number of participants who have streamed in and perform their various dances. They receive a gift of *tabu*, whereby the dance they performed and the singing become the property of the host.

The several-day celebration on Matupi was totally peaceful throughout. At the festivity in Nanuk, which only lasted one day, my intervention prevented major bloodshed without my being aware of anything at that time. As I was later told, it had been the custom in earlier times that participants in the ceremony, if they saw that they were strong enough, suddenly fell upon any enemies present from another tribe and killed them, which always brought about a major massacre. At Nanuk they had decided that day to kill the headman, Tonoe, who lived on the shore not far from Ralum, and who had come with a small retinue. My arrival delayed the attack, and the victim in question, for whom the presence of many old enemies seemed uncanny, had time to get away. I can still remember clearly the glowering look and the sullen silence of the natives armed to the teeth, so that a lengthy stay did not seem advisable to me either, the more so since I was accompanied by my wife and several officials of the New Guinea Company.

Several years previously such an attack had taken place in a neighbouring district, when more than fifty men had been killed. The incident is still talked about today by the older men, who were for the most part present as boys or youths. The Dawaun people from Blanche Bay had come along in great numbers. The *pukur a pal* was in full song on the uppermost platform of the *pal na pedik*. The Dawaun people thronged the building under the pretext of wanting to perform their dance, and with great speed untied the bands attaching the upper platform to the tree branches. As a result, the dancers suddenly felt the structure breaking up under their feet and plunged all the way down. Then began a great bloodbath in which many of the Dawaun people were killed, but about fifty of the other party also met their deaths. The following day, the bodies of these people were brought to the host of the celebration and for each one 50 to 100 fathoms of *tabu* were paid to the relatives. The slain Dawaun people formed the subsequent festive roast. According to the native accounts this bloody event must have taken place in the latter half of the 1860s.

So far the *ingiet* society might be regarded as simply a men's society for practising their superstitious customs. However, it had a far deeper influence in that it totally undermined the natives' morals, which were always only at a low level.

At the exhibitions that I have already partially described, the proceedings are fairly respectable, apart from some minor obscene scenes. In the

Plate 39 Group of men on Nukumanu

preceding gatherings, reserved for practising singing and dancing, it is quite different and, in the presentation that I had seen, the offensive part was discarded because of my presence, for fear of causing displeasure. However, if no white person is present, the natives let themselves go, and the gatherings are like nothing imaginable. Women without relatives and widows on their own must present themselves at the local *ingiet* rehearsals and the members fornicate with them without restraint. Since the rehearsals take a long time and many of the dancers remain on site, they roam the neighbourhood, plundering and stealing whatever they need from gardens and compounds. However, they are very careful not to take the property of other *ingiet*. They restrict themselves to those who do not belong to the society, who are labelled with the designation *a mana*. *A mana* or non-members are, without exception, people who have no relatives by whom they can be introduced or bought into the society, or who have found no rich friends willing to take on their introduction. These poor wretches lead an unenviable life, nobody paying them any attention; if they want to live, they have to grow their scant nourishment. To some extent they have no rights because they have no family connections to stand up for them when need arises. They are completely powerless against the *ingiet* people. When these approach the gardens and compounds of the *mana* on their raids they give a loud cry, *valeo*, and the *mana* immediately flee, abandoning their property. Sick people are persuaded to go to the assemblies, and have to pay shell money, ostensibly for the evil spirit that has caused the illness to be exorcised and rendered powerless. In short, the *ingiet* can do and say as they please, since nobody dares to resist them for fear of being enchanted and dying an excruciating death. What is more, the secrets, *pedik*, of the society are nothing more than a series of abominations which are carefully kept secret. Promulgation of the secrets was previously punished by death; today, when there is fear of the imperial administration, by payment of *tabu*. The local village magistrates, established by the administration, turn a blind eye as well, because in their hearts they are convinced of the power of the society, and fear their spells and exorcisms.

Yet the abominations are still not at an end. The earlier custom, that initiates must drink human blood, has, however, ceased. On the other hand, there are still a great number of the most obscene songs that are sung by young and old at the gatherings. Although I am obliged to mention highly indelicate matters in order to give a complete picture of the natives, I cannot persuade myself to write down an example of these songs. It is impossible to think of anything more filthy and crude. The natives, who otherwise do not have a tendency towards obscene language and gestures in their daily lives, are totally depraved on these occasions.

At initiation in a few *ingiet*, sodomy is performed before the eyes of those present. An old *ingiet* drops the *balana marawot* and steps back totally naked, smeared with lime from head to foot. He holds one end of a coconut mat in his hands offering the other end to one of the newly initiated and then they pull each other around for a while until they fall over each other and the abomination takes place. All the initiates must undergo this procedure in turn. I want to mention here that sodomy is not a deplorable custom in the eyes of the natives; it is regarded more in the light of a derisory treatment.

It takes years of acquaintance and absolute trust in the inquirer before a native can be persuaded to report these matters; not so much because he is ashamed and regards them as bad, since all the other natives do exactly the same, and his forefathers acted likewise. Should he have any scruples he takes comfort in the thought: 'it was ever so!' However, he is so thoroughly convinced of the power that dwells within the society that he is frightened of its magical powers above all else. These notes are based on extensive accurate accounts by natives, and have been variously confirmed throughout both by white missionaries and by the coloured teachers.

The imperial authority, at the instigation of rebukes by the Christian missionary societies, has recently undertaken to stop these excesses. It is questionable whether prohibition will have any effect; most probably what happened semi-publicly before will now continue in secret and the evil will be aggravated. Such a deep-rooted superstition will not be stopped straight away by an official order. First, the superstition has to be rooted out, and only the missionaries can do this, although not in a few decades. In Europe today, in spite of centuries of Christianity, many old superstitions still flourish, against which the Church can do nothing, and it will be the same out here. The abominations that spring from the *ingiet* may perhaps be restricted, and may, over the years, even be totally eradicated, but the sorcery connected with the society, and the call of the spirits, will still flourish for a long time and exert their influence, even though in secret.

In the Duke of York group, the *ingiet* society is just as universally spread as on the Gazelle Peninsula. Although Christian missions have been active there for about thirty years, the people are possibly even more strongly and more extensively involved in this cult of the most crass superstition than on the Gazelle Peninsula, although strongly campaigned against by white and coloured teachers. This is an example of how little success there is in getting to the root of these secret societies.

Before I leave the inhabitants of the Duke of York Islands and the north-east of the Gazelle Peninsula, I want to comment briefly on their totem system. In the Duke of York group, the influence of the original homeland, the southern half of New Ireland, is still recognisable in that each division has a particular totem sign. We find only two large groups, differentiated as *maramara* and *pikalaba*, who do not marry within the group but always into the other group. It is the rule here, too, that children belong to the mother's group. As an attribute each group has a certain species of *Mantis*; that of the *maramara* is called *kam* and that of the *pikalaba* is named *kogilele*. Veneration of these creatures does not occur.

The inhabitants of the north-eastern Gazelle Peninsula divide themselves similarly into two large groups, with the difference, however, that here, over the course of time, the names of the groups have been completely lost, and that they use the words *avet* and *diat*, or *tavevet* and *tadiat* – that is, 'us' and 'them' – as the sole designation. Insignia of both groups are unknown. Nevertheless, the division is effective; all those who belong to one group regard themselves as close relatives, and sexual relations within the group are seen as a great transgression, for which they have a special word – *pulu*. Here, too, the children belong to the mother's group.

Now that I have described the secret societies of the north-eastern part of the Gazelle Peninsula, I will turn to the Baining.

They are mountain-dwellers and gardeners, and, as far as one knows today, they are at a much lower level of development than their eastern neighbours. Elsewhere, I have expressed the view that the Baining form the original population, as far as one can speak of such at all, of the Gazelle Peninsula, and that the inhabitants of the north-eastern corner are far later immigrants. Whether or not this is so, both tribes have very little in common with each other in language, traditions or customs. It is, therefore, worthwhile to look more closely at their mask dances and their disguises, the more so since I have established that in many places the institution of the *duk-duk* is of very recent date, although I am not able to establish its origin with complete certainty. Since, in my opinion, those tribes that have the *duk-duk* today have migrated originally from the southern half of New Ireland, it can safely be assumed that they brought the basic elements of the secret society from there as well. How far these elements were influenced by neighbouring tribes can best be judged when their related institutions are compared with the *duk-duk*.

It only became known more recently that that type of secret society existed elsewhere on New Britain. Characteristic images from the south coast of New Britain, the area round Montague and Jacquinot bays, only become known in 1900 and 1901. These were interpreted as masks. At the end of 1901 I succeeded in authenticating masks from the South Cape region and, over time, other discoveries will probably be made, which will enable us to build a complete picture. Furthermore, the masks and dances of the Baining have been known to us for only a few years, since the Catholic mission succeeded in gaining a firm foothold in the mountain region, establishing missions and learning the language.

Father Rascher, who had the opportunity to make precise observations, reports on the Baining dances and customs such as mask-making, as follows:

After a brief greeting from the chief we hurried to the dance place. Broad clear paths led there from all directions.

With great noise men and boys carried colossal masks wrapped in dried leaves. Others followed in high spirits with decorated lances, dance sticks, and other items that are used only on these occasions. From the slopes of Vasserom (a high mountain) came the sound of singing accompanied by the dull tones of the *garamut* drum. The dance place was very broad and long, and cleared of all brushwood. Directly overhead stood a huge platform (*ririveigi*), about 15 metres high and 40 metres long, erected with bamboo poles. In front of the platform and connected to it, extended a 3- to 4-metre-wide table, also made from bamboo. Huge masses of cooked and raw taro, yams and bananas, which were either piled up or lay in gorgeous giant baskets and nets, had been put out on display. Each stave and crossbeam of the platform was artistically decorated with garlands of coconuts, bananas, nuts, sugarcane, and so on. In front of the table squatted the festively decorated women and children. They had smeared their entire bodies with ochre and slung their wealth of pearls round their necks and chests. In the middle of this bright throng the orchestra had taken its place. It consisted solely of women, one beating a wooden drum, several others pounding the end of a thick piece of bamboo onto the bare ground or onto stone, while another struck a board-shaped hewn piece of *gallip* wood with a short drumstick. As soon as we arrived, the women's round dance began. About ten to fifteen women, as well as several girls, tripped slowly and silently round in a circle. Their dance costume (*niski*), which covered them like a petticoat, is made from the leaves of a type of *Pandanus* (*bereharenga*) which is split into very fine fibres and twisted by a cord (*siska*). In places the *niski* are painted with egg yolk or red dye, which has a very pleasing effect on the eye. On a handle over the forehead they carried exquisite nets (*asangenaji*), sometimes six or seven at once, and of widely varying sizes. The nets rested on the upper part of the shoulders, and a piece of wild sugarcane was inserted to pull them out to their full length. There were various items in the nets, such as stones, taro, *Areca* nuts. Many dancers had fastened bright loincloths over the *asangenaji*. All held bunches of cassowary feathers or bouquets of fragrant plants or even new knives in their hands, and waved them about during the performance. Every dancer, young girls too, carried a child on their shoulders hanging on by clasping their hands round the head. The loud outcry of these small 'riders' aroused fear at times.

About 10 o'clock, four or five figures smelling of coconut oil (*kokor*) suddenly came into view. At the same instant, the spectators and guests, women and children, who had come from far away, poured onto the dance site. They arranged themselves according to villages. The fantastically decked-out dancers came closer. They supported themselves on lances as they came. Sometimes they walked bent over; then they straightened up, pulling their bodies in tightly and letting them out again, then they stood as if exhausted, panting and with legs sprawled out. On a string on their ankles they wore nutshells (*a chlam*), which rustled at each forceful step. A lance decorated with cockatoo and parrot feathers passed from the buttocks between each person's legs. The shaft of the lance was secured between the legs in a *tapa* sheath that hung from a narrow, painted *tapa* girdle which, in turn, was pulled through the skin at the end of the vertebral column, to hold the lance firm from behind. A fan of cassowary feathers was attached both in the middle of the buttocks and to the pubic area in front. On the front fan was always the stuffed head and neck of a cockatoo (*mareve*). They reached the dance place, stamping in a brisk tempo. The women, who up until now had paid silent homage to the dance, shyly withdrew, but at the same time new female dancers appeared and joined in the men's round dance. The latter, like the earlier women, went silently round in a circle. The musicians went an octave higher, the tone of the *garamut* quickly followed; the melody, which always moved in a minor key became, if possible, even more plaintive. At each new changeover of the dance the circling men and women reversed direction. Suddenly, cries rang out from the foot of the slope. Seventy to eighty men at a gallop hauled in a striped mask image, with shouts of joy and strenuously set it up by raising up the back (upper) part of the mask with bamboo poles and lying the front (lower) part on the dance stick which had been hastily fastened to the head of one of the dancers, who stood still during this scene. Then the dancer with this monster took a few steps forward, stamped and rustled and, amid the yells of the crowd, threw the mask to the ground and, after his lance or two new axes had been handed over to him, resumed the circle dance with the others. Meanwhile the spectators fell on the mask, ripping and cutting off the *tapa*, to take home. The first mask paraded measured 35 metres long.

I estimate the number of masks paraded in this way to be between sixty and seventy. As soon as the mask was thrown off the head of the dancer who, panting, stood there and stamped, he went around in the circle a few minutes longer and then, at the melody changeover, left the dance place and stamped off in a zigzag as if in a frenzy. Several men followed him in double-quick steps. As soon as they caught up with him, one of them held him fast while the others robbed him of his fine jewellery. If he were lucky enough to escape those in pursuit by adroit sidesteps and fast running, the whole audience applauded, and showed their joy with shouts and laughter. When a dancer left, another took his place, in the same costume, panting and stamping, to go through the same procedure. The mask dance gave the appearance of being an interlude. There were about twenty people with the special fixed lances. About half of them carried a short *sareigi* on their head, held by two cords, attached to the stick on which it stood upright. The face was wrapped in a piece of *tapa* which was fastened to the dance stick. Others held sickle-like *tapa* shapes, decorated in stylish patterns, on their heads by means of very large bamboos that tapered off in *sareigi* form. In front of the site where the dancers went round in their circle they stopped, stamping as though in a rage, while the musicians accompanied with a song. Then, suddenly, they dropped the *sareigi* and *ngoáremchi* which were immediately taken away by the spectators. Then the lances were removed from their bodies and each was handed two simple lances on which they leaned while moving round. Perspiration streamed from their bodies. Several boys stood a certain distance apart, outside the circle dance, chewing sugarcane. If one of the dancers held out his chest or back to them they spat saliva on them to refresh them. From time to time one of the dancers bent over again, stamped, drew in his body so that one could encircle him with two hands and count all his ribs, before standing upright again. All the dancers dragged their feet. Their whole body trembled from exhaustion, their faces were haggard, and their hearts were pounding. One fainted, and had to be dragged away. To revive him, a bamboo tube of water was held over his mouth, and so much was poured in that he came round.

The arrival of the headman formed the end of the dance. It was already past 4 o'clock. Men, women and children approached him as close as his toilet hut. A number of men and children carried a gigantic mask in front of him, followed by the honour guard; the chief followed behind, carrying a Nakanai lance in each hand. The splendidly decorated lance that he had attached to his buttocks was reverently held off the ground by two people, using forked bamboo. The procession moved silently uphill and down, onto the hillock. Now and again the headman bowed deeply to the ground, pulled his stomach in, stamped, and proceeded earnestly on again. When he arrived at the top, a *sareigi* was placed on his head, firmly bound under his chin, and the two lances were taken from him. Then the colossal *hareiga* (mask) was fixed onto the *sareigi*. About twenty men stood behind him to support the heavy thing with bamboo, so that it did not crush the wearer. He then stamped for several minutes, and then twelve dried, air-filled pigs' bladders were passed to him; he had to strike these one after another with the flat of an axe, with all his strength so that they really popped. At the ninth his strength failed, so that one of his trabants had to perform the favour for him. During the entire scene, many guests had approached, and watched the Herculean task of the chief, almost with a kind of devotion. His mask remained intact, it had been leant against a tree, and his dance decoration was not stolen, but was handed over to his people for safe-keeping. He then went to the platform and distributed the piled up taro, bananas, coconuts, etc. among the attending guests.

I want to add a few explanatory notes where the description Father Rascher has been kind enough to give me does not seem quite clear and distinct.

The dance that he has described is called *sarecha*. The colossal masks, with a circumference of 3 metres and often 45 metres long, are so heavy that they would crush a man if they were actually placed vertically on his head. They are supported and partially carried by men with long bamboo poles, so that the massive weight is distributed. This type of mask then is not actually worn by the dancer, rather it is carried by those accompanying him, and only leans to a certain extent on the dancer. This happens as follows. The *sareigi* or, as Father Rascher calls it, the dance stick, is fastened to the dancer's head. This expression is misleading; the *sareigi* is actually a conical hat of strips of bamboo covered with painted bark material. From its top soars a (sometimes long, sometimes short) bamboo pole, often similarly carefully covered with fine bark and painted.[1] The big masks (*hareiga* or *sarechi*) are raised upwards by the bearers, as Father Rascher describes, and laid on the *sareigi* whereupon the people armed with long bamboo poles raise the upper end by means of the poles, so that the mask rises steeply upwards from the wearer's head as high as the poles permit. The creation thus never stands vertically on the wearer's head, and its weight is rather borne by the numerous supporters; no man, not even the strongest, would be able to carry the upright mask.

Of course, not all masks are of such enormous size; there are also smaller ones which are put on the boys who participate in the dance, but they are similarly quite heavy in relation to the wearer. It is the small masks that are held in European museums because the very big ones are not suitable for transport to Europe. However, they are all of the same shape, construction and painted decoration.[2]

A second form of headdress is not so heavy. Father Rascher also describes it. It consists of the *sareigi* (dance hat) that ends in a long bamboo tube, on which the so-called *ngoáremchi* are fastened crosswise. In the *Mitteilungen des Dresdener Museums*,

1. See *Mitteilungen aus dem Ethnographischen Museum zu Dresden*, vol. XIII, plate 3, figs 1a, 2 and 3.

2. See *Mitteilungen aus dem Ethnographischen Museum zu Dresden*, vol. XIII, plate 6, figs 1 to 5.

volume XIII, plate 3, figures 1a and 1b, a *sareigi* is depicted with *ngoáremchi* hanging from it. This figure does not, however, accurately reproduce the relationship of both parts of the headdress. The *ngoáremchi* actually hang from the bamboo of the *sareigi* by means of two cords usually decorated with white feathers and down; these cords go from each end of the *ngoáremchi* and are attached to the bamboo of the *sareigi* in such a way that the shape is at right angles to the bamboo, one half rising from each side. The *ngoáremchi* often have a sleeve of bamboo tube in the middle, pushed over the bamboo of the *sareigi*. Here, too, both cords serve more as attachment and balance. Several *ngoáremchi* are always attached one above the other in such a way that the slightly bowed ends are directed upwards, not downwards as in the Dresden figure.

To balance the headdress on the head, partly so that it stays upright and partly so that it does not fall off, long bands of bark are attached to the *sareigi*, and held in the hands of the helpers. This headdress, while heavy enough, depending on the number of *ngoáremchi*, does not have the enormous weight of the *hareiga* or *sarechi*, and can therefore be worn upright on the head of the dancer, although not for long. In the *Mitteilungen des Dresdener Museums*, volume XIII, plate 4, figures 1 to 9, a number of *ngoáremchi* are excellently depicted. According to the natives these represent canoes.

As well as the latter headdress, there is yet a third kind which has many similarities with the foregoing. Father Rascher discusses it as follows:

> Another type of mask, which is likewise carried on poles (bamboo in the *sareigi*), is the *siengem*. These have a round shape. One ends in a long cassowary whisk, the other in a human or pig's head. The former is usually hung with feathers and fragrant plants.

In the often-quoted *Mitteilungen des Dresdener Museums*, volume XIII, plate 5, figures 1 to 5, such *siengem* are depicted. Attachment of these to the long bamboo of the *sareigi* is the same as for the *ngoáremchi*.

We are still not clear about the purpose and significance of the dances. Father Rascher believes that they took place partly to honour the dead and partly as a celebration at the time of ripening of the taro tubers.

Preparations for such a feast take a long time. First the bark material (*kambulucha*) has to be prepared. It is produced from the bark of the breadfruit tree (*bischa*) which is softened in water and beaten with pieces of wood to remove the pith. Choicer bark is used for the hat and for the *ngoáremchi*. For a mask of the form shown in figure 2 of plate 6 in volume XIII of the *Dresdener Mitteilungen*, great quantities of this bark material are required, particularly when the structure is 35 to 40 metres long. Preparation of the bark material is the men's work, as is the painting. The principal colours are red, yellow and black. The red colour is produced from a root. The scraped root is chewed, and the chewed mass is spat out into a coconut shell or onto a leaf; the sap is used as a dye. The black colour is produced from the resin of the *gallip* tree (a species of *Canari*). The resin is sprinkled on the fire where it produces a rich form of soot; this is caught on leaves covering the fire, and then scraped off the leaves. Yellow is produced from the nut kernel of a certain plant; the kernels are squeezed, and they use the yellow sap which flows out. The figures on plates 3 to 6 of volume XIII of the *Dresdener Mitteilungen*, and the reproductions of the drawings printed in the text, give a representation of the drawings, made with astonishing care and, I might also say, with artistic feeling. This is particularly the case when we observe the drawings of the *sareigi*, the *ngoáremchi* and the *siengem*. The drawings of the *hareiga* show less care.

What is the significance of these drawings? Once more we are confronted with an enigma that is difficult to resolve. The patterns are, however, traditional, and it is possible that the current artists have forgotten a large part of the original meaning. On the big *hareiga* or *sarechi* the painting always represents a face. During a visit to the Baining I was shown two of these drawings, with the comment that one represented a man and the other a pig. The difference was hardly noticeable; in any case, it would have been impossible for an inexperienced person to say which drawing represented a human face, and which a pig's head. At the most, one could distinguish the masks from the other decorations; thus, on the image with the alleged pig's head were added the cut-off tail and the genitalia of a boar; the image with the human face had ear-shaped appendages on the sides, which for their part needed explanation before they could be recognised as ears. That the drawings on plate 5, figures 3b, 4b and 5b of volume XIII of the *Dresdener Mitteilungen* should represent human figures can be guessed from the shape of the frame; but it is less clear that figures 1a, 1b and 2a should represent a pig's head. The *Mitteilungen* designate these images as snakes, where head and body have the greatest similarity; the Baining, however, maintain that it is a pig.

The composite form of the whole drawing offers even greater difficulty in explanation. Figure 2a of plate 5 and figure 2 of plate 6 in volume XIII of the *Dresdener Mitteilungen* show this very clearly. The drawing is composed of various systems of lines, triangles, circles and dots that do not bear the least resemblance to the items that they allegedly represent; for example, shellfish, *gallip* (*Canari*) trees, palm leaves, coconuts, and so on. The adjacent figure (fig. 108) could, if need be, indicate a face; but, according to the natives, it represents a club, despite there not being the least similarity to this object, and certainly nobody, even if he let his wildest fantasies roam free, would arrive at this explanation by himself. Perhaps it might be possible to recognise three stylised clubs: the middle one with the pommel downwards, those on either side with the pommels obliquely upwards, the whole thing surrounded by an ornamental band. Besides this, the separate drawings arranged in circles and bands have a particular special significance that I will reproduce from the Baining comments.

I want first to mention that I tended to regard the three circular shapes in the picture as eye ornaments. However, the person explaining immediately destroyed this illusion with the comment that 'eyes' in particular could not be painted. The explanation goes as follows:

The outer border of the band-shaped drawing, which to some extent frames the whole thing, represents fern (1), the inner margin of the same band (2) represents turtle vertebrae; the broken zigzag line which forms the middle of the band on the right side and which we find again as a surround of both drawings to the right and left of the central figure (6), are, according to the native, simply lines serving as decoration without representing anything in particular; the small, almost T-shaped drawings on the inner margin of the right band (4) are a type of insect that gnaws holes in the leaves of a certain type of tree; the decoration designated 5 indicates wooden clubs; the E-shaped figures (7) arranged in circles and bands represent *Nassa* snails; at position 8 the figure is called *kanagoal*, a word whose significance was unknown to Father Rascher, and was probably regarded by him only as the designation of this type of decoration; pattern 9 represents trees.

The nine images in figures 109 to 111 are photographic reproductions of various patterns on painted bark.

The explanations of the decoration are given by the Baining themselves; there can therefore be no doubt that the artists actually combine a certain idea with the drawing, although in most cases the connection remains unclear to us, since the drawing bears no resemblance to the object thought of. In figure a 1, small wedge-shaped ornaments are evident on a dark background, running diagonally across the field in nine consecutive rows, three to a row. These wedge-shaped objects represent a certain parasite that lives on trees. We find similar wedge-shaped drawings on other bark material, but in other forms and of different significance; for example, in figure b the short, wedge-decorated clubs (*holmetki*) designated by 1. We find the same figures in figure c 1 and 2, figure d 5, and figure f 3.

Figures a 3, b 2, c 3, d 2, f 1 represent the stomach, *a chusim*, or entrails; the cross-hatched figures inside the long ovals are the stomach contents.

The frame of the figures that represent a stomach

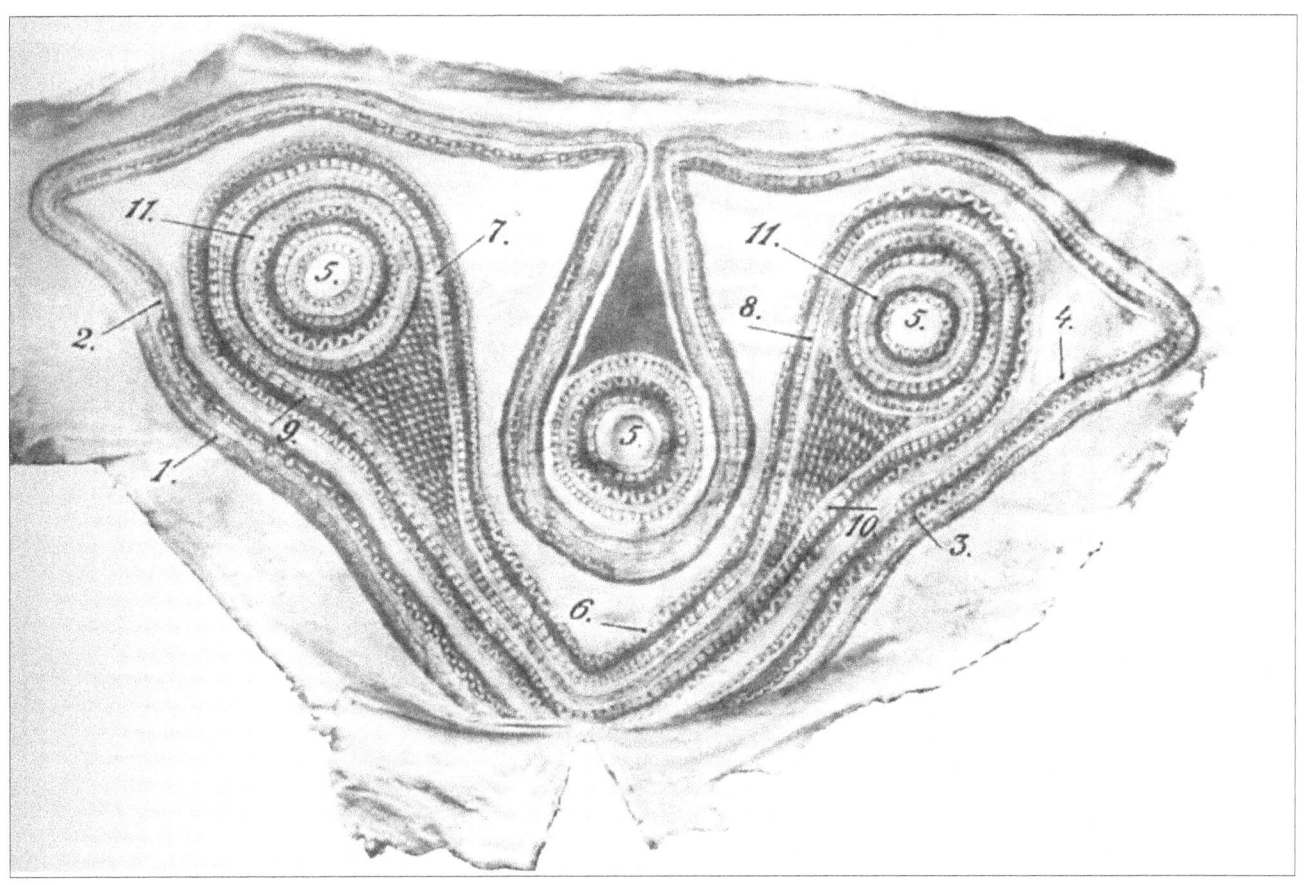

Fig. 108 Painted piece of bark of the Baining

or entrails consists of a band-like decoration that represents a chafer beetle larva, a favourite food.

Figure a 2, a stretched hook-like figure, represents tobacco pipes.

Figure a 4 is a commonly recurring drawing, which represents blossoms.

Figure a 6 represents fishbones. This drawing is relatively recognisable, but less so in figures b 3 and 5, figure c 5, and figure f 4, which are also supposed to represent fishbones.

Figures b 4 and 6 are various forms of net; we observe them again in figure c, bottom right-hand corner, and in figure f 2.

Figure c 4 is called *a onpemetka* and is an ornament without significance.

In figures c 7, e 2, g 2, i 3, and h 3 hands are represented, the arm as well in the last figure.

Figures d 3 and 4 represent the bamboo frame of one of the big headdresses which are covered with bark; the pattern is called *a lmihung*.

Figure e 1 indicates twisted fibres produced by the Baining from various fibrous material.

Figure f 5 is an imitation of chequered cloth that had been introduced by the settlers as a trade article.

Figures g 1 and 4 represent a small leaf-eating insect; the whole figure is the image of a frigate bird.

Figure h 1 is the representation of a particular fern, called *tadahir*.

Figure i could be regarded as a somewhat stylised head, perhaps that of a snake. However, it is an arbitrary arrangement of various ornaments in a row, and the Baining see no representation of a head in it. The drawing designated 2 represents scorpions, bordered on both sides by a simple line 1; in 3 we recognise hands again; lianas are supposed to be represented in 4 and 5, the two cross-hatched ovals are two stomachs with contents.

Although this explanation of various Baining drawings does not encompass all figures, it still gives us an indication of how inaccurate we are, when we give an interpretation of the ornaments of a primitive people from the similarity the drawing has to an object familiar to us. Not every circle is an eye decoration; a spiral may look so much like a coiled-up cuscus tail and yet represent something entirely different. The Baining artists are like small children who have a crayon or slate pencil put in their hands for the first time, and then draw figures on the paper or slate, which they say are people, dogs, pigs, trees, and so on, and which, just like the Baining drawings, bear little or no resemblance to the object that they are supposed to represent. The child unquestionably connects the representation of a man, a dog, and so on, with these drawings, and it may be just the same with the Baining who see a shellfish, a particular leaf, a human face, and so on, in these traditional drawings. This representation is so deeply ingrained that one can clearly read the bewilderment on the faces of those asked, who cannot understand that not every other person immediately sees the significance of the design.

The higher the level of design by the natives, the

Plate 40 Artistically laid out taro garden on Nukumanu

SECRET SOCIETIES, TOTEMISM, MASKS AND MASK DANCES

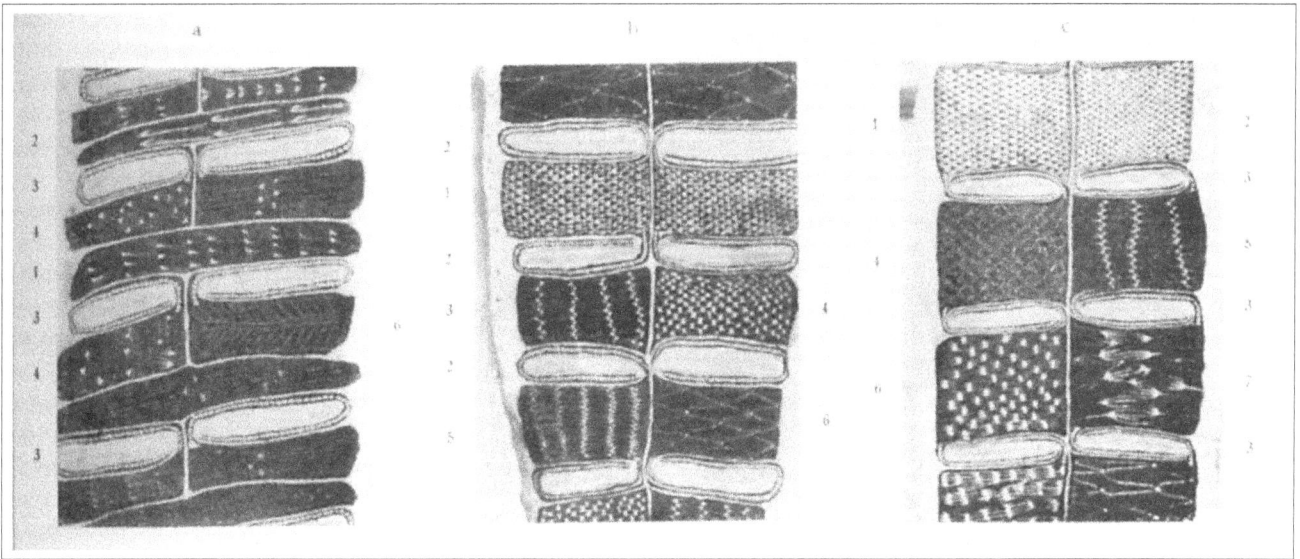

Fig. 109 Various patterns of painted bark

Fig. 110 Various patterns of painted bark

Fig. 111 Various patterns of painted bark

Fig. 112 Mask from Cape Orford

more clear the designs become, and one can, without difficulty, recognise the meaning of the object depicted. I have often wasted time on deciphering designs. However, since I have come into contact with the Baining, I have become very cautious, and have let a great part of my apparently quite sound explanations find their way back into the waste paper basket.

The pieces of bark furnished with drawings are stretched onto the frame when completed, giving form to the image. The frame consists of split strips of bamboo cane attached to one another by thin lianas or strips of rattan. The finished frame, which is very tough and strong throughout, is first wrapped in dried banana leaves, over which the bark pieces are laid and sewn together with thin dry lianas (*angelka*).

In Father Rascher's description, the attachment of the lances decorated with feathers is not quite clear. The skin above the buttocks on both sides of the vertebral column is grasped with the fingers of one hand and pulled over the backbone. The fold of skin between hand and backbone is pierced by a spear point or bone awl (today probably with a knife), and a band of bark is pulled through the hole formed, and this serves to fasten the lance. The procedure is very painful. It must often be done in the early years of childhood, since I saw eight- and ten-year-old boys with the wound already fully healed.

Other castigations of the flesh are also connected with the dance. The participants must fast rigidly for a period of five days before the ceremony; only betel chewing is permitted. During the fast, these people go to an isolated place in the forest, and avoid all association with their people. It can happen that for some reason the ceremony is postponed for one or more days; for example, as a result of a war disturbance, heavy rain, and the like. The participants then continue the fast, and it is no wonder that they are emaciated and exhausted on the day of the ceremony, barely able to carry out the strenuous activities connected with the presentation.

Father Rascher describes a second dance, called *a mabucha* by the natives, in which disguises are used. This dance takes place annually from April to May when the taro and *pit* (*Saccharum floridulum*) ripening season arrives.

Mabucha does not require nearly so extensive a preparation as that of the *sarecha*. In the subsequent description I am following the written and oral accounts of Father Rascher who was a frequent eyewitness. Since people often come from great distances to the *mabucha*, the dance usually begins when the day is already far advanced, often at nightfall. The accumulation of great quantities of foodstuffs, which are piled up on a table-like bamboo structure, is, here too, a characteristic appearance, for the Baining cannot put on a ceremony without a corresponding overfilling of the stomach that goes so far that they throw themselves on the ground like bloated boas, and in complete calm, almost in a type of debility, resign themselves to digestion. The dancers step around in a circle in front of the table-shaped structure, sometimes stamping, sometimes tripping lightly, always in time with the musicians (consisting of both men and women who strike bamboo sticks together). Everybody present takes part in the dance; the women carry their infants on their shoulders but are undecorated; the men paint their bodies partially with lime. During the dance they chew betel, consume great quantities of *pit* and bite into raw taro tubers. This pageant lasts three to four hours. Then youths from eight to sixteen years old appear, holding hands, and interrupt the rows of dancers, moaning horribly as if they were in great pain, twisting their bodies and adopting most peculiar postures; then leaping away with a loud howl to make way for another group. At the same time, they bite into raw taro tubers, eat pulled-off foliage, even human excrement. The

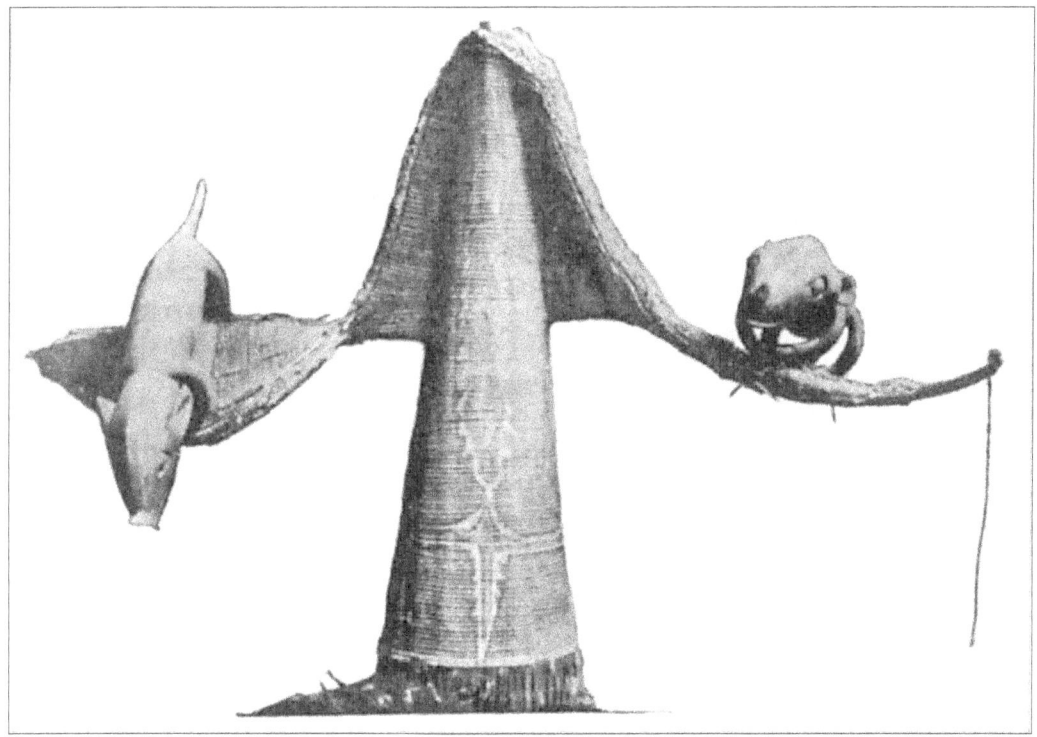

Fig. 113 Mask from Cape Orford

dance meanwhile is growing steadily more wild and rapid. Towards daybreak, the music suddenly takes on a raging tempo, and a number of young people appear in pairs. On their heads they wear conical hats covering their faces and extending onto their shoulders. Their bodies are shiny black from the oil and soot rubbed in, and a cloth of shredded banana leaves girds their loins. These figures, fifteen to thirty in number, are called *a ios prara* – spirits. They stride up, noiselessly and solemnly, and above their heads they carry a club and a number of switches bound together with long, tough, finger-thick plant stalks. They position themselves silently some distance from the dancers, and boys and youths immediately fall on them, rip a portion of the switches from their hands and attack them with all their strength. The switch must break with each blow; otherwise the spirit in his turn begins the castigation. This event does not last long, but always long enough to cause the participants bloody welts, which are rubbed immediately after the flogging by men who rush up with burnt lime, the universal medicine of almost all Melanesians. The scars of the switch blows remain clearly visible for a long time.

It is characteristic of this Baining mask dance that absolutely no secrecy is connected with it, neither in the preparation of the masks nor in the presentation of the performances. We rediscover many characteristics in far-distant secret societies – for example, mortification of the flesh by fasting, flagellation by switches, and so on – and the conical hat recurs in other places, so the interrelationship of all these manifestations can hardly be doubted any longer.

The previously described Baining dances and masks have, as we know, spread over those parts of the mountain range rising west of the deep-cut valley, stretching from Weberhafen south to Vunakokor. Whether the inhabitants of the mountain range extending eastwards to St George's Channel recognise the same customs, we do not yet know. No white person has yet reached their dwellings and villages; at St George's Channel one occasionally comes into contact with the inhabitants of this part of the Gazelle Peninsula, especially on the beach between Cape Palliser in the north and Cape Buller in the south. As far as can be judged today, these people have the greatest ethnographic similarity with the Baining, although they speak a somewhat different dialect. In body form they show the greatest resemblance; also, like their related tribes to the north, they have no canoes. It is possible they have adopted many things from their southern neighbours, south of Wide Bay, but whether they possess masks and mask dances, we do not yet know. However, it seems very probable that similar institutions might be encountered, since all the natives round about have them.

Unfortunately, we must, in the meantime, forsake this tribe and turn further to the south, to the far side of Wide Bay, the area south and south-west of Cape Orford. Although we encounter an entirely new ethnographic province here, the masks are still in evidence. One of these was purchased by the then Imperial Judge, Dr Schnee, during a coastal tour in 1900.

This mask is now in the Berlin Museum, and Herr von Luschan has described and depicted the mask in *Globus*, voll. LXXX, no. 1. I can do no better than repeat this description here verbatim and add the illustrations. After Herr von Luschan has

Fig. 114 Mask from Cape Orford

drawn attention to the fact that they are familiar there also with shields, in contrast to the fable that there were no shields in New Britain, he continues as follows:

> Likewise from there, Cape Orford, the Berlin collection also obtained several large dance masks that have a certain similarity to the well-known *duk-duk* masks, but are still completely novel and surprising in their style.
>
> One of these masks is shown in figure 1 (see fig. 112; author). For ease of understanding and also to give a reference point for its great size, it is placed on a plaster of Paris figure. The loin cloth photographed with it comes from New Guinea and is therefore not authentic, but it appears that quite similar loin cloths of fresh ferns are also actually worn with our masks.
>
> The most striking among our pieces is a large, almost circular, disc about 1.5 metres in diameter, attached like an umbrella. It rests on two staves on a high, woven cone, that has a thick crown of bunches of grass below, where it sits on the head. The tip of the cone carries a top-piece with two very large slightly canoe-shaped arched lobes that project far out far over the shoulders to left and right.
>
> A piglet carved out of wood, 45 centimetres long, and painted green, white, red and black, is fastened to each of these lobes. The ends of the lobes are connected to the rim of the umbrella by cords; in moving and dancing the piglets are tossed about in a type of see-saw motion.
>
> The technique of these masks is just as novel as their shape. To make them as light as possible in spite of their great size, they are made from only one completely spongy skeleton of thin switches and are clad in leaf strips and very light cylinders of pith.
>
> Figure 2 (see fig. 113; author) shows on a somewhat larger scale the cone-shaped crown piece with both big lobes and the piglet, and one can recognise the splendid patterns onto which the pith cylinders are sewn. The cone itself is painted green, white and black both front and back. I am unable to give any explanation of the unique pattern.
>
> The umbrella-like disc has three rough staves crossing in the centre, as a skeleton, and a thicker rod as a circumference. Seven thinner rods are added concentrically for further reinforcement. The upper surface, not visible when in use, has no decoration. The inner surface is all the more carefully decorated. It is covered throughout with large and small pieces of pith cylinders, as illustrated in figure 3 (see fig. 114; author). I am unable to interpret it, and I assume that it will gradually become more clear with other representations on such umbrellas. The resemblance to a broken cross is certainly only coincidental; on the other hand it is probably significant that a type of hand appears in the upper right and lower left, and that, corresponding with this, the pale rim strips are also dotted on the upper right and lower left.

At the beginning of 1901, a trading schooner of the firm of E.E. Forsayth brought a large number of masks from the same area. These had been made in the region between Jacquinot and Montague bays. Among them was a mask of the form described above, as well as a large number of new types that corresponded with the first-mentioned type both in technique and raw material. The unusual fragility of the material had caused major damage to several masks, but the grotesque forms, the careful workmanship and the splendid painting could still be recognised. The collection is now in the *Ethnographisches Museum* in Stuttgart. Unfortunately, the collector could not give any information about its use, and so, in the meantime, the beautiful material remains unintelligible.

I finally succeeded in shedding a little light on this situation, although, at the moment, only a very feeble one. In the Catholic mission, at the same time that Dr Schnee was collecting masks and, as far as I can remember, on the same occasion, several adolescent boys had been persuaded to go to the mission station. Here they were given over to a brother so that he could learn their language, and, once this was achieved, I was in a position to obtain several explanations about the masks.

The Sulka – the masks emanated from them – have many different masks, each having a particular significance. At the great mask ceremonies each mask has a particular function and bears an unique name.

A similarity with the *duk-duk* of the Gazelle Peninsula is unmistakable. In both places the members belong to a secret society of men, into which boys and youths are initiated. The women and non-members believe that the masks are actual spirits, *o inkuol*, that occasionally devour women and children. If women go onto the assembly places of the secret society members, this would lead to destruction of the unborn child and subsequent infertility. In order to warn the women that a mask is in the vicinity, the bullroarer, *vuvu*, is swung, and the frightened people, who believe that they are hearing the voice of a spirit, immediately disappear.

The mask storage place is a compound, *a vererei*, set apart in the forest. The men's masks are made and stored here. The masks leave from here to go to the villages and dance in the compounds.

The masks of the Sulka have a common mother, called *parol*. However, the mother never appears, but always dwells on the assembly place, because she cannot walk as a result of severe wounds. The unitiated believe that the *parol* makes all the big drums there, by hollowing out the wooden blocks from which they are made, with her teeth. All wooden blocks from which drums are to be made are therefore taken to the compound *parol a vererei*, or *parol karik* (*karik* = nest, birthplace), where they are hollowed out by the men. When the *kol* instruments are blown, the women must prepare food, which is carried by the men to the *parol karik*. When the drums are finally ready, they are beaten in a certain way for several days and nights without interruption, and women believe that the spirit *parol* is producing the sound by continually hitting her head against the side of the drum. The finished drum is then brought with dancing and celebration from the *vererei* to the compound for which it is intended.

Although all masks are designated by the common name *a hemlaut* (old man), a very special type of mask has a special right to this name. This is the type illustrated in *Globus* by Herr von Luschan. The broad umbrella disk represents the head of the spirit; the cone-shaped part is called *mneikeit*, and the two wing-shaped additions represent the arms, *kalaktiek*. A small figure sits on each arm, representing a girl and a boy and these are moved to and fro by strings that the wearer of the mask holds in his hands. The *hemlaut* mask is, like the other masks, roughly made first in the men's house. It is then taken at night to the *vererei*, where it is completed.

While this is going on, another mask, *a kaipa*, takes care of procuring the necessary food. The *kaipa* come into the gardens, armed with spears, chase out the women working there and, according to their needs, take as much produce, taro, yams, and so on, as they can carry, and drag their booty to the *vererei*. Now and then they come into the compounds, dance and leap about in front of the huts, and throw their spears powerfully into the doorsills. The *kaipa* are also called *kekiap* or *kékep*.

At celebrations, the *hemlaut* comes from the *vererei* to individual compounds, accompanied by members of the society, wildly yelling and gesticulating. Arriving in the compound, he first crouches on the ground, then suddenly springs up and begins a dance to the accompanying singing of his followers. While he is squatting on the ground, the little children are thrust towards him so that they touch him; this should ensure that those children thrive and grow big.

Often the *hemlaut* is also introduced into the compound through another mask, which is called *o sisu*. The *sisu* (plate 46) wears a conical mask top reminiscent of the *tubuan* of the Gazelle Peninsula. These masks run around rapidly, and the women begin a song in their honour.

The *o mongan* are other masks. They present themselves in the compounds with a number of rods, *a kansi*, which are made from supple vines. The inhabitants of the compound position themselves upright, hands raised above their heads, and the *mongan* then begins whipping them with his *kansi*. The *mongan* then pays the victim who has been bloodied a new loincloth, a spear or the like. Fathers bring their sons on this occasion and hold them up high in front of them for the *mongan* to thrash, so that they will develop strongly.

The *tutui* and his wife *lolisne* are masks that carry out all kinds of entertainment before ceremonies to make the spectators laugh. They approach people, tickle them and stroke them and finally run away with the drinking vessels. *Gitwungul*, *kulkan optek*, and *sungrum* and *silavik* are various masks about which I have so far not been able to learn anything of their significance or function.

The *tamanmanpoi*, or *tamalmalpoi*, have a little basket in their hand, with a species of wild lemon (*o poi*) and little pebbles (*o gul*) in a little pocket. At their approach the men grasp their shields and try to protect themselves against the lemons and pebbles with which the masks bombard them. When the ammunition has run out the masks dance out of the compound.

The whole mask cycle is concluded by the *lelwong*. This one wears a mask that covers the entire upper body. A snake curls out from the stomach region over the head and back so that the tail stands out behind. The dance of the *lelwong* concludes the ceremony.

The night before the ceremony the *o siêtam* carry out their mischief. These are boys and youths who break into compounds, beat against dwellings, rip out saplings, and break down empty huts while yelling with disguised voices. The women believe the children of the masks carry out this mischief. The *panvave* are another kind of mischief-maker.

Further westwards we again encounter secret societies and masks. As far as I could ascertain, these are connected with circumcision ceremonies; at least

Fig. 115 Mask from the circumcision ceremonies. 'Liebliche Inseln' and Möwehafen

this is the case on the French Islands, the Arawa Islands, and in the South Cape region east and west of Möwehafen. The mask illustrated from the Möwehafen region (fig. 115) has many similarities with the *duk-duk* mask of the Gazelle Peninsula. The cone-shaped hat is called *katumu*; the costume consisting of banana leaves covers the entire body and is designated as *kavala*. The masked form represents a spirit, *Mewo*, whose dwelling is a spacious house, *num*, which stands in the village but is separated from the other houses. This site is called *kamangulu*.

The ceremonies *kamurmur* or *kamutmut* take place at a certain time each year, and the boys have to buy themselves in by payment of shell money, *del*. During the ceremonies, the women must provide abundant good food, although they are not invited to participate. The prepared food is set down out at the outer limit of the ceremonial place, and collected from there by the men. On the Arawa Islands, there are a number of other masks besides those previously described, some appearing in the circumcision ceremonies, and some that function when a *tabu* is placed on coconuts. At the dancing in celebration of circumcision, the dancers wear mask-like headpieces decorated with bright feather combs (plate 47), astonishingly reminiscent of similar hats that I had the opportunity of seeing in the Finschhafen area of Kaiser Wilhelmsland. However, the latter headdresses were much finer because they used splendid bird of paradise feathers.

On the French Islands we encounter the same masks and headdresses, although in another form.

In the *Publicationen aus dem Ethnographisches Museum zu Dresden*, volume X, plate 8: 1 to 5, and volume XIII, plate 1: 1a and 1b such masks are illustrated. Volume X, plate 8, figures 6 and 7 show the form of the headpiece there without the usual feather decoration. The mask illustrated here (fig. 116) is a less common form and is similarly used in the circumcision ceremonies.

It is also characteristic of this whole area of western New Britain that the bullroarer plays a significant role in the circumcision ceremonies and, as in Kaiser Wilhelmsland and on Bougainville, it is regarded as the voice of a spirit, the sight of which is forbidden to women in all circumstances.

The bullroarer consists of a thin lancet-shaped leaf of wood about 24 to 30 centimetres long and 4 to 5 centimetres wide, fastened to a 4- to 5-metre-long pole by means of a cord about 3 metres long. To produce a humming sound the pole is swung in a circle – the more powerful the swing the louder the noise. I have never seen decorated bullroarers. The instrument is carefully stored in the men's houses and must not be seen by women. From this area, as a sacred instrument, we are familiar with the water flute which we also encounter far into the west in Kaiser Wilhelmsland. This consists of a bamboo tube, about 50 centimetres long, open at the top, and partially filled with water. Another bamboo tube, open at both ends, is stuck into this. The musician blows into the latter, and, depending on whether he sinks the blowing tube into the water or raises it clear, there arises a swelling or dying flute tone. The women must not see this instrument either; in their opinion it is the voice of a spirit.

Also, throughout the north-western half of New Ireland, on Sandwich Island, and the Fischer and Gardner islands we find a society that must be numbered among the secret societies, although its aims and purposes are far different from the secret societies of New Britain. This is the men's society that celebrates ceremonies in honour and memory of the dead at special sites, often extremely isolated.

As well as the secret activities, a public spectacle, called *malangene*, takes place with the participation of the entire tribe. (On the Gazelle Peninsula we find the same word as a universal designation for dance.) All other dances, and their number is uncommonly large on New Ireland, are, on the other hand, indicated by the common name *bot*. On the coast opposite Gardner Island the word *malangan* has the significance of an ordinary dance; the death dances are called *malangan bessa*.

These presentations take place annually from about the end of May to the beginning of July, and the masks and carvings used on this occasion are made during the rest of the year in the greatest secrecy in isolated places that are rigidly forbidden to be approached by women and children.

The ceremonies that take place, as we have said, to honour the dead obviously have to assume a more or less public character, according to the nature of the ceremony, since on this occasion the whole sib, the entire tribe, express their grief about those deceased. They are by and large the same everywhere, namely ceremonies consisting of great feasts and dancing, which are performed using head masks. Incidentally the hosts of the ceremony are, to a greater or less extent, expert at cloaking the preparations, the production of masks and carvings, in secrecy.

Above all, several of the carvings are never exhibited to the common people. They are displayed in a hut built for the purpose, and the site on which the hut stands is enclosed by a high, thick fence, inside which only certain people are permitted to go and to see the carvings. Entry is forbidden to women and children. Obtaining such carvings always entails great difficulty, for they are wary of bringing them out of the enclosure. This can be circumvented by putting these pieces into canoes at night, when no women are about, and taking them to a ship waiting nearby or, alternatively, chasing women away with sticks and clubs in order to remove the objects unobserved. Under these circumstances over-inquisitive women pay for their curiosity with their lives.

The carvings are of different types and serve different purposes. Although their use is, by and large, universally the same, their names differ in every region, which is not surprising with the wealth of dialects on the island.

From the works published in recent times about masks and carvings from the Bismarck Archipelago, all forms have become known. I refer here particularly to the excellent reproductions in volumes VII, X and XIII of the *Publikationen aus dem Königlichen Ethnographischen Museum zu Dresden*.

In volume VII, plates 11 and 12, and in volume X, plate 4, number 1 and plate 5, figures 1, 2, 3 and 4, masks are reproduced which are called *tatanua* in the north of New Ireland, and *miteno* in the Gardner Islands (fig. 117). This type has probably been designated as a helmet mask because it shows great resemblance to a Bavarian military helmet in its shape. These masks are purely dance masks; as with all other carvings, they are certainly made in secret and are only exhibited publicly on a ceremonial occasion, but there the secrecy is ended, for anyone can now admire them, and after the ceremony they are not kept especially concealed. These masks are put on the head so that they cover it completely, the body is wrapped in foliage from the waist on, and in front of the ceremonial house the masked ones present a dance that is generally a pantomime presentation of the encounter of both sexes. This dance, or more accurately the

Fig. 116 Kneeling mask-wearer from the French Islands

pantomime, is accompanied by the singing of all those present, with the accompaniment of beating the wooden drum or striking dry pieces of bamboo with thin wooden battens.

Volume X, plate 4, figures 2 and 3, and plate 5, figure 5 also show masks that are worn on the head, but serve a completely different purpose. These types of mask are called *kepong*, and on the Gardner Islands *vaniss*, and are dedicated exclusively to remembrance of the dead. Plate 48 shows a mask house at Labangerarum on New Ireland on a ceremonial day. On the lower shelf the dance masks, or *tatanua*, stand in a line; the *kepong* stand on the upper shelf. In the latter masks, it is characteristic that they have wing-like additions on both sides of the head, often in careful open-work carving, representing ears (see also figs 118 and 119).[3]

They do not dance with these masks. The male relatives of the dead, in whose honour and memory the *kepong* have been made, certainly put them on their heads, but they go silently with them from house to house in the village. In one hand they hold a small stick, and in the other a shell clapper, called *bondalok* (*lengleng* on the Gardner Islands), with which they announce their approach. Standing still outside each house they receive a small piece of shell money, probably a form of payment for the expenditure on the banquet requisite to the ceremony.

The shell clapper is also used in *tatanua* dances. Figure 120 (see also *Dresdener Publikationen*, vol. VII, plate 9, figs 1 and 2; vol. X, plate 1, figs 1, 2 and 3; and vol. XIII, plate 9, figures 1 and 1b,

3. The coloured design on the book-jacket represents the same mask as in fig. 119.

Plate 41 Village scene on Tauu

Fig. 117 *Tatanua* mask from New Ireland

plate 10, figs 1 and 2) are masks closely related to the *kepong*, but much larger and more carefully carved; they are called *matua*. Because they are too heavy to walk around with in the village, the relatives of the dead put them in their heads in front of the mask house and remain standing there; if the carvings are very big and heavy they kneel with them on their heads in front of the mask house.

When the *kepong* and *matua* come into view on the ceremonial site, a loud cry of grief arises from those gathered, and the names of the dead who are to be honoured by these carvings are called out aloud amidst weeping and wailing. The women tear out their hair, make loud lamentations, and behave as though they were insane with grief.

As well as the carvings mentioned, there is a further type that, as the incised peg at the lower end suggests, is fixed in the ground so it stands upright; they are a variation of the *matua* and are called *totok* (or *kulibu* on the Gardner Islands) (fig. 121).

On the Gardner Islands the *kulibu* are never shown in public; they stand in specially constructed shelters or huts that are surrounded by high thick fences, and can only be entered by certain men and youths. Volume X, plate 11, figures 1 to 7, and volume XIII, plate 10, figures 3, 4 and 5, plate 11, figures 1e, 1d, 1c and 1b, and figure 2 are carvings of the type described.

On the Gardner and Fischer islands, as well as in the regions of New Ireland lying opposite, yet another kind of carving is found, serving the same purpose as the *matua* and *totok*. These are carved boards partly in relief or in filigree, or in open-work carved beams, both often of great size. They are given the group name *turu* (plate 49), but further south-eastwards they are *vavál* and *kulipumu* (this latter designation is probably a dialectic variation of the word, *kulibu*). Volume X, plate 12, figures 1 and 2, plate 13, figures 1, 2 and 3, plate 14, figures 1, 2, 3 and 4; and volume XIII, plate 12, figures 4 and 5 depict carving of this type.

It must be noted here that the huts, *fu na totok* (plate 48), in which the carvings and masks are set up and publicly displayed, are called *mirir* on the Gardner Islands, and *aroniaro* further south-eastwards.

Manufacture of the dance masks, *tatanua* or *miteno*, is permitted to anyone who can accomplish it; however, the other carvings are done by special artists, of which there are several in every large village. In northern New Ireland these people are called *mata totok*; on the Gardner Islands they are *turu marre*. They make all *kepong* or *vaniss*, *matua*, *kulibu* and *turu* on commission. I have often sought the acquaintance of these people, partly to admire their truly astonishing artistry and partly also to obtain information from them about the aim and significance of the carvings.

With regard to the dance masks, *miteno* or *tatanua*, all agree that, to some extent, the classical form of male beauty in the eyes of the local natives is expressed in them. These concepts are admittedly diametrically opposed to those of an artistic European, and we therefore tend to regard the dance masks as grotesque and affected. A native of New Ireland would probably regard a Belvedere Apollo or a Canova Venus as an equally grotesque creation.

First of all the gigantic crest of hair on the *tatanua* is striking. This is actually only an imitation of the mourning hairstyle customary in former times. In earlier years, particularly on Fischer Island, I have seen such hairstyles several times, though not often. Like so many other things, this hairstyle too has disappeared over the years; today it is no longer found. This quite characteristic hairstyle was produced by the relatives of the dead letting their hair grow and be stained yellow by rubbing in burnt lime and dyestuffs. At the time of the funeral rites the sides of the head were shaved; only the central section from the forehead to the neck was allowed to remain. This was first fashioned into a central crest with two low shelves of hair one on either side of the crest, and then carefully pinned up and dyed yellow. The shaven sides of the head were then smeared with a thick paste of lime and more decoration added. Although today we are no longer in a position to admire this hairstyle in the living, the faithful imitation seen today in the *tatanua* gives us an idea of the extraordinary care with which the styling of the hair decoration was performed in earlier times. Only those young people who are able to lay claim to masculine beauty would have such a festive hairdo. Whoever felt that he had not been granted the facial features of a native Adonis or, probably was too lazy to go to the trouble connected with such a hairstyle, made himself a mask in which he tried to incorporate all the attributes of masculine beauty. Among these, as already mentioned, is the hairstyling. Also among male beauty belongs a large broad prominent nose, pierced ear lobes hanging down as far as possible, whiskers that are streaked

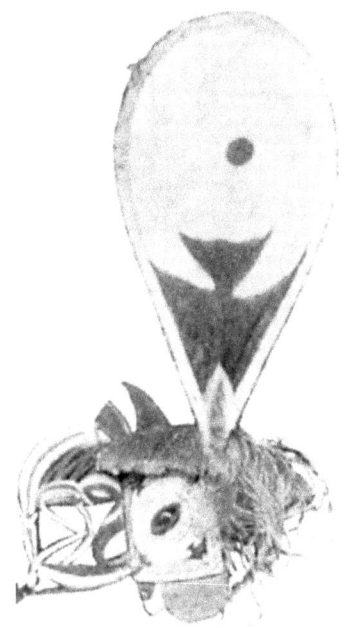

Fig. 118 Mask, New Ireland

with lime or bound together in tufts, and a large mouth with a healthy bite. The *tatanua* show us all of these attributes to the most extreme limits permissible.

Carvings, both in the form of masks and others prepared as signs of memorial to the dead, often reveal wide-reaching characteristics which are not content only with stylising the head according to the current attributes of beauty. The *mata totok* or *turu marre* gives free reign to its adulation of the dead person, it idealises him, as we might express ourselves in such cases. What is otherwise present in the carving as a fantastic embellishment, is inspiration through the spirit of the dead person, who reveals himself to the creator of the image in the form of the *manu* (bird) of the deceased. The *manu* of the dead person is the emblem of his tribe

Fig. 119 Mask, New Ireland

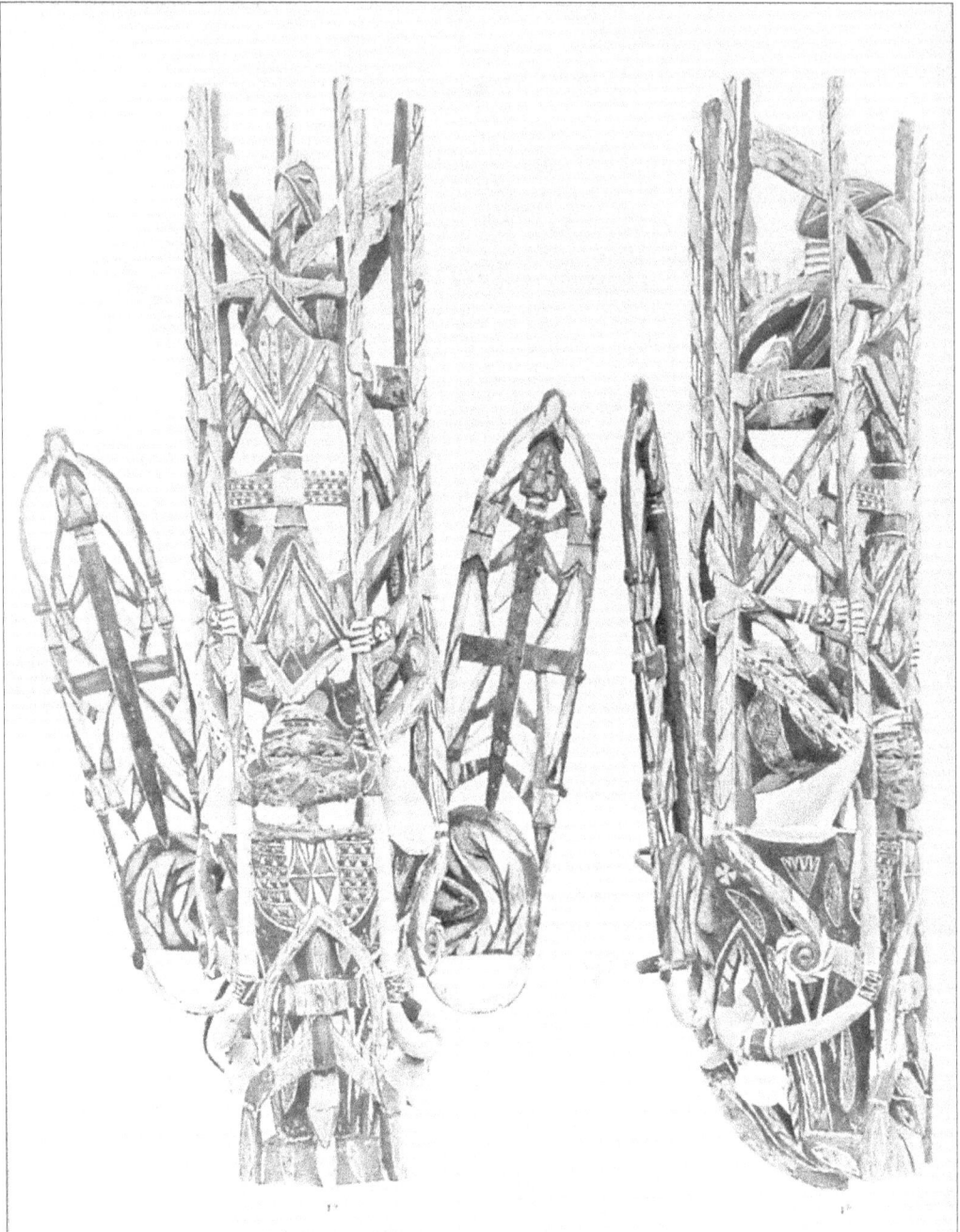

Fig. 120 *Matua* mask, front and side views. (Reproduced from *Publikationen aus dem Königlichen Ethnographischen Museum zu Dresden*, vol. XIII, plate 9. Dresden, Stengel & Co.)

or of his kin during his earthly life, his totem sign.

This totem sign of the deceased must never be missing from these carvings. It represents to some extent the family coat of arms of the dead person. Every New Ireland person has a certain type of bird or *manu* as a family insignia. The *manu* plays a major role in the life of the natives. A man and a woman who have the same *manu* must not marry or have sexual relations; this is regarded as incest and today is still punished by death. Only natives who have different *manu* may marry, and the offspring of the pair always inherit the *manu* of the mother. Members of the same *manu* combine as a rule in communal undertakings, while those with another totem do not take part. I know of an incident in which two natives, whose *manu* was the hen, decided to kill a white trader. There were not many men of this insignia in the neighbourhood; about fifteen could be assembled. These carried out the plan, killed the trader, and plundered his goods. All other natives, and these were quite numerous, did not take part in the deed, although they also did nothing to prevent it. Later, when a punitive expedition was mounted to propitiate the crime, and a number of prisoners were taken, the other natives offered, as the principal evidence of their innocence, that they had a totally different *manu* from the murderers – grounds which, to the officials unfamiliar with the local situation, must have seemed totally unsatisfactory.

Also, in wars among individual districts where there are often many warriors on each side, the parties divide according to the individual *manu*. It

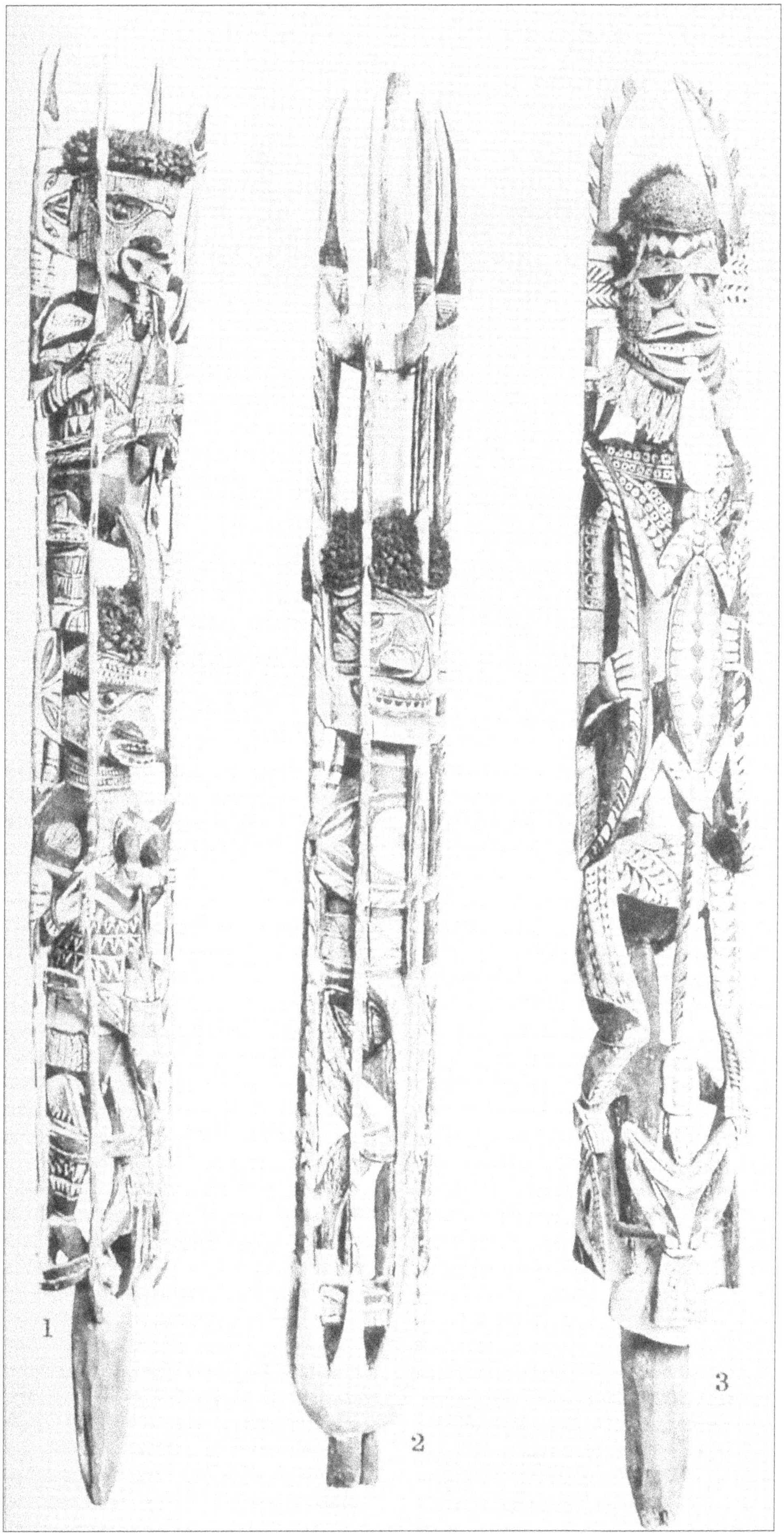

SECRET SOCIETIES, TOTEMISM, MASKS AND MASK DANCES

Fig. 121 *Totok* or *kulibu* carving. (Reproduced from *Publikationen aus dem Königlichen Ethnographischen Museum zu Dresden*, vol. X, plate 11, figs 1-3. Dresden, Stengel & Co.)

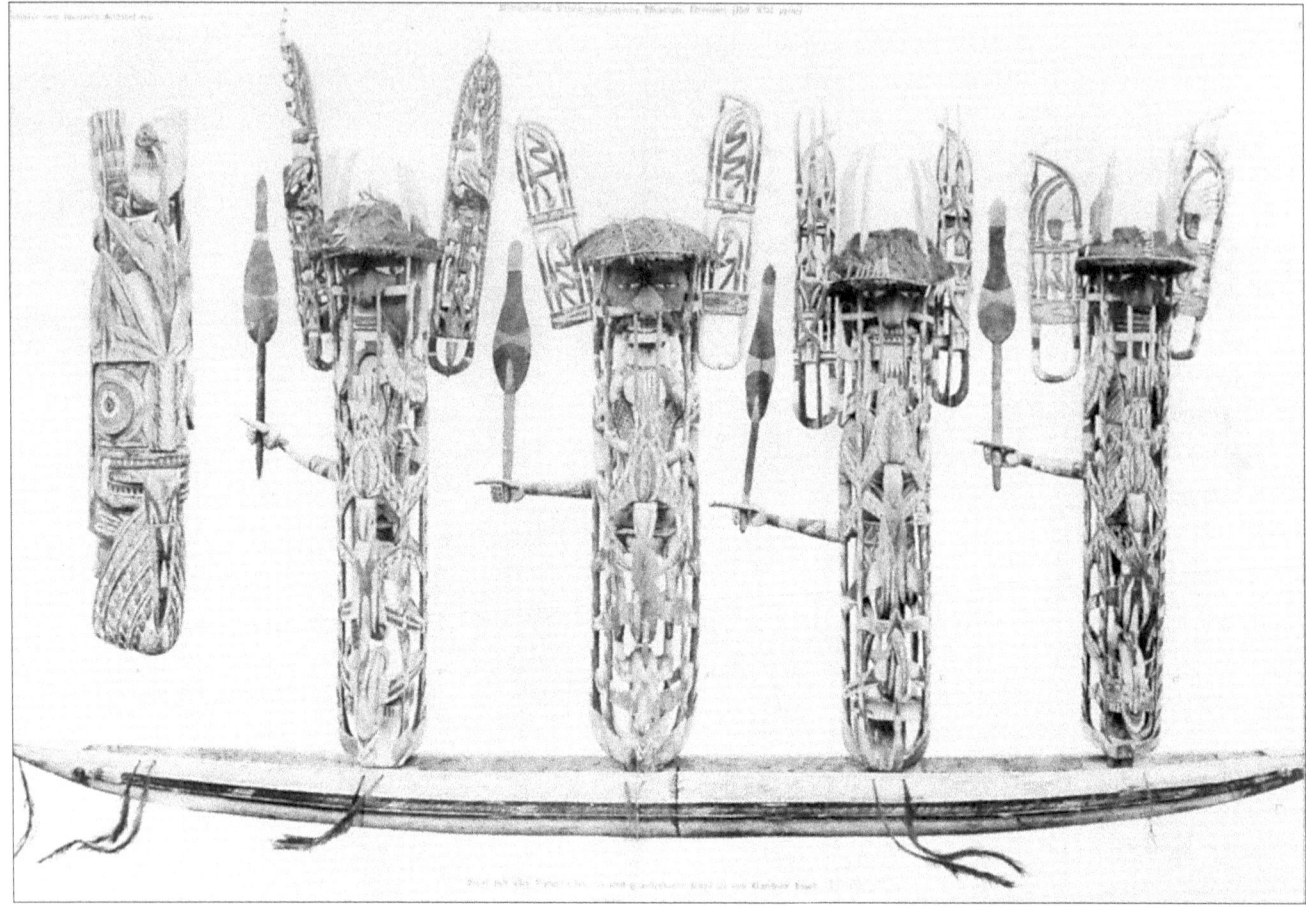

Fig. 122 Carving as a memorial to the dead. (Reproduced from, *Publikationen aus dem Königlichen Ethnographischen Museum zu Dresden*, vol. XIII, plate 11, fig. 1. Dresden, Stengel & Co.)

can happen that there is a group on each side with the same *manu*; in such cases these wordlessly avoid each other and endeavour to come hand to hand with a party bearing a different *manu*.

People who have the same *manu* regard themselves as closely related, even when personally they are total strangers; they reciprocally welcome one another into their houses, and host one another as if they had been friends or acquaintances for years.

Should a man and woman of the same *manu* be caught in a sexual act, the least consequence is the death of the woman, often the death is of both. It is always members of the same *manu* who come forward as avengers. Since the blood relatives of those dead seek vengeance in their turn, complicated situations often arise that seem impossible to unravel to the outsider unfamiliar with the *manu* institution.

On the previously mentioned large carvings, which depict the *manu* of the deceased, we find, on close examination, that other animal forms are represented, especially the snake, the lizard, shark and dolphin, pig, and so on. These animal images, often done with skilful accuracy, do not belong to the series of *manu* or totem signs, which are taken exclusively from the avian world, but are representations of evil spirits that fight the *manu* and are finally overcome by it.

Each carving therefore carries a particular story, illustrating the struggle of the *manu* with the evil spirit. The snake and the monitor lizard are the mightiest of all the evil spirits; but the good spirits, especially the hornbill and the pigeon, exercise their powerful protection, so that the evil spirits are unable to harm those who have these two birds as their *manu*. For this reason we often see both of these good spirits on carvings together with the evil spirits.

Several carvings are exclusively decorative pieces, although honouring a particular *manu*. There are a great number of stories and legends about the *manu*. Sometimes they have achieved this, sometimes they have accomplished that, and the carvers endeavour to present these legends in a pictorial manner. So long as we have not succeeded in revealing this treasury of tales, the significance of the carvings will remain a mystery to us. It will also be very difficult for us to recognise the basic story in the carving. Thus, years ago, from the Gardner Islands, I obtained a carving that in essence represented two birds, which sat with their heads turned towards a circular opening, about 20 centimetres in diameter, in the centre of the carving. The edges blended into foliage and a coiling snake. Quite by accident I learned the significance of this.

Two pigeons sat by a pool of water to quench their thirst. They had flown a long way and were very thirsty, and so they refreshed themselves at the water and noisily drank a drop from time to time. However, the snake was watching them, and slowly and silently crawled nearer, to catch the pigeons. As the pigeons bent down once more to drink a drop of water, they were able to look between their legs because their heads were bent and their eyes were looking downwards, and so they saw the snake and flew away.

By itself, the tale is of little significance; when the carver took it over, it was up to him to present the figures in question and the finer details. He therefore carved a broad wooden rim around a circular hole in the centre of his work, representing the pool of water; he then placed the two pigeons on either side, and finally, he depicted the snake, whose thwarted plan was alluded to by its separation from the birds.

On the Caen Islands (Tanga), St John (Aneri), and in the Siara district on the eastern side of southern New Ireland, which is in contact with these islands we find, albeit in variation, not only the totem idea but also the use of masks in places, although the latter form only a type of supplement in the big dance ceremonies.

All the inhabitants of these districts have certain animals as totems, here too bearing the name *manu*, although they are not exclusively birds (*manu*). They are the *manlam* (sea eagle), *am bal* (pigeon), *an dun* (black and white flycatcher), *angkika* or *angkäkä* (species of parrot), *am pirik* (species of parrot), *tagau* (gull), as well as *fumpul* (the dog) and *fumbo* (the pig).

Here, it is not only strictly enforced that possessors of the same totem may not marry, but a man is also not permitted to marry, for example, a woman who has just any totem. Rather, the men marry as follows:

Tagau always marries a woman from the *manlam*; *angkika* marries likewise only *manlam*; *am bal* marries any totem; *am pirik* marries only *angkika* and *am bal*; *an dun* marries *manlam*, *tagau*, *angkika* and *am bal*; *fumpul* marries any totem, as does *fumbo*, although with the exception of *manlam*.

Just as on New Hanover they believe that they can recognise individual totems from the lines on the hand, so too in the regions mentioned above they also have certain features from which they can recognise to which totem the person in question belongs: namely, they maintain that *tagau*, when stepping out, always starts with the left foot; *manlam* on the other hand with the right; *angkika* has thick calves and thin fine ankles, *am bal* on the other hand has less pronounced calves and thick ankles; *an dun* has allegedly thin upper arms and more muscular forearms; *fumpul* can run rapidly for a long time.

The animals that serve as totems are not distinguished or venerated in any way; they are eaten like any other animal.

Sexual relations between men and women having the same totem sign is punished by death. The children always inherit the mother's totem sign. At ceremonies and gatherings of any kind, and also in the very frequent feuds, all members of one and the same totem silently stick together, and only in this way can the natives easily recognise the members of the same totem group.

On Tanga earlier, masks were customary; among others these have also been reproduced in the *Dresdener Publikationen*, volume XIII, plate 15, figures 1, 2, and 3, as splendid illustrations. During my last visit to Tanga, in 1903, I was unable to obtain further specimens. They are no longer made, I was told; the older people who knew how to make them have died, and the younger people, who for the most part have hired themselves as labourers on distant plantations, neglected to learn how to make them. A specimen brought to me revealed this most strikingly; it was sloppily made, decorated with bright scraps of material, and not even approximately similar in form to the old masks. From the older people I have gathered information on the use of masks, which do not play the role here that they do in northern New Ireland.

The masks are designated on Tanga as *tedak*, and they are used in conjunction with a long shirt-like garment made from the bark of the breadfruit tree, a garment worn also on Nissan and Buka (*Papua Album*, vol. II, plate 42). The masks have nothing to do with honouring the dead; they are used during the great feasts to celebrate completion of the planting, or more accurately, harvest season. The mask-makers are called *anterere*. Among their following I always used to find a number of younger islanders who were learning the technique. On Tanga the masks are made, away from the village, in a little house in the forest; these huts are called *borong fel*, and the entry of women is forbidden on pain of death, just as the sight of the masks is especially prohibited to all women before the day of public presentation. The wearers of the masks are likewise unknown to the women, and remain so; the women regard them as incarnate spirits. At a ceremony, first a single mask appears, shows himself to the participants, both men and women, then disappears to summon a second mask. After they have both shown themselves, they go off to collect a third mask, and so it continues, until all the masks are gathered on the ceremonial site, where they present a group dance and then silently disappear, to remove the *tedak* in the *borong fel*.

On Aneri they have no characteristic masks. From coconut shells, however, they make a type of spectacles, to which they attach a flowing beard of plant fibres. These are used in the same way as on Tanga.

On Gerrit Denys (Lihir) masks are still known today; these are very close in form to the masks from the Gardner and Fischer islands but, as on Tanga and Aneri, are neither connected with the ancestor ceremonies, nor with the totem. They are

Fig. 123 Stone figures from southern New Ireland

3. The masks from Bougainville in the *Berliner Museum* do not match the description above. They are identical in part with the first type of Nissan mask (Fig. 125), and partly consist of several (four or five) wooden boards bound together with rattan. The largest two, in front, show a face painted in white, red and black. Nose and eye brows are rolls

simply named *malangene* (that is, dance) and they are actually mask costumes purely and simply, for various dance ceremonies. However, what has been said about masks on Tanga and Aneri is valid for these masks as well. Masked people likewise show themselves here to the public and represent certain spirits, creating terror in the uninitiated (plate 50).

In southern New Ireland, in the Laur district, the natives make (or more accurately, made, since due to the influence of the Christian mission, the custom has now completely disappeared) human figures out of chalk, designated by the name *kulab*, which can be regarded as ancestor figures (fig. 123). As soon as a native died, whether man, woman or child, one of the closest relatives went to a certain place where there was a chalk outcrop. He took a piece large enough to form the figure, and worked on it with his primitive tools until it had the rough incomplete form of a human. Male and female figures were the same in all contours; only the abnormally proportioned sexual organs

served as a differentiation. Children's figures were produced correspondingly smaller; the sculptures representing adults were seldom more than 70 centimetres tall. These representations of the dead were stored in a special hut that could not be entered by women, although they occasionally gathered in front of it and set up a lament over the loss of their relative. After a certain period these ancestor figures were quietly removed by the men and destroyed.

A lot of new information about masks and totem customs in New Ireland will come to light when these things can be studied in detail on site. The preceding is to be regarded only as a short summary that can be very broadly expanded by more detailed observations. However, here, too, one will have to be swift, for much has already disappeared, while other things are in the process of disappearing, and, since the population is dying out, it will presumably be only a short time before there is nothing more, at least nothing reliable, to be discovered about these things either.

I come now to the secret societies on Bougainville, Buka and Nissan. The few masks that I saw on Bougainville consisted of arched, black-painted wooden boards on which was carved a prominent nose; there were openings for eyes and mouth. Against the black background, there were decorations in relief, painted red and white, imitating the painting customary for dances.[3] No special reverence appears to be given to these masks.

In the Nissan group the masks are far more carefully prepared; one can probably assume that the New Ireland influence is felt via St John and Pinepil. A framework of strips of bamboo, enveloping the entire head, is covered with bast, onto which an artistic face is formed from the crushed nut of *Parinarium laurinum*. An artistic wig of moss or plant fibres is attached. The ears are marked by thin carved boards which stick out, exactly as in the New Ireland masks (fig. 125). This is one kind of mask used there; another represents a face carved out of wood, on the black background of which the usual facial sketching is carefully copied with red and white lines. The wigs on these masks are made from human hair, and show the usual hairstyle of the region. With these masks belongs a characteristic shirt-like robe with sleeves of brown-coloured, thinly beaten fibre from the breadfruit tree. This is put on over the body, and extends to the heels.

On the island of Buka similar masks are used, although in a somewhat different form.

From time to time the men meet in an isolated spot in the forest, where they clear a small area and erect small huts. This site is called *tálohu*, and the women are strictly forbidden to go there. On the *tálohu* the masks and bark costumes are prepared. During the manufacture, boys and youths must bring food to the *tálohu*, and sometimes also prepare

Fig. 124 Mask from Bougainville

SECRET SOCIETIES, TOTEMISM, MASKS AND MASK DANCES

Plate 42 The surviving population of the island of Tauu

it there. For recreation there is dancing and singing. The disguise is used solely as a means to extort all kinds of property. The uninitiated, in particular, are told that the spirit *kokorra* (*Papua Album*, vol. II, plate 42) hides in the costume. Then, when they see the presumed spirit, they hastily throw aside everything they are carrying at the time, and flee as rapidly as possible. Naturally, the men gather up the goods thrown away, and regard them as their property. This behaviour is continued for several weeks, during which time the men remain on the *tálohu* where the women and uninitiated believe that they are serving the spirit *kokorra*. To reinforce this belief, the men on the *tálohu* know how to create all kinds of horrible noises, which the uninitiated believe to be spirit voices.

In northern Bougainville, we find a similar institution that is apparently an extension and completion of the previously described one. On Bougainville this is called *rukruk*, and sometimes *burri*. The details are as follows: from time to time, the older men select from friendly families in the neighbourhood a boy or youth who has not yet been brought into the *rukruk*. Headmen usually choose more than one youth, but the number chosen is rarely greater than four. It is a particular honour to be chosen by a headman. Those selected are called *matasesén* after their selection, and as such during the period of the *rukruk* they belong to the selectors, who are called their *marau*. The *marau* leads his *matasesén* to an isolated place in the forest where a spacious hut has been erected, called *áhbassa*; the site is the *áhbassa burri*. The balloon-shaped hats, which the *matasesén* wear, are stored in the hut, which incidentally serves as a sleeping place for the *marau* and the *matasesén*. These hats, called *hassebou*, are made by certain old men, and the *marau* pays each manufacturer a string of *viruan* (shell money), spears, bows and arrows, and so on. The *matasesén* must remain at the *áhbassa burri* until their hair has grown so long

of plant fibre covered with a black mass. The ears consist of painted wooden boards (Fig. 124). (Editor's comment)

Fig.125 Mask from Nissan

that when forced into the *hassebou* it holds the hat firmly on their heads. (plate 51 shows a group of *matasesén*.) As soon as this is the case, the *matasesén* can leave the site and visit their relatives and home village, but they must never show themselves to women without the hat, and must always return to the *áhbassa burri* in the evening. If they want to bathe, this is done at night on the beach or in the mountain rivers at isolated spots. Throughout the entire time, the *matasesén* work for their *marau*, establishing large gardens for them. They are treated quite strictly overall, and when they lack food the relatives must provide the necessaries and set them down outside the high fence of the *áhbassa burri*. Should women come onto the site, which probably never happens, they are killed. They are also killed if they see a *matasesén* accidentally without head covering, and are caught.

Such cases must not be too rare, for human life does not have much value on Bougainville. As a consequence, it is understandable that the women stay as far as possible away from the location of the *matasesén* and their gardens. The women are told that on the *áhbassa burri* the *matasesén* communicate with spirits called *ruk*. There are two different spirits, a male called *ruk a tzon* and a female called *ruk a tahol*. These spirits make a noise that sounds so terrible to the women's ears that they throw their goods away and rush off as fast as they can. Naturally the *marau* and *matasesén* take the things thrown away. The fearful noise is of itself harmless enough, since the instrument creating it is a bullroarer attached to a thin cord that is swung round the head with great speed. It is obvious that the bullroarer is a secret that remains strictly concealed from the women, and one that a visitor gets to see only with the greatest difficulty. The deep humming sound that the instrument creates is audible over a great distance in the forest, especially when several are swung at once.

Finally, when the hair on the head completely fills the *hassebou*, a great feast is put on inside the *áhbassa burri*, to which the fathers and male relatives are invited. This feast lasts for several days; dancing and singing alternate with feasting. The men prepare all the food; it is still strictly forbidden for women to approach, and the supposed spirit voice of the *ruk* keeps them at a respectful distance. At the end of the feast the parents of the *matasesén* give the *marau* gifts, consisting of two or three pieces of *biruan*, spears, bows and arrows and other goods. At the feast place the *hassebou* are taken from the youths and burnt, and the long hair of the *matasesén* is cut off and then wrapped in leaves, tied into a bundle and stored in their huts. As a rule, a single long lock is left hanging from the neck and the end of it is decorated with beads or a shell. After the haircut, the *marau* lead their *matasesén* back to their villages, and this is an occasion for further festivities. On their return, a mast or tall pole is erected in an open space in the village. This mast, decorated with foliage and paintwork, is climbed by a *marau* who then calls the *matasesén* by the names they will be known by from then on; the old name disappears into oblivion. This mast is called *kukun a solo*. Following the naming it is pulled out, cut up and burnt. After the *ruk-ruk* ceremony the *matasesén* usually choose a wife. From now on they are regarded as adults, and take part in all the adult ceremonies.

Almost involuntarily a comparison of the *ruk-ruk* of the Solomon Islanders with the *duk-duk* of the Gazelle Peninsula comes to mind. It is not only the almost identical name that leads to such a comparison. Just as with the *duk-duk* a unique ceremonial site, the *taraiu*, is dedicated for the participants, so with the *ruk-ruk* it is the *tálohu*, two words that have the greatest similarity in otherwise very different languages. Exclusion of women from all ceremonies on the ceremonial site is common to both, as is the pretence that participants talk with spirits on the ceremonial sites. The female spirit, *ruk a tzon*, corresponds with the *tubuan* which is regarded as female, and the male spirit *ruk a tahol* with the male *duk-duk*. Terrifying the women and appropriation of the goods thrown away is a common feature, as is the killing of women when they by chance penetrate the secrecy. The burning of the *hassebou* and the burning of the *duk-duk* costume is a further parallel and, were we in such a position of trust with the *ruk-ruk* as we are with the *duk-duk*, we would assuredly discover many further similarities.

In common with the *ingiet* of the Gazelle Peninsula, various illicit sexual practices are carried on at the gatherings of these secret societies. Sodomy is performed without shame, and nothing wrong is seen in it. Our ideas of morals are so far removed from the concepts of the natives, who only see something as evil or unjust when it causes harm to the common good, that moral aberrations such as sodomy are regarded in their eyes as harmless games. This is also evident in that, although moral misdemeanours such as adultery or incest as a rule are punished by death or at least by a heavy fine, sodomy goes free, worthy of a smile at most.

We find the totem system in the German Solomon Islands, just as in the Bismarck Archipelago.

On Buka the whole population falls into two main classes, which have the hen and the frigate bird as their insignia, and are correspondingly named *kéreu* and *mánu* from the names of the two birds. A *kéreu* can marry only a *mánu*. Relations between two people of the same sign are regarded as incest. The children always inherit the sign of the mother. In northern Bougainville they have the same two insignia, the hen, *atóa*, and the frigate bird, *manu*. In southern Bougainville, the same situation exists, but with the difference that a greater number of birds serve as group insignia, and that the possessors of the same group insignia are not named after the bird in question but have an unique group name. The members of the clan that has the pigeon (*baólo*) as its insignia are called *baumane*; those that have the hornbill (*popo*) are called *simäa*; those that have the cockatoo (*ána*) are called *bánahu*; those that have the frigate bird (*mánua*) are called *talapuini*; those that have the *tigenou* are named *hanapare*; those of the *kápi*, *talasaggi*; those of the *tálile*, *habubúsu*. Members of one clan marry only members of another clan, but here too there is a fixed rule that the children belong to the mother's clan.

There are no outward and visible clan signs, yet the members recognise one another, and regard themselves as closely related.

It is clear that the secret societies are a characteristic feature in the spiritual life of the Melanesian. We have seen in the *duk-duk* that it has spread to the Gazelle Peninsula only in relatively recent times. But we should not conclude from this that all secret societies are of recent date; on the contrary, they are probably very old, and possibly have a common origin. However, over the course of time, the secret societies in the different regions have evolved in different ways and, if the natives had been left in peace, would possibly have developed even further and taken on new forms. They all have much in common; even minor details are the same in widely separated regions, and the more one gets to know them, the more one becomes convinced that they share a common origin.

This will become clearer to the reader when he compares the following brief description of the secret societies existing on the other Melanesian islands with the extensive description of the societies in the Bismarck Archipelago.[4]

In the southern Solomon Islands, we encounter the *matambala* on the island of Florida, the *tamate* on the Banks Islands, and the *qatu* in the northern New Hebrides. From New Caledonia we know of disguised people in certain ceremonies, whose masking is almost identical with that of the *tamata* of the Banks Islands. Similarly, the *nanga* from Fiji, although somewhat different, can probably be included here.

The *matambala* on Florida would probably have been brought from the large island of Ysabel. Young and old, married and single are accepted; a man who does not belong to the society is not on the same level as the men who are members. The women and children, and the uninitiated, *matavonovono*, believe that the initiated ones communicate with spirits; the shrill calls and unexplained noises that emanate from the ceremonial site are not human to their ears; the forms that appear are not men.

The Banks and Torres islands appear to be the principal sites of the societies whose members are called 'the spirits', *o tamate*, *netmet*. The societies are particularly numerous in the Torres group, and there are some people who belong to four or five of them. The principal society is the *tamate livoa* from Mota. Another society differs by having a special dance and has a unique society- or club- house; this society, the *qat*, predominates on the Banks Islands, and is unknown in the Torres group.

All the *tamate* societies have a certain leaf or flower as a visible emblem. The wearing of this emblem is restricted to members, and transgressions are severely punished. Besides the great *tamate*, the most powerful group, there are numerous smaller local societies of more recent date, having as a rule a bird for their insignia. The assembly place of the great *tamate* is called the *salagoro* and, like the *taraiu* of the Gazelle Peninsula, it is an isolated place in the forest, not far from the village. The path branching off to it is proclaimed by a special sign as a 'forbidden route'; no woman and no uninitiated person would dare to take this path; strangers from other districts are from time to time allowed. The mask hats and costumes are stored on the *salagoro*; the building there contains nothing extraordinary. The only remarkable thing is the apparatus that makes the noise which the uninitiated regard as a spirit voice. It consists of a smooth flat stone on which the stalk end of a fan palm leaf is rubbed; the fan-shaped leaf is then swung, creating the characteristic sound whose pitch and volume can be altered at will. The bullroarer, such a carefully guarded secret in northern Bougainville, is a familiar instrument on the Banks Islands.

The *matambala* on Florida was destroyed by the influence of Christianity. We know little about it; it is, however, known that Florida people on the Banks Islands recognised the *tamate* there as identical with their own *matambala*. On the Banks Islands, the *tamate*, like the *duk-duk* of the Gazelle Peninsula, still remains, in spite of Christianity.

To be accepted into the society of the great *tamate*, the individual in question first has to bring a pig, which is offered to the members; then he has to undergo a certain period of fasting. When he is conducted onto the *salagoro* he must make payment; he then stays hidden for a number of days and may subsequently help in the daily preparation of food. This period varies; in several societies the new member stays hidden for 100 days and then helps equally as long with the cooking. During the first hundred days he may not wash, and becomes so encrusted with dirt that he becomes unrecognisable; it is then said, 'He is so dirty that he is invisible!'

Beyond the actual ceremony, the *salagoro* is the usual assembly place for the members. When a ceremony is pending, the far-sounding noise of the *linge tamate* signals the beginning of the mysteries. New masks and costumes are made, and the masked members visit the villages and take without retribution what they need of field and garden produce,

4. I have taken the following excerpts substantially from Codrington's outstanding work, *The Melanesians, their Anthropology and Folklore*.

and frighten women and children.

The people of the New Hebrides, neighbouring the Banks group, also have *tamate* societies. On Aurora, Araga and Ambryn there are secret assembly places and masks. On Ambryn, Dr Codrington was taken to such a place, and shown a mask that was made from a skull and furbished with long hair and pig tusks.

The *qat* society differs from the *tamate* society in that it does not have a fixed assembly place; its main feature is the dance. The *tamate* perform the current dances but the *qat* itself is a dance or, more accurately, it is danced. When a certain number of novitiates are available, they are led to an isolated and enclosed space. Here they stay, unwashed and rubbed only with ash, for a long time while they learn the dance and the accompanying song by which all movements are governed. Before this, however, they have to present an entry gift. Although the spirit *qat* is honoured to some extent by the dance, the inception has no religious significance. The hat worn during the dance is also named *qat*. The neophyte learns a difficult dance that requires long and often repeated practice, not so much on account of complicated figures but because of the rapidity and precision of the dance steps. These are directed by a song and the beating of a bamboo stick; the song is intoned with a deep and gentle voice. These songs are known only by those initiated; they lack any deeper meaning. Here is a translated example:

> Mother, fetch my bow so that I can kill a hen, a flying hen! Mother, bring the bow here, so that I can shoot the hen!

The words of this song, if one can call it that, are endlessly repeated.

When the appointed time approaches, the new dancers and the initiates appear with tall hats on their heads. The hats are pointed, and rest on the shoulders. Over the course of time they have gradually become so high that lines are attached to the sides to hold them upright and it becomes impossible to dance with them. One is reminded automatically not only of the *duk-duk* masks but also the characteristic dance presentations of the Baining on the Gazelle Peninsula.

In the northern New Hebrides the *qatu*, as well as similar institutions, is based especially on Maevo, Omba and Araga. All that is known of Omba is that there, they use a hat in the form of a shark; there are more extensive accounts from the other islands.

On Maevo, there are several *qatu* but one of them, the *qatu lata*, is the main one. Initiation consists of patient endurance of drudgery and hardship, but no secrets are imparted; then come the song, the dance and the preparation of costumes. Not far from the village is erected a dense enclosure in which the novitiates spend about thirty days, unwashed and only sparingly fed. The insignia of membership is the flower of a plant, called *nalnal*. Those initiated take a new name but retain their earlier name as well. Also, they become *tari* and *vula*; the young people, usually called *tileg* and *goa*, become *tari-koli* and *vula-ngoda*. Women must not see the novitiates before they have returned to public life. Transgression is punished by death. Those newly initiated finally appear, blackened by soot and dirt, but no non-member must see them in this condition; they must first wash and clean up.

The great secret of the society is the preparation of the *qatu* hat that again brings to mind the *duk-duk* and other New Britain masks.

On Araga the institution is called *qeta*. New recruitment is carried out every five or six years. The neophytes are housed in small huts erected for this purpose, on a site where visiting is prohibited to all non-members. They stay here for a certain period while they learn a particular song and a dance; the period of isolation is indeterminate. After a few days the initiated leave the site, and food now becomes very sparse, each neophyte receiving only a small amount each day. As a rule, the isolation lasts for five months, from the time when the yam shoots are put in the ground until the ripening of the tubers. During this period the neophytes may not wash. When the first ripe yams are dug up, the youths go to the water and wash themselves; only then can they return to their villages and be seen by the women again. They are now *tari*, and this word is added to their names; for example, Liu becomes Tariliu, Suluana becomes Tarisuluana, and so on.

The *matambala* on Florida is traced back to a native named Siko, who is supposed to have brought it from Bugotu on Ysabel. The ceremonies took place every six to ten years. On a particular part of the island there was a site where all non-members were strictly prohibited from going. Within this forbidden zone were twelve divisions, each with a sacred house. Two of these buildings were so holy that nobody went inside them or even went near them; in these houses stood wooden carvings of birds, fish, crocodiles and sharks, and images of men, sun and moon.

The ceremonies began as a rule when the *Canari* nuts began to ripen and the first fruits were harvested. The nuts were cut open first in one particular house of the twelve, and this was continued in the other houses, in a certain order. The women placed baskets in rows on the path at the first new moon after the ripening of the nuts; and, from morning till night, the men filled the baskets with nuts. The following moon was called the 'moon of the sweeping clean'; that is, all paths within the sacred zone were cleaned and swept, to show that they were now ready for the *matambala*, and were consecrated to it.

On the day of the initiation, the members went

to the small huts that had been erected on the beach for this purpose; they took their friends who wanted to join the society. The novices had to stay in the huts without daring to enter the actual sacred site, *vunu tha*, where, meanwhile, the members were using bamboo cane to make the objects called *tindalo*. These had different shapes; one called *voi* consisted of a 10 feet long and 9 feet tall wall of tree bark, decorated and painted. Several men, concealed behind, carried this wall into the open, where the women could look at the image. Another was called *koitaba vunutha*, and was so big that eighty to 100 men could hide in it; they carried the structure to the beach where everyone could admire it.

After the paths had been swept, the *matambala* people cut the bamboo canes necessary for their structures. Different lengths of tubing were bound to one another and a conical frame was prepared, and covered with the painted flower cuttings of the sago palm. These structures were presented after the completion of the public activity, and the non-initiated believed that they were spirits.

A type of initiation ceremony consisted of each neophyte clasping a tree trunk, and, while in this position, being touched on six parts of the body with a glowing wooden firebrand. Afterwards they were *matambala*, or people of Siko, the founder of the society. The celebration lasted for about three months; during this period, the *matambala* carried out their bad behaviour, plundered the neighbourhood and terrorised the women. The latter had to prepare numerous dishes, and the *matambala* collected them by swinging the bullroarer, *buro*, and striking bundles of coconut leaves against a stick. As soon as the women heard the noise created by these instruments, they quickly slipped into their huts and pushed the food outside through a small opening in the wall. On these excursions the men's bodies were wrapped in foliage so that they could not be recognised.

As in island Melanesia, we are also familiar with a number of secret societies in New Guinea, which have many similarities with the societies of the Bismarck Archipelago and the Solomon Islands. They share a characteristic feature, that elsewhere is found only on the western end of New Britain and on the French Islands, namely the admission of youths into the company of grown-ups through circumcision. We indeed recognise a relationship with the *ingiet* society of the Gazelle Peninsula, although no circumcision takes place there, and consequently the ceremonies are significantly abbreviated and correspondingly modified.

Dr Schellong and missionary Bammler have given us closer acquaintance with the *balum* ceremonies of the natives around Finschhafen. Just as in the Solomon Islands, here too the bullroarer plays a major role as a creator of the sound that is regarded by the non-members as a spirit voice. From the accounts of the two named above, it is clear that here too we are dealing with a men's society, and that the uninitiated are permitted to see only certain public presentations by the society. If we go further westwards, to Astrolabe Bay, we find in the Usa customs an institution very close to the *balum*.

Further westwards, from the Bertrand and Guilbert islands onwards, we find the *parak* institution on the mainland opposite, reaching, via Berlinhafen, roughly as far as the village of Serr.

Everywhere here, certain houses are reserved for the society (*Papua Album*, vol. II, plate 11); in the eyes of the uninitiated they are the dwellings of spirits, with which only the initiated can communicate. The sinister voice of the spirits sounds from these houses, either having the procurement of dinner in mind or chasing women away so that the members can enjoy their meal undisturbed.

The secret societies play a role also in Dutch New Guinea. The familiar 'temple' in Tobadi on Humboldt Bay (*Papua Album*, vol. II, plate 2) is none other than the men's clubhouse, where the youths have to stay for a while. Only the members are allowed to enter this house. Although I was allowed to go in, I clearly saw that everyone was keen to get rid of the inquisitive foreigner as quickly as possible. The novitiates present hid in dark corners or behind matting walls, and nobody wanted to part with the numerous drums and other items present, in spite of the most enticing offers; these above all did not appear to be intended for public display. As well as this clubhouse, there is a men's assembly house in Tobadi, a large, carefully constructed building which, however, is apparently in the nature of a communal house. Naturally, entry to this house too appeared to be forbidden to women, although it was completely open right round, so that anyone could see from outside whatever was going on inside; whereas the 'temple' had thick mat walls, and even the door was constructed in such a way that the opening left the interior of the building invisible.

Although they do occur, we have no extensive knowledge of secret societies in British New Guinea. Professor Haddon, in an essay on the dances of the Torres Straits (*Archiv für Ethnographie*, vol. VI) describes the initiation ceremonies for admission of boys to the men's society on Mer, where entry is forbidden to non-initiates and women. On these occasions masks are used, and one of the secrets that the new members learn involves their being told the names of the various masks. The sharing of this secret with a non-member results in the death of both parties.[5]

All these accounts of the secret societies of the Melanesians and Papuans justify some quite definite conclusions. They are a universal privilege of the men; the customs of the society are kept as a great secret from all non-members and especially from all women; what is shown in public is clothed in the form of a spirit manifestation; the noises that sound from the ceremonial sites are the voices of spirits which communicate there with the members; the masked people are not representations, but are spirits in the eyes of the non-initiated; as a rule, the new members have to undergo a series of privations and physical suffering, either extended fasts or demeaning activities or direct bodily abuse; a payment is almost always connected with the initiation (where money is known, as, for example, on the Gazelle Peninsula, this is the most convenient and easiest means of payment; where they do not have this, offerings of food of every kind takes its place). The members of the societies have not only social but, more especially, material advantages as well; they accumulate not only a financial fortune but they ensure an ever-renewable, luxuriously appointed free table for the rest of their lives. No religious motive can be recognised in any of these societies. Spirits and spirit voices dwell on the societies' ceremonial sites; in the natives' minds spirits reveal themselves to the public, but those initiated know that it is all an empty charade, and nowhere is there any trace of a veneration of the spirits or higher beings. When, for example, on the Gazelle Peninsula the cult or, as one might probably more accurately say, the high esteem, of ancestors is expressed by their skulls being dug up, displayed publicly and ceremonies put on in their honour, the *tubuan* has profited from this custom because their owners understood, like cunning financial people, that there was money to be made from this story. We know that in many regions of the Gazelle Peninsula the *tubuan* and *duk-duk* institution is of relatively recent date, but the natives say that the skull veneration is much older.

This should make our ethnologists much more cautious in their general inferences. To many ethnologists the native stands at the same level that he occupied a thousand years ago. But this is not the case universally; evolution is also recognisable among the people of nature. It is not regular, it moves erratically and, not infrequently, results in a retrograde movement, to come back onto the right path only after a long reversal; but it always brings out new developments that are sometimes of long, and sometimes of short, duration according to whether favourable or hostile elements are making themselves felt.

We have a series of reports from the Melanesian islands concerning the totem system, at our disposal. Codrington, whom I am following here also, reports that on the islands and island groups discussed in his book, the southern Solomons, the Banks and Torres islands and the northern New Hebrides, the natives are divided into two or more classes, and that marriage within the same class is not allowed. Maternal rights are here universally predominant, and form the basis on which social relationships are built. In the Solomon Islands, this division into classes is not, as far as we know, universal; just as the maternal right is not exclusively authoritative; for example, on the islands of Ulava and Ugi, and in parts of San Christoval, Malaita and Guadalcanar. Within these regions, the languages also form an unique grouping, just as peculiarities in ornamentation and in the appearance of the natives themselves are unmistakable. In general, these kinds of marital classes exist almost everywhere in Melanesia, although not everywhere with special names, nor with special insignia.

On the islands of Aurora and Maewo, the nearest New Hebridean island neighbours of the Banks Islands, there are two divisions, which distinguish themselves internally as *ta tavaluna* (from the other division). Besides these, there are divisions named for the place of their origin. Another division names itself after the octopus – *wirita* – and has its base originally on Bugita. The members catch and eat the octopus just like other natives; but, when a man from another division intends to catch *wirita*, he takes a member of the *wirita* division with him to Bugita, where the latter stands on the shore and calls, 'So and so (naming the native) wants to catch *wirita*!'

On Omba the two divisions are called '*wai wung*'; that is, bundle of fruit, or part of a bundle of the same fruit, such as the banana, as if all members belong to a common stock.

On Florida and the surrounding islands there are more than two divisions. On Florida alone there are six, which are called *kema*. Each *kema* has an independent designation, namely *nggaombata*, *manukama*, or *honggokama* (eagle), *hongokiki*, *kakau* (crab), *himbo* and *lahi*. Each *kema* has one or more *buto*; that is, objects that the members must keep away from, that they dare not eat or see, or that they are forbidden to approach. If the *buto* is a living thing, it is sometimes eaten and sometimes not; the *kakau* division, for example, may not eat the crab, nor likewise a certain species of parrot (*Trichoglossus massena*); on the other hand, the members of the *manukama* division are allowed to eat the eagle (*manukaka*), but may not disturb the wild pigeon. The *nggaombata* do not eat the flesh of the *Tridacna* shellfish; the *lahi* eat no white pork.

Indeed Codrington seems to see no totem in this situation, nor any vestiges thereof; however, if we compare them with similar institutions – for example, on New Ireland or on Bougainville – it is clear that here we find a feature widespread in Melanesia: that certain classes are named after certain objects, and that these objects are held in a fairly high degree of veneration. Wherever the

5. In the intervening time Professor Haddon has made new and comprehensive studies of these subjects, which unfortunately are not available to me, but indicate that the secret societies are widespread in British New Guinea.

Plate 43 The *tubuan* renders the last rites to the deceased

Polynesian element was enforced in Melanesia, the totem system invariably weakened, or was lost completely; the former situation occurred on Florida.

In his book *Among the Headhunters*, Woodford comments as follows:

> During my last residence on Guadalcanar, it came to my knowledge that an extensive and widespread system of 'castes' or *totems*, for want of words to better express my meaning, exists upon this and some of the adjacent islands. The name for them on Guadalcanar and upon Gela or Florida is *Kema*, upon Savo, *Ravu*. At Veisali, on the west end of Guadalcanar, the word used is *Kua*.
>
> I could find out very little about them. Their influence is, however, powerful. The natives told me that a man might not marry a woman belonging to his own caste. They are not confined to tribes speaking one language, but, as in some of the instances I cite below, natives belonging to tribes speaking a different language will be found to belong to the same caste. I can conceive it due to the protection afforded by these castes that certain natives can pass freely backwards and forwards between tribes at open war, as occurred to my knowledge last year, when severe fighting was taking place between the island of Savo and the west end of Gauldalcanar; or that natives are enabled to remain in a village when others have had to leave on account of anticipated attack by another village.

Woodford then named a number of these *kema* or *ravu*, that are in part identical with those named by Codrington, namely *Gambata, Kiki, Lakoli, Kakau, Tanakindi*, and thinks that there are a lot more of them.

Dr Fison in Fiji believes that he has seen traces of an earlier totem there. For example he met a native who was teaching his son to worship the rat; on being asked why he was doing this, he answered, 'Because the rat is our father!'

On several Polynesian islands also, we find vestiges of an institution that I can only interpret as a totem. Thus, in Samoa, every significant family has some animal that is not eaten and cannot be called by its usual name in the presence of family members but has another designation. It does not seem impossible that the Polynesians, on their wanderings from west to east stretching over a long period of time, intermingled with the Melanesians, especially marrying their women and adopting part of their institutions. Particularly through marriage with Melanesian women, the totem system, which plays such a significant role in the life of the natives, would also be implanted in Polynesia.

The esteemed Governor of British New Guinea, Sir William MacGregor, set up investigations in various districts of his jurisdiction into existing totem customs. In his annual report of 1897-98 he presented the result of these investigations, that totemism still plays a significant role throughout the east of New Guinea. It extends westward as far as Mairu (Table Bay) and then suddenly disappears. It is fairly widespread along the east coast;

however, no traces had been found on the Mambare River, although it is possible that the system is also known there.

No trace of totemism was found in the central districts, but it was certainly on the Fly River, although not to the same degree as in the east.

In the east the totem symbol of the mother is passed down to the children, but not everywhere. In the west, the reverse is more often the case. Sir William believes that this is a consequence of the higher status that the women occupy in the east compared with the women in the west. The totem system in the west is generally in the process of dying out. The current younger generation appears to know little or nothing about it. On the other hand, in the east totemism will maintain its influence for a long time yet.

On the island of Tubetube (Engineer group) the inhabitants are divided into six tribes which have six different emblems. Members who have the same emblem regard one another as close relatives. In almost every case the first question directed at strangers or visitors is, 'What is the name of your bird?' or, 'What is the name of your fish?', because the totem emblems are either birds or fish.

Men and women of the same totem cannot marry; the children have the mother's emblem. The animal, be it fish or bird, never serves as food to the totem member, nor can others kill it without incurring the displeasure of the tribe who carry the animal as their totem.

On the island of Kivai the name for totem is *muru mara*. Here the totem insignia is passed from father to son. Men and women of the same insignia may not marry; however, after marriage, the women take the sign of their husband. The totem emblem can be neither killed nor eaten.

In war and during certain dances, the man's totem sign is painted on his chest or on his back, and no warrior attacks an enemy who is painted with his own totem sign. Beyond their village, natives are always greeted cordially by wearers of the same emblem.

The population of the Kadawarubi tribe (Ture-Ture and Hawatta in the western district) have nine different emblems. The natives here do not kill or eat their totem animal, and its killing by others is always an occasion for quarrelling and conflict. Marriage is permitted only if the totem signs of the couple are different. The wife does not eat or touch the husband's totem insignia, and he behaves likewise towards his wife's totem emblem. The children as a rule inherit the father's totem sign, but it can happen that, when a married couple has several children, a few of them will inherit the father's sign, and others that of the mother.

The natives on Saibai have five totem emblems. Marriages take place only between people of different insignia; but in this district the totem emblems are eaten. The members of the same totem unite both in work and in discussion.

Through the extensive investigations of Messrs Spencer and Gillen into the Australian tribes, published in two very interesting volumes, *The Native Tribes of Central Australia* and *The Northern Tribes of Central Australia,* the secret societies of the Australians have become more familiar to us. It would be going too far to give an extract here from both these valuable works, but it is worth noting that these secret societies contain many of the features that we found among the Melanesians.[6]

In the Solomon Islands, as in the Bismarck Archipelago and New Guinea, time will offer us many valuable accounts in which this characteristic feature of the spiritual life of the Melanesians and Papuans will become clearer. What I have given in the preceding pages shows up the large holes that still need to be filled, and an interesting and profitable field is thus opened up for the activities of later investigators in this region.

The institution that we designate by the name 'totem' and that we find so extensive among our Melanesians has in recent years been the object of extensive investigations. In particular, people have sought to establish its origins. The reports of the English researchers Spencer, Gillen and Howitt on the customs of the Australians, have brought to light a great number of different theories, and these are discussed comprehensively, especially in the English specialist literature. I believe that all these debates are moving in a circle of thought that is totally foreign to the natives, and that, in order to investigate the origin of this characteristic institution, we must refrain from all such spiritual speculation, and attempt to separate the true core from the later additions and intermingling with other customs. With the Australians this seems very difficult, because here a thousand-year association appears to have taken place between two major tribes that were originally totally different in their traditions and customs. In the Bismarck Archipelago, where indeed extensive mixing with other tribes is recognisable, it seems rather more possible to reach a satisfactory answer to this question. I want to make my own position clear in the following:

Wherever we find the totem system in New Britain, New Ireland, New Hanover, the Admiralty Islands, and the German Solomon Islands, its purpose is always the same, namely the sharp division of different groups that inherit a particular group insignia from the mother, and whose members are not permitted to enter any marital relationship within the group. These groups are differentiated as a rule by having adopted a certain animal as a group attribute, namely birds (for example, cockatoo, pigeon, hornbill, and so on), and inheriting this attribute from the mother at birth. On the Gazelle Peninsula and on southern New Ireland,

6. Howitt's work, *The Native Tribes of South-East Australia*, also gives extensive accounts of secret societies; however, it seems to me that in Australia the secret societies have lost a large part of their originality probably as a result of the mixing of two races – a crinkly-haired race (very close to the present inhabitants of the archipelago) that took the eastern part of Australia and was the original owner of the secret society, and a smooth-haired or curly-haired race that had their homeland in the west.

we find an even more primitive form, in that the entire population falls into two groups which are designated simply as 'we' (or ours) and 'they, them' (theirs). I believe that in this I am seeing a primitive form of the whole system. If we go still further back to a time when even this simple split did not exist, we find the earliest population at a level where marriage did not yet occur. In earliest times, congress between both sexes was totally free and unfettered within the tribe, and it is understandable that in this situation the children followed the mother, since in most cases the father was probably hard to identify. Over the course of time, such incest must have proven disadvantageous and disastrous; the tribe lost strength and resistance, and succumbed in the struggle for existence. In this situation, it seems to me that the knowledge must have spread quite rapidly: our women are not giving birth to sufficient of the next generation for perpetuation of the tribe; or the natives are of poor quality and are not in a position to promote the general well-being; consequently our own women are not fit and we need to acquire them from other tribes. This insight led to stealing of women, for we might probably assume that in that far-off time each tribe or each society formed a segregated group that was at war or feuding with the neighbours. Woman-stealing is therefore the foundation for that which we now call marriage, although the stolen ones were probably the common property of the tribe, just as their own tribal women were. Woman-stealing must necessarily have led to a segregation into classes. Let us imagine that two neighbouring tribes stole each other's women; in tribe one there would soon be many women from tribe two, and vice versa. Now, if a member of tribe two wanted to take a woman from tribe one, he ran the risk of seizing a girl born of a woman stolen from his own tribe; that is, a mother who, in his opinion, was not in a position to bear strong, healthy children. There was probably little time or opportunity for genealogical discussions between robber and robbed, and it becomes obvious that one looked for certain signs and peculiarities to prevent poor quality; that is, related, women from being introduced into the tribe.[7] On New Hanover, they apparently regarded the lines on the palm of the hand as such signs of recognition and only later succeeded in connecting the lines with particular designations or attributes. In New Guinea, as we have already seen, the totem sign was painted on the body to indicate group membership. On the Gazelle Peninsula, the original form remained; whoever was born from a woman who originally belonged to 'us', belonged henceforth also to 'us', in the sense that it was not desirable to have sexual relations with such a woman because the tribe would be weakened. However, since everything that prejudiced the strength or well-being of the tribe had to be avoided, the prohibition against sexual relations with descendants from the same tribe built up over time. In the most primitive and simplest situation initially two groups arose. The situation became more involved when several tribes carried out woman-stealing with one other, and here the designation of each individual group by a particular sign probably had its origin. The choice of birds in particular as such attributes, can be explained, I believe, from the idea that most other animals were the dwelling of evil spirits with which nobody wanted to be involved. Several years ago, I undertook investigations into the totem system on the west coast of New Ireland. Here I found specified as a totem a bird that I had not found mentioned elsewhere, namely the heron. In the village there were five men and youths and two women who belonged to the heron totem, and I was immediately astonished that all of them differed, in varying degrees, in their external appearance from the other villagers. In some the skin shade was paler, in others the scalp was surprisingly different in that several had almost smooth hair. Extensive enquiries brought to light one old man with surprisingly smooth, grey hair who explained that his mother had been shipwrecked in a canoe many years ago. She had been taken as a wife by the village headman and, when she gave birth to children, these had been designated with the totem of 'heron'. The marriage produced two sons and two daughters, and the current herons stemmed from the latter. Several years later, in the same village, I learned that one of the women had died childless, and that the other had been married into Gardner Island opposite, and therefore the heron totem had probably been planted further afield. It is certainly still present on its original spot but cannot be inherited through the female line because this no longer exists. It is clear that the shipwrecked woman originated from islands far to the east, whose inhabitants have smooth hair, perhaps Ongtong Java or the Gilbert Islands. These types of involuntary voyages cannot be deemed rarities. The mother's racial features were partially transmitted to the offspring, however, since she originated from a region where the totem system was unknown, her offspring of necessity had to possess a totem sign, and this was resolved simply by bestowing an as yet unused sign on the children. That they are expert in helping themselves in other ways is demonstrated by a case I know of from the island of Buka. I know two women there who were shipwrecked about twenty years ago in a canoe from Aoba in the Gilbert Islands. Both women were taken as wives by Buka islanders, and, since the men have the totem sign '*manu*' (frigate bird), the offspring, who could never inherit the father's totem sign, were simply given the second totem sign occurring on the island, *kéreu* (hen), implicitly implying that a *manu* man could marry only a *kéreu* woman and their offspring belonged to the kéreu.

Of course there are also regions where the

7. The word 'totem' according to Powell (*Man* 1902, no.75) is a word from the Algonquin language spoken by Indian tribes in parts of Canada and the United States. According to Powell, it is derived from a root which meant 'clay' or 'loam'. Among the Algonquin Indians, clay or loam was used to paint the face or body with the heraldic sign of a certain group of people. If an Algonquin Indian asked another, 'What is your clay?' – that is, what is your colour or what is your weapon sign or heraldic design – he would use the designation 'totem'. I believe that I am seeing a proof of my assumption that natives originally used certain signs by which all those who belonged to the same group were made easily recognisable.

totem system is not conducted so rigidly; that is, where the totem sign is not inherited exclusively from the mother by the children, but where the latter, by choice of the parents or relatives, receive the totem sign of either the mother or the father. In these cases, we can almost always assume with certainty that there had earlier been a mixing with other tribes who did not know the totem system and had therefore adopted it, but had not drawn the consequences as sharply as in regions where the totem system was indigenous. We find, for example, in the Solomon Islands that, the further south and south-east we go, the more modified is the totem system, through the influence of the immigrant Polynesians. In particular, the inheritance of the mother's sign has in many cases totally disappeared, and the children inherit the father's insignia. We find the same in Australia, as I have already remarked, most probably evoked by those tribes that inhabited the present western Australia, and did not know the totem system, mixing with the totemistic tribes of eastern Australia. We find the same thing in New Guinea, and, on the Admiralty Islands we can observe that one of the tribes rigidly carries out the totem system, while the two other tribes are very lax in the consequences of the system, probably because the custom had been forced upon them, and is still regarded as something foreign, to which they need not be very strict in their adherence.

It must further be borne in mind that, over the course of time, all sorts of other customs have become connected with the totem system, so that it is very difficult for us today to pick out the real core from a long series of complicated customs and ceremonies. Sorcery and belief in spirits have done their bit to embellish the originally simple system with additions and outgrowths, so that it has become almost unrecognisable. This has undoubtedly required a very long period of time, for the native does not sacrifice lightly a tradition or custom that, like the totem system, has such trenchant effects on all aspects of public life. Thus, for example, Christianity has not succeeded so far in shattering the system, although it has been possible to restrict polygamy here and there, and to introduce the Christian system of marriage, though only under constant supervision on the part of the missionaries, and always in conjunction with the established wife purchase.

IX   Stories and Fables

The treasury of stories and fables among the natives varies greatly in range on the various islands. Fantasy has not developed equally in all places: here, the luxuriant twigs and blossoms flourish; there, they are stunted and barely recognisable.

The most impoverished are probably the Baining. They plant their taro and otherwise care little about the way things are. The Solomon Islanders, too, appear to be far behind the inhabitants of the Gazelle Peninsula in this aspect.

However, on New Ireland stories and fables flourish luxuriantly and, with the exception of the Baining, this is so throughout New Britain. Of course, our knowledge is small; white people have not yet come into closer contact with very many of the tribes, and do not know their language, both of which factors are essential for gathering the storehouse of fables.

I regard any classification of these native tales according to content as premature, because of the paucity of material available, and accordingly, I lay them before the reader in all their bright array.

The natives of the north-eastern Gazelle Peninsula believe that the world and everything in the world were originally created beautiful and good by *To Kabanana* (*To Kabinana*). Then there came an evil spirit that spoiled everything that To Kabanana had created, including humans. His name differs in the various districts, the most common being *To Karavo* or *To Korvuvu*; however, he is also designated as *Puruqo*, *To Poruqo* and *To Purukelel*.

One day, To Kabanana sent out a boy to fetch a firebrand for the workers. The boy did not want to go, and To Kabanana asked him, 'Why don't you want to go?' However, the boy did not answer.

Then the snake said, 'Well then, I shall go and fetch the firebrand!' And the snake hurried away and brought the firebrand to To Kabanana.

He then said to the snake, 'You, snake, will always live, but you, shore people, will die!' Then he added, 'You, snake, eat fruit, birds, wallabies and mice in the forest, and you will live on those (eternally); they (shore people), on the other hand, will become ill and die.'

One day, To Korvuvu wanted to eat a man. He killed him at night, cut him up, and ate him. When the people heard that To Korvuvu had eaten a man, they said to one another, 'To Korvuvu is destroying the people, he strikes them dead, and eats them.' But they did not dare to attack him because he was far greater in strength than they. He continued doing evil. One day he was catching lice on a boy's head; suddenly, he bent towards the boy's ear, cut it off, and ate it on the spot. The boy asked To Korvuvu, 'What are you eating?' To Korvuvu said, '*A kubika na moramoro*' after which he confessed that he had cut off his ear and eaten it, and, bursting out laughing, he added, 'It tastes marvellous!'

The boy then ran crying to To Kabanana and complained about To Korvuvu. To Kabanana, however, only said angrily, 'Why did you go to that savage?'

To Kabanana's wife gave birth to a son. When he got bigger she sent him to a small island with a sling to kill pigeons. He went immediately, sat in his boat and rowed with his hands since there were yet no paddles. In the evening he paddled back to the mainland. On the way a shark came, struck the canoe, and ate the boy. To Kabanana and his wife wailed and lamented night and day over the death of their son, having looked in vain for him everywhere. However, the shark had eaten only the body of the boy, and one day the uneaten head was washed up by the waves. To Kabanana spotted it, brought it ashore and buried it. The mother stayed constantly by the grave, weeping and wailing. One day she noticed that something was growing up from the grave. When the soil was carefully shovelled aside, they clearly saw the eyes, nose and mouth of the skull which had put out roots. To Kabanana said to his wife, 'Let us watch, we will see what happens!' Over time the shoot turned into a tree which bore fruit. One day a ripe fruit fell; somebody opened it and ate it. More fruit continued to fall; all were eaten and found to be good and tasty. The tree that grew in such a wondrous way out of the boy's skull was the coconut palm.

One day To Kabanana, To Korvuvu and a small boy went to the sea with nets to catch turtles. To Kabanana and To Korvuvu held the net while the boy was supposed to drive turtles into it. As they drew the net together in order to see their catch, they spotted a piece of *pit* (unopened bud of a species of *Saccharum*) in it. They removed it and said, 'What a stupid thing!' The net was lowered into the water again, and the boy made a noise to drive turtles into the net, but again they found the piece of *pit* in the net. Again they threw it far away. When they had positioned their net a third time and the piece of *pit* was still the only catch, they marvelled and said to one another, 'This is a completely mysterious catch!' This time they did not throw it away but took it home and planted it. Soon the *pit* grew up into a large bush. One day To Kabanana, To Korvuvu and the small boy were going for a walk. Suddenly they saw a woman emerge from the *pit*, sweep the yard, make fire and prepare food. The three were very astonished at this, and said to one another, 'Who is that, who sweeps, fans the fire and cooks?' When the woman heard the whispering, she disappeared immediately back into the *pit*. The three then went into the yard and ate the meal prepared by the woman. Days later, they saw the woman again, and when she had swept the yard and done the cooking they rushed her and held her fast. To Korvuvu said, 'This is my wife!' To Kabanana said that she was his sister, and the boy called her mother. Finally To Korvuvu took her as his wife; she bore him many children, boys and girls who then populated all the land.

Simolo, a Nakanai woman, was working one day in her garden and while she was pulling out the weeds a man from Ulavun approached her. He stood behind a bush and smoked a *suk* (tobacco wrapped in a leaf). The Nakanai woman, who did not know about smoking tobacco, marvelled at it, and asked what it was. The stranger smoked on and, astonished, the woman went up to him, saw how the smoke came out of his mouth and asked if he would give her the *suk*. Her wish was granted, and the woman tried to smoke. When the smoke appeared she was very happy and said to the man, 'Let us get married.' Then they both went to Ulavun (the volcano, The Father) and sat up there smoking and stamping, so that the ground shook and the mountain spewed fire. The Nakanai people living at the foot of the mountain saw this and were very surprised. They looked in vain for the missing Simolo. One evening Simolo and her husband came down from the mountain and entered the village. Simolo was smoking, and when the villagers saw this they asked her, 'Who gave you this wonderful thing?' and she pointed to the stranger. But the people said to one another, 'Let us do it too!' and they ate (smoked) the *suk* and enjoyed it. The man climbed up the mountain again with Simolo, but sent her back with tobacco seeds so that her people could cultivate the plant. The seeds grew, and since then tobacco has been grown in all gardens. The man, To Ulavun, fetched Simolo again, and led her as his wife to the top of the mountain where they have remained, smoking, ever since.

Simolo, who was a real woman, had a son by the snake To Ulavun. When he had grown, his parents said to him, 'Leave here and seek another mountain for your home.' He went away and chose as his dwelling another mountain, to which he gave his name, Bamus (South Son). He remained up there, smoking and spitting out fire and rocks so that villages in the valley were devastated and people were killed. Only a few escaped to Wittau and Tiwongo.

On one occasion all the volcanoes, Langulangu, Kaije, Vunakikiu, Koponawat, Matalaka and Kokomba went to Nakanai to attend the dance of Bamus and Ulavun. When they had reached Sambai they bathed and adorned themselves, then floated further on their rafts. Having arrived at Nakanai they attended the dances. First, they watched Ulavun's dance and, when it had finished they said that it was no good. Nor did they think that the dance of Bamus was any good. Afterwards, To Ulavun and To Bamus gave the foreign volcanoes gifts of *Areca*, betel and shell money. They did not favour Vunakikiu, on the pretext that he was a bad man. To Vunakikiu was very angry, and said to the favoured volcanoes, 'Go home, off you go, I will follow you.' And so they went away. The angry To Vunakikiu bored his tail into the mountain Likuruanga (North Son) and the mountain swayed and shook, fell into the sea and smoked no more. The Nakanai people then hurried up there, held Vunakikiu fast and gave him gifts of *Areca*, betel and shell money, whereupon the earthquake stopped and he went home.

In the opinion of the Nakanai people, the inhabitants of Ulavun are ugly and deformed. They talk about them in the following way:

The inhabitants of Ulavun and Imbane one day caught a *wengi* (a mythical sea monster) and roasted the flesh. A woman ate it first and immediately her mouth convulsed, the lips swelled and the mouth remained open. The nose grew larger, broad and flat. All children born to the woman resembled their mother, and, since all the women had eaten the *wengi*, all their offspring were deformed. Since that time they have been ashamed, and no longer come down to the shore.

STORIES AND FABLES

Plate 44 Dancers, representing spirits

One day Tolangabuturu saw a pigeon. He followed it from tree to tree and tried to catch it, but always it evaded his grasp. Finally it flew over the sea and Tolangabuturu got into his canoe and followed it. After a long journey, he reached an island and discovered that it was inhabited only by women. This seemed uncanny to him, and he climbed a tree to hide. But the shadow of the tree fell on a spring, and when one of the women came to it she saw the silhouette of Tolangabuturu and discovered his hiding place. He pleased her at first sight and, to keep him for herself, she collected water in empty containers for the other women, so that they would not have the opportunity of discovering the treasure. When all the women went away to amuse themselves on the beach with the turtles, the woman crept to the tree and called to Tolangabuturu to come down. She took him to her hut and concealed him there, but eventually the other women discovered his presence and everybody wanted to have the new arrival. This was an occasion for great quarrelling and strife, for the initial discoverer regarded Tolangabuturu as her exclusive property; but finally they came to an agreement and he became the common property of all the women, who looked after him most solicitously to the end of his days.

One day Tokadol found a boy and a small girl in the forest. They had run away from their mother because she was angry that the children had eaten her mangoes. Tokadol took compassion on the little ones and took them to his hut, but his wife, Limlimanavin, was not in agreement, for the little girl aroused her jealousy; and she threatened to eat the boy. Tokadol, however, prevented this, but while he was away one day the wife carried out her plan and ate the boy. She hid his head in the bush, where it was found by Tokadol. He was very angry, ran home and torched his hut, so that his wife would burn with it. Tokadol had thrown the boy's head into a waterhole, where the spirit of the burnt woman visited it. Tokadol now felt very lonely and forsaken, and pined for the boy. The spirit of Limlimanavin awakened the head to life, and brought the boy to Tokadol, who was overjoyed, and forgave his wife because he regarded her innocence as proven.

Ja Dapal had an evil, jealous husband from whom she finally ran away to find safety on a rock in the sea. But the tide rose; soon the water reached her waist, then her neck, and gradually rose higher and higher. Her husband stood on the beach and called to her to come back to shore, but, although the water had already risen so high that she had to jump up from the rock from time to time to keep her head above water, she called back that she would come only if he fetched her. Since the husband did not wish to do this, she finally had to die.

To Kabanana is the inventor of the big fish-trap. He also taught To Poruqo how to make it. One day To Kabanana had to go off to a compound, and left To Poruqo behind to continue working on the basket while he was away. After a short time this got boring, and for recreation he began to throw his spear at different objects. In the end he threw it at the fish-trap as well, and when To Kabanana returned he found it partially destroyed. Indeed he scolded To Poruqo but he had to prepare the trap himself.

Then he showed his companion how to use it, and also taught him how the fish should be prepared and baked. Then he went into the forest. To Poruqo prepared the fish he caught, as he had been told, ate some of them and packed the rest into a basket to take to To Kabanana in the forest. On the way, he spotted a beautiful bird, and tried to knock it out of the tree by throwing stones. When there were no more stones available, he threw the baked fish at the bird, but of course in vain. Thus, through his thoughtless activity, he ruined what his companion with thought and care had planned.

To Kabanana and To Poruqo noticed that, in the mornings when they went outside their huts, somebody had already laid prepared food outside. When this continued, To Kabanana lay in hiding and discovered that it was a woman who made them this gift. Each of them wanted to acquire the benefactor, and To Poruqo was loud in his demands; but To Kabanana finally succeeded in persuading him that he alone had a right to the woman, and she became his wife. Over time the couple had many children, and finally To Poruqo married one of the daughters. Based on this, there are always useful and useless men in the world, and both must see how they can get along together.

One day, the wallabies went onto the reef to fish. As the tide rose, most of them went back to shore, but one hopped from stone to stone and jeered at the fish swimming by. It did not notice that the water was rising higher and higher until, finally, surrounded by the sea on all sides, it was marooned on an isolated rock far from shore. Then it began to wail, and implored the fish to carry it to shore, but the fish said, 'Earlier you ridiculed and insulted us; now see how you can get to land without us.' Luckily the turtle came by, and was touched by the pleas of the wallaby. The wallaby settled on the turtle's broad back and entwined its front legs round its neck to get a better grip. The turtle swam to the beach; but on the way the wallaby gnawed at its saviour's shell, where it covered the neck between head and trunk. When the turtle noticed this, it began in turn to gnaw at the front legs of the wallaby, so that they became shorter and shorter. When they reached the beach the wallaby sprang down from the turtle's back and called to it, 'Look at your neck! How ugly and wrinkled it has become!' The turtle replied, 'Look at your front legs; how short they have become.' Since that time the turtle has no shell between head and trunk and draws his head back to protect this region; ever since then the wallabies have had short front legs.

Long ago the *kau* (*Philemon cockerelli* Kl.) had the bright plumage of the *mallip* (*Lorius hypoenochrous* H. R. Gr., a species of parrot), which had the simple grey plumage of the other. One day the *kau* went to bathe, and laid his bright garment carefully on the shore. The *mallip* came along, and laid his grey costume down before he stepped in to bathe. He saw the bright plumage and crept towards it to admire the splendid decoration. Unobserved, he adorned his own body with the iridescent feathers, and when he was ready he called to the *kau*, 'See how beautiful I am!' The *kau* was very angry and called upon him to put the costume back, but the *mallip* laughed and flew away. Incensed at this, the *kau* grabbed a lump of earth and threw it after the *mallip*. The clod hit the *mallip* on the head, and ever since then he has a grey-black fleck on his beautiful red head. The *kau* then had to slip into the dull garment of the *mallip*, and he has not yet succeeded in retrieving his stolen property.

The following legendary tales date from more recent times:

When the volcanic eruption occurred in Blanche Bay in 1878 and the small, flat Vulcan Island was formed, people in the village of Karavia opposite claimed to have seen spirits in human form on the island, going to and fro in the rising steam. After the eruption of the small undersea crater to which the island owes its existence, they disappeared as quickly as they had come. Old people still alive will not let this story die, and are firmly convinced that those who appeared on that occasion were the children of Kaije.

In 1901 the Bremen Lloyd steamer *München* ran onto a sandbank in the harbour when putting to sea from Matupi, and was refloated only after several hours. It so happened that on that evening there occurred a quite severe earthquake, and the Matupi people declared that the steamer had run up onto the tail of Kaije, who was lying on the sea floor in the form of a crocodile. Angered by this, Kaije had swung his tail to and fro thus causing the earthquake.

The Sulka folk, through their extraordinarily developed fantasy which sees spirits and spirit activities everywhere, understandably have a great number of tales, of which we know only the smallest fraction. For the following, I am grateful to Brother Hermann Müller of the Catholic mission, who has recorded them from the accounts of his Sulka pupils.

Long ago the Sulka did not know about fire. They ate all their meals raw, as nature had presented them. Night, too, was unknown at that time, and crickets, which chirp at night, did not exist; neither did the *kau* bird, which greets the dawn with his cries and whistles.

One day a man by the name of E Makong (Emkong) was lopping boughs off a tree on the bank of the Makong River. His *kienho* (an item of jewellery) fell into the water, and he climbed down the tree, laid his stone axe and loincloth on the grass and leapt into the water to retrieve his lost ornament.

When he reached the bottom of the river, to his astonishment he found himself in a compound, where many people ran up to see the stranger. A man approached him and asked his name. 'E Makong is my name,' he replied, whereupon the questioner answered, 'Oh, then you are my namesake, for I too am called E Makong.' Then he led him into his yard and offered him a new loincloth. Greater still was the astonishment of E Makong when he saw fire for the first time, and he was overcome with great fear. Cooked bananas and taro were set before him, but at first he did not want to eat anything. After a long hesitation he finally tasted it; the cooked food pleased him and he ate to his heart's content.

Gradually evening approached and it began to get dark, and the crickets sang their little song. He was very frightened and believed that he was going to die. But his fear grew extreme when detonations sounded all round him and the people were transformed into snakes which curled up and lay down to sleep. His namesake soothed him and said that he should not be frightened since this was their normal custom. It would soon be day again and they would turn back into humans. As he said this he gave a loud report, turned into a snake and lay down to sleep. E Makong was now alone in the dark among a lot of snakes, and afraid; but finally weariness overcame him and he fell asleep.

When the *kau* began to pipe and whistle, he awoke and saw that day was gradually breaking. Loud reports began to sound around him and the snakes assumed human form.

Makong, the host, then wrapped the night, fire, several *kau* birds and crickets into a little pack, which he gave to his guest to take home with him. Then he led him along the way. Makong soon found himself on the surface, and climbed onto the bank. He laid the fire in a field of grass, and, as it began to burn and crackle and the flames flared high in the air, all the people ran up in fear. Makong, whom they believed had drowned, then stepped forward, recounted his experiences and explained the use of fire to his people. He unpacked everything else and let the crickets and *kau* birds fly away, but, gradually as it became pitch-black night, the fear of the people knew no bounds. However, he pacified them, and over time the people grew accustomed to the new state of affairs.

Earlier the moon shone and burned just like the sun. A small bird (*a vit*) came, took mud, flew with it to the moon and threw it in its face. Since then the moon has darkened and does not burn; the flecks of mud are still clearly visible.

The *vong* (cassowary) used to be able to fly, just like the other birds, but he lost this ability in the following way.

One day it rained heavily. The *vong* sat in a tree

and let the raindrops run off. Along came the little bird *a vit*, and spoke to him as follows, 'Grandfather, raise your wing in the air a little so that I can slip under and protect myself from the rain!' The good-hearted *vong* granted the little one's request straight away and the *vit* slipped nimbly under the wing. But he was a mischievous rogue and took needle and thread and sewed the upper wing of the *vong* firmly to its body. When he had finished he spoke again, 'Grandfather, let me slip under your other wing, since it is dripping through here.' The *vong* was quite happy and the *vit* hid under the other wing, which he fastened with needle and thread just like the other wing.

When the rain had stopped and the sun was shining again, the *vit* said to the *vong*, 'Let's fly away, for the weather is fine again!' and he quickly slipped out of his shelter and flew away. When the *vong* wanted to follow he noticed to his horror what the *vit* had done; try as he might, he could not spread his wings and fly away. He fell to the ground, and since that time he has had to remain permanently on the ground.

The *vong* was very angry and called to the *vit*, 'Just you wait, I will cast a spell on your droppings and then you will die.'

Now when the *vit* had to relieve himself he settled in the top of a tree so that his droppings could not fall on the ground to be bewitched by the *vong*, but would remain in the tree. But the droppings, hanging from a branch, gradually stretched into a long thread and transformed into a creeper, *a gilengœi*, with beautiful red flowers.

(This fable with slight variations is also known on the Gazelle Peninsula.)

The *vukameak* is a recluse among the birds, and he sits silently with his bill pinched together, alone in his hole in the rock. One day the other birds decided to do everything they could to make the *vukameak* laugh. They tried everything possible; the crow striped his whole body with charcoal, the *gumbul* ate earth, the *gau* made warts on his bill, but all was in vain, and nothing made the *vukameak* laugh. Without a change of expression he watched the crazy behaviour with bill tightly closed. Last came the green parrot; he had smeared his entire body with excrement, and presented himself in front of the *vukameak*. When the latter saw him, he finally had to laugh, opening his beak to do so. At the same moment something fell out, and the parrot was quickly on hand to catch and swallow it. When this had left the parrot through excretion and fell to the ground, a taro sprouted from it. The people found the plant, tended it and raised other taro plants from it. Thus, the taro gradually spread throughout the villages.

In two different neighbouring villages there lived two brothers of the same name. One, *Nut vulau* (Nut the elder), had two wives and many servants; the other, *Nut sie* (Nut the younger), was unmarried. He lived with his grandmother in a compound and had only ten servants.

One morning Nut sie got up, took his fishing spear, and went fishing. When he had caught three *vulaupun* he made his way home with them. On the way, his brother's two wives met him, and when they saw the handsome young man they found him pleasing. They said to him, 'Your brother's taro are drying, he has sent us to catch crabs.' He handed them his fish and said, 'Take these fish and prepare them for your husband.' They took the fish and went back home with them, but gave their husband only the crabs that they had caught, and ate the fish themselves.

Another day when Nut vulau was working with his people he sent his wives again to the sea to fetch salt water and catch crabs. Nut sie, who had gone fishing again, met them once more on the way home and again the women lusted after the handsome youth. He asked them, 'Did you give my brother the fish?' They answered in the affirmative, whereupon he again gave them fish for their husband. They met several times, and each time repeated the same routine as at their first meeting.

One day Nut vulau was again hard at work with his servants, and the women were sent to catch crabs as usual. Nut sie, who had also gone fishing, met the women again and, since they were now quite accustomed to him, they pestered him at length until he consented to have sexual relations with them. He painted the genitalia of his brother's two wives with a coloured design. One day the elder brother noticed the drawing when one of the wives sprang over a fence, and his suspicion was immediately aroused. But to be more certain he set to and had a boat made, and, when it was ready, he ordered his wives and several of his people to go to sea in it. He remained on shore; as the women climbed into the boat he saw the designs clearly. Under the pretext that a storm was coming he called the boat crew back and made them land.

He then had whitish coconuts (*a sil*) brought down and new unpainted loincloths produced. He summoned all the people and gave them each a nut and a cloth so that they could make a design on both and then give them back to him. Nut sie received a nut and a garment also, but his designs were poor. When all the drawings had been returned Nut vulau inspected them, but none matched the pattern on the women. However, he had his suspicions about his brother, and had him draw another design. This time the pattern precisely matched those on the women, and now Nut vulau knew the perpetrator. Immediately he prepared for war, and his servants had to make weapons and shields. Nut sie and his servants also prepared for war. They made fine shields, painted them with bright colours and hemmed them round the edges; they also made handgrips on the reverse side. However, Nut vulau's servants were very unskilled; their shields were ugly, and lacked hand-grips, so that they had to grasp them by the edges and hold them.

The grandmother, the old Tamus, wept and said, 'Nut vulau will come with his servants and attack us!' Nut sie replied, 'Let them come, we will acquit ourselves well.' Then the old woman made a spell from lime, which she smeared on the warriors. Nut sie spoke to his servants, 'We will remain in our two houses and await the enemy; nobody will go outside. When the enemy arrives and I go outside, you will all follow me but we will stay close together, nobody will go off to the flanks.'

When the enemy arrived and drew nearer, Nut sie stepped out of the house and danced in front of the entrance swinging his shield. When Nut vulau saw his brother's shield he was astonished at its beauty and said angrily to his servants, 'You don't understand anything; look at my brother's shield, how beautiful it is.' Meanwhile the servants of Nut sie all came out into the open, threw lime at the enemy and the battle began. As a result of the advice given, it ended with the total defeat of the attackers; all were killed, only Nut vulau survived. The victors looked at the shields of the slain and laughed; but Nut sie called to Nut vulau, 'Go and get new warriors, we will do the same to them as we did to these.'

Nut vulau then assembled new warriors and attacked his brother again, but it turned out the same as the first attack, his people were killed and he alone survived.

Early next morning, at the cry of the *kau*, Nut sie got up and climbed a *vanga* tree. Calling in all directions he summoned the land and then went to inspect it. On returning home he said to his grandmother and his servants, 'We will leave here and go to a new homeland.' They made ready for the journey, took taro, bananas and other fruit, tied up their pigs and laid everything beneath the *vanga* tree. The following morning they set out, and soon came to a beautiful land where they settled.

Later, Nut sie cherished the hope of getting married, and he decided to carry off one of his brother's wives. For this purpose he built a great bird, *ngaininglaut*, out of wood; it was hollow inside. When the bird was ready he slipped inside and flew away. The bird's wingbeat was like the rushing of the wind and trees were uprooted. He climbed high in the air and from above he saw his brother's gardens. Then he flew back home, went to his grandmother and said, 'I looked down on my brother's gardens, and I shall fly there to fetch one of his wives for myself.' The grandmother gave good advice, saying, 'Be careful! Do not fly close to the ground, and do not alight on low trees lest your brother kill you.' Nut sie got into his bird and flew away.

Nut vulau was working with his servants when the bird came flying along. There was a roaring and blustering like a heavy gale and the banana plants were torn out of the ground and trees crashed down, so that the servants threw themselves on the ground in terror. Nut vulau, however, recognised his brother, and said, 'I know you! I saw you in a dream! You have come to steal my wife.' Nut sie flew to the wife, took her by the hand and flew away with her. She was very frightened but he calmed her and took her to his grandmother. At first the grandmother was not pleased, but she settled down over time. The woman bore Nut sie many children, and the tribe soon grew very large.

The grandmother, Tamus, created the sea and covered it with a stone to keep it hidden. Her two grandchildren soon noticed that their food tasted better because she had cooked it with salt water. One day they spied on the old lady as she went to the sea to moisten their food with sea water. When she had done this, to her horror she spotted her grandchildren and shouted to them, 'Now the sea will destroy us all!' Then the sea flowed out in all directions, forming islands and bays and straits, and so it stayed to this day.

The following story about obtaining salt, half fable, half true, probably belongs here.

On the shore one of the Tumuip tribe had a house, which was split in two by a dividing wall. Only boys and youths could enter the front part of the hut; not married people. Only the owner of the house could enter the rear part of the house. Here a large fire burned under a framework on which lay a big piece of tree bark. The women drew sea water from the ocean and poured it into bamboo tubes placed at the hut entrance. The owner of the house poured the sea water onto the bark above the fire; meanwhile he chewed ginger and spat this onto it. The fire was maintained until the tree bark was crusted with salt. Then the people came to buy the salt, *ralminmin*. Salt is regarded as a great delicacy; it is also given to the pigs because it makes them big and fat. However, people avoid touching the *ralminmin* with their fingers, because they believe that skin diseases can develop from it.

In a certain place lived two *mokpelpel*, Kanmameing and his wife Lelmul, who ate everybody. The surviving inhabitants therefore decided to move away, and got into their boats to seek a new home. At this place there was a woman called Tamus, who was in an advanced stage of pregnancy, and the voyagers did not want to take her with them. But she was resolutely determined to go, and clung to a boat with her hands at the departure. They pushed her back and yelled, 'The time of your confinement is near and you would only be a burden to us on the journey.' Tamus went sadly back to the shore and built a dwelling out of *kejang* (a tall type of grass). Here she gave birth to a son, and when he had grown somewhat she left him in the house while she worked nearby. However, she told him never to talk or laugh lest Kanmameing and Lelmul hear him and come to eat him up.

One day as she went to work, she gave her son a *púpál* (a species of *Dracaena*) for him to play with in her absence. The boy looked at it and said to himself, 'What shall I make out of this plant, a brother or a cousin? I know, I shall make a cousin!' During these words he had held the plant behind him, and he suddenly felt as if somebody had scratched his hands. He looked round in amazement and saw a handsome boy standing behind him. At first the latter was shy and said nothing, but soon a casual conversation was in full swing. The mother heard it and, believing that her son was talking loudly to himself, she called to him, 'Be quiet, or the two *mokpelpel* will come and devour us.' The boy named his cousin Pupal, because he had been created from a *púpál*; however, he did not share the event with his mother immediately, and decided to keep Pupal hidden from her for a while. He therefore went to her and said, 'Mother, I want to erect a dividing wall in our hut, and then you can live in one part while I stay in the other.' The mother agreed with this, and the boy divided the hut with a wall. Then Tamus' son went to his mother again and said, 'Mother I am hungry; bring me sugar cane and bananas!' The mother brought them. Now, when the two boys were sucking out the sugar cane, the mother heard all the noisy eating and called, 'My son, is anybody with you? I can hear a lot of noisy eating.' – 'I am alone, mother, and I alone am eating so noisily,' answered her son. Then, when the pair drank water, the mother heard a lot of swallowing. However, in answer to her questioning, the boy protested once more that he was completely alone.

This went on for a while, and the mother had no idea of the presence of Pupal. At the son's request, Tamus allowed him to lay out his own garden, and then both boys were able to work together and talk to their hearts' content, joking and laughing without the mother hearing them. One day when the mother unexpectedly brought the son his food, she saw to her great astonishment the strange, handsome boy and, full of amazement, she said, 'Who is this, and where does he come from?' The son replied, 'Mother, do you remember the *púpál* that you gave me as a toy one day? This handsome boy came out of it!' Now the mother knew the secret and from then on all the onerous barriers in their relationships could be brought down. However, she was concerned that the two *mokpelpel* could easily discover them, and warned the two boys, 'Children, do not talk so loudly, otherwise the *mokpelpel* will find us and devour us.' But the children answered, 'Oh, we are not frightened! Let them come, we will destroy them.' Tamus was astonished at this self-confidence in the two boys, and worried about it a lot when she was alone.

But the pair were very serious about killing Kanmameing and Lelmul. However, they kept their plans secret at the start, but made all the necessary preparations.

First they build a dwelling, *a rik*, for Tamus, and a men's house, *a ngaulu*, for their own use. Then they made shields and spears, and practised throwing the spears. Their initial shields, however, were made from soft wood, and so they made fine new shields from the wood of the *guip* tree, and hung them up in the house. Next, they felled *msa* trees, and used the trunks to erect a barricade in front of the entrance to the compound. At this point they invoked very hot weather, so that the bark of the *basika* tree became very hard; they next invoked heavy rain so that the bark of the *msa* tree became very slippery. The mother, who did not know what all this was for, looked on in amazement, and finally asked what they actually intended to do. 'We want to kill the two *mokpelpel*!' answered Pupal. Tamus warned, 'Children, do not annoy those two.' But Pupal continued, 'Just let them come, we will be ready for them.'

When all their preparations were complete, the two boys climbed into a swing that they had made in a tree on a slope not far from their compound. They swung here and called with loud voices, 'Oh Kanmameing and Lelmul! Oh where are you hiding? Come and eat us!' But in her hut Tamus shook with fear. Lelmul, who was outside while her husband was in the house sharpening his teeth, was first to hear the youths shouting. She went to her husband and said, 'Can't you hear? We are being called. Who can it be? Haven't we eaten all the people around here?' Kanmameing then took both his fangs, put them in his mouth, and set off in the direction from which the call came. Lelmul followed him. With his two fangs, he cut down the bushes on both sides, and made a wide path.

Meanwhile Pupal said to his companion, 'Stay in the swing and call again!' Meanwhile he climbed down, took several lances and lay in ambush. When the giants were close he called, 'Come down quickly! They are here. You take the woman, I will attack the man.' When the *mokpelpel* came, and tried to climb the barricade, they slid down and fell on the ground; a big piece of wood fell down on Kanmameing. Pupal then stepped forward, and Kanmameing sprang up and tried to catch him with his fangs to devour him. Pupal was agile, however, and slipped between the giant's legs. Meanwhile Tamus's son had thrown his lance at Lelmul and pierced her right through. While she was still struggling on the ground he wanted to finish her off, but Pupal called to him, 'Leave her and come and help me!' He hurried up quickly, and they both threw their well-aimed spears at Kanmameing, but only after he had been pierced many times did he fall to the ground. The two lying on the ground, were killed stone dead with much derision and many insults. Then Tamus was summoned, and the youths said, 'Look, they are both dead.' With great jubilation, a huge fire was made, and the dismembered corpses of the *mokpelpel* were burnt.

They cut off Lelmul's breasts, laid them in a coconut shell which they floated in the sea, saying, 'Go to the people who went away from here, and when they ask, "Have the *mokpelpel* slain Tamus, and are these her breasts?" continue floating on the water. But if they ask, "Did Tamus give birth to a son, and did he kill the *mokpelpel*, and are these the breasts of Lelmul?" sink immediately.'

The coconut shell floated away and came to the people who had left. They looked at the shell with the breasts and asked, 'Has Tamus been killed by the *mokpelpel* and are these her breasts?' The coconut shell made a sign of denial and remained afloat on the water. Then the people asked, 'Did Tamus give birth to a son who killed the *mokpelpel*, and has he sent us the breasts of Lelmul?' Immediately the shell sank, and the people then cried joyfully, 'Now the two giants are dead! Let us go back to our old home!' They immediately prepared for the voyage and set off in their canoes. When they reached their homeland, the two boys did not want to let them land. They threw stones at them and Tamus's son called out, 'You did not want to take my mother with you when her baby was due; when you fled from here you pushed her back. Now *we* do not accept *you*; go back where you came from.' However, the people would not be intimidated, but landed and again lived happily in their homeland.

Two brothers lived together in a village. The younger was very clever, and could turn himself into a cockatoo by using a magic spell that he knew; the elder, on the other hand, was a braggart, did not understand sorcery, and knew no spells. Not far from this village, an old married *mokpelpel* couple had settled. Their hut stood beneath a coconut palm, and their property consisted of a large pig. One day Blakas (as he was called, because of his skill,) turned himself into a cockatoo, and in his favourite form cried, 'kah, kah, kah', and flew into the coconut palm beneath which stood the *mokpelpel*'s hut. He bit off a nut and let it fall onto the hut; it fell through the roof into the hut. The elderly woman said to her husband, who could not see well because of his age, 'A cockatoo is perched in the coconut palm; go outside and chase him away.' The old man went outside, struck the trunk of the palm, clapped his hands, then came back inside, saying, 'He has flown away.' Then the cockatoo again bit off a nut, and it fell through the roof and into the hut. The elderly woman became angry, and again sent her husband out to chase away the cockatoo. The old man did exactly the same as before, then came back inside and said, 'He has definitely gone away this time!'

But it did not last long, and again a coconut flew into the hut. The old woman sprang up enraged, scolded her husband and yelled, 'You old fool, you can't see anything any more; the cockatoo is indeed still there.' With these words she rushed outside, but was very surprised when she looked up and spotted a man at the top of the palm tree, for Blakas had quickly assumed his human form. Amazed, the elderly woman called out, 'That is no cockatoo; it is a man!' and turning to her husband she ordered him, 'Climb up and bring him down so that we can eat him.' The old man then climbed up, but when he had reached Blakas and was in the process of grabbing him, the latter stepped on his head and knocked him down, calling to the woman, 'There is one that you can eat.' In her anger the woman immediately seized hold of the one that had fallen and devoured him, without first checking who it was. Then Blakas called to her, 'You have eaten your own husband.' Then he changed into a cockatoo again, cried, 'kah, kah, kah,' and flew away back to his garden, taking a number of coconuts with him. In the garden he assumed human form, scraped the coconuts into taro leaves and took them home. When he got there he began to eat, and his brother asked him what he had there. He gave some to his brother, who ate it with great pleasure, and asked where it came from. Blakas then told of his adventure and added, 'Had it been you, they would have devoured you!' The brother answered, 'Who would be afraid of your *mokpelpel*?' – 'Good,' said the other, 'Go and try it.' – 'I will go first thing in the morning,' replied the elder brother.

The following morning he set out along the path to the *mokpelpel*'s hut, crept to the coconut palm and climbed up it without being noticed. His brother, Blakas, who loved him very much and knew well that great danger threatened him, went meanwhile into the forest, and with his magic drum called the dogs, wild pigs, wallabies, biting ants and other animals together, and led them all in the direction of the *mokpelpel*'s hut where he hid with them. Meanwhile, the one up the tree had plucked off a coconut and thrown it down. The *mokpelpel* looked up, spotted him and called out, 'Are you still there? I thought that you had gone. Just you wait, I will get you down and eat you.' She thought that it was the same visitor as the previous day. The one up the tree answered, full of confidence,

Plate 45 The *mabucha* dance of the Baining

'Climb up to me; I will knock you down.' The old one climbed up, grasped his foot and pulled him down; his struggles were of no use, he could not free himself. Once down on the ground, a life and death struggle began. The *mokpelpel* fastened her fangs into his body, and threatened to devour him. Blakas, who was watching the struggle, realised that his brother was on the point of being overcome, and he began to beat his drum. The *mokpelpel* started up, but already all the beasts who had been summoned had fallen upon her, and she had to get away as quickly as possible.

'You see,' said Blakas to his brother, who was shaking all over, 'if I had not come quickly, the *mokpelpel* would have eaten you.' – 'Oh,' said the latter, 'I would have finished her off. Didn't you see what she did, out of fear?' He meant, what he himself had done. But Blakas had seen everything, and did not believe a word. Then they tied the *mokpelpel*'s pig, took anything else of use from the hut and went home with their booty.

There was once a boy who suffered greatly; his name was Loel. His mother had died; he lived in the compound of his father, who had remarried. His father and stepmother were very miserly, and gave the poor boy nothing to eat; he had to look for his own food. Often when they were both eating, he would ask if they would give him something, but the request was always in vain. If he asked his father for something, he would refer him to his stepmother. If he asked her, she would refer him to his father, and so it went on every day, even though he begged and pleaded so pathetically.

One day Loel had set bird lime and caught several birds, which he prepared. When they were cooked, he began to eat them. Earlier, his parents had given the usual mealtime reply. As he was eating, they saw that it was something tasty and they went up to him. His father said, 'Son I have worried myself to death about feeding you; give me a piece of your birds.' Loel replied, 'Get something from your wife!' Then the stepmother came with the same request, but she was given the answer, 'Get something from your husband!'

Then the parents became very angry, and went out to summon evil spirits to eat their son. Meanwhile Loel sat on his bench, expecting no harm. A bug crawled up and bit him. He turned round angrily, to see what had bitten him. How surprised he was to see a bug, which began to speak, 'Why are you so angry, and why do you shower abuse on me? Listen to what I have to say to you. Your father and stepmother have gone to fetch evil spirits to eat you.' Then the bug crawled away. Loel, however, was not very frightened, because he could turn into a grasshopper (*loel* = grasshopper). He quickly did so, chewed a hole in a piece of wood, and crawled inside.

Soon he heard his parents coming with the evil spirits, and, when they could not find him, they called out, 'Loel, where are you?' – 'Here I am!' he called from his hiding place. They searched the entire house but found nothing; during the search they had thrown out the piece of wood in which Loel was hiding. Again and again they called out, 'Loel, where are you?' and again and again came the answer, 'Here I am!' In time this became so boring for the evil spirits that they ate the father and the evil stepmother.

The following story has a lot in common with a previous one that talks about the origin of fire. It goes as follows: Mugowan was paddling in a canoe on the Mewlu with several of his friends. On the way he skewered a fish with his fish spear, but the fish swam away with the spear and disappeared in the flood. Then Mugowan sprang out of the canoe and dived under the water to retrieve his spear. When he reached the bottom he suddenly found himself among many spirits who were sweeping the bottom, and, when they saw him, they rushed up to see the stranger whom nobody knew, and they asked one another, 'Who might this be?' Among them, Mugowan recognised his uncle, Koutol, who, when he spotted his nephew, recognised him; but they both kept quiet until Koutol finally said, 'Don't you know him? This is Mugowan.' The spirits asked him, 'Are you dead, then?' But Mugowan remained silent. Finally they said, 'You are a living person!' And Koutol added, 'Go! When you are dead you will live here among us.' Then the spirits guided him on the way back, and he climbed out. Meanwhile his friends had been looking for him. When they saw him climbing out they spoke joyfully to him, but he could not speak because he had been speaking with spirits. They laid him in the canoe, took him to the mouth of the river, chopped wood and made a big fire. They laid him beside it until he became warm. Then they said to one another, 'If we stay here the Saktai will attack us and kill Mugowan; let us go to the island where we are safer.' They did this, and when they arrived they prepared food, but Mugowan did not want to eat anything. The following morning they paddled back home in their canoe and called Mugowan's wives and children. They were inconsolable and spoke reproachfully, 'Why did you dive in after your spear!' Mugowan began to speak again and said, 'When we die, we go to the bottom of the Mewlu and live there. Whatever we say up above they can hear down below, while up above we can hear nothing of what they say down below. It is a splendid place, with many pigs, breadfruit, coconuts and betel nuts, bananas and all good things.'

From the Admiralty Islands we know, from the mouth of the native, Po Minis, a great number of stories which I will set down here.

The name, Tjaw'mu (not Tshebamu) is the designation for the high, universally visible mountain range occupying part of the main island north of the island of Ndruval. It is said of Tjaw'mu that, ages and ages ago, it was in the process of growing higher. Getting bigger and bigger, it would finally have grown into the sky, had a snake, which was lying on its crest not prevented it. The snake had noticed this secret growth and forbidden the mountain from doing it. Now that the mountain realised that his secret, which had remained undetected under cover of continuous night, was discovered, it suddenly became daylight and the mountain grew no further. Then the mountain spoke to the snake, 'I wanted to climb into the sky, but you forbade me. Your language will now become different, and mine will become different, and our descendants will all speak different languages.'

They tell the following story about Mount P'unda in the Usiai region, not far from Tjaw'mu mountain: In early times two giants, the sons of Nimeï and Niwong, the progenitors of the islanders, wanted this mountain to tower up to the sky. They dragged huge boulders up to the top, and piled them one on another. However, a snake lived in the caves and crevices on the mountain. It was unnoticed by the giants, but the snake had noticed their intention, and decided to foil them. It slithered out of its hiding place, and ordered one of the giants from henceforth to work for it, but it allowed the other one to haul stones as before. However, he was annoyed that his friend had been taken away, and the following night he loaded himself up with a mighty boulder and went away with it. By daybreak he had reached the Papitálai region and decided to erect the boulder as a boundary marker. With great force he threw the boulder on the ground and called out, 'Sea, divide the land! One part for those two (the snake and the other giant); one part for me!' Immediately the sea rushed in from north and south, meeting at the foot of the boulder, which can still be seen today, in the region of Papitálai, and is called Tjaretánkor (= land cut).

The giant who had remained with the snake was frightened, and said to it, 'Why have you banished my friend? You are a snake, not a man; you are not a companion of equal birth.' The snake felt put down by these words, and wanted to demonstrate its superiority to the giant. It said, 'Go, fetch your meal and cook it; I want to watch.' The giant went away, took his net and began to catch fish, which he took back to the snake. Then the snake said, 'Prepare your fish; I want to see how you start.' The giant took a fish, laid it in the sun to let it dry, and then ate it half-raw. The snake laughed at this and said, 'You are truly an evil spirit; you would even eat me.' The giant became angry and replied, 'My father is no evil spirit, I am a human child!' But the snake replied in a tone inspiring trust, 'Crawl into my stomach!' And it opened its mouth wide. The giant summoned up his courage and crawled inside.

He found firewood within, and pieces of wood for rubbing together. He saw taro, sugar cane and many good things, causing his heart to leap for joy. He dragged a little of everything into the daylight, rubbed the sticks to make fire, on which he roasted the taro, and sucked the juice of the sugar cane while he waited for the taro to cook. When the meal was ready, the giant and the snake tasted it, and the snake said, 'Whose meal is better, yours or mine?' And the giant had to admit that the snake's meal was better.

Since the snake guarded the compound exclusively, all the work fell on the man, who had soon had enough, and reviled the snake. When the snake heard this, it asked, 'Why are you insulting me? Had I not been here you would already have been dead. Through the good food that I have provided for you, you have grown strong. See, I will go away and you will remain on our land.' Then the snake wriggled down to the shore and swam through the sea to a distant land.

The last part of the previous tale describes the appearance of produce and fire, and how the latter is used. The land and its inhabitants originate from Nimeï (husband) and Niwong (wife). They both came originally in a canoe from far across the sea. According to another, less widespread, tale the islanders trace their form to two parrots, Asa and Alu. They sat side by side in a tree, and it irked them to be so alone. They decided to make a man, and Asa sewed a human figure together out of leaves. When it was completed, he let it fall onto the ground, and immediately the figure changed into a living man. Asa told him to go inland, build a house, and create a woman out of leaves, the same way that he had done the man. He would then have many children with her.

The great spirit above the clouds was originally completely alone. Then he noticed on earth forty men from Laues, who were scuffling together and hurling insults back and forth. He plaited a large disc from rattan with a rope attached, and lowered the disc to the ground. During the night he climbed down the rope, laid the sleeping men on the disc, and climbed back up. He used the rope to pull up the disc and the sleeping men. He laid them on their beds and hid the disc in the top of a tree. Then he closed up his house, and went into the forest to prepare sago for the men. When he had prepared a sufficient quantity, he hid it in the forest and went back home. When he got there, he spoke to the forty men but they were very frightened. He tried to calm them down, and then went back into the forest. Meanwhile the group became hungry and sent one of their number out to get food. When he reached the forest he saw the prepared sago hanging from the trees, and hurried back. However, he said to his companions, 'My brothers! This evil spirit is going to devour us; in the forest he is chopping up garnishes that he will eat as well as us.' They were very frightened and wailed in grief. Then a dog said to them, 'Why are you weeping?' They replied, 'We are frightened because your master is preparing side dishes in the forest and is going to eat us up.' Then the dog took pity on them and said, 'Look, there is the disc that you were pulled up in, and there is the door.' The men pulled the disc out of the top of the tree, lowered it on the rope and slid one behind the other down to earth. Thirty-nine escaped, only the fortieth remained behind and said, 'When you arrive, you must come to an agreement between our two groups, for we will certainly begin a fight among ourselves.'

When the spirit returned and found only one man, Po Tjutju, he asked, 'Where are our people?' Po Tjutju replied, 'They have gone into the forest.' However, the spirit realised what had happened, and said, 'Do not lie to me!' Then he grabbed a stick and began to thrash Po Tjutju, who was sitting on a drum. Po Tjutju sprang onto a bamboo bed but there too the blows rained on his back. He sprang onto the fireplace, vainly seeking refuge, and finally he made a leap through the open door, constantly pursued by the angry spirit who thrashed away at him without stopping. Then Po Tjutju made a leap into the air where the wind caught him and carried him gently to the ground like a leaf. When his friends saw him coming, they ran to meet him. He said, 'Brothers! The dog is kind, he has saved us. You had little to put up with, while I have endured a hard struggle. I sat on the drum and he beat me; the drum boomed. I leapt on to the bamboo bed and he beat me so that it rattled. He beat me at the fireplace, and it blazed; he beat me in the open doorway and shining light arose.'

The spirit was very angry, and plaited a new disc to let down to earth. Then the moon stood in front of the doorway and the shadow of the disc left an imprint on the moon's shining disc.

Another story about the origin of the spots on the moon runs as follows: Two women were busy laying out a garden plot. When night fell they rested from their work, and roasted taro tubers on the embers. When they wanted to scrape the tubers, they found that they had forgotten to bring the shell fragments that they used for the purpose. Right at this moment the moon rose; they grabbed it and used it to scrape their roasted taro. However, after the work was done the moon followed its usual path. The following evening the two women did exactly the same as the previous evening, but this time the moon played a mean trick on them, and the women were very angry. As it went away they called out, 'You are a miserable devil; your face is blackened. You have served as a shell scraper, the black from the charred taro is sticking to your face. You will never be able to wash away the stain of disgrace.' Since then the moon has borne the indelible black spots on his disc.

Once a boy fashioned a female figure out of sand on the beach. A spirit entered the sand figure and it stood up. Whenever the boy came to the beach it lay down, but when he went home it stood up. Finally the boy was enticed to have sexual relations with the figure, and the spirit twisted his neck until he died.

On the island of Patuam, one of the Horne Islands, the sand figure is visible to this day.

An evil spirit entered a banana. Po Ueïe ate the banana and the spirit killed him. His arms and legs were convulsively pulled together; his liver and intestines hung from his belly.

Two women, one of whom was pregnant, went to catch crabs. When the hunt was over, they returned home, and on the way the pregnant one gave birth. When the evil spirit heard the baby crying, he went to the women and said, 'Come with me to my cave.' When they reached it, the spirit killed a pig and roasted taro tubers. When these were ready he ate them all up, but threw the entrails and taro remains to the women. They felt that they had been scorned by their host and said, 'You are a scoundrel, to offer us such food.' To which he replied, 'I have already eaten pig and taro, it is your turn now!' and he ate them up.

Once a person took a pig's trotter, hid it in his carry basket and took it into the forest, where nobody lived and where there were no compounds. He threw the trotter on the ground and immediately a pig stood on the spot. He said to it, 'Multiply!' and immediately a second pig appeared. He continued the spell, and in the end he had a large number of pigs.

An evil spirit named Po Pékan lived in his compound called Káli. He had four eyes and ate all humans without exception. Two boys went along a winding path and got lost; finally they came to Po Pékan's compound and stood half-hidden in a corner. Po Pékan was busy building a canoe. Two of his eyes were directed towards his work; the other two roved unceasingly in all directions. He noticed the two boys, laughed with joy at seeing them, and called, 'Come out, do not be afraid. Sit down and be my guests.' He set food before them, then suddenly fell on them, pressed their eyes out, killing them, and then ate them. When it was over he beat the death drum and the neighbours said, 'The evil spirit of Káli has eaten a man again.'

An evil spirit from Péhëu lay hidden. Two men were returning at night from fishing. One lay down to sleep, the other carried the gear ashore and then wanted to relaunch the canoe. However, he pushed against one end in vain, for the evil spirit held fast to the other end. He renewed his effort fruitlessly, for the invisible evil spirit always foiled his attempts. The man flew into a great rage over this, seized an axe and destroyed the canoe. Then, when he wanted to go into his house the evil spirit attacked him. He cried loudly for help, but the spirit held his mouth closed and said, 'Eat my h…!' [Probably *hoden:* balls (Translator)]. The man answered, 'Who would want to eat your h…? Your h… are stale.' Then the spirit said again, 'Eat my h… as a man eats a fish,' but the man still refused. Then the spirit said, 'If you won't do as I tell you, I will eat you up. Come, follow me to my compound.' The spirit lay down to sleep and commanded, 'Look for lice!' When he had fallen fast asleep the man bound him fast to the bed frame by the strands of his hair, and escaped, climbing Mount Ndr'tjun and singing, 'The evil spirit from Péhëu wanted to eat a man. Where is the man that he wanted to eat? The spirit is bound fast by his hair!'

When the spirit awoke and tried to stand up, he had to drag his bed frame behind him, and since it was heavy he flew into a rage and cried, 'I am a fool, blinded by stupidity; why did I not eat the man straight away. Oh, his tongue, what a morsel, my mouth waters at the thought!' And, beside himself with rage, he crushed his h… and died.

An evil spirit from Ndritápat went to Loniu. Two women were night-fishing by torchlight and discovered the spirit in the form of a child, on the shore. Full of compassion, they took him to their huts, set food before him and killed a pig. They gave the entrails to the child and said, 'Take them to the sea, slit them open and wash them.' The child went off, assumed his real form on the beach, washed the entrails and ate them. Then he cut off a finger and returned to the huts in the child's form. When he got there he said, 'Mother, the fish stole the entrails from me and bit off one of my fingers.' The two women answered, 'Never mind, there is enough pork left for you.' They set it in front of him, and while they were watching he ate slowly, like a normal man, but when their eyes were elsewhere he greedily swallowed large chunks. When a piece of pork fell on the ground, they sent the child out to wash the sand off in the sea. When he had gone the women said, 'One of us should follow, to see what the child does.' One of the women did so, and when she reached the beach unnoticed, she saw from her hiding place that the child had turned into a horrible devil whose hair hung down in long strands. Terrified, she hurried back to her friend and called, 'Let's flee, otherwise the evil spirit will eat us up. We thought that he was human, and raised him, but he is an evil spirit.' They hurriedly ran away, and when the evil spirit returned, he looked around for them in vain. He grew very angry, slit his belly in rage, and died.

Ten fruit were in their husks, but when it grew dark they fell from their husks onto the ground, took on human form, bathed in the sea, sang and enjoyed themselves. A man came along, saw the swimming forms, whose bodies were as pale as albinos, and beckoned the young women. As they approached, they pleased him greatly, and he said to them that they should all be his wives and go back to his hut with him. Nine of the young women agreed, but the tenth refused, and when the man wanted to force her, she cried, 'I am the wife of no man; I am a fruit!' However, the man laughed and said, 'Oh, you are not telling the truth. Follow me!' But the young woman said, 'Look, I will climb up the tree!' and she did so. When she got up there, she slipped into her husk and turned back into a fruit.

Previously, the men of Háüm had breasts while the women had beards. One day they organised a race; the women came first, the men last. Then the spirit who ruled Háüm said, 'This is not right. From now on the men will have beards and the women breasts.' Had he not brought about this change, it is evident that up to the present day women would have given birth to children but the men would have raised them. However, everything turned out for the best.

An old woman was already very old and wrinkled. Once both of her sons went fishing, while she went to bathe. While bathing she stripped off her skin and appeared as a young, smooth-skinned woman. She went home in this form, and soon her sons returned. They were very astonished, and one said, 'Is this our mother?' However, the other said, 'Good, she will be your mother, and my wife.' Their mother overheard this and said, 'What did you say?' and they replied, 'Nothing! We said that you are our mother.' But she answered, 'Do not tell lies! One of you said that I was his mother, while the other said that I was his wife. Had it turned out the way I wanted, we would have grown up and become old and grey, then we would have stripped off our skins and become young men and women again. After your comment, we will grow old and grey, but then we will die.' She took her skin, put it on again, and became once more the wrinkled old woman. From then on humans have grown old and died. Had the two sons spoken otherwise, humans would have become rejuvenated and lived forever.

The spirit entered a large fish, which stirred up the sea so that a great flood poured over the island of Lóniu. All the Lóniu people drowned in the flood, as punishment for their illicit sexual activity.

In former times there was no fire on earth. A woman sent out the sea eagle and the starling, ordering them to bring fire down from heaven to the earth. They both flew into the sky and the sea eagle brought the fire down to earth. Halfway, however, he became tired and handed the fire over to the starling. The starling put it across the back of his neck, but the wind blew and fanned the fire so that the starling was scorched, and turned into a small black bird. The sea eagle, however, remained big. Had the fire not scorched the starling, then it would still be as large as the sea eagle today.

A man from Sauch (a place on the main island) went fishing. An evil spirit saw him and gave chase, to kill and eat him. However, the man fled into the bush. On his flight a tree opened in front of him and he slipped inside, upon which the tree closed round him. The pursuing spirit no longer saw the man and went away. When he had gone, the tree opened again and the man stepped out into the open. The tree said, 'Go to Sauch and catch two white pigs for me.' The man went away and caught one white pig and one black one, but striped the latter white with lime to deceive the tree. Then he brought the two pigs to the tree. However, on the way the lime coating had fallen off the black pig, and the tree realised that the man wanted to cheat him. He said, indignantly, 'You are ungrateful! I sheltered you from the evil spirit, but you sought to deceive me. From now on when an evil spirit chases you I will not open up to protect you, and you will die. Had you done as I asked, then every time you were attacked by an evil spirit while going fishing, I would have opened up and sheltered you, but now I will never again open to protect you.' And so the tree no longer offers protection to the man when he is pursued by an evil spirit.

A maiden named Nja Sa sat inside her house. Her parents had pierced her earlobes and had gone off into the garden. The evil spirit had seen them depart, slipped into the house and called out, 'Come, Nja Sa, I am your suitor.' Nja Sa peeped out through a hole and recognised him. She said, 'You are the evil spirit.' However, he kept up his assertion and called, 'Let down the ladder!' The maiden did not obey, and the spirit began to dig out the poles on which the house rested. Nja Sa screamed for help, and her parents rushed back to her cries. They saw the evil spirit, which had made himself as small as a child, and said, 'It is only a game.' However, Nja Sa told the truth. Her father grew very angry, grabbed a club and thrashed the evil spirit. However, the latter gave him a severe wound with one of his tusk-like teeth, so that the man had to cease the thrashing and the evil spirit was able to escape.

A woman cut off her finger while working, and caught the blood in a shell. Three days later the blood changed into two eggs, and a snake slithered from one and a bird from the other. The bird flew away and lay in wait for fish; the snake slithered into the forest and caught a possum. When the sun had gone down, they both came home; the bird brought fish to the woman, but the snake brought nothing. The bird said to the woman, 'Let us go away!' and he carried her up into a tall tree. He brought the hut up there as well. The snake searched for a long time in vain. He finally discovered their location and called out, 'Mother, brother, how can I get up to you?' The bird replied, 'Climb up!' The snake coiled upwards around the tree, but when it had climbed up the bird grabbed an axe and severed its head from the body, which fell down, but came to life again and resumed the ascent. However, up above, the bird raised the axe and cut up the snake into small pieces that fell down to the ground. Several became fish, others became snakes.

Hi Kalemuindr and Po Samitanpun paddled out to sea to catch turtles. The woman sat in the canoe while the man dived to the sea floor. He let himself down by a long rattan rope that he attached round his body, with the other end made fast to the canoe. While the man was below, the woman fell asleep, the rope broke and the canoe drifted out to sea. The chief Halives and his people noticed it. They paddled out to it, found the woman asleep and asked, 'Where have you come from?' She replied, 'I have come from the west. My husband and I went fishing for turtles, but while he was diving I fell asleep and the west wind has driven me to you.' Halives made her his wife and took her to Jap (Halives' homeland).

When Po Samitanpun surfaced, he did not find his canoe, and swam ashore. He carved a bird out of wood and sent it off with the words, 'Fly to Jap and search for your mother!' The bird flew to Jap but did not find its mother but numerous crabs instead. It ate some and grew strong. Then it flew back and reported, 'Father I did not find my mother.' The father said, 'Come closer to me,' and when the bird obeyed the father sniffed his breath and cried angrily, 'Yes, just as I thought, you have not found your mother; but you have eaten crabs.' When the bird heard this reproach, it flew away enraged. Po Samitanpun then carved a sea eagle and said to it, 'Fly away and find your mother! She is called Hi Kalemuindr, and when you see her, say to her that she should come to me.' The sea eagle flew away to Jap and perched on a tree there. It shook the tree so that the fruit fell to the ground, and when the women heard it they ran to gather the fruit. When they returned to the village, laden, Hi Kalemuindr asked if someone would give her some of the fruit; but the women refused, and said, 'Do you not have legs? Go yourself, and get fruit!' She went to the tree with some other women. The sea eagle heard her name and immediately flew down to the ground, caught Hi Kalemuindr by the leg and flew away with her. On the way the sea eagle dropped down so that the water wet the leg of the woman, who cried out, 'My son, my son, I am falling into the water!' The sea eagle replied, 'Do you trust the strength of my talons so little?' It rose higher, and took the woman to Po Samitanpun. However, instead of being grateful he showered the sea eagle with reproaches, and said that it wanted to harm the woman at sea. The sea eagle was enraged at this and flew away.

Had injustice not been done to the sea eagle, it would have continued to bring back those shipwrecked on distant islands. However, Po Samitanpun had done so great a wrong that shipwreck victims nevermore returned, but had to remain wherever they had gone ashore.

Long ago on the island of Lou (St George Island) there was a great flock of *tjauka* (*Philemon coquerelli*). One day while the Lou people were at work, a man attempted to rape a woman, but a *tjauka* who witnessed this deed called out loudly, 'A man of Lou is doing evil!' and when the man realised that he was found out, he stopped his action and went home angrily. To get his revenge he distributed betel nuts throughout Lou as payment for wiping out all the *tjauka*. The Lou people caught all the *tjauka* in nets, and only one succeeded in hiding. It then sucked up all the water on Lou in its beak and carried it to Lom'ndrol on the main island. Since then Lou has been arid, while Lom'ndrol has an abundant water supply. *Tjauka* are no longer found on Lou, but they are numerous among the Moánus.

A number of Pitilu people went to Mbutmanda to catch turtles. The Papitálai people attacked and killed them all, except Po Toui, who hid. The canoes were taken away by the victors. Po Toui then decided to swim home. However, the sea sapped his strength, and he was close to drowning. He called to the spirit of his brother, and a shark came and carried him on his back to Pitilu. His brother's spirit had entered the shark and hurried to the aid of Po Toui.
The Moánus believe that their spirit guardians occasionally enter sharks to come to the aid of those in trouble at sea. Likewise, the spirit can enter a sea eagle to give a prompt warning to a village threatened with danger. If a Moánus sees two sea eagles fighting or restlessly flying around, he does not continue his journey but goes back home.

Plate 46 The *gifu* mask of the Sulka tribe

X Languages

It was only in recent times that a little light was shed onto the involved linguistic relationships of the archipelago. The Wesleyan missionary Dr G. Brown was the first to study the language of the Duke of York Islands, and his *Dictionary and Grammar of the Duke of York Islands* (Sydney 1883) published in only a small number of autotyped copies, provided the first information on one of the languages of the archipelago. This was followed a number of years later by the far more detailed and more extensive work of the Wesleyan missionary R. Rickard, published as an autotype in 1889 under the title, *A Dictionary of the New Britain Dialect and English, and of English and New Britain, also a Grammar*. Both works showed the intimate connection of the two languages, and the Wesleyan mission soon found that in southern New Ireland the language was so closely related to both these languages, that the north-eastern Gazelle Peninsula language could be used without difficulty in their schools. Meanwhile the Catholic missionaries, whose settlements on the Gazelle Peninsula had spread extraordinarily rapidly over a large part of the Gazelle Peninsula since 1890, under the leadership of the extremely capable and hard-working Bishop L. Couppé, had also undertaken a study of languages, and in 1897 there appeared in volume 2 of the third annual edition of the *Zeitschrift für afrikanische und ozeanische Sprachen*, an extensive grammar of the language of the north-eastern Gazelle Peninsula by Father B. Bley, which he followed up in 1900 with a language dictionary, published in Münster by the mission press. I would also like to mention that in this work, for some unknown reason, the chapter on adverbs, that Father Bley had covered in detail, has been significantly curtailed. Both works complement and expand the earlier publication by missionary Rickard. Then, in 1903, the autotype publication of a grammar of the Baining language by Father M. Rascher appeared, in which is given a further valuable contribution to the study of the languages of the archipelago. An updated edition of this valuable work followed in 1904, in the *Mitteilungen des Seminars für Orientalische Sprachen zu Berlin*, annual volume VII, section I.

For the following information I am grateful to fathers B. Bley and M. Rascher who, in spite of the great workload resting on them, very kindly obliged me by preparing a short summary of their earlier investigations. From this a presentation of the languages of the Gazelle Peninsula is given in a rounded form, with the addition of studies on the related southern languages of the Sulka and the Nakanai, and the language of the Duke of York group in the north.

Although the darkness previously hanging over the interrelationship of the Bismarck Archipelago languages is, through these studies, beginning to lift, there is still infinitely more in this area to be investigated and defined, but the eager enthusiasm directed at this situation by the missions' guarantees that this area of research will not be neglected.

1. The Languages of the Coastal Dwellers of the Northern Gazelle Peninsula

An homogeneous language exists among the coastal natives along virtually the entire northern coast of the Gazelle Peninsula, from Cape Birara to Massawa, including the island of Massikonápuka. Although these coastal dwellers are undoubtedly of common origin, and, according to currently accepted opinion, have crossed from the southern end of New Ireland to the north coast of the Gazelle Peninsula as plundering tribes; pushing the original inhabitants – the Butam, Taulil and Baining – into the interior, or occupying the coastal strips that the latter had forsaken on account of volcanic eruptions, these coastal dwellers still feel little affinity towards one another. More often, hostilities have reigned between most districts and villages on the coast since time immemorial, and fear of being attacked and captured, or of being eaten, hinders any approach between them. This favours maintenance of purity and further development of the various dialects that were probably brought in with immigration from New Ireland,

and which all represent only different idioms of the language family held in common with the inhabitants of southern New Ireland. For these coastal dwellers, related by origin, traditions and customs, there is no common tribal name that we can assign to their language, in the way we speak of the Taulil language, or the Nakanai, Baining or Sulka languages, but they must be known simply as the languages of the coastal inhabitants of the northern Gazelle Peninsula.

According to a rough estimation by the former imperial magistrate, Dr Schnee, the total number of natives, heavily decimated by war and epidemics, who speak these languages today is only 20,000, or at most 30,000.

The greatest majority of these speak the melodious so-called Matupi or north coastal dialect, whose boundary actually begins about the middle of Blanche Bay near the villages of Dawaun and Kararoia, and extends along the coast to include Matupi Island, then stretches along the entire north coast from the village of Nonga to the middle of Weberhafen. From Weberhafen this dialect moves inland on the Gazelle Peninsula, extending over the entire area south of the Varzinberg, incorporating the districts of Napapar, Tombaul and Tamaneiriki.

On the coast of Blanche Bay, from Schulze Point to Kabakaul and inland as far as the Varzinberg, the so-called Blanche Bay dialect is spoken. This differs from the previous dialect both in the pure and harder consonants, *b*, *d*, *g*, compared with the gentler sounding *mb*, *nd*, and *ng*, of the former, and through several not-exactly beautiful-sounding variations in word form. Apart from the more uneven pronunciation, which sounds as though the people had blocked their noses while having their mouths half-open, a simple comparison of several words (Table 1) shows which part has the greater euphony.

We meet a further dialect in the villages at the foot of Mother and North Daughter; in Bai, Nodup, Korere and Tavui, towards Cape Stephens. This has the hard *b*, *d*, and *g* in common with the Blanche Bay dialect, but differs from it and the other dialects in many word forms, and sounds very broad, while adding an *i* to many word forms; for example, see Table 2.

This dialect prevails also on the north coast of the island of Uatom; moreover it is pronounced in almost a singing tone, and the hard terminal *p* changes mostly into a *v*. For example:

	north coast	northern Uatom
hedge	*a liplip*	*a livilivi*
yam	*a up*	*a uvu*
fire	*a iap*	*a iavi*

Finally, from the middle of Weberhafen in the districts of Ramandu, Massawa, and on the island of Massikonápuka, we have the so-called Baining shore dialect, or s–dialect. It has the latter name because, as well as having deviating word forms it differs from the other dialects particularly in the frequently occurring s-sound, again demonstrating a great affinity with the language of southern New Ireland.

A few examples:

	north coast	Baining coast
stone	*a vat*	*a vas*
earth	*a pia*	*a pissa*
knife	*a via*	*a vissa*
to sit	*kiki*	*kiskis*
to go out	*irop*	*siropo*
little	*ikilik*	*sikilik*
to deceive	*vaogo*	*vassere*

On the boundaries of both dialects, at Cape Livuan and on the island of Urar, both the north coastal and Baining shore dialects are spoken.

Seventeen letters suffice for writing the language: *a*, *b*, *d*, *e*, *g*, *i*, *k*, *l*, *m*, *n*, *o*, *p*, *q*, *r*, *t*, *u*, *v* (= *w*), to which the letter *s* must be added, because of the Baining dialect and essential foreign borrowings.

Table 1

	Blanche Bay dialect	north coast dialect
canoe	*a wagga*	*a oanga*
my child	*kaugu bul*	*kaningu mbul*
banana	*a wuddu*	*a wundu*
thing	*a maggit*	*a mangit*
to give	*tăbar*	*tambar*
women	*a wadān*	*a warenden*

Table 2

	north coast dialect	Nodup dialect
sea	*a ta*	*a tai*
path	*a ga*	*a gai*
no	*pata*	*patai*
where from?	*mamāve?*	*memēvei?*

The sounds *c, h, f, z, x* and *ch* are foreign to this language. The *s, c, z* and *tz* in foreign words and also *sch*, are, as in the Baining shore dialect, pronounced as *t* by the natives; thus 'Jesus', 'Moses', 'sacrament' become *Jetut, Motet*, and *takrament*. In the Baining shore dialect the *s-* sound is not pure, but is strongly mixed with the *h-* sound.

F and *pf* in foreign words become *p* in the mouth of the natives (for example, *Jotep* instead of Joseph); and *ch* becomes *k* (for example, Achab to *Akap*).

The sounds *b, d*, and *g* at Matupi and on the north coast are always *mb, nd*, and *ng*, and whereas *g* in the Blanche Bay dialect designates the pure hard *g*, it is only a more intensive *ng* in the north coast dialect – almost *nk*.

Among the vowels, *a* is by far the dominant one, and is almost as common as all the others put together. But although a certain monotony is created, the other vowels are fortunately distributed in such a way that the speech in general – assuming naturally that it is well pronounced – must be regarded as melodious, and one might with some justification be astonished that such a primitive people can possess such a fine language.

One becomes even more astonished in studying the grammar, both by its richness in form and by the clever manner in which missing forms are circumvented or substituted.

This language shares with all the Melanesian languages the article *a* for all genders, for the definite article 'the' and also the indefinite 'a' (while *ta* indicates 'any'). Also, the personal article *to* in front of men's names and *ia* in front of women's names, is a common occurrence in the Melanesian languages, in similar form.

A surprise is the triple genitive form of the substantive, formed by the particles *kai, na*, and *i*; the first expressing actual ownership, the second determination or subject, the third belonging to the whole or family property.

Examples:
a pal kai ra tutane, the man's house;
a pal na tutan, the men's house;
a pal na kāpa, the tin house;
tama i ra tutan, the man's father.

The dative is formed by the prepositions, *ta, in, an*; and the accusative, apart from the mostly euphonically essential form of the article, *ra*, is the same as the nominative.

The triple form of multiples: dual, triple and plural, provides no difficulty in the substantive, because they are formed simply by prefixing the numerals two and three and the plural particles *a lavur* and *a umana* (the former being the absolute plural: all of their kind; the latter the relative plural: representing several in speech).

The situation is more difficult with the pronoun, in which the inclusive and exclusive form must be differentiated in the dual, triple and plural, depending on whether the people spoken to are incorporated or not. An outline might illustrate this more easily.

Singular	Dual
I. *iau*, I	I. (inclus.) *dor*, we two (you and I)
	(exclus.) *amir*, we two (another and I)
II. *u*, you	II. *amur*, you two
III. *i*, he, she, it	III. *amutal*, the two
Triple	Plural
I. (inclus.) *datal*, we three (you two and I)	I. (inclus.) *dat*, we all (you and we)
(exclus.) *amital*, we three (two others and I)	(exclus.) *avet*, we without you
II. *amutal*, you three	II. *avat*, you all
III. *dital*, the three	III. *diat*, they all

We have an abundance of forms here, far exceeding that of European languages, but also establishing a brevity and precision of expression that is scarcely possible in another language. Equally numerous are the forms of the reflexive pronoun:

iau mule, I myself,

dor mule, we two ourselves,

datal mule, we three ourselves, and so on, and of the possessive pronoun. In the latter, in all numbers and persons, besides the objective and substantive forms, a special form for determination or personal use is differentiated from possession. Here too we provide a plan, for the sake of clarity and brevity:

Singular
Possession	Determination
I. *kaniqu*, mine	I. *aqu*, for me
II. *kou* (*koum*), yours	II. *amu*, for you
III. *kana* (*kaina*), his	III. *ana*, for him

Dual
I. { *kador* / *komamir*	I. { *Ador* / *amamir*
II. *komamur*	II. *Amamur*
III. *kadir*	III. *adir*

Triple
I. { *kadatal* / *komamital*	I. { *Adatal* / *amamital*
II. *komamutal*	II. *amamutal*
III. *kadital*	III. *adital*

Plural
Possession	Determination
I. { *kada* (*kadat*) / *komave* (*komavet*)	I. { *ada* (*adat*) / *amave* (*amavet*)
II. *komava* (*komavat*)	II. *amava* (*amavat*)
III. *kadia* (*kadiat*)	III. *adia* (*adiat*)

The forms in brackets are the variations of the substantive form from the adjectival; where no special form is given, both are the same. For illustration of possession-indicating and determination-indicating pronouns, several illustrations follow:

They say: *kaiqu pal*, my house, but *aqu nian*, the food meant for me; *komave boroi*, our pig (possession), but *amave boroi*, pork meant for us; *kou paip*, your pipe (possession), but *amu tapeka*, tobacco for you, destined for your use; *kana rumu*, his spear (possession), but *ana rumu*, spear destined for him, by which he might be killed; *kana market*, his weapon, but *ana bol*, the bullet meant for him.

It is interesting, and in accordance with most Melanesian and several Micronesian (Gilbert Island) and Papuan languages, that in designations of relationship, body parts and several prepositions, the possessive pronoun is added as a suffix. For example:

tamaqu, my father	*tama i dor*, our two fathers
tamam, your father	*tamamamir*, etc.
tamana, his father	*amamamur*
naqu, my mother	*naqu i dor*
nam, your mother	*nam a mamir*
nana, his mother, etc.	*nan a mamur*
turaqu, my brother	*a limaqu*, my hand
turam, your brother	*a limam*, your hand
turana, his brother, etc.	*a limana*, his hand, etc.
piraqu, near me	*taqu*, in me
piram, near you	*tam*, in you
pirana, near him, etc.	*tana*, in him, etc.

The relative pronoun is replaced sometimes by the personal pronoun, sometimes by the indicating *nam* or *ni*, sometimes by the particle *ba*.

The indefinite pronouns *di* and *da* for 'one' are probably abbreviations of the personal *diat*, 'she' and *dat*, 'we', while the indefinite 'it' is reproduced by the personal pronoun third person singular *i*; for example, *i bata*, 'it is raining'.

The adjective can stand either before or after the substantive, and in the former case is connected to it by *na*, and in the latter by *a*, and takes the substantive form.

Examples:

a gala na pal	a big house
a pal a gala	a big house
a bo na tutan	the good man
a tutan a boina	the good man
a lalovi na davai	a tall tree
a davai a lalovina	a tall tree

An actual gradation of the adjective does not occur, but there is a substitution for it, sometimes by juxtaposition, such as: *qo i boina, nam i kaina*, 'this is good, that is bad' (that is, this is better than that); or in the form: *i boina ta dir*, 'he is the good one of the two' (that is, the better); or: *i gala taun diat par*, 'he is big above them all' (that is, the biggest), or in similar circumlocutions.

Numerals, as almost throughout the South Seas, are based on the five or ten system. 'Five', *a ilima*, comes from *lima*, the hand. From 5 onwards the basic numerals are repeated with the prefix *lap* or *lav*, and from 10 on they are put together:

1	*tikai*	6	*a laptikai*
2	*a urua* (or *evut*)	7	*a lavurua*
3	*a utul*	8	*a lavutul*
4	*a ivat*	9	*a lavuvat*
5	*a ilima*	10	*a vinun* (or *arip*)
11	*a vinun ma tikai*	40	*a ivat na vinvinun*
12	*a vinun ma evut*	50	*a ilima na vinvinun* etc.
13	*a vinun ma utul*		
14	*a vinun ma ivat* etc.	100	*a mar*
		200	*a ura mar*
		300	*a utul a mar*
20	*a ura vinun*	400	*a ivat na marmar*
21	*a ura vinun ma tikai*	1000	*a mar na limana*, i.e. a hundred times the hands, or *a vinun na marmar*, i.e. ten times a hundred
22	*a ura vinun ma urua* etc.		
30	*u utul a vinun*		

2000, *a tutan ot*; that is, a whole man, or so many times 100 as there are fingers and toes on an intact man (assuming that the latter still has all his limbs, which is quite often not the case).

The scheme shows how impractically long these numbers are (for example, 948 = *a lavuvat na marmar ma ra ivat na vinvinun ma ra lavutul*), and how little they are suited to rapid usage in trade and commerce. In actual fact, the natives need few dealings with numbers in their life. Where they have not been educated in schools and taught to count, they have so little numerical skill that in counting up to 5 or 10 they have to use the fingers of one or both hands to help them to form and retain a number picture. The larger numbers: tens, hundreds and thousands, are used only when counting strings of shell money, which occasionally run into the hundreds and thousands. This is carried out extraordinarily slowly and carefully, with fingers and toes used as aids.

Wherever in life more rapid counting is required, unique counting methods are available. For eggs, a brood of young birds, pigs or dogs, the native uses *a keva* instead of *ivat* for 4, *a ura keva* for 8, and *a utul a keva* for 12; similarly for 5, *a vinar* instead of *ilima*, for 10 *a ura vinar*, for 15 *a utul a vinar*, for 20 *a ivat na vinavinar*, and so on.

For fruits that are bound into bundles, he calls a bundle of 4 *a varivi*, 8 *a ura varivi*, and so on; a bundle of 6 *a kurene*; 12 *aura kurene*, or *a naquvan*, a dozen; 120 *a pakaruot*.

He counts smaller shell money after *nireit* – that is, every six shells; he names larger ones after that part of the body up to which they reach.

Every eight slender strips of bamboo used for making fish baskets are called *a kilak*, and accordingly sixteen are *a ura kilak*, twenty-four *a utul a kilak*, and so on.

By doubling the cardinal numbers, the distributive numbers are obtained, such as *tikatikai*, each one; *a evaevut*, every two; *a ututul*, every three; *a ivaivat*, every four; *a ililima*, every five; *a laplaptikai*, every six, and so on.

By placing the causative particle *va* in front of the cardinal numbers, the ordinal numbers are formed; for example, *a vaevut*, the second – that is, 'that which makes it become two'; *a vautul*, 'that which makes it become three' – that is, the third; *a vaivat*, *a vailima*, and so on.

The substitution of numeric adverbs is characteristic. Since there are actually almost no real numeric adverbs, so-called numerating adverbs are formed by prefixing the causative *va*, in the sense of, 'to do something once', 'to do it twice', and so on; for example, *i vautul me* means 'he has tripled it' – that is, he has done it three times. *I vailima me*, 'he has quintupled it', and so on.

The natives lack all understanding of precise fractions and thus lack precise names.

With verbs, as well as the transitive and intransitive there is often a third form as well, in which the object, when it is a third person singular personal pronoun, is already included, and thus does not need to be specifically expressed. For example, *oro* (intransitive) to call, *ora* to call him or it; *virit* to fish, *virite* to fish for him or it; *qire* to see, *qure* to see him or it.

Another feature of the verbs that is a characteristic of most South Sea languages consists of doubling them. They are either partially or completely doubled, be it to indicate the intensity of treatment or of frequent occurrence, or to make transitive intransitive.

Time and mode of the verb are not expressed by verb alteration but by particles, and often do not coincide with those of European languages, as the following scheme shows.

I. Present

Singular	Dual
iau vana, I am going	*dor (amir) vana*
u vana, you are going	*amur vana*
i vana, he is going	*dir vana*

Triple	Plural
datal (amital) vana	*da (ave) vana*
amutal vana	*ava vana*
ditaI vana	*dia vana*

II. Completed Present
iau ter vana, I have (already) gone
dor ter vana,
ditaI ter vana, etc.

III. Just begun Past
iau bur vana, I have just left
dor bur vana, etc.

IV. Narrative Past
iau qa vana, I went
dor qa vana, etc.

V. Pluperfect
iau qa ter vana, I had gone, have already been gone a long time
dor qa ter vana, etc.

VI. Future

Singular	Dual
ina vana, I shall go	*dor (amir) a vana*
una vana, you will go	*amur a vana*
na vana, he will go	*dir a vana*

Triple	Plural
datal (amital) a vana	*dat (avet) a vana*
amutal a vana	*avat a vana*
ditaI a vana	*diat a vana*

VII. Future Anterior
ina qa vana, I shall have gone, or will certainly go
dor a qa vana, etc.

VIII. Future Presumptive
na ter vana, he will probably have gone
dir a ter vana, etc.

Through the particle *vala*, a so-called habitual form is obtained. For example:

iau vala vana, I often go, have the habit of going
iau ter vala vana, I have often gone, etc.

In a similar way, through *tiga* a daily form is obtained: *iau tiga na vartovo* = I come every day for lessons.

In all its forms the imperative coincides with the future: *una vana*! go! *avat a vana*! go (plural)!, and so on.

Unfortunately, a real conditional is lacking, as well as the entire passive voice. In the former, one is aided by the particle *ba* in front of the indicative form, and in the latter by circumlocution with the active; for example, instead of 'I am hit', one says, *dia kita iau*, they hit me or, *i kita iau*, he hits me, or similar.

The above scheme has already shown how the conjugation particles form complete replacements for our auxiliary verbs, 'to be', 'to have', 'to become', 'may', and so on, in so far as these serve for the construction of time and manner. For 'to be', when it designates the relation of the predicate to the subject, a corresponding personal pronoun serves each time. For example:

a bul i gala, the boy, he big;
a ura bul dir gala, the two boys, the two big;
a utul a bul ditaI gala, the three boys, the three big;
a umana bul dia gala, the boys, all big.

In spite of the apparent lack, in reality this language deviates so little that it almost never lacks a substitute form.

Still with the verb, besides the causative prefix *va* mentioned above, which signifies 'to allow' or 'to make' what the action of the verb does, we want to mention the prefix *var* in the formation of the reciprocal, occurring in similar form in a whole series of Melanesian, Polynesian and Papuan languages. Examples:

tur, to stand; *vatur* to permit, or to cause to stand;

gala, to be big; *vagala*, to enlarge;

ubu, to strike; *varubu*, to strike one another, to fight;

vul, to insult; *varvul*, to insult one another.

Of the remaining word forms, adverbs of place deserve special mention, as much for their individuality as on account of their frequent use. In them, rest and motion must be precisely differentiated, as well as direction to the speaker, whether on the shore or forest edge (or conversely on the open sea), whether straight over the person addressed, whether over yonder, up above or down below is intended. Thus:

uro, outwards	*ura*, downwards
aro, yonder	*ara*, under
maro, from outwards	*mara*, from below
urie, to the edge of the forest	*urike*, towards the shore
arie, on the edge of the forest	*arike*, on the shoreline
marie, from the edge of the forest	*marike*, from the shore
urama, upwards	*ubara*, downwards to you
arama, up above	*abara*, down below near you
marama, from above	*mabara*, from below near you

The adverbs of place often replace prepositions, such as:

arama ra balanabakut, in the sky;

ara ra pia, on the earth;

aria ra pui, in the forest;

uria ra pui, to the forest.

They are usually also used where the indication of place has been done using a substantive with a preposition or in some other way. For example, *arama raul a davai*, 'on the tree'; *abara piram*, 'near you'.

As far as the real prepositions are concerned, their small numbers can be explained as due both to their replacement by adverbs, and the significance and manner of construction of many verbs that require no preposition. Thus, here too, the lack is only ostensible.

In the numerous interjections for the expression of astonishment and wonder, like *aipua! ua! gaki!*; of pain, like *vele!*; of compassion, like *rabiavui!*; of joy over the new moon or the presence of a lot of fish in the basket, like *kuo! kuo! kuo!* and other sentiments, this language can indeed measure up against others.

On the other hand, it is very modest in sentence construction. In simple sentences, the sentence parts can indeed be partially inverted and placed at the head for emphasis, but for longer sentence structures, or for coordinating or subordinating composition of sentences, both precise particles and the actual conditional form of the verb are missing.

If we compare the vocabulary of this language with that of European languages we must be amazed on the one hand by its great wealth and on the other hand by its great poverty. This language is uncommonly rich in names and designations for objects and processes, and in technical expressions from the daily life of the natives. Every plant, every forest tree, each one of over a hundred varieties of banana, each one of the numerous species of taro and creeper, every bird, every type of fish, every minute part of their huts, their canoes, their fishing baskets, has a special name. Every technique in house construction, fishing, and so on, has a short, precise technical expression that, because of its absence in our languages, we can reproduce only by a circumlocution of varying length. Often words coincide in a certain sense with European ones, but the slightest nuance, another situation, another object, requires yet another totally different verb.

On the other hand, the dearth of expressions from the area of the abstract, of spiritual life, morals, and above all from everything that passes beyond the horizon of notions in the natives' daily lives, is very great. Above all, many general concepts, such as 'plants', 'animal', 'human', 'person', are missing. Others indeed exist, but do not correspond generally with ours, as, for example, bird, *a beo*, which also encompasses everything that flies, like beetles and butterflies. Mental powers and activities like comprehension, thought, volition, belief, are idiomatically never expressed in the abstract by the substantive, but always concretely by verbs: *matoto*, to understand; *nuk-vake*, to remember; *meige*, to desire; *nurnur*, to believe. However, in this area the language is still capable of modification, and permits – for example, by doubling the verbs – many new word constructions for abstract concepts. However, it will be necessary for the young people to become accustomed to the use of the abstract. The same applies to the area of morality.

It is obvious that the natives can have no expression for totally unknown or only unclearly felt ideas, such as gratitude, chastity, humility, modesty, and so on, but, here too, many a new word can be formed grammatically correctly, corresponding to

Plate 47 Dance at a circumcision ceremony. South coast of New Britain

the meaning of the word in European languages, while transposing it from the concrete into the figurative sense. But where this is not possible, one ought not to shy away from enriching and complementing such a beautiful language by introducing the simplest possible foreign words. One would fervently hope that in our German colonies German words would be introduced for missing words, rather than English, which has unfortunately occurred too often up till now.

For comparison with other South Sea languages, a list of a few common words follow, and as an example of speech, a translation of the Lord's Prayer.

a tutan, the man
a vavin, the woman
tamana, his father
moki! (address) my father!
nana, his mother
gaki! (address) my mother!
a limana, his hand
a matana, his eye
a taligana, his ear
a ta, the sea
a tava, the water
a oaga, the canoe
a en, the fish
a vat, the stone
a davai, the wood, the tree
a tabaran, the soul of the dead
a balanabakut, the belly, the firmament, the heavens
boina, good
kaina, bad
mat, dead
ogor, strong
laun, to live
tur, to stand
ki, to sit
a mal, the clothing
a luluai, the headman
a pal, the house
a vudu, the banana
a lama, coconut tree and coconut
a kian, the egg
a vuaina, his fruit
a pap, the dog
a boroi, the pig
vua, to lie
vana, to go
kakaile, to sing
malagene, to dance
pil, to leap
ean, to eat
kita, to strike
kul, to buy
log, to steal
qori, today
nabug, yesterday
karaqam (*ieri*), tomorrow
narie, the day before yesterday
oarie, the day after tomorrow
dari, so
a kapiaka, the breadfruit tree

The Lord's Prayer

Tamamavet nam u ki arama ra balanabakut. Boina da ru ra iagim. Boina na vut kou varkurai. Boina di torom tam ara ra pia, veder di torom tam arama ra balanabakut.

Qori una tabari avet ma ra amave nian na bugbug par. Una nukue komave magamagana kaina ta nidiat, dia ter vakaine avet. Qaliak u beni avet ta ra varlam. Ma una valauni avet ka ra kaina. Amen.

2. The Duke of York Language

Lying between New Britain and New Ireland, the Duke of York group forms a natural connection between these two islands. One therefore easily tends to believe that the earlier migrations from southwestern New Ireland to New Britain, especially in view of the imperfect vessels, all followed their natural route through the Duke of York group, and that therefore this island group was again a starting point for the various migratory expeditions, and that the language there was virtually the mother of the various northern Gazelle Peninsula dialects, which had gradually evolved and branched from it. Only a more intensive study of the Duke of York language seems to demonstrate that this can hardly be the case.

In any analogy, such a number of basically different elements are brought to light, mainly in the word forms and less so in the grammatical constructions, that one has to accept a completely independent development of the Duke of York dialect. On the other hand, as far as grammatical construction is concerned, the main similarity is with that of the northern Gazelle language, and the rules of the latter can almost all be applied to the former, with little alteration. Thus, without doubt, the Duke of York language belongs to the same idiom as the various dialects of the north-eastern Gazelle Peninsula and the south-western coast of New Ireland.

Moreover, in the Duke of York group, from island to island and occasionally from village to village, variants exist, based more or less on neighbouring dialects. Thus in Nakukur, woman = *a tebuan* (according to G. Brown's dictionary), while on the island of Mioko and on the northern Gazelle Peninsula it is *a vavina*; whereas on Nakukur the latter word signifies only the female of animal species.

'Long', *iok*, *iokana* on Nakukur, is *tia*, *tiaina* on Mioko. Likewise, *divai* 'tree' and *make* 'sun' are *nai* and *kake* on the latter island. A great many words are originally different from those of the northern Gazelle language, such as those in Table 3.

A very large number of totally similar words with the same meaning as those of the northern Gazelle Peninsula demonstrate the original relatedness of both dialects; see, for example, Table 4.

With other words the similarity is immediately apparent. For example, see Table 5.

In many words of course the relationship does not leap so easily to the eyes, and it is only discovered when one goes back to the root of the words; for example, *make* ('sun', 'heat') is called *keake* on the northern Gazelle. The root of them both is *ke*; in the latter case it is doubled to *keake*, and in the former case it is changed into the perfect participle by the prefix *ma*, and is found in similar forms in the Baining s-dialect in *maqes* ('sun'), or as the adjective in *maqe*, and *makeke*, 'dry'. It is the same with *ninogon* and *nagnagonai*, 'laughter'; *akaka* and *kaina*, 'bad'; *veum* and *varubu* (root *um* = *ub*), 'to fight'; *teglik* and *taiqu* (root *ta*), 'brother'; *tunalik* and *matuana*, 'nephew'; *vekankan* and *varqanai*, 'to agree', 'to be happy', and others.

This dialect has the broad *ai* in several words like *tai* (sea) in common with the dialects of Nodup

Table 3

	Duke of York	northern Gazelle Peninsula
house	*ruma*[1]	*pal*
six	*nom*	*laptikai*
ten	*noina*	*vinun*
breadfruit	*bare*	*kapiaka*
to eat	*utna*	*kaikai* (*nian*)
bird	*pika*	*beo*
long	*iokana*	*lolovina*
man	*muana*	*tutan*
thing	*lig*	*maqit*
shell money	*divara*	*tabu*
spirit, image, shadow	*nio*	*tulugean*
as	*len*	*veder*
the demonstrative	*kumi*	*qo*
	kuma	*nam*

Table 4

ki, to sit	*pia*, earth	*pidik*, secret
tur, to stand	*bug*, day	*aman*, outrigger
laun, to live	*vo*, paddle	*tamana*, his father
mat, dead	*kiau*, egg	*nana*, his mother
gala, big	*burut*, alarmed	*bata*, to rain
vana, to go	*daka*, pepper	*dur*, dirty
pula, blind	*liplip*, fence	*kalagar*, parrot
lama, coconut	*tutun*, to cook	*lagun*, border
up, yam	*barman*, youth	*vat*, stone
via, knife	*dodo*, stiff	

1. This word coincides with the Malayan *ruma* (house), and corresponds with *luma* (house) in the Buka language.

Table 5

	Duke of York	northern Gazelle Peninsula
wood	*divai*	*davai*
to sleep	*inep*	*diep*
wind	*vūvū*	*vuvu*
fishing net	*bene*	*ubene*
bath	*nirariu*	*niiu*
small	*liklik*	*ikilik*
seed	*patikina*	*patina*
to do	*pet*	*pait*
mango	*kai*	*koai*
to cough	*kogo*	*kaogo*
ripe	*mo*	*mao*
to sing	*kelekele*	*kakaile*
pig	*boro*	*boroi*
canoe	*aka*	*oaqa*
soul	*tebaran*	*tabaran*
for, on account of	*kup, kupi*	*up, upi*
louse	*nanut*	*ut*
close to	*matiti*	*matatai*

Table 6

| Singular | Dual | Triple | Plural | |
			on Nakukur	on Mioko
iau, I	*dar* (inclus.)	*datul* (inclus.)	*dat* (inclus.)	*det*
u (*ui*), you	*mir* (exclus.)	*mitul* (exclus.)	*meat* (exclus.)	*met*
i, he, she, it	*mur*	*mutul*	*muat*	*mot*
	diar	*ditul*	*diat*	*diat*

and Tavui at the foot of Mother volcano; likewise the word *toto*, instead of *bebe* (butterfly).

Several identical or similar words probably originally had the same meaning but gradually became shaded to more or less related concepts, such as:

Duke of York	northern Gazelle Peninsula
taurara, virgin	widow, quarrel because of adultery
vavin, female animal	woman
tebuan, woman	*tubuan*, old woman
vinun, ten men	ten in general
utul, three pairs	three individuals
kuren, four fruits	*kurene*, half a dozen

The word *par* (all) here has the reversed form *rap*, just as *diradira* (flying squirrel) is reversed into *ridarida* in other places.

A brief overview of grammatical forms will show us on the one hand the great relationship of the northern Gazelle dialects with those of the Duke of York group, but, on the other hand also their differences, occurring particularly in the particles of construction.

To begin with, as on the Gazelle Peninsula, seventeen letters suffice for written representation of the language, and the letter 's' has had to be added because of introduced foreign words.

The article *a* for all genders, and the personal article *to* is again common to both. Also, a special article is available for female personal names, but here it is called *ne* instead of *ia* or *ja*; for example, *Neling* becomes *Jaling* on the Gazelle Peninsula.

Exactly as on the Gazelle Peninsula, besides the singular, they differentiate a triple multiple-form, dual, triple and plural, and the triple genitive with *na*, *i*, and *kai* deviates only insofar as the posses-sive genitive has *a nu* instead of *kai*. The preposition *tai* for forming the dative on the Gazelle Peninsula corresponds with *karom* here, and has the same meaning. The dual is formed with *ru* and the triple with *tul* instead of *ura* and *utul* on the Gazelle Peninsula. Also, the plural has two forms, with *in* or *kum*, as in *a in ruma* or *a kum ruma*, 'the houses'.

With regard to the adjective, in both its formation and its placement to the substantive and the designation of differences in gradation, there is no difference in treatment from that on the northern Gazelle Peninsula.

The personal pronoun is almost the same as on the Gazelle Peninsula. Table 6 indicates variations.

Also, the reflexive pronouns are formed, as there, by doubling the preceding form or adding *ut* (Gazelle Peninsula *iat*).

The possessive pronoun is likewise differentiated by a doubling: indicating possession and indicating assignment. The former is indicated in Table 7, the latter in Table 8.

The possessive pronoun is added also to several prepositions as a suffix:

tag, to (at) me	*nag*, near me (for me)
tam, to (at) you	*nam*, near you (for you)
tana, to (at) him	*nana*, near him (for him)

Finally, it is added to certain substantives, but in a more extensive way than on the Gazelle Peninsula. As well as to those substantives indicating relationships, body parts or parts of a whole, like those in Table 9, the possessive pronoun can also be added as a suffix to a whole number of other words, such as those in Table 10, and:

a divaraig, my shell money, but also: *a nug divara*;
a marig, my body decoration;
a pinapamig, my garden;
a lamaig, my coconut;
a akaig, my canoe.

The relative pronouns are, as on the Gazelle Peninsula, replaced by personal pronouns, or by pronouns indicating ownership, or can be left out completely.

The interrogative *ooi*? 'who'? and *aua*? 'what'? correspond to *toia* and *uva* on the Gazelle Peninsula.

However, the demonstratives, *kumi*, *kuma*, *kumia*, and *bi*, are different.

The numerals are:

on Nakukur	on Mioko
1 *ra*	1 *ra*
2 *ruadi*	2 *ruo*
3 *tuldi*	3 *tul*
4 *vatdi*	4 *vat*
5 *limadi*	5 *lima*
6 *nomdi*, or *limadi ma ra*	6 *nom*[2]
7 *limadi ma ruadi*	7 *talaqarua*
8 *limadi ma tuldi*	8 *lakatul*
9 *limadi ma vatdi*	9 *latakai*
10 *noina*	10 *noina*
20 *ru noina*	20 *ruo noina*
50 *a lima na noina*	50 *a lima na noina*
60 *a nom na noina*	60 *a nom na noina*
100 *a mar*	100 *a mar*

Ordinal numbers

Nakukur	Mioko
the first, *a mukana*	*a muqana*
the second, *ra i patap*	*dina*
the third, *ru i patap*	*dituina*
the fourth, *tuldi i patap*	*datavavat*
etc., etc.	the fifth, *datalalima*
	the sixth, *datanonom*
	the seventh, *datalakarua*
	the eighth, *datalalima*
	the ninth, *datalakakai*
	the tenth, *nonodet*

Table 7: Indicating possession

Singular	Dual	Triple	Plural
a nug, mine	*a nudar*	*a nudatul*	*a nudat*
a num, yours	*a numir*	*a numitul*	*a numeat*
a nuna, his	*a numur*	*a numutul*	*a numuat*
a nudiar	*a nuditul*	*a nudiat*	

Table 8: Indicating assignment

Singular	Dual	Triple	Plural
agag, for me	*amadar*	*amadatul*	*amadat*
amam, for you	*amamir*	*amamitul*	*amameat*
ana, for him	*amamur*	*amamutul*	*amamuat*
	amadiar	*amaditul*	*amadiat*

Table 9

tamag, my father	*nakug*, my mother
tamam, your father	*nam*, your mother
tamana, his father	*nana*, his mother
matag, my eye	*limag*, my hand
matam, your eye	*kapig*, my blood
matana, his eye	etc.

tug or *natig* } my child

2. 'Six' on Buka is *monom*; on northern Bougainville, *tunom*; and in the Shortland Islands, *onomo*

Table 10

rumaig, my
rumaim, your } house, but also: { *a nug ruma*, my
rumaina, his   *a num ruma*, your } house
                                      a nuna ruma, his

Distributive numbers are formed by duplication of the cardinal number

Nakukur	Mioko
every 1, *rauravin*	*rara* or *lapara*
every 2, *ruruvin*	*rurua* or *laparua*
every 3, *tultulavin*	*tultul* or *lapatul*
every 4, *vatvat na vin*	*vatvat* or *lapavat*
every 5, *limlim na vin*	*limlimo* or *laplima*

Variations here from the northern Gazelle language are a special kind of counting for pairs, where the first five numbers almost coincide with the cardinal numbers of the Gazelle Peninsula, but on the other hand they do not disown their pure Polynesian origin. Thus they are:

1 pair, *kai*	in Samoan, *tasi*
2 pairs, *urua*	in Samoan, *lua*
3 pairs, *utul*	in Samoan, *tolu*
4 pairs, *luvat*	in Samoan, *fa*
5 pairs, *tilim*	in Samoan, *lima*
6 pairs, *ma nom*	in Samoan, *ono*
7 pairs, *ma vit*	in Samoan, *fitu*
8 pairs, *tival*	in Samoan, *valu*
9 pairs, *tiva*	in Samoan, *iva*
10 pairs, *tikina*	in Samoan, *sefulu*

Most of the other varying forms of numbering for fruit, shell money, eggs, animals and humans are quite different from equivalent numbering methods on the Gazelle Peninsula; thus, here, *a inagava* is a 200-shell piece of money; there, on the other hand, it is four eggs or youths.

In the verbs, the transitive suffixes *tai* and *pai* correspond with *tar* and *pa* on the Gazelle Peninsula. The ending *tau* is perhaps the similar-sounding preposition: 'on', 'over'. The causative prefix *va* also exists here, and *ve* corresponds with the prefix *var* in forming the reciprocal.

With regard to the partial or total doubling of the verbs, the same rules apply as on the northern Gazelle Peninsula.

In conjugation the verb remains unaltered. In the present tense only the pronoun precedes the unaltered verb (see Table 11).

According to the Reverend G. Brown, the perfect should be expressed by inserting a long *a* between pronoun and verb. This seems erroneous to me; I rather believe that it is the particle *ta*, as in the Nodup dialect, where *ta* is also used instead of *tar* or *ter* on the Gazelle Peninsula. As it seems, the particle of the perfect is used less often here, and narrates mostly in the present, if the past already stems from the rest of what is said.

The imperative coincides with the forms of the future tense (see Table 12), and the conditional is like the indicative, and is differentiated only by the particles *ba*, 'so that', 'if'; *duk*, 'perhaps'; *kaduk*, 'lest'.

The entire passive voice, with the exception of a few perfect participles, is missing and, as on the Gazelle Peninsula, is replaced by circumlocution with the active voice.

The small number of prepositions is based both in the significance that no preamble is required and in the use of adverbs which often take the place of prepositions. The most essential real prepositions are *ko*, *kon* 'from'; *karom*, 'to', 'at'; *ma*, 'with', 'from', 'through'; *na*, 'by', 'for'; *ta*, *tan*, 'in', 'at'.

Of all types of word, adverbs deviate the most from those of the northern Gazelle Peninsula; only very few are totally the same, like *na bug*, 'yesterday'; *na taman*, 'outside'. Yet others are not totally dissimilar in form, and are perhaps originally from the same stem, although no longer with the same meaning, like:

Duke of York	Gazelle Peninsula
urin, to this place	*urie*, to the shore
urog, away, from	*uro*, over there
unata, unaga, upwards	*urama*, upwards
amaganate, above	*arama*, above
una pia, on the ground	*ura ra pia*, to the ground
ura bugbug rap, all day	*ra bugbug pa*, all day
iu, ioi, maia, yes	*maia*, yes
pate, my	*pata*, no

The adverb *nakono* (on the shore) corresponds to the adverb with the same meaning on the island of Uatom: *naono*.

The following are totally different:

Table 11: Present

Singular	Dual	Triple	Plural
ian van	*dar van*	*datul van*	*dat van*
ui van	*mir van*	*mitul van*	*meat van*
i van	etc.	etc.	etc.

Table 12: Future

Singular	Dual	Triple	Plural
ag van	*dar a van*	*datul a van*	*dat a van*
un van	*mir a van*	*mitul a van*	*meat a van*
in van	etc.	etc.	etc.

Duke of York	Gazelle Peninsula
kumari, today	*qori, ieri*
kumi ut, nadirik, now	*qoko*
unaburu, naboroa, tomorrow	*karaqam, nigene*
umera, uragra, the day after tomorrow	*oarie*
ulogra, three days ago	*naria liu*
gen, igen, apart	*arirai*
lelavai, leloa, why? how? how?	*dave?*
lenkumi, lenkuma, lenma, so	*dari*

The conjunctions *ma, bulug, kaduk, ba*, correspond to the Gazelle Peninsula words: *ma*, 'and'; *bula*, 'also'; *kan*, 'lest'; *ba*, 'when', 'if'. *Ku* corresponds probably to the end-syllable *ka*, 'only'. On the other hand, *kuma*, 'because', differs from *taqo* on the Gazelle Peninsula.

Since interjections often vary even from village to village, there are deviations from those on the Gazelle Peninsula, like *au!* instead of *aipua*; *a peu!* instead of *ra biavi!* and others of lesser significance for the comparison of both dialects.

In any event, this brief comparison shows that in spite of the great similarity of both languages, and the consequent original affinity, basically different elements are nevertheless present in the Duke of York language; searching for their origin would still be an interesting project in further language investigation.

3. The Baining Language

Just as the Baining is different from neighbouring tribes in his physiognomy, traditions and customs, he differs also in language. This deviates in many ways from the great Melanesian family of languages.

A general feature of Melanesian languages is the presence of a triple; the Baining language lacks this. It has merely three numbers: singular, dual and plural. Formation of the pronoun, which is so painfully precise in most Melanesian languages, is less advanced here. There are no inclusive and exclusive forms, and furthermore a proper possessive pronoun is missing for words that indicate relationships or body parts. The Baining language recognises no difference in possessive pronouns and does not append them to the substantive, but always places the possessive pronoun in front of the substantive.

A further, and probably the most significant feature of the Baining idiom consists, in my view, in that it is an inflected language. The word endings are altered to express the different numbers.

The vocabulary is totally divergent from that of the Melanesian languages known so far, right down to insignificant exceptions.

The grammatical outlines of the Baining language are as follows.

I. Phonetics

The Baining alphabet has 22 sounds:
1. vowels: *a, e, i, o, ä, ö*;
2. consonants: *b, ch, d, g̃, g, h, k, l, m, n, p, r, s, t, u, v*.

Vowels and umlauts are the same as those in German.

Note in regard to the pronunciation of consonants:
a) *b* must always be pronounced by sounding an *m* in front; for example, *a bieska*, is pronounced *a mbieska*, 'the wound'.
b) *ch* sounds far more gentle than our 'ch'; somewhat like the German 'g' as the terminal sound after 'a', 'o', 'u' in 'Lug' with the assonance of 'ch'.
c) *d* has, like *b*, an epenthesis, *n*; for example, *a dulka*, is pronounced *a ndulka*, 'the stone'.
d) *g̃* corresponds to the 'ng' in 'long'; for example, *g̃oa*, is pronounced *ngoa*, 'I'.
e) combines the two sounds *g̃g*; for example *a gunarka*, is pronounced *a nggunarka*, 'the pencil'.

Note: If the vowel following *g̃g* (=g) drops off, the pronunciation of the *g* becomes *g̃* for example, *a muga*, 'the tree', *a mug̃*, 'the trees'.

f) *h* is pronounced like our German 'h'. But, it has the characteristic that at the beginning of a word and as a medial sound it can be replaced by an *s*; for example, *a hur* or *a sur*, 'the fences'. *h* is never a terminal sound, except when a vowel follows; for example, *ka tes*, 'he is eating'; *ka te ut*, 'he is fighting against us'.
g) *k* does not have the hard palatal plosive sound as in German; it sounds almost like our 'g' at the beginning of a word.

k between two vowels changes to 'ch' in the third person singular personal pronoun; in other cases usage decides it. For example, *a choátka cha mit*, 'the man he goes away', but on the other hand *g̃oa aka*, my friend.

h) *p* between two vowels must be changed into *v*; for example, *g̃u tav a mug̃* instead of *g̃u tap a mug̃* 'I am felling trees'.
i) *t* between two vowels is usually changed into *r*; for example, *g̃oa rar* instead of *g̃oa tar*, 'I am bathing'.

II. Lexicology

The Baining language is founded on the following five basic rules:
1. The noun-substantives are divided into several groups distinguishable by suffixes.
2. All the other classes of words, with the exception of adverbs, prepositions,

conjunctions, interjections, and sometimes verbs, when related attributively or predicatively to a noun, adopt the syllables corresponding to the noun, in all numbers.
3. The words (substantive, adjective and pronoun) of the first and second groups, designating creatures endowed with intellect, have an unique pronoun for the third person plural (*ta*, *ti*, *tu*).
4. All designations for creatures without intellect, in the plural, belonging to the first and second groups, and the singular and plural of words of the third group regardless of whether or not they concern rational beings, have just one pronoun (in the singular and plural), namely *g̃a* or *g̃et* (*g̃eri*).
5. Words of the first group have a special possessive pronoun in the singular and plural (*a – a ra*).

The words of the second and third groups have the same possessive pronoun for singular and plural, namely *at*.

1. The Article

a) The definite and indefinite article is *a* (*ama*) in singular and plural, for all cases; for example, *a ika*, 'the bird', plural *a ik*; *a muga* 'the tree', plural *a mug̃*.
b) The article is placed in front of nouns, adjectives, numerals, the possessive pronouns, 'ours', 'yours', 'theirs', and the three persons of the dual. For example:
   a nanki, the woman
   a mer g̃oa, I am well ('well I')
   a ratpes, we
   a ur a luan, our clothes
   a g̃en a luan, your clothes
   a ra a ruis, their children
   a un a chip, our two spears
   a oan a lat, your two gardens
   a ien a vrika, their two slingshots
c) A number of words, mostly those expressing a relationship or parts of the body, occur without articles, and only in conjunction with the possessive pronoun. For example:
   gu mam, 'my father'; *gu nan*, 'my mother'; *goa ren*, 'my body'.

2. The Substantive

a) The Baining language has three numbers: singular, dual and plural.
b) No unique suffix in the plural form corresponds to the suffixes of the singular of the first and second groups.
c) Only one special form of the dual suffix (*iem*) supports the various suffixes of the first group.
d) Similarly, only one special form of the dual suffix (*im*) supports the various suffixes of the second group.
e) Also one of the dual as well as the plural supports the various suffixes of the second group.

Plate 48 Mask house on New Ireland. In the lower row, ordinary dance masks (*tatanua*); in the upper row, totem masks (*kepong*)

Annotations:
1. Suffixes of the first group in the singular: *acha, cha, ka, ga*
    Suffixes of the second group in the singular: *eichi, chi, ki, gi*
    Suffixes of the third group in the singular: *ini, eit, bit, igl, um, em, bem, ar, as, us, es.*
2. Most words of the first and second groups can take the derivative syllables (suffixes) of the third group.

Observations on the three numbers:

A. Singular

Mam, 'father'; *nan*, 'mother', and several others have no singular ending.

B. Dual

1. The dual in the first two groups is formed by appending the ending *iem* or *im* to the stem, depending on the ending of the substantive, to its stem. For example, *a igelka* 'the boy', stem: *a igel*, dual: *a igeliem*; *a igelki*, 'the girl', dual: *a igelim*.
2. Each of the various suffixes of the third group, with the exception of *as*, has its own dual ending, which is appended to the stem of the word:

ini	singular	*iram*	dual
it, eit, bit	singular	*ihim*	dual
igl	singular	*igrim*	dual
ar	singular	*isum*	dual
em (um, bem)	singular	*am, bam*	dual
as (us)	singular	*ihim*	dual

C. Plural

a) In the words of the first and second group:
   Formation of the plural occurs by omitting the singular ending (suffix). For example:

   a vaska singular, 'breadfruit tree', *a vas* plural
   a leichi singular, 'the door', *a lei* plural

b) In the words of the third group:
   Each of the six classes is aided by an unique plural suffix, as evident from the summary in Table 13.
   Examples: *a larini*, 'the small garden'; *a lariam*, 'two small gardens'; *a larirag* 'small gardens'.

Annotation:
The suffixes of the third group each have a specific meaning. For example:
a muñini, 'the sapling';
a muñigl, 'a small piece of wood';
a muñem, 'a piece of wood', and so on.

Declension

a) Genitive

The subjective and objective genitive relationship is expressed by a corresponding possessive pronoun. For example:

a	*choatka*	*a*	*a*	*chipka*
the	man	his	the	spear
a	*choata* (irregular plural)	*a ra*		*chip*
the	men	theirs		the spears
a	*choariem*	*a ien*	*a*	*chiviem*
the two men		the their both	the	spears
a	*nanki*	*a r*	*a*	*niska*
the woman		to her	the	kilt
a	*nankina*	*a ra*	*a*	*nis*
the women		to them	the	kilts

Annotation:
The corresponding possessive pronoun varies in form according to the different groups of the substantive.

b) Dative

There is no unique dative particle. The dative is expressed by circumlocution as in pronouns and prepositions. For example:

Thu   tal   a   arepki   hair   Paskam
I am carrying the axe to Paskam.
The   chur   a   savireicvhi   ra   ltigi
You are giving the people the gift of fire.
Nemka a   a   hinki? Ka   goa   hinki
Who owns the knife? It is my knife.

3. The Adjective

The attributive adjective can stand before or after the substantive.
In both cases it has *ama* or *a* as a joining particle.
a) Where the adjective is in front of the substantive, it is the unaltered determinative word with the preceding article, both in the singular and in the plural. For example:
   a mrer a choatka, or, better,
   a mrer ama choatka, 'the good man'

Table 13

ini	singular	*iram*	dual	*irañ*	plural
it, eit, bit	singular	*ihim*	dua	*isiñ*	plural
igl	singular	*igrim*	dual	*igriñ*	plural
em, um, bem,	singular	*am, bam*	dual	*ap, lap*	plural
ar	singular	*isum*	dual	*isuñ (itnek)*	plural
as, us	singular	*isim*	dual	*isiñ*	plural

a mrer ama nanki, 'the good woman'
a mrer ama nankina, 'the good women'

b) Where it stands after, the substantive retains its article and the objective is bound to it by the simple article or its expanded form (*ama*); moreover the adjective itself undergoes certain further alterations, according to how it stands in relation to a substantive of the various groups. For example:

a choatka ama vucha, 'the man the bad'
a nanki ama igelki, 'the woman the small'
a choariem ama viem, 'the both men the both angry'
a nanim ama igelim, 'the both women the both small'
a lapki ama pelki, 'the cockatoo the small'
a lavim ama plim, 'the both cockatoos the both small'
a choata ama hlur ta, 'the men the big they'
a nankina ama vu r a, 'the women the angry they'
a lav ama pel ẽet, 'the cockatoos the small they'

c) Where the subject is a pronoun and the predicate an adjective, the latter always stands in front of the pronoun. For example:
a vu ẽoa, 'angry (am) I'
a vu cha, 'angry he (is)'

4. The Numeral

The numerals up to and including 5 are simple; the rest are compound.

1 = *a choanáska, a choanaski*, etc.
    a giẽsacha, a gigsichi, etc.
2 = *a rekmeneiem* (first group)
    a rekmeneiem (second group)
    a odochim   (second group)
    a onpim   (second group)
3 = *a dopgues*
4 = *a ratpes* or *a baẽeigi*
5 = *a ẽarichit*
6 = *a ẽarichit a demka*, etc.
7 = *a ẽarichit dat demiem*, etc.
8 = *a ẽarichit dat demẽer ama dopgues*
9 = *a ẽirichit dat demẽer ama ratpes*
10 = *a garichigrim*.

Annotation:
Numbers above 10 are not customary.

5. The Pronoun

a) Personal

See Table 14.

b) Possessive

See Table 15.

c) Indicative

1. *a, ära, aiet, la*, 'that, this'
They always follow the substantive, without any alteration.
2. *lucha*, singular (first group), *luicha*, singular (second group), 'this, that'
liema, dual (first group), *lima*, dual (second group)
lura, plural (first and second group) for persons

Table 14: Personal pronouns

ẽu, I	*un*, we two, the both of us
ẽoa, I, me, to me	*ut*, we, us
ẽi, yoẽ, you, tẽ you	*ẽen*, you, you
ẽie, you	*ta, ti, tu*, they, for persons (first and second groups)
ka, ki, ku, he	*ẽa, ẽet*, they, for persons (third group) and things (first, second and third groups)
kie, chie, she	
chie, she (object)	
ẽa, ẽet, ini, it	

Table 15: Possessive pronouns

goa, mine	*a ien*, their two
gu, mine	*a ut*, our
gi, your	*a ẽen*, your
a, his	*a ra* (persons, first and second group)
a t, her	*a t*, their (persons third group; and things, first, second and third groups)
a ẽet, his, her	
a un, our two	
a van, your two	

lugera, plural (first and second group) for non-rational beings

lina, lira, luma, etc., for the third group singular.

Annotation:

lucha can stand before or after the substantive. When it is in front, it is connected to the substantive by the expanded article *ama*; for example, *lucha ama dælka*, 'this stone'.

Where it stands after, it follows the substantive without any connecting particle; for example, *a dælka lucha*, 'this stone, the stone there'.

d) The interrogative

nemka? singular, first group, 'who?' *nemiem?* dual, first group; *nemta?* plural, first group

nemki? singular, second group 'who?' *nebim?* dual, second group; *nemta?* plural, second group

nemŋet? plural, first, second and third groups, 'who?' in words designating non-rational beings.

Annotations:

1. *nemka*, used substantively, is always placed in front; for example, *nemka cha rekmet nini?* 'Who did it?' *nemka*, used adjectively in the sense: 'what kind of..' is always placed following; for example, *a nanki nemki?* 'What kind of woman?' *a ik nemget?* 'What kind of bird?'
2. *nemka* also has all the derivative forms of the three groups.

a igacha? singular, 'what?' 'what kind of?' (first group)

a igichi? singular, 'what?' 'what kind of?' (second group)

a igiem? dual (first group)

a igim? dual (second group)

a igiŋet? plural for all three groups

Annotations:

a igacha, like *nemka*, can take all the derivatives of the three groups.

e) The indefinite

ta, ti, tu, 'one', actually 'she'

sichik, tarak, 'another'

bak, 'anybody'

Annotation:

sichiak and *tarak* have definite suffixes for the second and third groups, as does the substantive.

6. The Verb

1. Various types of verb are differentiated in the Baining language:
   a) those that have the personal pronoun in front
   b) those that have the personal pronoun following
   c) those that are formed from a substantive or adjective and a preposition. Prepositions and pronouns follow the substantive.
2. The Baining verb, like the noun-substantive, has three numbers: a) singular, b) dual and c) plural, and each one has three persons.
3. Also, the Baining verb has three tenses: present, future and perfect.
4. In the present and future tenses, the actual stem of the verb does not undergo any alteration, except for many abbreviations.
5. In the perfect, the stem sometimes remains unchanged, and sometimes is abbreviated, or undergoes changes of sounds.
6. Temporal difference (future and perfect) is expressed by the particles *i, ik, ip*, for the future, and *sa* for the past.

Paradigms of the verb

a) Verb with preceding pronoun

Present

Singular	Dual	Plural
ŋoa tes, I eat	un tes	u tes
ŋie tes	oan tes	ŋen tes
ka tes	ien tes	ta tes
kie tes		ŋa tes.
ŋa tes		

Future

Singular	Dual	Plural
ik ŋoa tes	iv un tes	iv u tes
ik ŋie tes	iv oan tes	ik ŋen tes
i ka tes	iv ien tes	i ta tes.
i kie tes		
ina ŋa tes		

Perfect

sa ŋoa tes	sa oan tes
sai ŋie tes	sa ien tes
sa cha tes	sa u tes
sai chie tes	sa ŋen tes
sa un tes	sa ra tes

Imperative

ŋie tes or sai ŋie tes, 'eat'
ŋen tes or sa ŋen tes, 'eat'
u tes or sa u tes, 'let us eat'

b) Verb with subsequent pronoun

kudas ŋoa, 'I do not want to'	kudas uin
kudas ŋi	kudas iem or im
kudas ka	kudas ut
kudas ki	kudas ŋen
kudas ini	kudas ta
kudas un	kudas ŋet

Future

i chudas ğoa, etc.

Perfect

sa chudas ğoa, etc.

c) Verb formed from a substantive and a preposition

Present

a chreika vra ğoa, 'I am fasting', literally: 'the fasting to me'
a chreika vrei ği
a chreika vra cha
a chreika vrei chi
a chreika vra un
a chreika vra uin
a chreika vre iem
a chreika vra ut
a chreika vra ğen
a chreika vra ra

Future

i a chreika vra ğoa

Perfect

sa a chreika vra ğoa

7. The Preposition

Prepositions are:

ba, bark, barak, for
bedeğ, up to
da, in, on, at, near
mar, met, at, on, in, through
men, through
mirk, about
munkrup, in the middle
pa chlichi, in the middle
n, nama, in front of, with, out of
nair, through, from
namen, from, out of
nanir, after, about
narak, after, during
nav, from, out of
navr, from, out of
gel
gelem
gelemna na } near, in the vicinity, during
gir
girna
p, pet, per, in, over, behind, with, to, after
pr – rut, under
t, tik, tichem, in front of
tuar – tuar, this side, that side
la, over, on account of, with
sair, to

sak, after, behind
sar, sarem, after, at, to

8. The Adverb

1. Adverbs of time

lära, now
la, leip, today
biga, tomorrow
biga d'oarik, early tomorrow
areip, one day
a aber na aren, often
mas, always
nauir, at first
sies, mäka, again, once more

nasat, afterwards
da arenkaris, at night
da a chorévetki, in the moonlight
sa unun, in the evening
da niracha, by day
da niracha a a ren, at noon

2. Adverbs of place

a, ära, ti, here
na ri, from here
koa? koari? koaridi? where to? where?
na choari? where from?
pusup, above
men a evet, on the earth, on the ground

ámuk, there
d'eğerkiğ, on the beach
da rik, outside
da ra ren, inside
imak, below
na imak, from below
ávano, over there
pa unes, in the shade
pa chöol, in the bush

3. Adverbs of manner

perhet, sa chap, enough, ready
ğu ikağ, I am quick
mavik, bad
tachorära, tachorá, so
meni, over, past
ia? iva? eviva? why?
neik, naka, only, merely

sa na? how?
pa, almost
manep, deeply
duchup, useless, futile
a chasna? how many?
malei, maden, very, strongly, firmly

4. Adverbs of negation

koasir, not, no
kuku, no, absolutely not
as koasir, as kuku, not yet

5. Adverbs of affirmation

e, echerer, yes
kachoia, yes of course
saka, all right

lucha iet, that is it
lura iet, those are they (people)

6. Adverbs of possibility

ari, ani, perhaps
aekoa? koa? perchance?
ei, if

9. The Conjunction

ai – da, when
i, because
den – den, both – and
tika, also
kan, 'and', for combining persons and things in the singular (first group)
chien, 'and' for combining persons and things in the singular (second group)
i ari, that about
i kurima, lest
ten, 'and', for combining people (first and second groups)
da, 'and', for combining verbs and substantives
dat, dap, and, but
koarik – koarik, either – or

10. Exclamation

aria, get away, come on, at work
ai, ae, quite right
kové? is that so?
vai, u, to call someone
achai, cry of amazement
sóka, finished, cry when job finished
ave, yes, naturally

Vocabulary

1. Substantive

a ioska, ghost of the dead
a n'racha, sun, day
a váldagacha, star
a rmriki, rain
a évetki, earth
a lochúpki, village
a éska, path
a chavilki, island
a dælka, stone
a chánki, ashes
a ltígi, fire
a eichí, water
a ruchanépka, sea
a mæga, tree
a chălbăga, bark, skin, hide
a nat, taro
a áchavetka, banana
a avesemka, betelnut palm
a rlépka, flea
a choátka, man, husband
mam, father
nan, mother
a uémka, child
a rŭăcha, brother
a nánki, woman
a lŋiéska, headman
a rsavracha, slave
a cháchracha, Baining
a óveska, head
a lámsacha, coconut palm
a alimki, sugarcane
a vlemka, pig
a dága, dog
a nevága, mouse
a cháelka, wallaby
a máracha, crocodile
a lápki, cockatoo
a áneska, parrot
a chaivichi, bush fowl
a gárumki, cassowary
a husúpka, sky
a chorévetki, moon
a arenki, night
avípki, adder
a líbicha, fish
a choigoiga, butterfly
a étki, louse
a chasiŋem, hair
a sākāncha, eye
a chrimki, nose
a sdémki, ear
a richit, arm
a richígl, hand
a rika, finger
a éleiŋit, leg
aŋeleiľígl, foot
a avetki, house
a arepki, axe

2. Adjective

a hlur, big
a dlok, strong
a mer, good, beautiful
a haru, old
a igel, small
a chlak, weak
a iámes, green, young
a lua, white
a vlu, short
a chloi, black
a gilál, red
a uis, cold
a vu, angry
a miľiés, rotten
a bup, full
a balu, ripe
a aretkína, wise

3. Verb

támen, táchen, tuchun, to speak
teiŋ, to sing
nen, to request
su, to teach
kal, to prohibit
kak, to tell a lie
drem, to know (how to), to be able to cause to fall, bring down
tit, to go
iachu, to fear
mes, to eat angered by
neiŋ, to drink
breiŋ, to sleep
tas, to lie
snes, to call
main, to dance
a iámes, to live
sal, to give birth
rekmet, to make, to do
tal, to fetch, to carry
iŋip, to die
túma, to laugh
lu, to see
pin, to come
nem, to send
sep, to fall
máravit, to stand
hap, to catch
tap, to
miŋ, plaŋ, to kill
rkur, to give
rbur, to be irritated,
knak, to weep
nari, to hear
nin, to cook
suau, to thieve
sep, to fall
tu, to set up
tălăk, to ruin
tănĕg, to hold
rĭgŭs, to rub
tat, to help
tmătnă, to work

Examples of speech

The Lord's Prayer

See Table 16.

Conversation

See Table 17.

The Spider and the Fly

See Table 18.

4. The Sulka Language

At first glance, on skimming briefly over a vocabulary, the Sulka language appears to have a great affinity with the Gazelle Peninsula language, since you find a multitude of totally similar-sounding words, like *mat, kagal, matmat, momo, mi, kor, lul, mama, taktak, kaur*, and so on. But when one compares the meanings of these words, not the slightest similarity

Table 16: The Lord's Prayer

A	ut	mam,	luɡ̃ia	va	husup,	i	ti	achu	ɡi	a	arenki,	i	kie	n
You	our	Father,	the	you	in the skies,	that	one	fears	your	the	name,	that	it	comes

ɡi a lɡ̃ichi, i ti nari ɡelem ɡ̃i vra évetki, rachoar ti nari ɡelem ɡ̃i va
your the word, that one obeys to you on the earth, as one obeys to you in the

husupka. Lei ɡ̃ie vana ut ta ur a smeski, ɡ̃ie reɡ̃ev a ur a
sky. Today you present us with the to us the food, you discharge from us the

vuɡ̃et, tachoar u reɡ̃ev a ra a vuɡ̃et, ti ralak sut; kurimai ɡ̃ie
evil things, as we discharge from them the evil things, they do evil to us; not may you

rut naut savra vuɡ̃et, dap ɡ̃ie ra ut namena vuɡ̃et. Amen.
lead us into evil things, but you take away us from the evil things.

Table 17

Goa ak, koa gie drem, ama eska samet ma Sankt Paul?	My friend, do you know roughly the way to Saint Paul?
E, goa dremacha.	Yes, I know it.
Gie ren da gie nagoa.	Come, go with me (literally, 'you to me').
Kudas goa, mácha cha ruchun, ik gun nacha savra lat.	I can't, (my) father said, I had to (go) to the garden with him.
Gie n di iv lei ik gu chureigi rama suiki.	Come, and I will give you a gift of tobacco today.
Ari gu mam ka hirin nagoa.	Perhaps my father will be angry with me.
Ai iv uri ravlag, da un tit ságel mácha, ik goa ruchun nacha, i gun neigi.	When we both come back, we will go to (your) father, I will tell him that I (was) with you.
Kure du goa it nanir goa ga-teichi.	Wait while I fetch my arm-basket.
Gie kag satmit, dav as goa ruchun mena mugaiet.	Go quickly, and I will sit down (meanwhile) on this tree.
Sa lugoaiet.	Here I am (again).
Gie tal goa luanigl, di gie uir.	Wear my garment and go ahead.
Gu ruir.	I am going in front.
Koa ama eska cha tit pit?	Does the path climb high?
Luära cha tit meni da sa amá-mano cha tit pit.	It is flat-going now, but later it climbs.
Koarich ama eska cha tit pra chöol, da choarik pa inim, da choarik pra ratem?	Does the path go through the jungle, or through bush, or through grass?
Echerer, ka tit pa chöol, da vra inim.	Yes, it goes through jungle and bush.
Koar ama eichi chirna nama eska?	Is there any water near the path?
E, ma Navi da ma Rivun.	Yes, the Navi and the Rivun.
Navi ära gelemna, a leichi meneichi.	Here is the Navi, a bridge crosses it.
Nemka cha rach a leichi ära?	Who built this bridge?
A chavilkiruemka.	The whites.
Koar ama lba ra mat navracha seichi?	Did the coastal dwellers help them?
Kuku, mäitika ama chavilkiruemka.	No, the whites alone (built it).
A muga nemka ära ama gaunipka?	What kind of tree is this tall one, here?
Ka ama galipka.	It is a *galip*.
Koa cha tu a gam?	Does it bear fruit?
Echerer, ka cha tu.	Yes, it does.
Koa gen tes get?	Can you eat them?
Ka u tes get.	We eat them.
Koar ama ich i choasir ga tes ama galip?	Don't the birds eat the *galip*?
Ka ama gaman gen ama marag ga tes get.	The pigeons and the hornbills eat it.
Koar ama aber nama gaman gelemgen?	Are there many pigeons where you are?
E, ka a malei naget.	Yes, there are a lot of them.
Karak preigi, a ika nemka ära cha knak?	Quiet (be silent), what bird is that, calling?
Ka ama barbaruoichi.	It is the *barbaruoichi*.
J chie nana?	What does it look like?
A chloigi.	It is black.
Koa ama hlurki?	Is it big?
Ka ama hlurki rachoar ama chaivichi.	It is as big as the bush hen.

Table 17

A sinepki chien ama slageichi
The Spider and the Fly

A sinepki chie msem a r a his.	*Kie tuchun: Slaḡeihi, ḡie dlu, i kurimai*
A spider she spun her strands.	She said: Fly, you be careful, lest
ḡie tit savet ḡoa his. Ari	*diḡ si ḡi a ichivaret praḡet. Dav ama slaḡeichi chie*
you go into my web. Perchance	entangle your wings in it. But the fly she
tuma di chie tuchun: Naka ama	*dlok ḡoa, nach lei ik ḡoa ralak*
laughs and she says: Only (but) the strong	I am, and only today, now shall I destroy
saḡet. Kie tit di diḡ sa	*a r a ichivaret praḡet. Kie prer*
it. She went (in) and they entangled themselves	her wings in it. She defended (herself)
malei, i kie chuvik, dai duchup.	*A sinepki chie ḡaḡ sagelemki di chie*
fiercely, so that she would get free, but in vain.	The spider she went to her and she
pligi samra r a his.	
killed her in her strands.	

Table 19

	On the north coast	Among the Sulka
momo	means to drink	wart
mari	means to love	to watch a dance
kaur	means bamboo	strong
kor	means quantity	to marry
mat	means dead	to bake
lul	means to request	to flow
mama	means low water, reef	to yawn
kal	means to dig	coil, bracelet
kangal	means rooster feather	fugitive
pal	means house	to originate from
vatvat	means stony	to sew, to mend
vuvu	means wind; to blow	piece of wood with a cord
vo	means paddle	to fly
pui	means forest	fire
tuk	means up to	alone
taktak	means to take; mocking song	to admire, etc.

remains, and one must wonder how such a large group of words, quite independent from those of the Gazelle Peninsula, have retained the same phonation. Comparing only, see Table 19.

To deduce a connection of the Sulka with the inhabitants of the northern Gazelle Peninsula based upon the similar sound of these and a whole quantity of other words would be just as wrong as trying to draw a conclusion on the connections of the Sulka with European peoples based upon the fortuitous presence of several pure Latin-sounding words like *pater, panem, mea, vis, vim, vi, vas, mulier, inopia*, and so on, or pure German-sounding words, like *Speck, Speer, Tor, laut, tot, Lohn, Kot, Kuckuck, lang, leer, Saus, Lilie*, and so on, in the Sulka language. Nevertheless, it would still be an interesting task for linguists to trace the steps in the gradual evolution of these South Sea languages, and to find out how, following natural universal rules of language, such a great number of identical-sounding words could be formed independently, and with different meaning by the Sulka folk, in whom, despite obvious differences from the Gazelle inhabitants, a certain similarity in physique and in traditions and customs cannot be denied. This task will be lightened as soon as the languages of the surrounding tribes from New Britain, southern New Ireland, and the northern Solomon Islands are examined in greater detail. It will then also be established whether the Sulka were the original inhabitants of New Britain or where they immigrated from.

I have been able to isolate only the few similar or identical words in Table 20 that have the same meaning as in the northern Gazelle language, from the already fairly complete word collection of Brother Hermann Müller (from the Catholic mission).

Therefore, even words that are similar elsewhere throughout the South Seas, such as *tamana*, 'father'; *matana*, 'eye'; *limana*, 'hand'; *taligana*, 'ear'; *mat*, 'dead', differ here.

Frequent liaison is very characteristic of the Sulka language – not, as in French, the liaising of the terminal consonants with the following word,

LANGUAGES

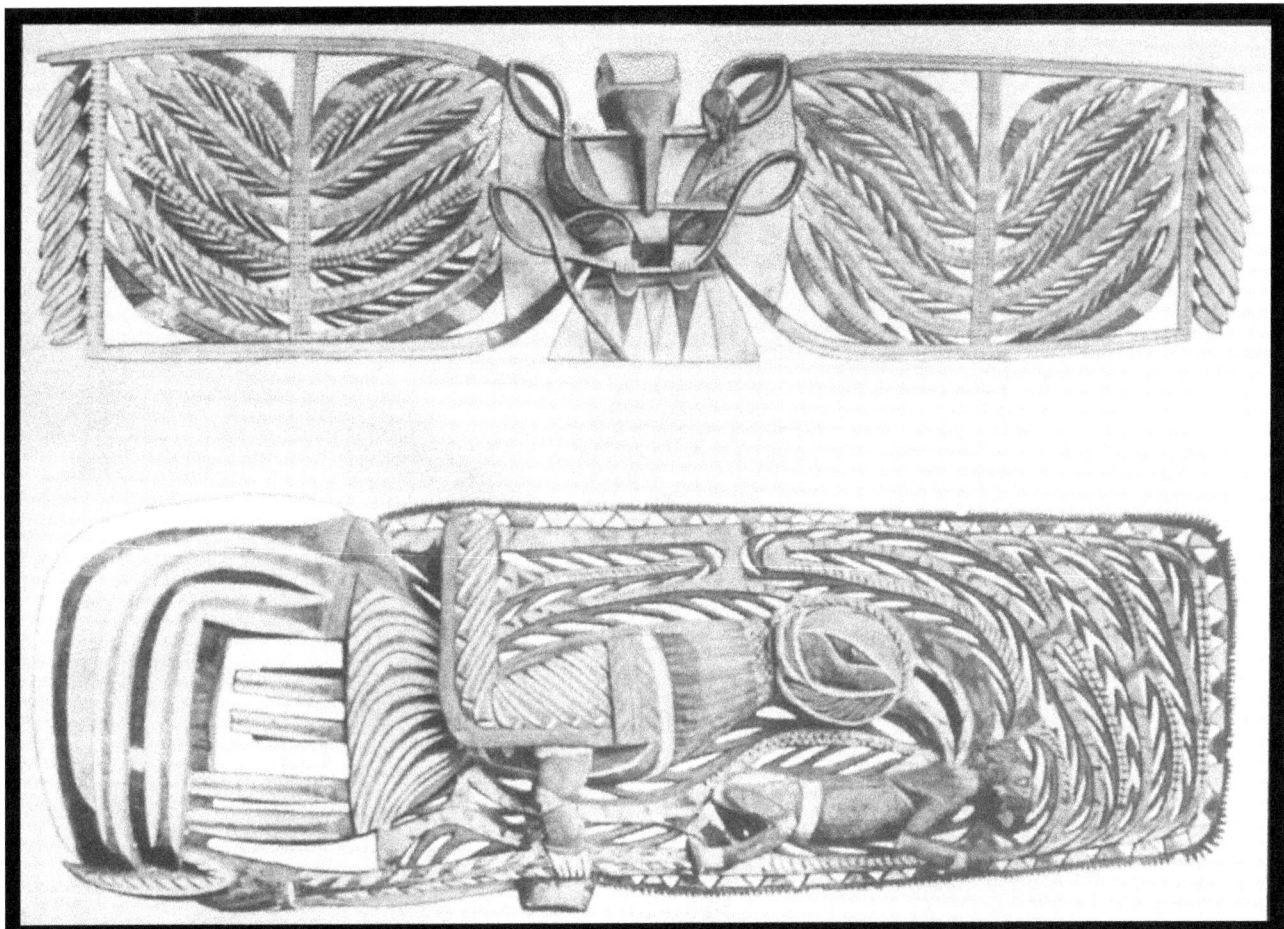

Plate 49 *Turu* carving from the Fischer Islands. (Reproduced from *Publikationen aus dem Königlichen Ethnographischen Museum zu Dresden*, vol. 10, plate 12)

Table 20

	northern Gazelle Peninsula	Sulka
tobacco	*a iuka (a suk)*	*a suku*
papaya	*a tapeka*	*a pepeka*
betelnut tree	*a buei*	*a vhui* (or *a bhui*)
Cordia subcordata (tree)	*a kanau*	*a kanau*
his mother	*nana*	*ka nan*
sand	*a veo*	*a vai*
to grind	*tau*	*tau*
to blow	*vuvu*	*huhu*
canoe without outrigger	*a mon*	*a mon*
from, hither	*ka, kan*	*kan*

Table 21

ka lpek (his head)	is spoken	*kal pek*
ta kpum (he caught hold of)	is spoken	*tak pum*
kua nvur (I wade through)	is spoken	*kuan vur*
a ktarkup (the first)	is spoken	*ak tarkup*
a to mhel (something)	is spoken	*a tom hel*
a lkiek (ginger)	is spoken	*al kiek*
ka kmeneng (his feather)	is spoken	*kak meneng*
ila nhar (his foot)	is spoken	*ilan har*
ta sma lgam (he does it well)	is spoken	*tas mal gam*
kua kha (my thigh)	is spoken	*kuak ha*

but rather the coupling of the first of two initial consonants to the preceding word ending in a vowel. For example, see Table 21.

On account of their many plosives – *t*, *p*, and the deep gutteral *k*, and the equally common aspirate *h* – the language sounds somewhat chopped up,

Table 22

a gi̥ sie (coconut palm and nut)	pronounced roughly	*ak sie*
a gi̥ tiek (the hand)	pronounced roughly	*ak tiek*
ka ku̥li (his fat layer on the stomach)	pronounced roughly	*kak li*
ku̥mau (damp, cold)	pronounced roughly	*k'mau*
mḁngar (to dry)	pronounced roughly	*m'gar*
kḁmua (to cough)	pronounced roughly	*k'mua*
nga tḁ mat o reak (they roast taro)	pronounced roughly	*ngat mat o reak*

Table 23

Standing alone	As subject	In the dative
nduk, I	*kua*, I	*makruk*, to me
in, you	*ia, ii*, you	*makòrin*, to you
en, he, she, it	*ta*, he, she, it	*makor*, to him
mua, we two	*mo (mu)*, we two	*makmua*, to us two
mui, you two	*mi (mea)*, you two	*makmui*, to you two
min, the two	*min (ngin)*, the two	*makmin*, to the two
mur, we	*ngur (ngu)*, we	*makmur*, to us
muk, you	*mu (mug)*, you	*makmuk*, to you
mar, they	*ngar (nga)*, the	*makmar*, to them

Table 24

ku tït, my father	*mo tït*, our two fathers	*ngor tït*, our father
i tït, your father	*mi tït*, your two fathers	*mu tït*, your father
ka tït, his father	*ngin tït*, their two fathers	*ngar tït*, their father

but otherwise it is no less pleasing to the ear than that of the northern Gazelle Peninsula.

Another characteristic of the Sulka language are the silent vowels in normal speech; pronounced only in singing or slow speech, and indicated in writing by subscripting a small 'o' below the vowel in question; for example, *koni* (to sing) is pronounced *ko̥ni*. (See also Table 22, overleaf.)

The common article, definite and indefinite, is *a*, and the personal article, for men's and women's, and place and river, names, is *e*.

The Sulka language does not recognise a true genitive, but copes by using the possessive pronoun, as shown in the following examples:

a vlom ka ngaurat, 'the woman her basket', instead of 'the woman's basket';

la reip nga kro ngaurat, 'the women their baskets';

e Veigi ka lpek ka kroir, literally 'Veigi his head his hair', instead of 'the hair on Veigi's head'.

The dative is formed in the singular and plural by means of *makor* 'to him': *Ku en makor e Kakau*, 'I give it to Kakau'. *Ku en makor a lo vlom ri*, 'I give it to the women there'.

The accusative is the same as the nominative: *Kua vuokom a vul*, 'I see a mountain'. *Ta klang e Nut*, 'he gives a gift to Nut'.

For multiples there are only two forms here to differentiate: dual and plural; the triple is lacking in the Sulka language. By placing the numeral *lo*, 'two' in front of the substantive, the dual is formed; for example, *a ho*, 'the tree', *a lo ho*, 'the two trees'. Similarly the plural arises by placing *kro* or *o* in front, whereby the substantive assumes the plural form, mostly differentiated from the singular form. For example:

a vip, the banana	*a kro vip*, the bananas
a morek, the pig	*a kro morek*, the pigs
a silang, the fish	*a kro* (or *o*) *singol*, the fishes
a ho, the tree	*a kro hi*, the trees
a ringmat, the village	*o ringmat*, the villages
a gi̥ sie, coconut palm	*a kro ges*, coconut palms
	o mea, the people

Only the adjective used in the predicate has the real adjectival form, whereas the adjective used in the attributive takes the substantive form, and the latter must agree with the substantive in number. For example:

a ho ta hok, 'the tree is high', compared with;

a ho a hogor, 'a tree, a high one';

a lo ho a lo hogor, 'the two high trees';

a hi a kro hogui, 'the high trees';

a silang ta la ut, 'the fish is big';

kua vuokum a silang a lautar, 'I see a fish, a big one'.

The comparative – that is, actually the expression of dissimilar grades of attribute– appears as a juxtaposition, as in the language of the northern Gazelle Peninsula. For example:

E Piia ta hok, va e Tabak ta kun, 'Piia is big and Tabak is small' – that is, Piia is bigger than Tabak; or: *E Piia a hogor, va e Tabak a gi kunur*, 'Piia is a big person and Tabak is a small person'; or: *E Tauvam ta laut manang e Kaple*, 'Tauvan is big far from Kaple' – that is, bigger than Kaple. *E Got ta ia mang ur*, 'God is better than us.'

The personal pronoun varies depending on whether it belongs as subject of a sentence or stands alone (Table 23).

Murua, attached to the lone-standing form, gives the reflexive pronoun: *duk murua*, 'I myself', *in murua*, 'you yourself', *en murua*, and so on.

The possessive pronouns

kua, my	*ma*, our two	*ngoa*, our
ila, your	*mea*, your two	*mula*, your
ka, his	*ngina*, their two	*nga*, their

Kua ngaulu, 'my house', *ila ngaulu*, 'your house', etc.

In front of substantives indicating relationship, the possessive pronoun has varying forms (Table 24).

In address one says, *tita!* or *tito!* or *titou!* 'my father!'

Likewise:

ku nan, my mother	*ku nopia*, my brother
i nan, your mother	*i nopia*, your brother
ka nan, his mother	*ka nopia*, his brother

In address one says, *ina!* or *ino!* 'or *inou!* 'my mother!'

The demonstrative

Standing alone:	In combination:
en do, this, that	*to*, this, that
en min, these two	*die*, these two
en druk, these, those	*ri* or *ruk*, those

The interrogative

erie? who? *erie min?* which two? *erie mar?* which?

a nie (subst.)? what? *a ni* (adj.)? what kind of?

nia or *ninia?* what would you like? how?

The relative pronoun is alternatively replaced by the demonstrative, as in:

A	ngokol,	kua	vuokom	namo,	tiur.
The man,		I	saw (him)	yesterday,	has died.

The impersonal pronoun 'it' is formed by *ta* (third person singular).

Ta keirik, 'it is raining'. *Ta sluk*, 'it is dark'. *Ta vurmik*, 'there is lightning'. *Ta kulang*, 'it is thundering'. *Ka vurgim a kolkha*, 'much sun for it'; that is, it is very hot.

Numbers, for the Sulka, are also based on the five-system; *a gitiek*, 'the hand', means 'five' and *a lo gitiek*, 'the two hands', 10. Yet their use of numbers barely reaches 20. In counting they repeat, incorporating the four fingers of the hand in sequence: *tang ta, tang ta, tang ta, tang ta*, and the thumb is called *a gitiek ta*. Then for 6, 7, 8, 9 *tanga ta* is repeated four times once more, and for 10 *a lo gitiek*. But besides this, they also have definite designations for each individual number:

a tiang	1	*a gitiek he hori orom a tiang*	6
a lo	2	*a gitiek he hori orom a lo min*	7
korlotige	3	*a gitiek he hori orom korlotige*	8
korlolo	4	*a gitiek he hori orom korlolo*	9
a gitiek	5	*a lo gitiek*	10
		a mhelum	20

As the outline shows the numbers are even more incomplete and clumsier than those on the coast of the Gazelle Peninsula, and therefore more unsuitable for commerce and trade, which can be explained by the low requirement for use of numbers in the daily life of the Sulka.

As on the north coast of the Gazelle Peninsula, here too we find transitive, intransitive and objective verbs, although the latter have no special form but every transitive verb, used without an object, already incorporates the object 'him, it'. Here, as there, several unconnected verbs can be placed side by side, as in:

kamik hala, to laugh eating;

onit langlar, to gaze upwards lying down;

vo käti, to cry out, flying;

sir paneng, to stand waiting;

kul es, to take it and put it down.

Doubling of the verb here means only multiples of treatments without otherwise altering the character of the verb.

The very convenient causative prefix is missing here; on the other hand, a prefix *mo* is available for forming the reciprocal:

mokla, to pelt one another;

mongami, to invite one another;

momeng, to order one another.

A plural form of certain verbs is characteristic, as in:

el, to lay it down; *ilik*, to lay them down

kul, to take it; *lol*, to take them

pis, to come; *pagis*, to come (from the plural)

Formation of time and manner occurs not through alteration of the verb, but by different particles and altered forms of the pronoun, as the outline will demonstrate.

It is noteworthy that the Sulka distinguish only two time periods, the present and the future. For the past, they use the present, but in speech the former must be made recognisable by some means.

Conjugation

I. Present	II. Future
	Singular
kua ngoi, I am going	*ngua k ngoi*, I shall go
ia ngoi, you are going	*ngea k ngoi*, you will go
ta ngoi, he is going	*na k ngoi*, he shall go

Dual

mu ta ngoi, we are both going	*ma k ngoi*, we shall both go
mi ta ngoi, etc.	*mea k ngoi*, etc.
ngin da ngoi	*ngin ak ngoi*

Plural

ngu ta ngoi, we are going	*ngur ak ngoi*, we shall go
mu ta ngoi, etc.	*mu ak ngoi*, etc.
nga ta ngoi	*ng'ak ngoi*

Imperative

ngoi! go!	*mi ngoi!* go, both of you!	*mu ngoi!* (you plural) go!

Habitual form

Singular	Dual	Plural
ku ma ngoi	*mo ma ngoi*	*ngo ma ngoi*
i ma ngoi	*mi ma ngoi*	*mu ma ngoi*
ma ma ngoi	*ngin ma ngoi*	*nga ma ngoi*

Conditional form

ku pa ngoi	*mo pa ngoi*	*ngo pa ngoi*
i pa ngoi	*mi pa ngoi*	*mu pa ngoi*
na pa ngoi	*ngin pa ngoi*	*nga pa ngoi*

Optative form

First style

kua ngoi	*mua ngoi*	*ngur ngoi*
ia ngoi	*mi ngoi*	*mu ngoi*
na ngoi	*ngin ngoi*	*ngar ngoi*

Second style

nduk kam ngoi	*mua kam ngoi*	*mur kam ngoi*
in kam ngoi	*mui kam ngoi*	*muk kam ngoi*
en kam ngoi	*min kam ngoi*	*mar kam ngoi*

Negation

Present

Singular	Dual	Plural
k'lo ngoi, I am not going	*mu t'lo ngoi*	*ngu t'lo ngoi*
i lo ngoi, you are not going	*mi t'lo ngoi*	*mu t'lo ngoi*
t'lo ngoi, he is not going	*min d'lo ngoi*	*nga t'lo ngoi*

Future

ngu loa ngoi	*ma loa ngoi*	*ngur a loa ngoi*
nge loa ngoi	*mea loa ngoi*	*mug a loa ngoi*
na loa ngoi	*ngin loa ngoi*	*nga a loa ngoi*

Habitual form

kum lo ngoi	*nom lo ngoi*	*ngom lo ngoi*
im lo ngoi	*mim lo ngoi*	*mum lo ngoi*
ma lo ngoi	*minm lo ngoi*	*ngam lo ngoi*

Conditional form

ku p'lo ngoi	*mo p'lo ngoi*	*ngur p'lo ngoi*
i p'lo ngoi	*mi p'lo ngoi*	*mu p'lo ngoi*
na p'lo ngoi	*min p'lo ngoi*	*nga p'lo ngoi*

Optative form I

kua lo ngoi	*mua lo ngoi*	*ngur lo ngoi*
ia lo ngoi	*mi lo ngoi*	*mu lo ngoi*
en lo ngoi	*min lo ngoi*	*ngar lo ngo*

Optative form II

nduk kam lo ngoi	*mua kam lo ngoi*	*mur kam lo ngoi*
in kam lo ngoi	*mui kam lo ngoi*	*muk kam lo ngoi*
en kam lo ngoi	*min kam lo ngoi*	*mar kam lo ngoi*

Negation in the imperative

nge or kam ngoi! don't go
mi or kam ngoi! you two, don't go
mug or kam ngoi! don't go

There is no interrogative form; a question can only be recognised from the tone of the affirmative form or from interrogative words.

The infinitive is very common, with 'to' represented by *kam*. *Ta mnur kam eitiek*, 'he knows how to write'. *K'lo pat kam kie*, 'I do not know how to write'. *Ta ngoi kam eiha*, 'he is going to work'.

The Sulka language is rich in prepositions, except that their meaning and use does not correspond with that of other languages, making it impossible to translate them universally. In each individual case we must use yet again another preposition, and vice versa. For example, in the sentence: *ta l'gam eakam e Veigi* (that is, 'he makes it after Veigi'), the preposition *eakam* means 'after'. But in the sentence: *ngu ta ktiegim a lut eakam o reak* ('we are weeding the garden for the taro'), *eakam* means 'for'. Finally, in the sentence: *o usiel nga ta girap eakam o hi* (that is, 'vines are climbing up on the trees' or 'against the trees'), it can mean 'on' or 'against'.

A similar situation occurs with other prepositions, like *kim* 'by', 'at', 'to', 'on account of', 'over'; *ma* 'about', 'with' 'in', and so on.

The conjunction is not much more frequently used than on the coast of the Gazelle Peninsula, except that here they have the contradictory 'or', *ee* or *oe*.

On the other hand, there is again a great abundance of interjections, and there are repeatedly shuddering or bleatingly uttered, long-drawn-out vowels, that we designate by a ~ over them.

iakō! iokō! cry of pain		*upuò* wonder	
ōhe! hōe! reluctance, unwillingness		*iu! iu!* joy	
jejejeje! amazement		*suvurum i kela!* sympathy, compassion	
vui! hui! st! shout			
jiji! danger		*vango! vangō!*	during battle
ho! hā!	before the attack	*pimo! pimō!*	
vavava!		*muso! musō!*	

The Lord's Prayer in the Sulka language

Ngur tit, in do ia vle kua ma volkha. Mur kam teiver ila munik. Ila kambung en kam pis. Mur kam titing eakam in mo ku mie, en'gar nga ma titing eakam in kua ma volkha.

A kolkha tieti klang ur orom ngo lol. Kikiangoi mang'ur ko, ngu ta lgam nong le iar, eng'ur ngo ma kikiangoi man gar, nga ta lgam nong le iar ngang ur. Nge or ia nglum mur ma mamas, va halger mur makor a tongman nong a iar. Amen.

Supplement

Side-by-side comparison of Sulka, O Mengen and Tŭmuip words

The O Mengen and the Tu̱muip are friendly neighbouring tribes of the Sulka. Their languages show similarities only here and there with the Sulka language. But the O Mengen language too has many assonances with the language of the northern Gazelle Peninsula.

It will certainly interest the reader if we append to the above outline of the Sulka grammar a short compilation of Sulka, O Mengen and Tŭmuip words (Table 25, overleaf) from the very industrious mission brother Hermann Müller's collection, which has already offered a valuable glimpse into the word forms and several grammatical constructions of both the latter languages.

5. The Nakanai Language

The Nakanai people do not appear to be closely related either to the inhabitants of the northern coast of the Gazelle Peninsula nor to those of the interior, the Baining. Rather, almost everything: physique, traditions and customs, communal life in the villages, and so on, points to a relationship with the Papuans of New Guinea. Comparison between the languages of the Nakanai and the northern Gazelle inhabitants also shows this difference. I cannot say how far the relationship with the Papuan languages extends; it is significantly different to the language of the northern Gazelle Peninsula.

Surprising first of all in the Nakanai language is the strong accentuation and stressing of certain syllables that, in the pleasant form of most words, adds to the melodious sound, if they are not too drawn-out, as happens from time to time. In words like *sodāni* (one plants it); *tinge usināni* (up to that time); *natuna tasamōni* (only son); *sonando* (around); *tauluvēni* (pretty); *palilina* (sick); *nosiāna* (to prohibit); *tausināte* (lay it there); *suntāno* (to kneel); *sinōpe* (broom) and others, one might almost imagine that one is hearing one of the melodious Romance languages. On the other hand, with the juxtaposition of vowels, like *sa'o*, 'jug'; *so'ēli*, 'to bury'; *sā'e*, to climb up; *pō'o*, 'beginning', 'origin'; *u'ūna*, 'his finger'; *vi'i*, 'fat'; *hu'u*, 'to call'; *a'ásu*, 'to match'; *no'ōse*, 'jealous'; *pa'ālis*, 'thief', 'to steal', and others, one could assume relationship with the Samoan language. One may add to this the aversion to the 'r', indeed the almost total absence of it, as in Samoan. Where the Nakanai language has words that contain an 'r' in the language of the Gazelle Peninsula, either the 'r' is totally absent, or it changes into an 'l', as in Table 26.

This sound occurs so often that this language has been called the 'L-language'. Perhaps this can be traced back to the transformation of the 'r' into 'l'. The 'r' is peculiar only to very few words, like *tamatūtur*, 'sleepy'; *giri*, 'hungry'; but my informant from the northern Gazelle Peninsula, whom I thank for these notes, also gave several of these, occasionally in the form with 'l' instead of 'r', like *kalakěla*, instead of *geragěra* with the same meaning: 'to be happy'.

The numeral group from 1 to 10 also shows great similarity with Samoan, as the outline below will demonstrate. In addition, the word *laulau* for 'leaf' recalls the Samoan *lau*, 'leaf of a tree'.

The Nakanai language appears to have absolutely no connection with the languages of the Sulka, the O Mengen or the Tŭmuip on the south coast of New Britain. Only the words, *a uamba* ('the axe') and *a visso* ('the knife') that we heard during our first visit to the O Mengen at Waterfall Bay, seem to have found their way across New Britain.

The term for 'sago', *a labia*, almost coincides with the term used in the New Ireland language, *a bia*.

In spite of the vast difference in character, a great number of words show great similarity or even complete identity with words from the language of the peninsula. Words like *pitimulu* ('to smoke'), *tobe̅ni* ('tabu'), *obéne* ('fishing net'), *galamu* ('*garamut* drum') and others, may perhaps in small part have been introduced by the Gazelle Peninsula people annually gathering shell money, but mostly they hark back to relationships of older date; see, for example, Table 27.

Even more surprising is the similarity and, in places, total correspondence, in grammatical forms.

Table 25

English	Sulka	O Mengen	Tumuip
man	*a ngokól*	*a punúngata*	*nōbung*
woman	*a vlom*	*a vail ta*	*nōlo*
child	*a kalsie*	*a goita*	*kotik*
mother	*ka nān*	*nɨname*	*tēnon*
brother	*ka nopia*	*tein* or *taun*	*dīek*
sister	*k'ētim*	*lɨnipi*	*devín*
uncle	*ka kāk*	*vɨn*	*ulōv anon*
soul	*ka múnu*	*kaununa ta*	*don*
body	*ka vŭok*	*merɨna ta*	*nēon*
head	*ka'lpek*	*kuruna ta*	*blālum*
eye	*ka kīek*	*matɨna (kana ta)*	*ngomtan*
ear	*ka ngēla*	*longana ta*	*palieng ndólgan*
mouth	*ka gu*	*kaúna ta*	*ndálien*
nose	*ka vorngap*	*inapogɨna ta*	*mblōdun*
tongue	*ka naperei*	*memeˋna ta*	*tamlon*
arm	*ka ktiek*	*kamɨna ta*	*lalman*
foot	*ka nhar*	*kaina ta*	*kean*
blood	*ka iindiel*	*savaluna ta*	*matómlon*
vein	*ka spang*	*loloi ta kie*	*kahem*
men's house	*a ngaulu*	*ginga ta*	*ndɨnu*
family house	*a rik*	*vail ta*	*bále*
mat	*a tamneng*	*tamneng ta*	*ratámeneng*
taro	*a iok*	*mɨ ta*	*lāmuop*
yam	*a tu*	*kolɨva ta*	*mbungian*
banana	*a vip*	*pɨr tua*	*mau*
sugar cane	*a kil*	*tuˋ tia*	*ne kunkun*
coconut	*a gisie*	*lamas tia*	*kálme*
garden	*a lūt*	*guˋr ta*	*lero*
tree	*a ho*	*veaga ta*	?
leaf	*a mīr*	*launa ta*	*raro*
blossom	*ka ngeihi*	*pɨna ta*	*búngen*
fruit	*ka mīt*	*péna ta*	*vúēn*
breadfruit	*a iangmeil*	*meiga ta*	*membiria*
canari nut	*a kaisiep*	*kangail tia*	*kangali*
Carica papaya	*a pepeka*	*teteka ta*	?
canoe	*a langeil*	*mananga ta*	*nuang*
paddle	*a pārai*	*kotɨanga ta*	*lopōte*
spear	*a mūs*	*juò ta*	*nodie*
shield	*a gólie*	*galéi ta*	*hedige*
slingshot	*a iān*	*tɨva ta*	*télva*
path	*a ngoi*	*gɨɛ ta*	*nsal*
compound	*a ringmat*	*mangkuna ta*	*vatōno*
dog	*a guéla*	*goíva ta*	*nē pap*
pig	*a morek*	*giɛ ta*	*mbuo*
mouse	*a vogor*	*vogɨr ta*	*me*
crocodile	*a iāme*	*iamɛ ta*	?
fish	*a silang*	*siláng ta*	*mpe*
earth	*a mie*	*magal ta*	*ndan*
mountain	*a vŭl*	*tuguˋr ta*	*manɨr*
sea	*a mau*	*piléi tia*	*nde*
water	*a si (a ii)*	*mɛ ta*	*nuje*
sand	*a vai*	*vuai ta*	*nkin*
stone	*a kóri*	*vanga ta*	*mper*
sun	*a kolkha*	*kei ta*	*nega*
moon	*a kienho*	*ina ta*	*nekang*
wind	*a ngausgi*	*isonga ta*	*ilúk*
rain	*a kus*	*kuɛ ta*	*nier*
fire	*a pui*	*pui tia*	*niu*
my faher	*ku tit*	*máma*	*mimaio*

your father	*i tit*	*tamān*	*mimem*
his father	*ka tit*	*tamān*	*mimam*
my brother	*ku nopia*	*teig*	*dieo*
your brother	*i nopia*	*teim*	*dieka*
his brother	*ka nopia*	*tein*	*diek*
my name	*kua mŭnik*	*jaig tia*	*sáieving*
your name	*ila mŭnik*	*jan*	*sáievim*
his name	*ka mŭnik*	*jāna ta*	*sáien*
my garment	*kua iet*	*māla ta ko*	*kapinge aning*
your garment	*ila iet*	*māla ta koen*	*kapinge anim*
his garment	*ka iet*	*māla ta kīe*	*kapinge anon*
my belly	*kua virik*	*siaig tia*	*búgheling*
your belly	*ila virik*	*sian tia*	*búghelim*
his belly	*ka virik*	*siāna ta*	*búghelon*
I	*nduk (kua)*	*jeo (ia)*	*io*
you	*in (ia)*	*goen (no)*	*ike*
he, she, it	*en (ta)*	*i, e, ti*	*bita*
we two	*mua (mu)*	*isuo (mamuo)*	*kuta*
both of them	*mui (mi)*	*imuo*	*kuma*
the two	*mun (min, ngin)*	*luo*	*turu*
we	*mur (ngu)*	*iz (mam)*	*kusier*
you	*muk (mu)*	*mo*	*ikom*
they	*mar (nga)*	*re (ri)*	*ti*
to eat it	*ēm*	*kain ītia*	*īn i*
to drink it	*eiviem*	*īn ītia*	*inūn i*
to strike him	*ospum*	*sp ītia*	*tul i*
I am drinking it	*ku eiviem*	*ia īn ītia*	*ta unūn i*
he eats the taro	*t'em a iok*	*e kain e mā ta*	*t'in la muop*
one	*a tiang*	*(tia) kĕn*	*dēnan*
two	*a lo*	*(tia) lŭo*	*ro huru*
three	*korlotige*	*(tia) molēg*	*horum detu*
four	*korlolo*	*(tia) toŭl*	*horumo horum*
five	*a gitiek*	*ta ne lim*	*ko līem*
six	*a gitiek he hori orom a tiang*	*kana kĕn*	—
seven	*a gitiek he hori orom a lo min*	*kana lŭo*	—
eight	*a gitiek he hori orom korlotige*	*kana molēg*	—
nine	*a gitiek he hori orom korlolo*	*kana togŭl*	—
ten	*a lo gitiek*	*kana lim* or *tángau na ta*	*līem*
twenty	*a mhelum*	*a gigi tia ken*	*tamdil*
what?	*a nie?*	*tár tia?*	*mene?*
what is that?	*a nie to?*	*tar tīgie?*	*mene na?*
who?	*erie?*	*tejo?*	*amo?*
who is this?	*erie tie?*	*té gie?*	*amo na?*
what is his name?	*ka munikerie?*	*iána ta nē tie?*	*saien amo?*
where?	*tam?*	*jē tie?*	*aua?*
where to?	*ngamriem?*	*mangeili?*	*ta noa?*
where from?	*tam?*	*ngeitie?*	*tōa?*
why?	*kaman?*	*to mer?*	*moho?*
how many?	*la nēr?*	*tia pīe?*	*ko ne vai?*
good	*ia*	*pe*	*mēpka*
bad	*la ia*	*soail*	*mēblik*
big	*laut*	*vúlo*	*mēpur*
to live	*ktal*	*mat*	*mēmar*
to die	*iur*	*mait*	*mer*
to sit	*orsang*	*tar*	*ndun*
to sleep	*ōnit*	*kenda*	*lēr*
to go	*ngoi*	*la*	*pu*

Table 26

	northern Gazelle Peninsula	Nakanai
brother	*turana*	*tuana*
casuarine	*a iára*	*a iala*
pig	*a borói*	*a bolo*
to smoke	*pítmur*	*pitimúlu*
wooden drum	*a gáramut*	*a galamu*
dead person	*a vírua*	*a vilúlua*

Table 27

	northern Gazelle Peninsula	Nakanai
dead	*mat*	*mate*
woman	*vavina*	*tavine*
fire	*iap (iavi)*	*oāvi*
son	*natuna*	*natuna*
youth	*natnatina*	*natatuna*
to weep	*tangi*	*tangi*
come here!	*mai!*	*maivele!*
hair	*īvuna*	*īvuna*
ear	*taligana*	*taligana*
eye	*matāna*	*matāna*
mother	*nāna*	*tināna*
pig	*boroi*	*bolo*
fruit	*vuaina*	*vuana*
sea	*ta (tas)*	*das*, etc.

A is the definite and indefinite article for all genders. On the other hand, a special personal article does not appear to exist, except in names that they have adopted from their friends on the Gazelle Peninsula.

Corresponding here to the possessive genitive with *kai*, is one with *manei*; for example, *a māvo manei Saēka*, 'the taro of Sāeka'.

Also, a genitive with *na* exists, with the same meaning as on the north coast, like *a vua na obu*, 'the fruit of the tree'; *a malala na obu*, 'the blossom of the tree'.

Besides the singular, the personal pronoun has the triple plural, and in the dual, triple and plural it has inclusive and exclusive forms as well, as the scheme shows:

eau, I	*aetau*, we two (inclus.)	*aetaolu*, we three (inclus.)
o, you	*amilu*, we two (exclus.)	*amiteu*, we three (exclus.)
i he	*amulu*, they two	*mumataina*, they three
	sulue, the two	*isou*, the three
	sauluvèn, we (inclus.)	
	amito, we (exclus.)	
	nunu, you	
	sou, they	

Correspondingly, the suffix possessive pronoun is common here, just as on the Gazelle Peninsula:

susungu, my wife
susum, your wife
susuna, his wife
a dalangu, my blood
a dalam, your blood
a dalana, his blood

natungu, my child
natum, your child
natuna, his child
a mangalingi, my stomach
a u'ungu, my finger
a ingu, my hair
a lamingu, my back
a inangu, my body

Counting is based on the 10 system.

1	*tassa*	6	*pantassa*
2	*lua*	7	*badilua*
3	*tolu*	8	*baditolu*
4	*iva*	9	*alasue*
5	*lima*	10	*savulu*

11 *savulu timana tassa*
12 *savulu timana lua*
13 *savulu timana tolu*, etc.
20 *savulu lua*
21 *savulu lua timana tassa*, etc.
30 *savulu tolu*
100 *savulu savulu*

In conjugation of the verb, three tenses are differentiated: present, past and future.

Present	Past
eau ini, I am drinking	*eau ini osi*, I have drunk
o ini, you are drinking	*o ini osi*, you have drunk
i ini, he, she, it is drinking	*i ini osi*, he has drunk

Future
ina ini, I shall drink
na ini, he will drink

The imperative in the singular coincides with the simple infinitive form of the verb. I do not have examples of the dual, triple and plural forms.

Negation is achieved by placing *boa*, or *saboa*, in front of the verb.

It seems that here too, as on the Gazelle Peninsula, verbs can be doubled, but, here, doubling does not occur so frequently.

Also, the prefix *va* is the causative prefix in front of verbs here; for example, *davut*, 'to ache', *vadavutisi*, 'to cause pain'.

The prefix *ma* serves to form the reciprocal, like *lobe*, 'to insult'; *mailobe*, 'to insult one another'; *maubi* or *masi*, to fight with one another'.

The entire passive voice, with the exception of a few perfect participles, seems also to be missing here, and to be replaced by circumlocution with the active form.

It is unfortunately not possible for me to go into greater detail about the verb, nor to be able to establish general rules on the other types of word, due to the small number of notes that I was able to make during a trip.

With the numerous adverbs, it was surprising to me that the same word, *alisa*, was used for 'the day before yesterday' and 'the day after tomorrow', while 'yesterday' and 'tomorrow' (*alavi* and *savulo*) are precisely differentiated.

In adverbs of place I feel able to conclude, at least after a few examples like *tana*, 'there', 'yonder'; *utano*, 'outwards'; *usala*, 'above'; *umasala*, 'upwards', that there is differentiation by use of separate forms and also between rest and movement, as on the Gazelle Peninsula.

For language comparison we add a small group from the Nakanai vocabulary and follow this with several examples for characterisation of euphony as well as sentence construction. In pronunciation it must be pointed out that the 's' is always pronounced like 'ss'.

the man, *a bibi*	to fetch, *ala*
the house, *a luma*	to give birth, *susuási*
the coconut, *a niu*	to give birth, *alaia*
the sun, *oasu*	to swim, *soavutu*
the moon, *a gama*	to fall, *bosa*
the rain, *a davo*	to wake up, *mailutu*
the wind, *a vivíli*	to straighten, *salipili*
the ashes, *a pipísa*	to ask, *suale*
the flesh, *a osovīni*	to fear, *lae*
the image, *a bōka*	to kill, *guāle*
shadows (spirit), *a lagalāna*	to serve, *osovīni bellapósa*
the village, *a ūbu*	to fast, *maniōto*
the spear, *a gāta*	to see, *ite*
decorated spear, *a*	to anger, *abutu*
the pearl, *a masilai*	to go, *polo*
the object, *a góulu*	to laugh, *poli* or *palipōli*
the slave, *a sousani*	
the stranger, *a sovasīla*	to know, *sa'āvi* or *saviusi*
the dog, *a būse*	
poor devil, *a livisea*	to remain, *patimōni*
the shark, *a pōio*	to stay, *patimōni*
the turtle, *a bōnu*	to buy, *ōli*
the lime, *a oāvu*	always, *asuosi*, or *tukasi*
good, *milimili*	now, *seideitunka*
beautiful, *kuba*	in the evening, *panga lavilāvi*
bad, *lumu*	
heavy, *māva*	by day, *panga malāta*
light, *malamāla*	by night, *panga lodos*
small, *kamumua*	in the afternoons, *panga tanaósi*
true, *seitōlo*	
full up, *masuluōsi*	quickly, *tototo*
weary, *balis*	why? *ili*?
red, *tasoso*	what? *sava*?

Plate 50 Masked men from Lihir

no, *ue*
so, *vate*
and, *e*
to speak, *voilei*
to sit, *ungu*
to stand up, *lisi*

yes, *maili*
with, *a*
oh woe! *uina!*
cry of astonishment, *homo!*

Esina savallo? What is your name?
Vatelli? What is your name?
O poli ili? Why are you laughing?
A obu a lili i totola. The plank is hard.
A mangalingi i davut. My body aches.

Goulu mineo kubana. Your object is beautiful.
Mu pidi a vivili divi. Sing, to bring the wind.
Saboa pulu. It is still not ready.
Bili Saeka a mavo. Give Saeka a taro.
O lae siva? What, are you frightened?
Soro bainini, mumaivéle. Boys, come here!
O ma lei lae lou! Don't be afraid!
O mamu tabosa! Thou shalt not kill!
O mamu malolo osi! Thou shalt not commit adultery!
O mamu pa'a li! Thou shalt not steal!
O mamu manasi! Thou shalt not bear false witness!

XI Cultigens and Useful Plants, Domesticated and Hunted Animals

The natives of the Bismarck Archipelago and the German Solomon Islands are certainly not exclusively vegetarian, yet the plant kingdom provides them with the greater part of their nutritional needs, and since they have a particular name for each plant, they obviously make the most extensive use of the products of the plant kingdom.

They put the Europeans to shame by their knowledge of plants. They can, with the greatest confidence, name several hundred plant species, and distinguish numerous varieties. Thus the inhabitants of the north-eastern Gazelle Peninsula, for example, know over seventy various species of banana, although the distinguishing characteristics are so subtle that even an experienced botanist would have to be very attentive before he would be able to recognise them.

It is true that many of the products of the plant kingdom virtually grow into the mouths of the natives. However, as a rule, he must also, like everywhere else in the world, obtain his daily bread by the sweat of his brow, although a benevolent nature takes care that his exertions in this direction are extremely tolerable. Many of the principal food plants require regular cultivation and careful tending, which the gardener carries out almost continuously, from setting out his plot right until harvest, while other plants yield an abundant harvest from year to year without special exertion.

The following can be designated as the main food sources: taro and yam tubers, *batatas* or sweet potatoes, bananas and breadfruit, as well as coconuts where they exist, and numerous other fruits, root crops, and vegetables as well.

Taro and yam require careful preparation of the soil. In the forest regions the undergrowth and medium-sized trees are felled and burned; very large forest giants are burned round their trunks, so that they lose their foliage and cast only small shadows; then the ground is cleared and all weeds and roots, and so on, are removed and burned on the spot. If the ground is stony, the stones are removed and piled up at the edge of the plot. In grasslands, the soil is deeply dug so that the grass roots can be removed. Where white settlers are established, the native today often uses iron spades where earlier a stick was used exclusively. This was about 2 metres long, 6 to 8 centimetres wide, somewhat tapered at one end and usually carved from the outer hard wood of a species of palm. In using it, with the tapered end they dig a number of deep holes around the clod to be removed, then finally dig the stick in deeply, and use this lever to break the clod completely free and turn it over. To lighten the work they often choose the side of a hill as the garden site, and begin breaking up the soil from below; repeated cultivation of such surfaces finally creates a vertical wall 2 metres tall, often more, at the upper edge. When the plot is broken up, individual clods are smashed, grass roots are gathered and flung far behind them. These then dry in the sun before being gathered up and burned.

Very rarely does the native plant the same crop in his plot for two or more consecutive years. One crop is the rule; the plot is then abandoned or another type of food crop is planted – one requiring less work and using up the soil to a lesser degree: for the most part bananas. Banana trees frequently bear throughout the year, especially when the plot is weeded from time to time. In the end the *alang-alang* grass overgrows the bananas, and the garden becomes grassland once more. The abandoned gardens lie fallow for years, until their fertility is called upon again.

Such a system of agriculture obviously requires extensive stretches of land to provide a relatively small population with food, but for the present there is no lack of ground and soil, besides which the native thinks nothing of it, if his garden is often 5 to 10 kilometres from his village. In such a case he builds a hut in his garden to provide him with shelter while working there.

In establishing their plots, caring for the cultivated plants and weeding the soil, the natives can certainly set an example to more advanced peoples.

Taro (*Colocasia antiquorum*, var. *esculenta*) occurs in two varieties, swamp and mountain taro, or more accurately taro that requires swampy or very damp soil in order to thrive, and taro that grows in less damp soil, on slopes and high plateaux. The strains are very numerous on the various islands. On the low coral islands the taro plant grows poorly, and it requires laboriously established plant nurseries, set deeply into the coral soil with an artificially produced humus layer in order to grow the desired tubers (see page 235).

The taro seedlings consist of the thin upper segments of the tubers or central stick with the adhering leaf stalks. These are placed in small holes 20 centimetres deep and about 50 to 75 centimetres apart. Making plant holes requires skill and practice; they use a sharpened planting stick, about a metre long. It is pushed into the ground and moved in all directions in a circle, partly to enlarge the hole upwards, and partly to compact the soil of the side walls. The seedlings are then gently pressed firmly into the bottom of the conical holes, which are not filled in but left open. During the first two months of growth, any earth or other rubbish that has fallen into the hole is removed from time to time. After about three months, all the leaf shoots, except one or two central ones, are broken off and from then on the plant requires no further care than weeding the garden and possibly a light breaking up of the soil.

After six or seven months the taro tubers are fully grown and can be harvested. With careful tending in good soil individual tubers can weigh 5 to 6 kilograms.

Planting season varies. In parts of the Gazelle Peninsula where the soil is inferior and where there are alternating periods of pronounced low rainfall and high rainfall, planting is carried out at the onset of the wet season. On Bougainville and on New Ireland where rainfall is fairly evenly spread throughout the year, and the soil is not so porous, planting is year-round.

Taro tubers have a significant nutritional value and stand above all other vegetables. An analysis of dry sections of taro from New Britain, reported in Volume II of *Tropenpflanzer*, yielded the following composition:

water	11.59 per cent
ash	2.33 per cent
fat	0.28 per cent
starch	56.988 per cent
nitrogenous material	2.85 per cent

Furthermore, both the tubers and the leaves of the taro plant have poisonous properties, which only disappear on roasting or boiling. The tubers are roasted over hot coals or baked between glowing stones; in areas where cooking pots are used – for example, on the Solomon and Admiralty islands – sliced tubers are also cooked in water. Grated or crushed taro tubers mixed with grated coconut are shaped into cakes, wrapped in leaves and baked between hot stones. Taro tubers are tasty and Europeans easily get used to them; in many areas taro totally replace potatoes.

Related to the taro plants are several species of *Alocasia* which are found growing wild everywhere. They are perennial plants whose leaves are frequently over a metre long and often having a central stem weighing 25 kilograms. However, because of its bitter taste and woody fibres, it is used only in times of necessity. On the low coral islands, like Nukumanu, Tauu and Nuguria, the varieties of *Alocasia* are cultivated to a greater extent, because they prefer poorer soil.

Yams (*Dioscorea*), like taro, require careful working of the soil, but do not tolerate very damp or swampy soil. Yam tubers take second place after taro as a food source, but are neither cultivated so much nor so widely enjoyed, probably because their nutritional value is low. The yam plant, of which there are as many cultivated varieties as wild species and varieties on all the higher islands, is a vine requiring a stick for support. A section of tuber with one or more eyes is placed in a hole in the dug-over soil, and the earth is heaped over it a little. Better results are obtained when the ground is deeply dug over, the earth heaped up and the seed tubers placed in the loose top of the heap. With good soil, and using the latter method, tubers weighing 30 kilograms are obtainable. The yam tubers are ripe after about six months, recognisable from the tops dying off. Yam tubers have an advantage over taro in that they can be stored for several months after harvest, whereas taro rots five to six days after harvest. Preparation for eating is the same as I have described for the taro tubers.

The numerous wild species of *Dioscorea* are eaten only when crops have failed; however, there are also wild species that are not unpalatable to the European taste and are often preferred to the cultivated species.

A tuber that in places is cultivated fairly widely, for example, in the north of New Ireland, is the *batata* or sweet potato (*Convolvulus batatas*). It is cultivated like the yam and prefers a leaner soil. A variety with white tubers and one with red tubers are most often encountered. For propagation it is sufficient to stick several twigs of the green top into the soil. The *batata* has little food value, and has a sweetish taste appealing to few Europeans.

Years ago the cassava or tapioca plant, *Jatropha manihot*, was introduced to the Gazelle Peninsula by settlers, and spread rapidly. Now fairly large gardens of it are found almost everywhere, and the floury tubers, roasted over charcoal are a popular food. That the plant has spread so quickly, is because it requires very little care, can be propagated in the simplest way by cutting off a stalk, and because with its thick foliage it covers the soil to such an extent that weeds do not become a problem.

Another food plant of great importance is the banana. It is found both in shore regions and on high mountains, in both rich and poorer soil, and, at any time of the year, in the banana plantations, giant bundles of fruit can be found in all stages of development. Cultivation is simple: a sucker is broken off the main root so that part of the root remains attached, and the rootlet is planted in a chosen spot. In the first four to six months, a banana plantation is occasionally weeded; after this the tree has developed so many leaves that the ground is shaded and weeds cannot grow so quickly. For about five to six years a plantation looks after itself with little care, and yields a large quantity of fruit during this time. The growing stem bears only once; after harvest of the bundle of fruit the subsequently barren stem is cut down, to avoid its hindering development of the sucker. In order to obtain large bundles of fruit, most of the suckers are destroyed while juvenile, and only two or three are allowed to grow. If the young shoots are not destroyed, then after two or three years in good soil a banana tree slowly forms a circle 3 to 4 metres in diameter, stem crammed against stem, but only bearing small bundles of fruit. Varieties are extremely numerous: I have already mentioned how many there are on the Gazelle Peninsula, the same goes for other islands. In several varieties the bundles of fruit reach an astonishing size; bundles of 60 kilograms are not infrequent in fertile soil. The ripe fruit of the individual varieties differ significantly from one another in form, size, taste and aroma. Bananas are eaten either in a fully ripened state, when they contain a lot of sugar, or they are roasted or boiled, and then contain more starch; the natives prefer the bananas in the latter form, because of their greater nutritional value.

The tree stem produces an excellent long, strong fibre, collected in many places for making strong cords and rope.

The leaves have many uses as well: a roof can rapidly be made from them for protection against rain or sunburn; they provide wrapping for food baked between stones; head coverings and loincloths are easily made from them, and they take the place of plates and bowls for serving food.

The coconut palm requires less care than the cultivation of the abovementioned food plants. The use of this very important tree has become almost proverbial among the South Sea islanders. However, there are many inhabitants of the Bismarck Archipelago and Solomon Islands who exist without coconuts, for the coconut palm thrives only on the shore regions and as far inland as the salt-laden onshore breeze is effective. Thus the inland inhabitants have no coconut palms. However, there are extensively inhabited stretches of shore where, in spite of quite a dense population, there are only small stands of coconut. As modest as the palm may be in terms of its needs, nevertheless in order to thrive its main requirements are air and light, particularly in the juvenile stage. Wherever the natives are too lazy to plant coconuts in abandoned taro or yam gardens, only small stands exist.

People often attempt to explain the wide dispersal of the coconut palm by the ripe nut falling into the sea, as may well happen occasionally, and, surrounded in a light fibrous material, floating on the water and being carried by currents from one island to another. The untenability of this theory becomes immediately clear to anyone who has travelled among the many islands populated by coconut palms. I cannot recall, in the course of my numerous voyages from one South Sea island to another (journeys that covered many thousands of miles) one single instance of a coconut ever coming into view carried on the sea, although, on reflection, this is not outside the realms of possibility, and nuts that have fallen into the water could reach other islands if the distance were only small. Sea captains who, over many years, have traversed these regions in all directions, do not remember any such instances either, even though their eyes scanned the surface of the sea from morning until late, and were used to detecting even the smallest object. Besides, there are many hundreds of miles of flat stretches of shore that are completely bereft of coconut palms, and it is not evident why coconuts, carried by the sea, should have avoided these stretches from time immemorial, to be cast ashore somewhere else in great numbers, when the current throws everything else ashore in these places. Again, there are islands which in their hilly, and in places mountainous, centre have good stands of coconut, but not a single palm on the beach. If one undertakes an investigation on the flotation ability of ripe coconuts, one finds that after a few days the fibrous covering has soaked up sea water like a sponge, so that the nut settles deeper, gradually losing all ability to float, and sinks to the bottom of the sea. Where coconut palms exist, they were probably always planted by human hand; and even where, today, uninhabited islands are found with large stands of coconuts, this is only an indication that the island was once inhabited, and became divested of humans for whatever reason. The legends of many islanders allude directly to the coconut being introduced by people who were, with the passing of time, venerated by those coming after as gods and legendary beings.

The great significance of the coconut palm for the natives lies in it, more than any other cultivated plant of the South Sea islands, being the basis for export trade, and thereby a foundation for development of the natives. It offers them the means, by way of the trade route, of satisfying those needs that constantly progressing culture tells them about and allows them to absorb.

It seems almost superfluous to report extensively on the uses of the coconut palm: accordingly it can be done in all brevity. The unripe nut yields 0.5 to 1 litre of a clear fluid, known as coconut milk, although it bears no resemblance to milk. This liquid makes a pleasant refreshing drink. The milk of the mature nut is less tasty. The frail gelatinous kernel of the unripe nut is a favourite delicacy everywhere. The hard ripe kernel serves as a foodstuff when fresh, or as an ingredient to dishes, in which case it is as a rule first grated. Cut up and dried, the coconut kernels form the export product copra, until now the principal export of the colony. The growing nut fills on the inside with a spongy white substance that is regarded by young and old as a delicacy. All natives know how to prepare the oil, although this is not customary everywhere; great quantities of oil are prepared in the Admiralty Islands and stored in huge containers to serve as a food additive when required. The hard nut shells are used as water, oil, and lime containers. Pieces of shell serve as drinking vessels, scrapers, spoons and armrings; on the Tasman Islands they make small discs, 6 to 7 millimetres in diameter, out of the shell, bore them through the middle and thread them on strings, alternating with white seashell discs. These serve as money.

The fibrous outer shell of the nut is separated from the woody part by hitting with a wooden maul. The fibre obtained is used for making yarn and cordage. Thousands of tons of this material are lost every year because the natives are too lazy to collect it. Pieces of the fibrous shell are used as paint brushes, and, with this primitive instrument, the native paints his carvings, masks, god images, house gables, and so on, with the finest decoration. On long journeys by land and sea the dried shell serves as tinder.

Baskets are woven from the leaves, and mats for various purposes. Almost everywhere that coconuts are grown, coconut palm leaves woven together serve as a roofing material; from the fine leaf ribs they make brooms, fish-traps and other kinds of trap. When night-fishing on the coral reef, dried leaves tied together serve as torches, whose glow attracts the fish. Immature centre leaves make a splendid vegetable, similar to cauliflower.

The wood of the coconut palm is very long-lasting, especially when it is kept away from dampness. It is used as posts and lathes in building, or as raw material for making clubs and spears.

In many districts, the flower cases are wrapped firmly and cut off before the flowers have developed; from the wound flows a sweet sap that is uncommonly nutritious, and on which suckling infants can be raised. After a short time this sap ferments, and becomes an intoxicating drink.

Of no small importance to the inhabitants of the various islands is the breadfruit tree (*Artocarpus*): twice a year it yields a great number of fruit whose flesh, roasted like seed kernels on a charcoal fire, provides a tasty meal. The breadfruit tree grows in a semi-wild state, and in places forms large stands whose shiny dark-green foliage gives an unique character to the vegetation. The trees grow as much as 20 metres high with a trunk up to 1 metre in diameter. The almost horizontal branches form a giant conical crown. The number of varieties is considerable, and the size of the fruit ranges from 2 to 4 kilograms. The shape of the fruit varies from spherical to a lengthy ellipse. In the Bismarck Archipelago and in the Solomon Islands are only the varieties with numerous seed grains the size of a chestnut imbedded in the flesh of the fruit.

The wood is soft, light and pale brown, and is used occasionally for canoe building. Cuts in the bark give a rich, milky-white sticky sap, which hardens rapidly and is used for caulking containers and canoes.

The cultivated plants previously mentioned provide the principal food resources of the natives. Besides these, however, the forest offers a great number of fruits of all kinds, with which the natives are familiar, and which form a supplement and give variety to the daily diet. Thus *Inocarpus edulis* provides numerous fruits that resemble our chestnuts when roasted. *Terminalia catappa* and species of *Canarium* provide nut kernels with a splendid flavour. *Spondias dulcis*, *Pometia pinnata*, *Carica papaya*, *Eugenia malaccensis*, various species of pandanus, and indigenous forms of mango provide juicy, tasty fruit that are not spurned by habituated whites either.

The sago palm also is of great importance in several places; for example, in the north of New Ireland and the west of New Britain. On Buka and Bougainville they obtain a flour very similar to sago from the pulp of the *Cycas* stem.

Several excellent varieties of sugar cane are found in almost all the natives' gardens as auxiliary produce, and likewise various plants whose leaves are prepared as vegetables, and appear also on the settlers' tables as spinach.

The shore-dwellers eat various species of seaweed, both raw and cooked.

Overall, there is no fruit that would not be more or less edible to a hungry native.

On all the islands apart from several low coral islands, they eat various varieties of the nut of the *Areca* palm as a stimulant, and in this connection they also eat the fruit and leaves of *Piper betle* together with unburned coral lime. Tobacco appears to have been known for a very long time by the natives of several places – for example, Buka – where they grow and process the special, not very fragrant, plant.

Native cooking is therefore richly garnished with vegetables, more so than the table of a European without means; and even when one or other crop occasionally fails, there are always sufficient others to prevent real deficiency. Thus, from these regions I do not know of a single case of starvation, or even the remotest resemblance of one. In comparison with the inhabitants of many other tropical lands – for example, India – the inhabitants of the Bismarck Archipelago and the Solomon Islands are in this respect to be envied.

Besides the indigenous products of the plant kingdom, each year more and more individually introduced plants are being established. Maize and watermelons, which I introduced to the Gazelle Peninsula in 1882, spread rapidly, also pumpkin, pineapples and, as already mentioned, tapioca. Orchard trees, which bear fruit only after long years, do not so easily find entry. The natives want to see a result of their industry as soon as possible, and do not readily comprehend cultivating a plant that only yields a visible benefit years later. It is, therefore, also difficult to convince them to plant out coconut palms, although they have been familiar with their nuts for a long time.

To satisfy their other needs, the plant kingdom provides the natives with a veritable wealth of products, which the native exploits in only a small measure, and which, with enough energy and labour, would be capable of making him prosperous, whereas usually he lives from hand to mouth.

Numerous trees provide wood for both canoe and house construction, and experience has taught selection of those woods best suited to the intended purpose. The tough, broad leaves of the different species of pandanus provide long-lasting roofing material, and from the leaf ribs they weave big and small mats, baskets and pouches. Crushed nuts of *Parinarium laurinum* serve as putty for caulking canoes, as a plastic material for reproducing faces on many masks, as an outer coat on dense matting to make it impermeable, and as a storage vessel for liquids, as, for example, the oil jugs in the Admiralty Islands.

Not only the coconut and the banana tree provide fibre; the natives know a number of fibre-producing plants besides these. Thus, on the Gazelle Peninsula, from the fibres of *Pueraria novo-guineensis* they produce the fine twine for making fishing nets. This fibre is not inferior to our best flax, yet it cannot be exported because the natives cannot be persuaded to produce sufficient quantities, although there is an abundance of this material. Several species of hibiscus likewise deliver an excellent fibre. Species of rattan, which make penetration into the forest so exceptionally difficult that they have been called 'bush lawyers' by the whites, are twisted together in threes or fours, according to length, to serve as anchor chain often up to 400 metres long; narrow strips of the outer hard bark serve as binding material.

There is an over-abundance of bright flowers, brightly coloured leaves and fragrant plants on all the islands, and the inhabitants use them most extensively as body decoration, and for decoration of their canoes, huts and ceremonial sites. They ensure that sufficient stock is always available, and plant red-flowered species of hibiscus, fragrant gardenias and bright-leaved crotons around their huts and villages. Their fields and gardens not uncommonly resemble a flower garden, for among the taro and yam plants they grow purple-leaved and multi-striped species of *Dracaena*, shining yellow and red coleus and numerous fragrant plants.

The native also obtains dyestuffs from the plant kingdom. Turmeric roots provide a yellow dye; soot and charcoal mixed with oil give a deep black. On Bougainville, various fibrous materials are dyed shiny red.

Plate 51 *Matasesén* from northern Bougainville

The list of useful plants would be incomplete if the various species of bamboo were not mentioned. They provide the material for building houses and huts; laid side by side and secured by cross-pieces, they make an excellent raft on which the natives often go for miles out to sea; across rivers and ravines they build light and safe suspension bridges and gangways; long and short pieces find use in carrying water; huts and gardens are surrounded by strong bamboo fences for protection; on New Hanover and northern New Ireland they make spear shafts from them; also, splendidly carved hair combs and boxes decorated with artistic branding for storing lime powder, are made from bamboo; the knowledge of making musical instruments from it is demonstrated by the large and small pan pipes of the Buka people and the splendid flutes of the Gazelle Peninsula, but in addition large and small pieces of cane serve as primitive drums; metre-long lathes of bamboo, bent over in the middle, serve as fire tongs; narrow strips of the hard outer layer provide knives with razor-sharp cutting edges, that I saw, for example, on Bougainville, being used for shaving; large and small fish-traps are made from thin, split strips of cane. In short, the native might often be quite helpless if he had no bamboo cane.

Ever since the Solomon Islands developed trade, a local species of palm, the ivory nut palm, *Coelococcus solomonensis, Warb.*, became of great importance because the hard ivory-like nut became a trading article. The palm prefers to grow in swampy ground; after a certain number of years a huge flower stalk rises out of the middle of the crown, and the numerous fruits come from this flower. After the fruit has ripened, the whole tree dies.

It must also be mentioned that the healing properties of many products of the plant kingdom are not unknown to the natives. Flowers, fruits, leaves, bark and roots of various plants are used by the indigenous medical specialists, and many of them fulfil their purpose. However, the injurious properties of many plants and parts of plants are also known, as are the effects of the various plant toxins. Many of the medicines and poisons, though, are merely magic potions, which have neither beneficial nor deleterious effects, but whose magical powers are regarded by the native as beyond all doubt.

Members of the animal kingdom find far less use. The number of mammals is small, and, apart from rats and mice, anything that runs on four legs provides a desired roast. The universally indigenous pig, existing both in the domesticated and the wild state, is never missing from any feast, even though in the Duke of York Islands and on part of the Gazelle Peninsula eating pork is forbidden to many men who belong to the *ingiet* society. There, the same prohibition covers turtles and sharks as well. The lower jaws of pigs that have been eaten, often intermingled with the lower jaws of men that have been eaten, are stored in the huts as souvenirs of great feasts.

Small bunches of bristles serve as an ornament, as do the big, abnormally curved, often ring-formed tusks that are held in high regard and are artistically displayed.

The flesh of man's real companion, the dog, is regarded everywhere as a delicacy, and its canine teeth replace our token coins in many places or are made into ornamental items. However, the dog is also trained to hunt pigs and marsupials.

The various species of marsupial, as well as the flying fox, are likewise not to be despised as a food source.

Of the reptiles, the turtle is the most coveted. The succulent flesh and the eggs are highly valued everywhere, as is the turtle shell, from which ornaments and jewellery, fishhooks, scrapers and spoons are made. Snakes are said to be eaten in a few areas; but this is probably the exception, for as a rule the natives are afraid of snakes, just as Europeans are. The same goes for species of lizard; in the archipelago the skin of the monitor is used as a drum skin for the familiar hourglass-shaped wooden drums.

The bird kingdom provides no great contribution to cooking, yet cannot go unmentioned. The domestic fowl is naturalised everywhere; both flesh and eggs are favourite foods. Of the wild birds, on New Britain the cassowary stands out; its flesh is very tasty. The bird's upper thigh bone is used for decorating spears; the spear points are armed by the sharp claws. Generally, the native eats any bird that falls into his hands. Bright bird feathers, especially parrot, rooster tail feathers, cassowary feathers and down, are put on as body decoration, headdresses, necklaces, and so on, and at festivities they are not lacking as effective ornamentation of many weapons, canoes, dance objects and the ceremonial site.

The sea offers wealthy treasures that do not go unnoticed. Numerous fish from the largest to the smallest serve to quell hunger, and experience has taught them to avoid those that have poisonous properties. Shellfish and snails as well as various molluscs are also eaten; however, the Melanesian is far more selective than the Polynesian, to whom everything in the sea appears to be a delicacy. Therein lies a significant difference, in that the Melanesian eats all seafood only when cooked, while on the other hand the Polynesian often eats them raw. Shellfish and snail shells in the natural and processed state provide material for all kinds of jewellery: they are used as coin tokens, and sharp axe blades are made from them. A round hole is bored through the side of the triton shell, which then serves as a far-sounding trumpet.

The insect kingdom is exploited to a small degree. Several species of grasshopper, cicadas and chafer beetle larvae are not rejected, and the head louse is universally regarded as a delicacy. These are collected reciprocally in a neighbourly fashion during leisure hours.

The reef-dweller known in *Samoa* as the *palolo* worm is also found in the Bismarck Archipelago. It is hunted here too; however, it is not regarded as such an extraordinary delicacy as it is in Samoa.

The mineral kingdom is less productive. As far as is known, metals occur exceptionally here and there, but the natives do not know how to mine them nor work them.

On the Solomon Islands and in the Admiralty group all kinds of pottery are made from clay. The Baining make bored-through clubheads out of hard basalt rock, while axe blades are made from similar material on all the islands. On Buka, heavy stone pestles are used for crushing hard nut kernels. Sharp slivers of obsidian are used for spear tips and dagger blades by the Admiralty Islanders. On New Britain and southern New Ireland they use egg-shaped sling-stones found in river beds and on the beach. Drill bits are made from hard slivers of quartz or obsidian in the Duke of York Islands. For the healer, larger sharp slivers replace the scalpel used by his European colleagues; such pieces also occupy the place of our razor blades, although today the civilised lager beer bottle has replaced the original material. Before the introduction of iron tools, the carvers made use of sharp slivers of obsidian, by the aid of which they produced finer objects than with the modern iron tools.

Everywhere that betel chewing is performed, burned powdered lime is used together with the *Areca* nut and betel pepper. The native paints his canoe inside and out with lime, and whitewashes his house with it on the Matty Islands. Lime slurry is rubbed into the hair and beard, partly to keep out vermin but rather more to make the hair paler. For dances, ceremonials and war expeditions the native paints his body with fantastic stripes, dots and circles, using either lime or burnt red ochre; for staining the teeth black they use types of earth containing manganese, which is a traded commodity because it does not occur everywhere. On southern New Ireland large and small ancestral figures in human form are made from a local chalk.

Salt is harvested in isolated places by evaporation (for example, at the south cape of New Britain); however, as a rule the native uses sea water as a condiment for his food.

XII History of Discovery

Knowledge of the initial discovery of the Bismarck Archipelago by whites is wrapped in mysterious darkness for us.

The voyages that were undertaken on the Pacific Ocean shortly after the beginning of the 16th century were most probably not the first of this kind. Even before the birth of Christ, Babylonians and Shebans were trading with Lanka (Ceylon), and from there they ventured as far as the Malayan island world and China. In the north-west of Shantung, in Shansi, Shensi and in Honan, according to Chinese translations, the foreigners had permanent trading settlements. They came in ships in the shape of animals, with two large eyes at the bow. They introduced the Babylonian monetary system, weights and measures, all kinds of sorcery and astrology, the twelve signs of the zodiac, and more of the same, into China. About 140 BC the first traders from Tarsus came to China via Alexandria and Eilat at the northern tip of the Red Sea.

At that time, sea voyages went south from Sumatra and Java, past Timor. It is therefore not improbable that many of the intrepid seafarers in their unsuitably constructed vessels and without present-day nautical aids, lost their way, and were washed up in regions that lay beyond the borders of the then-known world. The large island of New Guinea and the Bismarck Archipelago further to the east were most probably familiar to them, and likewise the coasts of western and northern Australia, although we have no reliable reports. One day, perhaps, it may be possible to draw conclusions on prehistoric immigrations from the collected sagas of the islanders. Many of the characteristic traditions and customs of the present inhabitants might be remnants of an early culture, transplanted into new ground by the original discoverers.

Migrations of people in Europe and Asia destroyed, among other things, trade and communication with the far east. The few accounts that had been brought back by intrepid travellers, bearing the stamp of the miraculous and fabulous, gained attention only in limited circles. The real knowledge of the seafarers and geographers of Greece, Rome and China has never been revealed to us, although classical authors give hints here and there which indicate at least that, many centuries ago, the human mind was already involved with these far-distant regions, whether as a consequence of imaginative speculations or the outcome of universally acknowledged facts.

After Vasco da Gama had rounded the Cape of Good Hope in 1497 the door was reopened to maritime discoveries. The courageous, far-sighted seamen of Spain and Portugal, and their successors the Dutch, French and English, whether it be the quest for glory, or for gold and treasure, proceeded to search for distant lands, and luck, accident or calculation must in time have brought to light what was previously hidden.

By 1511, the Portuguese Francisco Serrano had discovered the Moluccas. His friend and countryman, Fernando Magelhaens, after Serrano's death, endeavoured to persuade the Portuguese administration to outfit an expedition to take possession of the rich islands. Rebuffed by Portugal, he turned to Spain, which agreed to his proposals. Meanwhile, on 25 September 1513, Vasco Nuñez de Balboa had gazed from the heights of Darien on the immense sea that was later given the name, 'Pacific Ocean'. Magelhaens suspected that, south of the new part of the world discovered by Columbus, a sea passage must lead to the Pacific Ocean, and thereby to the Moluccas. Subsequent events showed that his assumptions were correct. Sailing through the Magelhaens Strait he traversed the Pacific Ocean between 28 November 1520 and 6 March 1521, and it is probable that it was on this voyage that he sighted the high land of 'New Guinea' (that is, the high mountain range on the island of New Ireland), which at that time, and for many years after, was regarded as part of New Guinea.

Alvaro de Saavedra, who, in 1527, sailed from New Spain across the Pacific Ocean to the Moluccas, again discovered what was then called New Guinea, and anchored on the coast for a whole month.

In 1529, after long struggles, the Spanish had relinquished to Portugal their claims on the

Moluccas, and not until 1540 did they resume their voyages from New Spain through the Pacific; this time with a view to settling the Philippines, discovered by Magelhaens. These undertakings, about which only brief accounts are available, encountered great difficulties. From Mexico it was, of course, easy to lay a course to the west, with help from the equatorial current and the east trade wind, whereas the return voyage along the same route, against wind and ocean current, caused numerous adversities. On these voyages the east coast of present-day New Ireland was not only sighted but also visited, because Abel Tasman asserts that on the old Spanish sea charts of that period he had seen the 'Cabo de Santa Maria' and the adjacent coast, the eastern tip of the present New Ireland.

Finally, in 1565 Andres Urdeneta succeeded in finding a route across the Pacific Ocean from west to east at about the 40° North latitude; he took 130 days for the crossing to Acapulco. Thus, the route across the ocean was laid down for seafarers for a long time to come.

The great aim of the Spanish had been achieved. The Moluccas, the Philippines, and the rest of the East Indian Spice Islands could be reached on a route across the Pacific, and linked to the motherland. All the other parts of the ocean not lying on the sea route north of the equator, remained ignored. In actual fact, it appears to have been the policy of the Spanish administration, very early on, to impede all further exploration of the Pacific Ocean. On the American continent, Spain was in possession of an immense empire that was already difficult enough to administer; the gold and silver mines of this empire offered a seemingly never-diminishing source of wealth, and neither greed nor ambition drove them to take possession of new unknown regions. The Portuguese also had attained their goal in the East Asian Spice Islands, and so it came about that although European settlements on the east coast of Asia and the west coast of America rapidly increased – settlements created as departure points for exploring the unknown Pacific Ocean – all the voyages for a long time passed along a definitively prescribed sea route, which was unfavourable for making new discoveries.

The viceroys in New Spain, however, conducted politics in their own right, and not always in accordance with the government in their homeland. They were besieged by adventurers of all ranks, whose ambition and greed had not been satisfied in the New World, and who for their part were pressing on to new undertakings that would lead to the fame and fortune of the participants. For these people the great southern land, the *Terra Australis incognita* designated on all the maps of the time, was the goal of all their efforts. Public opinion populated this unknown land with fabulous beings and immeasurable riches, although nobody could state exactly where this wonderful land was.

The *Terra Australis incognita* of the old cartographers is undoubtedly based on an inaccurate knowledge of present-day Australia, but it was given total reality in consequence of a theory of the learned geographers of that time, according to which, corresponding with the land masses of the northern hemisphere, there had to be an opposing land mass in the southern hemisphere, to maintain equilibrium with the former. In an old 10th-century manuscript by Macrobius there is a map on which the unknown southern land is already depicted. In later centuries it takes on more definite form, and on one map, dated 1536, now in the British Museum, it is called 'Java la Grande'. On all maps from the same century, particularly on the maps of the French, whose geographers played a leading role at that time, we find not only the coasts of western and northern Australia, but also the islands lying to the north. The English and Dutch geographers, on the other hand, tried to connect facts with the theory at the same time.

At the court of the viceroys, the impetus became stronger year by year. The magnificent southern land could, in everyone's opinion, not be too far away, and in 1566 the viceroy of the time, Lope Garcia de Castro, outfitted two ships to find the unknown southern land. Overall command was given to Alvaro Mendaña de Neyra, with Hernando Gallego assigned as navigator. Both ships, *Almirante* and *Capitano*, left Callao on 19 November 1566, and returned to Peru on 19 June 1568. During the voyage, on 1 February 1567, a group of islands was discovered. This was named 'Los Bajos de la Candelaria' (the earlier German Ongtong Java Islands or Lord Howe group). Sailing south from there, on 9 February the two ships anchored off the coast of an island that Mendaña named after his wife, Isabel (previously German, transferred to England a few years ago). Mendaña was thus the discoverer of the Solomon Islands, which he regarded as a part of the southern land. In 1896, the German warship *Möwe* named the cape first sighted by the expedition not far from their first anchorage, Cape Gallego, in honour of the original discoverer.

Fig. 126 Fragment of a map of the western hemisphere, by Th. de Bry (1596)

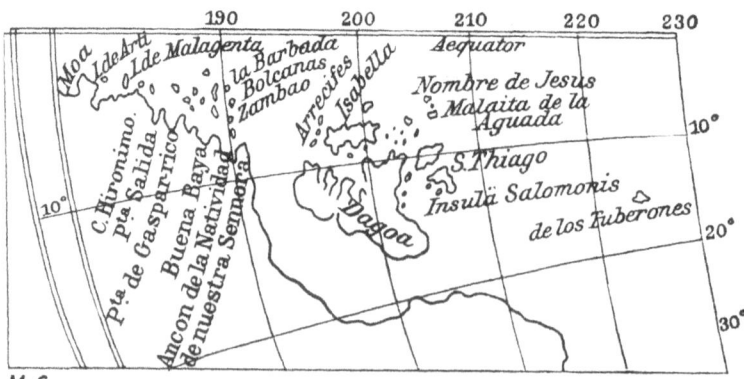

Mendaña was so convinced of the wealth of the land discovered by him that he pushed for a repeat of the expedition; but he achieved this goal only as an old man. However, on this second voyage, in 1595, he was not able to locate his earlier discovery; in the end, he reached the southerly situated Santa Cruz Islands, like his later follower, Pedro Fernandez de Quiros, who discovered the northern New Hebrides. Torres, Quiros's second-in-command, brings us back once more to the neighbourhood of the German South Seas possessions when, after separating from the commander-in-chief, he sailed westwards and discovered the strait between Australia and New Guinea that today bears his name. This significant discovery was kept secret by the Spanish, and only when the English occupied Manila in 1762 was Torres's report found there in the archives. Likewise, Mendaña's first journals were kept secret, and the later reporters, Herrera and Figueroa, gave such an incomplete and inaccurate account that the geographers of the time located the Solomon Islands too far to the east and then too far west, and later seafarers who actually sighted the groups were of the opinion that they had discovered new, hitherto unknown island groups. The French geographers Buache in 1781, and Fleurieu in 1790, established finally that the islands discovered by the English and the French at the end of the 18th century were identical to Mendaña's Solomon Islands.

Mendaña's discoveries have no significance for our German Solomon Islands of Buka and Bougainville

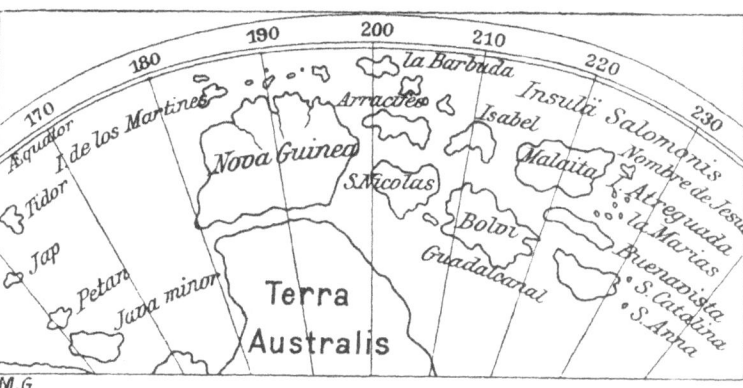

Fig. 127 Part of a map by Witfliet (1597)

– they were discovered about 200 years later. However, I have not been able to avoid the geographers' dispute over Mendaña's discovery because, as we shall see later, it strongly influenced the cartography of the Bismarck Archipelago.

With the beginning of the 17th century we see the power and influence of Spain already on the wane. The Netherlands had shaken off the Spanish yoke, and quickly decided that, if the trading of the hated papists could be hurt, there would be a possibility of winning back the Netherlands's southern provinces. Geography and hydrography were the subject of ongoing research, and, in Peter Plancius's nautical school in Amsterdam, they systematically studied how the Spanish and Portuguese possessions could be usurped. Jan Huyghen van Linschoten, who had spent fourteen years in the Portuguese territories and absorbed a wide knowledge, published

Plate 52 Coconut plantation at Ralum

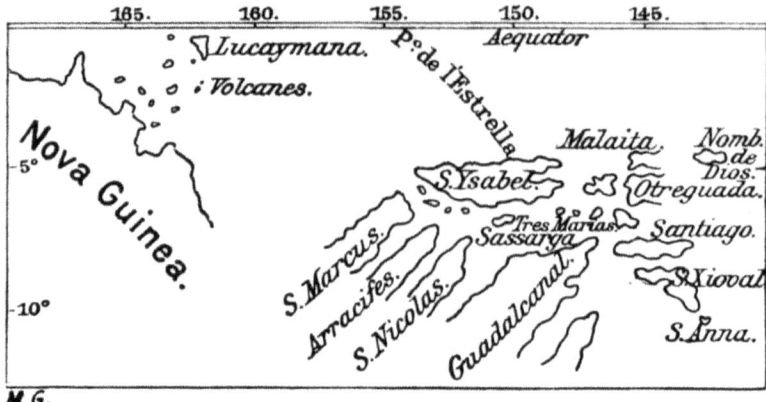

Fig. 128 (top) Part of a map by Herrera (1601)

Fig. 129 (above) Schouten and Le Maire's map

his observations in Amsterdam in 1618, and fired up his countrymen even further with his accounts.

In 1602, the Dutch East India Company had been founded, and its ships were soon sailing to seize the trade with Batavia, Bantam, Amboina, Banda and other places. However, at home opposition soon stirred against the company, which sought to monopolise all commerce, and, out of indignation against the rude allegations, Willem Corneliszoon Schouten and Jacob Le Maire fitted out the ships *De Eendracht* and *Hoorn* in which they embarked on their voyage in 1616.

This voyage by the two Dutchmen is of significance to our South Sea possessions, since after they had rounded Cape Horn and sailed through the

Fig. 130 *De Eendracht*, Schouten and Le Maire's ship. After an old copperplate engraving.

southern tropical zone they sighted low-lying land on 20 June, and sailed close inshore on 21 June. There were three or four small wooded islands with a coral reef stretching to the north-west. Two canoes came alongside, and both Schouten and Le Maire recorded that here, for the first time in the South Seas, they noticed bows and arrows in the hands of the natives. In the evening of the 22nd, they again sighted a number of small low-lying islands, which they named the Marken Islands.

On 24 June they sighted three low-lying islands in the south-west that seemed to be covered in trees; two of them were about 2 miles long, while the third was small. The coasts were steep and without any anchorage. This group was named the 'Groene Islanden' (the Sir Charles Hardy Islands or Nissan on the current charts). Sailing on, they discovered two further islands that we designate today as 'Green Islands' (Pinepil and Esau). Due to the onset of darkness they did not venture closer to these islands.

Meanwhile, west-a-quarter-north-west a high mountainous island had come into view ahead, and during the night they traversed the island-free gap, which according to Le Maire's statements was 15 miles (60 nautical miles). The high island was named 'Sankt Jan' from the calendar saint of that day.

On the morning of the 25th, they sighted very high land. St John was no longer visible, and they sailed towards the high land that conformed to the then-known profile of the north-eastern tip of New Guinea. We know today that the coastline encountered was the current New Ireland, in the vicinity of Cape Santa Maria.

The wind before and after was east-south-east and they were able to sail close inshore along the coast, but did not find an anchorage. The boats launched to pilot them were attacked by canoes of natives with slingshot stones, and the following day, the 26th, the ships were attacked so that firearms had to be used. Ten of the attackers were killed and three captured, while four canoes were seized and destroyed. Two of the prisoners were released on payment of a ransom, consisting of a pig and a bundle of bananas. The journal adds: 'They did not seem to be worth more.' The following day a pig was traded for several iron nails and other trinkets, thereby paving the way for peaceful contact, for on the 28th a beautiful large canoe came alongside with twenty-one natives who marvelled tremendously at the ship. They brought lime and betel, but made no offer to ransom the third prisoner, who was then released.

Only a few years ago, some 250 years later, quite similar events could have been played out on that same coast.

Sailing on, they discovered the offshore islands. However, they did not recognise the insular character of the current New Hanover; they also skirted east of the Admiralty Islands, which they designated as 'Hooch Landt'. Schouten designated the small islands offshore from the eastern end and the southern coast as 'Fünfundzwanzig Inseln', whereas contemporary charts frequently give them as 'Islas de la Magdalena', probably from accounts of earlier Spanish seafarers.

From here the enterprising seafarers directed their course to the coast of New Guinea, and during the subsequent voyage they did not come into contact with any further islands of the archipelago.

We are again indebted to the Dutch for further exploration of the archipelago. In 1642 the then Dutch governor of the East Indian possession, Anton van Diemen, fitted out two ships to look for the unknown southern land.

The expedition vessels consisted of the yacht *Heemskerk*, the flagship, and the *Zeehaen*. The former had a crew of sixty, and the latter fifty, the best seamen that could be recruited at that time in Batavia. Provisioning was reckoned on twelve to eighteen months.

Abel Jansz Tasman was the commander-in-chief; the commander of the *Heemskerk* was the master mariner Yde T'Jercxzoon Holman, or Holleman, from Jever in the present archduchy of Oldenburg. The *Zeehaen* was commanded by Gerrit Janszoon of Leiden, and Isaak Gilsemans, the probable draughtsman of the expedition, was on the same ship, as auxiliary. Aboard the *Heemskerk*, Abraham Coomans acted as Tasman's secretary. These people, together with the two first mates, formed the 'grand council' of the expedition, with Tasman as chairman. The first mate of the *Zeehaen* was Hendrik Pieterson, while on the *Heemskerk*, and with the title of 'pilot-major' it was Franz Jacobszoon Visscher from Vlissingen, a seafarer who had already made numerous important voyages in the service of the company.

Of the crew, the following are known by name: on the *Heemskerk*, Crijn Hendrikszoon de Ratte or de Radde from Middelburg, and Carsten Jurriaenszoon; the gunnery officer, Eldert Luytiens; the head carpenter, Pieter Jakobszoon, and his assistant, Jan Joppen; the quartermaster, Jan Pieterszoon, from Meldorf; and seaman Joris Claesen. On the *Zeehaen* were the second mates, Peter Duijts and Cornelius Roobol; the boatswain, Cornelius Joppen; seamen Pieterszoon from Copenhagen, Jan Tijssen, Tobias Pieterszoon from Delft, Jan Isbrandtszoon, and the ship's boy Gerrit Gerritszoon. The ships' surgeon, Hendrik Haalbos, was probably on the *Heemskerk*.

Although Tasman as an explorer cannot be placed alongside the great Spaniards and the Portuguese of the preceding century, nor the great Englishmen of the following century, he is nevertheless the most prominent personality in this field in the 17th century.

His original log has apparently been lost; a fair

Fig. 131 Tasman's chart

copy bearing Tasman's personal signature is held in the State Archives in the Hague, and was made available to a wider circle by Frederik Muller & Co. in Amsterdam in 1898, in a splendid display of facsimiles. An extract of this follows, as far as the islands of the Bismarck Archipelago are concerned, and covers the period from 22 March until 14 April 1643:

22 March: At noon we spied land ahead, about 4 miles off; in order to pass to the north of it, we steered firstly west by north and then west-north-west. Towards evening we sailed in a north-westerly direction close inshore. These islands are about 30 in number, but are very small, the largest no more than 2 miles long; all the rest are small and are surrounded by a reef. Another reef runs off to the north-west, surmounted by three coconut palms, which make it easy to see. These are the islands that Le Maire had indicated on his chart; they are about 90 miles from the coast of New Guinea. In the evening we saw land to the north-north-west.[1] We therefore set our course north-north-east, on the wind, to sail north of all the shallows, furled our foresails and continued thus until morning.

[Various coast representations follow in the manuscript, with signature.] We named these islands the 'Inseln von Onthong Jaua' on account of their great similarity with them; they are surrounded by reefs, and appear in this form when you have them in the south-west about 2 miles from you.

23 March. In the early morning we again made sail, and steered westwards, having the small islands that we had seen the previous day about 3 miles to the

1. The current Tasman Islands, or Nukumanu.

south. The wind was easterly and north-easterly, with cloud cover and trade-wind weather. At noon our position was latitude 4°31', longitude 177°18'; steered west-north-west, sailed 20 miles. During the night, at the end of the first watch we hove to, because we feared beaching on the island of Marcken, discovered by Le Maire.

24 March. In the morning the sails were set again and we steered westwards. Towards noon we spied land directly ahead; this land was very low-lying, and appeared to be two islands lying south-east and north-west of each other. The northernmost showed several similarities with the island of Marcken in the Zuyder Zee, as Le Maire says, for which reason he gave it the name Marcken. Noon observation gave 4°55' latitude and 175°30' longitude; kept a westerly course as far as we could estimate. We find, however, that a strong current is pushing us southward; we sailed 20 miles with an easterly and east-south-easterly wind and trade-wind weather with a light topsail breeze. In the evening we altered our course to the north, to pass north of the island. During the night we drifted becalmed, and closed on the forementioned island.

[The following page has a coastal representation with signature.] The island appears like this when it is west from you at a distance of 2 miles; Le Maire named the island Maercken because of its great similarity with this island.

25 March. In the morning watch we heard the sound of breakers on the beach; as it was still totally calm, the pinnace and the sea boat were launched to haul us free of the reef or shallows. However, sea and tide drove us a distance towards the reef. To our great chagrin, we found no anchorage. About 9 o'clock a canoe from the island came alongside, carrying seven people and about twenty coconuts. We traded a dozen of these for three strings of beads and four medium-sized nails; the coconuts appear to have grown wild, and were of poor quality. The people seemed rough and wild, with a darker skin than those of the islands where we had taken recreation. They were also less well-mannered, and were totally naked except for an apparently cotton cover of their sexual organs, scarcely big enough to conceal them. Several had short hair while others wore it bound up like the rascals in Murderers' Bay.[2] One of them wore two feathers on his head, like horns; another had a ring through his nose, although we could not establish what it was made of. Their canoe tapered sharply fore and aft like the wings of a seagull although not elegant in shape and in poor condition; they had arrows and two bows, and seemed to have no esteem for either beads or nails, nor to value them at all. Then the wind came from the south and fortunately helped us to get away from the reef. The canoe was paddled back to the beach. We saw a small canoe approaching, but it did not reach us because of a suddenly arising squall. A northerly course was then laid, to bring us out of the area of reef and shallows. The islands are about fifteen to sixteen in number, the largest being about a mile long while the rest seemed like houses. They all lay together, surrounded by one reef. The reef runs north-west from the islands; about a cannon-shot from the islands a grove of trees stands level with the water. Two miles further north-west is another small island, like a *toppershoetje* (a small seaman's hat). The reef stretches a further half mile to sea, so that in total it runs about 3 miles north-west from the islands. The noon position was 4°34'S latitude and 175°10'E longitude. Course north-west, sailed 7 miles. Towards noon the wind shifted to the north-west and then north. We altered course to the west, upon which the wind was from the north-north-east, and a gentle breeze sprang up, which altered our course to the north-west. During the night, with calm weather and a northerly wind we ran somewhat more to the west.

26 March. Fine weather and a calm sea with a light north-easterly breeze. Noon observation was 4°33' latitude and 174°30' longitude; westerly course, sailed 10 miles. We encountered a strong current going to the south, and we again set our course north-west. Variation 9°30' north-east.

27 March. Wind and weather as before. Noon observation 4°1' latitude, 173°36' longitude; course north-west by west, sailed 16 miles; at noon steered westwards to look for the islands lying east of the New Guinea coast, and then to reconnoitre the mainland coast by sailing close inshore. Variation 9°30' north-east.

28 March. Continuing fine weather; light easterly breeze and calm sea. Noon observation 4°11' latitude, 172°32' longitude; course west; sailed 16 miles. Towards noon we sighted land ahead, and at noon were still about 4 miles from it. This island lies at 4°30' S latitude and 172°16' longitude. It is 46 miles west and west by north of the island that Jakob Le Maire named Marken. At night we drifted in calm.

[Here the text has a sketch of the coast of the Green Islands with the comment:] Le Maire named these islands the 'Groene Eylanden' because they seemed beautiful and green; their form is as shown here when the east end is to the south and the west end to the south-west, from about 2 miles away.

29 March. In the morning we observed that the current was carrying us towards the island. Noon observation, 4°20' latitude, 172°17' longitude. Throughout the day we drifted in calm, so that in the last 24 hours we had travelled 5 miles south-west. In the middle of the afternoon two small vessels from the island came alongside; they had two wings

2. Moordenaers Bay in New Zealand where Tasman's vessels had been attacked by the Maoris.

or outriggers. Their paddles were small with thick blades; they seemed poorly made to us. One of the canoes carried six people; the other, three. When they were about two ship-lengths away, one of the six men in the one canoe broke one of his arrows, stuck one half in his hair and held the other in his hand, apparently indicating his friendship. These people were completely naked, and their bodies were black with crinkly hair like the Kaffirs, but not quite so woolly as the latter, nor were their noses quite so flat. Several wore white armbands, apparently made from bone, round their arms; others had smeared their faces with lime, and wore a piece of tree bark, about three fingers wide, on their foreheads. They had nothing but bows, arrows and spears. We called out several words from the vocabulary of the New Guinea language; however, they seemed to recognise only the word *lamas*, meaning 'coconut'. They pointed continually towards land. We gave them two strings of beads and two large nails, as well as an old tablecloth, in exchange for which they gave us an old coconut, the only thing that they had with them, then they paddled back to shore. Towards evening it was still calm, with a very slight breeze from the north-east; we sailed close inshore and had to launch our boats to keep us off the beach. At the end of the dogwatch we succeeded in escaping the island. There were two large islands and three small ones, the latter lying on the western side. Le Maire had named these islands the 'Groene Eylanden' (Green Islands). In the west-north-west we saw a further high island and two to three small ones; also, in the west we noticed very high land that appeared to be a continental coast; but only time will tell the truth of this opinion. Variation 9° north-east.

[At this point the text contains a coastal view of the island of St John, with the following note:]
A view of Sankt Jans Eylandt when it is about 2 miles distant to the north.

30 March. Fine weather with a light breeze from the north-east; still engaged with towing; we found that the current was taking us south. Noon observation 4°25' latitude, 172° longitude; course west; sailed or drifted 4 miles. In the evening St John's Island was 6 miles to the north-west.

31 March. Continuing good calm weather, with an easterly wind and calm sea. Noon observation 4°28' latitude, 171°42' longitude; course west; sailed 6 miles; at noon we hoisted the white flag and pennant, at which our friends on the *Zeehaen* came aboard and we have decided with them what can be seen more fully in today's resolution.

1 April AD 1643. We had the coast of New Guinea alongside at 4°30'S latitude, at a place that the Spanish call 'Cabo Santa Maria'. Noon observation 4°30' latitude and 171°2' longitude; westerly course, sailed 10 miles. Variation 8°45'.

2 April. Continuing good calm weather with variable breeze. We did our best to sail along the shore, which here extends north-west and south-east of St John's Island. North-west is another island, which we named Anthony Caens Island.[3] The island lies directly north of Cabo de Santa Maria. Noon observation 4°9' latitude and 170°41' longitude; course north-west, sailed 10 miles; we then had Cabo de Santa Maria to the south, which fixes it at 171°2' longitude. In the evening we ran under the shore so that we could make better progress with the land breeze. At four bells of the first watch we obtained a light land breeze and made our course along the shore.

[The subsequent four pages contain coastal views with the notes:]
View of the coast of Noua Guinea when sailing along it; this land is named 'Cabo de Santa Maria'
  View of the coast of Noua Guinea between Cabo de Santa Maria and Anthony Caens Eylandt.
  View of Anthony Caens Eylandt when it lies to the north.
  View of 'Gerrit de Nijs Eylandt'[4] lying two miles to the north.
  View of 'Visschers Eylanden' 4 miles to the east.
  View of the coast of Noua Guinea when sailing along it between Gerrit denys Eylandt and Visschers Eylandt.

3 April. In the morning we felt another slight land breeze; our course was still north-west along the shore. About 9 o'clock we saw a fully manned vessel coming from the shore; the vessel was curved at both ends like a *corre-corre* from Ternate. It lay quietly for a while beyond the range of our big ordnance, then paddled back to shore. Noon observation 3°42' latitude, 170°20' longitude; course north-west; sailed 10 miles. Towards evening a light breeze arose from the east-south-east. We continued north-west along the coast. This seemed to be very fine land; however, the worst was that we did not find an anchorage anywhere. During the night we had thunderstorms with rain and variable breeze.

4 April. We continued to sail along the coast, which here extends north-west by west and south-east by east. It is a fine coast with many inlets. We passed an island about 12 miles from Anthony Caens; both lie on a line north-west and south-east from each other. We named this island Garde Neijs. Noon at 3°22' latitude and 169°50' longitude; course north-west by west; sailed 9 miles; continuing variable light winds and calm. In the evening we had a land wind with thunder, and did our best to sail along the coast.

5 April. In the morning we still had a light land wind. Towards noon we reached another island about 10 miles from Gardenys in a line west-north-west and east-south-east from each other. On the beach of this island we saw several canoes that

3. After a member of the council of the Indies.

4. More correctly 'Arend Gardenijs'; after a member of the council of the Indies.

Fig. 132 *Heemskerk* and *Zeehaen*, Tasman's two ships. From an old copperplate engraving

5. All of these designations by Tasman are, for the most part, written incorrectly on later maps up to the present day, and should at least be written as above, especially if people wish to retain them.

Fig. 133 Natives of New Ireland. From a drawing in Tasman's log

were probably used for fishing, which was why we named this island Visschers Eilandt (Fisher Island). Towards noon we observed six vessels ahead, three of which paddled so close to our ship that we were able to drop two or three pieces of old sailcloth, two strings of beads and two old nails down to them. They did not seem to notice the sailcloth, and also barely noticed the other items. However, they pointed constantly to their heads, from which we gathered that they wanted turbans. These people seemed to be very shy, and judging from their behaviour were fearful of being shot; they did not come close enough for us to ascertain whether they were armed. They were very black, and totally naked apart from a few leaves covering their genitals. Several had black hair, others had hair of another shade. Their canoes had outriggers, and each held three or four people, but, because of the distance, it was not possible to discover further features. After they had paddled around the ship for a long time, they paddled to the beach, calling out to us, while we responded, although neither understood the other. Noon at 3° latitude and 169°17' longitude. Course west-north-west, sailed 10 miles; in the afternoon we had a light north-west wind.

6 April. In the morning there was no wind. In the middle of the forenoon we again observed eight or nine canoes coming from the same island; three paddled to the *Zeehaen* and five to our ship. Several held three people, others four, and one five people. When they were about two stones' throws away, they stopped paddling and called to us; we did not understand them but we beckoned them closer. At this, they paddled in front of the ship and loitered there for a long time, without coming alongside. Finally the boatswain took off his belt and held it out to them, whereupon one of the canoes came alongside. We gave them a string of beads, and the boatswain handed his belt over to them, in exchange for which we received only a piece of pith of a sago palm, the only thing that they had with them. Meanwhile, the other canoes had come alongside, as they saw that their friends had suffered no injury. None of the canoes contained weapons or anything they could have used to fight us. At first we had our suspicions that they were rascals who were plotting evil and looking for plunder, because they affected such great apprehension. Had our suspicions been well-founded they would have been warmly received, because we had already prepared measures necessary to repel them, although the cook had not yet prepared breakfast. We called out the words *anieuw*, *oufi*, *pouacka*, and so on (coconuts, yams, pigs, and so on), to them, which they appeared to understand, because they pointed towards the shore, as if they wanted to say, 'There they are'. Then, with one accord, they paddled swiftly back to the beach, as the wind had grown stronger; we did not see them again. These natives are dark brown, almost as black as Kaffirs; their hair has various shades depending on whether or not they have powdered it with lime; their faces are smeared with red dye except for their foreheads. Several wore a thick bone, the size of a little finger, through the nose. Otherwise they wore nothing on their bodies, except for several green leaves over their genitals. Their canoes were new, and neatly constructed, decorated fore and aft with carvings, and fitted with an outrigger; their paddles were neither very long nor broad, and tapered at the end. Towards noon the wind turned south-east, and we made our course west by north along the shore; observed latitude 2°53', longitude 168°59'; course west-north-west, sailed 5 miles; during the afternoon we made good progress. During the night we had a light offshore breeze.

[The next three pages contain views of the New Guinea coast, with the comments:]
View of the coast of Noua Guinea, when sailing westwards from 'Visshers Island'.

View of the coast of Noua Guinea up to this bight.
View of the coast of Noua Guinea or 'Salmon Sweers hoeck'[5].
View of a canoe of Noua Guinea, with local

natives (fig. 133).

7 April. In the morning we drifted without wind. Before noon twenty canoes came back, and remained in the vicinity of the ship, but outside cannon range, as on the previous day. After repeatedly making signs to them, they finally ventured alongside. They had nothing in their vessels, although one contained three coconuts, one of which we traded for a string of beads. Our thought was to get all three but they firmly refused to hand over the other two. Another had a shark, which we similarly traded for three strings of beads; a third had a dolphin, which one of our sailors traded for an old cap. Several had small fish that they threw to our people, but they were not worth eating. Eventually three or four of the people came aboard, looking at everything with great astonishment and walking round as though they were drunk – a peculiar characteristic, since in their small canoes they paddle for many miles out to sea without the slightest sign of seasickness, but on a big ship like ours they seem to be struck with dizziness from the movement brought about by ocean swells. They had neither weapons nor objects with which they could have attacked us. They appeared to feed themselves from fishing, as several carried eel spears (fishing spears). After they had spent some time on board, they left us and, with great commotion, paddled hastily to shore. We lay here during the afternoon, drifting in a calm. Further westward, the land becomes very low-lying, but the coast still stretches, unbroken, west by north and west-north-west. At noon we estimated 2°35' latitude and 168°25' longitude; course west by north; sailed 9 miles. In the afternoon we saw more high land west by north, and west of the previously mentioned point; and estimated that this land was about 10 miles away. We drifted becalmed, but soon found a light easterly wind and tried to approach the high land. The current along this coast is steadily in our favour, so that we proceed further westwards every day as we evidently advance over the water. We passed a large inlet during the night.

8 April. In the morning we reached the western side of the bight and four small low-lying islands. When we had passed these, we again reached three small islands, lying west of those that we had passed at noon. At noon we estimated 2°26' latitude, 167°39' longitude; the wind was south-east but variable; course west by north, sailed 12 miles; variation 10° north-east. South-west by west we had a low cape with two small islands to its north. From this cape the land begins to run gradually southwards. Towards 6 o'clock in the evening we had the two small islands to the south by west, and the next land visible, very low and flat, lay south-west by south, about 4 miles away. During the entire time we steered our course along the coast.

9 April. At sunrise in the morning we drifted becalmed; the land sighted in the south lay south-east by east, about 2.5 miles away, where the coast suddenly dropped away. We then had another low island to the south-south-west, about 2 miles away. Although we did our best to sail closely along the point in question, we were prevented by lack of wind. At noon, 2°33' latitude, 167°4' longitude; course west-south-west; sailed 7 miles, variation 10°. In the afternoon we again steered towards the point.

10 April. During the last 24 hours we have made good progress southwards. As a result of the calm and for other reasons, we attempted to go southwards as fast as possible, partly to explore the coast, partly to find a southern passage. At noon the southernmost point was east-north-east, and the northernmost north-north-east. At noon 3°2' latitude, 167°4' longitude; course southerly, sailed 12 miles. In the afternoon sailed further south; towards evening the wind became north-north-west. To come close in under the land a course was set east-south-east and south-east, and occasionally south; variable winds with rain bothered us a lot. But after midnight we again drifted becalmed on a smooth sea.

11 April. At noon we drifted becalmed, without being in a position to take a sighting. We still observed land before us to the north-east, i.e. the easternmost point; the westernmost point lay north-north-east and north by east ahead of us. At noon, 3°28' latitude and 166°51' longitude; course south-west by west half a point west, sailed 7 miles. In the second watch a light breeze from the north-north-east; altered course to south-east, close on the wind, but later it became calm again.

12 April. At three bells in the morning watch we felt such a strong earthquake that none of our crew, even though fast asleep, remained in his hammock; they all came on deck instantly with the greatest astonishment, in the belief that the ship had run onto a rock. It was just as if the keel had slid over a coral reef, but when we took soundings we found no bottom. There were further earthquake shocks later, but none as powerful as the first; initially we had calm weather, then heavy rain later; wind variable and occasionally still. We attempted to push as far south as possible. Towards 3 o'clock in the afternoon we had a light westerly wind. At noon, 3°45' latitude and 167°1' longitude; course south-south-east; sailed 6 miles. Then we sailed south-south-east and observed a small, round, low island in the south and west, about 4.5 to 5 miles away. Heavy rain and changeable weather at night.

[The three subsequent pages contain coastal views of New Guinea and Vulcan Island with the annotations:]

View of the coast of Noua Guinea in the large bight where we hoped to find a passage through to Cape Keerweer, but were deceived.

Plate 53 Grotto in raised coral rock on Mioko

View of Nova Guinea in the large bight close to the reef.

View of the coast of Nova Guinea, when sailing westwards between the coast and the volcanic island.

View of the volcanic island in the north-east.

13 April. In the morning a light north-easterly wind; observed high land with several mountains and low land between, from south-west by west to east-south-east. We appear to have found ourselves in a large bight. We did our best to go as far south as possible. At noon, 4°22' latitude, 167°18' longitude; course south-south-east, sailed 10 miles. Drifted in calm during the afternoon, without being able to strike bottom; the sea here is as calm as a river, without any movement, which makes us believe even more that we have found ourselves in a large bay; we will find the real situation with time. At night variable wind with occasional calm. In the evening a distinct mountain range to the south-south-west, towards which we set our course.

14 April. In the evening we saw land from east-north-east to south-south-west, and later in the west-south-west. We hoped, but in vain, to find a passage through; however, as we came closer, we found that it was a bight, and that the land was continuous to the south. Therefore in the afternoon we directed our course to west by south with a north-north-west wind, and between 3 and 4 o'clock in the afternoon we found a reef which lay right on the surface of the sea, and which we could scarcely pass, with the prevailing wind. The reef in question lies about 2 miles from the shore, as far as we could estimate. At noon, 5°27' latitude, 166°57' longitude; course south-south-west, sailed 15 miles; variation 9°15' north-east. Towards evening light wind from the north-north-east. At night, again drifted in calm.

I end the extract from Tasman's journal here, because from this point on it has no connection with the Bismarck Archipelago. However, if we follow his course, we observe that if on the 14 April he had succeeded in penetrating further south-west, then on this day or, with the same course, on the 15th at least, he would have discovered the straits between New Guinea and New Britain. Seen from the area where he was on the 14th, western New Britain, Rook Island and New Guinea appear to form a connected land mass.

A long pause in discoveries set in, right up until

Fig. 134 Facsimile of Tasman's log with his personal signature

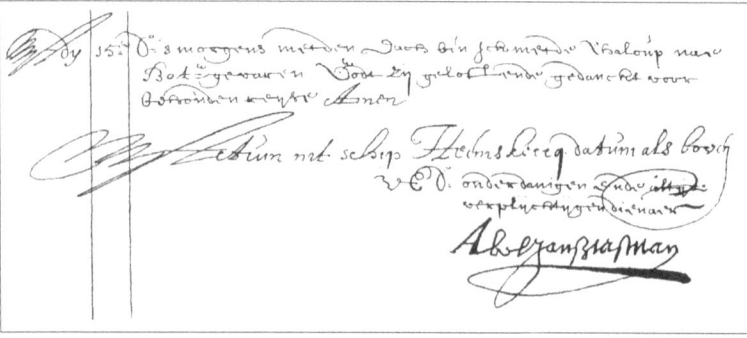

the end of the century. English, Dutch, French, Spanish and Portuguese were heavily occupied in siphoning off the treasures won in the East Indies and America from one another on the journey home. A form of official piracy, that promised easy pickings, flourished widely, and nobody found time for further exploration. Not until the end of the century did the desire for discovery reawaken, this time in England where the intrepid seafarer William Dampier drew attention by the publication of his adventures in America and the East Indies. The Earl of Oxford, at that time Lord of the Admiralty, was introduced to the well-travelled man, and finally appointed him commander of a South Seas expedition. On 26 January 1699, Dampier left the English coast in the ship *Roebuck*; we find him again on the west coast of Australia, which he had already visited once before. From here he turned towards Timor, and then steered eastwards between latitudes 2° and 2.5°S. About the 149th meridian he steered south, thereby avoiding the '*Hooch Landt*' of Schouten and Le Maire. However, on 16 February 1700 he encountered St Matthias, and then sailed between this island and Squally Island to the present New Hanover. On his map he indicated a portion of the small islands off the north coast of New Hanover, but he came as little as did his predecessor to the conclusion that New Hanover was an independent island.

From then on he steered a course along the coast, but somewhere between the present Gardner Island and Gerrit Denys Island he came into conflict with the natives, who attacked his ship with slingshots from their canoes. Dampier named the spot Slinger's Bay, and preferred to put further out to sea. He touched the small offshore islands, and approached the coast again only in the vicinity of Cape Santa Maria. Moving further south he discovered and named Cape St George, and after he had sailed round it he anchored in a fairly large bight stretching northwards; he named it St George's Bay. In the northern corner of the bay he observed huge clouds of smoke rising from a crater (volcano on the Mother peninsula). According to his map he must also have noticed the present Neulauenburg islands, since in the inner northern corner of his St George's Bay two small islands are shown in the location of that group.

Thus, William Dampier is the first European documented as having anchored in the Bismarck Archipelago.

Had Dampier arrived at another time of the year, say July, then wind and current would probably have driven him into the so-called St George's Bay, and he would have made the discovery that remained reserved to his later successor, Carteret, that this was a strait. However, he navigated the coasts of the present-day Neumecklenburg and Neupommern from 16 February until April, and, during this period, a strong current sets out of his assumed bay, due to the prevailing north-west wind. When Dampier left his anchorage, both a favourable wind and a favourable tide carried him along the south coast of New Britain. In Montague Bay, which he named, Dampier again came into contact with natives, of whom he gives a description that is still relevant today. However, he did not stop here but sailed along the coast until he found the Dampier

Fig. 135 (left) William Dampier. From an old engraving

Fig. 136 (below) Dampier's map

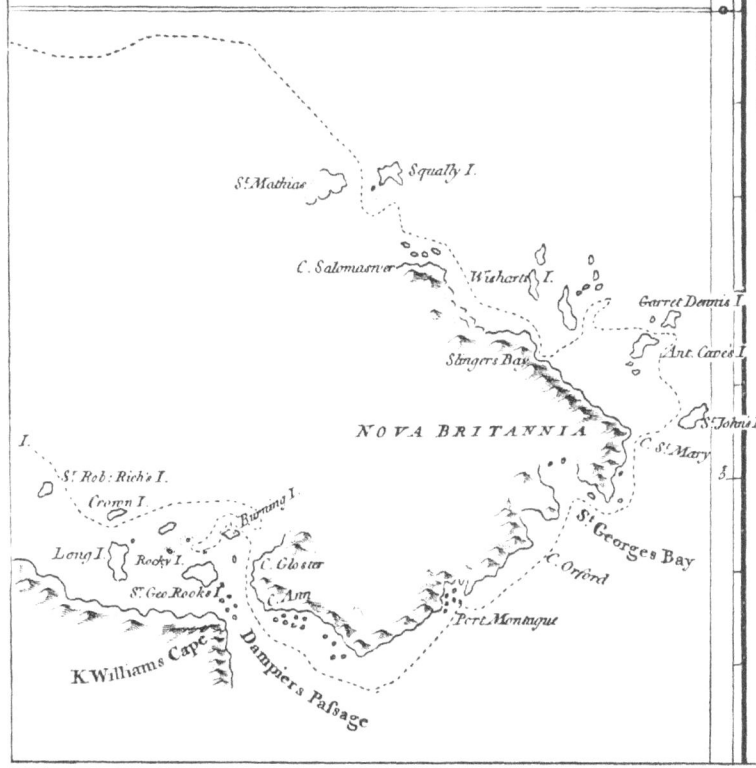

Strait, named after him, between a smaller island that he named Sir George Rook's Island, and the large main island, that he gave the name of *Nova Britannia*. His further course led him along the coast of New Guinea and, if we look at his chart we can recognise without difficulty the Ritter, Tupinier, Heyn, Lottin, Long and Crown islands. Thus, Dampier became the discoverer of the Bismarck Archipelago which, up until then, had been regarded as a part of the large island of New Guinea.

It is interesting that on his special chart of St George's Bay, and on his depiction of the western shore, Dampier shows a then-active volcano. The position of the volcano is approximately correct, although it has currently been extinct for a long time. It was probably extinct even during the time of Carteret, who does not mention it, even

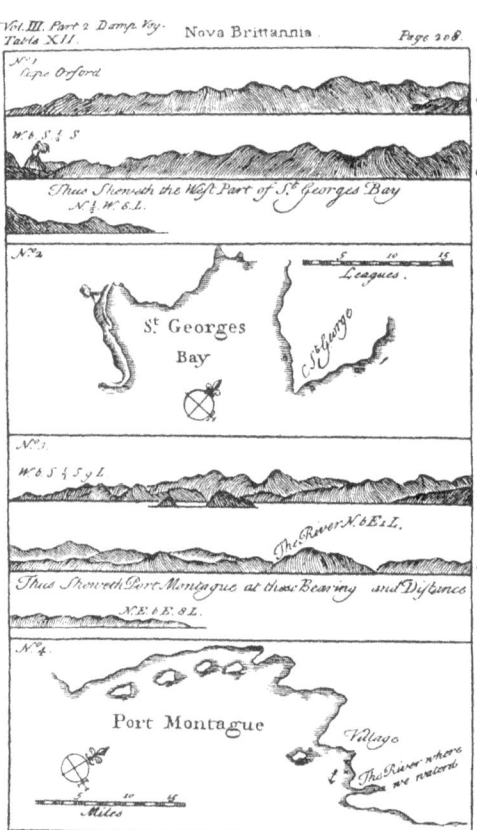

Fig. 137 Facsimile of Dampier's coastal survey of New Britain

though, during his long stay at the southern end of New Ireland, he would certainly have noticed the volcano opposite, had it been active at that time.

Once more, twenty-two years pass before a seafarer approaches the archipelago. In 1722 the Dutchman Jacob Roggeveen sighted the island of *Nova Britannia*, which he named *Neu Zeeland*. However, his voyage brings nothing new. On board Roggeveen's squadron as a sergeant of marines was a German named Karl Friedrich Behrens, a native of Mecklenburg. Behrens published his experiences of the voyage in Leipzig in 1738. He honoured his fatherland by calculating his longitude east and west of the meridian of his homeland, which is somewhat confusing to the reader.

Forty-five years later, in 1767, the Bismarck Archipelago emerges again out of its darkness, to be enriched again by a significant discovery. Between 1764 and 1766 the English administration had despatched the first of those epoch-making voyages of discovery into the South Seas, under Captain Byron, soon followed by the voyage of Captain Wallis and the three voyages of the famous James Cook.

All of these voyages, as well as the almost simultaneous expeditions of the French – Bougainville, Surville, La Perouse and D'Entrecasteaux – supplement our knowledge of the Pacific Ocean, and the current German possessions were also at that time further explored.

First of all, the expedition under Captain Wallis is significant to us. He was in charge of two ships, the frigate *Dolphin* and the much smaller vessel *Swallow* which was commanded by Lieutenant Philipp Carteret, who had previously been a member of the Byron expedition in 1764-65.

The *Swallow* was a so-called 'sloop of war' of fourteen cannon, with a crew of ninety men and twenty-two deck officers. She was totally unsuitable for the voyage for, as Carteret himself says, 'she was an old ship, in service for thirty years already and unfit for a longer voyage'. Besides, the outfitting was inadequate, and even the most essential items were missing. It sounds almost laughable when we read today that Carteret's formal request to the Admiralty to supply a portable forge and iron, a small boat and other small items that, from experience, he knew were essential, was bluntly refused because 'the fitting-out for the intended purpose is completely satisfactory'. Even rigging was provided only sparingly, and Carteret was overjoyed when he received 5 metric hundredweight of rope from the commander-in-chief during the voyage. It is small wonder, therefore, that the voyage, which lasted from August 1766 until 20 February 1769, was an almost uninterrupted sequence of all manner of difficulties. At the outlet of the Magelhaen Strait, the badly sailing *Swallow* lost the *Dolphin* from view (11 April 1767), and the unruffled Carteret decided to continue the voyage alone. Only rarely did he sight land; on 24 August 1767 he spotted the Carteret Islands, named after him. His description matches the present situation remarkably: 'The inhabitants are black, and woolly haired like the African negroes; their weapons are bows and arrows, and they own large canoes, which they navigate by means of sails.'

Nissan was sighted the following evening, and on the same day high land was discovered to the south. Carteret named it Winchelsea's Island in his journal, but on his chart he named it Lord Anson's Island. This is the first report on the northernmost of the Solomon Islands, the island of Buka. On the 26th, St John's Island was sighted and, shortly after, the raised land of *Nova Britannia*. They rounded Cape St George, and on 27 August wind and tide drove the ship into Dampier's St George's Bay. On the 28th their joy was great when they were able to anchor not far off the small Wallis Island. The crew's condition was demonstrated by the fact that, in spite of the efforts of the entire crew, they were unable to raise the anchor on the 29th; this was achieved only after renewed effort on the 30th. The *Swallow* was brought closer inshore and beached in the tiny English Cove to careen the hull, badly damaged by ship worm. They stayed here until 7 September, when they sailed several miles north to Carteret Harbour and anchored between a small island with a stand of coconut palms and the main island.

The voyage was continued on 9 September; outside they found strong east-south-east winds and a strong current from the south-east, which drove the *Swallow* deeper into St George's Bay, and Carteret discovered that the assumed bay was actually a broad strait, which he named St George's Channel. In the evening, they discerned the Duke of York Islands (today Neulauenburg) which Carteret, however, designated on his chart as Man Island, and they observed three high mountains, named the 'Mother and Daughters'. Carteret reports, 'The Mother is the middle and highest mountain, and behind it we saw giant clouds of smoke.' (These would be from the not yet totally extinct volcano, which Carteret could not see from his vantage point.) He named the northern point to his left Cape Stephens, and the current Cape Gazelle 'Cape Palliser'. Not far from Cape Stephens, he discovered another smaller island that he named Man Island; however, he left it unnamed on his chart. Wind and current took him along the coast of the newly discovered large island, which he named Nova Hibernia. On the 12th he sailed between Nova Hibernia and a small island, and gave the latter the name Sandwich Island. During a calm he received a visit from ten canoes with about 150 natives. They were shy and did not venture aboard. Carteret's description of the canoes and their crew is appropriate word-for-word today. In the continuation of the voyage they discovered the strait between New Ireland and New Hanover, presented for the first time as an island; the strait is named Byron Straits.

Early on the 13th they sighted the small islands already seen by Tasman, now christened Portland Islands, and on the 14th they had the small eastern islands of the Admiralty group in view. On the 15th, numerous canoes and natives came from the islands. They could not be persuaded to go aboard, behaved in a hostile manner, and finally attacked the ship with their spears. Carteret had to use his ordnance to dissuade them from further attacks. Continuing on, they encountered another group of them; they had to be put to flight, and a canoe containing all kinds of weapons and objects was seized. The hostile demeanour of the natives frustrated a detailed investigation of the islands, which he designated with the name they retain today.

In the evening of 18 September they again saw two small islands; one of them could be seen only from the masthead, and it was named Durour Island. They passed the second island during the night, and a lot of natives were seen running along the beach with torches; he named this island Maty Island ('Matty' is a later disfigurement).

With this, the Carteret discoveries in the Bismarck Archipelago came to an end.

The French too were busy in the South Seas at the same time as the English.

On 15 December 1766, Louis Antoine de Bou-

Plate 54 Waterfall in the Karo valley. Baining

gainville put to sea from St Malo with two ships, *La Boudeuse* and *L'Etoile*, under orders of the king. After he had discovered the southern border of the Louisiades he sailed north, and on 28 June 1768 he sighted the coast of a long high island to starboard. On the 30th he had come so close to the coast that he attempted to anchor. A boat was launched, which was followed by many heavily manned canoes but was not attacked. However, there appeared to be open sea ahead, and both ships continued their set course. On 1 July the boat was launched again to find an anchorage, and was attacked by ten canoes containing about a hundred natives. The island was named 'Choiseul' and the strait they sailed through still bears the name Bougainville.

After passing through the Bougainville Strait, they spied an extensive coast to the west, whose high mountain peaks were hidden in clouds. In the evening of 2 July the northern tip of Choiseul was still visible, but on the morning of the 3rd they saw only the coast of the land discovered the day before, whose height was astonishing. The northern tip of the island was named Cape l'Averdie; while the island itself was named after its discoverer, Bougainville.

Early in the morning of the 4th, they sighted land lying further to the west; the coast was less high, and between the southernmost point of the land and Cape l'Averdie they noticed a wide open stretch which was assumed to be a pass or a broad deep bight. On the far side of the presumed strait, or bight, the peaks of high mountains rose steeply, which led to the conclusion that the land must be an island. I will let Bougainville continue:

> In the afternoon three canoes pushed off from shore to reconnoitre our ship; each contained five or six negroes. They stopped just out of range, and only after an hour did our continuous entreaties succeed in bringing them closer. Several trinkets thrown to them, tied to pieces of wood, strengthened their resolve, so that in the end they came alongside and held up a few coconuts, crying '*Bouka, Bouka, Onellé*' over and over again. After some time we did the same, and this appeared to cause great joy. They did not stay long by the ship but indicated to us that they were going back to shore to collect coconuts. However, these treacherous people had gone scarcely twenty paces away when one of them fired an arrow at us which fortunately did not hit anyone. Then they paddled away as fast as possible, and we despised them too much to think about punishing them.
>
> These negroes were totally naked; they had short woolly hair, their ears were pierced and pulled down and many had their hair dyed red, with various parts of their bodies painted with white patches. To judge from the red stains on their teeth they appeared to chew betel, and we noticed the same in the inhabitants of Choiseul Bay, for, in their canoes, we found small bundles of leaves as well as *Areca* and lime.
>
> The island, which we named Bouka, seems very well populated, if we can draw a conclusion from the large number of huts and the numerous gardens. A fine plain against a hillside, completely planted out in coconut palms and other trees was a splendid sight to us, and I would have liked to have found an anchorage off the island, but wind and current were perceptably taking us north-west.

They hove-to during the night, but the following morning the island of Buka, which Carteret had named Winchelsea, or Lord Anson, the previous year, was already far to the east and south-east.

In the afternoon of 5 July the high land of New Ireland was discovered and on the 6th they dropped anchor on the western side, not far from the southern tip. The place was christened 'Baie de Praslin'; the same place that Carteret had named 'Gower Harbour' the year before. Here the crew recovered a little, and the journey was then continued along the east coast, since the existence of a strait in the west was then unknown to the French. Bougainville gave new names to the islands already discovered by his predecessors; for example, he changed St John into Bournand, the Caen Islands into 'Isles d'Oraison', Gerrit Denys into Bouchaye, Wishart Island into Souzanett, and so on, names that have already long since disappeared from the maps. Sailing on, he sighted Squally Island and St Matthias, and further to the west discovered the Isles des Anachorettes and the Echiquier Islands. His course then led him further along the coast of New Guinea.

In 1781, the Spanish warship *Princesa*, under Captain Maurelle, fleetingly touched the east coast of New Ireland and the Admiralty Islands and, travelling on, sighted the Hermit Islands.

At this time there arose the previously mentioned argument among the geographers about the position of the Solomon Islands. The French asserted the rediscovery of the group by their seafarers, while the English, on the other hand, laid claim to the fame of their people for having discovered new land, and moved the Solomon Islands, the existence of which, however, could not totally be denied, westward, north of New Guinea, where they were attempting to bring the discoveries of Dampier and Carteret into accord with those of Mendaña.

The Englishman Dalrymple was the principal proponent of this theory, and for further clarification, he presented a map in conjunction with his written evidence. The map is reproduced here. On it he ingeniously combined the islands of the present Bismarck Archipelago and the Solomon Islands into an island group that of course does not bear the slightest resemblance to the real situation. On the other hand, the French maps of

1785 and 1790 give the position and shape of the archipelago and the northern Solomon Islands with reasonable accuracy.

A consequence of this argument was the fitting-out of a further French expedition under Count de la Pérouse, which left its homeland in 1785. La Pérouse visited first the west coast of the Americas and the east coast of Asia, and reached Australia in September 1787, whence he began his second great voyage. However, he went missing in February 1788, and, on the order of Ludwig XVI, the two ships *Recherche* and *Espérance*, under the command of Bruny D'Entrecasteaux, were sent out in 1791 to search for the missing people. We are grateful to this expedition for valuable contributions to the knowledge of our archipelago.

It must be mentioned here that the English commodore Hunter, whose ship, *Sirius*, had stranded on Norfolk Island in 1790, and who was travelling with the Dutch ship *Waaksamhed* from Sydney to Batavia, on 23 May 1791 put into the small harbour, named Port Hunter after him, on the north coast of Duke of York (Neulauenburg) to take on water. He came into conflict with the natives, which was, however, finally settled, and on his departure as a gift Hunter left two English pointers, which were probably eaten immediately as dainty morsels. From Duke of York, Hunter saw huge volcanic eruptions on New Britain, in the present Blanche Bay. On the continuation of the voyage the *Waaksamhed* passed the Admiralty Islands, and Hunter thought he saw items of French uniforms on the natives. He had met La Pérouse in Australia and knew that he intended to visit these regions.

The Frenchman's disappearance without trace was still fresh in his mind, and, from a distance, the white body paint of the natives looked like the white uniform facings of the French marines to the commodore, who assumed that La Pérouse had foundered here. Hunter reported this supposition on his arrival in Batavia, from where it was passed on to the French Governor on Ile de France. The latter immediately despatched a frigate to inform D'Entrecasteaux's expedition in Cape Town. Hunter was in Cape Town at the same time as the two French ships, and it seems strange that not only did he not pass on his observations to the commander, but on the other hand maintained to friends that he knew nothing of the matter.

Nonetheless, D'Entrecasteaux went directly from Cape Town to Van Diemen's Land and, via New Caledonia, to the archipelago to carry out an investigation. They sighted the southern end of Bougainville on 10 July 1792, but heavy rain prevented closer investigation until the 13th. On the 14th the small islands at the north-western end of Bougainville were sighted, and on the 15th they were not far from the northern tip of Buka. Canoes of natives came out to the ship, and their

description by the naturalist, Labillardière, who was accompanying the expedition, is as apt as if he were describing them today. The contact with the natives was totally friendly.

On the morning of the 16th they passed Nissan, and Cape St George came into view about 1 o'clock. On the 17th they dropped anchor in the tiny Carteret Harbour and stayed there until the 24th without coming into contact with natives. Sailing along the west coast of New Ireland, they found themselves off the small islands between New Ireland and New Hanover on the 26th. Finally, on the 28th they sighted the eastern Admiralty Islands; La Vandola was reached on the 29th

Fig. 138 Dalrymple's map

Fig. 139 Part of a map put together in 1785 for orientation of the Count de la Pérouse

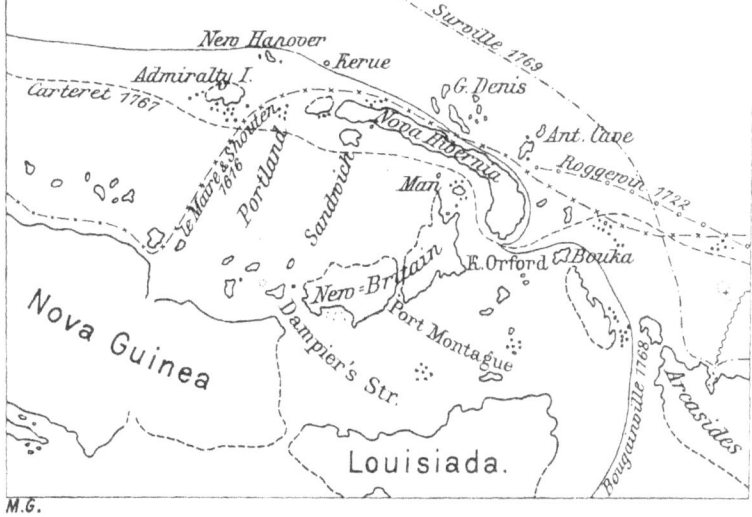

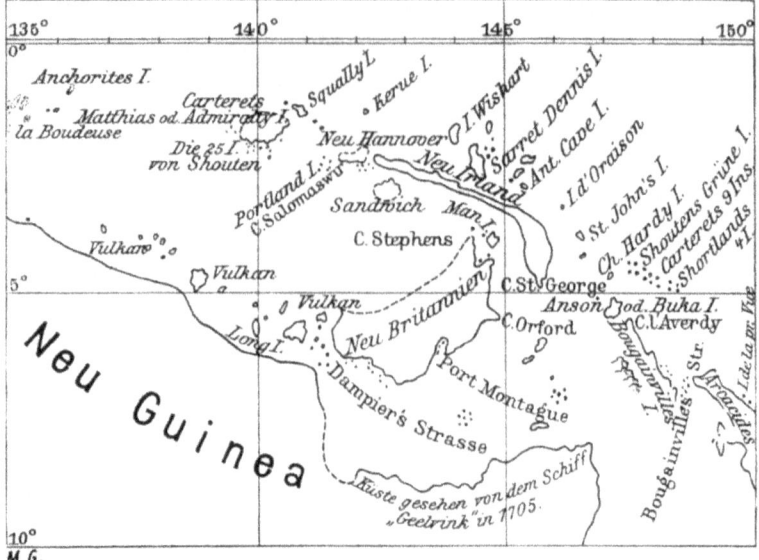

Fig. 140 (top) L.C.D. Fleurieu's map (1790)

Fig. 141 (above) Admiralty Islanders. After an engraving in D'Entrecasteaux's account of the voyage

and they got on peacefully with the islanders, who were, however, very thievish. They navigated the north coast of the main island on the 30th, and on 1 August the group was lost from sight. Contact was friendly everywhere; Labillardière accurately described the natives. However, no trace was found of the missing La Pérouse. Sailing on, they made contact with the inhabitants of the Hermit Islands, and then sailed to New Guinea.

Thus passed the expedition's first visit to the archipelago. After a voyage among the East Indian islands, along the west coast of Australia, and after visiting a number of new islands, the expedition approached the archipelago a second time, this time along the north coast of New Guinea.

Labillardière writes about this last visit:

> At daybreak on 30 June 1793 we discovered, northwest by west, a very high mountain, the flanks of which were furrowed by deep longitudinal valleys. This was Cape King William. Later we sighted the west coast of New Britain and steered towards it under full sail, so as to pass through Dampier Strait before nightfall. Since the sun was in our faces the lookout did not promptly spot a flat with

breakers, which we passed over at about 8 o'clock in the morning. We had believed that we were out of danger when again, three-quarters of an hour later, we found ourselves between two shoals that surrounded us on all sides to such an extent that, with the south-south-east wind driving us further and further in, it seemed impossible to pass through. The commander immediately ordered to go about; time was too short to carry out this manoeuvre and our ship drifted steadily towards the northern shoals ahead of us. Shipwreck seemed inevitable, when suddenly Citizen Giquel yelled from the masthead that he had spotted a passage which, although very narrow, seemed wide enough to allow our ship to pass through. Immediately steering for this pass, we finally got out of one of the most dangerous situations during the course of the expedition. We were, however, still not yet completely out of danger and, surrounded by many shoals, we were frequently obliged to alter course. However, we finally succeeded, luckily, in finding a path through the narrow channels.

Towards noon we had already travelled quite far into Dampier Strait; our latitude was 5°83'S, our longitude 146°24'E.

In direction the coast of New Britain ran from east 37° south, to east 61° north; our distance from land amounted to about 2,500 toises.

The island (Tupinier) on which Dampier had observed a volcano, lay to the west, about 38° north, about 7,600 toises away. This volcano was now extinct; however, 5,130 toises distant in the west 28° north we saw a small conical island (Ritter Island), which had shown no sign of subterranean fire during Dampier's time. From time to time, a thick column of smoke rose from the summit of this mountain; about half past three, great masses of fiery material were hurled out of the crater; they covered the eastern side of the mountain in a fiery glow and rolled down the slope until they fell into the sea, causing the water to boil, and white clouds of vapour to rise. At the time of the eruption, a dense cloud of smoke of many hues, but mostly copper-red, was thrown upwards with such violence that it rose above the highest clouds.

On the New Britain coast we saw numerous natives and several huts, which were erected on stones in the Papuan style.

We left the strait before darkness fell.

Sailing along the north coast of New Britain, we discovered several small previously unknown islands. During this journey the current was barely noticeable; at the meridian of Port Montague only did we drift quickly northwards, which led us to conclude that we were off a strait dividing New Britain in two. On 9 July we left this coast, after our exploration had been made more difficult by south-east winds and frequent calms.

For a long time our food had consisted of wormy

ship's biscuit and tainted salt pork, and therefore scurvy was very prevalent. Most of us had to refrain from drinking coffee, because it induced troublesome convulsive episodes.

On 11 July we sailed close by the Portland Islands. We sighted the eastern Admiralty Islands in the afternoon of the 12th, and about sunset on the 18th we sighted the Anchorites south-west by west.

About 7 o'clock on the 21st, our commander D'Entrecasteaux died from intractable diarrhoea, which had set in two days previously. Minor bouts of scurvy had afflicted him from time to time, but we were far from suspecting the severe loss that threatened us.

Several names of members of this expedition are preserved on current maps: D'Entrecasteaux, Willaumez, Dumerite, Cretin, Giquel, Huon, Kermadec, Riche, Duportail, and so on.

The real discoveries in the Bismarck Archipelago basically conclude with these two voyages by D'Entrecasteaux. The 19th century brought a series of more or less significant, isolated expeditions through which we become more closely acquainted with the coasts as well as with the land and people. Settlement followed only in the last quarter of the century.

After D'Entrecasteaux's expedition, it was again the French who explored the archipelago. The frigate *Coquille*, under Duperrey, visited the northern Solomon Islands, New Ireland and New Britain in 1824. Lesson, the naturalist, accompanied the expedition. Then, in 1825, we find the French admiral Dumont d'Urville on his first South Seas expedition, and again, on a second expedition, in 1838.

The Englishmen, Sir Edward Belcher in the *Sulphur* and Lieutenant Kellett in the *Starling*, visited New Ireland in 1840. In Carteret Harbour, where their ships anchored, they even met a native who spoke a little English, whom the sailors christened Tom Starling. The latter reported that, from time to time, ships from Australia touched on the coast, and that a certain amount of trading had developed. An American named Jacob Kunde, who visited the South Seas in 1834 aboard the clipper *Margaret Oakley*, gave his accounts of the contact at that time; however, these were not published until 1844. Captain Morrell of the *Margaret Oakley* had certainly behaved neither more cruelly nor more humanely in his dealings with the natives than had his contemporaries; however, his contact for the most part consisted of hostile encounters, in which the natives always drew the shorter straw.

Captain Keppel, in the English warship *Meander*, passed the Purdy Islands on 29 December 1849. On the 30th and 31st he came into contact with the Admiralty Islanders, and, although he described them as excitable and noisy, the contact was nevertheless peaceful. On 4 January 1850 he passed the Sandwich Islands, and sailed along the coast of New Ireland with the intention of visiting Hunter Harbour. This was unsuccessful, and instead, on 6 January they anchored not far away in Makada Harbour. The *Meander* remained in Carteret Harbour from 8 January until the 12th. Captain Keppel and several of his crew visited a village north of the harbour and admired the carefully laid-out, well-kept gardens. Although the natives seemed peaceful, one had to be very alert. One of the officers, who had gone hunting, allowed two natives to guide him back to the *Meander*. On the way, they tried to steal his pocket watch, and he threw one of the thieves into the water, and threatened the second with his rifle butt before compelling him to guide him on board. This minor incident is so typical that one would not be surprised today, if something similar were to occur.

The English warship *Blanche*, Captain Simpson, discovered Blanche Bay in 1872, and anchored in the inner corner behind Matupi in Simpson Harbour.

Plate 55 Forest path on the Gazelle Peninsula. Breadfruit and *canari* trees, bananas

At the same time, ships of the Hamburg firm Johann Cäsar Godeffroy & Sohn, established in Samoa, were occasionally visiting the archipelago from the Carolines, and the firm decided to open up the island group to trading. In 1873, the first traders were landed at Nogai at the foot of Mother, not far from Cape Stephens, and on the island of Matupi, by Captain Levison in the brig *Iserbrook*. The settlement at Nogai had to be abandoned after only four weeks on account of hostile behaviour from the natives, and the trader fled to his colleague on Matupi. Three weeks later, they had to flee from here as well, and seek sanctuary with an Englishman in Port Hunter, who was representing the interests of an English firm there. The following year Levison set up the first permanent German station at Mioko, Duke of York Islands.

The year 1875 greeted two scientific expeditions to the archipelago. *The Challenger*, commanded by Sir George Nares, with the scientific expedition led by Sir Charles Wyville Thomson, paid a formal visit to the Admiralty Islands from 3 until 10 March 1875. The ship anchored among small islands at the north-western end of the group, and since then the harbour has borne the name Nares Harbour. Contact with the natives was peaceful. The naturalist Moseley, who accompanied this famous expedition, gave comprehensive reliable accounts of conditions there. Our knowledge has not increased significantly since then.

The second scientific expedition was a German one, undertaken on the warship *Gazelle*, Captain von Schleinitz. It visited parts of New Hanover, New Ireland, the Gazelle Peninsula, and the island of Bougainville. The numerous German names on the map, like Bendemann, Dietert, Strauch, Rittmeyer, Steffen, Hüsker, and so on, stem from that expedition.

The same year also brought Christian missionaries to the archipelago. A Catholic mission had already been founded on Rook Island in 1852, but was abandoned after a brief existence. This time, a permanent station was founded at Hunter Harbour by the Wesleyan mission. The mission ship *John Wesley* anchored there on 15 August 1875 and, by the 16th, the missionary George Brown was marking out a building site. On 12 October, the first branch station was established at Nodup, at the foot of Mother, on the Gazelle Peninsula, and, several weeks later, two coloured catechists were stationed opposite on the coast of New Ireland.

Eduard Hernsheim founded a trading station at Makada in 1876; however, for health reasons, he transferred it to the small island of Matupi in Blanche Bay. The well-known Russian naturalist, Miklucho Maclay, visited the Admiralty Islands and several of the small western island groups the same year.

From then on warships of the various nations called in frequently, especially the ships of the English Australian squadron. The German warship *Ariadne*, Captain B. von Werner, made a visit in 1878, and subsequently, visits by German warships on the Australian station took place more and more frequently, to provide forceful backing wherever necessary to the aspiring German trade.

In 1879, the island of New Ireland was the stage for one of the greatest swindles of the century. In France that year, the Marquis de Ray established the colony 'Nouvelle France', which comprised all islands of the western Pacific that had not at that time been claimed by any power. The ship *Chandernagor* brought the first settlers, who landed at the south-east end of New Ireland. This miserable undertaking struggled on until 1882, when suddenly the great bubble burst, and the last of the cheated settlers, swindled out of their money, left the inhospitable coast. Thirteen million francs had been involved in this swindle, and numerous families were ruined.

Catholic priests who had accompanied the expedition and had, over time, seen through the swindle, moved to the Gazelle Peninsula. In 1881, Father Lanuzel set up a Catholic mission at Nodup, but had to abandon his station in 1883 as a result of dissension with the natives, caused by the activities of an Australian recruiting ship. However, the foundation of this station led to the Sacred Heart Missionary Society taking on the task, and proceeding with it.

The first plantation in the Bismarck Archipelago was established by the author in December 1882 at Ralum on the Gazelle Peninsula, and, in conjunction with this, the following year T. Farrell founded the trading and plantation firm which later experienced a significant upswing under the name E.E. Forsayth.

Since 1879, the plantations on various South Sea islands had, to a limited extent, recruited workers in the archipelago. In 1883, the rapidly flourishing sugar plantations, in Fiji and especially in Queensland, brought numerous recruiting ships to the islands, and these reappeared annually until the proclamation of the German protectorate. The labour recruiters did not exactly contribute to the pacification of the natives. Many were taken by force against their will to the distant work sites, and the newspapers of the English colonies continuously reported not only the trespasses and outrages of the recruiters, but also those on the part of the natives, usually leading to the murder of the whites, and the confiscation and destruction of the ships. The system threatened to destroy the fledgling colonisation completely, for native hatred extended gradually towards all whites, whether they were recruiters or traders and planters who had settled various coastal sites. Not a year passed by without a series of murders of whites. English warships, which would have had immediate grounds to step in because of the activity of English subjects, were very lenient towards both recruiters and natives. Cases are known where the unmotivated murder of English traders was regarded as compensated for, on the order of English warship captains, by forfeit of a few sacks of yams and several pigs, and the English press in Australia pointed with indignation to the behaviour of the warships sent out to protect colonial trade. However, the powerful Exeter Hall Party in England, which championed the natives in every case, exerted such an influence on the administration that public opinion could achieve nothing against it. Sydney newspapers of the period, although not otherwise favourably disposed towards the Germans, pointed with satisfaction to the energetic intervention of the German navy, which not only protected German life and property in those distant regions, but also extended its protection to English people and citizens of other nations, when there was no established administration.

As a consequence of the situation described above, the attention of European politics was directed more and more on the South Seas. Australia and New Zealand made various proposals to their domestic governments to seize possession of various groups, against which, strangely enough, the English statesmen of the time reacted coldly. The imperialism that blossomed so exuberantly later existed already among the people, but had not yet infected government circles. At the end of the 1870s, interest in overseas colonies had begun to stir in Germany too, and in the Reichstag the government introduced the Samoa bill, as a first tentative step; its intent was the seizure of the Samoan islands. At the time, England and America fully concurred that Germany should declare sovereignty over an island group where it demonstrably had the greatest and most extensive interests. How much humiliation, how much loss of human life, ships, and territory might the German nation have been spared if the short-sighted politics of a parliamentary party of the time, whose main driving force was opposition to the government in all things, had not caused the bill to fail. In subsequent years, it appears that the German statesmen had abandoned all further attempts to establish colonies. It was not revealed until 1884 that Prince Bismarck had deferred the matter, but not cancelled it.

On 19 August 1884, the German government ordered its general consulate in Sydney to have the German flag raised over the archipelago of New Britain and New Guinea. In November, the German corvette *Elisabeth*, Captain Schering, arrived at the archipelago from Sydney, and on 3 November 1884, the German flag was unfurled at Matupi and in subsequent days at Mioko and various places on the Gazelle Peninsula, after which both vessels, *Elisabeth* and *Hyäne*, set out on a voyage to the coast of New Guinea, to take possession of this as well for the German empire.

The English warship *Swinger* which had arrived at the archipelago to shadow the *Elisabeth*, took news of these events to Australia as fast as possible. Although it might certainly be assumed that Germany and England had made certain agreements in advance, since the south coast of New Guinea had been proclaimed an English protectorate on 6 November, there nevertheless developed an amusing hunt between both powers over who could validate their claims the fastest; on England's part also to appease public opinion, which regarded the occupation of the archipelago and part of New Guinea by the evil Germans as an added insult to the English empire. Germany unfurled its flag at various places as far as the east cape of New Guinea. England did nothing about this, but raised her banner over the same stretch as far as Cape King William, and the coast with its bright decoration of flags offered a muddle of various claims. On 29 April 1885 an exchange of notes over boundary regulations took place between the two states, and on 6 April 1886 they combined in an agreement over the boundaries of German and English spheres of influence in the western Pacific Ocean.

As a consequence of this demarcation, on 28 October of the same year, by order and in the name of His Majesty the Kaiser of Germany, the German flag was unfurled on the island of Choiseul by Captain von Wietersheim, commander of the cruiser *Adler*, and all islands of the Solomons group lying north of the designated line of demarcation were proclaimed as German protectorate. The islands of Isabel, Choiseul, the Shortland group, Bougainville and Buka, as well as various smaller groups lying to the north and north-east, were thereby incorporated into the protectorate.

On 17 March 1885, His Majesty the Kaiser bestowed an imperial letter of safe-conduct on a German company that had been constituted in Berlin on 26 May 1884 under the name of 'Neuguinea Kompanie', and, in the person of Dr Finsch, had travelled in the steamer *Samoa* and reported on the New Guinea coast between October 1884 and May 1885. Besides sovereignty, this letter guaranteed extensive privileges to the society. The first head of the protectorate, Admiral von Schleinitz, arrived at Finschhafen on 10 June 1886.

These events led generally to the expectation that development of the occupied lands would be rapid. However, it was subsequently shown that this expectation was incorrect.

On the Bismarck Archipelago (the new official name of the archipelago of New Britain), an imperial magistrate was installed soon after the arrival of the administrator, and the company installed a station manager to look after its rights. However, the island of Kerawara in the Neulauenburg group, which was designated as the seat of these officials, soon showed that it was in every way unsuitable as the seat of administration and, grudgingly, in 1889 the company resolved to transfer the station to the coast of the Gazelle Peninsula opposite. On 3 January 1890, General Director Arnold selected the site of the future settlement, and, on turning the first sod, christened it with the name Herbertshöhe. In February of the same year, the author of this book began breaking up the station on Kerawara and transferring it to Herbertshöhe. At the same time, the plantation was begun there, the first permanent settlement of the company in the Bismarck Archipelago.

It lies beyond the bounds of these brief sketches to recount the events in the archipelago at the time of the sovereignty of the New Guinea Company in detail. It is well known, that the company was in no way equal to the task set before it. Its own undertakings progressed only slowly. Many of them, after costly preparations, were abandoned as rapidly as they had been brought into existence. Foreign undertakings, if not made totally unfeasible, were restricted wherever possible by obstacles being placed in their path. In the Bismarck Archipelago in particular, where trading firms and settlers had been involved and had laid solid foundations for further development even before the constitution of the New Guinea Company, complaints increased daily, especially about inadequate protection of individuals and property. In most instances, imperial warships had to take over the police work that had been incumbent on the company, and many a settler was grateful to the willing and determined action of the commanders of those warships, enabling him to continue on in his hard-won post.

As the complaints about the company's administration increased, the company gradually came to realise that it was faced with a task whose resolution was beyond its capability. Negotiations were started with the German government, leading, after many difficulties, to the government assuming administration on 1 April 1899. The imperial safe-conduct letter of 17 May [*sic*] 1885 was rescinded, and the New Guinea Company received a settlement of 4 million Marks in compensation, payable in ten annual instalments; in addition, extensive land and mining privileges in Kaiser Wilhelmsland were granted to the company.

On his arrival, the first imperial governor, Herr von Bennigsen, chose Herbertshöhe as the future seat of the imperial authorities and the administration.

Attempts have recently been made to transfer the seat of the governor to the inner corner of Blanche Bay, Simpson Harbour. Wide-ranging objections were raised from many quarters against the practicality of this transfer, chiefly on account of the unhealthiness of the site and the total lack of a hinterland. The future will show whether these misgivings are justified.

In the last decade, the cartography of the Bismarck Archipelago has been advanced to an extraordinary degree by the undertakings of the officers of HIMS *Möwe*. A four-sheet, 1:100,000 scale map includes the Gazelle Peninsula and the coast of Neumecklenburg opposite, with St George's Channel and the Neulauenburg group in between. Also, a great part of northern Neumecklenburg is laid out in the same careful manner.

When this vast undertaking of mapping is completed, the Bismarck Archipelago will be ahead of all other island groups in the Pacific Ocean with regard to the precision of its coastal charting, and it is no more than fair that a picture of the small *Möwe*, the officers of which have given themselves a lasting memorial by this surveying, is added to this section.

For orientation of the reader, an overview map and several specific maps are appended to this work, designed by Dr M. Groll in Berlin based on the map in Sprigade and Moisel's *Grosser Deutscher kolonialatlas*. It would be highly desirable if, through local authority negotiations, perhaps through one of their appointed commissions, the names on the map of the *Kolonialatlas* were to be comprehensively revised. Not only would many place-names of coastal sites be able to be omitted without detriment to the whole work, but, above all, a correct style of writ-

Plate 56 HIMS *Möwe* in Peterhafen, French Islands

ing would have to be chosen. Thereby, one should operate universally by the definitive rules for writing such names: wherever a literary language already exists, as, for example, on the Gazelle Peninsula and on Neumecklenburg; a single rule cannot be imposed for our entire protectorate. Centuries-old names could, out of respect for the old seafarers whose names are thus revered, be quietly allowed to stand. Only in cases where no local designation exists, which is often enough the case, a new name must of course be chosen; otherwise it would be desirable for the local names to retain their prominence.

Index

Abgarris Islands 225
abortion, induced 34, 91, 120, 175
Admiralty Islands 131, 155f., 353, 361, 365
  anthropology 156ff, 163f.
  betel apparatus 163
  canoes 160
  cannibalism 173, 174
  character 157
  clothing 163
  coconut vessels 160
  division into tribes 157, 165
  fishing equipment 160
  kava 165
  knives 160
  legends 305f.
  manufacture of obsidian blades 165
  mourning decoration 163
  ornamentation 161f.
  population of (cf. Moánus, Matánkor and Usiai) 156f.
  pottery 158
  shell money 169, 173f.
  spoons 159
  villages and huts 160
  weapons 157f.
  wooden drums 164
  wooden vessels 159
adornment
  in the eastern islands 237
  in western New Britain 92-6
  of the Admiralty Islanders 161-3
  of the Solomon Islanders 214
  on Kaniet, Luf and Ninigo 197
  on New Ireland 129f.
  on St Matthias 142f.
  on the Gazelle Peninsula 61-7
  on Wuwulu and Aua 190
adultery
  among the Moánus 176

in the tribes of the north-eastern Gazelle Peninsula 29
Agomes (cf. Luf) 183, 191
agriculture 69, 71, 91, 169, 235, 341
Ahet (island) 160
Albatross Channel 116
Alim (island) 171
Allison Island 184, 191
Ambitlé (island) 111, 135
ancestor worship 38, 229, 284
Anchorite Islands (cf. Kaniet) 183, 192, 362
Andra (island) 173
Aneri 111, 117, 135, 137, 283, 284
Angriffs Island 115
anklets 96
anthropology 68, 87f., 106f., 117f., 141f., 156f., 163f., 183f., 208f., 228, 246
anthropophagy 118f., 173, 174, 211f.
aprons
  from Kaniet, Luf, and Ninigo 198f.
  of the Admiralty Islanders 162
  of the Solomon Islanders 190
Arawa 89, 91, 92, 93, 106, 200, 212
Arawa Islands 54, 88, 105f., 276
Archway Island 115
armlets
  from *Tridacna* shell 65, 131, 135, 214
  in the Admiralty Islands 162
  in the Caen Islands 135
  of the Solomons 214f.
  on Ninigo 197
  on New Ireland and New Hanover 131
  on St Matthias 143
  on the eastern islands 237

on the Gazelle Peninsula 65
on western New Britain 95f.
on Wuwulu and Aua 190
Arrove (island) 201
arrows
  of the Admiralty Islanders 158
  of the Solomon Islanders 218, 219f.
Astrolabe Bay 96
astronomy by the Moánus 168f.
Aua 143, 183f.
  population (see under Wuwulu)
Austronesian languages 87
Aveleng = Ross Islands
axes
  from Kaniet 197
  from Squally Island 153
  from the eastern islands 237
  from the Solomon Islands 217f.
  from western New Britain 102f.
  from Wuwulu and Aua 188
  of the Admiralty Islanders 158
  of the Baining 74
  of the Gazelle Peninsula 58
  on New Hanover 128f.
  on New Ireland 128f.

Bábase (island) 111, 135
Bagovegove (village) 202f.
baibai (musical instrument) 60
Baikai (island) 201
Baining 22f., 25f., 68f.
  agriculture 69, 71
  bark 73
  baskets 73
  birth 70
  body form 68

burial of the dead 70
carrying bundle 73
child slaying 70
clothing 73
cooking tubes 72
feasts 71
hairstyle 68
houses 72
languages 69, 72, 87, 311-40
legends 69
marriage 70
mask dances 265-7, 272-4
masks 267, 273f.
painted bark 73, 273
social organisation 68f.
spiritual beliefs 69f.
weapons 73f.
Baining Mountains 1, 8f., 22
Balakuwor (Credner Islands) 7
Balboa, Vasco Nuñez de 349
Balnatoman, see North Daughter
Bälz, Dr 246
Bammler, missionary 289
Bamus = South Son
Banks Islands 143
Banniu Bay 199, 204
Baraff 135
Barahun (island) 206
bark fabric 73, 95, 162, 197, 268
Batamma (island) 201
battle axes
  of the Admiralty Islanders 158
  of the Baining 74
  on the Gazelle Peninsula 58
Baudissin Island 116
beard styles 65, 95, 129, 152
Beehives (rocks) 6
Behrens, Karl Friedrich 360
Belcher, Sir Edward 365
Below, von 14
belts 65, 73, 95, 135, 143, 162, 196f., 214,

237
Bennigsen, Governor von 15, 88, 139, 165, 368
Berry Island 171
Betaz (island) 206
betel 72, 92, 145, 152, 161, 163, 188, 196
Bird Island 173
birth 33, 177, 231
birth, customs
  among the Baining 70
  among the Moánus 176
  among the Solomon Islanders 211
  among the Sulka 78
  in the eastern islands 231
  in the tribes of the north-eastern Gazelle Peninsula 33f.
  on Kaniet 192
  on Luf 194f.
  on New Ireland 121, 136
  on Ninigo 195
Bit (island) 111
Blanche Bay 3, 6f., 249, 252, 258, 365
Bley, Father 87, 311
blood-letting 51
blowpipe 96
Bo (district) 111
bone fractures, treatment of 51
Bougainville (island) 199-205, 363
  population, see Solomon Islands
Bougainville, Louis Antoine de 199, 203, 362
Bougainville strait 362
bows
  of the Admiralty Islanders 158
  of the Solomon Islanders 218, 220
Broadmead Island 171
Brown, missionary 76, 311, 366
Brown Island 77
Buchner, Professor 131
Buka 191, 204-6, 284, 361, 363
  population, see Solomon Islands
bullroarer
  among the Sulka 275
  in the Solomon Islands 286
  on the Gazelle Peninsula 61
  on western New Britain 61, 276
burial embellishments 38
burial of the dead
  among the Baining 70
  among the Sulka 80
  among the tribes of the north-eastern Gazelle Peninsula 34f.
  in the eastern islands 231f.
  of the Matánkor 173
  of the Moánus 179f.
  of the Solomon Islanders 211
  of the Usiai 169f.
  on Kaniet 194
  on Luf 194f.
  on New Hanover 122
  on New Ireland 122f., 136f.
  on Niningo 195
burial places 236
Butam 26, 74f.
Byron, Captain 360
Byron strait 114, 115, 116, 361

Caen Islands 50, 111, 135, 283
cannibalism, see anthropophagy
canoe sheds 104, 186, 196, 214, 235
canoes
  from Nakanai 103f.
  from New Ireland and New Hanover 132
  from the Duke of Yorks 46, 48
  from Uatom 46
  from western New Britain 103
  of the Admiralty Islanders 160
  of the French Islands 104
  of the Gazelle Peninsula 47f.
  of the Solomon Islanders 221
  of the Sulka 104
  on Kaniet 195
  on Luf 195
  on Ninigo 195f.
  on St Matthias 147, 148
  on Squally Island 151, 153
  on the eastern islands 235
  on Wuwulu and Aua 186
Cape Balli = South Cape
Cape Banniu 199f., 204
Cape Buller 26, 74, 273
Cape Cretin 92
Cape Friendship 200f.
Cape Gallego 350
Cape Gazelle 1, 3, 24, 361
Cape Giori 127
Cape Gloucester 1, 99, 105
Cape Hüsker 205
Cape Lambert 1, 9, 46
Cape l'Averdie 199f., 203f., 362
Cape le Cras 199, 202, 225
Cape Livuan 25, 46, 312
Cape Matantéberen 115
Cape Merkus (Mulius) 13, 15, 26, 91, 92, 105
Cape Moltke 200, 205
Cape Orford 2, 77, 274
Cape Palliser 2, 273, 361
Cape Pedder 88
Cape Quass 11, 12
Cape Queen Charlotte 144
Cape Raoult 91
Cape Roebuck 12, 26, 88, 106, 108
Cape St George 111, 114, 127, 359, 363
Cape Santa Maria 51, 111, 115, 117, 352, 355, 359
Cape Stephens 1, 312, 366
Cape Strauch 127
Cape Turner 77
Carola Harbour 206
Carteret, Philip 114, 183, 199, 221, 360-2
Carteret Harbour 114, 359, 365
Carteret Islands 199, 206, 360
catastrophic flooding in western New Britain 14
chest ornaments
  in western New Britain 95
  of the Solomon Islanders 214
  on New Hanover 131
  on New Ireland 130f.
  on the Admiralty Islands 131, 161
child murder 70, 91, 211
children, treatment and raising of
  in the eastern islands 231
  on Kaniet 192
  on New Ireland 121
  on the north-eastern Gazelle Peninsula 34
Choiseul (island) 362
Christian, F.W. 189
circumcision 79, 150, 152, 177
clothing
  of the Admiralty Islanders 163f.
  of the Solomon Islanders 214f.
  on Kaniet, Luf and Ninigo 196f.
  on New Ireland 121
  on St Matthias 142f.
  on Squally Island 153
  on the eastern islands 237f.
  on Wuwulu and Aua 190
clubs
  of Jacquinot and Montague bays 100
  of the Admiralty Islanders 158
  of the Baining 73f.
  of the eastern islands 237
  of the Gazelle Peninsula 57f.
  of the Solomon Islanders 220f.
  of the Sulka 99f.
  of the Tumuip 99f.
  of Wuwulu and Aua 186f.
  on New Ireland and New Hanover 126f.
  on western New Britain 100
Coconut Island 114
coconut money 238
coconut scraper 92, 145, 236
Codrington 287, 290, 291
coloured patterns on the Gazelle Peninsula 62
combs 93, 142f., 161, 197
Commerson Island 192
Commodore Bay 1, 12
conclusion of peace
  among the Moánus 178
  in western New Britain 89
  on the Gazelle Peninsula 29
cooking tubes of the Baining 72
counting with shell money 40f.
Couppé, Bishop 3, 311
Credner Islands 3
Crown Prince Range 199f., 201, 218f.
Crump, missionary 50
cultivated plants 71, 91, 145, 169, 190, 341-6

daggers 158
Dampier, William 114, 127, 139, 153, 359f.
Dampier Strait 14, 360
dances
  ceremonial 67
  erotic 124
  invention of 67
  of the men 67f., 124f.
  of the Solomon Islanders 213 (see also mask dances)
  of the Usiai 169f.
  of the women 67f., 125f.
  rehearsal of 68
  on New Ireland 124f.
  on the Gazelle Peninsula 66f.
  on Wuwulu and Aua 189
  profane 67, 125

INDEX

sale of 67
totemistic 125
war 125
Danneil, Dr 12, 215, 239
Dawaun (village) 263, 312
decorative scars
   in the Solomon Islands 212f.
   in western New Britain 96
   on New Ireland 129
   on the Gazelle Peninsula 63
Deep Bay 115
D'Entrecasteaux, Bruny 363
D'Entrecasteaux Islands 105
Deslacs (island) 17, 98
Dieterici Islands 202
Dietertberg 115
Diwarra 38, 41
Djaule (= Sandwich Islands) 114, 115
Dover Island 172
drill burr 41, 215, 218, 238
drum signals 59, 126
drums, see skin drums, and wooden drums
duk-duk 34, 38, 249-57
Duke of York group 17-19, 22
   population number 18f.
   surface area 18
Duke of York Islands = Neulauenburg
Dumont d'Urville, Admiral 365
Dungenun Point 206
Duperrey 365
Duportail Island 11, 26, 101
Durour Island 183, 361
dwarfs 82

Ealusau (island) 148
ear ornaments
   in the Admiralty Islands 161
   in the eastern islands 237
   in western New Britain 93
   of the Solomon Islanders 214
   on Kaniet, Luf and Ninigo 197
   on New Ireland and New Hanover 131
   on Wuwulu and Aua 190
eastern islands, see Nuguria, Nukumanu, and Tauu
   agriculture 235
   ancestor feast 232
   anthropology 228f.

   birth and childhood 231
   burial of the dead 231f.
   burial sites 236
   canoes 235
   clothing 238
   fishing 234
   household utensils 236
   houses 235f.
   language 229
   marriage 230
   money 238
   ornaments 237
   population 228-40
   puberty ceremonies 231
   religion 229f.
   social organisation 230, 233f.
   status of the wife 234
   tattooing 232f.
   weapons 237
   weaving 238-40
   wells 236
Eberlein, Father 76
l'Echiquier Islands 183, 362 (see also Ninigo)
Edge-Partington 196
Ehánu (island) 206
Ehüene (island) 206
Elemakunaur (district) 141
Elemusoa (island) 148
Elizabeth Harbour 115
Elizabeth Island 155, 171
Emanaus (island) 141
Emirau 139, 149, 153
Emperor Island 206
Emperor Range 199f., 205, 217, 219
Empress Augusta Bay 200, 205, 212
Emusaun (island) 141
Epiül (island) 206
Ernst-Gunther-Hafen 199, 204
Esau (Esow) Island 206, 352
Etalat (district) 141
Etongane (island) 141

Father (volcano) 11, 39
du Faure-Berg 15
Fead Islands 225
Fedarb Islands 171
Ferguson, Captain 202
Finni 135
Finsch, Dr 11, 96, 106, 367
Finschhafen 92, 96
fire-making 92
Fischer Island 111, 131, 132, 276, 278f.
fishing
   in the Admiralty Islands 160
   in the eastern islands 234f.
   in the Solomon Islands 221f.

   on Kaniet, Luf and Ninigo 197
   on New Ireland 133
   on St Matthias 145
   on Squally Island 153
   on the Gazelle Peninsula 43-6
   on Wuwulu and Aua 190
fishing spears 46, 133, 147, 160, 187, 190, 234
Fison, Dr 291
flutes 60, 145, 276
forbidden foods 76, 81, 138
Forestier (island) 17
Forsayth, E.E. 13, 207, 225, 274, 366
Foy, Dr W. 257
French Islands 17, 91, 92, 93f., 96, 98f., 102, 104, 276
Friedrich Wilhelmshafen 92
Frobenius, L. 257
Fromm, Father 257

Gak*tei* 76
Gallego, Hernandez 350
Gardner Islands 111, 115, 120, 131, 132, 276f., 279f., 282, 359
gatherings of the people on the north-eastern Gazelle Peninsula 28
Gazelle Peninsula 1-11
   coastal navigation 9f.
   economic significance 10f.
   inhabitants 19-76
   north-east, its inhabitants 22ff.
   birth 33f.
   body painting 61ff.
   burial of the dead 34-8
   canoes 47
   catching turtles 46f.
   childhood 34
   conclusion of peace 56
   dances 66f.
   decorative scars 63
   fishing 43ff.
   immigration from New Ireland 22-5
   jewellery 63-7
   judicial customs 29
   language 23f., 311-17
   marriage 29f.
   masks 43, 250f., 257f., 259
   medical knowledge 48f.
   musical instruments 58f.
   secret societies 249-57, 259-65

   shell money 38-41
   social organisation 28f.
   sorcery 52-5
   tattooing 63
   trepanation 49f.
   vuvuei feast 42
   warfare 55f.
   weapons 56f.
   plantations 11
   settlement 22f.
geographical nomenclature 17f.
Gerrit Denys Island 50, 111f., 359
geysers
   in the French Islands 17
   on the Willaumez Peninsula 15f.
Giglioli, Professor 128
Gilbert Islands 239, 242
Gillen 292
Giquelberg 15
Godeffroy and Son, J.C. 19, 366
Golau = North Son
Gower Harbour 362
Grabowsky 196
Green Island 172
Green Islands 352, 354
Guinot volcano 200

Haddon, Prof. 289
Hagen, Dr 106
Hahl, Governor Dr 12, 189
hair dyeing 61
hair ornaments
   on the Gazelle Peninsula 63f.
   in western New Britain 92, 93
   of the Matánkor 163
   of the Solomon Islanders 214
   on St Matthias 142
   on Wuwulu and Aua 190
hairstyles 68, 129, 142, 152, 161, 190, 215
Hanahan (district) 206, 209
Hanita (island) 173
Hannamhafen 15
Haréngan (island) 172, 174
Háuai (island) 173
Hayrick Island 155
headbands
   from the Gazelle Peninsula 65
   in western New Britain 93
headmen
   in Siara 136
   in the eastern islands 230, 233f.
   in western New Britain 89

on the Gazelle Peninsula 27f.
of the Moánus 176
of the Solomon Islanders 209
Heinroth, Dr 140
Hellwig 183f., 191
Henry Reid Bay 2, 76f.
Herbertshöhe 6, 19, 368
Hermit Islands 183, 191, 362f.
population, see Luf
Hernsheim & Co. 19, 116, 139, 140, 183, 366
Hetau (island) 206
Hixon Bay 11
Hohn (island) 203
Holmes River = Toriu
Horne Islands 171
household utensils 132, 144f., 153, 158f., 161, 188, 197, 216f., 236
Howitt 100, 292
Hulungau (island) 174
human sacrifice at burials 38, 80, 91
Hunstein 14
Hunstein Mountain 14
Hunter, Commodore 363
Hunterhafen (Port Hunter) 19, 363, 366
hunting 71, 91, 223
Huon Bay 96
Hus (island) 173
huts
in the eastern islands 235f.
in western New Britain 91
of the Admiralty Islanders 161
of the Solomon Islanders 213f.
on Kaniet, Luf and Ninigo 196
on New Hanover 131f.
on New Ireland 132
on St Matthias 143f., 147
on Squally Island 152
on Wuwulu and Aua 185f.

illnesses, customs during 52f.
ingiet 34, 52f., 65f., 76, 259-65
internal illnesses, treatment of 51f.
Islas de la Magdalena 353
Itasidl (district) 141

Jacquinot Bay 4, 11, 12, 26, 76, 100
Jacquinot Island 156
Jakupia 37
Jesus Maria Islands 155, 171
jew's harp 60
Johann-Albrecht-Hafen 17
judicial customs 29, 175, 176

Kabakaul 3, 312
Kabange Bay 252
Kabien Peninsula 116
Kabokon (island) 19
Kadakadai (district) 252, 259
Kaianu (district) 201
Kaije (volcano) 6, 22
Kaléu (island) 139, 140, 141
kamara 29
Kambair 249
Kambange (district) 75
Kaniet 183, 192
betel utensils 196
birth 192
burial of the dead 194
canoes 195
clothing 196f.
household utensils 197
huts 196
ornaments 197
population 192-7
population number 192
puberty ceremonies 192f.
weapons 196
Kapsu 116, 128
Karawat 3, 75
Karawia 250, 312
Kärnbach 183
Karo (River) 9
Karutz, Dr 187
Katitj (island) 205, 206
kava 165
Kavieng 115, 116
Kéa (island) 171
Keaop (island) 204, 209f.
Keppel, Captain 133, 365
Kerawara (island) 19, 252, 368
Kerué 139, 148
natives of 148-51
King, Lieutenant 153
King Albert Strait 199, 204, 205
Kininigunan 252
Kintjáwon (village) 173
kite fishing 222
Kobaiai (island) 201
Koch, Geheimrat Dr R. 15, 88
Kolvagát (village) 82
Kombiu, see Mother
Koromira (district) 201
Korónjat (island) 173
ko-t (spirit) 81, 172
Kubary 192, 246
Kumúli (island) 171
Kure (village) 115, 117
Kurumut (village) 111
Kusaie 143, 239

Labangerarum (village) 277
Lalobé (village) 163, 165
Lamassa (island) 114
Lambom (island) 114
lamentation for the dead 35, 122
Landip (village) 252
Langalanga = Hixon Bay
language
of Nakanai 87, 335-40
of Siara 136
of Squally Island 151
of the Baining 69, 72, 87, 322-8
of the Butam 76
of the Duke of Yorks 317-22
of the natives of the Gazelle Peninsula 23f., 311-17
of the O Mengen 335
of the Solomon Islanders 209
of the Sulka 87, 328-35
of the Taulil 76
of the Tumuip 335
of Wuwulu and Aua 190f.
Lanuzel, Father 366
Latau (island) 114
Laueáhafen 204
Laur (district) 115, 134, 252, 284
La Vandola (island) 174, 364
legends
from the Gazelle Peninsula 295-9
of the Admiralty Islanders 305-9
of the Baining 69, 330
of the Sulka 299-305
Lehon (island) 206
Le Maire, Jacob 352
Lerum (River) 81
Levison, Captain 366
Lihir (Lir) (= Gerrit Denys) 111, 118, 119, 134, 284
Limondrol (village) 171
line fishing 46, 133, 145, 160, 190, 197, 222, 234
Liot (island) 191
Liueniua 225f., 227
migration legends 227f.
Lólau (island) 171
Lolobau = Duportail Island
loloi (rolls of money) 38, 40
Lómpoa (village) 170
Londip (district) 75
Lóniu (village) 172, 173
Lord Anson's Island 361f.
Los Negros Islands 173
Los Reyes Islands 172

Lótja (village) 170
Lou (island) 164f., 171, 173, 174
Luf 183, 191
betel utensils 196
canoes 195
clothing 197
customs 194f.
huts 196
ornaments 197
population numbers 192
weapons 196
Lúhuan (village) 173
Lundis (district) 209
Luschan, Prof. von 18, 127, 183, 187, 215, 219, 274
luxuries (cf. also betel, kava, tobacco) 72, 92, 145

Mabirri 202
MacGregor, Sir William 107, 292
Magelhaens, Fernando 349
magic charms 63f.
magic potions
malira 53f.
pepe 54f.
taring 54
Maitland Islands 174
Makada (island) 19, 366
Malai Bay 172
Malakat (mountain) 140
Malakuna (district) 75
Malelif (island) 111
Malenaput (island) 111
Maletafa (island) 111
Mali = San Bruno
Malikolo 88
Malulu (island) 206
Malum (atoll) 225, 226
Mándrindr (island) 173
Man Island = Uatom
Manus (island) 191
Marankol 163
marawot, see *ingiet*
Marken Islands 352, 354f.
Marqueen Islands 225
marriage
among the Moánus 175
among the Solomon Islanders 210f.
in the eastern islands 230f.
in the tribes of the north-eastern Gazelle Peninsula 29f.
on Kaniet, Luf and Ninigo 194f.
on New Ireland 120f., 136
marriage contracting
among the Baining 70
among the Moánus 175, 176
among the Solomon

INDEX

Islanders 210
  in the eastern islands 230f.
  in the Sulka 77
  in the tribes of the north-eastern Gazelle Peninsula 30f.
  on New Hanover 120
  on New Ireland 120
marriage prohibition
  among the Moánus 175
  among the Sulka 77
  in the eastern islands 230f.
  in the Solomon Islands 210, 287
  in the tribes of the north-eastern Gazelle Peninsula 29, 265
  on New Ireland 120, 282
  on St Matthias 150f.
  on Siara, Tanga and Aneri 283f.
Marshall Islands 239, 242
Martin Islands 200f., 202
Masava (island) 8, 24, 46, 311f.
mask dances (see also *duk-duk*)
  of the Baining 265-7
  on New Ireland 276f.
  of the Sulka 78f., 275f.
masks
  from Aneri 284
  from Bougainville, Buka and Nissan 284f.
  from Lihir 284
  from Möwehafen and the Arawa Islands 276
  from New Ireland 277-9
  from Tanga 283
  from the French Islands 276
  of the Baining 267f., 273
  of the Gazelle Peninsula 43, 250f., 257-9
  of the Sulka 274f.
Masikonápuka (island) 9, 24, 46, 311f.
Massait = San Joseph
Matánkor 119, 157, 158, 161, 163-5
  character 168
  dwelling sites 172-4
  significance of the name 170
matasesén 285f.
Matehes (island) 205, 206
Matty Island 183, 361 (see also Wuwulu)
Matupi 6, 263, 312, 366
Matzungan (island) 204
Maur = San Francisco
Maurelle, Captain 362
Mausoleum Island 115

Mävlu (Powell River) 77
Mbúke (island) 170-2
Mbúnai (village) 170, 172
Mbutjoruo (island) 173
Mbutmanda (island) 172
mealtimes 92
medical knowledge
  of natives of New Ireland 50f.
  of natives of the Gazelle Peninsula 48-51
Meier, Father P.J. 165
Melanesian languages 87
men's houses 147f., 161, 214
Mencke, Bruno 139f.
Mendaña, Alvaro 350f.
Mérite (island) 17, 93, 98
migration legends
  from Liueniua 227
  from Nuguria 226
Miklucho-Maclay 366
Mioko (island) 19, 252, 366
mission
  Catholic 70, 116, 336
  of the Sacred Heart of Jesus 3, 366
  Wesleyan 116, 366
Mlol 81
Moánus 119, 157f., 161, 163f.
  astronomy 169f.
  birth 177
  burial of the dead 179f.
  character 168
  chiefdom 176
  dwelling sites 170-2
  judicial practices 176
  marriage 175f.
  naming 177
  puberty ceremonies 177
  songs 180f.
  sorcery 169, 175f., 178f.
  totemism 174
  trade 173f.
  war 177f.
Moila Point 199, 200, 205
mokpelpel (eater of human flesh) 81
Mologoviu (volcano) 203
money, see coconut money, shell money, teeth money
Montague Bay 12, 26, 93, 100, 101f., 359
Morrell, Captain 365
Mortlock Islands 207, 225
Moseley 366
Mother (volcano) 6f., 361
Móuk (island) 171f.
Mount Balbi 199, 202
Mount Below 14
Mount Bendemann 115

Mourning decoration 37, 62
Möwehafen 13, 26, 38, 89, 92, 276
Müller, Hermann (missionary) 76f., 330, 335
Mundua = Forestier
musical instruments
  of the Solomon Islanders 213
  on New Ireland 126
  on St Matthias 145
  on the Gazelle Peninsula 58-61
Musson (= Nissan) 135
Mutlar 2

Nabutu Bay 111, 114, 115
Nago (island) 115
Nakanai 12, 26, 39f., 87, 91, 92, 95-103
  language 87, 335-40
  people of 88, 89
name-giving
  among the Moánus 177
  among the Sulka 78
  among the tribes of the north-eastern Gazelle Peninsula 33
Namisoko = Duportail Islands
Nanuk (Credner Islands) 7, 263
Napapar (district) 311
Naraga (island) 91
Nares, Sir George 366
Nares Harbour 366
nasal ornaments
  in the Admiralty Islands 161
  in the eastern islands 230, 237
  in western New Britain 93
  of the Solomon Islanders 214
  on Kaniet and Luf 197
  on New Ireland and New Hanover 131
  on the Gazelle Peninsula 66
Naumaúma (district) 75
Naúna (island) 174
Nauru 239
Ndrel (village) 173
Ndréu (island) 171
Ndrilo (island) 173
Ndriol (villlage) 171
Ndrówa (island) 172
Ndruval (island) 163, 165, 172
Ndruwiu (island) 173
neck ornaments
  from the Gazelle Peninsula 65
  in the Admiralty Islands 161
  in western New Brit-

ain 95
  on New Ireland 130
  on Ninigo 197
  on St Matthias 143
Nehuss Point 199, 203
net fishing 45f., 133, 145, 160, 190, 197, 221-3, 234
New Britain 1-109
  central part 11f.
  earthquakes 1
  Gazelle Peninsula 1-11
  geological structure 1
  inhabitants 19-109 (see also Gazelle Peninsula and western New Britain)
  surface area 1
  volcanoes 1
  western part 12-17
New Guinea Company 11, 19, 367f.
New Hanover 114, 116, 359
  natives of 117-35 (see under New Ireland)
New Ireland 111-17
  anthropology 117f.
  birth 121
  burial of the dead 122-4
  cannibalism 118-20
  canoes 132f.
  carving 278-80
  character 118
  clothing 121
  dances 124-6, 276-8
  fishing 133f.
  houses 131f.
  marriage 120f.
  masks 277-83
  money 134f.
  musical instruments 126
  natives of 70-138
  ornaments 129-31
  puberty 121, 122
  secret societies 276f.
  stone figures 284
  totemism 280
  weapons 126-8
Ngówui (island) 171
Ninigo 143, 164, 183, 191
  canoes 195f.
  clothing 197
  customs 195
  household utensils 197
  huts 196
  ornaments 197
  population number 192
  trade 195
  weapons 196
Nissan 135, 199, 206, 284, 352, 361
  population, see Solomon Islands
Noanaur (island) 141
Nodup 366
Nonga (village) 311

Normanby Island 100
North Cape 111, 115
North Daughter (volcano) 6
North Son (volcano) 11
Nuguria 190, 225, 226
  immigration legends 226
  population, see eastern islands
Nukufetau 227
Nukumanu 190, 225f.
  population, see eastern islands
Nukuoro 226
Numanuma (village) 202f.
nunut (musical instrument) 126
Nusa 115f., 132, 243
Nusa Harbour 115, 132, 243
Nusalik (island) 115

O Mengen 76, 102, 335
obsidian, manufacture of blades from 165
Ongtong Java 207, 225, 227, 353
Open Bay 9, 11f., 76
ornamentation
  of the Baining 268
  on New Ireland 127
  on St Matthias 147
Otua (island) 201

Paanopa 239
Pahakáreng (village) 173
Pahalum (village) 81
painting of the body
  in the Admiralty Islands 161
  in the eastern islands 237
  in the Solomon Islands 215
  in western New Britain 93
  on New Ireland 129
  on the Gazelle Peninsula 61f.
Pak (island) 171, 172, 174, 175
Palaiai (island) 171
Palakukúr (village) 74, 75
Palamot (village) 171f.
Paleawe 12, 76, 99
Palúal (island) 172
pan flutes 60, 127, 213
pangolo (stringed instrument) 60f.
Papimbutj (island) 173
Papitálai (village) 170, 171-3, 174
Papuan languages 87
Papuans, origin of 106
Parroran (island) 206
Patúam (island) 171
Patúsi (village) 170

Pelau (island) 227
pele (shell money) 41f.
penis shell 142, 150, 162, 170
Pére (village) 170, 172
Pérouse, Comte de la 363
Peschel, Oskar 242
Peterhafen 17
Pflüger, Dr A. 15, 17
Phoon Islands 206
Pierson, missionary 124
Pinepil (island) 206, 212, 352
Pitilu (Pidelo) (island) 158, 173
plaiting 158, 217
Poam (island) 165, 174
Poauárei (village) 170
Poekálas (village) 173
pole buildings 91, 161
Polotjal (village) 173, 174
polygamy 32, 121, 175, 210
Polynesians, migrations of 240-6
Pónam (island) 173
Ponape 165, 189
Pongópou (village) 173
Popapu (island) 173
Port Breton 114
Port Hunter, see Hunterhafen
Port Praslin 114
Portland Islands 114, 361, 365
Potomo (island) 173
pottery 158f., 169, 216, 241f.
Powell 92
Powell Harbour 9
property 28f., 69, 175, 177, 210f., 233f.
puberty ceremonies 78, 121, 122, 177, 192f., 231, 275f., 285
Pulié River 13
Punro (village) 164
Purdy Islands 155, 365
purification ceremonies 78, 80
Putput = Rügenhafen
Putúli (island) 172
Pyramidenberg 15

Quiros, Pedro Fernandez de 351

Rabaul 6
Raluana 250, 252, 253
Ralum 6, 252, 263
Ramandu (district) 312
Rambutjo (island) 171, 172, 173, 174
Raoulberg 15
Rapitok (district) 75
Rascher (Father Mathäus) 9, 12, 25, 68, 69, 70, 76, 266, 267, 272,

311
Ratzel, Prof. 238
Rautan (island) 200
Rautan Strait 201
Ray, Marquis de 114, 366
Rebar (district) 75
religion, see ancestor worship, spiritual beliefs, sorcery
Réta (island) 172, 173
Rickard, missionary 311
right of succession 27, 175, 176, 234
ring money 215f.
Ritter Island 14, 364
Rocholl (surveyor) 3
Roggeveen, Jacob 360
Roitan (district) 141
Rook Island 29, 95, 360
Ross Islands 13
Rossel Range 111, 114, 117, 118, 123, 127, 131
Rotuma 226, 228
Rügenhafen (Putput) 2f.
Ruk-Ruk 285

Saavedra, Alvaro de 349
Sae (island) 192
St Andrew Islands 155
St George Island 171, 175
St George's Channel 2, 111, 249, 273
St John 111, 119, 133, 135, 206, 283, 284
St Matthias 139-41, 359, 362
  anthropology 141f.
  canoes 145, 148
  clothing and ornaments 142f.
  dance batons 147
  fishing equipment 145, 147
  foodstuffs and luxuries 145
  houses and domestic utensils 143f., 147f.
  musical instruments 145
  natives of 140-8
  weapons 145-7
  weaving 143, 148
St Patrick Islands 155, 172
St Paul (mission station) 9
Sal (island) 206
Salapio (island) 115
Sali (village) 164
salt harvesting 91, 347
San Bruno (island) 111
San Francisco (island) 111
San Gabriel (island) 155, 171, 174
San Joseph (island) 111
San Miguel (island) 172
San Rafael (island) 155,

174
sandals 235
Sandwich Island 114, 115, 127, 276, 365
Santa Cruz 143
Sapiu (village) 202
Saposá (island) 211
scar tattooing, see decorative scars
Schack, Commander 139
Schellong, Dr 289
Schering, Captain 367
Schleinitz, von Admiral 15, 199, 366, 367
Schleinitz Mountains 111, 115
Schmidt, Prof. W. 87
Schnee, Dr 170, 274, 312
Schouten Islands 156
Schouten, Willem Corneliszoon 352
Schulze Point 6, 312
Scilly Islands 9
secret societies 247-90
  in New Guinea 289f.
  in the New Hebrides 288
  in the Solomon Islands 211, 285
  in western New Britain 276
  of the Gazelle Peninsula 249-57, 259-65
  of the Sulka 275
  on Florida 287, 288
  on New Ireland 276f.
  on the Banks and Torres Islands 287
Serrano, Francisco 349
shark-catching 132f., 173
shell money
  in the Admiralty Islands 169, 174
  in the Duke of Yorks 38f., 40f.
  in the Solomon Islands 215f.
  on Aneri 135
  on Nakanai 41
  on New Hanover 134
  on New Ireland 41f., 134f.
  on the north-eastern Gazelle Peninsula 28, 38-41
shields
  from Nakanai 101
  from the French Islands 101
  from the South Cape 102
  from the Willaumez Peninsula 101
  in western New Britain 96, 100-2
  of the O Mengen 105
  of the Sulka 100, 104
shooting stars 53, 81, 229
Siara (district) 111, 115,

117, 129, 135, 283
Sikaiana 227
Simberi (= Fischer Island) 111
Simpson, Captain 365
Simpson Harbour 7, 366, 368
Sir Charles Hardy Islands 199, 206, 352
Sirot (island) 206
Sisi (island) 172, 173, 174
Siwisa (island) 170f., 174
skin drums
  on Kaniet 197
  on the Gazelle Peninsula 59
  on Wuwulu and Aua 189
skull deformation 26, 88f.
skull masks 257-9
slingshots
  in western New Britain 99
  of the Baining 73
  on New Ireland 127
  on the Gazelle Peninsula 56
Slinger's Bay 127, 359
Smith, Percy 242
social organisation of the natives 243
  in the eastern islands 230
  of the Baining 68f.
  of the Gazelle Peninsula 27f.
  of the Moánus 176
  of the Usiai 169
Sohanna (island) 204
Solomon Islands, German 199-207
  anthropology 208f.
  axes 217
  birth 211
  burial of the dead 211
  cannibalism 211f.
  canoes 221
  chiefdom 209
  clothing 214f.
  dances 213
  decorative scars 212f.
  domestic utensils 216f.
  fishing 221-3
  houses 213f.
  hunting 223
  jewellery 214
  languages 209
  marriage 210
  masks 284f.
  money 215f.
  musical instruments 213
  ornamentation 219
  population 208
  puberty ceremonies 285f.
  secret societies 211, 285
  songs 213
  tools 218
  totemism 210, 286
  trading 209f.
  weapons 218-21
songs
  of the *duk-duk* society 252f.
  of the Moánus 180f.
  of the Solomon Islanders 213
sorcery
  against illness 53, 54, 82, 178f.
  against theft 52, 84
  for protection during battle 66, 84
  in the eastern islands 230
  of the Matánkor 173f.
  of the Moánus 169, 175, 178f.
  of the Sulka 82-5
  on the Gazelle Peninsula 52-5, 260
  to awaken love 54, 65, 66, 82, 179
  to cause sickness or death 52f., 54, 83f., 86
  to give a good harvest 85
  to influence the weather 85
  to make one brave and strong 65
  to make weapons effective 56f., 58, 84
Sori (island) 173, 174
souls
  driving out of 80
  resting places of 36f., 81, 137, 172, 230
South Cape 1, 12f., 38, 91, 92, 93, 102, 103, 108, 276
South Daughter (volcano) 6
South Son (volcano) 11, 39
Sovie (island) 201
spears
  from Kaniet, Luf and Ninigo 196
  from the eastern islands 237
  from Wuwulu and Aua 186
  in the French Islands 98
  in western New Britain 98
  of the Admiralty Islanders 157f.
  of the Baining 73
  of the natives of the Gazelle Peninsula 56f.
  of the Solomon Islanders 218f.
  of the Sulka 98
  on Nakanai 98
  on New Ireland and New Hanover 127f.
  on St Matthias 145-7
  on Squally Island 153
  on the Willaumez Peninsula 98
Spencer 292
spiritual beliefs
  in the eastern islands 229f.
  of the Baining 69f.
  of the Matánkor 173f.
  of the Sulka 81
  of the Usiai 172
  on Kaniet 194
  on Ninigo 195
  on Siara, Aneri and Tanga 137f.
  on the Gazelle Peninsula 53-5
springs 236
Squally Island 139, 151f., 359, 362
staining of the teeth 61, 79f.
Stalio Island 201
Steffen Strait 114, 115, 116
Stettiner Bay 89, 103
stick-throwing on Wuwulu 189f.
stone figures 284
stone structures, prehistoric,
  in *Samoa* 244f.
  on Ponape 243
stoneware, prehistoric 243
Stoschberg 116
stringed instruments 60f.
Suf (island) 192
Sugarloaf Island 155
Suhm Island 174
Sulka 76-87, 95, 98, 99, 100f., 104
  blackening of the teeth 79f.
  burial of the dead 80
  canoes 103f.
  circumcision 79
  clothing 95
  clubs 99
  dwelling sites 77
  language 87, 330-5
  legends 86, 299-305
  marriage 77f.
  mask dances 78, 275f.
  masks 274f.
  intellectual and spiritual beliefs 81f.
  puberty ceremonies 78
  purification ceremonies 78, 80
  shields 100f.
  social organisation 77
  sorcery 82-5
  spears 97f.

Tabar 114, 118, 134
tabu, see shell money

Taguu (= Tauu) 225
Takumal (island) 171
Talele = Scilly Islands
Talvat (village) 252
Tamaneiriki (district) 75, 311
Tami Islands 91f., 104
Tanga (island) 111, 117, 135, 283
Tarawa 227
Tasman, Abel 129, 133f., 350, 353-8
Tasman Islands 225
tattooing
  in Siara 129, 135f.
  in the eastern islands 231-3
  on the Gazelle Peninsula 63
  on western New Britain 96
Taulil 25f., 74-6
Tauu 190, 225-7
  population, see eastern islands
Tava na tangir = Powell Harbour
Tavanumbattir, see North Daughter
Teeth money 215
Tekareu (island) 203
Tench Island 153
Teng (village) 173
terrace formation 12f., 27
Teworran (island) 204
Thiel, Max 164, 195
Thilenius, Prof. G. 192, 195f., 196, 225, 226, 228, 230
tidir (musical instrument) 60
Tikopia 226, 228
Tiliánu (island) 172
tinbut (musical instrument) = *tutupele*
Tingenataberan 36f.
Tingenavudu (district) 75
Tinputs (village) 204
Tjápale (village) 170
Tjawompitou (village) 170
Tjókua (island) 171
Tjovondra (island) 172
Tjuándral (island) 173
tobacco 72, 92, 344
Toboroi (village) 199, 201, 217
Toioch (island) 205, 206
Toiupu (= Mount Balbi) 202
Tolumean 37
Tombara 111
Tombaul (district) 311
Tong (island) 174
Tongilus = Cape Lambert
Tonilaihafen 200
tools 129, 145, 197, 218, 236
Topaia (district) 115
Toriu (river) 9
Torres 351

Torubea (island) 203
Torututa (island) 203
totem system, origin 292-4
totemism
  among the Moánus 174f.
  among the Solomon Islanders 210, 286f., 290f.
  in Fiji and *Samoa* 291
  in New Guinea 292
  in the New Hebrides 290
  in the tribes of the north-eastern Gazelle Peninsula 29, 32, 265
  on New Ireland 280
  on St Matthias 150f.
  on Siara, Tanga, and Aneri 283
Towi (island) 172
trap fishing 43-6, 134, 222
traps, manufacture of 43f.
trepanation
  in the Caen Islands 50
  in the Duke of Yorks 50
  on Gerrit Denys 50
  on New Ireland 50f.
  on the Gazelle Peninsula 48-50
Trobriand Islands 105f.
tubuan 35, 38, 248, 249-57
Tumuip 76, 79, 99, 335
Tupinier (island) 364
Turanguna, see South Daughter
Turtle-catching 46f., 91, 134
tutupele (musical instrument) 60
Tylor, E.B. 238

Uainkatou (island) 171
Uatom (Watom) 7, 24, 46, 47, 243, 246, 312
Ufe (island) 191
Ulavun = Father
Ulu (island) 19
Unea = Mérite
Urara (Urar) (island) 24, 46, 312
Urdeneta, Andres 350
Usiai 157, 158, 161, 163f.
  agriculture 169
  burial 170
  character 168
  crafts 169
  dances 169f.
  dwelling sites 172
  social relationships 169
  war 169
Utan (islands) 192
Utuan (island) 19

Vangalu (island) 141
Varzinberg = Vunakokor
vendetta 87
Violet Island 171
Virien (district) 252
Viviren (district) 75
Vleomen (river) 81
Vulcan Island 6
Vulvut (Henry Reid River) 77
Vunadidir (district) 75
Vunakokor 1, 3, 7, 22, 24, 74, 249, 257, 273, 312
Vunapope 3
vuvuei ceremony 42f.

Wairiki (district) 75
Wallace, Alfred 106
Wallis, Captain 235
Wallis Island 114
war conduct
  in the Admiralty Islands 169, 177f.
  in western New Britain 89
  on the Gazelle Peninsula 28f., 55f.
war ornaments 62, 93, 131, 162, 214
war paint 62
Warangoi 3, 22, 75, 252
Wasserhafen 118
water flute 276
Watu (village) 12
weapons
  from Kaniet, Luf and Ninigo 196
  from St Matthias 145-7
  from Squally Island 153
  from Wuwulu and Aua 186f.
  of the Admiralty Islanders 157f.
  of the Baining 73f.
  of the eastern islands 237
  of the Gazelle Peninsula tribes 56-8
  of the Solomon Islanders 218-21
  of the western New Britain natives 96-103
  on New Ireland and New Hanover 126-8
weaving 143, 148, 153, 238-40
Weberhafen 7f., 9, 22, 24, 39, 249, 258, 273, 312
Werner, Captain B. von 366
Western New Britain, natives of 87ff.
  anthropology 87f.
  canoes 103f.
  circumcision ceremony 276
  foodstuffs 91
  fortifications 89
  harvesting salt 91
  hut construction 91
  jewellery 92-6
  language 87
  luxury items 92
  masks 276f.
  skull deformation 88
  tattooing 96
  utensils 91f.
  village headmen 89
  warfare 89
  weapons 96-103
Whirlwind Reef 17
Wietersheim, von Captain 367
wife, her position
  among the Moánus 175
  among the Solomon Islanders 211
  among the tribes of the north-eastern Gazelle Peninsula 29f.
  in the eastern islands 234
Wild Island 174
Willaumezberg 15
Willaumez Peninsula 1, 12, 14, 15, 26, 39, 91, 92, 93, 95f., 101f.
Winchelsea Island 199, 360
Wittau 12
Witu = Deslacs
wooden drums on the Gazelle Peninsula 58f.
  in the Admiralty Islands 164
  in the Solomon Islands 213
  in western New Britain 89
  on New Ireland 126
  on St Matthias 145
Wooden swords from Wuwulu and Aua 187
Woodford 291
Woodlark (island) 106
worker recruiting 207f., 366
Wuneram (Wonneram) 111, 135, 206
Wuwulu 143, 183-91
  anthropology 184
  axes 188
  betel 188
  canoes 186
  clothing 190
  dances 189
  domestic utensils 188
  drums 189
  fishing 190
  foodstuffs 190
  games 189f.
  houses 185f.
  jewellery 190
  language 190f.
  origin 184f.
  population 183-91
  weapons 186f.

Yaming (island) 206
Yangaine (island) 206
Yelaule (island) 206
Yésele (island) 206
Yolása (island) 206
Ysabel Strait 116

Zeune Islands 201
Zöller, Hugo 11, 199, 202, 205, 214, 263
Zolloss (district) 205
Zweigipfelberg 15

INDEX

Islanders 210
  in the eastern islands 230f.
  in the Sulka 77
  in the tribes of the north-eastern Gazelle Peninsula 30f.
  on New Hanover 120
  on New Ireland 120
marriage prohibition
  among the Moánus 175
  among the Sulka 77
  in the eastern islands 230f.
  in the Solomon Islands 210, 287
  in the tribes of the north-eastern Gazelle Peninsula 29, 265
  on New Ireland 120, 282
  on St Matthias 150f.
  on Siara, Tanga and Aneri 283f.
Marshall Islands 239, 242
Martin Islands 200f., 202
Masava (island) 8, 24, 46, 311f.
mask dances (see also *duk-duk*)
  of the Baining 265-7
  on New Ireland 276f.
  of the Sulka 78f., 275f.
masks
  from Aneri 284
  from Bougainville, Buka and Nissan 284f.
  from Lihir 284
  from Möwehafen and the Arawa Islands 276
  from New Ireland 277-9
  from Tanga 283
  from the French Islands 276
  of the Baining 267f., 273
  of the Gazelle Peninsula 43, 250f., 257-9
  of the Sulka 274f.
Masikonápuka (island) 9, 24, 46, 311f.
Massait = San Joseph
Matánkor 119, 157, 158, 161, 163-5
  character 168
  dwelling sites 172-4
  significance of the name 170
matasesén 285f.
Matehes (island) 205, 206
Matty Island 183, 361
  (see also Wuwulu)
Matupi 6, 263, 312, 366
Matzungan (island) 204
Maur = San Francisco
Maurelle, Captain 362
Mausoleum Island 115

Mävlu (Powell River) 77
Mbúke (island) 170-2
Mbúnai (village) 170, 172
Mbutjoruo (island) 173
Mbutmanda (island) 172
mealtimes 92
medical knowledge
  of natives of New Ireland 50f.
  of natives of the Gazelle Peninsula 48-51
Meier, Father P.J. 165
Melanesian languages 87
men's houses 147f., 161, 214
Mencke, Bruno 139f.
Mendaña, Alvaro 350f.
Mérite (island) 17, 93, 98
migration legends
  from Liueniua 227
  from Nuguria 226
Miklucho-Maclay 366
Mioko (island) 19, 252, 366
mission
  Catholic 70, 116, 336
  of the Sacred Heart of Jesus 3, 366
  Wesleyan 116, 366
Mlol 81
Moánus 119, 157f., 161, 163f.
  astronomy 169f.
  birth 177
  burial of the dead 179f.
  character 168
  chiefdom 176
  dwelling sites 170-2
  judicial practices 176
  marriage 175f.
  naming 177
  puberty ceremonies 177
  songs 180f.
  sorcery 169, 175f., 178f.
  totemism 174
  trade 173f.
  war 177f.
Moila Point 199, 200, 205
mokpelpel (eater of human flesh) 81
Mologoviu (volcano) 203
money, see coconut money, shell money, teeth money
Montague Bay 12, 26, 93, 100, 101f., 359
Morrell, Captain 365
Mortlock Islands 207, 225
Moseley 366
Mother (volcano) 6f., 361
Móuk (island) 171f.
Mount Balbi 199, 202
Mount Below 14
Mount Bendemann 115

Mourning decoration 37, 62
Möwehafen 13, 26, 38, 89, 92, 276
Müller, Hermann (missionary) 76f., 330, 335
Mundua = Forestier
musical instruments
  of the Solomon Islanders 213
  on New Ireland 126
  on St Matthias 145
  on the Gazelle Peninsula 58-61
Musson (= Nissan) 135
Mutlar 2

Nabutu Bay 111, 114, 115
Nago (island) 115
Nakanai 12, 26, 39f., 87, 91, 92, 95-103
  language 87, 335-40
  people of 88, 89
name-giving
  among the Moánus 177
  among the Sulka 78
  among the tribes of the north-eastern Gazelle Peninsula 33
Namisoko = Duportail Islands
Nanuk (Credner Islands) 7, 263
Napapar (district) 311
Naraga (island) 91
Nares, Sir George 366
Nares Harbour 366
nasal ornaments
  in the Admiralty Islands 161
  in the eastern islands 230, 237
  in western New Britain 93
  of the Solomon Islanders 214
  on Kaniet and Luf 197
  on New Ireland and New Hanover 131
  on the Gazelle Peninsula 66
Naumaúma (district) 75
Naúna (island) 174
Nauru 239
Ndrel (village) 173
Ndréu (island) 171
Ndrilo (island) 173
Ndriol (villlage) 171
Ndrówa (island) 172
Ndruval (island) 163, 165, 172
Ndruwiu (island) 173
neck ornaments
  from the Gazelle Peninsula 65
  in the Admiralty Islands 161
  in western New Brit-

ain 95
  on New Ireland 130
  on Ninigo 197
  on St Matthias 143
Nehuss Point 199, 203
net fishing 45f., 133, 145, 160, 190, 197, 221-3, 234
New Britain 1-109
  central part 11f.
  earthquakes 1
  Gazelle Peninsula 1-11
  geological structure 1
  inhabitants 19-109 (see also Gazelle Peninsula and western New Britain)
  surface area 1
  volcanoes 1
  western part 12-17
New Guinea Company 11, 19, 367f.
New Hanover 114, 116, 359
  natives of 117-35 (see under New Ireland)
New Ireland 111-17
  anthropology 117f.
  birth 121
  burial of the dead 122-4
  cannibalism 118-20
  canoes 132f.
  carving 278-80
  character 118
  clothing 121
  dances 124-6, 276-8
  fishing 133f.
  houses 131f.
  marriage 120f.
  masks 277-83
  money 134f.
  musical instruments 126
  natives of 70-138
  ornaments 129-31
  puberty 121, 122
  secret societies 276f.
  stone figures 284
  totemism 280
  weapons 126-8
Ngówui (island) 171
Ninigo 143, 164, 183, 191
  canoes 195f.
  clothing 197
  customs 195
  household utensils 197
  huts 196
  ornaments 197
  population number 192
  trade 195
  weapons 196
Nissan 135, 199, 206, 284, 352, 361
  population, see Solomon Islands
Noanaur (island) 141
Nodup 366
Nonga (village) 311

Normanby Island 100
North Cape 111, 115
North Daughter (volcano) 6
North Son (volcano) 11
Nuguria 190, 225, 226
  immigration legends 226
  population, see eastern islands
Nukufetau 227
Nukumanu 190, 225f.
  population, see eastern islands
Nukuoro 226
Numanuma (village) 202f.
nunut (musical instrument) 126
Nusa 115f., 132, 243
Nusa Harbour 115, 132, 243
Nusalik (island) 115

O Mengen 76, 102, 335
obsidian, manufacture of blades from 165
Ongtong Java 207, 225, 227, 353
Open Bay 9, 11f., 76
ornamentation
  of the Baining 268
  on New Ireland 127
  on St Matthias 147
Otua (island) 201

Paanopa 239
Pahakáreng (village) 173
Pahalum (village) 81
painting of the body
  in the Admiralty Islands 161
  in the eastern islands 237
  in the Solomon Islands 215
  in western New Britain 93
  on New Ireland 129
  on the Gazelle Peninsula 61f.
Pak (island) 171, 172, 174, 175
Palaiai (island) 171
Palakukúr (village) 74, 75
Palamot (village) 171f.
Paleawe 12, 76, 99
Palúal (island) 172
pan flutes 60, 127, 213
pangolo (stringed instrument) 60f.
Papimbutj (island) 173
Papitálai (village) 170, 171-3, 174
Papuan languages 87
Papuans, origin of 106
Parroran (island) 206
Patúam (island) 171
Patúsi (village) 170

Pelau (island) 227
pele (shell money) 41f.
penis shell 142, 150, 162, 170
Pére (village) 170, 172
Pérouse, Comte de la 363
Peschel, Oskar 242
Peterhafen 17
Pflüger, Dr A. 15, 17
Phoon Islands 206
Pierson, missionary 124
Pinepil (island) 206, 212, 352
Pitilu (Pidelo) (island) 158, 173
plaiting 158, 217
Poam (island) 165, 174
Poauárei (village) 170
Poekálas (village) 173
pole buildings 91, 161
Polotjal (village) 173, 174
polygamy 32, 121, 175, 210
Polynesians, migrations of 240-6
Pónam (island) 173
Ponape 165, 189
Pongópou (village) 173
Popapu (island) 173
Port Breton 114
Port Hunter, see Hunterhafen
Port Praslin 114
Portland Islands 114, 361, 365
Potomo (island) 173
pottery 158f., 169, 216, 241f.
Powell 92
Powell Harbour 9
property 28f., 69, 175, 177, 210f., 233f.
puberty ceremonies 78, 121, 122, 177, 192f., 231, 275f., 285
Pulié River 13
Punro (village) 164
Purdy Islands 155, 365
purification ceremonies 78, 80
Putput = Rügenhafen
Putúli (island) 172
Pyramidenberg 15

Quiros, Pedro Fernandez de 351

Rabaul 6
Raluana 250, 252, 253
Ralum 6, 252, 263
Ramandu (district) 312
Rambutjo (island) 171, 172, 173, 174
Raoulberg 15
Rapitok (district) 75
Rascher (Father Mathäus) 9, 12, 25, 68, 69, 70, 76, 266, 267, 272,

311
Ratzel, Prof. 238
Rautan (island) 200
Rautan Strait 201
Ray, Marquis de 114, 366
Rebar (district) 75
religion, see ancestor worship, spiritual beliefs, sorcery
Réta (island) 172, 173
Rickard, missionary 311
right of succession 27, 175, 176, 234
ring money 215f.
Ritter Island 14, 364
Rocholl (surveyor) 3
Roggeveen, Jacob 360
Roitan (district) 141
Rook Island 29, 95, 360
Ross Islands 13
Rossel Range 111, 114, 117, 118, 123, 127, 131
Rotuma 226, 228
Rügenhafen (Putput) 2f.
Ruk-Ruk 285

Saavedra, Alvaro de 349
Sae (island) 192
St Andrew Islands 155
St George Island 171, 175
St George's Channel 2, 111, 249, 273
St John 111, 119, 133, 135, 206, 283, 284
St Matthias 139-41, 359, 362
  anthropology 141f.
  canoes 145, 148
  clothing and ornaments 142f.
  dance batons 147
  fishing equipment 145, 147
  foodstuffs and luxuries 145
  houses and domestic utensils 143f., 147f.
  musical instruments 145
  natives of 140-8
  weapons 145-7
  weaving 143, 148
St Patrick Islands 155, 172
St Paul (mission station) 9
Sal (island) 206
Salapio (island) 115
Sali (village) 164
salt harvesting 91, 347
San Bruno (island) 111
San Francisco (island) 111
San Gabriel (island) 155, 171, 174
San Joseph (island) 111
San Miguel (island) 172
San Rafael (island) 155,

174
sandals 235
Sandwich Island 114, 115, 127, 276, 365
Santa Cruz 143
Sapiu (village) 202
Saposá (island) 211
scar tattooing, see decorative scars
Schack, Commander 139
Schellong, Dr 289
Schering, Captain 367
Schleinitz, von Admiral 15, 199, 366, 367
Schleinitz Mountains 111, 115
Schmidt, Prof. W. 87
Schnee, Dr 170, 274, 312
Schouten Islands 156
Schouten, Willem Corneliszoon 352
Schulze Point 6, 312
Scilly Islands 9
secret societies 247-90
  in New Guinea 289f.
  in the New Hebrides 288
  in the Solomon Islands 211, 285
  in western New Britain 276
  of the Gazelle Peninsula 249-57, 259-65
  of the Sulka 275
  on Florida 287, 288
  on New Ireland 276f.
  on the Banks and Torres Islands 287
Serrano, Francisco 349
shark-catching 132f., 173
shell money
  in the Admiralty Islands 169, 174
  in the Duke of Yorks 38f., 40f.
  in the Solomon Islands 215f.
  on Aneri 135
  on Nakanai 41
  on New Hanover 134
  on New Ireland 41f., 134f.
  on the north-eastern Gazelle Peninsula 28, 38-41
shields
  from Nakanai 101
  from the French Islands 101
  from the South Cape 102
  from the Willaumez Peninsula 101
  in western New Britain 96, 100-2
  of the O Mengen 105
  of the Sulka 100, 104
shooting stars 53, 81, 229
Siara (district) 111, 115,

www.ingramcontent.com/pod-product-compliance
Lightning Source LLC
Chambersburg PA
CBHW040317240426
43665CB00031B/2972